Government and F
Middle East and N

The latest edition of this renowned textbook explores the states and regimes of the Middle East and North Africa. Presenting heavily revised, fully updated chapters contributed by the world's leading experts, it analyzes the historical trajectory, political institutions, economic development, and foreign policies of the region's nearly two dozen countries. The volume can be used in conjunction with its sister volume, *The Societies of the Middle East and North Africa*, for a comprehensive overview of the region.

Chapters are organized and structured identically, giving insightful windows into the nuances of each country's domestic politics and foreign relations. Data tables and extensive annotated bibliographies orient readers towards further research. Whether used in conjunction with its sister volume or on its own, this book provides the most comprehensive and detailed overview of the region's varied politics. Five new experts cover the critical country cases of Turkey, Lebanon, Jordan, Saudi Arabia, and Iran. All chapters cover the latest events, including trends that have changed remarkably in just a few years, like the gradual end of the Syrian civil war. As such, this textbook is invaluable to students of Middle Eastern politics.

The ninth edition brings substantial changes. All chapters also have a uniform, streamlined structure that explores the historical context, social and economic environment, political institutions, regime dynamics, and foreign policy of each country. Fact boxes and political maps are now far more extensive, and photographs and images also help illustrate key points. Annotated bibliographies are vastly expanded, providing nothing short of the best list of research references for each country.

Sean Yom is Associate Professor of Political Science at Temple University and Senior Fellow at the Foreign Policy Research Institute. He is a widely published expert on regimes and development in the Middle East and North Africa, and regularly travels to the region.

Government and Politics of the Middle East and North Africa

Development, Democracy, and Dictatorship

9th edition

Edited by Sean Yom

Routledge
Taylor & Francis Group

LONDON AND NEW YORK

Ninth edition published 2020
by Routledge
2 Park Square, Milton Park, Abingdon, Oxon, OX14 4RN

and by Routledge
52 Vanderbilt Avenue, New York, NY 10017

Routledge is an imprint of the Taylor & Francis Group, an informa business

First edition published by Westview Press in 1980
Eighth edition first published by Westview Press in 2017

British Library Cataloguing-in-Publication Data
A catalogue record for this book is available from the British Library

Library of Congress Cataloging-in-Publication Data
A catalog record has been requested for this book

ISBN: 978-1-138-35431-9 (hbk)
ISBN: 978-1-138-35432-6 (pbk)
ISBN: 978-0-429-42490-8 (ebk)

Typeset in Sabon
by Swales & Willis, Exeter, Devon, UK

Visit the companion website: www.routledge.com/cw/yom

For Zeynep'im, with love and flair, in between Reason and Rhyme

CONTENTS

PREFACE

Like past editions, this venerable volume introduces the reader to the historical development, domestic politics, and foreign policies of the varied countries constituting the Middle East and North Africa. However, this ninth edition marks a sweeping revision in two regards. Above all, with a bevy of new contributing experts onboard, this latest edition of *The Government and Politics of the Middle East and North Africa* incorporates major updates regarding the flurry of events that have rocked the MENA since 2015. Many new country experts join us, all on top of their fields – Imad Salamey (Lebanon), André Bank (Jordan), Kristin Fabbe (Turkey), Saeid Golkar (Iran), Sean Foley (Saudi Arabia), and Kira Jumet (Egypt). They, and the other authors, explore the dramatic transformations and popular struggles that have unfurled across the MENA states. Some parts of the region are churning; other parts are burning. Everything is changing.

Second, this latest edition is also the first to be paired with a sister volume from Routledge – *The Societies of the Middle East and North Africa*, a new text that engages all the economic, social, cultural, and environmental issues not covered in this book. To extract the most panoramic vista of the Middle East, both of these books should be carefully considered. Their shared goal is to provide research-friendly guidance for understanding the region's modern states and human societies. Both are edited by Sean Yom, who spearheaded the creation of the new *Societies* volume and has assumed primary authorship and editorial leadership of *Government and Politics* from Mark Gasiorowski, who adroitly edited the last two editions.

The structure of this book, *Government and Politics*, is designed to maximize clarity so that the broad audience – from students and researchers to journalists, policymakers, and travelers – can quickly gain expertise in any country they choose. The first two chapters provide an overview of the MENA. The first chapter reviews the political regimes, governing institutions, and historical milieu of the region, enabling readers to quickly grasp leading concepts and patterns. The second chapter adds thick context by showing how the geographic circumstances, economic struggles, and social dimensions such as identity, human security, youth bulges, and gender inequality are also influencing the nature of policymaking and state governance. The subsequent country-based chapters are arranged in geographic order from

West to East. Part I comprises North Africa, which geographically encompasses Morocco, Algeria, Tunisia, Libya, and Egypt. Part II entails the Near East, meaning Israel, Palestine, Syria, Lebanon, Jordan, Iraq, and Turkey. Part III includes the countries bordering the Arabian or Persian Gulf, meaning Saudi Arabia, Iran, Yemen, and the smaller Gulf kingdoms of Kuwait, Bahrain, Qatar, Oman, and the United Arab Emirates.

These country-based chapters have been heavily vetted and updated. Each follows an identical format involving six parts. First comes *historical background*, which provides an overview of the country's history and the antecedent facts that are vital to know to better understand its current politics. Second is *social and economic environment*, including the geographic, ethnic, and structural factors that shape the relationship between society and politics. Third is *political structures*, which highlight the core institutions, organizations, and organs that govern the distribution and exercise of power. Fourth is *political dynamics*, which describe the leading actors and recent events that are driving political change. Fifth is *foreign policy*, which discusses the determinants underlying the country's diplomacy, trade, investment, and military ties to other countries and global organizations. Sixth is *future prospects*, which forecasts the main trends that will characterize the country's future political development in coming years, including any ongoing conflicts, debates, and uncertainties. Finally, each chapter ends with an annotated bibliography that gives valuable references for further reading, including carefully curated online sources.

This volume was written with an eye towards accessibility and absorption, even for readers with little prior familiarity with the MENA region. All country chapters contain national maps, fact boxes giving key details, and helpful photographs to illustrate key points. Routledge also provides a companion website for this volume, not least because web links change faster than book editions can be published. There, discerning readers can find easier access to the data, organizations, blogs, databases, and portals cited in the bibliography ("Further Reading") sections. Finally, a note on transliteration: in an effort to make the text as readable as possible, spelling conventions for Turkish, Persian, and Arabic attempt to conform as closely as possible to the most popular Anglicized versions for each country. (Thus the same name may have different variants in different chapters, like Hussein versus Husayn, in an effort to honor what each country's specialists recognize as prevailing local standards.) For Arabic transliteration, diacritics are kept to a minimum except for 'ayn when convention demands.

In a time where global politics have become unpredictable and terms like "fake news" have run amuck in popular discourse, the need for rigorous scholarship is a moral imperative. In this milieu, *Government and Politics* is not merely another book on Middle East politics; it is a rich compendium of indisputable knowledge about the MENA's diverse countries authored by researchers who have devoted their entire lives to exploring and explaining the region. It is an immense undertaking – but a worthy one. For editorial assistance and proofing, I owe immense thanks to Nadia Farajallah, who intervened in a timely and gracious manner. As always, Joe Whiting and his team at Routledge deserve applause for steering this book through all the relevant production and publication processes.

LIST OF MAPS, TABLES, BOXES, AND PHOTOGRAPHS

MAPS

TABLES

BOXES

PHOTOS

LIST OF CONTRIBUTORS

Ariel Ahram is Associate Professor in Virginia Tech's School of Public and International Affairs, VA. His research focuses on politics, security, and environmental change in the Middle East and North Africa region. He is the author of *Break All the Borders: Separatism and the Reshaping of the Middle East* (2019).

André Bank is the Interim Director of the Institute of Middle East Studies at the German Institute for Global and Area Studies in Hamburg, Germany. He is also the head speaker of the international research network, International Diffusion and Cooperation of Authoritarian Regimes (IDCAR). His research on authoritarianism and conflict dynamics in the Middle East has been published in *Democratization, Journal of Peace Research, Middle East Critique,* and *Review of International Studies,* among other journals.

Lindsay J. Benstead is Associate Professor of Political Science and Director of the Middle East Studies Center at Portland State University, OR. She has served as Fellow at the Woodrow Wilson International Center for Scholars in Washington, DC, and as Kuwait Visiting Professor at Sciences Po-Paris. Her research interests include women and politics, public opinion, and survey methodology, and Middle East and North African politics. She holds a PhD in Public Policy and Political Science from the University of Michigan.

Jill Crystal is the Curtis O. Liles III Professor of Political Science at Auburn University, AL. She received her BA from Cornell University and MA and PhD from Harvard University. She is the author of numerous articles, chapters, and two books on the Gulf: *Oil and Politics in the Gulf: Rulers and Merchants in Kuwait and Qatar* (1995) and *Kuwait: The Transformation of an Oil State* (1992). Her research and teaching interests include Gulf politics, authoritarianism and democratization, policing, and political economy.

Tahani Elmogrbi is a Libya expert based at Culmen International, LLC, VA. She previously worked as a democracy and governance specialist with the United States Agency for International Development, as well as on issues of peacebuilding, conflict resolution, and property rights for nonprofit groups. She has an MA from the Elliott School of International Affairs (George

Washington University) and an MA in business from Hamline University, earned on a Fulbright.

Kristin Fabbe is Assistant Professor and Hellman Faculty Fellow at Harvard Business School, and affiliate at the Middle East Initiative at the JFK School of Government, Harvard Center for Middle East Studies, and Harvard Center for European Studies, MA. She is author of *Disciples of the State: Religion and State-Building in the Former Ottoman World* (2019) as well as numerous articles and chapters. Her research focuses on state-led development, political economy, forced migration, and identity politics in the MENA, especially Turkey.

Sean Foley is Associate Professor of History at Middle Tennessee State University, TN. His research focuses on the culture, history, and politics of the Middle East and the wider Muslim world. He is the author of *Changing Saudi Arabia: Art, Culture, and Society in the Kingdom* (2019) and *The Arab Gulf States: Beyond Oil and Islam* (2010).

Saeid Golkar is Assistant Professor in the Department of Political Science and Public Service at the University of Tennessee-Chattanooga, TN, and non-resident Senior Fellow on Middle East Policy at the Chicago Council on Global Affairs (CCGA). His research focuses on the comparative politics of authoritarian regimes, with an emphasis on the Middle East. His book, *Captive Society: The Basij Militia and Social Control in Iran* (2015), was awarded the Silver Medal Prize by the Washington Institute for Near East Policy.

Kira Jumet is Assistant Professor of Government at Hamilton College, NY. Her research focuses on protest mobilization related to the Egyptian uprisings, including the relationship between emotions and participation. She is author of *Contesting the Repressive State: Why Ordinary Egyptians Protested During the Arab Spring* (2017).

Azzedine Layachi is Professor of Government and Politics at St. John's University in New York City, NY. He has served as Associate Director of the Center for Global Studies, Executive Board member of the American Institute of North African Studies, Associate Editor of the *Bulletin of the Middle East Studies Association*, and President of the Northeastern Political Science Association. He serves on the Advisory Board of the Maghreb Center. He received his PhD and MA from New York University and BA from the University of Algiers. He is author of numerous books, chapters, and articles, including *Economic Crisis and Political Change in North Africa* (1998); *The United States and North Africa: A Cognitive Approach to Foreign Policy* (1990); and *Global Studies: The Middle East* (2010). He is currently finishing a book entitled *Algeria: History, People, and Political Struggle*.

Karim Mezran is Director of the North Africa Initiative and resident Senior Fellow at the Atlantic Council's Rafik Hariri Center for the Middle East, and adjunct professor at the School of Advanced International Studies (SAIS) at Johns Hopkins University, MD. His work has been widely published in English, Italian, and other languages. He is the author of *Negotiation and Construction of National Identities* (2007) and co-editor with Dr. Arturo Varvelli of *Foreign Actors in Libya's Crisis* (2017) and *The Arc of Crisis in the MENA Region: Fragmentation, Decentralization, and Islamist Opposition* (2018). He holds a PhD in international relations from SAIS at Johns Hopkins University.

Hamed Mousavi is Assistant Professor at the Faculty of Law and Political Science at the University of Tehran, Iran. He is currently a visiting professor at the Department of Political Science at Carleton University in Ottawa, Canada. His research interests include Israeli foreign policy, US foreign policy, and Middle East politics. He is currently writing a book on the role of ideology in Israeli foreign policy. He regularly appears as a political analyst on various broadcast media, including *CNN*, *BBC*, *Al-Jazeera* and *RT*.

Thomas Pierret is Senior Researcher at the Institute for Research and Studies on the Arab and Muslim World (IREMAM), National Center for Scientific Research (CNRS), Aix-Marseille Université in Aix-en-Provence, France. He holds a PhD in Political Science from Sciences Po-Paris and the University of Louvain. He was previously Senior Lecturer at the University of Edinburgh, and Postdoctoral Research Associate at Princeton University and Zentrum Möderner Orient in Berlin. He is author of *Religion and State in Syria: The Sunni Ulama from Coup to Revolution* (2013).

Glenn E. Robinson is Associate Professor at the Naval Postgraduate School in Monterey, California, and is affiliated with the Center for Middle Eastern Studies at the University of California, Berkeley, CA. He has authored or co-authored three books on Palestinian politics. His current projects include the forthcoming book *Global Jihad: A Brief History*, and a study on the impact of the information revolution on understandings and practices of Islam in Southeast Asia.

Imad Salamey is Associate Professor of Political Science and International Affairs at the Lebanese American University in Beirut, Lebanon. He is author of *The Government and Politics of Lebanon* (2013), *The Decline of Nation-States after the Arab Spring: the Rise of Communitocracy* (2017), and *Post-Conflict Power-Sharing Agreements: Options for Syria* (2018). His latest work examines the repercussions of contemporary transformations from national to communitarian political paradigms. He serves as policy advisor and monitoring consultant for various international and regional organizations.

Mira Sucharov is Associate Professor of Political Science at Carleton University in Ottawa, Canada. She is the author *The International Self: Psychoanalysis and the Search for Israeli-Palestinian Peace* (2005), and *Public Influence: A Guide to Op-Ed Writing and Social Media Engagement* (2019). She is co-editor (with Aaron J. Hahn Tapper) of *Social Justice and Israel/Palestine: Foundational and Contemporary Debates* (2019), and, with Eric Van Rythoven, of *Methodology and Emotion in International Relations: Parsing the Passions* (2019).

Gregory White is Mary Huggins Gamble Professor of Government at Smith College, MA. His research is located at the intersection of environmental studies, migration studies and security studies, focusing on North Africa and the Mediterranean. He is the author of *Climate Change and Migration: Security and Borders in a Warming World* (2011).

Stacey Philbrick Yadav is Associate Professor and Chair of Political Science at Hobart and William Smith Colleges, NY. She is author of *Islamists and the State: Legitimacy and Institutions in Yemen and Lebanon* (2013), and various other scholarly works on youth, opposition, and identity.

Sean Yom is Associate Professor of Political Science at Temple University, PA, and Senior Fellow at the Foreign Policy Research Institute. His research specializes on authoritarian regimes, political economy, and US foreign policy in the Middle East and North Africa. He is author of *From Resilience to Revolution: How Foreign Interventions Destabilize the Middle East* (2016) and various journal articles, book chapters, and popular essays. He is also author and editor of *The Societies of the Middle East and North Africa: Structures, Vulnerabilities, and Forces* (2019). He holds a PhD from Harvard University.

Political dynamics in the MENA region

Democracy, authoritarianism, and history

Sean Yom

LOCATING THE MIDDLE EAST AND NORTH AFRICA

A classic Arabic proverb holds that forgetfulness is the plague of knowledge. In the Middle East and North Africa (MENA), global audiences do not merely forget so much as exhibit chronic amnesia when stumbling across politics throughout the region. Breaking developments in these countries – policies, elections, protests, conflict, governance, revolution – frequently interrupt global headlines. Yet instead of unpacking these events in the same way as we might when discussing, say, American presidential elections or Brexit in the United Kingdom, observers too often fall back upon familiar tropes of an exotic Orient whose political dramas forever appear mysterious and irrational, given as they seemingly are waged by bearded sultans and veiled women speaking incomprehensible tongues. The poster depicted in Photo 1.1, for instance, nicely captures all the other iconic stereotypes associated with the region: the musical oud, the hookah pipe, prayer beads, palm trees, flying carpets, camels, pyramids, the Qur'an, mosques, tea kettles, crossed swords, and the Islamic crescent.

PHOTO 1.1
Popular images of the MENA region.

Source: iStock

To be sure, these are not fanciful inventions. They are cultural notions that can be physically located by casual visitors to the Arab world. (Except, perhaps, for the flying carpet.) The problem is when the imagery of such convenient symbols takes the place of gritty, concrete, and objective *knowledge* about political life – awareness gained only by discarding assumptions and biases about how people in the MENA behave, and instead matter-of-factly dissecting the institutions, policies, and personalities of each country on their own terms.

This book does just that, and therefore seeks to staunch the plague of forgetfulness. It makes the MENA *knowable* under the uncontroversial assumption that though politics is shaped by local circumstances, it expresses universal patterns of human behavior that can be studied and analyzed. As political scientist Harold Laswell memorably observed nearly a century ago, politics is the study of "who gets what, when, how." How individuals and groups interact, bargain, and struggle over the allocation of power and resources through the craft of governance therefore marks our imperative. The contributors in this volume take this charge seriously, and present an impressive corpus of political knowledge about the Arab world, Iran, Turkey, and Israel that, collected over many years through focused research and frequent travel, reveals the connections between the historical past, present circumstances, and future pathways.

At the same time, this exploration shows that the MENA is no monolith. This is a critical region at the crossroads of three continents, and includes nearly two dozen states and various stateless peoples. It is also a region of *opposites*. In the last decade alone, there have been both inspiring revolutions for democracy and brutal counterrevolutionary repression inflicted by dictators. Both republics (some elected, most not) and ruling monarchies – that rarest of regime types – occupy the reins of national power. Several states like Yemen and Libya have all but collapsed due to violence and war, while others like Morocco and Kuwait seem to embody resilience and stability. Extreme wealth and opulence flourish in some hydrocarbon-exporting Gulf states, like Qatar; not far away are humanitarian crises and grotesque poverty. Some countries like Jordan remain tenaciously pro-Western in their foreign policy, while others like Syria and Iran resist Western entreaties and hegemony. In many societies, a vibrant youth generation aspires for entrepreneurship and innovation, even as elderly norms and religious dictates impose conservativism and tradition. Some travelers to the region see a fantasy land where flying carpets, belly dancers, and bellowing mosques should thrive; others see Facebook groups, Twitter hashtags, and McDonald's in Mecca.

Understanding these politics requires drawing upon political science and international affairs, but all the contributors also incorporate insights from other disciplines as well, including history, anthropology, economics, sociology, and religion. To that end, this first chapter provides a broad overview of the MENA's regimes, parsing out the different types of institutions and structures that characterize political order. The next chapter takes a different approach and analyzes how structural forces – such as geographic constraints, cultural change, religious identity, gender roles, and economic development – also shape the social arena of politics. A thicker and richer version of this framework of understanding *societies* rather than government and politics also occupies this book's sister volume.[1]

The book proceeds simply. Every chapter beyond the first two explores a different country as a case study, including the still-stateless Palestine. Each follows an identical format. Authors provide the historical background, then social and economic context, next ruling political structures as well as the latest dynamics and events, afterwards the nature of foreign policy, and finally the outlook for the future. The arc of analysis is linear, moving from past to present to future, and each stage requires careful reading, detailed attention, and an open mind.

As a result, this book fulfills three goals. First, by delivering critical information about different countries in a consistent format, it makes a perplexing region more concrete, empirical, and knowable through the universal language of politics. It seeks to create familiarity from which expertise and knowledge flow. Second, it illuminates the diversity of the MENA countries. Far from a homogenous region, the MENA is a mosaic, and one can spend a lifetime studying its politics, as indeed the contributing authors have. Third, this volume accentuates the pace of large-scale change. For many readers, the cataclysmic ruptures and defining ideologies of yesteryear – anti-colonial movements, Arab Nationalism, communism and the Cold War, Arab-Israeli wars, the genesis of Islamism, the US-led invasions of Iraq – are emblazoned in history books rather than living memory. Yet for generations, events like these defined the politics of the Middle East and North Africa. Today, even the Arab Spring, the 2011–12 wave of regional uprisings that many likened to the 1989 Velvet Revolutions in Europe that helped end the Cold War, is fading into the backdrop. The rhythms of political transformation march on, and knowing them intimately must be a priority.

Where *is* the MENA? Maps 1.1 and 1.2 graphically depict this region, broken into two maps given its vast size. The entire region covers many countries at the intersection of Europe, Africa, and Asia.

The phrase "Middle East" has Western origins: it was invented as a geopolitical moniker by British and American strategists in the early twentieth century to describe the eastern area of the world distinctive from the "Far East" (i.e., China and other Asian countries on the Pacific Ocean). Traditionally, this meant the geographic region bounded in the north by Turkey, in the east by Iran, in the south by Yemen, and in the west by Egypt and the

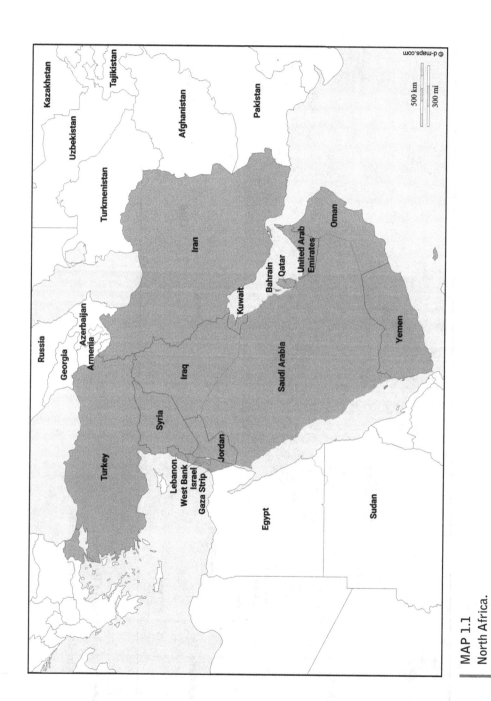

MAP 1.1
North Africa.

Source: adapted from D-Maps by Titanilla Panczel

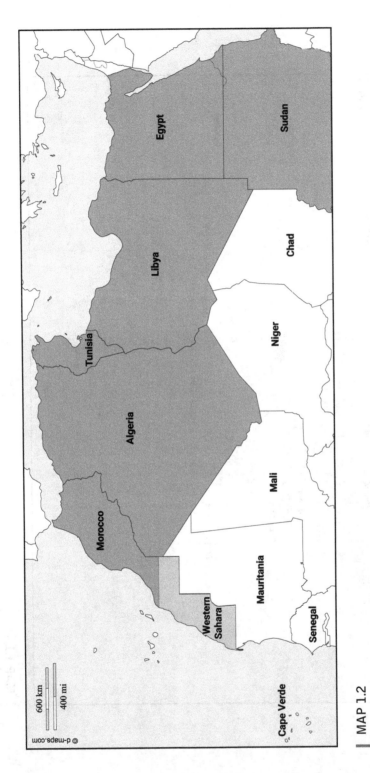

MAP 1.2
Near East and Arabian Peninsula.

Source: adapted from D-Maps by Titanilla Panczel

Red Sea. Today, the term "Middle East" or "Mideast" is frequently used by Westerners as a synonym to mean the entire Arab world, meaning not just this area but also all of North Africa, plus the three non-Arab countries of Israel, Turkey, and Iran.

That this wide-ranging area is now known by artificial nomenclature concocted by Anglo-American military elites hints at the enormous influence the West has played in shaping regional politics over the past century. This region lies in the middle part of the exotic East only from the Western imagination; from the perspective of, say, Japan or India, it could well be called the Middle *West*. Further, only in the past several decades have Arabic media begun using the literal translation of Middle East, *al-Sharq al-Awsat*, as an idiom for the region. For centuries, Arab geographers referred to the Arabic-speaking lands as *al-'Alam al-'Arabi*, or the Arab world. Likewise, until 1935 Iran was called Persia, while the main land area of Turkey is still known as Asia Minor or Anatolia. In this book, for the sake of simplicity, "Middle East" and MENA are used interchangeably to refer to the entire region depicted in Maps 1.1 and 1.2, that is, the Arab countries plus Israel, Iran, and Turkey. However, it is also fruitful to envisage the MENA as consisting of three subregions, each with its own distinctive geographic terminology: North Africa, the Near East, and Arabian (or Persian) Gulf.[2]

First, North Africa stretches across the uppermost zone of the African continent and includes Morocco, Algeria, Tunisia, Libya, Mauritania, Egypt, and Sudan. While Mauritania and Sudan are not covered in this edition, they represent indelible parts of this subregion and the Arab world. Of the remainder, Morocco, Algeria, Tunisia, and Libya share the closest social, cultural, and historical ties with one another. In Arabic, these four countries are called the *Maghrib*, which means literally "sunset" and figuratively "west." Morocco, Algeria, and Tunisia are often clustered together given their common French colonial past and post-colonial relations with France, which remains the most important external actor in this neighborhood.

Second, the Near East (a customary term used early on as synonym with Middle East) includes the lands east of North Africa but north of the Arabian (also known as the Persian) Gulf. This includes Israel, Palestine (i.e., the Palestinian territories, or the West Bank and Gaza Strip), Syria, Lebanon, Jordan, Iraq, and non-Arab Turkey. Mirroring the Maghrib, this subregion is known in Arabic as the *Mashriq*, which translates as "sunrise," or "east." Much of this area is also colloquially known as the Levant, a French-derived term that signifies a shared cultural and historical heritage since antiquity.

Turkey possesses its own civilizational heritage, and as a non-Arab country has its own unique trajectory of political development.

Finally, the Arabian Gulf touches Iran and all the countries in the Arabian Peninsula, which encompasses Saudi Arabia, Kuwait, Bahrain, Qatar, Oman, the United Arab Emirates (UAE), and Yemen. Also known as the Gulf states, these Arabian countries traditionally incubated close tribal and social bonds by virtue of their collective proximity. In Arabic media, they are termed the *Khalij* (literally, "gulf"). Though frequently classified as part of this subregion given its location, Iran is not an Arab country. The country formerly known as Persia carries its own storied identity and ancient past, including a lineage replete with empires and a political system unlike any other today.

Demographically, as Table 1.1 shows, the MENA countries wildly vary. National populations range from just a few million residents in tiny principalities like Bahrain and Qatar to closer to 100 million as in Egypt and Iran. Most are urbanized, although Morocco, Egypt, Syria, Iraq, Yemen, and Iran still have significant rural populations. Population density, measured as inhabitants per square kilometer, also varies; compare sparsely settled countries like Oman or Libya (3.6 persons per square kilometer) to extremely crowded places like the Palestinian territories, or Bahrain (1,918.5 persons per square kilometer). Most societies have experienced strong populational growth in recent decades, although birth rates have gradually declined. Syria has notably witnessed populational decline due to the flow of refugees outwards. The sources of demographic growth vary elsewhere; some countries have slightly higher birth rates, such as Egypt and Oman; some have seen enormous immigration by foreign workers (e.g., Kuwait, UAE); and some have received refugees fleeing conflicts like Syria (e.g., Jordan, Lebanon). The last column reveals an important but dreadful figure, the number of refugees living in the territory from other countries. Jordan, Lebanon, Turkey, and the Palestinian territories have the highest refugee populations, followed by Sudan and Iran. The Palestinian territories (in particular, the West Bank) represent a special case, as most refugees there are Palestinians who have held refugee status for many decades due to displacement from past Arab-Israeli conflicts.

TABLE 1.1

Demographics of the MENA, 2019

	Total population	Population density (per sq. km)	Urban population (% total population)	Population growth rate (annual)	Refugee population
Algeria	41,318,142	17.3	72.1	1.7	94,128
Bahrain	1,492,584	1,918.5	89.2	4.6	**
Egypt	97,553,151	98	42.7	1.9	232,617
Iran	81,162,788	49.83	74.4	1.1	979,435
Iraq	38,274,618	88.16	70.3	2.8	277,663
Israel	8,713,300	402.7	92.3	1.9	25,637
Jordan	9,702,353	109.3	90.8	2.6	2,896,162
Kuwait	4,136,528	232.1	100	2.1	**
Lebanon	6,082,357	594.6	88.4	1.3	1,468,137
Libya	6,374,616	3.6	79.8	1.3	9,342
Morocco	35,739,580	808	61.9	1.3	4,678
Oman	4,636,262	15	83.6	4.7	**
Palestine (West Bank & Gaza Strip)	4,684,777	778.2	75.9	2.9	2,213,963
Qatar	2,639,211	227.3	99.1	2.7	**
Saudi Arabia	32,938,213	15.3	83.6	2	**
Sudan	40,533,330	23.3	34.4	2.4	906,585
Syria	18,269,868	99.5	53.5	−0.9	N/A
Tunisia	11,532,127	74.2	68.6	1.1	**
Turkey	80,745,020	104.9	74.6	1.5	3,480,310
UAE	9,400,145	132.4	86.2	1.4	**
Yemen	28,250,420	53.5	36	2.4	270,898

Sources: World Bank (2019), *World Development Indicators*.

** denotes under 1,000 refugees.

Note: Refugees are those forcibly displaced from their home territories or countries who are either recognized in accordance with the United Nations High Commissioner for Refugees or granted refugee-like humanitarian protections and rights by their host territory or country.

UNDERSTANDING POLITICS: STATES, REGIMES, AND FOREIGN POLICY

The study of politics rests upon several foundational concepts. *States* are mostly synonymous with countries in common parlance, but in social science the term taps a deeper concept. In the classic Weberian definition, the modern state is an organized political community that possesses a monopoly over the legitimate use of coercion and commands sovereignty within a finite territorial space. That monopoly means that only the state can serve as ultimate arbiter over life and death within the population: no entity except the government can raise an army, make laws, close borders, execute persons, and commit other acts requiring force or violence. Sovereignty implies exclusive authority. States are sovereign insofar that within their boundaries, only they determine political and legal structures of authority, regulate social and economic relations (such as taxation), and formulate foreign policy toward other states. In theory, all modern states have the right of sovereignty; in practice, sovereignties are frequently violated by global powers in acts ranging from invasions and interventions to diplomacy and sanctions. Still, we distinguish modern states from old colonies or protectorates, as the MENA was prior to the 1950s, in that the former at least have a recognized expectation for sovereignty.

Every sovereign state has a government or *regime*, defined as the institutions and rules that determine access to key offices of state power. Many ways to classify regimes exist, but here the most convenient is through three categories: democratic, authoritarian, and hybrid.

a. *Democratic* regimes allow for free, fair, and regular elections with full adult suffrage. Those elections determine those who will occupy offices of legislative and executive power, and thus who makes policies. These regimes also promise the protection of civil liberties – such as religious, expressive, and press freedoms – under the rule of law. In addition, there must not be any unelected tutelary body, such as generals, priests, and kings, who can overturn the decisions of elected officials. Ideally, there is also accountability and transparency; citizens can redress their grievances through the judiciary and other constitutional mechanisms, and also hold their leaders responsible for abuses of power, such as corruption and other illegal actions.

b. *Authoritarian* regimes, also deemed autocracies or dictatorships, lack meaningful competition for power. For the typical citizen, elections do not exist, or else are so restricted that the incumbent leader or ruling party always wins. There does not exist any uncertainty about who will govern. Unlike democracies, opposition is banned outright or severely curtailed through repression. Elected bodies like symbolic legislatures and advisory councils do not have autonomy compared to the ruler – the president-for-life sitting astride a ruling party, the military general leading the *junta*, or the absolutist monarch who actively decides. Civic freedoms are restricted, minority rights are unprotected, and the threat of violence contains societal pluralism.

c. *Hybrid* regimes constitute a gray zone, and are also called competitive autocracies (or semi-democracies). Such governments combine institutional qualities of democracies and authoritarianism, making it difficult to put these cases squarely in either camp. Electoral contestation, legal opposition, and civic freedoms are ensured by law; there is no ironclad dictator ruling by repression. That said, the playing field of competition is grossly unfair due to rules that favor some powerholders and prevent the public from expressing its preferences. For instance, state violence can hamper citizens from participation; periodic elections are postponed or manipulated; civil society and the media face limitations; and judiciaries side with the executive to stifle change.

Democracies, autocracies, and hybrid regimes vary across one common institutional dimension – the structure of executive power, or who commands supreme authority. Most countries in the world today are *republics,* where the heads of government are public officials chosen by society to rule according to a constitution. In *parliamentary republics*, an elected legislature chooses a cabinet-based government whose head (i.e., prime minister, premier, or chancellor) is held accountable. The executive and legislative branches are interdependent. In some cases, a ceremonial president may represent the nation to the outside world as head of state (that is, the figurative embodiment of the country's sovereignty), but has little internal weight. In *presidential republics*, the head of government and head of state is the same figure – the president, who is directly elected to office rather than chosen by legislative results. The president wields the preponderance of power. The legislature is institutionally separate, but serves to check and balance the executive, as in the United States. Finally, some republics have popularly elected presidents who, as head of state, share policymaking powers in a compromise with governments led by a prime minister, the head of government. Presidents are usually the stronger actor in these *semi-presidential* systems, but not always. Table 1.2 shows how regime types and structures of executive power interactively align in MENA countries.

TABLE 1.2

Political regimes and power structures, 2019

	Year of independence	Current constitution, year adopted	Regime type	Power structure	National elections
Algeria	1962	1989 (last amended 2016)	Authoritarian	Republic (semi-presidential)	Parliamentary (every 5 years); presidential (every 5 years)
Bahrain	1971	2002 (last amended 2017)	Authoritarian	Monarchy	Parliamentary (every 4 years)
Egypt	1922	2014	Authoritarian	Republic (presidential)	Parliamentary (every 5 years); presidential (every 4 years)
Iran	1946	1979 (last amended 1989)	Authoritarian	Republic (theocratic)	Parliamentary (every 4 years); presidential (every 4 years)
Iraq	1932	2005	Hybrid	Republic (parliamentary)	Parliamentary (every 4 years); presidential (every 4 years)
Israel	1948	None (Basic Law established 1958)	Democratic	Republic (parliamentary)	Parliamentary (every 4 years); presidential (every 7 years)
Jordan	1946	1952 (last amended 2016)	Authoritarian	Monarchy	Parliamentary (every 4 years)
Kuwait	1961	1962	Authoritarian	Monarchy	Parliamentary (every 4 years)
Lebanon	1943	1926 (last amended 2004)	Hybrid	Republic (semi-presidential)	Parliamentary (every 4 years); presidential (every 6 years)

(Continued)

Libya	1951	2011 (last amended 2012)	Hybrid**	Republic (parliamentary)**	Parliamentary (electoral term unspecified)**
Morocco	1956	1962 (last amended 2011)	Authoritarian	Monarchy	Parliamentary (every 5 years)
Oman	1951	1996 (last amended 2011)	Authoritarian	Monarchy	Parliamentary (every 4 years)
Palestine (West Bank & Gaza Strip)	Not independent	None (Basic Law established in 2002)	Hybrid	Republic (semi-presidential)	Parliamentary (every 4 years); presidential (every 4 years)
Qatar	1971	2004	Authoritarian	Monarchy	Advisory assembly (as of 2019, never held)
Saudi Arabia	1932	1992 (last amended 2013)	Authoritarian	Monarchy	None
Sudan	1956	2005	Authoritarian	Republic (presidential)	Parliamentary (every 6 years); presidential (every 5 years)
Syria	1946	1973 (last amended 2012)	Authoritarian	Republic (presidential)	Parliamentary (every 4 years); presidential (every 7 years)
Tunisia	1956	2014	Democratic	Republic (semi-presidential)	Parliamentary (every 5 years); presidential (every 5 years)
Turkey	1923	1982 (last amended 2017)	Democratic	Republic (presidential)	Parliamentary (every 4 years); presidential (every 5 years)
UAE	1971	1971 (last amended 2009)	Authoritarian	Monarchy (federal)	Advisory assembly (every 4 years)

(Continued)

	Year of independence	Current constitution, year adopted	Regime type	Power structure	National elections
Yemen	1918 (North), 1967 (South)	1991 (last amended 2001; new constitution proposed in 2015)	Authoritarian**	Republic (presidential)**	Parliamentary (every 6 years); presidential (every 7 years)**

Note: Iran's British and Russian occupation ended in 1946, but it was never officially a colony or protectorate. Sudan's ongoing instability has removed its presidency, and in early 2019 installed a military council in its place.

** denotes situations of ongoing civil conflict throughout 2018–19, leaving future of executive power structure and elections unknown.

Foreign policy

Regardless of regime type, most governments today make decisions that not only shape their national societies, but also affect their relations with the regimes and governments inhabiting external states. Thus, we must understand not just domestic politics but also *foreign policy*. Foreign policy means the choices, strategies, and goals chosen by state leaders to achieve their goals vis-à-vis other states. The realm of foreign policy analysis is replete with important puzzles and newsworthy events to decipher: why, for instance, did Egypt make peace with Israel in 1978? Why did Iraq invade Kuwait in 1990? Why did Saudi Arabia intervene to suppress Bahrain's revolution in 2011? Why are some MENA regimes pro-Western and others antagonistic to Western interests? In sum, what determines how much a regime will decide to trade, invest, negotiate, engage, ignore, embrace, betray, or ally with its neighbors?

MENA regimes are no different than governments elsewhere in that their foreign policies firstly aim to perpetuate their survival and protect their core interests. Beyond that, foreign policies project their long-term objectives and values in ways that should enhance their reputation and security. As such, foreign policies typically originate from several sources. First, domestically, national constituencies, supporters, and groups within a country favor certain initiatives because it would benefit them. In this theoretical lens, the international behavior of states and regimes comes from the constraints and challenges that rulers face in governing at home. While such a lesson applies clearly to democracies – American presidents, after all, frequently campaign for votes with foreign policy promises, such as less interventionism or more human rights protections – it also applies to autocracies. Dictators cannot rule by force alone, and they need at least some coalition of supporters to legitimate and back their rule. The preferences of those domestic players may well diverge from their own interests, requiring some sort of compromise or adjustment that eventually is expressed in foreign policy. For instance, business moguls may desire for their king or lifelong president to make peace and strike trade deals with former enemies because it would mean greater profits and wealth.

Regionally, leaders also interact with one another within fixed patterns of conflict and cooperation. Most global regions constitute what political scientists call "sub-systems" within the broader international system, which are regulated by particular hierarchies and relationships. Often, regional sub-systems revolve around a major power that creates implicit rules of engagement and polices other countries by virtue of their larger size, economy, or military. In East Asia, for example, China plays this role. In other cases, regional sub-systems can feature recurrent types of conflict, often driven by the intervention of global actors that seek to dominate the region – a scenario the MENA matches. At the same time, the MENA sub-system has its own peculiar features, among them regional organizations like the Arab League, which since its 1945 founding has attempted to foster cooperation and unity among its members. In the Arabian Gulf, the Gulf Cooperation Council since 1981 has served as a weak security and economic alliance, although in the late 2010s it has become paralyzed with internal rifts. Intra-MENA geopolitics also have visible cleavages between regional powers that stem from conflicting interests and ambitions to dominate the regional space, such as the ongoing Saudi-Iranian rivalry, which has forced virtually all states to pick a side as part of their foreign policy.

Finally, internationally, regimes must also navigate their external relations under the constraints imposed by global rules and powerful actors, who may reward or restrict certain behaviors. In developing regions like the MENA, most countries have interacted with the global system under conditions of absolute asymmetry, meaning they have far less autonomy to select new policies than the handful of countries that stand as hegemons. Since the 1990s, for instance, the United States has interacted with Arab states and Iran with the assumption that only the US has the will and capacity to strategically intervene into the domestic affairs of these regions, and sanction or destroy perceived threats; there is no equivalent reciprocal threat that can be made back. Multilateral institutions like the United Nations also operate in the transnational realm, requiring countries to make important decisions regarding their stances and alliances. Globalization also presents a pivotal milieu: whether or not a country chooses to lower trade barriers, end old conflicts, and raise its visibility can reflect structural incentives to better integrate into the global economy and reap its networks of transnational finance, investments, and cultural flows.

To all these causes of foreign policymaking must be added one additional factor; namely the idiosyncratic logic of national leaders. Sometimes, foreign policy may stem not from any domestic, regional, or international factor but instead the particular beliefs of the president or king. For example, Iraq's invasion of Kuwait in 1990 may well have sprung from its authoritarian regime's desire for greater oil resources and to capture regional prestige. Or, it could have expressed the wildly grandiose aspirations of Saddam Hussein, who fancied himself as a pan-Arab leader who could unite the Arab world under a new, singular banner of anti-Western resistance. No matter the cause, foreign policy remains an integral component of every political system.

Democratic regimes

In the post-colonial era, democracy has been scarce in the MENA. Table 1.3 reveals Freedom House scores for political rights at five-year intervals from 1976 through 2018. While no quantitative metric is perfect, Freedom House's index helps capture long-term regime trends by taking into account the regularity and fairness of elections, the scope of opposition toleration and legality, and the effective functioning of government institutions. The scale runs from 1 through 7, and lower is better: scores from 3 to 1 denote democracies of improving quality, while 4 and above identify hybrid regimes and, near the maximum of 7, the most closed dictatorships. The table shows that Israel has consistently qualified as democratic, while Turkey has varied over time due to military coups and, today, overstepping by the government. It also conveys how the Arab Spring's success in Tunisia remarkably changed its political system, as its score has rapidly improved since the pre-2011 years. Minor variations over the decades in countries like Egypt, Jordan, Morocco, and Kuwait reflect periodic reforms that temporarily allow for greater individual freedom but ensure unelected rulers hoard power. Long periods of torpor also characterize the most closed dictatorships, such as Libya until the Arab Spring, Iraq under Saddam, and Saudi Arabia, Sudan, and Syria for decades; in such cases, there are few to no real improvements to the state of political rights, competition, and pluralism.

TABLE 1.3

Average Freedom House scores of political rights, 1973–2018

	1976–1980	1981–1985	1986–1990	1991–1995	1996–2000	2001–2005	2006–2010	2011–2015	2016–2018
Algeria	6	6	5.4	6.2	6	6	6	6	6
Bahrain	5.6	5	5.4	6	7	5.2	5.4	6.2	7
Egypt	5	4.5	5	5.6	6	6	6	5.8	6
Iran	5.4	5.5	5.4	6	6	6	6	6	6
Iraq	6.8	6.5	7	7	7	6.8	5.6	5.4	5
Israel	2	2	2	1.4	1	1	1	1	1
Jordan	6	5.5	5.2	3.8	4	5.2	5.4	6	5.3
Kuwait	6	4	6.2	5.2	4.6	4	4	4.6	5
Lebanon	4	5	5.8	5.8	6	5.8	5	5	5.3
Libya	6.2	6	6.4	7	7	7	7	5.6	6.7
Morocco	3.8	4	4	5.2	5	5	5	5	5
Oman	6	6	6	6	6	6	6	6	6
Palestine (West Bank & Gaza Strip)	5	5	5.4	6	5	5	5.2	6.2	6.5
Qatar	5	5	5.8	7	6.6	6	6	6	6
Saudi Arabia	6	6	6.4	7	7	7	7	7	7
Sudan	5.4	5.2	5.8	7	7	7	7	7	7
Syria	5.2	6	6.4	7	7	7	7	7	7
Tunisia	6	5	5.4	5.8	6	6	6.8	3.4	1.3
Turkey	2.6	3.75	2.4	3.6	4	3.2	3	3	4
UAE	5	5	5.4	6.2	6	6	6	6	6.3
Yemen	6.2	5.75	5.8	5.2	5	5.4	5.4	6	7

Source: Freedom House (2019), Freedom in the World. 1 = most free (e.g., liberal democracies); 7 = least free (e.g., closed dictatorships).

Note: Data for Palestinian territories begin in 1978. Yemen data from 1976 through 1989 is average of North and South Yemen.

Had Libya held together after the Arab Spring, it might well be considered democratic today, as it held early elections and began crafting a new constitutional framework before institutional rules collapsed and internal wrangling deepened. Egypt also experienced a brief window of democracy after 2011, until the July 2013 military coup implanted a new authoritarian regime. Given the brevity of these post-revolutionary experiments, the list of stable MENA democracies is few. Israel is a parliamentary republic led by a prime minister chosen by its legislature, the Knesset. Tunisia's post-Arab Spring political arena abides by a semi-presidential system that balances duties between a president and premier, the latter of whom is chosen by a capable parliament. Turkey featured various types of parliamentary republicanism until 2018, when it shifted to a presidential republic with a greatly weakened legislature. These countries present meaningful elections and civic freedoms, although they are not perfect. Grappling still with unresolved issues of religious and national identity, Israel's laws continue to discriminate against Arab citizens. Tunisia's young democracy has balanced power between Islamists and secularist parties, but its liberal constitution continues to be tested by local unrest and corruption. Turkish politics allows for regular multiparty competition, although increased suppression of dissent under the ruling Justice and Development Party and its long-serving leader, President Recep Tayyip Erdogan, has introduced authoritarian tendencies.

What explains the paucity of democracy in the Arab world and Iran? Arguments that Islam encourages despotism are ethnocentric and misleading, not least because the world's largest Muslim-majority country and third largest democracy is Indonesia. Further, polling organizations like the Pew Research Center and Arab Barometer consistently show that the vast majority of Muslims prefer democracy regardless of their religiosity – something also confirmed by the Arab Spring protests, which demanded freedom, voice, and above all elections. In truth, the longevity of authoritarianism has little to do with any alleged cultural barrier, and instead reflects matter-of-factly the strategies and techniques that autocratic rulers exploit to survive. Among these are institutions calibrated to squelch opposition, widespread intimidation and violence, adroit redistribution of oil wealth, and geopolitical support from global powers prioritizing stability over the uncertainty of democratic change.

Authoritarianism: the republics
Within the camp of authoritarianism, republics in Algeria, Egypt, Syria, and Sudan have historically revolved around dominant presidential figures. Prior

to 2003, Iraq fell into this category; before the Arab Spring, so did Tunisia, Yemen, and Libya. In such systems, parliaments cannot curb the executive and its control over the coercive apparatus, including the security services and the army. Some dictators inherit power. In Syria, Bashar al-Asad came to power in 1999 after the death of his father, Hafiz. Others seize power through coups, as Muammar al-Qaddafi did in Libya in 1969. Once ensconced, however, they do not leave quietly. Most refuse to hold meaningful elections, and instead only offer half-hearted plebiscites (as in Libya, Syria, Iraq, and Tunisia for decades) or else sabotage ballot boxes with such grotesque fraudulence and repression that the decimated opposition has no credible chance of winning. Former Egyptian president Hosni Mubarak swept his reelection in 2005 with nearly 90 percent of the vote, for instance, while in 1999, Ali Abdallah Salih of Yemen retained power with over 96 percent of all ballots. In 2007, Bashar Al-Asad was "re-elected" with a 99.8 percent margin of victory; in the purportedly more competitive 2014 elections, he still garnered nearly 90 percent.

Iran's Islamic Republic, the product of its 1979 revolution, represents a special case of theocratic presidentialism. The Iranian constitution allows for competitive parliamentary and presidential elections that often shows spirited contestation, but such contests are overshadowed by the tutelary power of Shi'a jurists who can screen candidates, dismiss the president, and, above all, select the *rahbar* (supreme leader) – the highest political and religious authority in the land. This dualistic system ensures that even if opposition forces win elections, unelected religious authorities keep superlative power to control the state and veto unwanted policies.

Two institutions secure republican dictatorships: hegemonic political parties and the coercive apparatus. In the post-colonial Arab countries, most presidential dictators headed party organizations that descended from the leftist and nationalist movements of the 1950s and 1960s. On paper, these parties existed to mobilize voters for elections, but as elections had little import, they supported the leadership in other ways. Ruling parties rallied popular opinion, unified bickering elites, and distributed patronage to supporters. For instance, Zine al-Abidine Ben Ali of Tunisia ruled for more than two decades through the Democratic Constitutional Rally, which had dominated politics under different names since the 1950s. After its rise, the Ba'th Party became deeply incorporated into Iraqi and Syrian state institutions, and helped burnish the long tenures of Saddam Hussein and Hafiz al-Asad. In Algeria, similarly, the National Liberation Front was the only party allowed until 1989, and all top political officials hailed from its ranks.

In most authoritarian MENA states (including the monarchies), the coercive apparatus serves as the linchpin. Its most visible manifestations are the intelligence services and the armed forces. The intelligence services (in Arabic, *mukhabarat*) operate to eliminate political threats through surveillance and intimidation at all levels – within universities, businesses, clubs, homes, even ruling parties. Not all methods are overtly violent; detention, harassment, and legal prosecution often prove sufficient to suffocate troublesome critics, such as human rights activists, religious groups, and trade unions. However, they are not invulnerable. Even the most rapacious intelligence and police forces can be overwhelmed by mass spontaneous revolts driven by citizens who no longer fear repression, as the Arab Spring showed. In addition, the military also plays an integral role in some republics. Inspired by Turkey's Kemalist ideology, many militaries in post-colonial Arab countries saw themselves as guardians of the state and hence above all reproach. That praetorian mentality meant that many presidents would come from military ranks, most famously Nasser of Egypt. Other officers-turned-leaders include al-Qaddafi of Libya, Salih of Yemen, Ben Ali of Tunisia, Hafiz al-Asad of Syria, and Mubarak of Egypt. The current Egyptian president, Abdel Fattah al-Sisi, is a former army general.

For this reason, most Arab militaries enjoy special privileges and big budgets. Tunisia under Ben Ali during 1987–2011 was a rare exception, as he relied more upon the intelligence services rather than the army for support – a preference that ultimately cost him dearly, as the military sided with protesters during the successful 2011 Jasmine Revolution. Closer to the norm are Algeria and Egypt, where the armed forces enjoy a huge independent domain of economic interests and institutional clout. When necessary, they can crack down upon large-scale threats. During its civil conflict in the 1990s, the Algerian military waged unending operations against Islamist militants, with nearly 150,000 perishing in the violence. In Syria, the military besieged the town of Hama in 1982 to dismantle the Muslim Brotherhood, killing 10,000; today, its tenacious loyalty and international support has helped keep the Asad regime in power despite the state of devastation in Syria. Most recently in Egypt, the army under President Sisi helped liquidate the Muslim Brotherhood after overthrowing the elected Islamist government in 2013, with the resulting unrest killing thousands of protesters.

Authoritarianism: ruling monarchies

Eight of the Arab countries feature monarchical regimes. Around the world, most monarchies are constitutionalized because the royal head of state reigns but does not rule, as in Spain or Japan. In the MENA, however, monarchies still reign *and* rule. In such systems, while there may be an elected parliament with a cabinet-based government led by a prime minister, the royal head (e.g., king, emir, sultan) holds almost all executive authority and can promulgate laws by decree. Moreover, royal authority is inherited through dynastic succession within the family, not contested by the public through elections. Abdication is rare, with one example coming from Qatar's al-Thani dynasty in 2013, when Emir Hamad vacated power in favor of his son, Crown Prince Tamim bin Hamad. Otherwise, succession lines are agnatic (i.e., based upon the male line) but vary in terms of which familial branches are favored. In Saudi Arabia, the throne has circulated among the elderly sons of the kingdom's founder, 'Abd al-Aziz ibn Saud, since his death in 1953; only after the passing of the current ruler, the ailing King Salman, will power pass to the next generation – most likely the current Crown Prince Muhammad bin Salman, the king's son. In Oman, Sultan Qabus captured his position in 1970 from his father, Sultan Sa'id bin Taimur. More familiar to Western audiences are succession lines in which the crown passes from father to son. King Muhammad VI of Morocco and King Abdullah II of Jordan both ascended to power after the deaths of their long-serving fathers in 1999, for instance.

Like their republican counterparts, monarchs keep tight grips over the coercive apparatus. By contrast, they have little need for dominant political parties, which serve little purpose as they cannot be voted out of office. Instead, they must reach out to supporters through other institutions. In Jordan, the king's court (in Arabic, *diwan*) serves as a shadow government, with a bureaucracy that consults with tribal *shaykhs* (chieftains) and other societal allies regularly. Within the larger royal families of the Gulf, rulers also employ the strategy known as dynasticism, or appointing their relatives to high-ranking positions in order to cement ties of familial loyalty. The UAE presents a unique monarchical form, as it is a federation of six royal families that collectively rule through a rotating council.

Furthermore, parliaments can coexist with authoritarian monarchies. The largely unelected assemblies in Saudi Arabia, Qatar, and the UAE do not count, as they have only consultative roles and their membership is almost exclusively appointed. Morocco, Jordan, Kuwait, Bahrain, and Oman legally tolerate elected legislatures where opposition forces can contest some seats, alongside royal allies jockeying for influence such as businessmen, tribal leaders, and elite brokers. Yet such legislative bodies have few powers. They cannot form committees to investigate royal spending, military affairs, or other privileged domains. They do not control the police or intelligence apparatus, and neither can they set foreign policy. Further, the highest offices of government on paper, such as the Prime Minister and the cabinet, are appointed by the monarchy, ensuring that no radical voices enter political circulation. The rulers of Bahrain and Kuwait also keep the premiership within the family, always assigning the position to a senior prince. If all else fails, monarchs can suspend parliaments altogether during periods of crisis, as Emir Jabir of Kuwait did between 1986 to 1992 and King Abdullah did in Jordan between 2001 and 2003.

The Arab ruling monarchies are commonly said to persist because they enjoy traditional legitimacy. However, dynastic absolutism has little cultural resonance in the modern Middle Eastern experience. Consider that in 1950, almost all the region lived under some type of kingship. Yet over the next thirty years, coups and revolutions exterminated royal autocracies in Egypt (1952), Tunisia (1957), Iraq (1958), North Yemen (1962), Libya (1969), and Iran (1979). Moreover, when citizens flooded streets during the Arab Spring, they called for democracy by elections, not a return to hereditary rule. In religious terms, royal absolutism also does not automatically flow from Islamic ideals. While the Hashemites and Alaouites descend from the Prophet's family lineage, and the House of Saud acts as custodian to the holy cities of Mecca and Medina, not even they claim a divine right to rule. Under Islam, the heavens do not appoint kings, who can no more speak to God than peasants. Leadership must instead be qualified on pragmatic grounds – to protect the Muslim community against foreign threats, for instance, or ensure commerce and public safety.

Hybrid regimes

In Lebanon, Iraq, Libya, and Palestine, hybrid regimes exist. These possess the electoral backbone of democracy, and even present political institutions that could theoretically govern fairly. Yet they are hobbled by serious institutional problems that preclude fair competition and political participation from occurring at the national scale. Those flaws can emanate from many sources, ranging from violent conflict to biased laws and rules that favor powerful elites.

For instance, Lebanon's semi-presidential republic allows for regular parliamentary elections, but its system embodies confessionalism: it allocates state offices and legislative seats to ethnic and religious sects according to a rigid formula to ensure balance. Competition occurs within these communities, but not across them, thereby creating a highly fractured landscape making governance difficult. However, many believe that overturning this system would spark the kind of communal warfare suffered in the 1975–90 civil war that killed 150,000. Lebanese politics also suffered from the country's occupation by its neighbors, with Israel only withdrawing in 2000 and Syria in 2005. In the Palestinian territories, the Palestinian Authority, which was established by the 1993 Oslo Accords as part of the vision of a two-state solution to the Israeli-Palestinian crisis, is technically a democracy styled as a semi-presidential republic. However, widespread corruption and abuses of power have marred internal governance, which has also been interrupted by frequent Israeli occupations and constraints. Moreover, the 2006 parliamentary elections resulted in Hamas' shock victory over the secular Fatah Party, the dominant group in Palestinian politics. This fractured the government, increased tensions with Israel, and did little to halt the flow of Israeli settlers into the West Bank, who number over 400,000 as of 2019.

In Iraq and Libya, fragmentation and conflict has impeded democracy. Both adopted parliamentary democracies after the downfall of their dictatorships due to foreign intervention, the former with the American-led invasion in 2003 and the latter with the 2011 NATO-led intervention in the Arab Spring. However, the post-war regime in Iraq did little to overcome tensions between the Shi'a majority, Sunni minority, and Kurdish community. Over the next decade, sectarian violence, flawed elections, and the Islamic State's bloody rise all worked to disconnect the Iraqi public's faith in the democratic process. Similarly, Libya's post-Qaddafi transition allowed for competitive elections until infighting between militia groups and political factions split the country into two competing governments in late 2014, each claiming legitimacy. Recurrent violence, including more recent attacks by the Islamic State and other extremist networks, has also hobbled the political system.

As a special note, as of 2019, Yemen remains in institutional limbo outside these categories of regime types. Its authoritarian republic under President Salih ended during the Arab Spring, but foreign pressures and internal skirmishes prevented democratic elections from creating a unitary successor regime. Its transitional government has been beset by the Houthi movement and countervailing separatism in the south, while the Saudi-led military intervention has destabilized the country, created the worst humanitarian disaster since the Syrian Civil War, and induced doubts that Yemen might ever be unified again.

This brief evaluation of different regime types unpacked the institutions, rulers, and processes. It describes the present circumstance. Yet as the introduction to this chapter invoked, we cannot comprehend the region's present without reaching back to the past to trace its long-term historical trajectory. The next section therefore tackles the region's modern political development, to provide a bird's-eye view of MENA politics as it has evolved over time.

REGIONAL POLITICAL HISTORY: EVENTS AND PATTERNS

The Middle East echoes with antiquity. The region gave birth to the great monotheistic faiths – Judaism, Christianity, and Islam – and many cities date back more than a thousand years and evoke the glory of empires past, such as Alexandria, Baghdad, Cairo, Damascus, Fez, Istanbul, Jerusalem, and Mecca. This heritage began in the Near East, which hosted some of the earliest recorded civilizations during the Bronze Age. The Fertile Crescent in present-day Iraq gave rise to the Sumerian Kingdom after 4,000 BC, while the Nile River nourished Ancient Egypt beginning about 3,200 BC. Other major civilizations included the Akkadians, Babylonians, Assyrians, and Phoenicians. In central Turkey, the Hittite Empire arose after 1,600 BC; after 1,200 BC, Greek colonists flocked to the Anatolian coast. The Kingdoms of Israel and Judah emerged around 1,000 BC. After 550 BC, the Achaemenids – the first Persian Empire – rose to prominence and from Iran expanded to the Levant, Turkey, and Egypt. Alexander the Great conquered these lands and left a Greek imprint that would last long after his death in 323 BC. Further west in present-day Tunisia, Carthage had emerged in 814 BC to rule over the western Mediterranean until its demise seven centuries later at the hands of Rome.

All these early civilizations achieved milestones in human history. Among them were settled agriculture and the cultivation of wheat; the first written alphabets, languages, and laws; and breakthroughs in mathematics, timekeeping, and metallurgy. The Roman Empire came to rule much of the MENA by the first century BC, and the Roman province of Judea, which today overlaps parts of Israel and the Palestinian West Bank, was the birthplace of Jesus Christ. In the twilight of Roman power in the fourth century AD, Emperor Constantine I legalized Christianity and moved the empire's capital eastward to Byzantium, known later as Constantinople (now Istanbul). Whereas Western Roman provinces in Europe collapsed by 476 AD, the Byzantine Empire would subsist for another millennium. Its only rival was the Sassanian Empire, also known as the Second Persian Empire, which occupied Iran, Iraq, and the eastern parts of the Arabian Peninsula.

The beginning of Islam and the Arab-Islamic Caliphate

As Europe underwent the Middle Ages, the story of Islam – the last great Abrahamic faith – began. Islam arose in the Arabian Peninsula. Whereas the south (present-day Yemen) saw small kingdoms come and go after 1,000 BC and the eastern shores fell under Persian influence, the western region, called the Hijaz, escaped external domination. The domestication of the camel around 3,000 BC made possible not only tribal nomadism but also commercial trade and travel, giving rise to towns like Medina and Mecca. In the latter, the year 610 AD saw a merchant named Muhammad receive a divine revelation. Revealing himself as God's last messenger, Muhammad and his teachings became the basis of Islam. The year 622 AD saw the *hijra*, or migration, of the Prophet Muhammad and his believers from Mecca to Medina, an event that also marks the beginning of the Islamic calendar. The Prophet eventually returned to Mecca and conquered much of Arabia before his death in 632 AD.

Thus began the epoch of the Arab-Islamic Caliphates, which for the next six centuries beheld various dynasties ruling over a massive empire. Each Caliphate represented not just a form of political governance but also Islamic unity. The title of the leader, Caliph, derives from the Arabic word *khalifah*, which means "successor" – successor to the Prophet as political and spiritual head of the Muslim community, or *ummah*. Yet who could succeed Muhammad was hotly debated. Many believed that Abu Bakr, Muhammad's father-in-law, was the rightful successor, whereas others preferred Ali, Muhammad's son-in-law and cousin. Most supported Abu Bakr, who after the Prophet's death became ruler of the first Caliphate, the Rashidun (632–661 AD), but discord lingered. Ali eventually ascended as the fourth Caliph in 656 AD, but many rejected his authority, creating turmoil and paving the way for a second Caliphate under the Umayyad dynasty, based in Damascus (661–750 AD). Most rejected calls to allow Ali's son, Hussein, to become Caliph; in turn, Hussein's faction refused to recognize Umayyad authority, holding Ali's descendants instead as the Prophet's legitimate successors. The followers of Ali became the Shi'a sect, whose various groups now represent 10 to 15 percent of all Muslims worldwide. Most of the opposing majority assumed the basis of what we now call Sunni Islam.

At the time of its collapse in 750 AD, the Umayyad Caliphate comprised not just the Middle East and North Africa but also much of Spain and Portugal, as well as present-day Pakistan, Afghanistan, and Central Asia. This was an area of six million square miles, or three times the size of the Roman Empire, although frequent rebellions meant that central authority was tenuous. The 'Abbasid Caliphate arose next, based in Baghdad (750–1258). While this Sunni dynasty technically lasted for five centuries, internal fragmentation worsened. The position of Caliph was reduced from political ruler to religious figurehead, and smaller dynasties controlled many areas. The Shi'a Fatimids, for instance, ruled Egypt from 969 to 1171. Despite such strife, the 'Abbasid era heralded a golden age for Islam in terms of commerce, medicine, science, philosophy, literature, and other achievements. The oldest degree-granting university in the world, the University of al-Karaouine, was founded during this period in 859 AD in Fez, Morocco; in 970 AD the Fatimids oversaw the creation of al-Azhar University in Egypt, which still serves as one of Sunni Islam's foremost centers of theological education.

The last 'Abbasid centuries saw migration and invasions. New Turkic peoples came from Central Asia, with most adopting Sunni Islam. Some bolstered 'Abbasid rule in Baghdad, while others headed toward Anatolia. Among them were the Seljuks, who captured most Byzantine lands save Constantinople by 1081 and later ruled much of Persia; and the Ottomans, who claimed a modest *beylik* (principality) in northern Turkey by the late 1200s – the seed of their future empire. In addition, European Crusaders, starting in 1096, pushed into the Mashriq, while from the east came the Mongols. Their sacking of Baghdad in 1258 ended the Caliphate.

Ottoman decline, World War One, and western imperialism

The story of the modern Middle East begins with the rise and fall of the last Islamic Caliphate, the Ottoman Empire. After 1299, the Ottoman Turks began enlarging their territorial reach in western Anatolia, eventually swallowing the last Byzantine remnants. By the time Constantinople fell in 1453, the nascent empire had spread across the Aegean Sea into present-day Greece, Bulgaria, and parts of Romania. Ottoman expansion continued, and in 1517 the ruling sultan proclaimed himself Caliph, reviving the ideal of the ummah. At its zenith in 1683, the Ottoman Empire extended from the MENA into central Europe, including the Balkans and Hungary, and nearly conquered Vienna. This period coincided with the rise of the rival Safavid Empire in Iran in 1501. Whereas the Ottomans prolonged the tradition of the Caliphate under Sunni Islam, the Persian Safavid *shahs* (kings) established Shi'a Islam as their state religion. The Safavid dynasty lasted until 1736; by then, Iran had solidified its status as the epicenter of Shi'a learning, doctrine, and authority.

Ottoman primacy waned starting in the 1700s, due to political infighting and competition with the Persian Safavid and European Hapsburg empires.

By the 1850s, industrializing Europe had eclipsed the Ottomans for technological, economic, and military supremacy. Several sultans attempted to arrest this alarming internal decay by ordering the modernization of political institutions, economic practices, and social life – the infamous *tanzimat* (reorganization). Still, Western pressure and nationalist awakenings forced the Ottomans to relinquish most of its European lands, and by 1912 they had lost all of North Africa to British, French, and Italian colonialism. London also took dominion over the Arabian Gulf by signing defense treaties with the tribal shaykhs ruling over the eastern coastal provinces, such as the Sabah dynasty of Kuwait, the Nahyan family of Abu Dhabi, and the Thani clan of Qatar – tribal families that, today, remain the ruling monarchies of their states. Iran suffered similar relegation. Its Qajar dynasty had arisen in 1794 with great aspirations, but over the following century Russian invasions and British trade pressures thwarted the ambitions of Persian shahs. Britain deepened its presence in the country after striking oil in southwestern Iran in 1908, the MENA's first large-scale oil discovery.

World War One heralded the age of Western dominion. By then, the Ottoman Empire covered just Turkey, the Mashriq, and parts of the Hijaz. Few Muslims still saw the sultans as true Caliphs, brandishing political and religious authority as successors to the Prophet. Qajar power in Iran was also greatly weakened through economic and political inertia. World War One sealed their fates, but was particularly traumatic for the Ottomans, who lost the conflict as part of the Central Powers. Famously, Ottoman lands in the Mashriq gave rise to the Arab Revolt after the British government persuaded tribal shaykhs to join its cause. Among these allies was Hussein bin Ali, the *sharif* (steward and protector) of Mecca, whose Sunni family – the Hashemite dynasty – descended from the Prophet Muhammad's tribe and clan. Sir Henry McMahon, a high-ranking British diplomat, promised Sharif Hussein that Britain would support an independent Arab kingdom after the war, once these Ottoman territories were liberated.

However, Britain and France instead colluded in the 1916 Sykes-Picot Agreement to divide the Mashriq amongst themselves. The 1920 San Remo Conference carved this area into mandates sanctioned by the League of Nations. The French assumed authority over Lebanon and Syria, while the British invented Iraq and Transjordan (later renamed Jordan) and administered Palestine (now Israel and the Palestinian territories). Britain chose two of Sharif Hussein's sons, Faysal and Abdullah, to be new monarchs of Iraq and Jordan, respectively. Mandatory Palestine was another matter, as tensions rose between Jewish and Arab settlers. In the 1880s, the

Jewish nationalist movement known as Zionism encouraged European Jews to emigrate to Palestine with the dream of creating a Jewish homeland. In 1917, British Foreign Secretary Arthur Balfour pledged support for that goal. Following the war, internecine violence escalated between Zionist settlers and the larger Arab population. After World War Two, Britain turned over the crisis to the United Nations, which partitioned Palestine into Jewish and Arab states in May 1948. Several Arab armies invaded shortly afterward. This first Arab-Israeli War ended with the independence of Israel, unsettled scores, and the exodus of seven hundred thousand Arab refugees – the Palestinians – many of whom left for adjacent countries like Jordan and Lebanon.

Such events encapsulated a wider pattern of political reformation from the 1920s to 1940s. In some cases, internal disturbances swept away old dynasties and created new political orders. In the Ottoman heartland of Anatolia, Kemal Ataturk led national resistance against the imperial government and foreign occupation. Abolishing the Islamic Caliphate, in 1923 Ataturk established the Republic of Turkey, which exemplified the new secularist ideology of Kemalism. In Iran, army officer Reza Khan deposed the enfeebled Qajars in 1921 and enthroned himself as shah of the new Pahlavi monarchy. By contrast, the Arab world coalesced into sovereign states through the hand of Western cartography. A few were claimed as colonies for settlement by European powers, such as Italian Libya, British Aden (in Yemen), and French Algeria. Most Arab countries, however, were protectorates, in that local authorities had to coexist with a European patron who held the strings of sovereignty through military basing, oil concessions, financial dependence, and other forms of territorial control.

Though brief, this age of Western colonialism left profound legacies. First, it etched out new boundaries without regard to preexisting ethnic cleavages and religious rifts. The hodgepodge societies of Iraq and Libya are testament to such map-making. Western powers also favored certain groups in divided societies, as the British did by privileging Bahrain's Sunni Khalifah family over the island's Shi'a majority; this had the effect of amplifying regnant tensions and planting the seeds for future sectarianism. Second, European powers radically transformed domestic politics by picking and choosing their favored rulers. For instance, in this pre-oil era, the small tribal dynasties of eastern Arabia like the Thani family of Qatar and the Sabah family of Kuwait struggled to regulate nearby tribes and rival merchants. By signing exclusive defense treaties with these clans, the British essentially transformed their tenuous claims to power into permanent rights. The French similarly transformed the Alaouite monarchy of Morocco, pacifying the last Berber rebellions by the 1920s and thus guaranteeing the dynasty's future.

Third, imperial policies prioritized stability over all else, encouraging routines of autocratic rule. In Algeria, French administrators poured resources into policing and settlement, displacing many local communities; in British protectorates like Jordan, the first national institutions were not universities and hospitals, but armies and bureaucracies designed to maximize social control. Colonial administrators gave little thought to economic development. Hence, agrarian countries like Iraq and Morocco not only remained impoverished but also suffered from extreme land inequality, with a wealthy elite owning most agricultural property. Fourth, oil exploration took off, thanks to major finds in Iran, Iraq, Kuwait, Bahrain, Saudi Arabia, and the Sultanate of Muscat (in present-day Oman). British and American companies controlled most oil production and lent their support to local rulers. For instance, the Kingdom of Saudi Arabia formed in 1932 after its contemporary founder, 'Abd al-Aziz ibn Saud, conquered other tribes, but only survived afterward through American recognition and royalty payments from American oil companies.

New sovereignty and post-colonial politics

These legacies made post-colonial state formation unpropitious. Some Arab countries gained independence before World War Two, such as Egypt (1922) and Iraq (1932), but most became internationally recognized states afterward. World War Two brought intense fighting to North Africa and parts of the Near East, while Russian and British forces occupied Iran to secure its oilfields. In the end, the war decimated European imperial powers, forcing them to abandon their overseas empires. In the Middle East, among the first to earn formal sovereignty were Jordan and Syria (1946); the last were Bahrain, Qatar, and the UAE (1971). North Yemen was already an independent kingdom, but South Yemen resulted from the British abandoning its Crown Colony of Aden in 1967. Not all decolonization was so anticlimactic: France fought a brutal war to retain Algeria during 1954–62, resulting in a million deaths.

At this post-colonial dawn, the kings and presidents of the Middle East and North Africa eagerly joined the new international system. Turkey, Iran, Egypt, Iraq, Lebanon, Syria, and Saudi Arabia were among the UN's founding members in 1945, and the Arab League was also created that year. Yet the real challenges to political stability would come not from the outside world but from within. While most MENA countries had the external appearance of statehood, internally many rulers stood on precarious ground and lacked mass support. Imperial habits meant they were more accustomed to upholding security through iron fists than allowing democratic participation, fostering economic inclusion, or rallying popular sympathies.

The result was instability starting in the 1950s, when a wave of secular leftist and nationalist movements mobilized across the Arab world and Iran. These movements drew upon the new urban middle class, such as army officers, teachers, students, lawyers, and engineers. The most vocal movement, the Arab Nationalists, desired to unify the Arab world, promote economic justice, and end subordination to the West. They targeted not only Israel but also enduring reminders of foreign humiliation, such as Franco-British ownership of Egypt's Suez Canal, British military bases in Jordan, and Libya's lopsided oil concessions to Anglo-American firms. A watershed moment came in 1952 when, in Egypt, a group of these Arab Nationalists led by Gamal Abdel Nasser upended the monarchy and seized power; four years later, Nasser nationalized the Suez Canal, leading Israel, Britain, and France to invade. Nasser's Egypt thus became the charismatic vanguard of Arab resistance against Western hegemony. Over the next two decades, more coups and revolutions would create new republics in Syria, Iraq, Algeria, Libya, and North and South Yemen. Oman nearly broke apart during the Dhufar Rebellion, while Iran's embattled Pahlavi monarchy survived only with American help.

As domestic political struggles abounded, so did superpower meddling. The Cold War saw the United States and Soviet Union see the region as a strategic chessboard connected to their wider global competition, and each sought to carve out their interests. Most of all, they wooed the loyalties of different regimes with offers of diplomatic, economic, and military support. For instance, from 1946 to 1990, the United States spent $92 billion in delivering economic and military aid to favored MENA clients and would-be allies, nearly double the amount it donated to sub-Saharan Africa and Latin America combined. Generally, the Arab Nationalist republics aligned themselves with the Soviet Union, which also supported the Palestinian cause, while the more conservative monarchies plus Israel looked toward the West. Neither superpower promoted democracy, and both accepted the autocratic abuses of these clients. Iran and Turkey were frontline states to this geopolitical discord. Iran, aligned with the United States and quietly supporting Israel, concentrated on Arabian Gulf security and its own development, at least until its revolution. Turkey had made great economic and military strides under the republican system created by Ataturk, and it served as a pro-Western bulwark within the Northern Atlantic Treaty Organization (NATO). The Turkish military protected this posture, given its status as the guardian of the state; indeed, it would undertake several coups from the 1960s through 1980s against civilian governments deemed threatening to national interests.

Above all, Arab conflict with Israel was a frequent flashpoint of foreign intervention and regional violence. The Arab-Israeli War of 1967 had titanic consequences, as Israel defeated a much larger pan-Arab force and began receiving significant US economic and military aid. Three Arab states lost Palestinian lands they had administered since 1948: Egypt lost the Gaza Strip; Jordan, the West Bank and Jerusalem; and Syria, the Golan Heights. Another Palestinian exodus occurred, with hundreds of thousands of refugees fleeing mostly to Jordan and Syria. The 1973 Arab-Israeli War ended in stalemate that further inflamed regional frictions. Magnifying such tension was ongoing terrorism by the Palestinian Liberation Organization (PLO) and other militant groups aligned with the Palestinian cause. Israel's pursuit of the PLO led to its 1982 invasion of Lebanon, then suffering from a vicious civil war magnified by Arab and Western interventions.

The 1970s and 1980s saw deepening entanglements and complications. The Arab members of the Organization of Petroleum Exporting Countries (OPEC) imposed an oil embargo against America in 1973 as retaliation for supporting Israel. As economic downturn struck the United States, the region's oil exporters experienced unprecedented wealth – fortunes that would reverse when oil prices crashed a decade later. Another major twist came shortly after the embargo, when Egypt and Israel signed their monumental peace deal in 1978 through the US-sponsored Camp David Accords. A more ambitious multilateral round of Arab-Israeli peace talks would follow in the early 1990s, resulting in the 1993 Oslo Accord between Israel and the PLO, and the 1994 Israel-Jordan Peace Treaty. In the late 1970s, though, the Egyptian-Israeli peace reverberated throughout the region; it shocked some and disappointed many in the Arab world.

Another shockwave came from the 1979 Iranian Revolution, which overthrew the Pahlavi monarchy and inspired new Islamist mobilization across the region. Arab nationalism and leftist movements had begun losing their allure in the 1970s, as the dream of a united pan-Arab state, Palestinian liberation, and economic prosperity stumbled against the backdrop of wars and stagnation. Nasser's death in 1970 was also a psychological blow. Many in the urban middle classes turned to Islamism, which held that political and social renewal required restoring conservative religious values and rejecting Western influences. The new Islamic Republic of Iran embodied this trend. Many nervous regimes in the Arab world reacted by repressing their Islamist movements, but such groups were not all the same. Moderate Islamists advocated peaceful and lawful change; today, Jordan's Muslim Brotherhood and Kuwait's Islamic Constitutional Movement are exemplars. More radical varieties pursued change through violence and terrorism. Hizbullah and Hamas are infamous examples that emerged during the 1980s, the former from the Lebanese Civil War and the latter from the 1987–91 Palestinian Intifada, or uprising, against Israeli occupation.

The Iranian Revolution also foreshadowed future regional conflict organized along sectarian lines. The Islamic Republic soured to neighboring Iraq, then led by the leftist-nationalist Ba'th Party under Saddam Hussein. The 1980–88 Iran-Iraq War killed nearly a million people and financially drained a region already struggling from low oil prices. America intervened by protecting oil tankers in the Arabian Gulf against attack; one confrontation with Iranian ships drew the United States into its largest naval battle since World War Two. A hobbled Iraq then invaded Kuwait in 1990. This precipitated the 1991 Gulf War, when a Western-led coalition liberated Kuwait and imposed wide-ranging United Nations sanctions on Iraq. Meanwhile, the unification of North and South Yemen in 1990 resulted in a period of civil violence. More hopeful was the 1989 Ta'if Agreement, which ended the Lebanese Civil War.

1990s to the present: American hegemony, the Arab Spring, and regional uncertainty

With the Cold War's sudden end in 1991, the United States assumed hegemony over much of the MENA. Indeed, the 1990s represented a time of gradual regional realignment after the rupture of the Gulf War, as America assumed the primary role as the guarantor of security for the region. The decade was not conflict-free even after the liberation of Kuwait; civil wars wracked newly unified Yemen and Sudan, the latter of which contributed to the eventual separation of South Sudan in 2011. Still, major initiatives all featured American fingerprints. For example, the United States helped guide the Oslo Accords, which called for a negotiated Arab-Palestinian peace through a two-state solution in which both Israel and the Palestinians would lead their own sovereign entities. The first step was allowing for self-government in the West Bank and Gaza Strip with the creation of the Palestinian Authority (PA) – a monumental event that resonated throughout the Arab world, where many had long seen the Palestinian struggle as the rare injustice that could draw everyone into consensus.

However, indivisible disagreements, such as the status of Jerusalem and territorial boundaries, as well as inconsistent Western support, blocked the implementation of this two-state solution under the Clinton administration. Frustrations boiled over during the costly Second Intifada in the early 2000s and resulted in Hamas's triumph in the 2006 Palestinian parliamentary elections, which split the PA. Israeli resistance to peacemaking also deepened after the Likud Party emerged as a dominant party in the early 2000s, resulting in more uncompromising Israeli demands. Needless to say, much like the Bush administration, the United States under President Barack Obama made little progress toward an Oslo-guided peace deal. More recently, the Trump administration all but admitted the two-state solution was dead in a controversial February 2017 meeting with Israeli Prime Minister Binyamin Netanyahu.

America's greater visibility in regional affairs also made it a target. Al-Qa'ida, a radical Islamist network founded by Arab veterans of the Soviet-Afghan War, orchestrated the 9/11 terrorist attacks in New York and Washington. In response, the United States and its allies launched a global war on terror beginning with the invasion of Afghanistan, where many of these militants were based. In 2003, the United States invaded Iraq, claiming Iraq had stockpiled weapons of mass destruction; when few such arsenals were found, the war's justification shifted to the need to promote democracy, as occupying forces toppled Saddam Hussein's dictatorship. Leaders in most other Arab countries, as well as Turkey, nervously sought to maintain political stability in a time of global interventionism. Notably, public opinion in almost every Arab society opposed the Iraq War. In some countries, such as Egypt and Saudi Arabia, regimes faced pressures to enact democratic reform by a Bush administration hoping to remake the MENA into a more liberal region, but most autocratic rulers successfully deflected such demands.

Geopolitically, Iran also began flexing greater muscle, pursuing nuclear enrichment programs while supporting Hizbullah in Lebanon, Palestinian Hamas, and Shi'a factions in Iraq. Perceiving this as a threat, the United States led the charge for intensifying international sanctions against Tehran. The result was a new "cold war" in the MENA starting in the late 2000s, often framed in sectarian terms as a coalition of Sunni Arab countries backed by Israel and the West aligned against the so-called "Shi'a Crescent" led by Iran. The 2015 Iran nuclear deal briefly changed this hardline narrative by proposing to lift sanctions in exchange for nuclear demilitarization, thereby helping Tehran end its isolation. However, in 2018, the Trump administration withdrew from the framework and re-imposed sanctions on Iran to the applause of many Arab states and Israel, returning the Arabian Gulf zone to a climate of near-war. Turkey sought to maintain guarded neutrality in these affairs; though no longer intending to join the European Union as many thought in decades past, neither did it wish to get drawn into broader conflicts.

The most momentous post-Cold War rupture, however, came not from foreign powers but from frustrated citizens and youths desiring economic and political change. In June 2009, fraudulent presidential elections in Iran elicited the youth-driven Green Movement, which held the largest protests the country had witnessed since the revolution. Then in December 2010, a Tunisian fruit vendor immolated himself in response to police harassment; that sacrificial act of defiance sparked a cascade of popular uprisings known as the Arab Spring. Protests, unrest, and resistance over the next couple of years spread like contagion and diffused like oxygen, as a combination of factors such as social media and grassroots activism gave rise to near-simultaneous confrontations between authoritarian regimes and popular movements in many countries. Demonstrations for social justice also burst forth in Israel and Turkey, the latter entering its second decade of governance by an Islamist party. Israel's own popular movements for social justice mobilized over a quarter-million protesters in August 2011 alone, aggrieved by declining living standards and political corruption.

Yet the Arab world remained ground zero, and it was here that the loudest explosions resounded. By 2012, autocratic presidents had fallen from power in Tunisia, Libya, Egypt, and Yemen, while Bahrain's monarchy narrowly avoided overthrow thanks to Saudi military intervention. What began as blooms of people power, however, turned into a darker winter. In 2013, a military coup in Egypt toppled the elected Islamist government, installing a harsher dictatorship. Libya's fragile new democracy splintered as its weak state fragmented into warring camps. So did Yemen, which also became subject to a 2015 Saudi-led military intervention that deepened its civil war and destroyed any semblance of domestic governance. Syria's revolution in 2011 was halted by the Asad regime's unrelenting repression, which resulted in eight years of internal warfare that butchered a half-million people and fueled the violent rise of the Islamic State terrorist group. The Islamic State's conquests in Syria and Iraq prompted Russia, Iran, and the West to intervene militarily, resulting in its defeat; as a corollary, the Asad regime retained power despite the displacement of nearly half of Syria's pre-war domestic population.

As the 2010s come to an end, political uncertainty looms over the MENA in two regards. First, the democratic aspirations of the Arab Spring have been largely unfulfilled, with only Tunisia having become a peaceful, stable democracy. In the other two democracies, namely Israel and Turkey, the same controversial political parties that formed the government a decade earlier remain political centerpieces – the Likud Party and AK Party, respectively. However, while the *supply* of democracy may be lacking outside of a handful of countries, the *demand* for it has not subsided. In most Arab states and Iran, youth-heavy societies continue to mobilize for various issues, discontent with the constraints placed upon their civic and social freedoms. In spring 2019, in fact, new national protest movements rocked the authoritarian regimes of Sudan and Algeria, two countries mostly untouched by the earlier Arab Spring. That this book and chapter are published before their stories are complete is testament to how unpredictable the politics in this region can be.

Second, the MENA has become strategically hewed by new axes of conflict in a way that encages many societies to violence and instability. Israel and many Arab states see Iran's expansion of its regional interests as a mortal threat, and this issue – not nationalism, the Arab-Israeli conflict, nor religion – has become the main agenda-setting item for their foreign policies. At the same time, many localized tensions persist as well, from the frosty Moroccan-Algerian affairs to the Saudi-Qatari rivalry. The Palestinian issue remains moribund. And while the United States is still the most formidable global power, the region is becoming increasingly penetrated by other external forces, among them Russia and China, whose governments sense an increasingly exhausted America reaching the limits of its influence.

CONCLUSION

The Middle East and North Africa is a vast and ancient region. Yet it is not unknowable: the economic structures, political institutions, and social forces shaping these countries today can be analyzed systematically, as this introductory chapter has made clear. Understanding the states and regimes residing in the region, as well as the historical legacies upon which they stand, is the first step towards breaking down the Orientalist wall.

However, politics does not only entail elites and governments bickering at each other. Structural factors also shape the political arena of every country. For this reason, the next chapter shifts gears and focuses less on *states* and more on *societies*, to unpack the geographic, economic, and social forces that impact entire national populations and thus also presage what political trends may crystallize in the future.

NOTES

1 Our sister volume is *The Societies of the Middle East and North Africa: Structure, Vulnerabilities, and Forces*, ed. Sean Yom (London: Routledge, 2019). Read together, both books provide the fullest, most balanced study of modern MENA states and societies.
2 For the sake of consistency, this body of water is referred to as the Arabian Gulf in this text, but is also frequently and rightly called the Persian Gulf in other texts.

FURTHER READING

For thorough histories of the Middle East, a plethora of options exist. The best references can be found among the following list: Ira Lapidus, *A History of Islamic Societies*, 2nd ed. (Cambridge University Press, 2002); Philip Hitti, *History of the Arabs*, 10th ed. (Palgrave Macmillan, 2002); Albert Hourani and Malise Ruthven, *A History of the Arab Peoples*, new ed. (Belknap Press, 2010); Peter Mansfield, *A History of the Middle East*, 4th ed. (Penguin, 2013); William Cleveland and Martin Bunton, *A History of the Modern Middle East*, 6th ed. (Routledge, 2016); James Gelvin, *The Modern Middle East: A History*, 4th ed. (Oxford University Press, 2015); Eugene Rogan, *The Arabs: A History*, rev. ed. (Basic Books, 2017); and Arthur Goldschmidt Jr. with Aomar Boum, *A Concise History of the Middle East*, 11th ed. (Routledge, 2016).

For modern political overviews that evaluate regional trends and make apparent the struggle for democracy, see R. Stephen Humphreys, *Between Memory and Desire: The Middle East in a Troubled Age* (University of California Press, 2005); Roger Owen, *State, Power, and Politics in the Making of the Modern Middle East*, 3rd ed. (Routledge, 2006); and Larry Diamond and Marc Plattner, eds., *Democratization and Authoritarianism in the Arab World* (Johns Hopkins University Press, 2014). Two works that take the perspective of popular movements and grassroots resistance as vectors of political change include Charles Tripp, *The Power and the People: Paths of Resistance in the Middle East* (Cambridge University Press, 2013) and John Chalcraft, *Popular Politics in the Making of the Modern Middle East* (Cambridge University Press, 2016). A contemporary look at civic and political activism can be found in Lina Khatib and Ellen Lust, eds., *Taking to the Streets: The Transformation of Arab Activism* (Johns Hopkins University Press, 2014), as well as Joel Beinin and Frédéric Vairel, eds., *Social Movements, Mobilization, and Contestation in the Middle East and North Africa*, 2nd ed. (Stanford University Press, 2013).

Most regional political primers emphasize the Arab world. However, excellent readers of the non-Arab countries abound. For Turkey, see Caroline Finkel, *Osman's Dream: The History of the Ottoman Empire* (Basic Book, 2007), and Douglas Howard, *A History of the Ottoman Empire* (Cambridge University Press, 2017). For Iran, consult Ervand Abrahamian, *A History of Modern Iran* (Cambridge University Press, 2008), and Touraj Daryaee, ed., *The Oxford Handbook of Iranian History* (Oxford University Press, 2014). For Israeli, political and historical references include Benny Morris, *Righteous Victims: A History of the Zionist-Arab Conflict, 1881–2001* (Vintage Books, 2001) and Daniel Gordis, *Israel:*

A Concise History of a Nation Reborn (HarperCollins, 2016).

For work on the region's geopolitics and international relations, see Louise Fawcett, *International Relations of the Middle East*, 5th ed. (Oxford University Press, 2019); Raymond Hinnebusch and Anoushiravan Ehteshami, eds., *The Foreign Policies of Middle East States*, 2nd ed. (Lynne Rienner, 2014); Fred Halliday, *The Middle East in International Relations: Power, Politics, and Ideology* (Cambridge University Press, 2005); and Tareq Ismael and Glenn Perry, eds., *The International Relations of the Contemporary Middle East: Subordination and Beyond* (Routledge, 2013). US-based readers should read Douglas Little, *American Orientalism: The United States and the Middle East since 1945*, 3rd ed. (University of North Carolina Press, 2008); Joel Migdal, *Shifting Sands: The United States in the Middle East* (Columbia University Press, 2014); and David Lesch and Mark Haas, eds., *The Middle East and* the United States: History, Politics, and Ideologies, 6th ed. (Routledge, 2018).

The Arab Spring is a major topic that still commands the attention of researchers. The best works on this include Marc Lynch, ed., *The Arab Uprisings Explained: New Contentious Politics in the Middle East* (Columbia University Press, 2014); Mehran Kamrava, ed., *Beyond the Arab Spring: The Evolving Ruling Bargain in the Middle East* (Oxford University Press, 2015); Fahed al-Sumait, Nele Lenze, and Michael Hudson, eds., *The Arab Uprisings: Catalysts, Dynamics, and Trajectories* (Rowman and Littlefield, 2015); Jason Brownlee, Tarek Masoud, and Andrew Reynolds, *The Arab Spring: Pathways of Repression and Reform* (Oxford University Press, 2015); Robert Worth, *A Rage for Order: The Middle East in Turmoil, from Tahrir Square to ISIS* (Farrar, Straus, and Giroux, 2017); and Asef Bayat, *Revolution without Revolutionaries: Making Sense of the Arab Spring* (Stanford University Press, 2017).

Online sources

The online world is filled with information – and disinformation (i.e., "fake news"). Reliable websites are becoming scarce, but the following provide a good start. The best sources for continuous news coverage include Middle East Online (https://middle-east-online.com), Al-Monitor (www.al-monitor.com), Middle East Eye (www.middleeasteye.net), Al-Jazeera (www.aljazeera.com/topics/regions/middleeast.html), Al-Bawaba Portal (www.albawaba.com), and the Arab Reform Initiative (www.arab-reform.net/). The best Western news sources include *The New York Times* (www.nytimes.com/section/world/middleeast), *Washington Post* (www.washingtonpost.com/world/middle-east/), BBC (www.bbc.com/news/world/middle_east), France24 (www.france24.com/en/middle-east), Reuters (www.reuters.com/subjects/middle-east), *The Economist* (www.economist.com/topics/middle-east), and *Foreign Policy* (https://foreignpolicy.com/channel/middle-east-africa/).

Excellent in-depth coverage of social affairs, cultural issues, and popular debates appear in dedicated research portals. These include: Fanack (https://fanack.com/); Al-Bab (http://al-bab.com); Middle East Research and Information Project (www.merip.org); Jadaliyya (www.jadaliyya.com); the Middle East Institute (www.mei.edu/policy-analysis); the Brookings Institution's Center for Middle East Policy (www.brookings.edu/center/center-for-middle-east-policy/); the Atlantic Council's MENASource Blog (www.atlanticcouncil.org/blogs/menasource); the Carnegie Endowment for International Peace's *Sada* (http://carnegieendowment.org/sada); Human Rights Watch's MENA Team (www.hrw.

org/middle-east/n-africa); and the regular publications of the Project on Middle East Political Science (https://pomeps.org).

There are three online sources of data heavily used in this volume. First, the World Bank's *World Development Indicators* is a treasure trove, highlighting almost all social and economic trends since 1960 (http://databank.worldbank.org/data/home.aspx). Second, Freedom House's political ratings and regime classifications are freely available, along with detailed information about each country (https://freedomhouse.org/). Third, for more geographic resources including an extraordinary array of maps, visit the Perry-Castañeda Library Map Collection (https://legacy.lib.utexas.edu/maps/middle_east.html).

Please note that URLs may change far more quickly than books can be printed; so if these exact URLs do not work, simply search Google or another engine by the titles of these websites and online resources.

The context of political life

Geography, economics, and social forces

Sean Yom

GEOGRAPHIC AND ENVIRONMENTAL CONTEXT

Like all regions, the social and political life of peoples across the Middle East and North Africa is the product not just of human choices, but also of the constraints imposed by the physical environment. Environmental and physical qualities weigh heavily upon development.

The MENA's defining ecological characteristic is aridity: this is a mostly hot, dry crescent of geography. It contains nearly two-thirds of the world's driest twenty-five countries, most of which receive well under 300mm (i.e., about 12 inches) of rain annually. Some, like Kuwait, get virtually no rain at all. Indeed, the MENA overlaps with the world's two largest deserts outside the Arctic and Antarctica. The largest, the Sahara, stretches across North Africa and is the size of the United States. The Arabian Desert occupies most of the Arabian Peninsula; within it runs the *Rub'a al-Khali*, or Empty Quarter, which is the world's longest contiguous sand desert. Another dry zone is the Syrian Desert, which includes parts of Syria, Iraq, Jordan, and northern Saudi Arabia. Smaller deserts include the Sinai and Negev, which overlie the border between Egypt and Israel, and the Dasht-e Kavir and Dasht-e Lut Deserts in Iran.

Of course, not all the region is arid, and its topography shows some variation. Several major river basins support productive valleys and ecosystems, such as the Tigris and Euphrates river system running across Iraq, Syria, and Turkey – the famed Fertile Crescent. The Nile Basin waters much of Egypt and Sudan. Vegetated steppes give way to some temperate zones in coastal North Africa and the eastern Mediterranean shores. In addition, snow can fall upon the region's rugged mountainous ranges, including the Atlas mountains in Morocco, Algeria, and Tunisia; the Taurus and Pontic mountains of Turkey; the Asir and Hijaz ranges of Saudi Arabia; Yemen's Hadhramaut region; and Iran's Zagros and Alborz mountains.

Human settlements have long adapted to this arid environment. Until the mid-twentieth century, most rural areas in the MENA featured one of two social structures: peasant villages clustered around common agricultural estates, or else tribal communities that migrated between oases and grazing grounds, as was practiced by Bedouin (e.g., fully nomadic tribes). In arable zones where agriculture formed the basis of economic production and social life, irrigation systems were rudimentary and seasons unforgiving. This subjected sharecroppers, tenants, and other workers to the mercy of powerful landowners, many of whom would later lose much of their wealth and status when post-colonial regimes in the 1950s sought to empower rural dwellers and reform landowning laws, as in Iran and Egypt.

In areas where farming was not possible, nomadism emerged as a logical response to ecological hardship. Where water was scant, herding animals like camels and sheep while on the constant move offered the best chance of survival. This agronomic divide between farming and pastoralism, peasants and tribesmen – *fellahin* and *badu* in Arabic – ineffaceably marked society. Tribal kinship still influences social and political networks in Libya, Syria, Jordan, Iraq, and the Gulf countries, even though most nomadic tribes have long settled and urbanized. However, not all rural populations in the pre-modern MENA adhered to this cleavage. For instance, small coastal strips engaged in maritime pursuits like fishing and shipbuilding. On the shores of the Arabian Gulf, pearling was also a major traditional industry among those living in what is now Kuwait, Bahrain, Qatar, and UAE.

Water accessibility also dictated the placement of major cities, which before the twentieth century almost always clustered around coasts and river valleys. Baghdad, founded in the late eighth century AD, lay in the Fertile Crescent between the Tigris and Euphrates Rivers. Dating back millennia to the pre-Islamic period, Istanbul straddles the Bosporus Strait and enjoys a Mediterranean climate. Cairo, more than a thousand years old and now the region's largest city with nearly 20 million residents, hugs the banks of the Nile River. Modern inland cities have come into their own only over the past century, when social life was no longer encaged by agricultural fertility and nearby water sources. Tehran, Ankara, Riyadh, and Amman – the capitals of Iran, Turkey, Saudi Arabia, and Jordan, respectively – are booming metropolises with millions of inhabitants; before the twentieth century, these were modest towns of barely thirty thousand people each, as the natural environment precluded large-scale settlement.

Urbanization, water, and climate change

Urbanization across the MENA has been steady and vigorous. Currently, more than two-thirds of the regional population live in urban areas. The World Bank estimates that the number of people residing in towns and cities jumped from just 44 million in 1960 to nearly 350 million in 2016, an annualized average rate of nearly 4 percent; today, only Egypt, Sudan, and Yemen have national populations where at least half still live in rural areas. Urbanization is a complex structural process with myriad effects on physical well-being, social inclusion, economic achievement, and political participation. Often overlooked are its ecological impacts, however, particularly in a region defined by aridity. Cities require water, but the MENA has few freshwater sources, including not just precipitation but also rivers, lakes, and aquifers. The United Nations Food and Agricultural Organization estimates that the MENA average for annual renewable water available per person is just 1,200 cubic meters – six times less than the global average of 7,000 cubic meters per person, and many times less than the average for other geographic zones, such as North America (20,300 cubic meters per person).

Compounding the problem, MENA countries annually withdraw over 70 percent of the region's total renewable water from aquifers and riparian zones for industrial and agricultural usage, severely desiccating the water cycle. A visceral example is the Jordan River, which Israel and Jordan have long overused for nearby agricultural projects. During summers, Bethany Beyond the Jordan – the holy site on the river where John the Baptist baptized Jesus Christ – becomes little more than a muddy trickle. Diminishing access to water may exacerbate internal conflicts in the future. In August 2009, for example, southern Yemen saw violent demonstrations against aggressive water rationing imposed by the government in response to prolonged drought, which left many areas without running water and forced some to buy private supplies at inflated prices. In these contexts, desalinization is not the answer to hydrological depletion. Desalinating seawater is an energy-intensive process that many countries cannot afford, and also produces chemical byproducts that shift the environmental burden to air and land-based externalities.

Partly for this reason, climate change will have disastrous ramifications for MENA populations. Ecological destruction and water exhaustion create severe downstream consequences for both rural and urban communities. In rural areas, it forecloses productive farming, increases the cost of basic goods, and encourages migration or refugee outflows to already-crowded urban areas. In urban environments, climatic downturns hit hardest the most vulnerable segments, in particular migrants, the poor, and children. People already without adequate water supplies, sewage access, and safe housing are unlikely to obtain it during unforeseen droughts and rising temperatures. Nutritional deficiencies, as well, can result from the loss of agricultural harvests and reliance upon expensive, processed food imports. Finally, apart from worsening community health, climate change can have dire political consequences. If floods or droughts destroy local food sources and cause the price of basic items like bread to skyrocket, dislocated citizens may take to the streets. Indeed, some do not find it coincidental that the Arab Spring protests occurred not long after agricultural and environmental catastrophes in 2009 caused global wheat prices to spike, resulting in costlier food supplies in Egypt, Syria, and elsewhere.

ECONOMIC CONDITIONS

Understanding the politics of the MENA requires unraveling its economic evolution. Economics entails analyzing how states and societies distribute scarce resources. Hence, who suffers poverty, who becomes prosperous, who obtains jobs, who dominates markets are all important aspects of a national economy. They reflect capacity of an economy to generate goods and services that ideally benefit everyone by improving overall standards of living and enhancing productivity. Economic development and political stability go hand-in-hand. Revolutionary episodes, such as the Arab Spring, are not waged by aristocratic elites; they are driven by citizens with material grievances that have long been neglected or marginalized.

Until recently, MENA economies were dominated by the state. Like other "late developers," a term coined by political economists for countries that began their modernization well after the start of the twentieth century, these countries sat on the global periphery when they became independent after World War Two. Despite leaders' promises to catch up to more advanced industrialized countries, colonial policies and geopolitical subordination left many sovereign MENA countries without financial capital, industrial assets, and infrastructure. Their economies were mostly agrarian, and had few industries. Some had developed a young oil sector, but Western firms controlled most of their petroleum production and exports.

For many post-colonial countries, the answer to this dilemma was state-led development. Late developers did not have the luxury of time to gradually evolve into industrialized states with competitive markets. By allowing political leaders and the machinery of government to dictate economic affairs, shortcuts could be made. Though such preferences for state leadership over free markets may seem anti-capitalist, most developing countries embraced government planning in the early stages of their modernization. Before World War One, the imperial rise of Germany, Russia, and Japan required swift state-driven industrialization; in the interwar decades, Latin American countries like Brazil and Argentina implemented similar reforms, as did Kemalist Turkey; and after World War Two, Asian countries like South Korea, Taiwan, and Singapore upgraded their economies and became competitive through state decision-making. The "invisible hand" of free markets did not come until much later; and so the experiment in the MENA began.

From early boom ...

Starting in the 1950s, many MENA regimes sought to achieve rapid economic development through frenetic, large-scale reorganization. Economic councils and planning ministries became leading agents in these modernization programs. Such state-directed policies flourished in most of the Arab world, as well as Turkey, Iran, and even Israel. Examples of such programs included the redistribution of rural lands held by wealthy elites; nationalizing companies and productive assets previously held by Western firms, from oil production to the Suez Canal; providing guaranteed employment in the public sector, namely jobs in the government and state-owned companies; and keeping food, gas, and other basic commodities cheap through subsidies. Exchange rates were also manipulated, with national currencies greatly overvalued in order to cheapen basic imports and protect local financing. Industries were created from scratch by government investments. The largest countries attempted the risky pathway of import-substituting industrialization (ISI). Under ISI, governments founded new industries, such as food processing, heavy mining, and machinery manufacturing. Those infant industries generated new jobs while producing directly for domestic markets, with foreign competitors blocked by tariffs and other trade barriers – hence the "import-substituting" aspect.

In many authoritarian states, a social contract came to surface. In return for political loyalty, citizens could access jobs in the swelling public sector and earn more social protections and services. Governmental provisions became embedded into the fabric of newly urbanizing societies, as leaders invested heavily in better education, health care, housing, infrastructure, and other public goods. Such central economic planning, however, also had the pernicious side-effect of discouraging regimes from developing efficient systems of taxation by which to extract domestic revenues. Taxation represents the ultimate act of state coercion, since it requires that citizens surrender a fixed portion of their wealth and property every year under threat of punishment. While oil-rich countries never needed to raise many taxes given their hydrocarbon riches, oil-poor countries like Jordan, Egypt, and Libya also refused to levy many taxes as part of the grand bargain between dictators and societies. A few countries bucked this trend, including Israel, Turkey, and to a lesser extent Tunisia.

At first, state-led development and this authoritarian social contract seemed to work. As Table 2.1 shows, the MENA reaped stunning economic dividends during the 1960s and 1970s. Many regional countries saw booming increases in their Gross Domestic Product (GDP, an indicator for economic size). Some even enjoyed sustained double-digit growth during these halcyon decades, such as Bahrain, Iran, Israel, Libya, Oman, Saudi Arabia, and the UAE. This is an incredible feat from an economic standpoint; for comparative perspective, consider that today in the United States, just 3 percent GDP growth annually is seen as a boom. Indeed, according to the World Bank, the MENA region's entire GDP grew by a world-leading annualized average of 5 percent during the 1960s and 1970s – double that of Europe, the United States, and Latin America, and higher than even Japan-led East Asia's second-highest rate of 3.15 percent.

... to bust

Yet with every boom comes a bust, and the MENA's crash was particularly harsh during the 1980s. As Table 2.1 shows, during that decade, GDP growth plummeted in almost every single country. Some countries, such as Saudi Arabia, even suffered negative economic growth over the decade. The region's collective GDP grew by just 1.3 percent from 1986 to 1990 – a far cry from the searing 6.2 percent growth rate recorded between 1976 and 1980. By then, the state-led developmental model reached its limits due to a confluence of shocks. The price of oil plummeted from more than one hundred dollars per barrel in 1980 to just thirty dollars per barrel in 1986, throwing the major energy exporters like Saudi Arabia into a financial tailspin. In turn, this exerted ripple effects on other Arab countries that exported both goods and workers to those oil-rich economies. Conflicts also surged;

TABLE 2.1

Average GDP growth rates by decade, 1960s–2010s

	1960s	1970s	1980s	1990s	2000s	2011–2018
Algeria	4.1	7.2	2.8	1.6	3.9	3.1
Bahrain	N/A	11.4	4.7	5.5	5.5	3.7
Egypt	4.3	9.5	5.4	4.7	4.9	3.1
Iran	11.6	6.2	−0.3	4.6	5.3	2.2
Iraq	6.9	9.6	−0.6	N/A	4.6	6.2
Israel	9.1	14.8	3.3	5.3	3.7	3.6
Jordan	N/A	15.2	2.5	4.3	6.3	2.5
Kuwait	6.7	2.3	−0.9	7	5.5	2.7
Lebanon	N/A	N/A	−42.5	9.7	5.2	1.7
Libya	24.7	6	3.4	2.5	4.3	5.5
Morocco	4.9	5.7	3.9	2.8	4.7	3.6
Oman	19.5	13.9	8.7	4.9	4.4	3.4
Palestine (West Bank & Gaza Strip)	N/A	N/A	N/A	16.5	1.7	4.6
Qatar	N/A	N/A	1.8	6.6	12.4	4.8
Saudi Arabia	6	14.2	−0.6	3.1	5.2	3.8
Sudan	1.1	4.3	3.4	4.4	7.1	2.8
Syria	7.8	8.6	2.8	6	4.7	−63.2
Tunisia	5.1	7.4	3.5	5	4.5	1.7
Turkey	5.7	4.7	4.1	4.1	3.8	6.6
UAE	N/A	12.6	18	5.5	4.2	4.2
Yemen	N/A	11.5	5.6	4.7	5.9	−5.9

Sources: World Bank (2019), *World Development Indicators.*

Note: All country data begin in 1961 except for Bahrain (1976), Egypt (1966), Jordan (1976), Lebanon (1989), Palestinian territories (1995), Qatar (1981), UAE (1976), and Yemen (1970). Yemen data before 1991 are average of North and South Yemen.

the Iran-Iraq War devastated both participants, while civil war demolished much of Lebanon.

Even in stable countries, though, the decisions of the past caught up with government planners. Demographic growth and urbanization had generated increasingly bigger and younger workforces, with more citizens all desiring the same opportunities as their parents' generation – university admissions, public jobs, decent housing, and social services. The sheer financial overhead of providing for these guaranteed benefits exceeded what cash-strapped governments could underwrite. Many were burdened by the cost of conflict, from the Arab-Israeli Wars to the Iran-Iraq War, and by borrowing heavily from foreign creditors, were mired in heavy debt. At the same time, they were unable to suddenly raise more revenues through domestic taxes, due to the political resistance this would spur.

Finally, the industries created by the old model were inefficient and struggled to grow. Creating new state-owned industries such as textile factories in Tunisia, chemical production in Egypt, or potash processing in Jordan was one thing; sustaining their long-term excellence through innovation in order to dominate global markets was something else. By contrast, other late-developing economies, such as the Asian Tigers – South Korea, Taiwan, Singapore, and Hong Kong – were able to gradually shift their industrialization strategy to become export-oriented, and hence move into advanced sectors such as electronics and automobiles. Only Israel and parts of the Turkish economy emulated this, and here such upgrading took much longer due to unique constraints. For instance, in Israel, the government constantly devoted a high portion of its resources to military defense, was obligated to accommodate steady waves of Jewish immigration from elsewhere, and uniquely could not trade with almost any of its Arab neighbors with which it was at war.

The 1980s, then, heralded an epoch of economic crisis. Many regimes teetered on bankruptcy, like those in Egypt, Morocco, Algeria, Tunisia, and Jordan. They turned to the World Bank and International Monetary Fund for emergency loans, but those funds came with "structural adjustment" conditions that required leaders to make unpopular cutbacks by imposing new taxes and lowering social spending, such as subsidies that kept food and fuel affordable. Some were also forced to stop overvaluing their currencies, a monetary policy that in some countries caused massive inflation. For instance, Turkey reported 140 percent inflation in 1980, Syria 60 percent in 1987, and Israel a whopping 450 percent in 1984. Under pressure from lenders and debtors, and hoping to integrate better into the global economy, many MENA governments attempted – at least rhetorically, when speaking with Western partners and donors – to shed their state-led development model and instead embrace market-based economics by privatizing their industries and cutting back on public spending. However, sudden layoffs and a sharp rise in living costs caused violent protests from citizens exasperated with their broken social contract. These "bread riots" rocked Morocco, Tunisia, Algeria, Egypt, Lebanon, and Jordan from the late 1970s through late 1980s, marking the largest disturbances in these countries since the Arab Nationalist and leftist awakenings in the 1950s.

One survival strategy in the Arab countries was political liberalization. A handful of embattled presidents and kings attempted to counter unrest by offering political reforms that improved civil freedoms and relaxed some repression, but nonetheless kept executive power safely in the hands of rulers. Thus after the 1980s, new parliamentary elections transpired in Morocco, Jordan, Kuwait, and Yemen, while Egypt, Syria, and Tunisia briefly enjoyed periods of greater toleration for pluralism and dissent. The other survival strategy was, in essence, to kick the bucket down the road by engaging in marginal economic changes combined with heavier repression. Some state-owned firms, such as transportation companies and heavy industries, were privatized; promises for future education, employment, and prosperity emanated as always from leaders, so long as citizens respected the rules of the political game. In the oil-exporting states, authoritarian officials believed that energy prices would swing high again, thus rescuing them from their fiscal doldrums.

Neoliberalism, unemployment, and uncertainty

The regional bust did end, but it would take another decade. The 1980s and 1990s hence represent something of a lost period for the MENA regional economy. In the 2000s, some countries continued to underperform due to sanctions, war, or isolation; this included Libya, Syria, Iran, Iraq, and Yemen. Other economies, particularly the Arabian Gulf kingdoms, latched on to rebounding oil and natural gas prices. Average crude oil prices rocketed from less than $16 per barrel in 1998 to nearly $150 in 2008, an all-time high. However, regimes in other countries reached implicit consensus that old developmental models were no longer completely viable, and some form of the "neoliberal" economics needed to be implemented in order to foster greater growth and integration with the globalizing world. The neoliberal economic agenda, endorsing the market-based prescriptions of the World Bank and International Monetary Fund, was the polar opposite of state-led development in that it treated government planning as the anathema rather than instrument of economic prosperity. Championed by a new generation of Western-educated technocrats, neoliberal reforms included floating exchange rates, slashing social and welfare spending, downsizing the public sector, raising more taxes for revenues, incentivizing private-sector employment, privatizing public firms, and instituting free trade and investment.

Various combinations of these reforms began to become implemented in the 2000s with mixed results. Israel, for instance, strengthened its economic fundamentals by transitioning to a diversified private-sector economy thanks to careful management, foreign aid, and strategic investments (especially in military arms and high-tech industries, both of which are now leading exports). Turkey also liberalized its economy and established a customs union with the European Union (EU), balancing its agriculture with manufacturing such as automobiles and electronics. In the Arab world, these transformations were more difficult to fully execute, with most leaders only half-heartedly pursuing these changes. One reason was political manipulation. For instance, officials often exploited privatization in countries like Morocco, Egypt, Tunisia, and Jordan, selling state assets and industrial licenses to crony investors in transactions that reeked of bribery and corruption. The larger reason, however, was that economic change requires too steep political costs. Laying off a quarter of civil or military employees, instituting strict income taxation, and halting subsidies to bread, fuel, and electricity do not merely expose societies to sudden privation; they also violate the old social contract. Of course, citizens who must surrender economic claims to a retreating state have *political* recourse: they can demand popular representation and democratic accountability. Yet the possibility of democratization alarms authoritarian regimes as much as financial insolvency.

Today, two decades into the twenty-first century, the MENA regional economy appears a patchwork of variation, much like its political regimes. First, consider the last column of data back in Table 2.1, which summates economic growth rates in the 2010s. Yemen and Syria have suffered contraction given their violence and breakdown; indeed, Syria's economy from 2011–18 contracted by nearly two-thirds, similar to the collapse of the Lebanese economy during the civil war of the 1980s. Most other countries continue developing but slowly, and certainly not at the breakneck speed of their historic boom during the 1960s and 1970s.

Second, the MENA economies also exhibit diversity in other ways. Table 2.2 presents several cruxes of variation. In terms of size, the region's largest economies are Turkey ($766.4 billion) and Saudi Arabia ($782.5 billion); they rank among the world's twenty biggest. They tower over the tiniest economies, including those of Bahrain ($38.3 billion), Yemen ($26.9 billion), and Palestine ($14.5 billion). Moreover, relative prosperity diverges sharply. GDP per capita, calculated by dividing the GDP value by the populational size, offers a basic way to measure average living standards. However, it does not mean income, nor does it take into account differences in the cost of living and inflation across countries. Thus, GDP per capita is also indexed to Purchasing Power Parity (PPP), which provides a more realistic way of capturing how much that relative wealth looks like when compared to the rest of the world. As Table 2.2 shows, GDP per capita (PPP) shows wide variance in the region. Qatar's figure of $130,475 makes it among the richest countries in the world. Indeed, the other affluent Gulf kingdoms and Israel ($37,972) far exceed less developed countries with severe poverty, such as Yemen ($2,377) and Sudan ($4,232). The same impoverishment likely holds true for Syria, although no reliable economic data has yet measured its war-time destruction. Critically, though, economists do not consider the MENA the most impoverished region. The World Bank has found that around 5 percent of the region's populace lives in extreme poverty, defined as subsisting on $1.90 or less a day – far lower than South Asia (over 16 percent) and sub-Saharan Africa (over 41 percent). In technical terms, the MENA is classified as middle-income.

Yet lack of extreme poverty does not mean the absence of hardship. What concerns most MENA countries is not so much absolute deprivation befalling entire societies, although genuine humanitarian crises like child starvation and disease epidemics exist in war-torn places like Yemen and Syria. Rather, it is *relative* deprivation, in which people can no longer achieve the economic goals and living standards to which they have become accustomed. This especially applies to urban citizens with enough education and mobility to realize that they have great potential – but are foiled by obstacles such as a lack of jobs, legal corruption, and political repression. Table 2.2 exposes the familiar problem of unemployment: too many people, too few opportunities. Most MENA countries suffer double-digit joblessness, with Palestine exceeding all others with nearly one-third of job-seekers unemployed. By contrast, the smallest Gulf kingdoms like Qatar and the UAE can ensure their tiny citizenries have easy access to state employment. Violence in Libya, Yemen, and Iraq have driven up their unemployment rates; the figure in Syria now is likely far worse than the pre-war 14.9 percent rate reported in 2011.

These official unemployment rates also underestimate because they do not count the informal sector, which includes economic activities unreported to the government, such as under-the-table jobs in retail, construction, and transportation (e.g., driving taxis). In addition, they do not count those who are so discouraged that they have stopped looking for work altogether. Worse, domestic unemployment remains high despite the fact that countries suffering from joblessness have seen hundreds of thousands of workers emigrate to seek employment abroad; that is, their labor markets struggle to

TABLE 2.2

Wealth, unemployment, remittances, and economic sectors

	GDP, in millions (current US$)	GDP per capita (current US$)	GDP per capita (PPP)	Unemployment rate (% labor force)	Remittances received (% GDP)	Agriculture (% GDP)	Services (% GDP)	Industry (% GDP)
Algeria	180,441	4,237	15,440	12.1	1.1	12.3	45.6	37.2
Bahrain	38,291	25,851	50,057	1.1	**	0.3	56.8	41.3
Egypt	249,559	2,573	13,367	11.4	10.1	11.5	53	33.8
Iran	452,275	5,491	19,557	12.1	0.3	9.5	54.4	34.9
Iraq	226,070	5,930	17,659	7.9	0.5	4.8	52.2	43
Israel	369,843	41,644	37,972	4	0.3	1.2	69.4	19.6
Jordan	42,371	4,278	9,433	18.6	11.1	4	63.9	25.4
Kuwait	141,050	30,839	67,000	2.1	**	0.5	40.9	58.7
Lebanon	56,409	9,257	14,684	6.2	13.2	4.2	74	13.6
Libya	43,587	6,692	11,469	17.3	N/A	N/A	N/A	N/A
Morocco	118,309	3,359	8,933	9	6.2	12.4	50	26.1

Oman	82,243	19,302	46,584	3.1	0.1	2.3	50.5	47.5
Palestine (West Bank & Gaza Strip)	14,498	3,095	4,896	30.2	14.8	3.2	63.4	19.6
Qatar	192,450	70,780	130,475	0.1	0.4	0.2	47.1	56.9
Saudi Arabia	782,483	23,566	55,944	5.9	**	2.5	50.9	45.5
Sudan	33,903	808	4,232	12.9	0.2	30.5	46.8	2.3
Syria (2015)	24,600	N/A	N/A	50	3.2	16	68.5	15.3
Tunisia	39,952	3,464	12,372	15.5	4.7	9.5	58.8	23.1
Turkey	766,428	9,346	27,956	10.9	0.1	6.1	53.4	29.2
UAE	424,635	41,711	69,382	2.6	N/A	0.8	55.6	43.6
Yemen	26,914	873	2,377	12.9	10.7	6	19.2	42.2

Sources: IMF (2019), *International Financial Statistics*; World Bank (2019), *World Development Indicators*. All figures for 2018 except Syrian data, which are estimates from 2015.

**denotes negligible values (less than 0.1).

provide opportunities even with the emigration safety valve. This is a worrisome problem in Morocco, Tunisia, Egypt, Palestine, Jordan, Yemen, which collectively have seen millions of citizens travel abroad for work. On the other hand, such emigration results in considerable remittance flows, or cash transferred by these expatriate workers back to their home countries (e.g., a Lebanese teacher working in Kuwait who sends his salary to his family in Beirut). As Table 2.2 shows, these cash streams constitute over 10 percent of the GDP in Egypt, Jordan, Lebanon, and Palestine.

One barrier to job creation comes from the inherited structure of most MENA economies. The three principal (but not only) components of most economies are agriculture and farming; services, such as administration, education, finance, and health care; and industry, such as mining, manufacturing, electricity production, and construction. As Table 2.2 shows, only a few countries still have sizable agricultural sectors that exceed a tenth of their GDP. Most rely upon services, which in many countries is still dominated by government employment. Many also present impressively large industrial sectors, but these figures can mislead. In Algeria, Bahrain, Iran, Iraq, Kuwait, Oman, Qatar, Saudi Arabia, and the UAE, the industrial sector revolves around a single activity – oil and gas production, not a diversified set of activities and products.

Herein lies the dilemma. Extractive industries like oil are highly mechanized and so employ few workers, but labor-intensive sectors like agriculture or industrial manufacturing see only inconsistent growth and are often uncompetitive when subject to foreign competition. At the same time, most MENA countries excepting the richest Gulf principalities cannot afford to continue paying their bloated public-sector payrolls in order to soak up their burgeoning workforces. For decades, civil services, government bureaucracies, schools and universities, and other state organs have been saturated with redundant employees, who carry prestige because they not only present decent salaries and lifelong job security but also pensions for perpetuity.

In this circumstance, neoliberal reforms require that these countries endure the pain of short-term shocks such as spiking unemployment and poverty, should such state-based economies be transformed overnight. This is easier said than done. Thriving economies driven by productive markets and private-sector firms exporting high-quality products do not appear overnight. They require a litany of other steps, such as attracting foreign investment, encouraging entrepreneurship, improving education, protecting legal rights through strong judiciaries, and eliminating the prestige of public-sector work. Such changes are not impossible, but they require transcending the entrenched social contract swapping security for loyalty. The absence of such changes means, for many MENA countries, continuing relative deprivation and the possibility of another Arab Spring.

Rentierism: oil and aid

Is petroleum the answer? Many see oil and natural gas reserves as black gold, the conduit out of poverty and a mechanism for long-term prosperity. And indeed, casual visitors to the wealthiest Gulf kingdoms like Kuwait, Qatar, and the UAE observe how these hydrocarbon exporters can hand out guaranteed jobs, free education, health care, and other cradle-to-grave benefits to citizens – so long as the price of energy remains high on global markets. In these environs, unemployment is seldom a problem. Indeed, these states have long attracted millions of expatriate workers from other Arab and Asian countries in order to fill worker shortages in the private sector. Fields like construction, retail, transportation, and household services are often starved for workers given that most citizens gravitate to more prestigious, government-oriented jobs. The UAE, and to a lesser extent Qatar, are also unique in having crafted small but advanced service sectors, in particular finance and consulting, that have drawn a rising number of Western expatriates.

Such states that derive substantial revenues from selling natural resources are known as *rentier states*. "Rent" in the macroeconomic sense signifies the productive value of a natural asset, once manipulated and extracted for outside usage. Oil fields, natural gas deposits, and gold veins all constitute examples of natural resource rents. However, regimes can also earn income from their inherent geographic location. Some countries have lucrative transit routes; Egypt charges a significant toll for every ship passing through its Suez Canal. Other countries, like Jordan, have long attracted foreign aid from international allies, who wish to keep these strategically placed countries and their pro-Western leaderships stable and secure. Notably, this does not apply to all MENA countries. For instance, Israel and Turkey have the most developed economies in terms of reliance upon domestic production and non-rentier revenues.

However, rentierism (i.e., financial reliance upon rents) can be as much a curse as a blessing, as Table 2.3 shows. Dependency upon external monies deters governments from developing adequate domestic taxation: why bother collecting taxes from citizens when money pours in freely from the outside world? As the data illustrate, there is often a negative correlation between tax revenues versus oil and gas revenues, as seen in Iraq, Kuwait, Oman, Saudi Arabia, Qatar, and the UAE. Indeed, the six Gulf kingdoms have virtually no

TABLE 2.3

Rentierism: taxation, hydrocarbons, foreign aid, and military spending

	Tax revenue (% GDP)	Oil and gas rents (% GDP)	Foreign aid, in millions (current US$)	Military expenditures (% GDP)
Algeria	37.2	14.5	189.2	5.7
Bahrain	1.1	3.5	**	4.1
Egypt	12.5	4.8	2,130.3	1.8
Iran	7.4	17	140.3	3.1
Iraq	2	38	2,907.5	3.9
Israel	24.6	**	3,500	4.7
Jordan	15.3	**	2,920.8	4.8
Kuwait	1.4	37.1	**	5.8
Lebanon	15.2	**	1,305.5	4.5
Libya	2.4 (2014)	38.4	431.9	11.4 (2014)
Morocco	26.4	**	1,884.9	3.2
Oman	2.5	23.4	**	12.1
Palestine (West Bank & Gaza Strip)	6.4	**	2,111.4	N/A
Qatar	**	17.9	**	2.5
Saudi Arabia	5	23.7	**	10.3
Sudan	6.3	1	840.4	3.2
Syria (2011)	14.2	21.6	335.5	4.1
Tunisia	21.1	1.7	775.8	2.1
Turkey	17.9	**	3,141.6	2.2
UAE	0.1	13.7	**	5.6
Yemen	N/A	1.9	3,234	5

Sources: World Bank (2019), *World Development Indicators*; International Monetary Fund (2019), *International Financial Statistics.* All figures for 2018 except Syrian data, which represent last available figures from 2011 prior to civil war, and Libyan data, in which tax revenue and military expenditure data represent last available figures from 2014.

**denotes negligible values.

Note: Foreign aid figures are for 2018 only. They include grants and loans given as part of development assistance, humanitarian support, strategic goals, and other declared purposes from foreign governments and multilateral organizations.

income taxation at all. By contrast, hydrocarbon-poor states like Morocco, Tunisia, Israel, and Turkey have comprehensive extraction schemes, with tax revenues representing between 18 to 26 percent of their GDP. This is on par with developed regions, such as the EU, where taxation equals 20 percent of GDP.

Although at first glance low taxation seems beneficial, it can leave perverse side effects. Citizens who must surrender their wealth to government desire political rights in exchange – "no taxation without representation," as the American Revolution put it. Some theorists believe that little to no taxation forecloses the desire for democratization, since there is no economic bargaining chip that citizens can use when advocating for democracy: "no taxation, no representation." Moreover, when volatility in global markets slashes oil prices, regimes have no tax revenues to fall back on. This can result in crisis. For example, Saudi Arabia's GDP per capita peaked at about $18,000 in 1981, well exceeding that of the United States; eight years in the wake of the epic oil price collapse, its GDP had plummeted to $6,000 – the same as Portugal's or Malta's.

Foreign aid is not the solution either. As Table 2.3 continues, many oil-poor states receive substantial economic and military assistance from external actors for various reasons. One is humanitarian. Turkey, for instance, has received several billion dollars of foreign aid for years due to the cost of accommodating nearly four million Syrian refugees. Jordan has also garnered a bump in aid for the same reason. Another reason is strategic, as foreign powers desire to stabilize and secure allied regimes. For instance, despite its oil wealth, Iraq still obtains significant Western assistance, not least as it has dealt with various terrorist and insurgent threats. Most of Israel's foreign aid comes from the United States as an annual military package exceeding $3 billion that includes top-shelf arms and technology. Egypt and Jordan represent special cases, as the United States has long delivered billions of dollars of economic and military assistance to both annually, given their geopolitical role as pro-Western clients that facilitate American interests. France has similar supportive ties with Morocco and Tunisia, while Saudi Arabia, Kuwait, Qatar, and the UAE have given billions to Egypt, Yemen, Morocco, and Jordan since the Arab Spring, largely to calm those autocracies and halt the tide of revolution.

Yet, much like hydrocarbon revenues, too much reliance upon foreign aid can also spawn fiscal dysfunction. Just like oil and gas rents, profuse aid monies can deter governments from developing adequate domestic taxation systems, something seen especially in Palestine and Jordan. Moreover, all types of rentierism can encourage governments to spend heavily on their coercive apparatus: after all, the money to pay soldiers and buy arms comes not from local taxes extracted from citizens, but from outside allies. Military spending as a percentage of GDP, shown in Table 2.3, partly turns on the availability of aid, oil, or gas rents. While this figure varies across countries, the regional average is 5.7 percent – *the highest in the world*, far exceeding that of the EU (1.5 percent), North America (3 percent), Latin America (1.2 percent), East Asia (1.7 percent), South Asia (2.5 percent), and sub-Saharan Africa (1.3 percent).

The effects of such heavy military spending on weapons, salaries, training, and other items means fewer funds for infrastructure, education, health care, and other public goods. This is not a new trend. In the MENA, such securitization began in the 1950s, rose with repeated wars and conflicts, and escalated in many countries as armies became incorporated into political and social life. This extends far beyond the Arab world; Turkey proudly has the largest military in NATO, while the Israeli armed forces compose a cultural and economic backbone in their state. Historically, this securitization peaked in 1980, when military spending reached 15 percent of the regional GDP and nearly 40 percent of all arms sold worldwide ended up in MENA countries. Yet the post-Arab Spring decade represents another peak, as regional conflicts (and in the authoritarian states, fear of domestic unrest) fuel another round of security-minded policies. Saudi Arabia was the world's top arms importer during 2014–18, for example, and in 2019 more than a third of all arms sold worldwide once again flowed into the region.

SOCIAL FORCES: IDENTITY, SECURITY, YOUTH, AND GENDER

Constrained by geography and pressed by underdevelopment, societies across the MENA face immense challenges moving forward. However, many economists believe they have an untapped source of immense potential – human capital, meaning the collective skills, habits, and knowledge accumulated across populations and especially driven by youth. Indeed, the drivers of political change are not merely elites and officials, but social forces shaped by multiple structures of opportunity. Understanding the human terrain of the region therefore requires engaging the most visible landmarks that prefigure everyday life. Here, four such vectors demand scrutiny: identity, particularly ethnicity and religion; human security; youth; and gender. They illuminate the contours of MENA societies.

Identity: ethnicity and religion

For individuals and groups, identity stands as a critical concept that can shed light onto political preferences, behaviors, and conflicts. While many definitions exist, identity can be conceptualized as one's self-conception as it relates to others, and which connote a particular set of expectations, norms, and purposes. There are many sources of identity, including nationality, tribe, ethnicity, religion, gender, culture, language, tribe, and other traits. People seldom have a single and immutable identity, as different affiliations can coexist. A middle-class Jordanian of Palestinian origin living in Amman who is an engineer by trade and also a member of the Muslim Brotherhood, for instance, presents multiple and overlapping self-conceptions.

While the study of identity politics occupies academic scholarship, one dimension is the propensity for contradictory or opposing identities to spark conflict. Sunni versus Shi'a, Christian versus Muslim, Moroccan versus Algerian, Israeli versus Palestinian, Eastern versus Western, poor versus rich, leftist versus conservative – many instantiations of conflict in the MENA today seem to reflect the tendency of different groups to see others as the interminable "Other" that must be fought, contested, or eliminated. Different theories exist to account for why identity-based conflicts can erupt, and in the worst cases produce horrific bouts of violence.

First, primordialists believe that identities express ancient hatreds that trace back many centuries, and are so culturally embedded into human existence that clashes are inevitable. Sunni-Shi'a sectarianism, according to this view, derives from not just doctrinal differences between these branches of Islam, but also the collective memory of millennial violence that are encoded into the social DNA of all Muslim societies. Conflict is a natural phenomenon. Second, instrumentalists argue the opposite. They suggest that while identities can express inherited traditions or beliefs, violence and contestation are not inevitable; rather, governments and leaders manipulate identity politics in order to drum up support for their own goals. Identities, in this sense, are simply an instrument in the toolkit of politics. For example, the Lebanese Civil War witnessed rampant violence between more than a dozen competing sects and communities, each led by elites who sought to maximize their power by attacking their foes. Once the international community incentivized peace through the promise of reconstruction and other rewards, those elites were convinced to demobilize and accept a nonviolent resolution, as if these communal identities suddenly lost salience.

Finally, constructivists contend that identities altogether are social inventions of people who constantly seek to create differences for various purposes; as such, they are malleable, and can be reinvented and reinterpreted in contradictory ways. For example, in 1962, Saudi Arabia intervened in North Yemen to back its monarchy against a pro-Egyptian military coup – a kingship following Zaydi Islam, a small sect within Shi'a Islam. A half-century later, the Saudi war in Yemen sought to destroy another Zaydi entity in the Houthi political movement; this time, however, the Saudi regime declared the Zaydi faith as heretical to Islam. In this instance, what counts as properly Islamic is clearly susceptible to manipulation in accordance with the subjective beliefs and political discourses of different leaders.

This debate remains unsettled. However, no matter the true cause behind identity-based conflict, the striking reality is that the MENA presents a dizzying array of different nations, groups, and communities predicated upon some articulated identity. Here, ethnicity and religion are easiest to dissect. Ethnicity and language are tied together for many in the region, and the five largest clusters are Arabs, Turks, Persians, Kurds, and Tamazight. Nearly two-thirds of the regional population speak Arabic as their primary language and can be considered Arabs in terms of ethnic origin. Outside the Arab countries, Arabs comprise small minorities in Israel, Turkey, and Iran. Turks are the next largest group, constituting about 17 percent of the regional population, mostly living in Turkey. The Turkic language tree is expansive and includes minority tongues spoken among Turkic minorities like the Azeris of northwestern Iran, the Qashqai of southern Iran, and the Turkoman of Syria and Iraq. The next largest group are Persians, who represent 10 percent of regional population and are primarily found in Iran.

The fourth largest are Kurds, who first coalesced as a cohesive group during Islam's golden age. At around 6 percent of the MENA population, they mostly reside in adjoining areas of Turkey, Iraq, Iran, and Syria. The fifth largest MENA community, at 4 percent of the regional populace, are Berbers, also known as Tamazight. They predated the arrival of Arabs and now extend across the Maghrib, with the largest communities in Morocco and Algeria. Many centuries of communal overlap have made it impossible to draw legible distinctions between Berber/Tamazight and Arab ethnicity. Tamazight identity is instead asserted through various Tamazight languages, collective memory, and cultural perceptions.

Beyond these five ethnolinguistic groups are other important populations. Hebrew-speaking Jews make up about 1 percent of the region's population but 75 percent of Israel's. Beyond this are other small but notable communities such as the Armenians in Syria, Lebanon, and Iran; Circassians in Turkey, Syria, Jordan, and Israel; and the Baluch in Oman and southeastern Iran (and, eastward, also Pakistan and Afghanistan).

In religious terms, the predominant faith is Islam. A common misconception holds that the region contains most of the world's Muslims. On the contrary, of the 1.8 billion Muslims around the globe, no more than 25 percent reside in the Middle East and North Africa. Within the MENA, over 90 percent of all peoples practice Islam, and of these more than two-thirds follow various schools of Sunni Islam while most of the remainder pursue some branch of Shi'a Islam. As a holistic religion, all of Islam shares common beliefs and practices. Islam has no organized church, emphasizing instead spiritual equality – all believers may read the holy Qur'an and worship the divine without any intermediary, such as a minister or pope. Muhammad himself was just a messenger, not a priest or vicar of God. Islam is anchored in five ritualistic pillars: the declaration of faith, prayer, almsgiving, fasting, and the *hajj* (pilgrimage to Mecca).

What divides the faith is doctrinal disagreements. Sunni Islam abides by the original Prophetic succession after the Prophet Muhammad's passing in 632 AD as discussed in the first chapter, beginning with Abu Bakr. It also holds that the *hadiths* (sayings) and *sunnah* (teachings) of the Prophet Muhammad provide ideal guidelines for religious praxis. Beyond this singular tenet, many different schools and legal canons exist. For instance, both Saudi Arabia and Jordan are mostly Sunni, yet the former enforces a puritanical interpretation of Islam called Wahhabism that bans alcohol, enforces gender separation, and impresses other conservative rules. The latter country is more tolerant and liberal, with a vibrant nightlife where neither gender segregation nor alcohol prohibitions hold. (The first Amstel Beer brewery opened outside Europe, in fact, was in Jordan in 1958.)

Around 20 percent of the MENA's Muslim population follows Shi'a Islam. Three countries have Shi'a majorities: Iraq (70 percent), Bahrain (70 percent), and Iran (over 90 percent). Further, sizable Shi'a minorities reside in Lebanon, Kuwait, Saudi Arabia, and Yemen. Shi'a Islam has different divisions. The largest are the Twelver Shi'a, who venerate as Muhammad's rightful successor his son-in-law, Ali, and 11 other subsequent descendants. The Alawis are a subsect of the Twelver branch in Syria, made prominent because the ruling Asad family hails from them. Non-Twelver branches include the Isma'ili and Zaydi, with the latter representing up to half of Yemen's Muslims. Beyond the succession issue, most Shi'a also diverge from Sunni Islam in their interpretation of the hadiths and sunnah, devotion to non-Prophetic religious figures, and belief in the *Mahdi*, or messianic savior of humanity.

Casting doubt on primordialist explanations of identity, Sunni-Shi'a conflicts are the exception rather than the rule in Islamic history. It seems that sectarian strife springs less from ancient hatreds, and more instrumentalist and constructivist means in which religious identity is manipulated and exploited for political goals. For instance, no Shi'a rebellion has shaken majority-Sunni Kuwait because its Sabah monarchy has treated Kuwaiti Shi'a as a protected minority with equal rights. The opposite characterizes Bahrain, where the Sunni Khalifah dynasty's marginalization of its Shi'a majority has bred frequent opposition, including the March 2011 revolution that nearly deposed it. In other words, Sunni-Shi'a conflict is conditioned not by the existence of these identities, but how institutions and policies shape relations between these communities.

A major topic of interest among scholars of Islam is the rise of political Islam, or Islamism, since the twentieth century. Islamists refer to organizations and movements that believe that the renewal of Muslim societies, and Islamic civilization broadly, requires rediscovering the conservative fundaments of the Islamic faith, before its perceived corruption by Western encroachment. This imperative for Islamization comes in many forms on the spectrum of Islamic ideology. The largest groups, such as the Muslim Brotherhood, tend to be moderate and peaceful, relying upon social mobilization, service provision, educational activities, and religious messages too. Political change requires participating in elections. Others mix such mobilizational activities with more militant methods in support of emancipating local Muslims, as in Hizbullah in Lebanon and Hamas in Palestine. Finally, the most extreme Islamists espouse a revolutionary creed embracing violence against perceived foes and advocacy for militant goals; the most visible examples include terrorist entities like Al-Qa'ida, as well as the more recent Islamic State in Iraq and Syria. Such extremist actors embody a subset of Islamism known as Salafism, which calls for returning all social, economic, and political life back to the ways of the *salaf* (ancestors), meaning the Prophet Muhammad. Most Salafi Muslims are peaceful, but the minority that violently attack symbols of modernity are deemed *jihadi* given their glorification of *jihad* (holy struggle) and brutal methods.

Not all of the region's Muslims are strictly Sunni or Shi'a. For instance, 75 percent of Omanis follow the eclectic Ibadhi offshoot of Islam. Sufi mystical orders also abound, although they are not tolerated everywhere. In Turkey, at least 10 percent hail from the Alevi community. Alevism is a syncretic, unique religion based somewhat on Shi'a Islam but also drawing on other traditions. Nearly a million Druze also live in Lebanon, Syria, and Israel, with their faith based somewhat on Islam but also incorporating other Abrahamic and non-Abrahamic ideas.

Most of the MENA's remaining population is Christian. The largest denominations are Copts, who constitute 10 percent of Egypt and 1 percent in Sudan and Libya; Maronite Catholics, who comprise about 25 percent in Lebanon; Syriac Christians (Assyrians), who made up around 2–3 percent in Syria and Iraq prior to their post-Arab Spring civil wars; and Armenian and Greek Orthodox communities spread across the Mashriq. Iraq also hosts a significant Chaldean (Catholic denomination) community, as well as the Yazidis, a small minority that is ethnically Kurdish and religiously non-Abrahamic. Lebanon has the highest proportion of Christians, with estimates ranging from 20 to 35 percent. A fair number of Palestinians also belong to the Catholic, Orthodox, and other Christian denominations.

The region's Jewish population lives almost wholly in Israel, and represents three-quarters of its overall populace. Within Israel, up to one-fifth of Jewish citizens are Orthodox or Haredi (ultra-Orthodox). More than a third self-identify as secular in terms of not adhering to many or most religious practices, such as honoring the Sabbath. The rest belong to the Conservative, Reform, and other Jewish denominations. Notably, prior to World War Two, 750,000 Jews lived in a thriving diaspora across Egypt, Iraq, Iran, Turkey, Yemen, and North Africa. Most emigrated to Israel after its creation, although small communities remain in Morocco, Tunisia, and Iran.

Human security

Apart from identity, human security represents the second important social dimension. The conventional idea of human security entailed that societies were more secure when free of physical dangers such as armed violence. This definition still holds weight, since it is easy to see why insecurity increases with exposure to conflict. For example, periodic but catastrophic waves of refugees created by regional wars, such as Syria's conflict, reveal the extent to which human life can be tragically uprooted across borders. Indeed, migration due to forced displacement is an unfortunately prevailing occurrence in more than a few populations throughout the MENA.

Since the 1990s and through the United Nations Development Programme, a newer view of human security has crystallized, one that takes into account a wider array of challenges that communities confront in real-time. Human security now means not just the absence of physical threats, but also the ability of peoples to flourish by attaining more humanistic goals of fulfillment, satisfaction, and dignity. Under this paradigm, true security requires having lives free from poverty, illiteracy, disease, oppression, and other harms that rob individuals and groups of their welfare. In other words, human security is *freedom* – freedom from want and privation, whether the sources are manmade or environmental.

Table 2.4 compares the MENA countries to other global regions on common measures of human security. It focuses upon three indicators of well-being: infant mortality, life expectancy, and adult literacy. Infant mortality, defined as deaths of those under one year of age per thousand live births, helps capture the extent to which families cannot access adequate medicine, nutrition, public safety, and other necessities due to economic, social, and political barriers. Life expectancy is a noisy measure, but hints at the developmental problems needed for biological longevity, including poverty levels, economic mobility, educational opportunities, healthcare access, and social equality. Finally, literacy helps expose the overall distribution of knowledge and education as measured by the ability of the adult population to read and write, in addition to the extent to which people have enrolled in schools.

Comparing infant mortality, life expectancy, and literacy, we see several patterns emerging in the data. First, as with past data, remarkable variation exists. On all these indicators, Israel and the Gulf rentier kingdoms, such as Qatar and Saudi Arabia, approximate or exceed levels seen in the EU and North America. Inversely, the most underdeveloped or war-torn countries, such as Yemen and Sudan, compare more to South Asian and sub-Saharan African levels. Just over two out of three adults in Yemen can read and write; almost everyone can in Bahrain, Jordan, and Palestine. Second, the MENA as a whole, as the regional comparison segment of Table 2.4 depicts, is neither the best-off nor worst-off geographic zone in the world. The regional average for infant mortality (19.3) and life expectancy (73.7 years) compare well to Latin America and East Asia. Regional adult literacy (79.6 percent) has declined over the past decade due to the accumulative effects of civil conflicts, which among other consequences result in the loss of schools and interruption of learning.

These deviating trends find validation through two additional indices used to evaluate human security. The first is the United Nations Development Programme's Human Development Index (HDI), a composite score based upon a combination of life expectancy, educational achievement, and per capita income. In the HDI scale, 1 is highest and 0 the lowest; the higher the score, the greater the level of human security. In 2018, some of the top performers in the world include Norway (.953), Singapore (.932), and France (.901); among the lowest tier were sub-Saharan African countries like the Central African Republic (.367), Liberia (.435). In the MENA, the

TABLE 2.4

Human security in the MENA versus global regions

	Infant mortality rate (per 1,000 live births)	Life expectancy upon birth (years)	Adult literacy rate (% people ages 15+)	Human development index (global rank) (scale 0–1)	Gini index (scale 0–100)
Algeria	20.6	76.3	79.6	.754 (85)	27.6
Bahrain	6.3	77	95.7	.846 (43)	N/A
Egypt	18.8	71.7	73.8	.696 (115)	31.8
Iran	12.8	76.2	86.8	.798 (60)	38.8
Iraq	25.3	70	79.7	.685 (120)	29.5
Israel	2.9	82.6	97.8	.903 (22)	41.4
Jordan	14.6	74.5	95.4	.735 (95)	35.4
Kuwait	6.9	74.8	95.7	.803 (56)	N/A
Lebanon	6.7	79.8	93.9	.757 (80)	N/A
Libya	10.6	72.1	91	.706 (108)	N/A
Morocco	20	76.1	68.5	.667 (123)	40.7
Oman	9.7	77.3	93	.821 (48)	N/A
Palestine (West Bank & Gaza Strip)	17.9	73.6	96.9	.686 (119)	35.5
Qatar	6.5	78.3	97.3	.856 (37)	N/A
Saudi Arabia	6.3	74.7	94.7	.853 (39)	45.9
Sudan	43.7	64.7	75.9	.502 (167)	45.5

(Continued)

	Infant mortality rate (per 1,000 live births)	Life expectancy upon birth (years)	Adult literacy rate (% people ages 15+)	Human development index (global rank) (scale 0–1)	Gini index (scale 0–100)
Syria (2015)	14.2	N/A	86.4	.536 (155)	35.8
Tunisia	11.2	75.9	81.8	.735 (95)	32.8
Turkey	10	76	95.6	.791 (64)	41.9
UAE	7.8	77.4	93.8	.863 (34)	N/A
Yemen	43.2	65.2	70.1	.452 (178)	36.7
Middle East and North Africa	19.3	73.7	79.6	.715	
European Union (EU)	3.4	81	99.1	.899	
North America	5.6	78.9	97	.852	
Latin America and Caribbean	14.9	75.7	93.5	.758	
East Asia and Pacific	13.1	75.6	95.7	.733	
Europe and Central Asia (non-EU)	11.4	73.2	98.9	.771	
South Asia	36.4	69	71	.638	
Sub-Saharan Africa	51.5	60.8	64.4	.537	

Sources: World Bank (2019), *World Development Indicators*; United Nations Development Programme (2019), *Human Development Report*. All figures for 2018 except Syrian data for infant mortality and adult literacy, which are estimates from 2015.

Note: Gini index scores not computed for regions.

highest-ranked country was Israel (.903), whereas the lowest was Yemen (.452). Much of the MENA, excluding these poles, falls in the middle part of global rankings. For instance, Lebanon (.757) runs almost equivalent with Brazil; Egypt (.696) matches with the Philippines.

These indicators underline the Middle East's status as a middle-income region. However, they also obscure the problem of *relative* hardship. It is one thing to starve without housing; it is another to eat but not regularly, to work but only seasonally, or to sleep under a roof but without sanitation. For this reason, many countries calculate their own poverty rates based upon what they determine are minimally acceptable standards. In 2017, for instance, 13.9 percent of all Americans lived under the poverty line established by the US Census Bureau. In Egypt, Iraq, and Turkey, internal estimates suggest that real poverty afflicts over 20 percent of the populace; in Yemen, war has thrust two-thirds of the population (as of 2019) under the poverty line. In Jordan, between 14 and 15 percent of all residents experience year-round poverty, but another 19 to 20 percent endure transient poverty due to having only seasonal income and short-term housing.

Another way to tap human security is inequality. Table 2.4 shows results from the Gini index, a statistical measure of income distribution within a society. Gini scores fall between the hypothetical extremes of 0 (perfect equality, where everyone earns the same income) and 100 (perfect inequality, where a single person earns all income). It is only a partial measure of inequality, but nonetheless usefully helps us compare countries against one another: the lower the number, the more that economic and social development has diffused equally across society. Among the most equal societies in the world are Iceland (25.6) and Finland (26.8); among the most unequal are South Africa (63) and Haiti (60.8). Where data are available in the MENA, countries generally cluster towards the higher end. Moderate inequality is recurrent across the region, although there is some variation. Saudi Arabia and Sudan have the highest Gini scores (and so most relative inequality) at 45.9 and 45.5, respectively.

In sum, the MENA shows a region of contrasts, with human security a prevalent challenge for most countries. Recurrent factors account for some of the worst cases of insecurity, such as conflict, inequality, and poverty.

Youth generation

A central dimension of social life in the MENA is its youthful nature. Nearly two-thirds of the region falls under the age of 30, split evenly between the 0–14 and 15–29 year age brackets. The median age of someone in the region is just 25 years old. In demographic terms, most societies feature generational structures with "youth bulges," meaning a disproportionately large pool of young people compared to older age cohorts. The problem is not an exploding population, as the overall MENA populational growth rate has slowed from 3.4 percent in the mid-1980s to just under 2 percent today, according to the United Nations Population Division. Rather, as the Arab Spring illustrated, it is that masses of young citizens have unfulfilled expectations regarding their political freedom, economic achievement, and social equality – and, as a result, become disenchanted, frustrated, and even rebellious in numbers that overwhelm their governments. Moreover, this demographic challenge is a double whammy. Currently, many regimes are struggling to cope with the desire for jobs, housing, and other aspirations held by millions of millennials leaving high school and college. Yet tomorrow, they will need to deal with the *next* generation of youth, as today's children mature and enter adulthood.

Table 2.5 clarifies the social and economic contours of this demography. First, the data show how much the very young, those aged 14 and under, represent in terms of populational structure. Iraq, Jordan, Palestine, Sudan, Syria, and Yemen are the youngest societies, as those aged 0–14 compose between 35 to 41 percent of their populations. By contrast, less than 14 percent of Qatari and Emirati societies fall in this youngest generational bracket. In regional comparison, 30 percent of the MENA's populace is aged 14 and under – the second-highest proportion in the world, trailing only sub-Saharan Africa. For all of today's difficulties, the future may augur greater crisis, as today's youngest grow up, finish school, and pursue employment. To appreciate this looming dilemma, consider that the next oldest segment, those aged 15 to 24, is highly literate, with most having at least primary education. As Table 2.5 continues, only Egypt, Iraq, and Sudan have youth literacy rates under 90 percent. Yet as the data indicate, these youth are also unable to find jobs. Collectively, the MENA presents a youth unemployment rate of 26.1 percent, meaning more than one-quarter of all youths seeking jobs cannot find work. This is the highest regional figure in the world, far exceeding that of North America (8.8 percent) and even South Asia (9.9 percent). This figure is also far above the overall adult unemployment rate in the region, which according to the World Bank is roughly 10 percent.

Amplifying the potential for political change and social mobilization driven by jobless, educated youths is the ubiquity of information and communication technologies. Table 2.5 shows the number of mobile phone subscriptions and internet usage across the region. These figures correlate with

TABLE 2.5

Youth, mobility, and technology

	Population ages 0–14 (% total population)	Literacy rate, youth total (% people ages 15–24)	Unemployment, youth total (% total labor force ages 15–24)	Mobile phone subscriptions (per 100 people)	Individuals using the Internet (% population)
Algeria	29.3	96.8	30	111	47.7
Bahrain	19.7	94.1	5	158.4	95.9
Egypt	33.5	88.2	32.6	105.5	45
Iran	23.7	98.1	28.4	107.2	60.4
Iraq	40.4	81.5	16.6	87.3	49.4
Israel	27.9	98.6	6.9	126.7	81.6
Jordan	35.5	99.1	37.2	100	66.8
Kuwait	21.1	99.1	13.9	172.6	98
Lebanon	23.1	99.1	17.4	72.3	78.2
Libya	28.2	99.9	41.9	94.4	21.8
Morocco	27.4	91.2	21.9	122.9	61.8
Oman	21.8	98.7	13.7	149.8	80.2
Palestine (West Bank & Gaza Strip)	39.6	99.4	46.9	81.2	65.2
Qatar	13.9	95.5	0.6	151.1	95.9
Saudi Arabia	25.2	99.2	25.8	122.1	82.1

(Continued)

	Population ages 0–14 (% total population)	Literacy rate, youth total (% people ages 15–24)	Unemployment, youth total (% total labor force ages 15–24)	Mobile phone subscriptions (per 100 people)	Individuals using the Internet (% population)
Sudan	40.8	70.9	26.7	70.7	30.9
Syria	36.6	96.4	N/A	84.2	34.3
Tunisia	24	96.2	34.8	124.3	55.5
Turkey	25	99.6	20.5	96.4	64.7
UAE	13.9	93	7.8	210.9	94.8
Yemen	39.9	90.2	23.7	54.4	26.7
Middle East and North Africa	30	90.8	26.1	106.8	55.2
European Union (EU)	15.4	99.7	17.1	123.5	80.6
North America	18.6	99.5	8.8	117.2	77
Latin America and Caribbean	24.9	98.4	18.7	107.5	62.1
East Asia and Pacific	19.8	98.7	10.1	116.4	55.1
Europe and Central Asia (non-EU)	20.8	99.7	19.1	127.3	66.4
South Asia	28.9	88.3	9.9	86.9	30.2
Sub-Saharan Africa	42.7	75.3	13.2	72	22.1

Sources: World Bank (2019), World Development Indicators; International Labour Organization (2019), ILOSTAT. All figures for 2018. Syrian data are estimates.

economic development and territorial size, with residents of poorer states like Sudan and the Palestinian territories, plus war-torn countries like Sudan and Yemen, featuring the lowest rates of mobile phone and internet usage. As expected, wealthier and smaller countries like Israel, Kuwait, and Qatar have extremely high penetration rates by these technologies; almost everyone in Kuwait, for instance, utilizes the Internet, while the UAE exhibits an astonishing ratio of more than two mobile phone subscriptions for every one person. On average, the MENA region is a well-connected one. Its mobile phone subscription rate of 106.8 per 100 persons exceeds South Asia and sub-Saharan Africa, and runs on par with Latin America; its 55.2 percent internet usage rate is equivalent to East Asia.

Such technological connectedness crucially affects politics, as it allows citizens to circulate images, learn new ideas, share strategies, and maintain social networks even in the face of repression. Starting in the 2000s, for instance, daring blogs by young activists created new spaces of online dissent, creativity, and entrepreneurship that caught many censors off guard. That technology can magnify youth mobilization is especially pertinent in dense urban areas, where students and young proponents have long supported popular ideologies and movements for change. The MENA has nearly forty cities with more than a million residents, and many became sites of tenacious protests during the Arab Spring. Youths in many urban neighborhoods not only thirst for greater economic mobility but also chafe from infrastructural shortcomings, among them housing crunches, air and noise pollution, sanitation problems, and power shortages. Paving over old cityscapes with expensive Western-style projects like gated neighborhoods and high-rise towers – as in the satellite suburbs of Cairo, parts of metropolitan Tel Aviv, and the megacity of Dubai – is not the answer, as these schemes ignore existing slums, exploit migrant workers, and reduce services available to other neighborhoods.

Gender

Gender represents another dimension of societal life with political implications. Imbalances between men and women persist in terms of equality, opportunity, and resources. In comparative perspective, the MENA scores poorly on many conventional measures of gender equality. The World Economic Forum's Global Gender Gap Index, for instance, measures female disadvantages compared to men across four indicators – economic participation, educational achievement, lifelong health, and political empowerment. The latest report from 2018 indicates the MENA as suffering unfortunately large gender gaps when compared to more developed regions. This pattern is found within hard data, as the regional comparisons of Table 2.6 show. The MENA's 72.6 percent female literacy rate ranks well above South Asia and sub-Saharan Africa, but also well below every other global region. The same middle-tier status holds for its 41.9 percent female tertiary school enrollment rate (that is, the percentage of eligible women who attend any kind of structured education after high school). This also marks a titanic increase from its 1990 rate of just 9 percent.

Where the MENA languishes is the female labor participation rate, or the percentage of women who enter the labor market. The regional rate of 21.7 percent – meaning, in essence, just one in five women seek employment – is lowest in global terms. Indeed, the abysmal rates of female job-seeking in Iraq (13 percent), Jordan (15.1 percent) and Yemen (6.2 percent) are among the lowest in the world. The situation is similar when comparing the proportion of seats held by women in national parliaments and advisory assemblies. Despite the reality that most legislatures under authoritarian regimes do not hold real power, the gender breakdown in these institutions leaves room for further reform and improvement. Regionally, 16.6 percent of all seats in national parliaments (even if they have little power) belong to women. This lags behind other regions, such as the EU (30.5 percent), Latin America (30.7 percent), and North America (22.9 percent).

What helps in many countries are gender quotas which sequester a fixed number of seats for women, by either allocating a fixed number of positions within the elected chambers for female candidates or else requiring parties to formulate candidate lists with gender parity. Algeria, Tunisia, Libya, Egypt, Iraq, Jordan, Sudan, and Palestine have all experimented with such mechanisms. Indeed, nearly a third of Tunisia's parliament is composed of women deputies, higher than most Western countries, while on the low end, virtually no women are represented in national legislative bodies in Oman, Kuwait, and Yemen.

As always, though, there exists significant variation within the MENA on these key indicators. Female literacy is well over 90 percent in over half of these countries, from Israel and Turkey to Jordan and Kuwait; but on the low end, the percentage of women who can read and write languishes at 55 percent in Yemen and 59 percent in Morocco. The same wide range goes for female tertiary school enrollment, female labor force participation, and parliamentary representation. Tunisia's democracy, notably, possesses a national legislature where women constitute nearly one-third of representation, a figure higher than most Western countries. To some degree, levels of economic

TABLE 2.6

Gender inequality in comparative perspective

	Female literacy rate (% females ages 15+)	Female tertiary school enrollment (% eligible women attending post-secondary education)	Female labor force participation rate (% females ages 15+)	Proportion of seats held by women in national parliaments or assemblies
Algeria	73.1	57.3	16.4	26.8
Bahrain	93	63.1	46.1	15
Egypt	65.5	34.8	24.7	14.9
Iran	80.8	65.5	17.9	5.9
Iraq	76	N/A	13	25.2
Israel	96.8	73.6	69.1	24.2
Jordan	97.4	33.9	15.1	15.4
Kuwait	94.9	42.7	58.8	3.1
Lebanon	91.8	45.8	26.3	4.7
Libya	85.6	N/A	27.3	15
Morocco	59.1	33.3	23.1	20.5
Oman	93.2	59.7	32.4	1.2
Palestine (West Bank & Gaza Strip)	95.2	52.5	20.7	12.9
Qatar	94.2	51	59	8.9
Saudi Arabia	91.4	68.5	24.6	20

(Continued)

	Female literacy rate (% females ages 15+)	Female tertiary school enrollment (% eligible women attending post-secondary education)	Female labor force participation rate (% females ages 15+)	Proportion of seats held by women in national parliaments or assemblies
Sudan	68.6	17.1	25.2	30.5
Syria	80.7	42.7	12.9	13.2
Tunisia	72.2	41.2	27.1	31.3
Turkey	93.6	73.4	37.5	17.4
UAE	95.8	36.9	52	17.5
Yemen	54.9	10	6.2	0.3
Middle East and North Africa	72.6	41.9	21.7	16.6
European Union (EU)	98.9	75.7	67.8	30.5
North America	98	99	67.7	22.9
Latin America and Caribbean	93.1	57.5	56.9	30.7
East Asia and Pacific	94.1	50.5	66.1	20.2
Europe and Central Asia (non-EU)	98.4	69.8	58.7	20.8
South Asia	62.2	22.8	27.8	18.3
Sub-Saharan Africa	57.1	7.9	62.9	24

Sources: World Bank (2019), *World Development Indicators*; United Nations Development Programme (2019), *Human Development Report*; United Nations Education, Scientific, and Cultural Organization (2019), *UIS.Stat*. All figures for 2018. Syrian data are estimates.

development correlate with trends in gender equality; the more industrialized and advanced the country, then the more likely women will enjoy equal access to schooling and employment. Conflict and violence disproportionately wreak havoc on women's health and opportunities as well, as seen in the data for Libya, Syria, and Yemen. However, there are limits to this developmental correlation. In oil-exporting Saudi Arabia, for example, over two-thirds of all eligible women pursue education after high school – but just one-quarter of all women seek jobs, the same as poorer Egypt. Kuwait, likewise, is a wealthy rentier state with 95 percent female literacy and where 59 percent of women enter the labor market; but women also compose just 3 percent of the parliament, one of the lowest rates in the region.

What accounts for gender inequality in the Muslim-majority Middle East? In historical terms, the region commands no monopoly on patriarchy. Patriarchy is a universal trait of almost every culture, and refers to social systems in which males enjoy inherent advantages in terms of authority and status over women, who suffer legal and informal subordination. It means male domination. Only in the last century have women around the world been able to attain political, economic, and social rights that approach those held by men. Some Western countries began this process early on, but the gender gap lingers. In the United States, according to the Pew Research Center, women still earn only 85 percent of men's pay for equivalent work, and so would have to work 39 additional days to earn the equivalent male salary. Moreover, few democracies anywhere exceed 40 percent female legislative representation, and most countries still await their first woman president or prime minister. Within Muslim societies, too, talk of gender equality is neither new nor taboo, and civic organizations devoted to furthering women's rights have existed for the past century, with many of the issues discussed – maternity leave, sexual assault, divorce rights – not unlike discourse in the West. During the Arab Spring, as well, women stood at the forefront of many revolutionary protests.

Historical context reveals the struggle for women's rights in this region as diverse and complex. Western imperialism brought with it deep prejudices against Islam, and many local voices resisted by advocating the authenticity of preexisting social practices like veiling. However, secular activists also began mobilizing for better schooling, legal rights, and suffrage. During the 1950s and 1960s, young women became leading members of the leftist and Arab Nationalist movements that swept the region. Dramatic improvements came during these decades, as state-led development expanded services, schooling, and employment in ways that incorporated many women. Such gains benefited urban more than rural communities, however, and linked gender advancement with authoritarianism. During their heyday, autocratic rulers in Tunisia, Iraq, Syria, Egypt, and other countries championed women's rights as a way to legitimate their power and prove they were more modern than Islamist alternatives. Where patriarchy especially thrived was in personal status and family laws regulating social relations, which persist today. Bias against women, for instance, manifests in unequal inheritance laws, rules regarding polygamy, divorce rights, and male guardianship. While some countries like Morocco, Tunisia, and Jordan have made strides in modernizing such laws, more conservative states like Saudi Arabia defend them with cultural reasoning.

Women's rights, hence, is not a straightforward issue. Now, even basic symbols of gender empowerment have become highly contested in some areas. For instance, prior to the rise of Islamism, many secularists saw veiling as repressive. The first Tunisian president, Habib Bourguiba, took inspiration from Turkey's Kemalism in banishing religion to the private sphere and virtually prohibited women from wearing the *hijab* (veil) in public venues. Today, however, many Islamists are women and see the veil as a form of empowerment against the repressive practices of secular dictatorships. Indeed, societal debates over gender equality are now highly politicized, with women's rights activists often taking opposing sides on issues. Such dynamism, however, disproves one of the oldest stereotypes about the Middle East – that unchanging cultural or religious values have locked women into positions of permanent subordination. Today, a new generation of young female activists is questioning the boundaries of male authority and aims to equalize their social, economic, and political playing fields.

CONCLUSION

This chapter probed the thick context of political life in the MENA. It unraveled the geographic context of the region, showing how environmental constraints and physical space have left deep imprints. It reviewed historical trajectories of economic development, tracing how state-led strategies and boom-and-bust cycles created wild swings of prosperity and privation that countries still face today. Financial crisis and unemployment problems haunt many. It then investigated four social issues – identity, human security, youth, and gender – to reveal the region's diversity and variance. There are multiple sources of ethnic and religious identity, while overall well-being spans the gamut of the human experience. Most countries face a demographic youth bulge, as technologically connected millennials and teenagers seek better lives. They also struggle to overcome gender inequality, although women's rights remain a promising point of contention and mobilization.

All these factors intersect with the political preferences, actions, and issues that mark governance and policymaking in the MENA. Having laid down this landscape, the subsequent chapters systematically explore the concrete histories and politics of most countries mentioned. They bestow extraordinary detail onto actors, institutions, events, and processes that drive forward the political pathway of each country.

FURTHER READING

This chapter covered myriad issues, and fortunately the scholarly world has kept abreast. First, a widening literature has addressed environmental issues, in particular how communities and states have attempted to engage, manipulate, and react to changes in their physical space. Among them are Alan Mikhail, *Water on Sand: Environmental Histories of the Middle East and North Africa* (Oxford University Press, 2013); Edmund Burke and David Yaghoubian, eds., *Struggle and Survival in the Modern Middle East*, 2nd ed. (University of California Press, 2005); and Dorte Vener, ed., *Adaptation to a Changing Climate in the Arab Countries: A Case for Adaptation Governance and Leadership in Building Climate Resilience* (World Bank, 2012).

The study of economic development in the MENA has spurred a virtual industry of historical analyses and policy-related writing. The authoritative primers include Melani Cammett, Ishac Diwan, Alan Richards, and John Waterbury, *A Political Economy of the Middle East*, 4th ed. (Routledge, 2015); Rodney Wilson, *Economic Development in the Middle East*, 2nd ed. (Routledge, 2010); and Clement Moore Henry and Robert Springborg, *Globalization and the Politics of Development in the Middle East*, 2nd ed. (Cambridge University Press, 2010). Since the Arab Spring, many new volumes have arisen to stress the structural problems of

unemployment, deprivation, poverty, and other ills. These include Magdi Amin et al., *After the Spring: Economic Transitions in the Arab World* (Oxford University Press, 2012) and Ahmed Galal and Ishac Diwan, eds., *The Middle East Economies in Times of Transition* (Palgrave Macmillan, 2016).

Though these works tend to emphasize the Arab world, there is excellent non-Arab scholarship as well: for Israel, see Paul Rivlin, *The Israeli Economy from the Foundation of the State through the 21st Century* (Cambridge University Press, 2010); for Turkey, Şevket Pamuk, *Uneven Centuries: Economic Development of Turkey since 1820* (Princeton University Press, 2018); and for Iran, Suzanne Maloney's *Iran's Political Economy since the Revolution* (Cambridge University Press, 2015).

Identity, human security, youth, and gender command impressive interdisciplinary research agendas. For identity, poignant looks at ethnic and religious (especially Islamic) identities include L. Carl Brown, *Religion and State: The Muslim Approach to Politics* (Columbia University Press, 2000); Michael Cook, *Ancient Religions, Modern Politics: The Islamic Case in Comparative Perspective* (Princeton University Press, 2014); Will Kymlicka and Eva Pföstl, eds., *Minority Politics in the Middle East and North Africa: The Prospects for Transformative Change*

(Routledge, 2018); and Heather Sharkey, *A History of Muslims, Christians, and Jews in the Middle East* (Cambridge University Press, 2017).

The study of human security has generated a growing scholarly lineage as well. The landmark work is the UNDP's *1994 Human Development Report* (Oxford University Press, 1994). Regional analyses include Ashok Swain and Anders Jägerskog, *Emerging Security Threats in the Middle East: The Impact of Climate Change and Globalization* (Rowman and Littlefield, 2016) and Anders Jägerskog, Michael Schulz, and Ashok Swain, eds., *Routledge Handbook on Middle East Security* (Routledge, 2019).

For deeper analyses of youth and youth activism, see Asef Bayat, *Life as Politics: How Ordinary People Change the Middle East*, 2nd ed. (Stanford University Press, 2013); Bessma Momani, *Arab Dawn: Arab Youth and the Demographic Dividend they Will Bring* (University of Toronto Press, 2015); and Samir Khalaf and Roseanne Saad Khalaf, eds., *Arab Youth: Social Mobilisation in Times of Risk* (Saqi, 2012).

Gender and women's rights are the subjects of innumerable volumes too, including Valentine Moghadam, *Modernizing Women: Gender and Social Change in the Middle East*, 3rd ed. (Lynne Rienner, 2013) and Nikkie Keddie, *Women in the Middle East: Past and Present* (Princeton University Press, 2008). Contemporary studies of female activism include Maha El Said, Lena Meari, and Nicola Pratt, eds., *Rethinking Gender in Revolutions and Resistance: Lessons from the Arab World* (Zed Books, 2015), and Leila Ahmed, *A Quiet Revolution: The Veil's Resurgence, from the Middle East to America* (Yale University Press, 2011).

Online sources

Voluminous research materials exist online for all the issues perused here. For instance, regarding environmental and ecological issues, the UN Food and Agricultural Organization's regional portal has a variety of data and publications (www.fao.org/neareast/en/). The FAO's water database also tracks water stress and water scarcity around the world, including the MENA (www.fao.org/nr/aquastat/). There are also a rising number of regional blogs and websites dedicated to conjuring more attention around environmental degradation and climate change. The best are EcoMENA (www.ecomena.org/) and Green Prophet (www.greenprophet.com/).

Economics may be the dismal science, but online sleuthing can produce enriching data. The World Bank's World Development Indicators comprise the primary source of quantitative data in this chapter (http://databank.worldbank.org/data/home.aspx), alongside the International Monetary Fund's datasets (www.imf.org/en/Data). These track thousands of social and economic indicators for every country in the region since 1960. The ILO also follows and investigates employment trends (www.ilo.org/global/lang–en/index.htm). The World Bank's MENA Economic Monitor (www.worldbank.org/en/region/mena/publication/mena-economic-monitor) and the Gulf Labour Markets, Migration, and Population Programme by the Gulf Research Center (http://gulfmigration.org/) also provide up-to-date policy briefings and breaking developments. Finally, data from the UN Human Development Index, and broader discussions of human security, can be found through the UNDP's relevant portal (http://hdr.undp.org/en).

For identity-based issues, Pew Global contains a multitude of global surveys and opinion polls, and some of them regularly ask individuals in the region about their views on nationality, religion, and other affiliations (www.pewglobal.org/). The

Arab Barometer survey project, which also queries individuals about family, tribal, national, and religious attachments, presents all of its data and results online (www.arabbarometer.org/).

For youth-oriented research, the region's most popular blogs can be found on Feedspot's listing (https://blog.feedspot.com/middle_east_blogs). There are also many youth surveys undertaken by regional organizations that help illustrate the generational gap; these include the Asda'a Burson-Masteller's Arab Youth Survey (www.arabyouthsurvey.com) and the Silatech Index (www.silatech.org). Another excellent source is the Arab NGO Directory (https://arab.org/directory/), which lists nearly 4,000 non-profit organizations and advocacy groups based in the Arab world. For data related to gender equality and women's rights, one fruitful source is the World Economic Forum's Global Gender Gap Index, which as mentioned in this chapter maps out various aspects of gender inequality (www.weforum.org/reports/the-global-gender-gap-report-2018). Other useful materials exist on the Harvard Kennedy School Women and Public Policy Program's Gender Action Portal (http://gap.hks.harvard.edu/) and the UN-Women's digital library on gender equality issues (www.unwomen.org/en). The World Bank also has a useful portal for gender-related data (www.worldbank.org/en/topic/gender).

Please note that URLs may change far more quickly than books can be printed; so if these exact URLs do not work, simply search Google or another engine by the titles of these websites and online resources.

North Africa

Morocco, Algeria, Tunisia, Libya, and Egypt

Kingdom of Morocco

Gregory W. White

INTRODUCTION

Morocco has a multifaceted history and complex political arena. Its political system rests beneath a ruling monarchy that, in the post-colonial era, receives close support from global powers – principally, the United States and former colonial power France – as well as regional actors. Ostensibly this is because of Morocco's perception of serving as an oasis of moderation and stability. In the aftermath of the 2011 Arab Spring, the government trumpeted the "Moroccan exception" – i.e., that Moroccan society, political norms, and institutions somehow made the country immune to the turmoil that was happening throughout the region. Yet, although the regime was not toppled *à la* Ben Ali in Tunisia or Mubarak in Egypt, the country has nonetheless experienced economic, political, and social strains that require urgent attention and domestic reforms in the coming years.

Morocco is also a kingdom accustomed to navigating through swirling geopolitical winds and regional pressures. Its position in the northwest of Africa has nurtured a rich, complicated relationship with the world: oriented towards Africa to the south, the MENA region to the east, and Europe and the United States in the global north. Perhaps the single most complicated aspect of modern Morocco is its claim to the Western Sahara territory. For its part, the Moroccan monarchy has claimed authority over what it calls the "southern provinces" since 1975; Rabat argues that this fulfills longstanding sovereignty that dates back hundreds of years. The territory is rich in resources, and continues to be a key pawn in a regional and global stalemate over sovereignty and international influence.

Box 3.1 provides vital data for this country.

BOX 3.1 VITAL DATA – KINGDOM OF MOROCCO

Capital	Rabat
Regime type	Authoritarian (monarchy)
Head of state	King Mohammed VI (since 1999)
Head of government	Prime Minister Saad Eddine Othmani (since 2017)
Legislative institution	Bicameral parliament, with elected 395-seat lower house (Majlis al-Nuwaab, or House of Representatives)
Female quota	Yes: women can run for any seat, but 60 are reserved exclusively for women through a national proportional representation system
Percentage of seats held by women	20.5%
Major political parties (share of seats in most recent general elections, 2016)	Justice and Development (31.6%), Authenticity and Modernity (25.8%), Istiqlal (11.6%), National Rally of Independents (9.4%), Popular Movement (6.8%), Socialist Union of Popular Forces (5%), Constitutional Union (4.8%)
Population	35,739,580
Major ethnic groups	Arab-Berber (99%), other (1%)
Major religious groups	Muslim (99%), other (1%)
GDP per capita	$3,359 ($8,933 at Purchasing Power Parity)
Unemployment rate	9%
Youth unemployment rate	21.9%
Major economic industries	Mining (especially phosphate), tourism, aerospace, automotive, food processing, textiles, construction, energy, agriculture, and fishing
Military spending as % GDP	3.2

HISTORICAL BACKGROUND

What is today known as Morocco remained largely cut off from the Roman Empire, primarily by the mountains of the Rif and the Atlas range. Nonetheless, the Romans established important settlements in Tingis (Tangier) and Volubilis. Islam reached Morocco in the early eighth century, as Arab-Islamic power spread into the area and across the Strait of Gibraltar into the Iberian Peninsula. For centuries, several dynasties dominated northwestern Africa: the Idrissids, who founded Fez in the 780s; the Almoravids, who established Marrakech in the eleventh century; the Almohads, who reigned during the fall of Muslim Spain; the Merenids; the Wattasids; and the Saadians. The completion of the Christian Reconquista of Spain in 1492 changed the region's political economy and society. The extension of Christian control into North Africa transformed the trans-Sahara slave trade and prompted the emergence of Christian enclaves on the Mediterranean coast, Melilla and Ceuta. Both *presidios* exist to this day and are prominent entities in Moroccan, Spanish, Mediterranean, and European politics.

Both the Saadians and, in turn, the Alaouite dynasty in the seventeenth century ultimately repulsed Ottoman imperial ambitions. Sultan Moulay Isma'il established Meknes as the capital in the late seventeenth century, and the Alaouites have ruled Morocco until this day.[1] The dynasty claimed descent from the Prophet, and as such carried (at least in the eyes of its supporters) a Sharifian sense of nobility and legitimacy. By the nineteenth century, however, the kingdom was largely in decline. The French occupation of Algeria in 1830 was met with virtually no response from the sultanate. In 1856, a treaty with Great Britain opened the country to trade and gave Britain control over the Strait of Gibraltar. Spain seized control of more coastal islands and unoccupied rocks in the mid-nineteenth century to complement its inland control of the territories of Ceuta and Melilla. Internal rebellions and unrest, long a feature across Moroccan lands, increasingly tested the frail authority of the Alaouite sultan.

From 1873 to 1894, Moulay Hassan as ruler briefly reestablished some authority and power, but the moment was fleeting. After his death, the country fell into deeper difficulties, largely owing to mismanagement by his son, 'Abd al-Aziz. By 1904, Spain and France had effectively divided the country. By 1908, many different Moroccan groups and rural forces were waging open revolt against 'Abd al-Aziz. His brother, Moulay Hafid, replaced him.

Moulay Hafid further indebted the country to European lenders. At the same time, dissident tribes in Fez besieged him, and the embattled sultan turned to France for military, political, and economic assistance. On March 30, 1912, Moulay Hafid signed the Treaty of Fez, establishing a French protectorate over most of Morocco. The French colonial presence retained the basic structure of the royal government. The administration of French

Marshal Hubert Lyautey ruled through a policy of co-optation and direct administration. Moulay Hafid signed official decrees in his own name and remained the ostensible authority, but Lyautey as Resident-General retained the unmatchable coercive power of French troops. Lyautey imposed a doctrine of selective pacification; rather than rule directly through military occupation, Lyautey carefully targeted rebellious tribes, communities, and groups in strategic areas that posed the most peril to French economic and political interests, and to the Alaouite crown.

In other ways, however, in striking contrast to France's direct colonial occupation and effective annexation of Algeria, colonialism in Morocco left many domestic institutions relatively intact. Privileged classes were preserved, especially the commercially dominant Arab bourgeoisie in the cities of Fez and in the southern Sousse, as well as Tamazight tribal notables. (This chapter uses "Tamazight" to refer to Morocco's indigenous peoples rather than "Berber.") Further, unlike Tunisia's experience under its French protectorate, internal social evolution in Morocco was modest. Upwardly mobile lower-status groups did not infuse sectors of the traditional elite with fresh blood, and few Moroccan elites received a French education.

At the same time, Spain colonized the north and, of course, controlled Spanish Sahara to the south. Although the Anti-Atlas (or Lesser Atlas) tribes in the south offered opposition, Tamazight communities in the northern Rif Mountains displayed the strongest resistance to European colonialism. The most famous figure was 'Abd al-Krim al-Khattabi, who attempted to establish an independent Rifian republic that espoused a mix of nationalism, tribalism, and Salafi Islamist fervor. His forces delivered a humiliating defeat to a superior Spanish army at the Battle of Annual in 1921. Nonetheless, the Spanish ultimately suppressed the Rif population by 1926, with colonial forces (including a young Francisco Franco) making extensive use of mustard gas.

The Geneva protocol prohibiting the use of gas was signed in 1925; Spain signed the treaty, but clearly flouted its terms. As such, the campaign was brutal. Legend has it that Franco himself once returned from a raid with the bloody heads of Tamazight tribesmen as trophies. The French also intervened after 1925, lending well over 100,000 troops alongside heavy artillery and battle tanks to the campaign to liquidate the indigenous uprising. Today, 'Abd al-Krim's resistance is annually celebrated as a source of national honor, a complicated deployment of Moroccan nationalist symbols given the fraught relationship between the Tamazight communities of the Rif – still an economically marginalized region – and the Alaouite monarchy claiming to embody the entire Moroccan nation.

Nationalism and independence

Despite the suppression of the Rif, a Moroccan national independent movement still gained shape. A turning point came on May 16, 1930, when French colonial authorities issued an infamous *dahir* (decree), establishing a separate system of customary law tribunals in Tamazight regions of the country. This "Berber Decree" was part of a French effort to isolate the rural areas from the anti-colonial nationalism. Empowered to deal with civil matters, these tribunals created an artificial division between Arab and Tamazight peoples by removing the latter from the national system of Muslim jurisprudence on civil matters. In May 1932, a coalition of traditional elites, radicalized younger advocates, and lower middle-class activists formed the Kutla al-Amal al-Watani (National Action Bloc), the first overtly nationalist party in the country. The bloc sought a reform plan that called for autonomy and an end to colonial efforts to divide and conquer by crafting a distinctive Tamazight identity through the Berber Decree and other colonial machinations. Nonetheless, French officials (and Sultan Mohammed ben Yusef, or Mohammed V, the titular head of the Alaouite dynasty) ignored the plan. In 1943, the National Action Bloc had attracted more members and evolved into the Istiqlal (Independence) Party.

After World War Two, the Istiqlal enjoyed strong urban support, and a tacit alliance with a monarchy increasingly resistant to French impositions and authority. The party was challenged, however, by powerful rural Tamazight chieftains allied with the French, by some traditionalist elements in the cities, and by the heads of some religious brotherhoods. During the late 1940s, the Istiqlal transformed itself into a broad-based independence movement. As the alliance between the Istiqlal and the monarchy became more overt and began to challenge French hegemony, colonial authorities took action. In August 1953, the French sent Mohammed V and his family, including his son Hassan, into exile in Madagascar and replaced the king with a more docile relative. But Mohammed V became a martyr in the eyes of the population, and the nationalist movement was catalyzed into an all-out fight for independence.

In large part because of the turmoil in neighboring Algeria, a quick political settlement was achieved. Mohammed V's return from exile in the fall of 1955 marked the end of colonial rule. On March 2, 1956, the French regions were joined with the Spanish-controlled areas, and France formally granted independence. In 1957, the country was proclaimed an independent kingdom.

The monarchy emerged as the major beneficiary of independence. Indeed, Morocco is notable because its struggle for independence revolved around the reinvigoration of a monarchy that had been ineffective and dissolute prior to (and during) colonial rule. In time, the population revered Mohammed V for his perceived *baraka,* or religious blessing, among other qualities. Upon independence, the country enjoyed a sufficient level of institutional stability and a reasonably effective political leadership. The political parties, with the Istiqlal in the lead, provided necessary cadres for the new government. The urban resistance forces were incorporated into the police, and the Army of Liberation, one of the last groups to recognize the monarchy, was absorbed into the Royal Armed Forces.

Within five years, however, the relationship between the king and the political parties disintegrated. Mohammed V, who changed his title from sultan to king, was unwilling to become a constitutional figurehead. The internally divided Istiqlal leadership was unwilling to accept the secondary role envisioned by a monarchy desiring more authoritarian powers. Rural pushback, especially from the restive Rif, again reared its head, resulting in forceful suppression efforts by the Moroccan military. Tension between the conservative and radical wings of the Istiqlal reached a breaking point in 1959 and a new left-wing party emerged, the National Union of Popular Forces (UNFP). In February 1961, however, these deteriorating relations were interrupted by the king's death after minor surgery. He was succeeded by his son and Crown Prince, Hassan, who was enthroned on March 3, 1961.

Ruling as King Hassan II, the new royal leader quickly introduced a constitution that was approved in a referendum in December 1962. This began the customary practice of promulgating and revising constitutions – a recurring theme of Moroccan politics. Though it would be revisited and reconfigured later numerous times, the constitution solidified the king's power and gave him the authority to dissolve the legislature and exercise unlimited emergency powers. The Alaouite monarchy's autocratic consolidation was proceeding apace. Facilitating that consolidation was Hassan's constant encouragement for the creation of weak, pro-regime parties, such as the Constitutional Institutions Defense Front (FDIC) and a conservative

Tamazight party, the Popular Movement (MP). Additionally, Hassan never hesitated to invoke states of emergency and assume full power.

One notorious security incident in October 1965 seared the country. Moroccan security forces abducted Mehdi Ben Barka, the popular UNFP leader, in Paris; Ben Barka had been sentenced to death in absentia because of his criticism of King Hassan's rule. Although his fate was the subject of speculation for years, with Hassan and other state voices feigning ignorance, the release of official documents after the king's death in 1999 indicate that Ben Barka was tortured to death with the connivance of French and US intelligence agencies. Thus began a period of sharp repression against party activities and opposition sentiments, which through the late 1960s resulted in a rising number of political prisoners – and consequently increased grumblings against the regime.

Coups, repression, and Western Sahara

The elimination of political opposition failed to prevent – or perhaps prompted – two attempts by military officers to assassinate the king: one in July 1971 at Skhirat, a coastal town between Rabat and Casablanca that hosted a major royal palace, and another in August 1972. The Skhirat episode was a bloody affair, with rebellious army forces attacking the palace when King Hassan and a large entourage were celebrating his birthday.

The second coup attempt was more dramatic, and provided the country with its second most notorious political episode after the Ben Barka affair: the death of General Mohammad Oufkir. In fact, Oufkir is known to have been present at Ben Barka's 1965 torture and murder. A longtime ally of Hassan and holder of several high-level government portfolios, Oufkir was also by the king's side during the 1971 Skhirat coup attempt. Afterwards, for reasons still debated, he conspired to overthrow the king. In August 1972, he ordered Moroccan fighter planes to strafe the king's royal jet as it returned from Europe. Hassan survived the attack, and by the evening the general lost his life though under conflicting accounts – the official narrative held that he committed suicide, but others suggest he was executed. Regardless, security forces imprisoned the general's family in a notorious desert prison, Tazmamart. Indeed, hundreds of military personnel and other accused coup participants or plotters were rounded up after each coup attempt. Oufkir's kin were finally released in 1991, when Tazmamart closed, but only allowed to leave the country in 1996.

Once the king felt confident that he had reestablished control of the military after the coup attempts through aggressive purges and other internal reorganization, he basically ignored the parties. Differences between the Istiqlal and the UNFP reemerged, with internal divisions within the UNFP as well. By the end of 1972, a Rabat-based faction had gained sway and renamed itself the National Union of Socialist Forces (USFP). The USFP would later play a central role in parliamentary political life in Morocco, but for now the country would continue its political period of heavy-handed repression and censorship under a ruling monarchy dominated by its personalistic incumbent.

By the mid-1970s, Hassan slowly began to liberalize trade with Europe. Morocco did not go as far as Tunisia in its pursuit of *infitah* (economic openness), which would mean the end of much state-led developmental programs, but Hassan combined his ability to outmaneuver opposition parties with liberalization measures that created the impression of change. He redistributed nationalized land from French colonial landholders, giving the land to the peasantry in an effort to increase support. He also promulgated ambitious development plans.

Hassan also launched foreign policy initiatives that brought Morocco into conflict with Spain. Fishing disputes in 1973 (and which continue today with the European Union) flared into the Spanish Sahara crisis of 1975. In November 1975, King Hassan organized the *Al-Massira Al-Khadra*, or "Green March," in which approximately 350,000 civilians assembled on the southern border with the territory and staged a short symbolic march into the disputed territory. The event is celebrated annually as a national holiday. Since the northern two-thirds of the territory had large deposits of prized phosphates, as well as oil and uranium reserves, the king's actions seemed to portend economic gains. This deployment of Moroccan nationalism mobilized popular support and raised the king's political fortunes. Since the Istiqlal and the USFP supported reintegration of the territory as part of their own platform, Hassan was able to co-opt much opposition sentiment. Known as "the southern provinces" within Morocco, the Western Sahara is discussed further below.

Severe droughts ravaged the economy during the late 1970s, devastating the agricultural sector and encouraging urban migration. World phosphate prices also began a decline during this period. After placing strong emphasis on phosphate exports to earn foreign exchange, the decline in revenue forced the government to incur more debt to underwrite its steep budgetary commitments, especially in its public employment and subsidies. Public investment in development projects declined, and overt popular discontent reemerged in the late 1970s, with unemployment reaching as high as 35 to 40 percent among youth. Several major episodes of bread riots erupted in the early 1980s, including mass protests in 1983. In the aftermath of the 1979 Iranian Revolution, militant Islamists opposed to the established political order also emerged. With the Moroccan army now mired in the Western Sahara against resistance by the Polisario Front – the local resistance movement that demanded the Western Sahara's complete independence – the cycle of unrest motivated by economic privation and popular mobilization and followed by harsh security measures continued.

The post-Cold War, post-Hassan decades

In December 1990, more anti-austerity riots, associated with the structural adjustment reforms sponsored by the Bretton Woods institutions, the World Bank and International Monetary Fund, unsettled the country. Further, Hassan had sent a contingent of soldiers to the Arabian Gulf to join the anti-Iraq coalition, prompting much domestic criticism from a population that generally evoked sympathies with Saddam Hussein and his anti-Western rhetoric. The king adroitly navigated the criticism by allowing protests, with as many as 300,000 people filling the streets of Rabat. The EU, Saudi Arabia, the United States, and international financial institutions rewarded the king's stance with debt relief and enhanced foreign aid. Disturbances continued, with riots in April and November 1991 led by Al-'Adl Wal-Ihsane (Justice and Charity), an Islamist association banned for its strong advocacy of Islamization.

During the early 1990s the political system was paralyzed by *attentisme* – "a wait and see" stalemate. King Hassan was visibly unwell and traveled to New York to receive medical treatment. In July 1995, things began to open further. Hassan permitted USFP leader Fqih Basri to return to Morocco after 30 years of exile. In 1996, as mentioned earlier, Hassan allowed General Oufkir's family to leave the country. And in September 1996 a referendum for the fifth constitution since independence created a bicameral *majlis*, or parliament, with a directly-elected Chamber of Representatives and a new upper house, the Chamber of Councilors. In November 1997, the first election under the newly recapitulated constitution was held, inaugurating *alternance* – i.e., alternating (and presumably accountable) governments created by parties winning parliamentary elections, although this still left untouched the monarchy's vast powers. The opposition had argued for years that, if given a fair opportunity, it would do well in an election. And it did. In March 1998, Hassan appointed the USFP's leader Abderrahmane Youssoufi to the post of prime minister, a move that allowed the opposition to form and lead the cabinet-based government for the first time, although many domains of policymaking remained far out of reach, particularly regarding foreign policy and domestic security.

In the end, a full assessment of Hassan's ability to rule under *alternance* was rendered impossible by illness and, ultimately, his death on July 23, 1999. His son, King Mohammed VI, acceded to the throne. Mohammed quickly distinguished himself by presiding in a less draconian fashion than his father. He immediately sacked Hassan's notorious minister of interior, Driss Basri. Moreover, the new king began to nurture discussions of human rights. He tolerated a climate that began to allow exposés of the human rights violations from the *années de plomb* (years of lead, so-called due to the brutality of repression) of his father's reign. Early on, Mohammed was also dubbed the "king of the poor" because of his trips throughout the country and his willingness to wade into crowds. Some even called him "Al-Jawal" – the Moroccan word for the ubiquitous cell phone – because of his frequent circulation and mobility.

In 2002 Mohammed publicly married a commoner, a Fez-born engineer named Salma Bennani. This was in stark contrast to his father, whose wives never appeared in public. Though there is no provision for the formal titling or status of Queen in the Moroccan monarchy, Princess Lalla Salma assumed a visible role in many social and charitable activities.

After the terror attacks of September 11, 2001, the promise of political liberalization promises began to slow, as the palace increasingly circumscribed the power of the *majlis*. To be sure, elections in September 2002 marked a significant moment in the post-Hassan era, with the Islamist Justice and Development Party (PJD) performing very well, becoming the third-largest party after the Istiqlal and the secular USFP. Despite irregularities and the king's selection of a nonparty technocrat as prime minister, Driss Jettou, the elections were trumpeted by some observers as the most competitive contest yet held. The 2002 elections also included a female quota, guaranteeing that women would hold 30 parliamentary seats.

Shortly thereafter, on May 16, 2003, the political and social landscape of Morocco was rocked by bombings in Casablanca that killed 45 people. In a royal speech on May 29, Mohammed declared the "end of the era of leniency." Following attacks on the Atocha train station in Madrid on March 11, 2004, in which Moroccan nationals were implicated, the political system tightened still further, with antiterrorism legislation passed later that year. The *majlis* also passed for the first time anti-immigration laws against sub-Saharan immigrants; these were cast in strict security terms, capitalizing on the zeitgeist of the period and mirroring similar legislation in European countries.

Concomitant with this tightening were two further developments. First, in January 2004, Mohammed created the Equity and Reconciliation Commission (IER) to formally investigate the human rights violations of the past – the first such step taken by any country in the Middle East and North Africa. Criticized for its circumscribed purview, underestimation of the number of victims, and unwillingness to name perpetrators, the IER nonetheless publicly investigated rights violations of the Hassan years and released its report in March 2006. The report stated that several hundred people had been illegally killed and over nine thousand subjected to human rights abuses during Hassan's reign. It also called for both reform of the judicial system and compensation for victims. Some dismissed the investigation as political theater, but others argued that it provided some closure for the victims and their families.

A second development was progressive reform of the family code, known in Arabic as the *Mudawana*. In a balancing act with conservative interests, a royal commission announced the changes in 2004 after several years of negotiation and deliberation. The new law reduced men's ability to treat their wives as property, required a man to inform his wife that he was seeking a divorce, and stipulated that he must get permission from a judge before taking a second wife. The legal age for marriage was increased from 15 to 18. Not surprisingly, some reactionary figures and conservative religious voices espoused their resistance. Yet women's groups also criticized the reforms. Given that four out of five rural women are illiterate and lack significant socioeconomic power, the right to divorce can lead to severe deprivation and ostracism, a social reality some believe should be addressed legislatively.

The September 2007 elections marked an additional turning point in Moroccan politics, demonstrating a significant consolidation of electoral reforms. That said, turnout was only 37 percent, a sharp decline from 52 percent in the 2002 election and 58 percent in 1997. The king appointed Istiqlal leader 'Abbas al-Fassi to be the new prime minister. By 2009, al-Fassi appeared to have fallen out of favor. Former deputy interior minister Fouad Ali al-Himma – a close friend and senior advisor to the king – organized a new party called Authenticity and Modernity Party (PAM) to contest municipal elections. PAM would continue its ascent and remains a major force in legislative elections today.

The Arab Spring and the Moroccan exception

Moroccans joined the entire world in watching the events of the 2011 uprisings in Tunisia, Egypt, and elsewhere. While convention continues to refer to the "Arab Spring," in Morocco this can be especially awkward: the monarchy and outsiders have long cast Morocco as Arab, but its Tamazight identity may be as strong as, if not stronger than, its Arabism. To be sure, Morocco was beset with many of the same concerns of people elsewhere in the MENA (and beyond): rising food and energy prices, stagnant economies, widespread youth unemployment, rising inequality, political corruption, and authoritarian governance. One might have even predicted that in terms of social and economic indicators Morocco would have been far riper for turmoil than, say, Egypt or Tunisia.

Though the monarchy managed to avoid full upheaval, Moroccans protested vigorously – although their target was not so much the king as affluent elites, in particular prominent business moguls and government officials. At least two Moroccans followed the lead of Tunisia's Mohamed Bouazizi and immolated themselves. By February, unrest had coalesced around the organization of a day of protest, which came to be known as the February 20 Movement. The February 20 protest was followed by smaller, regular protests. The movement comprised a heterogeneous assortment of associations covering the spectrum – from leftists and Tamazight activists, to feminists, to Islamists from the banned Justice and Charity Movement.

In a preemptive move, Mohammed gave a speech on March 9, 2011, in which he established a royal commission to work on a package of reforms that would strengthen the *majlis* (with the prime minister automatically coming from the largest party in parliament, rather than being handpicked by the king), as well as a deeper respect for human rights, independence of the judiciary, gender equality, and full recognition of Tamazight languages. The commission released its findings in June, followed by a hasty referendum on July 1, the ninth in the post-independence era. As with past referenda rolled out by the palace, the yes vote according to official figures was absurdly high: 98.5 percent.

The opposition's frustration with the referendum process was compounded when national elections scheduled for fall 2012 were moved up to November 25, 2011. The new elections resulted in a victory for the PJD. The Istiqlal placed second, followed (in order) by the National Rally of

Independents (RNI), the PAM, the USFP, the Popular Movement, the Constitution Union, the Progress and Socialism Party (PPS), and the rest to a smattering of smaller parties and quota lists. The February 20 Movement and other Islamists and leftists had called for a boycott, but turnout was 45 percent, a respectable increase from the 2007 figure. Abdelilah Benkirane of the PJD became prime minister in January 2012 and formed a coalition government with the Istiqlal, the Popular Movement, and the PPS. The PJD's first term as lead party, however, resulted in little structural change, as the palace retained control over the reins of power and periodically reshuffled ministerial portfolios to keep parties off-balance.

Still, much was made of the so-called "Moroccan exception," the notion that something enduring or special about Moroccan society enabled the regime to dodge the revolutionary bullet. Such narratives often invoked monarchism, such as the Alaouite dynasty's religious legitimacy, expressed by its descent from the Prophet and the traditional Islamic honorific given to Moroccan kings – *amir al-mu'minin* (Commander of the Faithful). Other explanations include the eschewal of single-party government in the post-independence era (even as the parties were weak vis-à-vis the palace); the allowance of a moderately robust press, with a few starkly drawn red lines concerning the Western Sahara and the monarchy; the gradual reforms concerning Tamazight identity and the *Mudawana*; and the king's willingness to more fully expose human rights abuses committed during his father's rule. Others point out that strong security measures – and the population's fear that clamor for deeper change could tip into a more turbulent situation – helped maintain relative calm. The February 20 Movement, for its part, was quickly repressed by the security services.

New mobilization: 2016 and Hirak Rif

Moroccan political history continues to be inscribed in cycles of mobilization and political contestation today. In October 2016, another round of parliamentary elections occurred, with the PJD again winning a majority with 125 out of 395 seats in the House of Representatives. This time, however, the pro-regime PAM took a close second with 102 seats, followed by the Istiqlal (46 seats) and pro-regime RNI (37 seats). Yet Benkirane was unable to form a government afterwards, largely due to the intransigence of the PAM and RNI. This resulted in the king simply picking another, hopefully more pliable politician from the PJD, Saad Eddine Othmani, as premier. The new Islamist-led government predictably came together in spring 2017, with new elections not due until 2021.

October 2016 also saw protests erupt over abusive police practices that resulted in the death of a fish vendor in the Mediterranean city of Al Hoceima, within the Rif region. Mouhcine Fikri's 1,000 pounds of swordfish had been confiscated by authorities because it was caught out of season. When Fikri climbed into a garbage truck to retrieve the fish, the trash compactor was turned on – allegedly on orders from a police officer – and he was killed. The grisly video went viral, spurring protests across the Rif. The resulting Rif Movement, or Hirak Rif, emerged to protest economic injustice, inequality, and *hogra* – the daily disdain and injury experienced by many working citizens at the hands of corrupt elites and officials. The mobilization also exploited the symbols of the Rif, from its past historical resistance to its strong Tamazight identity. The regime, however, responded with concerted coercion, with most protest leaders intimidated and arrested. In summer 2018, several major figures of the Hirak Rif, including a vocal activist named Nasser Zefzafi, were sentenced to twenty years in prison. Other protesters were given sentences of 2–15 years.

Though the mobilizational campaign was temporarily stifled, the years afterwards were marked by continuing political tensions. The PJD-led government grew increasingly unpopular, while social forces from different parts of the country, from unemployed university graduates to underpaid teachers, mounted their own campaigns of demonstrations. Yet the regime's political reactions have remained as stolid as its economic solutions, with each outburst of popular frustration treated with a combination of police repression and vague reform promises.

SOCIAL AND ECONOMIC ENVIRONMENT

Morocco's physical geography is remarkably diverse, from the relatively fertile, sun-drenched Mediterranean and Atlantic coasts to the snowcapped Atlas Mountains and Sahara desert areas of the east and south. The beauty of the country's natural patrimony has impressed Moroccans and foreign travelers for ages. In recent times this has been the source of crucial foreign exchange, as tourists have traveled to Morocco to explore its culture and varied landscape. There are multiple major urban centers, each with a distinctive provincial heritage, such as Rabat, Casablanca, Marrakech, Fez, Tangier, Meknes, and Agadir (Map 3.1). In social terms, while Tamazight identity and heritage saturate Moroccan society (Tamazight and Arabic both being official languages), almost all Moroccans are Sunni Muslim.

Morocco has been plagued by chronic drought in recent decades, undermining efforts to engineer economic growth. The challenges of the water

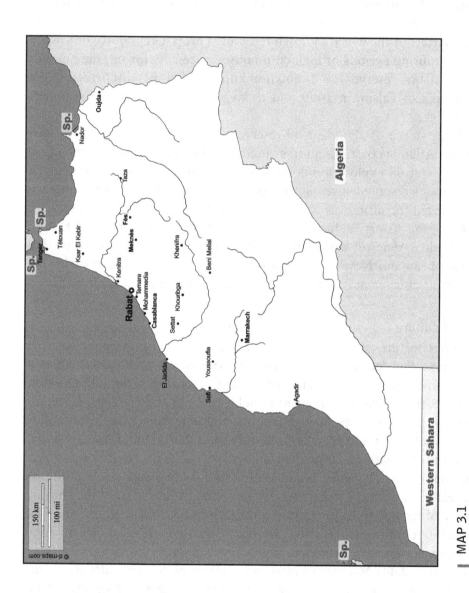

MAP 3.1

Kingdom of Morocco. Major rivers and cities shown. "Sp." indicates Spanish territory. Western Sahara (disputed territory) not fully displayed.

Source: D-Maps.

deficit are profound in a country where the preponderance of the population works on the land and the government has devoted considerable resources to hydrologically-intensive sectors such as irrigated agriculture, phosphate mining, and high-end tourism. The country claims deep-sea fisheries off the Atlantic coast. It also has enormous phosphate resources – as much as three-quarters of the world's known reserves. This is a key source of foreign exchange during periods of high commodity prices. As for oil, the amount of hydrocarbon reserves is a "known unknown." Oil was discovered in the eastern area of Talsint in 2000, but it was determined to be not commercially viable.

The existence of abundant oil reserves in the Western Sahara – as well as off the Atlantic coast – is another matter. Oil extraction has promise economically, yet oil-exploration contracts lack sufficient legal standing given the territory's disputed sovereignty; companies operating in the region have been targeted for protest as well as sanctioned by the European Parliament and European Court of Justice. The United States Department of Energy acknowledges that oil claims in the region are controversial. Nevertheless, European and North American firms continue to make plays with the Moroccan government in Rabat for contracts concerning these oil fields.

Political culture

A primary feature of Moroccan political culture today is public distrust of the state. For decades, Moroccans have viewed the political system as a coercive instrument rather than a basis for cooperative action, an emotion that has been expressed in frequent popular protests and marches. A second feature is the informality of high politics and elite power. In many policy domains, political authority is derived only secondarily from formal political offices. Instead, patterns of neopatrimonialism – a heavy reliance upon personal relations of dependence and exploitation – dominate political life. A third feature is political stalemate, or *attentisme*, resulting from the chronic inability of many opposition parties and factions to work with one another. This facilitates the monarch's power, wherein *lèse-majesté*, or criticism of the monarchy, is expressly forbidden.

The formidable Ministry of Interior broods over domestic affairs; it controls or has a hand in policing, national security, judicial processes, media and information, electoral mechanisms, and even foreign affairs. As such, it reports more to the palace than it does the formal government. Its role is especially apparent during periods of intense monitoring and policing, such as the clampdown after the 2003 Casablanca attacks, the post-Arab Spring emergence of the so-called Islamic State of Iraq and Syria (ISIS) which brought heightened suspicions over youth activism and radicalized Islamism, and the Rif protests of 2016. Fears of terrorism are regnant. In 2014 an increasing number of Moroccans were heading to Syria and Iraq, and authorities expressed concern that they would return home to launch attacks. In August and September 2014, Spanish and Moroccan authorities made arrests in the Spanish enclave cities of Ceuta and Melilla, as well as Melilla's neighboring Moroccan town of Nador; officials said the suspects were terrorists recruiting jihadists to fight for ISIS.

Judicial and administrative institutions reflect French and Spanish colonial influences. The country is administratively divided into 19 provinces and two urban prefectures, Casablanca and Rabat. The provinces are further divided into 72 administrative areas and communes. A governor appointed by the king heads each administrative area. The Supreme Court is composed of four chambers: civil, criminal, administrative, and social. The king appoints all judges, with the advice of the High Judicial Council. Moroccan courts administer a system strongly influenced by French and Spanish legal systems, with elements of *shari'a* – retooled and reinterpreted for modern purposes – expressed in various codes and courts as well. A separate system of courts administers the Judaic religious laws for Jewish citizens, although today there is only a small remnant of the country's once-prosperous Jewish community.

Economic conditions

Economic growth remains uneven for a lower middle-income country. The average annual growth in GDP per capita between 2000 and 2010 was 3.8 percent; in 2018, the overall GDP growth rate was 3.4 percent, representing a bit of a slowdown from its average pace in the 2000s, in which the economy expanded at 4.7 percent annually, on average. However, economists estimate that 7 to 10 percent annual growth is considered necessary to reduce unemployment and especially poverty, which in rural areas is estimated to increase 20 percent. According to government estimates, the average individual annual income ranges from $2600 to $3000. Illiteracy is highest in the Arab world, with the most optimistic surveys holding that a third of the national population (and informal estimates suggesting closer to a half) cannot read and write. Female illiteracy is among the worst in the MENA, and in rural areas may be as high as 80 percent. The country ranked 123 out of 189 countries in the United Nations Development Programme's 2018 Human Development Index, and 123 out of 189 countries in its 2018 Gender Inequality Index.

Government-held foreign debt as a percentage of GDP fell from a high of 112 percent in 1987 to 48 percent in 2010 – a positive trend. But it began to increase and stood at 65 percent by 2019. Exports of goods and services as a percentage of GDP also increased to over 35 percent. This is a concerning feature of the economy, as it remains vulnerable to exogenous shocks such as international conflict, economic recession in Morocco's major European trading partners, or downturns in commodity prices. For example, the 2008 global financial crisis and subsequent crisis in the Eurozone had profound reverberations in Morocco, as Western tourists steered away from trips abroad and European demand for Moroccan exports fell sharply.

Agriculture remains a significant economic contributor; more than one in three employed Moroccans works in this sector today, although this figure has been gradually declining since the 1990s. Indeed, the relative importance of agricultural production has diminished, partly due to growth in other sectors and partly due to the nature of land ownership and exports. In some areas, wealthy landlords own the best, most arable land and have been slow to fully modernize practices. Although the productivity of the high-end sector exceeds that of subsistence farming, agricultural exports have dropped significantly since the 1990s. Traditional markets in Europe were limited by the EU's Common Agricultural Policy, and then hit hard by Greece's admission to the EU in 1981 and Spain and Portugal's in 1986. The EU became self-sufficient in the citrus, olive oil, and wine that Morocco had long exported north. Indeed, some Moroccans have ironically commented their farms enjoyed easier access to Europe during colonialism.

Another limiting factor is drought. Morocco has long experienced regular drought, but it has become chronic in recent decades. According to the UNDP, the average number of "hot" days in Morocco has increased by 21.5 since 1960. The frequency of "cold days" has decreased significantly in all seasons since 1960. Particularly worrisome is the fact that droughts are increasing during the winter, when the Mediterranean region accumulates most of its precipitation. Future climate projections for Morocco are dire. The mean annual temperature is projected to increase by 1.1 to 3.5 degrees Celsius by the 2060s and 1.4 to 5.6 degrees Celsius by the 2090s. By the 2090s annual precipitation is also expected to drop by 10 to 40 percent, including a 10 to 30 percent reduction during the wet season, from October to April, and a 10 to 40 percent decrease during the dry season, from May to September.

The principal crops are wheat, barley, maize, beans, and chickpeas. In addition, there is a large government-owned sugar beet sector. However, livestock productivity and crop yields remain low, and to meet domestic consumption needs the country imports many food products and commodities from the EU and, since signing the US-Morocco Free Trade Agreement in 2004, from the United States. For its part, the fishing sector offers some promise, although export markets for the main product, sardines, are highly competitive. Since the 1970s, the government has sought to develop the deep-sea fishing fleet that plies the Atlantic waters. European boats – principally Spanish – also want to fish in Morocco's territorial waters, causing sharp diplomatic disputes. Accords have been signed in 1995, 2005, 2014, and 2019, but only after acrimonious rounds of diplomacy, with the European Parliament often blocking agreements because of solidarity with Spanish boats and protests over Western Sahara. Chronic overfishing also raises questions about long-term ecological sustainability.

Morocco's major physical industries, such as manufacturing, are concentrated in the Rabat-Casablanca region along the western Atlantic seaboard. Light manufactures such as textiles and leather are also major components. While industrial production decades ago was dominated by low value-added goods, such as various phosphate outputs and oil refining, in recent decades trade agreements and business integration with some European firms has allowed for more valuable production lines within manufacturing. For instance, aerospace and automobile factories are now operating in the kingdom, although their impact on reducing unemployment has been limited given that such industries are reliant more on technology rather than labor. Facilitating logistical and export networking with Europe is Tanger-Med – a massive port complex (now the biggest in Africa) built in the Mediterranean city of Tangiers.

Finally, tourism remains extremely important. The government aggressively markets Morocco as a romantic destination to high-end travelers, celebrities, and adventure-seekers; luxurious world-class hotels and top-notch golf courses are found throughout the country. Despite the profound contradiction presented by the country's hydrological challenges, the government continues to promote tourism and has welcomed direct foreign investment. The tourism sector has rebounded impressively from the 2008 fiscal crisis. Moroccan cities and attractions have been glamorized in prominent global media, from travel publishers like *Lonely Planet* to the *New York Times*. Moroccan locales have also hosted foreign movie productions, with Morocco chosen to stand in for other Middle East countries in Hollywood film sets.

On the other hand, the hot tourism sector has created a housing boom in cities such as Marrakech, Fes, and Tangiers that in turn has squeezed locals. "International gentrification" is occurring, with Western retirees driving the market. Some foreign investors buy and renovate traditional Moroccan houses, known as *ryads,* in the old *medina* (medieval quarters) areas of cities around the country. This renders housing prices unaffordable for local residents, who relocate to suburban and exurban zones.

In a broader sense, the real estate market expresses one of the major problems of the Moroccan economy today – inequality. Major cities are no strangers to luxurious hotels, estates, restaurants, and other well-to-do establishments, but their slums and surrounding rural areas host deep poverty. A notable symbol of this incongruity is the Bank of Africa skyscraper in Rabat, a futuristic luxury tower that began construction in late 2018 but whose rental costs will far exceed the means of most Moroccans.

POLITICAL STRUCTURES

As head of not only the 400-year-old Alaouite dynasty but the Moroccan state itself, the king is the supreme authority – the *amir al-mu'minin,* the Commander of the Faithful (not to mention, constitutionally, the commander-in-chief of the armed forces). He also stands at the center of the *Makhzen,* a word that literally means treasury but colloquially in Morocco refers to the overlapping networks of elites who hold political power and economic wealth by virtue of either their positions in government offices or else their proximity to the all-powerful palace. The monarchy and the four most important ministries needed to maintain social and political control (Interior, Justice, Foreign Affairs, and Islamic Affairs) occupy the apex of this system. Though these ministries of sovereignty belong to the cabinet-based government created by parliament, its ministerial heads are anointed by the king.

The Alaouite king's authority is based on not just the ancient nature of the monarchy but also the religious role traditionally played by the dynastic head as head of the Islamic community. Like other monarchs, his imagery saturates political life and culture – from currency (Photo 3.1) and textbooks to mass media, billboards, and even car decals. Because of his noble religious ancestry and the attendant nobility and legitimacy ascribed to him, some observers believe the Moroccan king satisfies the aspirations of Muslim subjects. Mohammed VI, like his father and grandfather, is venerated by many Moroccans who view him as *sharif* (descendant of the Prophet) and a dispenser of God's blessing. His standing as a religious leader is said to defuse the potency of political Islamism.

PHOTO 3.1
Moroccan currency (dirham) with king's image.

Source: Pixabay. Public domain.

On the other hand, such philosophical and mystical qualities of legitimation did not foreclose the two coup attempts in the early 1970s against King
Hassan, nor has it precluded major periods of popular unrest and social
frustrations driven by perceptions of inequality, injustice, and deprivation, as
in the early 1980s and today since the Arab Spring. The monarchy's security
and stability hence also depend upon not just the brute force of repression
but also its ability to manipulate rival factions, such as parties whose leaders
and followers can be bribed into obeisance or threatened into subordination.

Indeed, alongside institutional manipulations, another source of royal
supremacy is the fact that the monarchy is the nation's most prominent dispenser of patronage. The king is the lead shareholder in what for many years
was known as the Omnium Nord Africain Group (ONA), a massive holding
company with subsidiaries in virtually every productive sector in the Moroccan economy. In 2010, ONA merged with (and now holds the name of)
the National Investment Corporation (Société Nationale d'Investissement,

or SNI). This accounts for the massive increase in King Mohamed's personal fortune since taking the throne in 1999. In 2015, *Forbes* estimated his net worth as $5.7 billion, making him one of the richest individual royals in the world and one of the wealthiest men in Africa.

Using royal patronage and the financial heft afforded by SNI, Mohammed has been able to balance and dominate aspiring political and economic elites through the promise of contracts, appointments, inclusion, payments, and other goods. Some within the king's inner circle are longstanding friends and advisors, such as Fouad Ali al-Himma. Others recruited into the Makhzen are young technocrats, often engineers or businesspersons trained in the West, whose emphasis on efficiency and growth make them often agnostic to the question of democracy and thus well-suited to carrying out important policy tasks, such as implementing World Bank programs or evaluating industrial performance in accordance with foreign investment goals.

Party system

Though the political system is dominated by the Makhzen and monarchy, Morocco's political party landscape is integral to understanding its structures. The country's parties frequently change and adapt, but there are some constants. On the loyalist right wing are parties known as the Coalition for Democracy: the National Independent Rally (RNI), the Popular Movement (MP), the Constitutional Union, the National Democratic Party (PND), and the Authenticity and Modernity Party (PAM), founded in 2008. The MP is a Tamazight movement, founded by resistance leaders in 1958 to counter the preponderance of the Istiqlal. The PND is a party of rural notables, such as major landowners. The RNI and PAM are often perceived as "palace parties" given that their founders and key members are well-known associates of the monarchy and, therefore, ostensibly loyal to the king.

A second formation is the generally left-leaning opposition: the Istiqlal, the National Union of Socialist Forces (USFP), and the Progress and Socialism Party (PPS). Each is affiliated with a trade union – the USFP with the Democratic Workers Confederation (CDT), and the Istiqlal with the General Union of Moroccan Workers. These bases of labor afford these parties credibility among working-class and middle-income Moroccans.

The third political formation is headed by the moderately Islamist Justice and Development Party (PJD), which has held the prime ministerial post and has technically led the government after electoral victories in 2011 and 2016. The PJD has emerged as the leading force in parliament. In the aftermath of the March 2003 bombing, the PJD took a lower profile in the September local elections. In 2004, the party elected a moderate, Saad Eddine Othmani, as its leader; he was replaced by Abdelilah Benkirane in 2008. Othmani returned as leader in 2017. The PJD runs on a platform of social justice, transparency, and anti-corruption. Importantly, the party focuses on *moral* corruption, rather than the economic corruption endemic to the Makhzen.

In addition to the PJD, there are several smaller Islamist groups committed to non-violent methods, such as al-Badil al-Hadari (Civilized Alternative) and Harakat Min Ajli al-Umma (Movement for the Nation).

Another major Islamist entity, the Justice and Charity Movement, is illegal and officially outside the Moroccan political process; nevertheless, authorities somewhat tolerate Justice and Charity so long as it does not directly question the king's powers. The movement mixes Sufi mysticism with Salafi theology and combines it with Muslim Brotherhood–styled social activism. Its founder, Abdesslam Yassine, was placed under house arrest throughout the 1980s and 1990s for condemning the monarchy as insufficiently Islamic and too beholden to Western interests. Yassine famously wrote an open letter to Hassan with the non-reverential salutation "My brother." In May 2000, as part of the opening after his father's death, Mohammed VI released Yassine, who eventually died in December 2012. Mohammed 'Abbadi is the organization's secretary-general. While outside the political process, Justice and Charity's followers are estimated to be more numerous than those of the moderate and officialized PJD.

The military and security structure

While today the Moroccan military remains an important organ of the monarchy's autocratic rule, it posed a serious threat to royal power during the early 1970s by virtue of the two coup attempts and wider conspiratorial planning. It is unlikely such actions would be repeated, not least due to frequent efforts by the palace to ensure fealty among its commanders. As with other elements of the Makhzen, the most loyal and useful military elites are handsomely rewarded. Notably, shortly after assuming the throne in 1999, Mohammed launched an inquiry into corruption within the armed forces; he backed off when it became apparent that the military would not countenance such examination.

The expanded size and combat experience of the army fighting the Polisario Front in the Western Sahara adds to the perceived sense of military threat against Morocco. Although resolution of this conflict continues to elude the parties to the conflict, the military Makhzen continues to resist being diminished. Contending with demobilized military units may in any case be a difficult source of pressure on the economy. According to the World Bank, Morocco spent nearly $4 billion (or 3.2 percent of its GDP), on its military in 2018. Much of such expenditures are devoted to maintaining armed forces capable of cooperating with European partners when necessary on important foreign policy matters.

The frontline institutions responsible for maintaining domestic order in Morocco include the civil police, royal gendarmerie, and specialized services such as the border police. As with other autocratic states, the Moroccan regime also maintains sizable and secretive intelligence services that untrammeled authority to monitor domestic activities; the most pertinent is the General Directorate for Territorial Surveillance.

POLITICAL DYNAMICS

Political rhythms in Morocco are controlled through the Makhzen at the apex of royal power – despite the pluralism and, at times, dramatic confrontations that play out between political parties within parliament. King Mohammed and the monarchy as an institution do not visibly promulgate, as that role is carried out by the cabinet-based government and its prime minister; but savvy Moroccans know well the many areas of state power that remain off-limits to premiers and parties, and are instead guarded closely by the palace. Indeed, discerning observers understand that at any given period, there are two currents of politics in Morocco: the visible public face involving parliamentary committees and cabinet meetings, where policies are discussed and controversies debated; and the invisible dimension involving the royal palace, as the king, royal advisors, security officials, and other powerful elites maneuver to push through major initiatives and oversee the political arena.

This puts inordinate emphasis on the king and his royal entourage, as well as the schemes that intertwine ambitious elites within the Makhzen as they climb the political ladder and seek royal favor. This also throws attention, for better or for worse, upon the personal life of the king himself, although there remain strict rules in the press that ban overt criticism or judgment. For instance, the country's social media and political salons were roiled in gossip after March 2018, when it appeared the king and Princess Lalla Salma had divorced. The established media could not publicly comment on their personal relations until July 2019, when their divorce was officially acknowledged by royal authorities. More recently, King Mohammed has spent increasing amounts of time abroad rather than in the kingdom, sometimes due to health (as in his February 2018 heart surgery in Paris) and sometimes due to personal and other unknown reasons, given his penchant for vacationing abroad. In Moroccan social media and other uncontrolled venues of gossip, some have raised speculation that the king may abdicate rather than rule until death like his father. This throws spotlight onto his son and Crown Prince, Moulay Hassan, who reaches adulthood in 2021.

Civil society

Below the regime and parliamentary scene, Morocco has a vibrant civil society where different organizations and movements have shaped the agenda of public discussion.

Within civil society, important actors include the National Union of Moroccan Students (UNEM) and various labor unions. Since the 1960s, the UNEM has been extensively involved in radical activities directed against the government. In recent years, student activism has taken on a decidedly Islamist cast, with supporters of Justice and Charity and other Islamist currents frequently active in street activities. Recent protests by unemployed graduate students and teachers, among other professional sectors who feel economically deprived, have garnered media attention. Students have been key players in the February 20 and Hirak Rif movements, and indeed today's generation of young activists – raised on social media, mostly Western-oriented, and open to learning from the failures and successes of activism elsewhere – have been quite savvy in poking holes in official authority, testing the boundaries of repression, and raising popular attention.

The Moroccan trade union movement acquired coherence and solidarity as a result of its struggles against colonialism. The Moroccan Workers Union (UMT) was the sole trade union confederation until 1960, when the Istiqlal organized a rival union, the General Union of Moroccan Workers. In the late 1970s, the CDT, a socialist-oriented union with ties to the USFP, overtook the UMT in prominence and militancy. However, despite the UMT's historic role and the CDT's occasional success in opposing the government, the political climate remains unreceptive to the development of a vigorous labor movement. High levels of unemployment undermine the effectiveness of unions as well. So, too, does the geopolitical environment: Morocco's liberal trade relations with the EU and the United States over the decades require a relatively docile (controlled) labor movement.

The country's nongovernmental organizations proliferated during the early 1990s, in the aftermath of the Cold War and Hassan's gradual, managed opening of the political system. Organizations devoted to women's rights, human rights, education, health care, AIDS, and Tamazight rights have all staked claims on the political process and the opening of the country's political system. This has also provided the space for the emergence of the February 20 and Hirak Rif movements in recent years, despite the harassment and sharp repression. In sum, while many organizations struggle, Morocco nonetheless has a relatively vibrant civil society in comparison to other MENA countries.

Women's groups are especially significant and active, and indeed Morocco has been a major site of Arab feminist movements since the 1990s. In January 2014 a major gain was achieved when the parliament voted unanimously to amend Article 475 of the penal code. The article, which stipulated that a rapist could escape prosecution if he married his underage victim, had achieved notoriety in April 2012, when 16-year-old Amina Filali committed suicide after she was forced to marry her rapist. The new code mandates a prison term of one to five years for the convicted rapist. In 2018, parliament passed another law that sought to combat violence against women, but was only half-praised by advocates because it lacked substantive enforcement mechanisms.

Starting in the 1990s, Morocco's journalism scene took advantage of political liberalization by generating a flurry of independent publications. The retraction of many political reforms since the early 2000s, however, has cowed much of the press back into obedience. Indeed, multiple Moroccan publications and newspapers have been shuttered, fined, or intimidated by crossing the oft-fuzzy lines of intolerance during Mohammed's reign; the typical triggers for government penalties or legal crackdowns are stories that infringe too uncomfortably upon royal affairs, or else irk officials in some way by implicating Morocco's image, accusing elites of corruption, or offending conservative religious sensibilities. Though different from the leaden days of Hassan when endemic censorship held, these roving limitations still hold today. In 2009, for instance, the well-known weekly *TelQuel* was temporarily banned after asking readers to gauge the performance of Mohammed over his first decade of rule; though almost all answered positively, the very act of publicly evaluating the stature of a sitting monarch infuriated the palace. Throughout the 2010s, Moroccan journalists still faced fines or arrests for their work, and a long list of defunct papers and websites attests to the success of government pressures.

At the grass-roots level, social media provides an important source of information and civil power, and has given many Moroccan readers and writers a much-needed outlet. Mobile technology abounds today, and two-thirds of the population reported using the Internet in 2019. At the same time, security services have learned how to harass and disrupt online activity, with local websites critical of the government often shut down and/or their organizers subjected to legal proceedings. In recent years, the Moroccan government has sought to combat its online critics by supporting its own quasi-official or conservative media outlets.

Radical Islamists

Morocco has experienced periodic confrontations with radical Islamism that often halt normal politics and spark heightened states of alert or repression. Such groups recruit in urban slums and disseminate arguments via inflammatory sermons, which indirectly pressures non-violent Islamist movements, such as the PJD. In recent decades, analysts tend to place radical Islamism under the rubric of Salafia Jihadia (Jihad for Pure Islam) movement, founded in the early 1990s by Mohammed al-Fizazi and led by many Moroccan veterans of the Soviet-Afghan War. Among its leading preachers is Mohamed Abdelwahab Rafiki, alias Abu Hafs. Abu Hafs was jailed in 2003 after the Casablanca bombings, but released years later on a royal pardon. At its height, estimates of the movement's strength ran to a few thousand members, but many of its most vocal or active members have been captured by the Moroccan intelligence apparatus. One of Salafia's major cells, al-Sirrat al-Moustakim (Straight Path), claimed responsibility for the Casablanca attack. Another current is al-Takfir Wal-Hijra (Exile and Flight).

The Moroccan Islamic Combatant Group (MICG) also remains salient, though fading as much of its leadership has been eliminated since the Casablanca attacks. Tied to Al-Qaʿida in the Islamic Maghrib (AQIM), the MICG networks are mysterious to analysts outside the intelligence community. In any case, the government has taken a resolutely hard line against radical Islamism, to the extent that Morocco participated in the extraordinary US rendition program in the so-called Global War on Terror.

Morocco has also had to grapple with the deep instability throughout the Sahel precipitated by Muammar al-Qaddafi's fall in late 2011 and the release of military arms into Chad, Niger, and, especially, Mali. The short-lived declaration of Azawad as a sovereign territory in 2012 in northern Mali provoked some fears as it threatened to host AQIM's operations. The Moroccan regime has not hesitated to portray militants in the Western Sahara as tied to such radical Islamism in order to justify its policies there.

More recently, an estimated 1,600 Moroccans joined the Islamic State of Iraq and Syria (ISIS) during the Syrian civil conflict. Some were killed, but those known fighters who returned were immediately arrested and imprisoned. The number of young Moroccans who joined ISIS signals not only stagnant economic opportunities but the latent specter of extremism.

FOREIGN POLICY

In its external outlook, Morocco has tried to balance various imperatives: close strategic ties with Europe and the United States, ongoing and deepening regional ties with other Arab (but especially Gulf) states, and increased orientation towards sub-Saharan Africa, all the while dealing with instabilities in the Sahel and the Western Sahara crisis.

The immediate focus remains Europe. Morocco's interests in the Mediterranean stem from geopolitical and economic realities as well as historical conditioning, meaning that ties are very close, but not without problematic tangles. Morocco's formal association with the European Economic Community dates back to the 1960s, with trade agreements, association accords, and "Neighborhood Policies" in regular renegotiation. In 1987, Morocco even applied to join the EEC – which was quickly rejected by the European Commission. Over the decades, Morocco has received extensive financial assistance from the EU in exchange for cooperation on trade, security, and immigration control.

Not surprisingly, France attracts considerable diplomatic energy. Relations are not always smooth given sensitivities about the colonial past and current disparities of power and resources. For its part, France sees Morocco as a linchpin in its African policy, while conversely Moroccan diplomats see France as the centerpiece of their international sponsorship. The French media pay especially close attention to Moroccan affairs, and vice-versa. Some French senior citizens even retire in Morocco, attracted by low housing costs and perceptions of a simpler lifestyle. Enterprising Moroccans speak of building assisted-living communities for retirees, a potential source of foreign exchange and employment in the health-care sector.

Relations with Spain are a different story. Former Spanish dictator Francisco Franco and King Hassan had a working relationship, with mutual interests in keeping their respective authoritarian structures intact. Nonetheless, despite some tension over competition with Spanish agriculture and fisheries, Moroccan-Spanish relations improved steadily after the 1970s. Spanish-Moroccan relations were cemented by Hassan's visit to

Spain in September 1989 and by the signing of a friendship treaty in 1991 during Spanish King Juan Carlos's visit to Rabat. In addition, Madrid and Rabat have collaborated on such projects as underwater electricity links, financial-sector ties, and the Maghreb-Europe Gas (MEG) pipeline. Spain ranks as one of Morocco's top two trade partners, alongside France.

However, Spanish public opinion has long criticized Morocco's stance on the Western Sahara. As Spain began to experience dynamic economic growth in the 1990s, a condescending attitude toward Morocco deepened. In Spanish political culture, Morocco is a foil that represents the past that Spain seeks to leave behind: absolutist, backward, and undeveloped. By the late 1990s, tension between the countries had become palpable on an array of issues, including drug smuggling, access to deep-sea fisheries, border security, the status of Ceuta and Melilla, and immigration. This was exacerbated by the 2004 Madrid train bombings, in which Moroccan nationals were implicated. In 2015, a Madrid judge ruled under Spain's universal justice law that 11 Moroccan former officials should stand trial on charges of genocide in the Western Sahara. Judge Pablo Ruz specifically called for seven of the officials to be arrested and extradited to Spain. Morocco offered no official response to the indictment.

These hiccups notwithstanding, since the early 1980s, the Moroccan military has collaborated closely with NATO, conducting bilateral exercises with France, Spain, and the United States. In summer 2004, the George W. Bush administration proffered the kingdom "non-NATO ally" status, elevating Morocco to an august club that includes key American strategic partners like Australia, Egypt, Israel, Japan, Jordan, and Pakistan. The designation entitles Rabat to priority delivery of defense items (e.g., military weaponry, vehicles, aircraft, and ammunition) and access to more generous loans. Morocco also cooperates closely with NATO and the US Africa Command on anti-terror initiatives in the Sahel.

With respect to the MENA region, Morocco played a provocative role under King Hassan. Morocco had a robust diplomatic presence in the region independently and through the Arab League. Viewed as moderate, Morocco quietly nurtured close relations with Israel, though much of its Jewish community left for the new state after 1948. King Hassan met with Israeli prime minister Shimon Peres in July 1986, the first public meeting between Arab and Israeli leaders since the 1981 assassination of Egyptian president Anwar Sadat. Hassan also helped advocate the multilateral peace tracks between Israel and Arab countries after the 1991 Gulf War. After the collapse of the Oslo peace talks and the second Palestinian Intifada in the early 2000s, diplomatic relations quietened. King Mohamed, as well, has proven far less aggressive in spearheading regional initiatives than his father, and on the Palestinian issue Morocco allows others to lead the way.

Historically, Morocco's primary antagonists in the Arab world were Algeria and Libya given their proximate rivalries and the Western Sahara issue. Relations with Libya quickly improved for the better after al-Qaddafi's downfall in 2011. However, Moroccan-Algerian ties are still strained, with their mutual border closed since 1994 and often militarized in response to tit-for-tat aggression and insults between the two autocracies.

Further east, Morocco has nurtured its warmest ties with other Arab monarchies. In May 2011, in the context of the Arab Spring, the Gulf Cooperation Council (GCC) floated the idea of adding Morocco (along-side Jordan) into the regional grouping – a geographically bizarre idea but one that made sense given the collective desire to halt the tides of revolution and keep the common structure of authoritarian monarchism alive. The proposal was never formally converted into an invitation, however, but Morocco still nurtures close diplomatic and financial ties with the kingdoms, especially Saudi Arabia. Saudi Arabia provided Morocco with several billion dollars of funds after the Arab Spring, particularly through investments and other channels of foreign aid. Morocco conversely joined the Saudi-led military intervention in Yemen which began in 2015, though its contributions were small.

Otherwise, Morocco's regional outlook under King Mohamed has been pragmatic, if predictable – participate as needed in major initiatives or Arab League meetings, but not standing as the forefront of any bold and controversial moves. Of equal certainty is the moribund Arab Maghrib Union, a short-lived idea conceived in 1989 to create a sub-regional grouping with Algeria, Tunisia, Libya, and Mauritania. Given Algeria and Morocco's chronic animosity – not to mention Libya's post-2011 disintegration – the idea remains stillborn.

What King Mohammed's reign has introduced is more sustained cooperation with sub-Saharan Africa. Morocco in no way competes with major investors on the continent (such as China, the US, India and France), but Mohammed has made extensive state visits to several sub-Saharan partners. This is strategic – especially concerning the Western Sahara – but it also reflects a genuine emphasis on "south-south" cooperation. By turning southwards into the African continent, Morocco can pursue a geopolitical vision of future diplomacy, trade, and ties distinct from its north-bound European outlook and its eastward Arab framework.

Western Sahara

The status of the Western Sahara demands special attention. The United Nations considers it a "non-self-governing territory" yet does not identify an "administering power" in the same way it does for, for example, American Samoa (US), French Polynesia (France), or Bermuda (UK). Despite the rise of Sahrawi nationalism in the 1950s and 1960s, Spain did not relinquish control until the Madrid Accord of November 14, 1975, when Spain ceded the colony to Mauritania and Morocco, setting the stage for the Green March. Spain withdrew its last troops in February 1976, and the next day the Polisario Front declared the area the Saharan Arab Democratic Republic (SADR). It also initiated a guerrilla war against Morocco and Mauritania. Morocco responded by deploying troops and erecting a massive defensive wall. By the mid-1980s, over 80,000 Moroccan troops were deployed in the territory, but by then the Polisario had gained the support of Libya and Algeria, the latter of whom provided a safe haven to its fighters.

In 1984, the SADR won a diplomatic victory by becoming a member of the Organization of African Unity (OAU). In November 1984, Morocco left the OAU in protest – an absence that persisted for 34 years until January 2017, when Morocco rejoined the renamed African Union (AU). Despite its readmission, Morocco remains diplomatically isolated regarding the Sahara, with which it shares AU membership despite not recognizing it as a country. Other AU members and many countries around the world do recognize the SADR, but no major power does, including the United States, China, Russia, and EU.

Since a cease fire in April 1991 and the Security Council's establishment of the UN Mission for the Referendum in Western Sahara (MINURSO), the United Nations has tried to get both sides to agree to a referendum, but with little success. Episodic peace talks over the decades have made no appreciable progress. In November 2010, a violent clash at the Gdeim Izik camp in Western Sahara between Moroccan security forces and local residents led to nearly a dozen Sahrawi deaths. Today, even with Morocco's 2017 readmission to the AU, stalemate persists.

FUTURE PROSPECTS

Morocco emerged from the Arab Spring in a relatively stable position, but like much of the MENA, a present calm does not portend future durability. The monarchy retains a strong grip over the political system, which nonetheless has become more diverse with the parliamentary ascent of Islamists.

Further reforms may occur, but they will ultimately hinge upon the views and strategies of the royal center. Economically, the country continues to become more tightly interconnected with external markets, with trade and investment flows from Western, Arab, and African states. China is also growing in its representation in the Moroccan market. Nevertheless, the problem of unemployment will need attention, given the large numbers of jobless youths.

In the years to come, the greatest variable is the uncertain status of King Mohammed VI, who turned 55 in 2019 and remains leader of a complex authoritarian system but with a style that has befuddled observers. The general trend since the Arab Spring has been one of increasing unwillingness or inability to attend to political matters, leaving such work to his associates. Yet many question whether parliament and its parties could govern in the absence of royal power, and monarchism remains integral to Moroccan political beliefs. The constitutional line of succession paves the way for his son, Crown Prince Hassan, to assume the throne. Until then, the country will confront environmental, social, economic, and political challenges from an array of directions. The Western Sahara remains a constant source of crisis and controversy.

NOTE

1 As the most distant Arab country from the historic cradle of Islam in the Arabian Peninsula, and the traditional centers of past Islamic Caliphates, Morocco has developed many unique cultural specificities. Moroccan Arabic, for instance, is among the most distinctive of all national Arabic dialects. In Moroccan Arabic, the honorific title "Moulay" means lord or prince, and today is reserved almost exclusively for members of the Alaouite dynasty. Women of the royal family carry the noble title of "Lalla," which roughly translates to lady or princess. In the other Arab royal families outside of Morocco, members carry the titles of Amir and Amira – more conventional terms meaning prince and princess, respectively.

FURTHER READING

An excellent comprehensive history is Susan Gilson Miller, *A History of Morocco* (Cambridge University Press, 2013). An accessible non-academic primer is Marvine Howe, *Morocco* (Oxford University Press, 2005). More deeply, colonial Morocco is analyzed in Edmund Burke, *Prelude to Protectorate in Morocco* (University of Chicago Press, 1976), and Janet Abu-Lughod, *Rabat: Urban Apartheid in Morocco* (Princeton University Press, 1980). Richard Pennell's *Morocco* *since 1830: A History* (New York University Press, 2001) is valuable, while the French entry and pacification campaigns are covered in Douglas Porch, *The Conquest of Morocco*, 2nd ed. (Knopf, 1982). A French-language classic is Abdallah Laroui, *Les origines sociales et culturelles du nationalisme marocain (1830–1912)* (Centre Culturel Arabe, 1993). Jonathan Wyrtzen, *Making Morocco: Colonial Intervention and the Politics of Identity* (Cornell University Press, 2015) examines the lasting impact of French occupation and its political manipulations. Senem Aslan, *Nation-Building in Turkey and Morocco: Governing Kurdish and Berber Dissent* (Cambridge University Press, 2015) explores the construction of national identity in the context of minority rights.

For deep historical analyses of the political system, see James Sater, *Civil Society and Political Change in Morocco* (Routledge, 2007); and Abdellah Hammoudi, *Master and Disciple* (University of Chicago Press, 1997). John Waterbury, *The Commander of the Faithful* (Columbia University Press, 1970) is a legendary work on the nature of elite politics. A classic French-language work is Remy Levau, *Le fellah marocain: Défenseur du trône* (Presses de la Fondation Nationale des Sciences Politiques, 1985).

For contemporary analyses of Morocco's political stability, authoritarian monarchy, and popular opposition, there are many books. Scholarly entries include Merouan Mekouar, *Protest and Mass Mobilization: Authoritarian Collapse and Political Change in North Africa* (Routledge, 2016); Michael Willis, *Politics and Power in the Maghreb: Algeria, Tunisia and Morocco from Independence to the Arab Spring* (Oxford University Press, 2014); Bruce Maddy-Weitzman and Daniel Zisenwine, *Contemporary Morocco: State, Politics, and Society under Mohammed VI* (Routledge, 2012); Mohamed Daadaoui, *Moroccan Monarchy and the Islamist Challenge: Maintaining Makhzen Power* (Palgrave Macmillan, 2014); and Ellen Lust-Okar's *Structuring Conflict in the Arab World* (Cambridge University Press, 2005).

For more controversial treatments (and critiques) of the monarchy, see Gilles Perrault, *Notre ami le roi* (Gallimard, 1992); Malika Oufkir and Michéle Fitoussi, *Stolen Lives: Twenty Years in a Desert Jail* (Hyperion, 2001); and Catherine Graciet and Eric Laurent, *Le Roi prédateur* (Le

Seuil, 2012). King Hassan II's own perspective is presented in his memoirs, *Hassan II: La mémoire d'un roi, entretiens avec Eric Laurent* (Plon, 1993).

For historical analyses of Islam and Moroccan culture, see Henry Munson, *Religion and Power in Morocco* (Yale University Press, 1993); Dale Eickelman, *Knowledge and Power in Morocco* (Princeton University Press, 1985); and Elaine Combs-Schilling, *Sacred Performances in Morocco* (University of Chicago Press, 1989). Islamism has also attracted attention; among the best works are Malika Zeghal, *Islamism in Morocco: Religion, Authoritarianism, and Electoral Politics* (Markus Wiener, 2008), and Ann Marie Wainscott, *Bureaucratizing Islam: Morocco and the War on Terror* (Cambridge University Press, 2017). Brian Edwards' *Morocco Bound* (Duke University Press, 2005) offers a stimulating analysis of America's cultural and political relationship with the Maghrib.

Moroccan social issues, including minority rights and gender, also have inspired an impressive literature. Studies on the role of women include Fatima Mernissi, *Dreams of Trespass: Tales of a Harem Girlhood* (Perseus, 1994); Mounira Charrad, *States and Women's Rights: The Making of Postcolonial Tunisia, Algeria, and Morocco* (University of California Press, 2001); and *The Moroccan Women's Rights Movement* (Syracuse University Press, 2014). Accounts of Morocco's Jewish community are provided in Emily Gottreich, *The Mellah of Marrakesh: Jewish and Muslim Space in Morocco's Red City* (Indiana University Press, 2007) and Aomar Boum, *Memories of Absence: How Muslims Remember Jews in Morocco* (Stanford University Press, 2013). Katherine Hoffman's *We Share Walls: Language, Land and Gender in Berber Morocco* (Wiley-Blackwell, 2008) examines Tamazight issues. The Western Sahara is carefully documented and discussed by John Damis, *Conflict in Northwest Africa* (Hoover Institution Press,

1983), and Stephen Zunes and Jacob Mundy, *Western Sahara: War, Nationalism and Conflict Irresolution* (Syracuse University Press, 2010).

Analyses of Moroccan economic development are available in Gregory White, *On the Outside of Europe Looking In: A Comparative Political Economy of Tunisia and Morocco* (State University of New York Press, 2001); Shana Cohen, *Searching for a Different Future: The Rise of a Global Middle Class in Morocco* (Duke University Press, 2005); David McMurray, *In and Out of Morocco: Smuggling and Migration in a Frontier Boomtown* (University of Minnesota Press, 2000); and Natasha Iskander, *Creative State: Forty Years of Development and Migration Policy in Morocco and Mexico* (Cornell University Press, 2011). The politics of inequality and urbanization is expertly engaged in Koenraad Bogaert, *Globalized Authoritarianism: Megaprojects, Slums, and Class Relations in Urban Morocco* (University of Minnesota Press, 2018).

Online sources

Starting points for online research include the government's press agency (www.map.ma/en) and official website (www.maroc.ma/en), which provide little by way of objective news but intriguing windows into what Moroccan officials see as important. The National Company for Radio and Television (www.snrt.ma) began a website in the early 2000s devoted to Moroccans living abroad; it streams daily news clips in Spanish, Tamazight, French, and Moroccan Arabic. Other pro-government outlets include *Le matin du Sahara* (www.lematin.ma) and *Le360* (http://fr.le360.ma/). The official TV station 2M is also available (www.2m.ma). Radio Méditerranée Internationale is a Tangiers-based radio station available online (www.medi1.com); it plays a fun, eclectic mix of music (Moroccan, American, African, Middle Eastern, and European) and broadcasts official news in Arabic and French.

More independent reportage can be found in *Telquel* (https:/telquel.ma), *L'Économiste* (www.leconomiste.com), and *Al-Sabah* (www.assabah.press.ma). *Lakome* remains active despite being repeatedly blocked by the government for its critical analysis during the Arab Spring (https://lakome2.com/). Several parties have their own newspapers, too. For instance, the Istiqlal publishes news in *Al Alam* (www.alalam.ma), while the USFP's news is available online at (www.libe.ma). An English-language online daily that generates interesting content is *Morocco World News* (www.moroccoworldnews.com), which for English readers may be the best portal to Moroccan happenings given that almost all Moroccan publications appear in only Arabic, French, or both.

Please note that URLs may change far more quickly than books can be printed; so if these exact URLs do not work, simply search Google or another engine by the titles of these websites and online resources.

People's Democratic Republic of Algeria

Azzedine Layachi

INTRODUCTION

With its past reflecting the struggle for national identity, Algeria in the twenty-first century reflects its Arab identity, the culture of the indigenous Berber (Tamazight) tribes, and other cultural traditions percolating inwards due to its central location on the Mediterranean. Algeria's political struggles today embody the battle for power in the context of an aging post-colonial state. Political reforms made after 1989 resulted not in democratization, but conflict and civil war. Perhaps because of this traumatic violence, Algeria did not experience a large-scale uprising during the 2011–12 Arab Spring as neighboring Tunisia and other Arab countries did.

However, in February 2019, the country experienced another uprising – albeit peaceful this time – as many thousands of people took to the street to protest against a fifth term of the incumbent president and to demand a fundamental overhaul of an autocratic regime that long revolved around the ruling party and armed forces. For the first time since the Islamists-led unrest of the 1990s, these institutions face a mass challenge. Discontent also stems from rising inequality and privation; despite some development fueled by oil rents, economic growth has still left behind much of society, while corruption and prosperity permeated political elites. The 2019 popular movement not only ended President Bouteflika's 20-year tenure but also inspired unprecedented anti-corruption crackdowns against some of the most notorious figures. As of autumn 2019, ongoing mobilization continues to pressure the entire authoritarian system and its powerholding structure, while the military leadership remains reluctant to accept calls for democracy. This leaves the future uncertain.

Box 4.1 provides vital data for this country.

BOX 4.1   VITAL DATA – PEOPLE'S DEMOCRATIC REPUBLIC OF ALGERIA

Capital	Algiers
Regime type	Authoritarian (semi-presidential republic)
Head of state	(Interim) President Abdelkader Bensalah (since April 2019)
Head of government	Prime Minister Noureddine Bedoui (since March 2019)
Legislative institution	Bicameral parliament, with elected 462-seat lower house (*al-Majlis al-Sha'bi al-Watani*, or People's National Assembly)
Female quota	Yes: women can run for any seat, and there are variable requirements for women to compose up to half of all parliamentary candidates in each electoral district
Percentage of seats held by women	26.8%
Major political parties (share of seats in most recent general elections, 2017)	National Liberation Front (26%), National Rally for Democracy (14.9%), Movement of Society for Peace and Front for Change coalition (6%), Rally for Hope (4.2%), Future Front (4.1%), Algerian Popular Movement (3.7%)
Population	41,318,142
Major ethnic groups	Arab-Berber (99%), other (1%)
Major religious groups	Muslim (99%), other (1%)
GDP per capita	$4,237 ($15,440 at Purchasing Power Parity)
Unemployment rate	12.1%
Youth unemployment rate	30%
Major economic industries	Petroleum and natural gas, petrochemicals, mining, food processing, light industries
Military spending as % GDP	5.7

HISTORICAL BACKGROUND

Until the sixteenth century, the Maghrib region of North Africa consisted of autonomous and independent tribes. The Berbers, or Tamazight, are the oldest inhabitants. The Phoenicians established themselves in the twelfth century BC, followed by the Romans in 146 BC and the Vandals centuries later. In 533 AD, Algeria was annexed by the Byzantine Empire, and in the seventh century came its conquest by the Islamic Caliphate. After being ruled by several of the Arab-Islamic dynasties, Algeria in 1518 became part of the Ottoman Empire. In 1830, Algeria was conquered by the French, who controlled and occupied these lands until 1962.

Throughout recent centuries, the Arab-Islamic tradition served as a powerful unifying tool in Algeria's struggle against foreign domination, most notably in the war for independence against France from 1954 to 1962. Nonetheless, French colonialism deeply instilled Algeria with French values and culture, at least among its urban and commercial classes. Today, Algerian politics is split between Western-oriented elites and the masses who identify more strongly with their Arab, Berber, and Islamic cultures.

France is often credited with the definition and consolidation of Algeria's modern state, but elements of statehood existed under the Ottoman Empire. It took France more than 40 years to conquer and subdue the whole country, and its so-called "civilizing mission" dramatically transformed the region. In colonial Algeria, the European settlers were mostly peasants, working-class people, army officers, and bureaucrats who profited from the prosperous arable land along the coast. By 1900, more than 150,000 Europeans had settled in Algeria, and the indigenous population had lost its independence and most land through seizure, expropriation, and property laws favoring the settlers. Moreover, by 1900 more than three million indigenous Algerians had died from mass repression and disease. France's imperial policy engendered antagonism among indigenous Algerians and gave rise to a nationalist movement.

The nationalist struggle

Algerian nationalists resisted colonialism, and the most prominent anti-colonial figure was Amir 'Abd al-Qadir. However, by 1847 the French had crushed his incipient movement and sent him into exile in Syria. In the 1850s the French government declared the territory part of France, and Algerians officially became French subjects, though not citizens. The extension of French authority and repression triggered more nationalist revolts in the 1870s, but these were suppressed and followed by more land confiscations, onerous taxes, and tighter control. These and other punitive actions intended to terrorize the Algerians into submission and procure land and money for colonization. French atrocities were documented in several eyewitness accounts and in reports such as one issued by a French royal commission in 1883, which stated:

> We tormented, at the slightest suspicion and without due process, people whose guilt still remains more than uncertain. [...] We massacred people who carried passes, cut the throats, on a simple suspicion, of entire populations which proved later to be innocent ... [Many innocent people were tried just because] they exposed themselves to our furor. Judges were available to condemn them and civilized people to have them executed.... In a word, our barbarism was worse than that of the barbarians we came to civilize, and we complain that we have not succeeded with them![1]

Early Algerian resistance movements, such as Jeunesse Algérienne and Fédération des Elus Musulmans, desired the full assimilation of Algerians into the French community without surrendering their Muslim identity. However, when the demand for equality went unanswered, a number of parties called for independence in the 1920s. In early 1954, the Comité Révolutionnaire d'Unité et d'Action (CRUA) was created by dissidents from earlier movements, ex-soldiers in the French army, and miscellaneous groups of activists. In October 1954, CRUA was transformed into a political organization, the Front de Libération Nationale (FLN) and its military arm, the Armée de Libération Nationale (ALN).

On November 1, 1954, the FLN issued its revolutionary proclamation calling on all Algerians to rise and fight for their freedom. Brutal irregular warfare and vicious fighting continued until a cease-fire agreement was signed in Evian, France, on March 19, 1962. The Evian Accords stipulated a national referendum on independence that was to include both European settlers and indigenous Algerians. On July 1, the overwhelming majority voted for independence; Algeria became officially independent on July 5, 1962.

Post-independence Algeria

Soon after independence, serious divisions within the nationalist leadership threatened the success of the revolution. The absence of a unifying revolutionary ideology plus factional squabbles carried over into the post-independence period. The earlier tactical unity that supported the FLN's efforts for independence broke down, and a vicious power struggle began. The three major contestants were the Algerian provisional government, the *wilayat* command councils (regional governing structures), and the army (ALN). Factional rivalries would remain an intrinsic feature of Algeria's post-independence politics, up to today.

On September 26, 1962, the Algerian National Assembly elected Ahmed Ben Bella as prime minister. His government was formed from the ranks of the military and close personal and political allies, and he soon was elected president as well. A new constitution gave the president considerable powers, while preserving the FLN's hegemony as the ruling political party. The most pressing task of the new government was to restore normality to the war-torn country. The mass exodus of Europeans had caused a severe shortage of highly skilled workers, technicians, educators, and property-owning entrepreneurs. It would take years before national campaigns emphasizing mass education and industrialization could generate the labor force necessary to fill this gap. The economy remained moribund until the late 1960s.

The concentration of power in the hands of President Ben Bella caused fragmentation within the leadership. Ben Bella owed his position to his status as "historic chief of the revolution." He had been a key figure in the struggle against French colonialism. Now, however, he struggled to manage various rivalries manifest by the ousting of traditional leaders, unpopularly attacked the national trade union, the Union Générale des Travailleurs Algériens (UGTA), and failed to transform the FLN into an effective mass party. He was overthrown on June 19, 1965, in a bloodless coup by Colonel Houari Boumédiène, who had helped put him in office in 1962.

The transition was smooth and efficient. All political power was transferred to Boumédiène and his military-dominated Council of the Revolution. The constitution and the National Assembly were suspended, and Boumédiène was named president, premier, and defense minister. He relied on the support of the *mujahideen* (veterans of the independence war) and technocratic elite drawn partially from the military. The new regime promised to reestablish the principles of the revolution, end corruption and personal abuses, eliminate internal divisions, and build a socialist economy based on state-led industrialization and land reform.

A new national charter, approved by referendum in June 1976, reaffirmed Algeria's socialist orientation, again recognized the FLN as the only legal party, and maintained the authoritarian system. A new constitution, approved by referendum in November 1976, reestablished the national legislature (Assemblée Populaire Nationale, or APN). A month later, Boumédiène was elected president with more than 95 percent of the vote in a shallow plebiscite. In the parliamentary elections of February 1977, all candidates were FLN members, but at least by now the FLN had broadened its base to incorporate different social forces. The diverse membership of the new assembly, which reflected many underrepresented classes, and its high proportion of industrial and agricultural workers, were lauded.

Boumédiène died suddenly in late 1978 of a rare kidney ailment. His legacy included a consolidated state, stable political system, rapidly growing economy drawing upon import-substituting industrialization (ISI) strategies, an extensive state-centered socialist program, and an expanding petroleum and gas industry. He also left a political vacuum. Rabah Bitat, the National Assembly president, was named interim president until a special FLN congress, following the army's recommendation, selected Colonel Chadli Bendjedid as presidential candidate. He was elected to office in January 1979. Through a policy of "change within continuity," President Bendjedid consolidated his power and took full control of the state through its twin pillars of authority – the FLN and the military.

The mid-1980s raised tough challenges, including a declining economy due to the inefficiency of state-owned industry, neglect of the agricultural sector, increasing unemployment, and the fallout from the global oil price crash. In response, Bendjedid initiated economic liberalization, which included a shift in domestic investment away from heavy industry and toward agriculture, light industry, and consumer goods. State enterprises were broken up into smaller units, and some state-owned firms were privatized. Subsidies were reduced, and price controls were lifted. The fiscal deficit was reduced by cutting government spending, and an important anti-corruption campaign was launched. Other changes included opening the economy to limited foreign investment, expanding and revitalizing the private sector, shifting away from the Soviet Union and toward the West in strategic considerations, and lowering Algeria's once high profile in global and Third World affairs.

However, despite their progressive intentions, Bendjedid's economic reforms exacerbated an already dismal situation. They increased unemployment, raised prices, and reduced industrial output. The upper class profited from economic liberalization while the burden of reform fell mostly on the masses. An already wide generation gap increased further between the elites, who based their legitimacy on their revolutionary anti-colonial credentials, and the masses, 70 percent of whom were under the age of 30 and had no memory of revolution. By the late 1980s, Algeria was highly polarized.

In October 1988, the crisis exploded in the most violent public demonstrations since independence. Weeks of strikes and work stoppages were followed by six days of violent riots in several cities, targeting city halls, police stations, post offices, state-owned cars, and supermarkets. It was a demonstration against the leadership, corruption, declining living standards, increasing unemployment, food shortages, and persistent inequality and alienation. The riots were quickly suppressed by the military; hundreds of rioters were killed, and a state of siege was declared. These and the ensuing reforms constituted the most important changes in post-independence Algeria. Today, some historians even call this event the "Algerian Spring," a forerunner to the wider 2011–12 Arab Spring uprisings.

The political system and ruling elite were severely shaken by sudden popular mobilization, and Bendjedid promised sweeping changes. Constitutional amendments approved in a referendum in February 1989, and other reforms, included separating the FLN from the state, a reduced role for the military in politics, restructuring the executive and legislative authority, strengthening the presidential power, eliminating the ideological commitment to socialism, free local and national elections, and more associational freedoms. By the time campaigning opened for the country's first multiparty elections in 1989, 62 parties existed, some of which were led by exiled dissidents and historic independence war figures, such as Ahmed Ben Bella (Movement for Democracy in Algeria) and Hocine Aït Ahmed (Front of Socialist Forces, or FFS).

The first multiparty elections for local and regional offices, held on June 12, 1990, delivered a shock. A new Islamist party, the Front of Islamic Salvation (FIS), secured 853 of the 1,520 local councils (55 percent) and 32 of the 48 provincial assemblies (67 percent). The FLN won only 487 local and 14 provincial constituencies. In the first multiparty parliamentary elections of December 26, 1991, the FIS won 188 seats out of 430 in the first round, followed by the FFS with 25 seats and the FLN with an embarrassing 16 seats. The ruling party's humiliation and the astonishing Islamist support among the underserved and youths instigated a harsh response from above – military intervention, in which the army canceled the vote, forced Bendjedid to resign, and banned the FIS.

In this period of crackdown, the promise of democratic opening was retracted under justification that Islamists gaining power was too destructive an outcome. The military pursued a strategy of violent repression. Thousands of alleged militants were imprisoned in desert camps, scores were killed, and civil war ensued. For several years, with parliament suspended, the regime was unable to assemble a civilian government that commanded the confidence and respect of all Algerians. Independence war hero Mohamed Boudiaf was invited to return from exile in Morocco and lead the country in January 1992; however, he was assassinated six months after his appointment as president. He was followed by Ali Kafi's one-year symbolic president. The appointment on January 31, 1994, of retired general Liamine Zéroual as president stimulated some hope for improved economic and security conditions. In the first presidential election in 1995, Zéroual won a six-year term with 61 percent of the vote. It was hoped that his electoral legitimacy would help end the long crisis, but violence persisted between the armed forces and Islamist militants, including not just the FIS but also new insurgent movements, including the Armed Islamic Group (GIA).

A 180-member National Council of Transition (CNT) was established as an advisory body in the absence of a working parliament. It was filled with representatives of parties, trade unions, managers' associations, professional organizations, and other civic associations. As attempts at dialogue with jailed FIS leaders failed, the state turned to even firmer repression of radical Islamists while opening up to moderate opposition parties, both religious and secular. In January 1995, most opposition parties (including the FIS) met in Rome, and agreed on a platform for resolving the crisis. The initiative failed when the government rejected the plan.

In 1996, new constitutional amendments reinforced the powers of the president and prime minister and created an upper parliamentary chamber, the Council of the Nation, with one-third of its members appointed by the president and the rest indirectly elected. The amendments also declared Islam the state religion, prohibited the creation of parties on a "religious, linguistic, racial, gender, corporatist or regional" basis, and outlawed the use of partisan propaganda based on these elements. Elections in June 1997 produced Algeria's first multiparty parliament. The main winners were the FLN and the National Democratic Rally (RND), a nationalist, conservative party created to support Zéroual. The FLN, the RND, the Movement of Society for Peace (MSP), a moderate Islamist party, and Ennahda (Movement for Islamic Renaissance), also a moderate Islamist party, formed a pro-government majority coalition that secured 21 ministerial posts, seven of which went to Islamists. This coalition survived until 2012, when the Islamist MSP joined the opposition in a failed bid to capture more votes in the wake of the Arab Spring.

President Zéroual, who had faced strong resistance from military hardliners when he attempted a discreet dialogue with the jailed FIS leaders, resigned in early 1999. Former foreign minister Abdelaziz Bouteflika became the FLN candidate favored by the military. Two days before the vote on April 15, 1999, the other six presidential candidates withdrew, angered by electoral irregularities. Bouteflika, the only candidate, won by 73 percent of the vote, with support from the military and the FLN, RND, and MSP. It was a triumphant return from a self-imposed exile; he was previously closely tied to Boumédiène but also accused of corruption.

The civil conflict in the 1990s grew vicious, as Islamist militants and the Algerian military engaged in a bloody spiral of violence. By 2001, an estimated 200,000 people had been killed. By then, however, the armed forces seemed to have gained the upper hand. Security improved markedly after an amnesty program called the National Concord – approved by referendum in September 1999 – invited armed Islamists to give up arms and avoid prosecution. The first to take advantage of this was the Army of Islamic Salvation (AIS), an element of the FIS. The Concord was not part of a comprehensive solution but a useful judicial action that enabled alleged terrorists to demobilize peacefully. Another amnesty program, the Charter for Peace and National Reconciliation, was approved in September 2005 by referendum, prompting more rebels to surrender and others to be released from jail.

This amnesty helped effectively end the civil war. Yet it was widely criticized, not only for preventing the prosecution of rebels who had committed grave crimes against civilians, but also for absolving the regime's military and intelligence agents responsible for similar offenses. Furthermore, many of those who surrendered returned to armed rebellion by joining the radical Salafist Group for Preaching and Combat (GSPC), which officially declared its allegiance to Al-Qa'ida in 2006 and renamed itself Al-Qa'ida in the Islamic Maghrib (AQIM). AQIM therefore served as the regional franchise for Islamist-inflected terrorism in Algeria, Mauritania, Morocco, Tunisia, and Mali; one brazen episode was a massive January 2013 attack at a natural gas facility near the southern town of In Amenas. The resulting hostage crisis and siege killed dozens, including 37 foreign hostages.

Excepting these events, Algeria's past civil strife is slowly fading into the background, but history looms large over all of Algerian politics. The revolutionary anti-colonial war was the violent forge of the Algerian nation, producing the FLN and a militarized state that often invokes the specter of instability and disunity to justify security measures. Memories of the 1990s have also hung over politics, with some suggesting that such fears of repeating such traumatic violence explains why Algerians did not mobilize like other Arab countries during the 2011–12 Arab Spring. Yet many Algerians, including the large youth generation, are no longer willing to accept these excuses in their demands for social justice, economic mobility, and political pluralism, and the coming years will require a system that prizes seniority, elitism, and status to accommodate such popular discontent.

More recent events, including the 2019 popular uprising, are covered in the Political Dynamics section, and demonstrate the extent to which institutional and historical legacies continue to influence state-society relations.

SOCIAL AND ECONOMIC ENVIRONMENT

Algeria is located in the center of the Maghrib sub-region of the MENA (Map 4.1). It is only a few hundred miles from the southern coast of France and even closer to Spain and Italy. Its strategic importance stems from several factors, including its vast territory (it is the largest country in Africa), linking sub-Saharan Africa to the Mediterranean; its 1,200 kilometers (about 750 miles) of Mediterranean shoreline; vast petroleum and gas reserves; and mineral resources, including phosphate, coal, iron, lead, uranium, and zinc.

Algeria's 91,935 square miles of land is 85 percent desert. Two ranges of the Atlas Mountains divide it into three regions: the Tell, along the Mediterranean lowlands on the coast; the High Plateau, south of the Tell and north of the Sahara; and the Sahara, the largest region. Only 3.2 percent of Algeria's land is arable, located mostly in the northern lowlands. The Tell region has mild, rainy winters and hot, dry summers, though the coast is quite humid. On the High Plateau, summers are hot and dry, and winters are colder, with rain in some areas and regular snowfall on some mountains. The Sahara is hot by day and cool at night, with rainfall rare. In the spring, a hot, dry wind from the south, the Sirocco, causes strong sandstorms.

Currently, more than three-fourths of Algeria's more than 41 million citizens live in northern cities and towns. The rest live in the rural interior and southern desert. The population is young, with 29.3 percent under 15 years of age and, in total, 70 percent under the age of 30.

Culture and identity

Most Algerians are Sunni Muslims of Arab-Berber stock. Arabic is the official language, though French is widely spoken and used in politics and business. In 2004, the Tamazight language spoken by most Algerian Berbers became a second national language. While Algerians exhibit the same

MAP 4.1
People's Democratic Republic of Algeria. Major rivers and cities shown. The capital is commonly spelled Algiers in English, but on this map, and others, is alternatively transliterated as "El-Djazaïr."

Source: D-Maps.

intermingling of Arab and Berber ethnic stock as other North African countries due to many centuries of coexistence, identity became politicized in the post-colonial decades due to the state's pro-Arab bias shown in education, language policy, and cultural expressions. Extensive "Arabization" programs and the masses' identification with Islam and the Arab ethnos also conflict with many economic and political elites' secular outlook and ideology. Some of this tension dates from the colonial era, when the French used secularization to fracture the country. The elite-mass divide remains a constant source of hostility and mistrust, and political and military leaders are uncomfortable trusting the public. That distrust reappeared in response to the emergence of opposition parties in 1989 and was apparent during the popular uprising in 2019.

Still, tolerance for limited dissent and discourse has emerged. Since the late 1980s, the leadership has increasingly recognized the validity of popular participation and political discussion. In the late 1980s and early 1990s, remarkably open and candid debates occurred over the National Charter (the country's ideological roadmap) and the restoration of local and national representative legislatures, evolving into a controlled liberalization program that permitted the emergence of competitive political parties. Such early efforts bore fruit when later groups, such as the 2019 popular movement, rejected mild pledges of more inclusion by the regime and instead demanded to overhaul the entire system of governance.

Algeria is a Muslim country with a primarily secular state that has long seen economic development and social regulation as its exclusive domain. Islam is part of the cultural and political tradition dating back at least to the independence war, when the revolutionary rhetoric of the FLN drew upon the unifying force of religion to strengthen national cohesion and opposition to colonial rule. Algeria's national seal as adopted in 1976 features the Hand of Fatima – a traditional Islamic symbol – rising in front of mountains sandwiched in between industry and agriculture, with the Islamic crescent juxtaposed in front (Photo 4.1).

Islam also contributed to a uniquely Algerian form of socialism under Boumédiène. Conservative policies regarding personal, family, religious, and moral affairs have predominated, despite sweeping secular and modernizing policies in the economic sphere. The populist version of Islamism that arose in the 1980s and 1990s in virtually every segment of Algerian society finds its roots in this conservativism, but added to it more radical demands for political change.

Economic conditions

Upon assuming office in 1965, President Boumédiène began an extensive industrialization program and established government control over most, if not all, foreign trade, manufacturing, retail, agriculture, utilities, and banking.

PHOTO 4.1
National Seal of Algeria.

Source: Pixabay. Public domain.

All major foreign business interests and most major domestic industries were nationalized. By the early 1970s, almost 90 percent of the industrial sector and more than 70 percent of the industrial workforce were under state control. From 1970 to 1973, nearly 45 percent of capital investment went to the industrial sector; about 40 percent went to social and economic infrastructure, and only 15 percent went to agriculture. The "Agrarian Revolution" of 1971 aimed to create a system of cooperatives. However, with insufficient funding and infrastructure, agriculture declined as a percentage of gross national product. In the second four-year plan (1974–77), the agricultural sector and small to mid-sized industries were encouraged, but the emphasis on heavy industry remained unchallenged. However, due to poor design, many large-scale projects failed to provide an effective impetus for national development. In general, industrialization was driven more by nationalism than by technical considerations of efficiency or cost.

Such cycles of experimentation required the government maintain a steady source of hydrocarbon income from its ample oil and gas production. However, declining energy prices in the 1980s left the country with frequent food shortages, exacerbated by growing dependence on food imports and an ever-increasing rate of urbanization. President Bendjedid's economic reforms aimed at breaking down massive state enterprises into manageable entities, with the hope of stimulating the private sector. However, the global collapse of oil prices in 1986 destroyed these initiatives and further undermined the oil-dependent state to finance its bloated employment payrolls, generous subsidies, and social services. The October 1988 riots, among other grievances, expressed public anger over the rising cost of living caused partly by retreating state protections.

Amidst the crisis, Algerian planners implemented modest reforms, recognizing the limits of state-led development, with its emphasis on ISI and public spending. For instance, restrictions on foreign and domestic investments were relaxed, money and credit laws were restructured, contract laws were revised, the central bank was given more independence, and the banking system was modernized to facilitate trade finance. Privatization was entertained. Yet these changes did not stop the economic decline and high unemployment persisted while living standards declined. A massive foreign debt, unpredictable global prices, and a high level of external dependence (on both food imports and petroleum-product exports) left the country dangerously vulnerable. A growing black market began to fill the empty shelves of the public distribution networks, corruption and private appropriations of state funds by some officials multiplied, and political and social challenges went unaddressed.

Economic programming was difficult in the early 1990s in the context of the overturned elections and civil violence. Structural adjustment programming from the World Bank and International Monetary Fund in 1994 provided a narrow neoliberal agenda of policy goals, whose insistence on further cutting state spending was resisted by the largest labor union (the UGTA), professional associations, public-enterprise managers, small entrepreneurs hurt by high interest rates and currency devaluation, and import-export businesses whose informal monopolies were threatened by change. Nonetheless, the economy stabilized by 2000, inflation decreased from 30 percent in 1995 to 2 percent in 2006, and the fiscal budget and trade balance produced surpluses as oil and gas prices rebounded in global markets. The external debt, which had reached $33 billion in 1996, was almost totally paid off by 2012. Sustained economic growth returned in the 2000s, bouncing from a nadir of –2.2 percent in 1993 to 5 percent in 2008, and registering over 3 percent throughout the 2010s.

Yet such aggregate results carried a heavy social cost. The currency was devalued by 40 percent, and many consumption subsidies were drastically cut. More than 500,000 workers were laid off by 1998, and youth unemployment leapt. Social inequality increased, with less than 20 percent of the population controlling more than 50 percent of the country's wealth. In spite of this, the 2010 Human Development Report placed Algeria among ten countries designated as "top movers" – i.e., countries that achieved the greatest improvements in human development when compared to their 1970 levels – and ranked it 96 out of 187 countries. (In 2018, it crept up to 85 in the world).

In the early 2000s, aiming to prime growth, the government invested around $500 billion in employment generation, low-income housing, and infrastructure. An additional $262 billion investment plan for 2015–19 focused on health, water, and transportation infrastructure, while $90 billion went into developing new hydrocarbon fields in an effort to revitalize declining production. On the other hand, the privatization of public enterprises remained far from its professed goals. A plan to privatize the first bank, Crédit Populaire d'Algérie, was postponed indefinitely, and a decision to open Sonatrach, the only public hydrocarbons company, to private capital was also canceled due to domestic opposition.

Agriculture remains a central part of the economy, contributing over 12 percent of GDP and employing more than 10 percent of the national workforce. Despite the privatization of state collectives, updated agricultural banking, and irrigation funding, however, drought remains endemic and threatens the sector's future. Otherwise, hydrocarbons dominate the economy in terms of financial contribution. Algeria is a rentier state: oil and gas products account for over 96 percent of all exports and typically between 35 to 50 percent of all government revenues. The decline of oil prices in 2014 raised new concerns about the viability of continuing market-oriented economic policies if rentier income could not be assured. Indicating its ability to still exert muscle, in 2018 the government barred the import of 851 products, including meats, cheeses, certain fruits and vegetables, carpets, cell phones, home appliances, and more than 360 medicines and medical devices – a policy that caused supply shortages but aimed to reduce import costs and favor local producers, in a modest throwback to the heyday of ISI.

Commitments to economic diversification and financial liberalization, in line with a rhetoric emphasis on market competition, often crash into the political requirement to maintain welfarist protections in line with the old social contract. During the 2011–12 Arab Spring, the government began a five-year program worth $286 billion of investments for infrastructure, low-income housing, and job creation. Such massive initiatives, funded by oil and expanding the public sector, run antithetical to structural reforms. It also contributed to rising inflation, which increased steadily from 4 percent in 2010 to nearly 8 percent in 2018 before cycling down. Such populist impulses have also disappointed by failing to create adequate jobs for educated youth; youth unemployment reached 30 percent in 2019, well over the overall jobless rate of 12.1 percent. Indeed, maintaining high economic growth remains a challenge today; as the 2010s closed, Algeria's annual GDP growth rate diminished to well under 2 percent.

The instinct to satiate popular demands through state expenditures not only requires steady income from hydrocarbon exports – itself dependent upon high global energy prices – but also results in budget deficits. Under a strong pressure to reduce its fiscal gap, the government in the 2010s gradually implemented incremental tax increases for gasoline, cigarettes, alcohol, and some imported goods, although it refuses to cut spending in education, healthcare, and low-income housing. Public debt and banking reforms have also dragged on. Inversely, frequent efforts to attract more financing and investments from the Arabian Gulf, Turkey, and Asia by relaxing legal requirements have been more successful. By 2019, for instance, Chinese investments in construction and other sectors had overtaken other European countries, and some officials believe that future Chinese trade deals and industrial partnerships are critical to Algeria's economic future.

Such efforts go hand-in-hand growing partnerships with multilateral institutions desiring greater access to Algerian markets, from the EU (with which Algeria signed a free trade agreement in 2002) and the World Trade Organization, which Algeria cannot join until it commits to another round of policy shifts away from state-led developmentalism. To satisfy these stakeholders, Algerian officials committed to some short-term changes after the mid-2010s; among them was the depreciation of the Algerian dinar to boost exports, develop renewable energy, encourage private entrepreneurship, and consider ending many subsidies.

In addition to slowing economic growth and high unemployment, corruption is also endemic. Most high-level cases involving powerful political and business figures, who often siphon off funds and wealth from large-scale government programs for development, remained unresolved by a lack of persecutory will and cover-ups.

POLITICAL STRUCTURES

Algeria's independence left in place an authoritarian political structure controlled by the FLN. This party-based structure then evolved into a triangular system of government in which the military (and its subsidiary, the Department of Intelligence and Security, known as DRS), the FLN, and the state bureaucracy share power and continually compete for it. In the last twenty years, a new force made its way into the political system: a group of powerful business magnates who prospered during the reign of President Bouteflika, and whose brother Said served as its relay in the upper echelons of the political system. Much as Moroccan analysts speak of the Makhzen, Algerian observers call this self-maintaining system of autocratic rule *le Pouvoir* (power).

For decades after independence, the constitution concentrated major powers in the executive branch; the president's role as head of state, commander of the armed forces, defense minister, and head of the FLN ensured his power. The FLN was recognized as the "only authentic representative of the people's will" and controlled all mass associations from 1968 to 1989. All this changed after the social upheaval of the late 1980s, when Algeria's political structure began to evolve toward a more competitive, pluralistic polity, albeit one where *le Pouvoir* still retained a virtual monopoly over state power.

Political liberalization and its limits

After several decades of closed authoritarian rule highlighted by the FLN hegemony and military supremacy over the civilian power elite, political reforms starting in 1989 altered the configuration of the state and opened the way for political liberalization. Constitutional reforms promised a "state of law" and removed all references to the socialist commitment. They deprived the FLN of its single-party status and of its official role as the "guardian of the revolution." The 1989 Political Associations Law extended the right to form political parties to all organizations committed to national unity and integrity, and explicitly prohibited parties of specifically religious, ethnic, or regional character. However, this last preclusion was laxly enforced. An amendment in 2011 added restrictions on obtaining and using funds from abroad, something which seriously hindered the operation of local offices of global nongovernmental organizations, particularly those oriented toward human rights. The new law allowed also the formation of independent associations and media outlets.

Promises to pluralize and liberalize politics have remained subordinate to the authority of the president, though. He has the power to appoint and dismiss the prime minister and all other nonelected civilian and military officials; he alone can initiate constitutional amendments and may bypass parliament with national referenda. Informally, presidential power before and during Abdelaziz Bouteflika's first term (1999–2004) was still subordinate to the military, but after a showdown with the army, which almost cost him a second term, Bouteflika managed to wrest some concessions from the military, notably less outright interference in politics.

The military and the presidency

The Algerian military (Armée Nationale Populaire) has remained a constant, if inconsistent, force in Algerian politics, at times quite visible, at others more discreet. In the early years of independence, the military, endowed with organizational capacity and technical competency, quickly occupied the power vacuum left by traditional and religious forces, whose power bases were almost completely undermined by the revolution.

The Algerian army has always presented itself as the "guardian of the revolution" and guarantor of the country's integrity and stability. Historically, it has maintained a discretionary role, interfering when conditions necessitated to ensure stability and security. Following the suppression of the October 1988 riots, the army quickly retreated from politics. However, the Islamist challenge served as an occasion for the military to reassert its historically predominant role. With little faith in the government of Bendjedid, the army, in January 1992, overturned the parliamentary elections won by the Islamists. During the 1990s civil war, the army operated with impunity. It carried out massacres and failed to prevent mass killings by Islamists.

Officially, the military establishment is committed to a democratic project and a republican form of government. In the 2004 presidential election, it announced for the first time that it would not play a role in choosing the next president. Despite a lack of full support from the military, Bouteflika won with a wide margin against an unorganized and divided opposition. When he sought a third term and a constitutional amendment ending term limits in 2009, the army did not seem to mind. With no real rival candidate and the army's tacit acquiescence, he won a third term with 90 percent of the vote.

In April 2013, Bouteflika suffered a stroke that left him paralyzed and confined to a wheelchair; yet a year later, he was elected for a fourth term. Those who voted for Bouteflika saw him – and the system he headed – as guarantor of stability, security, and unity at a time when conflict and violence wracked other parts of the MENA, and terrorist threats roved across the Maghrib. This heralded a shift in the underlying structure of the regime; by 2015, Bouteflika's clique had dismantled the mighty DRS, which had become powerful enough to act almost like a parallel government since 1990, after a long power struggle with its chief, Mohamed Mediène (known as "Toufik"). In the months preceding this event, several military and security leaders were dismissed, pushed into retirement, or arrested following an obscure armed incident in July 2015 near the coastal residence of the president.

For its part, the military had started working to professionalize itself and reduce its open interference in politics and economics; this had followed the sudden retirement in August 2004 of the Chief-of-Staff General Mohamed Lamari. This allowed Bouteflika to appoint new individuals to top positions and start asserting the preeminence of civilian leadership over the military. Perceived as a close associate of President Bouteflika, General Ahmed Gaïd Salah was appointed army head in August 2004, and Vice-Defense Minister in September 2013. In April 2019, he became the main political actor, presiding over the dismissal of the president and managing the state response to the historic mass protests that started in February. That event also marked something else – the military's indifference, or even support, for Bouteflika's toppling as demanded by the popular uprising, which suggests a recalibration of the regime's underlying balance of power between the military, FLN, and elite elements in the near future.

The Islamists

For the Algerian leadership, the Islamist movement has been a constant source of agitation. Recognizing the powerful message and capabilities of the movement, the regime has alternated between suppressing and befriending Islamist voices. The Ministry of Religious Affairs was established to control the mosques and oversee the appointment of imams (prayer leaders). However, urban growth during the 1970s and 1980s led to a rapid proliferation of independent mosques and neighborhood associations, which the government could not contain. The call for greater religious piety during those decades formed the foundation of the Islamist movement, and was accompanied by extensive voluntary social work and charitable acts in areas such as education, garbage pickup, and aid for the poor, sick, and elderly. These social services fostered a loyal and extensive mass base which the Islamists mobilized once political parties were legalized in 1989. Although several Islamist organizations emerged, the Front of Islamic Salvation (FIS) became the only national challenger to the FLN. The FIS was led by Abbassi Madani, a moderate Western-educated university professor, and Ali Belhadj, a high school teacher from a poor urban neighborhood, known for his fiery rhetoric and radical views.

Despite its victory in the 1990 municipal and 1991 legislative elections, as well as its impressive capacity for popular mobilization, the FIS was critiqued for having profited from the discontent of unemployed youth in urban slums and for lacking the technical capabilities to lead an effective government. However, it presented an alternative to the existing regime at a time when there was none, and its electoral success reflected a large protest vote. Following the crackdown in the early 1990s, the FIS became increasingly radical. Internal splits separated its pragmatists from hard-liners, particularly as new transnational connections coalesced with the global Salafi movement. After the FIS was banned in 1992, most of its leaders were imprisoned or in exile, but many also defected to more radical Islamist groups.

The most prominent of the newly radicalized Islamist opposition were the Armed Islamic Group (GIA), the Armed Islamic Movement, the Islamic Salvation Army within the FIS, and the aforementioned Salafist Group for Preaching and Combat (GSPC). They engaged in daily terror campaigns, killing security personnel and civilians, including journalists, professors, poets, doctors, union officials, opposition party leaders, citizens suspected of cooperating with the state, women not abiding by Islamist commandments, and foreigners. They also destroyed infrastructure, including telephone centers, public utility vehicles, and schools. State countermeasures also left scores of people dead, hundreds jailed, and thousands missing.

Nonviolent, moderate Islamist parties were allowed to partake in national politics in the mid-1990s, but support for them declined steadily, due partly to the general irrelevance of opposition parties and partly to internal discord within the two leading entities, the Movement of Society for Peace (MSP) and Ennahda. In the 2002 elections, the MSP lost 31 of its 69 seats, and Ennahda kept only 1 of its 34 seats. However, a breakaway party from Ennahda, Harakat al-Islah al-Watani (Movement for National

Reform, or Islah), obtained 43 seats. Overall, the number of seats controlled by the Islamists declined from 103 to 82. In the November 2005 municipal elections, Islamists obtained only 7 seats. Similarly, in the May 2007 parliamentary elections, the Islamists lost 22 of the 82 seats they had won in 2002. For all its aging status, the FLN and its allied National Democratic Rally (RND) obtained 136 (down from 199 in 2002) and 61 (up from 47) seats, respectively.

Today, the Islamists remain an increasingly marginalized force in politics, bound by ugly memories of the 1990s and restricted (like all opposition) by the authoritarian regime. In the 2012 parliamentary elections, the government legalized 21 new parties in order to further fragment the opposition. The resulting vote suffered a paltry 43.1 percent official turnout rate. While FLN split into opposition factions, the MSP had withdrawn earlier from the ruling coalition to create instead an eclectic alliance with the Movement for National Reform and Ennahda – Green Algeria. Yet despite attempting to emulate the success of Islamists in Morocco, Tunisia, Egypt, and Libya in the aftermath of the Arab Spring, the alliance only obtained 49 seats, or about 10 percent of parliament, compared to the FLN's resounding capture of nearly half of the legislature.

In the 2017 elections, the Islamists did not do much better. After the dissolution of the Green Algeria Alliance, MSP formed a new coalition with the Front for Change (FC) and won 33 seats, while Ennahda allied itself with smaller Islamist groups to win just 15 seats. Altogether, the Islamist parties have 67 seats, merely 8 seats more than in the 2012 elections, suggesting that the Islamist "moment" in Algeria has come and gone.

Civic associations

In the wake of political liberalization of 1989, civic associations proliferated and became a vibrant part of Algerian political life. Many organizations – mainly those of journalists, women, and human rights advocates – played a significant role in Algeria's brief democratic experiment from 1989 to 1991 and have continued to actively challenge the regime since then.

In spring and summer 2001, a series of protests against the regime erupted in the Kabylie region, east of Algiers, following the killing of a young man imprisoned by the paramilitary gendarmerie. From these events was born the Citizen Movement, a unique mobilization started by grassroots traditional village and tribal leadership structures. It bypassed the two Berber-based parties, the FFS and the Rally for Culture and Democracy (RCD) whose 15 demands included the recognition of Berber as a national and official language. Notwithstanding its cultural demands, the Citizen Movement targeted the entire regime. The bulk of the Berber movement was opposed to both Islamism and the regime. While most of the demands of the Kabylie movement were not met, the Berber language was eventually made an official national language. However, this did not end mounting secessionist ambitions led by the Berber Movement for the Autonomy of Kabylie (MAK).

Beyond this movement, the civil society that was mobilizing in the late 1980s and early 1990s fell victim to the resilient authoritarian rule, which, after quelling radical Islamism, muzzled other opposition voices through repression, co-optation, infiltration, and control. However, peaceful protests and localized riots over a host of issues continued and intensified in recent years; they affected several towns and many professional sectors, including education, health care, civil service, the legal sector, several industries, and even the security services. The protestors' demands have been various and often disruptive.

One strong showdown involved environmental demonstrations in early 2015 in southern towns against ongoing exploration for shale gas. The deadliest confrontations were those in the southern region of Ghadaia (about five hundred miles from the capital), which pitted Arab, Sunni youth against the Mozabites, a Berber ethnic community. This conflict has been attributed to changed local demographics and socioeconomic mutations over the last 20 years, which have caused major imbalances in the distribution of wealth and employment between the two groups. In the Saharan city of Tamanrasset, another Berber group, the Tuareg, started mobilizing in early 2018 to express similar grievances of injustice, isolation, and deprivation from the benefit of the country's resources.

POLITICAL DYNAMICS

The dynamics driving Algerian authoritarianism since the violence of the 1990s are one of elite schemes and institutional change. After coming to power in 1999, President Bouteflika tried to further the return of normalcy by holding regular elections. In the parliamentary elections of May 30, 2002, to the surprise of many observers, the FLN won 199 seats, up from 69 in the previous parliament and 15 in the 1991 elections. The 2002 elections were marked, however, by people's growing apathy toward the political process in general and political parties in particular, both religious and secular. Voters had lost faith in many of the parties created since 1989 because of their internal dissention and their marginalization within the political process.

Additionally, some opposition leaders had been co-opted through election to parliament or appointment to high office, reducing both their popular appeal and their ability to oppose the regime.

Apathy, however, continued to grow and was resoundingly expressed in the 2007 and 2012 parliamentary elections; the first had a mere 35 percent voter turnout rate, the lowest in Algeria's history, and the second had a 43 percent turnout. Turnout plummeted back to 38 percent in the 2017 contest, suggesting that many Algerians place little trust in parliament, active parties, and other visible institutions of politics to become drivers of political and economic reform. Currently, parliamentary life in Algeria – for all its overshadowing by the military and autocratic presidentialism – speaks to this. The 2012 and 2017 elections essentially created a two-party legislative organ under the FLN and RND; in the latter, these pro-government parties won 164 and 100 of the 462 parliament seats. Many believe their victory was akin to a plebiscite (at least among those who bothered to vote) on the need for security and stability in light of the troubles afflicting in Libya and Egypt, Islamist extremism spreading across the Sahel (especially nearby Mali and Mauritania), and the graphic conflicts exploding in Yemen and Syria.

The missing spring in 2011

When the Arab Spring began in Tunisia in December 2010, the situation in Algeria was already tense due to dire socioeconomic conditions and lasting political malaise. On January 3, 2011, riots broke out in Algiers and other major cities, following rumors that the prices for basic food staples were about to rise again due to new regulations. These riots focused on the rising cost of living due to diminished state subsidies and the stagnant, low minimum wage. The rioters were also angry at shortages of affordable housing, failing educational and health systems, rampant corruption, cronyism, and nepotism in the bureaucracy and public companies.

While protests had become almost a daily occurrence across the country – mostly over local problems or professional issues – those of January 2011 were not limited to a single locality; they took place simultaneously in several cities. In contrast to the Tunisian and Egyptian protestors, the demonstrating Algerian youth were not supported by labor unions, political parties, or civic associations. The riots lasted only four days and ended as soon as the government announced a low price ceiling on basic food, tabled impending market regulations, and promised to address grievances about jobs, housing, marginalization, and the contempt (*hogra*) bureaucrats and security agents showed for everyday citizens. As in the past, rentierism enabled the Algerian government to pacify popular unrest with bursts of social spending.

Yet on February 12, 2011, a peaceful protest demanding political change began in Algiers, led by the newly created National Coordination for Change and Democracy (CNCD), which included small political parties and a few civic associations. It demanded democracy, an end to the state of emergency imposed since 1992, the liberalization of the political and media fields, and the release of people arrested during the January 2011 riots. However, this movement was short-lived, as it was not able to assemble a significant force of protestors due to heavy security restrictions and its failure to attract enough people.

In all, then, the Arab Spring left Algeria unmoved. Several reasons explain this, including Islamist violence of the 1990s, which was still fresh in public memory; the belief that Algeria's security forces would not hesitate to repress a popular revolt, as they had in 1988 and the 1990s; the absence of a single leader against whom to focus the protest, like Zine al-Abidine Ben Ali in Tunisia and Hosni Mubarak in Egypt; and the inability of the opposition to create a wide and sustained mass movement capable of uniting activists across a geographically sprawling country.

However, in spite of this, a growing number of other types of protests and localized riots continued in several towns and villages and many professional sectors. Strikes led by independent unions (i.e., those not affiliated with the UGTA) occurred regularly in the education, health, and legal sectors, the civil service, and several industries, including the parastatal oil and gas company Sonatrach. The strikers' demands included pay raises to keep up with inflation, parity with public-sector salaries (which had increased by 25 to 50 percent), improved work conditions, and better health insurance and pension programs. Another, sad form of protest also became prevalent: suicide, especially by self-immolation, apparently in emulation of Mohamed Bouazizi, who set himself on fire in Tunisia in December 2010, initiating the Arab Spring. The growing number of these suicides has generated neither public interest nor the concern of government officials. A final form of protest involves the growing phenomenon of illegal migration to Europe via the sea. This dangerous form of exit has caused many deaths, yet remains an attractive alternative for many people with no hope of a decent life in Algeria.

Since the Arab Spring, the government's response to such restiveness has entailed lifting the longstanding state of emergency laws, a promise of yet another constitutional reform, changes in the electoral system and media laws, and greater gender balance in political institutions. Twenty-one new parties were legalized for the 2012 elections, further diluting the power of both secular and Islamist parties, and a new women's quota system was established. This allowed 145 women to be elected to parliament in May 2012 – accounting for 31 percent of the 462 deputies, up from a mere 7 percent in the previous parliament; after the 2017 contest, women represented nearly 27 percent of all seats.

However, parliamentary elections have not halted the rising apathy and disconnect felt by many citizens when participating in politics. Support for opposition parties has been steadily dwindling, and turnouts for the past several elections have been abysmal. Most people, especially youth, had lost faith in the political elite as the twin crises of economic sluggishness and leadership succession during the 2000s unfolded. The democratic reform measures announced after 2011 were met with cynicism by an incredulous audience for whom the country's fundamental problems appear as not the product of bad policy choices, but deeply embedded in the nature of its political and economic systems.

After 2014, further signs of worrying decay and discontent could be seen. Global oil prices suffered a mini-shock that year, resulting in steep declines in hydrocarbon revenue. High youth unemployment, weak industrial production, a persistent housing crisis, and external pressures for austerity and cutbacks all converged upon policymakers. Increased attacks by armed groups belonging to AQIM and other extremist networks, amplified by worsening violence in neighboring Libya and the Sahel countries, raised new worries about insecurity. And yet, localized protests and small-scale, grassroots citizen movements continued to sprout daily.

Catching up with the Arab Spring: the post-Bouteflika era

In February 2019, 82-year-old President Bouteflika announced that he would run for an unprecedented fifth term, a fact that most Algerians recognized meant he would retain power indefinitely given the uncompetitive nature of presidential elections. For various reasons, this announcement interrupted the climate of political apathy and created an almost revolutionary momentum in the streets of most urban centers.

The popular movement began as a virtual coalition of young citizens, including students, lawyers, engineers, and other civic activists, organized spontaneous protests and demonstrations. The key motto of these multiple, overlapping, and unarmed uprisings was, in colloquial Algerian Arabic,

Tetnahou Ga'a (You Will All Depart). Far more Internet-savvy and globally connected than the political elite, this new generation of Algerian protestors demanded that Bouteflika stand down, among other social and economic claims. By early March, an estimated several million Algerians had participated in these burgeoning marches and strikes. Under intense pressure, Bouteflika surrendered on his fifth term intentions and announced that he would simply preside over the election of a new leader.

As ministers were shuffled and protests continued, popular demands grew increasingly firm, as many demonstrators recognized the tendency of *le Pouvoir* to maintain itself. Activists responded by rejecting Bouteflika's concession and instead called for his removal – something the military, under the leadership of General Ahmed Gaïd Salah, facilitated by invoking Article 102 of the constitution and declaring the president incapacitated. On April 2, Bouteflika submitted his resignation and was replaced by Abdelkader Bensalah, the president of the parliament's upper house, the Council of the Nation. As acting president, Bensalah announced that a presidential vote would be held in 90 days, as constitutionally required, in July 2019. Again, this plan was rejected by the protest movement, which feared a combination of FLN and military scheming to ensure Bouteflika's replacement with simply another autocratic elite. The Algerian military attempted to invoke its historic role as guardians of the nation, indicating that it was seeking to avert the chaos and violence witnessed in other countries of the region. In June 2019, authorities canceled the July 2019 presidential elections, citing a lack of viable candidates.

Meanwhile, other moves were unfolding. As a last act before resigning in April 2019, Bouteflika appointed a new government of mostly technocrats with the hope of appeasing the street protests, led by Prime Minister Noureddine Bedoui. Among its first actions was a campaign to arrest prominent political and business magnates for corruption. Among the affiliates of Bouteflika ensnared were former Prime Ministers Ahmed Ouyahia and Abdelmalek Sellal; Mohamed Loukal, the incumbent finance minister and former head of Banque d'Algerie; and several business tycoons and influence peddlers linked to the circle headed by the president's brother, Said Bouteflika. These include the famous Kouninef brothers, Issad Rebrab, Ali Haddad, Omar Haddad, and the father-son duo of Mahieddine and Nacer Tahkout, among many other luminaries and oligarchs popularly seen as having accumulated their wealth unjustly.

Such anti-corruption measures did not succeed in quieting the protests. The social movement demanded instead an entirely new regime, one not led by veteran political operators who had failed them for years. Even the judicial offensive against corrupt officials was perceived by some as suspicious justice administered by the same system that had allowed for years such a state of affairs in the first place. For others, it was simply part of the perennial battle between the various clans that have constituted *le Pouvoir*, and whose cohesion as a power coalition seems to have collapsed. Learning from the failed transition in Egypt, where the fundamentals of the old systems (including the military) have remained in place, protest groups suggested drafting a new constitution through a national conference that would decidedly exclude current members of the government, military, and ruling parties. They also pointedly rejected many established opposition and Islamist trends hoping to partake in the demonstrations.

As expected, the armed forces resisted this proposal for a clean slate and regime change that would create a second Algerian republic. A truly representative and democratic system would destroy its prerogatives and power. However, because the protests were peaceful, well-organized, and spontaneous, it was difficult to respond with customary coercion and repressive force. Images and videos of the protests, widely available on social media, showed a calm ambiance where demonstrators of all walks of life, professions, and ages expressed pride in being Algerian and vowed to prevent a repeat of the failed transitions of Egypt, Syria, and Libya.

The result was continued political stalemate throughout summer 2019, albeit one largely free of violence. Officials tolerated most protests, understanding that excessive repression frequently backfired for other autocratic regimes during the Arab Spring. They also continued espousing an anti-corruption stance by arresting moguls and politicians linked to Bouteflika. Unsatisfied, the protest movement suggested a slate of prominent lawyers, intellectuals, and human rights advocates with whom military authorities could negotiate in order to organize new presidential elections and install democratic reforms. However, the military leadership refused to participate in any process of political change that would result in its institutional demise.

In the closing months of 2019, the most pressing tasks remained resolving the political crisis and, perhaps more important, ameliorate crushing problems of job creation and economic lethargy. Many technocrats do want to enact serious – albeit stringent and painful – reforms, but consensus on the form, depth, and timing of reform remain elusive. Also, fears about the potentially negative consequences of severe economic change for an already discontented population continue to produce hesitation and inconsistency, especially given the instinct of policymakers to simply reach for the toolbox of welfarist spending in response to major unrest. In this conjuncture, the state is caught in the difficult position of having to resolve serious socioeconomic problems while opening Algeria's economy to global capital, enacting more austerity measures, maintaining strict budgetary discipline, and rebuilding its damaged legitimacy.

FOREIGN POLICY

Algeria's revolutionary tradition has strongly influenced its foreign policy. Its anti-colonial revolution against France was extended to encompass a challenge to imperialist powers worldwide. This lent Algeria a prominent position in the Maghrib, the Arab region, and the developing world more broadly. Pursuing an independent, if often abrasive, course in its foreign policy, Algeria acquired an influential role in world politics during the 1960s and 1970s – a role that far exceeded its resources and capabilities. However, internal economic and political problems restricted Algeria's foreign policy, as strategic, economic, and political interests in its region began to take precedence. As evidenced by the dramatic reversal of the government's position on the 1990 Iraqi invasion of Kuwait, Algeria's foreign policy has slowly come to reflect the course of pragmatism, one more concerned about not disturbing the status quo than creating bold initiatives or aligning itself against global majorities.

Algeria's relations with its Maghrib neighbors were strained after independence and remained so throughout the 1970s, especially with Morocco, whose conservative ideological orientation conflicted with Algeria's socialist orientation. In the 1980s, however, political and economic liberalization in Algeria drew the two countries closer, and relations improved dramatically, only to deteriorate again in 1994 after Morocco accused Algeria of supporting an armed Islamist attack in a Marrakech tourist hotel and imposed visa requirements on Algerian visitors. Algeria responded by closing the common border. It was later found that the attack was orchestrated by a French-based network which recruited young Frenchmen of Moroccan descent for armed operations in Morocco. The Western Sahara issue remains a major point of contention between Morocco and Algeria, with the latter aiding the Polisario Front. The potentiality for hostility is a major reason why the Arab Maghrib Union (UMA) between Algeria, Libya, Mauritania, Morocco, and Tunisia has never succeeded beyond its proposal stage.

Despite its membership and founding role in the Organization of African Unity (OAU), Algeria is still much more closely affiliated with its Arab neighbors and southern Europe than with the African countries to the south, except on issues concerning instability and insecurity in the Sahel region, with which Algeria shares more than 1,000 miles of border. It remains involved in the successor organization, the African Union (AU), more out of tactical considerations than genuine commitment. Algeria hosted the 1999 OAU summit, assumed the OAU presidency for one year, and committed itself to an active role in conflict resolution in Africa – mediating a peace agreement in 2000 between Ethiopia and Eritrea, and another in 2015 between Tuareg rebels and Mali's government – and in negotiations with the industrialized countries over African debt. In 2006, it held in Algiers an AU meeting of experts on migration and development which adopted a Draft African Common Position on Migration and Development which was a set of shared policy recommendations.

After the OAU was succeeded by the African Union in 2001, President Bouteflika became involved in the New African Partnership for Africa's Development. In July 2009, Algeria hosted the second pan-African cultural festival; the first had been held in 1968.

Well before the 2012 conflict that left first Tuareg rebels and then Islamist groups in control of northern Mali, Algeria had served as a mediator between Malian Tuaregs and their government. It favored a negotiated solution, but the United Nations Security Council in October 2012 called for joint military action by Mali's neighbors – including Algeria – if a peaceful solution to the conflict could not be found. Algeria feared such a development because it risked creating an influx of refugees and aggravating instability within its own borders. However, in the end, and to the consternation of many Algerians, it acquiesced to the French use of Algerian airspace for a military offensive against the Islamist rebels in northern Mali in January 2013.

Algeria's policy toward the Sahel region in general, and Mali in particular, has been characterized more by discreet diplomatic actions aiming to resolve issues through negotiations and influence rather than the flexing of its military power as a regional heavyweight. It appears that Algeria, which stands officially by its long-held principle of non-interference in the domestic affairs of neighboring countries, has been mostly concerned with how an unpredictable military intervention might affect its own security along its long Sahelian borders.

Algeria has been an active member of the Arab League since independence in 1962, but its involvement in Middle Eastern affairs has been limited mainly to supporting the Palestinian cause. Algeria's historical and ideological commitment to self-determination has fostered a strong affinity with the Palestinians. The Iraqi invasion of Kuwait in August 1990 and the subsequent retaliation by Western coalition forces produced substantial popular support for Iraq, leading the government to quickly backpedal from its initial neutral position. In the context of the Arab Spring, Algerian officials grew concerned about the spread of popular upheavals, especially in Libya and Syria. They opposed foreign intervention in both, and did not warm up to the new Libyan leadership until well after al-Qaddafi had been deposed.

Political and economic liberalization at home and a moderate foreign policy have substantially improved Algeria's relations with Europe and the United States in recent decades. In January 1981, Algeria mediated the release of the American hostages held in Iran. Western powers likewise have tolerated the resolutely authoritarian nature of the Algerian state, which has moved toward the West in its economic orientation and affiliation. Europe's energy demands and the common fight against Islamist violence ensure Algeria's dense cultural, diplomatic, and military ties with its European allies.

France is Algeria's most significant foreign partner. More than 20 percent of all Algerian exports and imports head to or originate in France, the single largest destination within the EU, which claims over half of all Algerian exports. There are close to two million Algerians living in France, and many Algerians speak French, creating tremendous cultural overlap. However, French-Algerian relations have not always been cordial. Algeria's high level of dependence on France and its desire to be free of that dependency have complicated relations between the two countries. France's support for Morocco on the Western Sahara issue, in contradistinction to Algerian support for the Sahrawi self-determination movement, have caused repeated frictions. As with many countries, however, diplomatic relations are largely determined by economic ties, in this case by gas and oil exports, which have always flowed north. Indeed, Algeria regularly ranks as among the top five largest sources of natural gas for the EU, and maintains a free trade agreement with the EU, although it will likely be renegotiated due to unfavorable political requirements.

Perhaps the most sensitive issue in French-Algerian relations is that of Algerian emigration to France. French policies toward Algerian immigrants have been less than consistent, and popular sentiment in France has generally been biased against people of North African origin. Xenophobic flare-ups between French nationalists and Maghrib migrants have become common, and are reported widely in the Algerian media. The issue of immigration implicates the deeper problem of historical memory tying the two countries together. Algerians and their government were unhappy with a 2005 law passed by the French parliament that described the French colonization of

Algeria as positive. The Algerian government requested a repeal of the law and a formal French apology for colonization and the brutality that accompanied it. The law, which jeopardized a planned treaty of friendship between the two countries, was later repealed. Since Algeria's independence in 1962, French leaders have not consistently acknowledged France's colonization of Algeria and its savage repression. However, in September 2018, French President Emmanuel Macron formally acknowledged the culpability of French authorities in the use of torture in Algeria. In the previous year, while campaigning for the presidency, he called the colonization of Algeria a "crime against humanity." However, he stopped short of offering a formal apology about France's colonial actions in Algeria.

Its close French association notwithstanding, Algeria's wide range of contacts qualifies it as one of the few countries in the world to maintain a truly independent position in the international arena. Throughout the most difficult years of the Cold War, Algeria remained actively involved with both the Soviet Union and the United States. During the Bouteflika era, Algeria balanced its relations with Europe by increasing interaction with the United States. The events of September 11, 2001, provided the United States and Algeria with a newfound affinity: the fight against Islamist extremism. Algeria became a key American partner in the war against armed Islamist groups, notably because of its experience in fighting them and its robust intelligence on their recruitment and training networks. However, many Algerians still hold a negative attitude toward the United States because of its support for Israel, the 2003 invasion of Iraq, and its perceived role in the conflicts in Syria and Yemen. If Algeria retains its current course of foreign policy pragmatism, it will likely keep open the possibility of more strategic and economic cooperation with the United States.

FUTURE PROSPECTS

Algeria faces many urgent problems, including the legacies of its revolutionary war and its 1990s internecine bloodshed. On the economic front, the government faces external pressures to better align the country with global markets, as well as internal pressures for greater employment opportunities and living standards for the young and educated populace. Politically, the authoritarian system has been historically shaped by a small elite, while the military and security establishments brooded over policymaking and maintained significant control over society. Changing both the economy and the political system have now become an urgent task as the country wrestles with a serious economic downturn, a leadership succession crisis, and a restless youth in search for a new beginning for the country.

Currently, Algeria's popular uprising and consequent political struggle mean that the future leadership could be potentially far different than during the past two decades of Bouteflika's presidency. Yet given ingrained military resistance and elite privilege, while there is the potential that conservative forces can hijack any transition; arguably, this is what transpired in the early 1990s. However, what was missing then is what could crystallize now – a united core of reformists and activists, who can guide the political system through any legitimacy crisis. The current momentum, if well managed, might usher in real change. Many imagine a hypothetical Algerian democracy where *le Pouvoir* is dismantled, with the FLN surrendering its dominant party position and the military retreating to its barracks. That new constitutional order would be characterized by democratic processes, accountability of all office holders, an independent judicial system, a free press, and a competitive but responsive economy that relies upon neither hydrocarbon rents nor widespread corruption to create job opportunities of the young.

NOTE

1 Cited in Pierre Nora, *Les Français d'Algérie* (Paris: Julliard, 1961), 88.

FURTHER READING

A historical primer for modern Algeria is James McDougall, *A History of Algeria* (Cambridge University Press, 2017), and the aging but accessible Phillip Chiviges Naylor, *Historical Dictionary of Algeria* (Scarecrow Press, 2006). More specifically, on Algeria's war of national liberation, the best account remains Alistair Horne, *A Savage War of Peace: Algeria, 1954–1962* (Penguin Books, 1979). Competent interpretations also can be found in David Gordon, *The Passing of French Algeria* (Oxford University Press, 1966); and Alf Andrew Heggoy, *Insurgency and Counterinsurgency in Algeria* (Indiana University Press, 1972). The war's psychocultural consequences are treated in Frantz Fanon's *The Wretched of the Earth* (Grove Press, 1963) and *A Dying Colonialism* (Grove Press, 1967). An excellent publication with French and Algerian contributors is Mohamed Harbi and Benjamin Stora, eds., *La guerre d'Algérie, 1954–2004: La fin de l'amnésie* (Robert Lafont, 2004).

Critical analyses of French colonialism and its effects may be found in Pierre Bourdieu, *The Algerians* (Beacon Press, 1962); and James McDougall, *History and the Culture of Nationalism in Algeria* (Cambridge University Press, 2008). Interrogations of post-colonial history begin with John Ruedy, *Modern Algeria: The Origins and Development of a Nation*, 2nd ed. (Indiana University Press, 2005). A polemical account sympathetic to the Boumédiène regime and its socialist policies is found in Mahfoud Bennoune, *The Making of Contemporary Algeria, 1830–1987* (Cambridge University Press, 1988).

Elite-based perspectives include William B. Quandt, *Revolution and Political Leadership* (MIT Press, 1969); John P. Entelis, *Algeria: The Revolution Institutionalized* (Westview Press, 1986); John P. Entelis and Phillip C. Naylor, eds., *State and Society in Algeria* (Westview Press, 1992); and Rachid Tlemçani, *Élections et élites en Algérie: Paroles des candidats* (Chihab, 2003).

Analyses of contemporary Algerian politics, including the role of Islamism, can be found in Azzedine Layachi's many works, including: "Political Liberalization and the Islamists in Algeria," in *Islam, Democracy and the State in Algeria*, eds. Michael Bonner, Megan Reif, and Mark Tessler (Routledge, 2005); "Reinstating the State or Instating Civil Society: The Dilemma of Algeria's Transition," in *Collapsed States: The Disintegration and Restoration of Legitimate Authority*, ed. I. William Zartman (Lynne Rienner, 1995); and "Reform and the Politics of Inclusion in the Maghrib," *Journal of North African Studies 5*, 3 (2001): 15–47. See also Andrea Liverani, *Civil Society in Algeria: The Political Functions of Associational Life* (Routledge, 2008); Martin Evans and John Phillips, *Algeria: Anger of the Dispossessed* (Yale University Press, 2007); Amar Benamrouche, *Gréves et conflits politiques en Algérie* (Karthala, 2000); and François Burgat and William Dowell, *The Islamic Movement in North Africa* (University of Texas Press, 1993).

On the civil conflict of the 1990s, the following are noteworthy: Habib Souaidia, *La sale guerre* (Découverte, 2001), which presents a strong indictment of the Algerian military in particular and the regime in general; Nesroulah Yous, *Qui a tué à Bentalha* (Découverte, 2000); Luis Martinez, *The Algerian Civil War, 1990–1998* (Hurst & Co., 2002); and Hugh Roberts, *The Battlefield Algeria, 1988–2002: Studies in a Broken Polity* (Verso, 2002).

Studies of Algeria's economic development include several more of Azzedine Layachi's studies, including: "Algeria: Crisis, Transition and Social Policy Outcomes," in *Social Policy and Development: The Middle East and North Africa*, eds. Massoud Karshenas and Valentine Moghadam (Palgrave Macmillan, 2006); "Domestic and International Constraints of Economic Adjustment in Algeria," in *The New Global Economy: North African Responses*, ed. Dirk Vandewalle (St. Martin's Press, 1996); and "The Private Sector in the Algerian Economy," *Mediterranean Politics 6*, 2 (2001): 29–50. Dedicated monographs to the subject are few, but the best implicate the role of oil and gas rentierism to the distorted trajectory of development. See, for instance, Ali Aissaoui, *Algeria: The Political Economy of Oil and Gas* (Oxford University Press, 2001); and Miriam Lowi, *Oil Wealth and the Poverty of Politics: Algeria Compared* (Cambridge University Press, 2011).

Treatments of the military include I. William Zartman, "The Algerian Army in Politics," in *Soldier and State in Africa*, ed. Claude E. Welch (Northwestern University Press, 1970); John P. Entelis, "Algeria: Technocratic Rule, Military Power," in *Political Elites in Arab North Africa*, eds. I. William Zartman et al. (Longman, 1982); and Hugh Roberts, *Commanding Disorder: Military Power and Informal Politics in Algeria* (IB Tauris, 2002). The best works on Algerian foreign policy include Nicole Grimaud, *La politique extérieure de l'Algérie* (Karthala, 1984); Robert Mortimer's articles in *African Studies* (March 1984) and *Current History* (1991, 1993, 1994); and Jeffrey James Byrne, *Mecca of Revolution: Algeria, Decolonization, and the Third World Order* (Oxford University Press, 2016).

Questions of culture, women, and society are treated in Ali El Kenz, *Algerian Reflections on Arab Crises* (University of Texas Press, 1991) and Natalya Vince, *Our Fighting Sisters: Nation, Memory and Gender in Algeria, 1954–2012* (Manchester University Press, 2015). A penchant take on Algerian national identity and its construction can be found in Laurie A. Brand, *Official Stories: Politics and National Narratives in Egypt and Algeria* (Stanford University Press, 2014). The following works deal with the Berber question: Amar Ouerdane, *La question berbère dans le mouvement national algérien: 1926–1980* (Septentrion, 1990); Ernest Gellner and Charles Micaud, eds., *Arabs and Berbers: From Tribe to Nation in North Africa* (Lexington Books, 1972); Azzedine Layachi, "The Berbers in Algeria: Politicization of Ethnicity and Ethnicization of Politics," in *Nationalism and Minority Identities in Islamic Societies*, ed. Maya Shatzmiller (McGill University Press, 2005); and Hugh Roberts, *Berber Government: The Kabyle Polity in Precolonial Algeria* (IB Tauris, 2013).

Online sources

Algeria remains one of the lesser researched countries in the MENA and Arab world, due to its past conflicts and perceived inaccessibility to many social scientists. Still, there are resources online to spearhead further sleuthing. News portals and informational websites include Algerie360 (www.algerie360.com); *El-Watan*, an independent newspaper (www.elwatan.com); and *ElKhabar*, another independent daily (www.elkhabar.com). The official government press outlet is the Algérie Presse Service (www.aps.dz/en/).

In addition, human rights monitors offer reliable reporting, including Algeria-Watch (https://algeria-watch.org/) and Human Rights Watch's portal (www.hrw.org/middle-east/n-africa/algeria). The World Bank's country portal provides economic data and briefings (www.worldbank.org/en/country/algeria/overview). Outside media also closely track political and economic events, including France24's Algeria coverage (www.france24.com/en/tag/algeria/), Al-Jazeera's country page (www.aljazeera.com/topics/country/algeria.html), and Middle East Eye's country portal (www.middleeasteye.net/countries/algeria). AllAfrica's country site also usefully aggregates news headlines for easy sifting (https://allafrica.com/algeria/).

Please note that URLs may change far more quickly than books can be printed; so if these exact URLs do not work, simply search Google or another engine by the titles of these websites and online resources.

Republic of Tunisia

Lindsay J. Benstead

INTRODUCTION

In early December 2010, Tunisia appeared to be the same island of authoritarian stability it had been for decades. Then a young man named Mohamed Bouazizi set himself on fire in front of a government office in Sidi Bouzid, a town in Tunisia's interior. Bouazizi, who worked on the streets as an illegal fruit-and-vegetable vendor, was angry because a police officer had confiscated his wares, and local officials refused to hear his complaint. His desperate act sparked protests that spread quickly to other towns and the capital of Tunis. President Zine al-Abidine Ben Ali promised reforms, but it was too late. Less than two weeks after Bouazizi died, Ben Ali fled to Saudi Arabia, becoming the first Arab leader ever overthrown by peaceful mass protests.

Of the Arab countries that experienced popular mobilization in the Arab uprisings, only Tunisia has become a nascent democracy. In the 2011 Constituent Assembly elections, the formerly banned Islamist Ennahda (Renaissance) Party won a plurality. By January 2014, the assembly had passed a constitution, and later that year, Nidaa Tounes (Tunisia's Call), a secular party established in 2012, won a plurality in parliament and the presidency. In 2018, local and regional elections – the first since the Ben Ali era – also took place, with women winning half the seats in local councils. Tunisia's political landscape is therefore remarkable in the dramatic changes it has witnessed in the last decade alone, with another round of parliamentary and presidential elections occurring in fall 2019. However, Tunisia also faces unprecedented challenges as it struggles to strengthen democratic institutions, grapple with transitional justice issues, and maintain security along its volatile border with Libya. The government must also invest in more focal efforts to enhance economic growth and local development, which have yet to take place since the revolution amidst a booming youth populace and rising unemployment.

Box 5.1 provides vital data for this country. Note that Tunisia held presidential elections in September 2019 and parliamentary elections in October 2019. Both results were received too late to have been included in this data box, which instead reflects Tunisian politics as it appeared in summer 2019 following the natural death of President Essebsi.

BOX 5.1   VITAL DATA – REPUBLIC OF TUNISIA

Capital	Tunis
Regime type	Democratic (semi-presidential republic)
Head of state	(Interim) President Mohamed Ennaceur (since July 2019; mandate ended after September 2019 elections)
Head of government	Prime Minister Youssef Chahed (since 2016, but likely to change after October 2019 legislative elections)
Legislative institution	Unicameral parliament, with 217 elected seats (*Majlis Nuwaab al-Sha'b,* or Assembly of Popular Deputies)
Female quota	Yes: parties must run candidates lists with parity between men and women
Percentage of seats held by women	31.3%
Major political parties (share of seats after general elections in 2014; does not reflect October 2019 legislative elections)	Nidaa Tounes (37.6%), Ennahda (27.8%), Free Patriotic Union (4.1%), Popular Front (3.6%), Afek Tounes (3%), Congress for the Republic (2%)
Population	11,532,127
Major ethnic groups	Arab (98%), European (1%), other (1%)
Major religious groups	Muslim (99%), other (1%)
GDP per capita	$3,464 ($12,372 at Purchasing Power Parity)
Unemployment rate	15.5%
Youth unemployment rate	34.8%
Major economic industries	Mining (especially phosphate and iron), tourism, textiles, agriculture, food processing, petroleum and refining
Military spending as % GDP	2.1

HISTORICAL BACKGROUND

Understanding Tunisia's apparent exceptionalism as the birthplace of the 2011–12 Arab Spring and its own democratic experiment begins with a look at its history of continuous state-building. Successive rulers under the Islamic empires, and the French – and later Tunisian – governments left many institutions of authority, administration, and responsiveness largely intact, culminating in the development of a strong, centralized state that allowed the country to escape civil conflict after Ben Ali was overthrown. Coupled with the country's small geographical size and flat topography, the scarcity of tribalism and other sub-national allegiances, and the predominance of Sunni Arabs as the predominant ethnolinguistic group, Tunisia is also relatively homogenous, with a strong national identity.

Ottoman rule

At the crossroads of Africa, the Middle East, and Europe, modern-day Tunisia was originally populated by indigenous Amazigh, or "free people," who lived in tribally organized societies. These communities mixed with and absorbed many influences and invaders, developing the cosmopolitan identity for which Tunisia is known. The Phoenicians, originally from the region of modern-day Lebanon, chose a site near Tunis to establish the city of Carthage in the eighth century BC. Romans brought Christianity, leaving some of the finest examples of their architecture and artwork from the second and third centuries AD.

By the mid-600s AD, Arab invaders brought Islam and the Arabic language to the region and incorporated Tunisia into the Umayyad Caliphate based in Damascus. Successive Tamazight (i.e., Berber) dynasties were also prevalent in the Maghrib region stretching to what is now Morocco, starting the general process of communal intermingling. Over the next several centuries, governments based in Tunis exercised authority over northern and coastal areas of Tunisia where much of the population was located. Even after the Ottoman Turks took control of the areas in 1574, anointing the administrative province of Tunis as their political centerpiece, governors in Tunis, known as *beys*, continued to enjoy substantial independence and to control an area roughly equivalent to modern-day Tunisia.

By the early 1800s, the European scramble for colonies, backed by new military technologies, tipped the regional balance of power in Europe's favor. The Ottoman sultan invested large sums to modernize the economy, administration, and military. Across the empire, Ottoman governors initiated similar reforms to defend their independence against both the Europeans as well as the Ottoman government. Borrowing to fund these reforms generated debt that made the region's governments even more vulnerable to European control. In Tunisia, France's influence grew after it occupied Algeria in 1830.

Internal events in Tunisia under Ottoman authority were groundbreaking, if underappreciated at the time. Elites and activists based mainly in Tunis, for instance, orchestrated the 1861 Constitution, the first such written document in the Islamic world; the purpose was to reduce the bey's absolute powers, create legislative accountability, promote financial transparency, and modernize the legal system. Khaireddin Pasha, a local reformer, led the Tunisian government as its chief minister in the 1870s, so impressing the Ottoman sultan with his progressive initiatives that he served afterwards as the Grand Vizier for the entire empire in Istanbul.

In an effort to protect investments in Tunisia and shield Algeria from Italian and British ambitions, French forces marched across the Algerian border in 1881 and turned Tunisia into a French protectorate.

From French protectorate to independence

The bey maintained his position under the protectorate, but a French resident-general wielded the real power behind the throne. A French adviser stood behind each Tunisian minister, and France had control over Tunisia's foreign policy. However, colonial administers also did not destroy local economic, political, and social institutions to the degree that they did in Algeria. To be sure, the French saw territorial mastery over Tunisia as important to their overall imperial position in the Maghrib, but Tunisia never had the same commercial and symbolic importance as Algeria did. Interested more in simply ensuring local stability, they safeguarded many roads and agricultural technologies that had in some cases existed since Roman times, laying the foundations for modern infrastructure in several key sectors; they also created educational institutions that exposed a select group of elite young Tunisians to European values.

At the same time, Tunisia was converted in mercantilist fashion into a producer for French markets. French elites expropriated or claimed the best agricultural land, manufactured goods that pushed out many traditional workshops, and turned the civil service into a *de facto* French institution. Such incorporation into the colonial empire required the construction of a robust centralized authority, one whose administrative capacity to tax, regulate, and monitor far exceeded social resistance. As such, the French employed a combination of coercive firepower, legal manipulation, and political pressures to eliminate provincial rebellions and revolts, including those by tribal leaders, rural notables, and the religious voices at Al-Zaytuna, the leading educational institution of Islamic theology. Such efforts to unify the protectorate helped create the perception of national homogeneity that observers often espouse today, for it meant Tunisia entered the twentieth century with few real centers of autonomy outside the French-led administrative apparatus, lacking for instance powerful rural tribes that could overturn urban authority or an ensconced class of Islamic leaders with national appeal.

Nonetheless, a proto-nationalist movement drawing upon educated Francophile Tunisian activists began to stir in the first decade of the twentieth century, partly as a consequence of interaction with France and the rise of nationalism throughout Europe and the Ottoman Empire. This group, the Young Tunisians, did not demand full independence. Rather, they criticized France for not honoring its promise to help Tunisia develop in ways that would benefit Tunisians. Following World War One, the Destour Party (from the Arabic *dustur*, or "constitution") took up these same themes but remained an elite-oriented entity rather than a mass-based organization.

In 1934, a young, French-trained lawyer named Habib Bourguiba led a breakaway faction of younger party members. Their new party, the Neo-Destour, sought to become more than an elite vehicle of intellectual debate; their goal was to create an aggressive anti-colonial movement that focused on social and economic issues and demanded independence. After World War Two, party leaders built the Neo-Destour into a national party, mobilizing Tunisians across classes, regions, and ideologies. Among Bourguiba's colleagues were figures that would prove central to Tunisian politics in future decades, among them Ahmed Ben Salah and Salah Ben Youssef. Another key event was the establishment of the Union Générale Tunisienne du Travail, the Tunisian General Labor Union (UGTT), by Farhat Hached in 1946. The UGTT, like the Neo-Destour, became a major source of Tunisian nationalist activism given its massive outreach and base connecting it to Tunisian workers. Its power to mobilize wage-earning Tunisians around themes of justice and sovereignty was such in 1952, when the French temporarily ceased negotiations for independence and cracked down on the Neo-Destour, Hached was assassinated.

Allied with the UGTT, the Neo-Destour built popular support for its cause. These two groups instigated strikes, mass demonstrations, and small-scale violence to influence French public opinion and maintain pressure on the government. In 1955, an exhausted France more interested in maintaining its Algerian position granted Tunisia internal autonomy, and in March 1956,

Tunisia declared its independence. Bourguiba became prime minister in 1956 and then president in 1957, announcing Tunisia as a republic and abolishing the bey. An immediate challenge emerged from Ben Youssef, however, who commanded his own faction within the Neo-Destour. Whereas Bourguiba was still envisaging the type of republican political order he desired, Ben Youssef's close ties with Arab Nationalism and in particular Egyptian Nasserists pulled some Tunisians into a more radical direction.

The struggle over the heart of the Neo-Destour was heated; while many UGTT supporters backed Bourguiba, as did most of the educated elites, many Tunisians from rural areas as well as religious groups joined urban ideologues in embracing Ben Youssef. The Sfax party conference in November 1955 allowed Bourguibists to expel Ben Youssef and his followers from the party, but this also instigated a period of internal violence replete with Youssefist insurgents operating in the rural south and competing propaganda. The French also lent their military support and policing assistance to Bourguiba several times, hoping to stabilize the newly independent country. In January 1958, Ben Youssef went into exile abroad, but continued to denounce Bourguiba; he was assassinated in mysterious circumstances in 1961 in West Germany.

Tunisia under Bourguiba, 1956–1987

With the Youssefists suppressed, Bourguiba and the Neo-Destour went about creating the modern Tunisian state. Although Bourguiba had rallied a broad coalition in the struggle for independence, the Neo-Destour was deeply divided by the time that goal had been achieved. Bourguiba and his allies represented a progressive wing of the party that reflected the influence of French socialism and its secular values. They pursued pragmatic policies that would generate growth and distribute it more equitably. To their left, more rigorous socialists wanted the government to adopt a development strategy based on state control of the economy. To their right, a religiously conservative wing was suspicious of Bourguiba's secularism and European orientation.

To legitimize the regime, Bourguiba sought to reorganize and centralize the Tunisian state apparatus, eliminating social resistance and possible opposition groups. One part of this authoritarian consolidation required expanding the Neo-Destour party such that it became hegemonic within politics. By the early 1960s, the ruling party counted over 350,000 members spread across nearly 1,000 branches in the country; the organization had a presence in every sector, thanks to its close partnership with the UGTT, and membership was a prerequisite for professional or political advancement. Needless to note, no other political party was tolerated. As a peak actor, the Neo-Destour was able to incorporate interests and representation from many major fields, from the UGTT to the national student movement and industry organizations, allowing Bourguiba to also closely monitor the country's public discourse.

Economic modernization was another aspect of Tunisian state-building. Massive investments in education, infrastructure, public employment, and social services allowed the regime to impose a sort of autocratic discipline upon an urbanizing society, while simultaneously creating the kind of autocratic social contract seen in other nondemocratic states in the MENA during this time – security and prosperity in return for political obeisance to an autocracy with little tolerance for dissent, opposition, or pluralism. This strategy also required secularizing state and society, eliminating Al-Zaytuna as a center for Islamic theology and folding almost all religious authority into the state bureaucracy and ministerial institutions. Bourguiba sought to instrumentalize Islam. He was perhaps biased towards the French notion of a secular republic; for instance, he discouraged fasting during Ramadan on the grounds that it hurt the economy. Yet he also believed that Islamic discourse and principles were important insofar that they could help his single-party dictatorship control public discourse and legitimate its standing among the conservative and pious.

Finally, in addition to secularization, Bourguiba also implemented a policy of state feminism. Bourguiba passed by decree a Personal Status Code (PSC) in 1956 that extended many new rights to women, outlawed polygamy and the guardian system, and gave women the right to ask for divorce. This made Tunisia the most liberally progressive country in the Arab world at the time in terms of the personal rights and freedoms afforded to women. Some modernist Islamic thinkers of the day supported women's emancipation, arguing that it reflected Islamic teachings. Other conservative leaders, however, including Rached Ghannouchi, who founded the Islamic Tendency Movement (MTI) in 1981, criticized the code as a violation of Islam. (Ghannouchi later accepted the PSC in 1988 as a condition of release from prison, where he was being held as a political prisoner.) Despite opposition, the PSC fueled social changes that altered women's roles in politics and the economy and contributed to the democratic transition that followed the 2011 Jasmine Revolution. Today, partly as a result of those changes, women in Tunisia have among the highest levels of political representation and labor force participation in the Arab world.

In the early 1960s, concern about lingering political opposition and the failure of the private sector to stimulate economic development prompted Bourguiba to adopt centralized planning and assume a larger role as an owner in the industrial and agricultural sectors. In 1964 the Neo-Destour changed its name to the Destourian Socialist Party (PSD), and Ben Salah was appointed as Minister of Planning and Minister of Finance to oversee this vast new economic framework, which made state control and collective planning central elements. Politically, the regime became even more repressive; party and state became indistinguishable, and there were few independent civil society organizations (CSOs) left that had not been co-opted into the ruling party. The socialist era failed to produce long-term growth, however, and in 1969, Bourguiba sacked Ben Salah and retracted some of the most aggressive collectivization measures.

Yet the economic crisis, the government's abrupt turn from left to right, and deepening authoritarianism created new pockets of dissent. Within the PSD, liberals argued that the party needed to become open to a wider range of views. When Bourguiba installed his allies in the PSD's Political Bureau and orchestrated his election as president for life in 1974 through a vote of the National Assembly, he made it clear that he was not prepared to share power. Further, among left-wing forces, a wide range of socialist ideologies had gained popularity on university campuses and in the trade union. As economic inequality increased, leftist activists turned the trade union into a militant opposition force. The UGTT, which alongside the Neo-Destour served as the vanguard for the Tunisian nationalist movement, began divorcing itself from the ruling party. While Bourguiba ensured that pliable, conservative labor leaders still reported to the PSD, the rank-and-file of the UGTT became disillusioned from the president's growing intolerance to workers' demands. Finally, a small collection of Islamic scholars established an informal group called the Association for the Safeguard of the Qur'an (ASQ).

This marked the beginning of Islamism in Tunisia as a recognizable political current. The ASQ represented the large number of Tunisians who had never been comfortable with Bourguiba's secularism, including pious citizens for whom the promise of economic success and political emancipation never materialized under a single-party dictatorship that had just failed in its socialist economic experiment. At first, Bourguiba tolerated the ASQ as a counter to militant left-wing groups as long as it focused on cultural and religious issues. But as those leftist forces gained traction by emphasizing economic and political grievances, particularly on university campuses and among the UGTT rank-and-file, it became harder for the ASQ to remain on the political sidelines. Islamist leaders began to support this opposition's demands for democratic reform, human rights, and economic protection. This marked the beginning of a working relationship between Islamists and secular democrats that deepened over the next three decades.

By the early 1980s, Bourguiba and the PSD had lost much of their historic legitimacy. Security forces had fired on striking workers and arrested much of the UGTT leadership in 1978 in a riotous massacre still memorialized by the labor movement today. Two years later, Libyan-backed rebels tried to ignite a rebellion by attacking the town of Gafsa. The party had become a rigid administrative machine led by an aging president and a clutch of self-interested elites jockeying to succeed him. In a bid to restore public confidence, Bourguiba allowed non-PSD candidates to run in legislative elections and legalized the Tunisian Communist Party (PCT), the Movement of Democratic Socialists, and the Popular Unity Party in a shallow bid for pluralism.

However, electoral rules in the 1981 parliamentary elections made it nearly impossible for opposition candidates to win seats in the National Assembly. Only the National Front, a coalition of the PSD and the national union, succeeded in doing so. The government refused to legalize the MTI. The economy added to popular frustrations, as Tunisia was buffeted by the same financial hardship that befell the entire MENA during this period. Bread riots erupted when debt forced the government to raise prices for basic commodities in 1984, the product of aggressive austerity measures required by an emergency loan from the International Monetary Fund. By 1985, the government's crackdown on the union and inability of the secular opposition parties to build broad support had created a void, one that the Islamists filled by creating a grassroots organization that worked on university campuses and in secondary schools and underprivileged neighborhoods. Bourguiba responded with a fiercely repressive campaign to destroy the MTI, some of whose members deployed violence to advance its agenda.

Ben Ali's Tunisia

By the fall of 1987, Tunisia was immersed in a dual crisis of economic recession and political paralysis. On the night of November 7, Bourguiba's prime minister, Zine al-Abidine Ben Ali, invoked Bourguiba's senility to justify a bloodless coup. (Under house arrest, Bourguiba passed away in 2000.) Afterward, Tunisia passed through an ever more repressive era during which the number seven, for November 7, the ruling party's color purple, and images of Ben Ali became symbols of the political order. Unlike Bourguiba, Ben Ali was not a long-time politician with extensive networks in the ruling party or anti-colonial credentials. He was a military man whose rise to power coincided with the escalating strife with Islamists.

In his first year came the promise of democratic opening. Ben Ali amnestied thousands of political prisoners, invited exiles to come home, met with opposition party leaders, eliminated the presidency for life and the state security court, ratified the United Nations anti-torture convention, and relaxed press restrictions. He talked about the importance of political competition and freedom of conscience and expression. In 1988, he began a program of political liberalization, signing a National Pact between the government and sixteen political parties and organizations, including the MTI of Ghannouchi. To reflect this new spirit of inclusion and reform, and the declining appeal of socialism, the PSD changed its name to the Democratic Constitutional Rally (RCD). But real change was not to be. While Ben Ali's initiatives earned praise at home and abroad, the April 1989 elections ended the honeymoon. The presidential election was the first since 1974, and Ben Ali ran unopposed.

In the months leading up to parliamentary elections, Ben Ali refused to modify the electoral code to give the opposition parties greater opportunities to compete. He also set the opposition parties against one another by proposing that they all run with the RCD on single lists and split the seats in parliament on the basis of a predetermined formula that would not allow the opposition to gain more than 25 percent of the seats. Hoping to participate in the first elections, the MTI reiterated its rejection of violence and changed its name to Ennahda (Renaissance) to comply with a rule forbidding religious references in party names. Despite these reforms, Ben Ali and his hardliners remained uncertain about Ennahda's strength and intentions. The 1989 election results reified their fears. The RCD won over 80 percent of the vote, but, due to electoral rules, received all 141 seats in the National Assembly. None of the legalized secular parties won seats. Allegations of fraud were rampant, but Islamists still officially won 14 percent of the national vote and more than 30 percent of the urban vote. They too received no seats, but their appeal was undeniable: even with the electoral deck stacked against them, Ennahda's message of renewal and unity through religiosity and Islam resonated.

The regime's reaction was to retract its earlier promises and enact harsh repression. Ennahda was banned, and its leadership (like Ghannouchi) driven into exile or else languishing in prisons. The internal security apparatus grew larger, as Ben Ali poured money into the Interior Ministry and its intelligence units in order to impose Stasi-like surveillance across society. Spying and informants, dirty tricks, opposition arrests, torture – these became the hallmarks of the government Tunisians had hoped would lead them toward democracy. The government also controlled society through the economy, which was dominated by Ben Ali, his wife Le la Trebelssi, and other close families. Economic coercion was widespread, as well-connected families could force others to sell property, while opponents of the regime could be barred from government jobs or lose access to bank accounts or loans.

What typified this period especially was a shift away from reliance upon the ruling party and other institutional mechanisms. Unlike the Bourguibist years, in which state-building entailed establishing a hegemonic party apparatus whose organizational links gave key sectors of society some proximity to the president, the Ben Ali era was marked by increasing personalism and corruption. Ben Ali's family, and their close circle of cronies and advisers, shunned the RCD as a mass-mobilizing party. The glue of authoritarianism was not the careful inculcation of obeisance and identity through political outreach, but instead widespread repression, alongside a healthy dollop of patronage and bribery to grease the wheels of favoritism.

Ben Ali played to his strengths as a former security chief. Algeria's civil war, brought on by the victory of an Islamist party in 1990 elections, stoked fears that violence would spread to Tunisia, which justified the prohibition of Ennahda. While repression intensified, the government also tried to create the appearance of reform. In 1994 and 1999, Ben Ali allowed non-RCD candidates to run for president. However, the electoral rules and the conduct of the elections made it impossible for anyone else to pose serious competition. Similarly, changes in the electoral code created the impression of reform in the National Assembly, which became a bicameral parliament in 2002. In reality, the rules continued to pit opposition against each other, while newspapers self-censored for fear of arrest or shutdown. In May 2002, the government organized a referendum that raised the maximum age for the president and abolished his term limits. In a vote denounced widely for its fraudulence, 99.5 percent of the voters purportedly approved these changes. The reforms also granted the president immunity from prosecution.

To be sure, dissent existed. In October 2005, Ennahda, and a host of leftist secular groups such as Progressive Democratic Party (PDP), Congress for the Republic (CPR), and Ettakatol, established the October 18 Coalition for Rights and Freedoms in Tunisia. This collective expressed its commitment to a democratically elected government, and demanded the release of political prisoners. Critically, Ennahda and its secularist opposition counterparts agreed to work with one another under the common basis of a Tunisian identity. In 2010, an unrelated "silent" protest for Internet freedom took place in Tunis, in which participants wore white. Still, Tunisia seemed an unlikely place for a revolution, as its relatively tame official politics gave visitors little indication of how much of the public had diverged from Ben Ali and his regime. All this changed on December 17, 2010, when Mohamed Bouazizi set himself on fire in front of a government office in Sidi Bouzid, setting into motion a spontaneous and leaderless explosion – the Jasmine Revolution – that began the Arab Spring.

The Jasmine Revolution and transition

In addition to signs of some opposition, the years prior to the Jasmine Revolution reflected structural antecedents. First, the security argument Ben Ali used in the 1990s no longer worked. There was no organized Islamist threat in Tunisia, and by 2000, Algeria's civil war had abated. Second, the economy struggled, as high unemployment and stagnant income growth posed the primary challenge. Officially, the government backed neoliberal economic policies with the support of multilateral financial institutions and foreign investors. Selective privatization, increased foreign investments, and more trade with the European Union – all implemented by a new generation of technocrats with little patience for socialism – abounded. Yet most Tunisians saw little of these paper gains in GDP. In the late 2000s, the UGTT continued to chafe; wildcat strikes and worker unrest were regular occurrences, and labor protests broke out in several towns across the rural south between 2008 and 2010.

After Bouazizi's self-immolation, marchers and bystanders used cell phone cameras to record protesters and clashes with security forces. When they posted the videos on Facebook pages, Al-Jazeera broadcast the images back to a national audience, creating a shared experience, a common narrative that cut across classes and regions and ultimately spread to other countries. Social media also made it impossible for the regime to hide its response. Twitter allowed protesters to share information and helped participants navigate away from security forces, aiding the movement of people in Tunis, where opposition converged. Ben Ali publicly sought to assuage the uprising by promising to reduce prices and not to run for reelection. But, his offer was too little, too late: when the commander of the army said he would not order troops to fire on protesters after they had overwhelmed recalcitrant police and security forces, Ben Ali and his family fled to Saudi Arabia. With Ben Ali's departure, the RCD and the security apparatus collapsed. Yet unlike in Libya, where high-ranking officials fled as the regime collapsed, members of Ben Ali's government did not. Nor did social order break down. Prime Minister Mohamed Ghannouchi, a technocrat who had been Tunisia's prime minister since 1999, claimed the interim presidency, but stepped down the next day due to technicalities and was replaced by the Speaker of Parliament, Fouad Mebazaa, who remained in office until December 2011.

With most Tunisians accepting governmental continuity for the sake of building a new political order, rapid changes occurred from January 2011 onwards. The interim government granted amnesty to political prisoners, invited exiles to return, froze the RCD's assets, and began legalizing new parties, including Ennahda. The government also created commissions that began designing political reforms and investigating the former regime's crimes. In February, activists organized themselves into a Committee to Safeguard of the Revolution, which pressured the government to develop a democratic reform plan. Beji Caid Essebsi, a Bourguiba-era official, served as Tunisia's prime minister until December 2011, moving on issues gridlocking the transition. The interim government legalized Ennahda as a party and accepted the opposition's plan for reforming the constitution before holding presidential elections. The government also established several new commissions to oversee major legal, political, and institutional changes. Still, major problems remained, including mistrust between secular parties and the reinvigorated Islamist trend led by Ennahda, which was quickly rebuilding its networks and membership across the country. The UGTT, women's movements, human rights activists, and secular parties like Ettakatol feared Ennahda's goals of Islamizing Tunisia; some accused Islamists of wishing to roll back gender parity and the gains of the revolution for the sake of imposing theocracy.

These tensions resulted in concerted bargaining, debates, and pacts between Ennahda and other major organizations in preparation for elections to the Constituent Assembly – the body charged with writing a new constitution, and which would be chosen in the country's first free and fair elections in October 2011. Extended negotiations produced some shared agreement among all groups; for instance, the governing commission voted to exclude from the elections RCD officials, and retained the closed-list proportional representation electoral system. The commission and Ennahda also agreed that the new electoral code should require all party lists to offer an equal number of male and female candidates. By October, nearly a hundred legal parties were campaigning for votes in an unprecedented showing of true pluralism.

In the October 2011 elections for the Constituent Assembly, 54 percent of eligible voters cast ballots. Just over 40 percent of those voters supported Ennahda, and the party obtained 37 percent of the 217 seats. The other winners were the major secularist parties, as the CPR obtained 29 seats and Ettakatol secured 20 seats. These three winners were all members of the October 18, 2005 coalition, and despite their ideological differences regarding religion and secularism within the Tunisian republic, agreed to form a coalition called the troika. No single party won more than 37 percent of seats, which meant a constitution could not be passed without compromise among the Islamists and secularists. This helped keep highly polarizing issues like the role of religion in politics from tearing society apart and derailing the transition. The troika agreed that Moncef Marzouki, a renowned dissident and leader of CPR, would be interim president of the republic; Mustapha Ben Jafar, of Ettakatol, would serve as Constituent Assembly president; and Hamadi Jebali, representing Ennahda, would be prime minister.

Crisis and consolidation

In the subsequent years, the Islamist-secularist coalition would be sorely tested by social tensions and political crisis. In 2012, the Libyan government requested that Tunisia extradite Baghdadi al-Mahmudi, Muammar al-Qaddafi's former prime minister; while President Marzouki refused, Prime Minister Jebali approved the request. The two leaders also clashed on issues relating to the Central Bank and the Constituent Assembly's authority. For its part, the Constituent Assembly began writing a new constitution through six commissions; the new document would need two-thirds majority support to pass. Yet as soon as drafting began, legislators bogged down on the role of religion. Islamists and secularists marshaled their forces in the streets and campuses as a cycle of protest, counter-protest, and restiveness commenced.

One issue was the place of Islam. Article 1 of the old constitution declared the country as a sovereign republic with Islam as its official religion. Whereas many in Ennahda desired to inscribe shari'a as the sole source of legislation and further underscore the Islamic aspects of Tunisian identity, their opponents argued this was antithetical to the secular basis of the Tunisian republic. Related disagreements over blasphemy consumed many debates. Another issue was women's rights. Many were concerned about potential rollbacks of the rights they had achieved since the 1956 PSC and later reforms, including in 1993, when women married to non-Tunisian men gained the right to pass Tunisian citizenship on to their children. Whereas some Ennahda drafters desired to describe men and women as "complementary," secular opponents rejected any linguistic distinction that fell short of equality. They pointed out, as well, that women composed 27 percent of the Constituent Assembly, a level higher than most other Arab parliaments.

Progress came slowly, and Ennahda in pivotal moments backed down on these two flashpoint issues; its leader, Ghannouchi, repeatedly championed the importance of compromise and learning in his public interactions with other political figures. Still, social tensions peaked. Amplifying secularist fears was the rise of grassroots Salafi groups demanding radical Islamization, and a rising spate of terrorist violence that shocked the public. The assassinations of two prominent leftist critics, Chokri Belaïd and Mohamed Brahmi, by Salafi radicals enraged many secularists, and pressured Ennahda to back down on its religious demands for fear of further escalating the conflict over national identity. In summer 2013, the troika government experiment nearly collapsed altogether; the toppling of the Muslim Brotherhood government in Egypt instigated many Tunisians to call for similar military action against Ennahda.

Further complicating matters was the rise of Nidaa Tounes, a new party led by Essebsi and which counted among its members many political elites and secularists either affiliated with, or supportive of, the Ben Ali regime. More than CPR and Ettakatol, Nidaa Tounes attacked Ennahda relentlessly, building support among urban Tunisians who were tiring of the political crisis. As paralysis deepened, a new civil society coalition called the National Dialogue Quartet stepped in to mediate the extreme disagreements. The Quartet comprised the UGTT, the Tunisian Human Rights League, the national lawyers' association, and the industry and commerce confederation – all CSOs with longstanding credibility and respect. The Quartet, which later won a Nobel Peace Prize for its efforts, negotiated a compromise that saved the democratic government. Under its stabilizing hand, the Constituent Assembly passed the post-revolutionary constitution in January 2014, which President Marzouki promulgated and declared as the final victory over the Ben Ali dictatorship. Elections for the now fully permanent parliament and presidency were scheduled for the end of the year.

The October 2014 parliamentary elections featured as surprising a result as the contest three years earlier. In the first polls following the ratification of the constitution in January, Nidaa Tounes won 38 percent of seats to Ennahda's 28 percent. Ennahda's loss, while not decisive, was the result of perceptions it had not governed effectively. No other party won more than 4 percent of the vote; CPR and Ettakatol were hence marginalized. Marking its commitment to compromise, Ennahda further decided not to run a candidate in the November 2014 presidential elections, which became a two-way race between Essebsi of Nidaa Tounes and Marzouki of the CPR. The former won by a 56–44 split. At the same time, Essebsi maneuvered the newly empowered Nidaa Tounes party to bargain with Ennahda in parliament, choosing to form a governing coalition with the Islamists despite his earlier denunciations.

Thus began the second phase of Tunisian democracy – the post-constitutional era of a new government featuring Ennahda and Nidaa Tounes, and where Islamists and secularists coexisted, if uneasily. In the years since, many new problems have come to prevail in Tunisian politics. The most urgent is widespread unemployment, particularly among youths; perceived inequality of development, particularly between Tunis and the poorer rural areas, have caused many protests. Another is transitional justice. In June 2014, the government created the Truth and Dignity Commission to investigate, prosecute, and provide restitution for victims of state-perpetrated human rights violations under the Ben Ali regime. Yet after Essebsi's election, the government offered an unpopular law offering amnesty to officials in exchange for truth-telling and some restitution; this caused many voters to sour both on Nidaa Tounes and Ennahda. Although the tribunal received over 62,700 complaints – many for economic corruption – and held 12 televised sessions, its work was hampered by numerous roadblocks by the Essebsi government and led to few trials. The commission issued its final report in March 2019, with many victims feeling that the process had not lived up to their hopes for justice.

President Essebsi died of illness in July 2019. Parliamentary and presidential elections were originally scheduled for fall 2019, but Essebsi's passing pushed up the presidential contest to September, while the legislative elections remained set for October 2019. This writing precedes those events, and the swings of Tunisian public opinion make it difficult to predict the winning parties and personalities. However, the more important constant is that Tunisian voters have consolidated their democracy, with few questioning the viability of electoral politics. All major political factions, from Ennahda and Nidaa Tounes to the UGTT and its civil society partners, accept democratic rules. Indeed, the September 2019 presidential elections constituted the most crowded democratic competition in Tunisian history, with 24 candidates representing all ideological backgrounds vying for office. A later runoff will determine the presidential winner between the top two candidates, Kaïs Saïed and Nabil Karoui.

SOCIAL AND ECONOMIC ENVIRONMENT

Over 11 million Tunisians live in an area slightly larger than the state of Georgia – nearly 70 percent in urban areas along the northern and eastern coasts (Map 5.1). The urbanized areas closer to the Mediterranean coast, known in Tunisian Arabic as the *Sahel* and which include Tunis, are far more populated and developed than the rural interior and southern areas, collectively termed the *Dakhil*. Tunis is the capital and dominant city: it represents the vast majority of the country's wealth, contains its centralized government institutions, and expresses the same problems of inequality and discord as can be found elsewhere. Its downtown promenade evokes the architectural and spatial feel of its French colonial designers (Photo 5.1).

Overall, Tunisia has very little oil, despite being flanked by Algeria and Libya, two of Africa's largest oil and gas producers. The country's small size and narrow resource base leave Tunisia no choice but to pursue growth through foreign investment, tourism, and exports to global markets. Yet this accident of geography is also a blessing. Lack of oil is more conducive to democratic development because the government must tax its citizens, who can then hold the government accountable. Taxation also reduces foreign interference and facilitates women's workforce participation. These factors have helped Tunisia experience a successful revolution and make its successful democracy.

At the same time, Tunisia's economy has struggled to sustain high growth. Like many countries in the region, Tunisia's government has difficulty securing sufficient foreign investment. It has few competitive export-oriented industries outside light sectors like textiles and agricultural goods, as well as its phosphate resources. Tourism remains a major income earner, but suffered during the post-revolutionary period due to several terrorist attacks and perceptions of Tunisian instability.

Society and culture

Bourguiba's state-building strategies contributed to Tunisia's commitment to education. Today, Tunisia's adult literacy rate is nearly 82 percent. For youths aged 15 to 24, literacy exceeds 96 percent. At the same time, the highly educated population creates challenges. Like other Arab countries, Tunisia's demography has a pronounced youth bulge. A quarter of the population is under 14, and in total well over half are younger than 30. Youth unemployment nearly

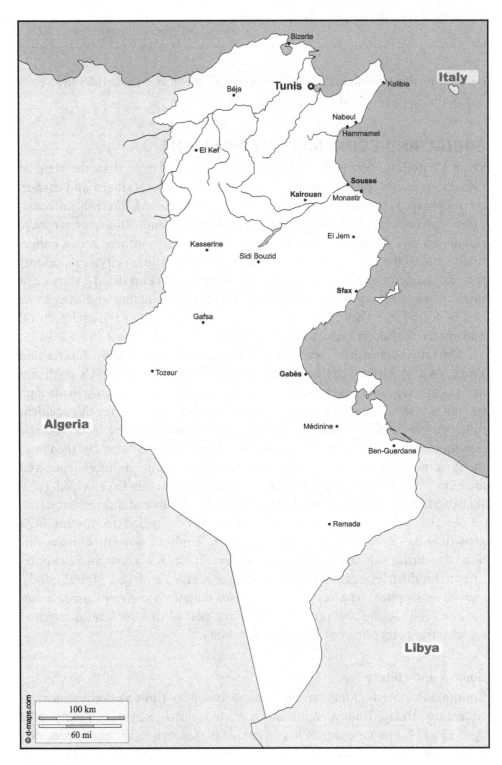

MAP 5.1
Republic of Tunisia. Major rivers and cities shown.

Source: D-Maps.

PHOTO 5.1
Downtown Tunis

Source: Pixabay.

reached 35 percent in 2019, one of the highest rates in the MENA, and far greater than its nearly 16 percent overall jobless rate (also among the highest in the region). The economy's failure to generate jobs and living standards that meet their expectations is a powerful source of tension. It made young people one of the primary constituencies in the revolt against Ben Ali, and it makes job creation a primary challenge for the current and future governments.

Tunisia's population is also more homogeneous than that of its Maghrib neighbors. Arabic-speaking Sunni Muslims compose 98 percent of the population. Ottoman and French state-building policies and urbanization long ago eliminated tribes as meaningful political actors or sources of identity for most Tunisians. Because tribes were weak, Bourguiba was also able to liberalize women's rights in 1956, which only further served to privilege urban elites and to consolidate his power. Notably, nearly 2,000 Jewish Tunisians live in Tunis and on the island of Djerba, while Tamazight communities also abound.

Ethnic and religious homogeneity does not mean that Tunisian society is free of cleavages. Region and family play important factors in politics. Because Bourguiba and many of his allies came from the Sahel, that region became synonymous with political power in the post-independence period. Indeed, development policies under both Bourguiba and Ben Ali concentrated Tunisia's modern economic activity along the coasts. This bias generated strong grievances among Tunisians in the Dakhil, particularly as the impoverished south possessed much of Tunisia's mineral resources such as its phosphate mines, but it is important to note that the resentment was not purely economic. More conservative Tunisians in the interior resented a condescending domination by coastal elites whose values and lifestyles frequently seemed more European than Tunisian.

These tensions between the coast and the countryside helped spark the rebellion against Ben Ali. They also played a role in Ennahda's October 2011 electoral victory. At first glance, the competition between Ennahda and secular parties would seem to indicate that the most important cleavage in post-uprising Tunisia is between religious and secular citizens. To some extent this is true. However, this split maps onto a deeper divide between less affluent Tunisians from interior regions who tend to support the Ennahda and more privileged citizens from major urban areas in the northern Sahel who more often support secular urban parties, including Nidaa Tounes.

POLITICAL STRUCTURES

Prior to the Jasmine Revolution, the Tunisian constitution described the state as a republic with executive, judicial, and legislative branches, and which allowed Tunisians to vote in elections for the president, parliament, and local mayors and municipal councils. In reality, the president wielded unchecked power, sitting atop the ruling party which, during its Bourguibist apex, was a highly structured, mass-mobilizing organization led by an adroit political leadership and anchored by party cells in every neighborhood and village. Because Tunisia did not have a constitutional court, and because the government appointed judges, the judicial branch could never declare a law unconstitutional.

Yet other parties have played critical roles in the country's development. Prior to the Jasmine Revolution, various groups characterized Tunisia's political opposition. The oldest was the Tunisian Communist Party (PCT), founded in 1934. Although the government outlawed the party in 1963, during Tunisia's period of single-party rule, it continued to exert a strong influence in the leftist opposition, particularly among student groups and the UGTT. After the end of the Cold War, the PCT changed its name to the Ettajdid (Renewal). The Popular Unity Party represented a vague mingling of socialist and Arab nationalist ideas. Finally, the Progressive Socialist Rally was established in 1983 by a group of young leftist activists; Ben Ali legalized it in 1988 as part of the National Pact. In 2001, the party changed its name to the Progressive Democracy Party (PDP). Ettakatol was another leftist entity; its formal name is the Democratic Forum for Labor and Liberties, and it was created in 1994 by Mustapha Ben Jafar. In 2001, Moncef Marzouki created the CPR, basing it on human rights ideals. Many of these democratic voices participated in the October 2015 opposition coalition.

Post-revolutionary structures

Tunisia is a unitary semi-presidential republic with a president as the head of state, Prime Minister as the head of government, and a unicameral parliament endowed by its 2014 constitution. Participating in that parliament are a plethora of political parties as discussed in the historical background section and earlier. The judiciary also gained considerable independence under the post-Ben Ali constitutional framework. With the security apparatus of the Ben Ali years dismantled, the civil police operate under strict guidelines now, although reports of police abuses have gradually risen since the mid-2000s, suggesting the need for greater accountability at the community level. In 2018, shortly before Tunisia held its first municipal and regional elections, parliament passed the Local Government Law, which increased and defined the powers of local government and increased the funds they control. This has helped promote development in poorer regions and improve regional equity, though far from the wishes of many Tunisians.

Unlike in many Arab countries, Tunisia's military has never been an important political actor. It has limited control over the economy and limited direct influence over politics due to its historical origins. Unlike Algeria, Tunisia's nationalist struggle against the French was not militarized. Bourguiba's emphasis during the formative years of Tunisian political order was placed upon party-building and mass mobilization, not militarized control over the nation. Ben Ali's rampant repression likewise relied more upon its civilian security apparatus, including the civil police and enormous domestic intelligence directorate. In both autocratic periods, the Tunisian military was relegated to border defense; its budgets were typically small, its arms antiquated, and its officer corps treated with a combination of suspicion or wariness. Partly for these reasons, the Tunisian armed forces neither raised arms to defend Ben Ali during its downfall nor intervened again during the subsequent political transition – a far cry from Egypt, where the army never exited the political scene and ultimately dictated the end of post-Arab Spring democracy.

POLITICAL DYNAMICS

Since 2011, Tunisian political space and its more democratic politics have been dominated by three major forces: Ennahda; Nidaa Tounes; and leftists, of which CPR and Ettakatol are most visible. In the past, Tunisia's authoritarian government sustained itself through co-optation, divide-and-conquer tactics, and strategic alliance-building. Today, most of the country's parties still struggle to overcome this institutional culture of personal rivalries and winner-take-all understandings of what it means to exercise power and shape institutions. These dynamics undermine the growth of parties that can inspire voters, especially young ones, to join the political process. This is a problem common to all new democracies, but promising signs include the various compromises made between Ennahda and its secularist counterparts during the 2011–13 period of constitutional drafting alongside CPR and Ettakatol, and the 2014–18 period of coalitional governance with Nidaa Tounes.

Recent politics within the ruling Nidaa Tounes party illustrate the problem of fragmentation well. Well before Essebsi's passing in July 2019, the Nidaa-led government frequently experienced shuffling due to internal disputes and battles. The movement itself split into several groups after 2014 over tensions about who would succeed the elderly Essebsi. Some backed his son, Hafedh. Others did not. Mohsen Marzouk created Machrouu Tounes (Project of Tunisia), while Prime Minister Youssef Chahed created Tahya Tounes (Long Live Tunisia). Slim Riahi, a businessperson and political figure, accused Chahed and others of plotting a coup against Essebsi, and became leader of his own political grouping under the umbrella of Nidaa. These three politicians were among the more than two dozen running in the September 2019 presidential elections.

Ennahda, still under the leadership of Ghannouchi, saw the dissolution of cabinets under the Nidaa Tounes government and its breakup into multiple factions as a source of instability. Ennahda also criticized all parties, including itself, for lacking distinct economic programs which can address regional disparities and local development and calls for a constitutional court to spell out the powers of the various institutions. Ennahda emerged as the country's most popular opposition to the secular regime in the mid-1980s. Ben Ali's repression prevented Ennahda from playing a major role in the 2011 revolution, but the speed with which it built its organization after Ben Ali's departure, and its victory in the first elections to the Constituent Assembly in 2011, demonstrate the party's ability to mobilize the grassroots and the popularity of its religious ideology.

Ennahda has also sought to develop a broad base through flexibility and learning. It elected a female member of parliament in 2011, Souad Abdel Rahim, who does not wear a headscarf. Her election exemplified the party's moderate nature and its efforts to appeal to a wider swath of society. During the 2012–13 debates over the constitution, Ennahda also compromised repeatedly on issues involving shari'a, blasphemy, and women's rights. Likewise, in summer 2016, Ghannouchi declared that Ennahda would separate its activities from purely religious and spiritual undertakings and instead operate purely as a political party – in other words, an internal separation between religion and politics. While some Tunisians remain suspicion of all Islamism, others see this as evidence that Ennahda has learned from its dealings in Tunisian politics and adapted to an environment that cherishes its secular heritage, unlike other settings in the MENA. Indeed, the movement refuses to apply strategies taken from other contexts or from abstract ideological programs. In separating religion and politics, its spiritual guides seem to have concluded that while education and social work can Islamize society more effectively than government edicts, the Islamists involved in government itself should focus purely on the task of effective governance and policymaking.

More radical Salafi groups have also emerged in the 2010s, taking advantage of the political vacuum after the Jasmine Revolution. The Islah (Reform) group is the most moderate, but still advocates a strict version of shari'a and an Islamic state albeit through nonviolent means. Another is Tunisia's chapter of Hizb al-Tahrir, a transnational Salafist organization that rejects the legal political process and supports the restoration of an Islamic Caliphate. It gained legal status as a party in 2012, and pressured Ennahda heavily to backtrack on its compromises with secularists. After Ghannouchi rejected their entreaties, they continued to organize protests.

Finally, Ansar al-Shari'a (Supporters of Shari'a) is a terrorist organization established in spring 2011, and initially staffed by Tunisian veterans of the Soviet-Afghan conflict. Ansar grew to encompass as many as a thousand militants, and carried out various terrorist strikes, including the assassinations of leftists Belaïd and Brahmi in 2013. Though banned by the government, excoriated by Ennahda, and targeted by the military, Ansar retains a militant network and still attracts sympathy from radicalized Tunisians. Importantly, Tunisia has been a target of Salafi terrorism even after the 2013 political killings. In March 2015, gunmen attacked the Bardo National Museum; in June 2015, a terrorist attacked a tourist resort in the coastal city of Sousse, killing more than three dozen people. In July 2018, Al-Qaʻida in the Islamic Maghrib (AQIM) killed six Tunisian troops in an ambush near the border zone with Algeria.

Civil society organizations

Civil society organizations play a vital role by articulating public demands during the transition and channeling social discontent that might otherwise have been expressed in more destabilizing ways. Tunisian CSOs have deep roots. The UGTT is the centerpiece; not just a labor union but also a social movement and political actor, the UGTT predates independence and has long hosted various currents and trends of opposition. Its partnership with the Neo-Destour helped lay the foundations of post-colonial Tunisia, and its divorce from the ruling party ushered in the Ben Ali period through an increased atmosphere of social unrest and labor strikes. In addition to the UGTT, Tunisia possesses a powerful student movement that has nurtured more radical leftist ideologies and groups. The national lawyers' association has also maintained a space of autonomy from the government, even during the authoritarian era. Representing over 100,000 private-sector firms is the national industry and commerce confederation, known by its French acronym UTICA. The business counterpart to the UGTT, the confederation had more controversial dealings with the Bourguiba and Ben Ali autocracies, but nonetheless also advocated for democracy after the revolution.

Likewise, in 1976 activists created the *Ligue tunisienne des droits de l'homme* – the Tunisian Human Rights League (LTDH), which was the first human rights league in Africa and the Arab world. Relations between the LTDH and the government improved when Ben Ali came to power and initiated some of the reforms that the LTDH had demanded. The relationship deteriorated as Ben Ali's repression intensified in the 1990s. In 1992, the government passed a law that required organizations to admit anyone who wanted to join (specifically so that the RCD could infiltrate CSOs). For the rest of Ben Ali's rule, the LTDH struggled with the challenges created by internal dissension and the government's efforts to freeze the organization's activity, and many of its members, including Moncef Marzouki and

Mustapha Ben Jafar, found themselves under repressive watch. The LTDH, alongside the UGTT, UTICA, and the national lawyers' association, comprised the Quartet that helped sustain Tunisian democracy after its summer 2013 crisis.

Women's organizations have also made critical contributions to Tunisia's development, helping to expand women's rights on the foundation of Bourguiba's 1956 PSC, achieving key reforms to the Code in 1993, and promoting women's advancement in politics and the labor force. Tunisia pursued "state feminism," during which the authoritarian regime saw the expansion of gender equality as conducive to its efforts to undercut opposition, support national development, and legitimate its nondemocratic political order. As part of this policy, the regime supported the National Union of Tunisian Women, the primary, albeit government-controlled, women's organization. After Ben Ali came to power, Tunisian women established two independent organizations. The Association of Tunisian Women for Research on Development became a center for the study of women's economic and social status and established active partnerships with global women's organizations. The Association of Democratic Women became an influential voice for gender equality, democracy, social justice, and secularism. These concerns inevitably generated ties to other opposition organizations.

Since the Jasmine Revolution, the capacity of Tunisian feminists and women's rights advocates to ally themselves with other CSOs and mobilize protests in response to worrisome restrictions has helped keep the political spotlight on issues of gender. Tunisian legislators throughout the decade have been consistently exposed to grassroots demands to continually push the frontiers of gender equality further. For instance, in 2018, parliament passed a new law establishing equal inheritance for daughters and sons and allowing Muslim women to marry non-Muslim men; Tunisia is the first Arab country to commit to this.

One healthy constant has been strong representation for women in politics, particularly since the Jasmine Revolution. Two women stood among the more than two dozen candidates who ran in the September 2019 presidential elections. Tunisian women have also been strongly represented in the legislative branch. In 2004, the RCD implemented a 25 percent party quota for women in parliament and in local councils, then increased the national quota to 30 percent in 2009. Consequently, on the eve of the revolution, 28 percent of the parliamentary representatives were female, due to RCD dominance. In response to the 2014 Constitution, which commits the state to promoting gender parity in elected assemblies (Article 10), the 2018 municipal election law included a gender quota establishing vertical and horizontal parity for women on party lists in the country's closed-list proportional representation (PR) electoral system. As a result, women won forty-seven percent of seats in local councils in May 2018. At the national level, the requirement that parties present lists with gender parity have likewise resulted in a high proportion of the Tunisian parliament comprising women, with men securing just two-thirds of all seats.

FOREIGN POLICY

Three basic goals have historically guided Tunisia's foreign policy, and continue to shape the new democracy's view of its Arab neighbors and the international system alike: (1) maintaining independence without building a strong military, (2) preventing other actors in the Arab world from meddling in domestic affairs, and (3) prioritizing robust economic linkages, including attracting foreign aid and investment.

Tunisia has pursued these goals with a resolutely pro-Western foreign policy. Even during the independence struggle, Bourguiba intended to make France the country's most important long-term partner. He also fostered ties with the United States because he recognized that the United States could pressure France to grant Tunisian independence and provide development assistance. Bourguiba never tried to play the United States and Soviet Union against each other for the sake of extracting aid. He also viewed pan-Arabism as a threat to Tunisia's sovereignty. As early as the mid-1960s, Tunisia advocated a two-state solution in Palestine. Yet these positions and Tunisia's small size left the country vulnerable, particularly after Algeria opted for a socialist development strategy and closer ties to Soviet Bloc countries and al-Qaddafi made Libya a bastion of pan-Arabism. Bourguiba needed to defend Tunisia's independence, but he did not want to pay the economic and political costs required to build a strong military. Courting French and US commitments to Tunisia's security, he provided deterrence without requiring large military expenditures.

These policies served Tunisia well. France and the United States provided substantial economic, political, and military assistance after independence. Ben Ali sustained this by playing up Tunisia's strategic importance, particularly in the battle against radical Islamism starting in the 1990s as Algeria descended into violence. Tunisia's business and political elites also oriented themselves towards France, with many studying abroad and perceiving themselves as equally cosmopolitan as Arab. In the latter years of Ben

Ali's rule, however, his relations with both countries grew slightly strained. Algeria's war had calmed, and Ben Ali had eliminated Islamism as a threat inside Tunisia. Yet as his repression became more brutal, corruption became more visible, and economic growth slowed, he no longer provided a firewall against an imminent Islamist threat. In the fall of 2010, WikiLeaks released American diplomatic cables that provided a frank description of corruption, repression, and mismanagement under Ben Ali.

Tunisia's relationship with the United States after the Jasmine Revolution has been strong, not least because the Obama Administration became a strong proponent of the new democracy. When protesters firebombed the American embassy and school in 2012, a travel warning was imposed and allegations swirled that the Ennahda government was too soft on right-wing Islamist groups. However, the Tunisian government repaired the damaged property, and the warning was removed, and the United States continued assisting Tunisia's government with the promise of generous economic aid. After the election of Nidaa Tounes in 2014, the deteriorating security situation in Libya, and the attacks on tourists at the Bardo museum, Tunisia signed a non-NATO ally agreement with the United States, joining a select group of other strategically vital Arab countries in this circle such as Jordan, Kuwait, and Morocco.

Tunisia rhetorically expresses a strong commitment to Maghrib unity, as expressed in the preamble to its 2014 constitution, but efforts to establish the Arab Maghrib Union (UMA) have remained frozen due to conflicts between other member states (particularly with Moroccan-Algerian relations). Tunisia's small size and narrow resource base give it a particularly strong interest in economic integration, but inter-Maghrib trade accounts still for only a tiny portion of its total economic exports and imports; Europe remains the financial and economic elephant in the room. In 1995, Tunisia became the first Maghrib state to sign an association agreement with the European Union; this culminated in Tunisia becoming the first southern Mediterranean country to join the European Free Trade Area in 2008, which granted Tunisia greater access to European markets and financial assistance. However, Tunisia also had to lower tariffs on imported European manufactured goods, a policy that took a heavy toll on the country's manufacturing sector.

In the 2010s, Tunisian governments have exhibited greater interest in facilitating more trade and investment with the United States as a complement to its reliance upon European commerce, with two-way trade between the two countries peaking at nearly a billion dollars in 2016. Both the United States and the European Union have given Tunisia substantial economic aid – partly to incentivize its democratization, and partly to help stabilize it. Through 2018, post-Arab Spring Tunisia had recorded nearly three billion dollars of foreign aid via grants and loans from both its Western patrons.

On geopolitical grounds, France has seldom wavered in its belief that a stable Tunisia, under any type of non-Islamist government, fulfilled its broader interests in having reliable Maghrib partners. French leaders and ministers repeatedly expressed confidence in Bourguiba and Ben Ali to govern Tunisia well, and during the Jasmine Revolution, the French government embarrassingly offered security assistance to Ben Ali to help quell the spreading protests. Since then, however, the French have realigned their perception and sought to ensure Tunisia remains free of violent extremism – this is important also because like Morocco and Algeria, there is considerable northward labor migration from Tunisia to France, and daily cross-cultural traffic between the two countries.

Since 2014, Tunisian officials have clamped down hard upon radical Islamists. ISIS created a presence in neighboring Libya and orchestrated the Sousse terrorist attack in 2014. Border security with Libya, and eliminating homegrown Salafi violence, remain areas where the Tunisian government continues to secure aid from France. Western support may be particularly crucial to ensuring Tunisian national security in the coming years. As one example, advanced military equipment and intelligence may be needed to securitize the Tunisia-Libya border. That Tunisia supplied more foreign fighters to ISIS than any other country is a frequent fact recounted in security discussions within Tunis. With many slowly returning, Tunisia remains in a state of alert, raising questions about the balance between security and democracy as the country looks to the future.

FUTURE PROSPECTS

After more than a half-century of authoritarian rule, Tunisia is now maturing as a competitive democracy. Yet it is not without its challenges. On the one hand, the conditions that fostered the birth of the Arab Spring are likely to continue supporting its democratic consolidation. Tunisia's history has given it a strong state capable of providing services and a cohesive national identity. Civil society is organizationally vibrant, and will continue to fight to hold the government accountable. On the other hand, important obstacles lie ahead. Issues of transitional justice, economic growth, and national security require further attention; the youth demographic and demands for dignity and employment today resonate, not least because they do not differ from the grievances of young Tunisians on the eve of the Jasmine Revolution.

Still, the desire to maintain a free society runs strongly throughout the public, despite social tensions and political strife over hot-button issues since 2011 that have been modestly contained through compromise. In recent years, succession questions within Nidaa Tounes and the ideological evolution of Ennahda as a political party have dominated political debates. After the presidential and parliamentary elections in fall 2019, these and other parties will continue to evolve through the crucible of democratic competition. With a healthy degree of other civic organizations and mobilizational activities, the future of Tunisian politics will be marked by pluralism and competition.

FURTHER READING

For general historical overviews of Tunisia, see Kenneth J. Perkins, *A History of Modern Tunisia*, 2nd ed. (Cambridge University Press, 2014); and Christopher Alexander, *Tunisia: Stability and Reform in the Modern Maghrib*, 2nd ed. (Routledge, 2016). A sweeping argument for Tunisia as an "exceptional" country can be found in Safwan Masri, *Tunisia: An Arab Anomaly* (Columbia University Press, 2017), while a countervailing perspective rests in Michel Camau, *L'exception tunisienne: variations sur un mythe* (IRMC, 2018).

On development and politics under Bourguiba, see Lisa Anderson, *State and Social Transformation in Tunisia and Libya, 1830–1980* (Princeton University Press, 1986); Norma Salem, *Habib Bourguiba, Islam, and the Creation of Tunisia* (Croom Helm, 1984); Derek Hopwood, *Habib Bourguiba of Tunisia: The Tragedy of Longevity* (St. Martin's Press, 1992). Excellent studies of the Neo-Destour and 1950s through 1960s can be found in Charles Micaud, *Tunisia: The Politics of Modernization* (Frederick Praeger, 1964); Clement Henry Moore, *Tunisia Since Independence: The Dynamics of One-Party Government* (University of California Press, 1965); Lars Rudebeck, *Party and People: A Study of Political Change in Tunisia* (Almqvist and Wiksells, 1967); and Mounir Charfi, *Les Ministres de Bourguiba: 1956–1987* (L'Harmattan, 1989). The oft-ignored perspective of rural Tunisians is discussed in Samir Radwan, Vali Jamal, and Ajit Ghose, *Tunisia: Rural Labour and Structural Transformations* (Routledge, 1991).

On development in the Ben Ali era, particularly the uneven efforts of the regime to implement neoliberal reforms and the failures to generate economic growth across all sectors, see I. William Zartman, ed., *Tunisia: The Political Economy of Reform* (Lynne Rienner, 1991); Emma Murphy, *Economic and Political Change in Tunisia: From Bourguiba to Ben Ali* (St. Martin's Press, 1999); Stephen J. King, *Liberalization against Democracy: The Local Politics of Economic Reform in Tunisia* (Indiana University Press, 2003); Melani Cammett, *Globalization, Business Politics and Development: North Africa in Comparative Perspective* (Cambridge University Press, 2007); and Eva Bellin, *Stalled Democracy: Capital, Labor, and the Paradox of State-Sponsored Development* (Cornell University Press, 2002).

On regime dynamics under Ben Ali, in particular repression and personalism as strategies of control, see Lisa Anderson, "Political Pacts, Liberalism, and Democracy: The Tunisian National Pact of 1988," *Government and Opposition* 26, 2 (1991): 244–260; Susan E. Waltz, *Human Rights and Reform: Changing the Face of North African Politics* (University of California Press, 1995); Nicole Grimaud, "Tunisia: Between Control and

Liberalization," *Mediterranean Politics* 1, 1 (1996): 95–106; Sadri Khiari, *Tunisie: le délitement de la cite – coercition, consentement, résistance* (Editions Karthala, 2003); John P. Entelis, "The Democratic Imperative vs. the Authoritarian Impulse: The Maghrib State between Transition and Terrorism," *Middle East Journal* 59, 4 (2005): 537–558; Beatrice Hibou, *The Force of Obedience: The Political Economy of Repression in Tunisia* (Polity Press, 2011); and Derek Lutterbeck, "Tool of Rule: The Tunisian Police under Ben 'Ali," *Journal of North African Studies* 20, 4 (2015): 813–831. The best historical work on the Tunisian military remains Lewis Ware, *Tunisia in the Post-Bourguiba Era: The Role of the Military in a Civil Arab Republic* (Air University Press, 1986), while Ben Ali's policies on the armed forces are explored in Hicham Bou Nassif, "A Military Besieged: The Armed Forces, the Police, and the Party in Bin 'Ali's Tunisia, 1987-2011," *International Journal of Middle East Studies* 47 (2015): 65–87.

On the Jasmine Revolution and transition to democracy, there are innumerable studies that have explored every aspect of Tunisia's experience since 2010. The best analyses include: Laryssa Chomiak, "The Making of a Revolution in Tunisia," *Middle East Law and Governance* 3, 1-2 (2011): 69–83; Alfred Stepan, "Tunisia's Transition and the Twin Tolerations," *Journal of Democracy* 23, 2 (2012): 89–103; Michelle Angrist, "Understanding the Success of Mass Civic Protest in Tunisia," *Middle East Journal* 67, 4 (2013): 547–564; Sami Zemni, "The Extraordinary Politics of the Tunisian Revolution: The Process of Constitution Making," *Mediterranean Politics* 20,1 (2015): 1–17; and Ian Hartshorn, *Labor Politics in North Africa: After the Uprisings in Egypt and Tunisia* (Cambridge University Press, 2019). Another comparative perspective with Egypt is found in David Ottaway, *The Arab World Upended: Revolution*

and Its Aftermath in Tunisia and Egypt (Lynne Rienner, 2017). The economic dimensions of post-revolutionary Tunisia, including its difficulties, are tackled in Hayat Alvi, *The Political Economy and Islam of the Middle East: The Case of Tunisia* (Palgrave Macmillan, 2019). An entertaining grassroots vignette appears in Helene Aldeguer, *After the Spring: A Story of Tunisian Youth* (IDW Publishing, 2019).

On the evolution and struggle over women's rights in Tunisia, old studies have been enriched by an veritable efflorescence of new work since the Arab Spring regarding the scope of patriarchy and boundaries of gender equality. Examples include: Emma C. Murphy, "Women in Tunisia: A Survey of Achievements and Challenges," *Journal of North African Studies* 1, 2 (1996): 138–156; Mounira Charrad, *States and Women's Rights: The Making of Postcolonial Tunisia, Algeria, and Morocco* (University of California Press, 2001); Mounira Charrad and Amina Zarrugh, "Equal or Complementary? Women in the New Tunisian Constitution after the Arab Spring," *Journal of North African Studies* 19, 2 (2014): 230–243; Andrea Khalil, "Tunisia's Women: Partners in Revolution," *Journal of North African Studies* 19, 2 (2014): 186–199; and Lindsay J. Benstead, Amaney A. Jamal, and Ellen Lust, "Is It Gender, Religion or Both? A Role Congruity Theory of Candidate Electability in Transitional Tunisia," *Perspectives on Politics* 13, 1 (2015): 74–94.

On political Islam, the best comprehensive studies of Ennahda are newer works benefiting from increased access to key officials and Islamist voices – Rory McCarthy, *Inside Tunisia's Al-Ennahda: Between Politics and Preaching* (Cambridge University Press, 2018), and Anne Wolf, *Political Islam in Tunisia: The History of Ennahda* (Hurst, 2018). Historically, the evolution of Islamism in Tunisia is studied in Marion Boulby, "The Islamist Challenge: Tunisia since Independence," *Third*

World Quarterly 10 (1989): 590–614; John P. Entelis, ed., *Islam, Democracy and the State in North Africa* (Indiana University Press, 1997); Mohamed Elhachmi Hamdi, *The Politicisation of Islam: A Case Study of Tunisia* (Westview Press, 1998); Alaya Allani, "The Islamists in Tunisia between Confrontation and Participation: 1980-2008," *Journal of North African Studies* 14, 2 (2009): 257–272; and Malika Zeghal, "Competing Ways of Life: Islamism, Secularism, and Public Order in the Tunisian Transition," *Constellations* 20, 2 (2013): 254–274.

Online sources

Since 2011, many newspapers and creative outlets have emerged to take advantage of the free media space. By contrast, prior to the Arab Spring, reliable online sources for Tunisian research were few; researchers thus have a bounty of online knowledge about Tunisian politics through which to browse. Useful Internet resources for tracking news and developments include Tunisia Live (www.tunisia-live.net), an English-language site established after the revolution by journalists; Nawaat (www.nawaat.org), a forum established in 2004 to provide an outlet for dissident voices under Ben Ali, and still a fantastic place for critical analysis; and La Presse (https://lapresse.tn/), which has a vast amount of digital information. Other useful streams include Tuniscope (www.tuniscope.com/), AlChourouk (www.alchourouk.com/), and the older Assabah (www.assabahnews.tn/).

Structured analysis, including brief research entries, also proliferate online, and are devoted to monitoring and evaluating the Tunisian government's latest policies. *Tunisia Monitor* at the Carnegie Endowment for International Peace is the best example (https://carnegieendowment.org/specialprojects/Tunisia-Monitor/). Another is the International Crisis Group's Tunisia portal (www.crisisgroup.org/middle-east-north-africa/north-africa/tunisia). The World Bank's country website on Tunisia has many economic and financial data and reports as well (www.worldbank.org/en/country/tunisia/overview).

Please note that URLs may change far more quickly than books can be printed; so if these exact URLs do not work, simply search Google or another engine by the titles of these websites and online resources.

State of Libya

Karim Mezran and Tahani Elmogrbi

INTRODUCTION

As the 2010s close, Libya is at a political crossroads, nearly a decade after the Arab Spring removed the regime of Muammar al-Qaddafi from power. The very existence of a unitary Libyan state is in doubt due to institutional fragmentation and widespread insecurity. The experiment of the unity government – the Government of National Accord (GNA), a product of the 2015 Libyan national accords – has failed to satisfy competing factions, despite being recognized by the international community as the executive body for national governance. A rival government nominated and supported by the House of Representatives (HOR), an assembly elected in the summer of 2014 and also recognized by the international community as the legitimate legislative body for Libya, continues to operate independently. It is supported by a coalition of armed groups self-defined as the Libyan National Army (LNA) and led by Field Marshal Khalifa Haftar. The difficulty of crafting compromises amenable to both sides has resulted in ferocious power struggles, violent clashes and campaigns, and the disintegration of political authority.

On a daily basis, militia infighting and rising extremism have begun to take their toll on the social fabric, creating a climate of uncertainty and violence. The collapse of political order represents a stark break from the way that Muammar al-Qaddafi governed for 42 years. Qaddafi's reign was characterized by hollow institutions, international isolation, and a rentier economy; Libyans have begun participating in democratic politics, and whether democracy can survive depends largely upon the durability of any future reconciliation between warring sides. After an overview of the historical evolution of the country, this chapter will introduce and discuss the major institutions, social structures, and economic forces struggling on the ground to create a new, more stable, and pluralistic state.

Box 6.1 provides vital data for this country.

BOX 6.1   VITAL DATA – STATE OF LIBYA

Capital	Tripoli
Regime type	Hybrid (parliamentary republic)
Head of state	President Fayez al-Sarraj (since 2016)
Head of government	Prime Minister Fayez al-Sarraj (since 2016)
Legislative institution	Unicameral parliament, with 200 elected seats (*Majlis al-Nuwaab*, or House of Representatives)
Female quota	Yes: parties must run candidates lists with parity between men and women for the 80 (out of 200) seats contested through list-based proportional representation
Percentage of seats held by women	16%
Major political parties (share of seats in most recent general elections, 2014)	None, as parties were forbidden from competing in 2014. However, parties competed in 2012 for the now-defunct General National Congress; these included the National Forces Alliance (48.1%), Justice and Construction (10.3%), Union for the Homeland (4.5%), and National Front (4.1%)
Population	6,374,616
Major ethnic groups	Arab-Berber (97%), other (3%)
Major religious groups	Muslim (96.6%), other (3.4%)
GDP per capita	$6,692 ($11,469 at Purchasing Power Parity)
Unemployment rate	17.3%
Youth unemployment rate	41.9%
Major economic industries	Petroleum, petrochemicals, aluminum, iron and steel, cement, food processing, textiles
Military spending as % GDP	11.4% (2014; no reliable data since then)

HISTORICAL BACKGROUND

In the earliest days, the area that is now Libya was visited by Phoenician sailors, who established trading posts along the coastline. Subsequently, control of part of the area fell to Alexander the Great and later to the Egyptian kingdom of the Ptolemies. Rome annexed Cyrenaica and Tripolitania, and both became part of the Roman Empire. Eventually, Pax Romana prevailed, and Libya enjoyed a long period of prosperity and peace. In the seventh century, the Arabs arrived from Egypt, and most of the native Berber tribes embraced Islam. The Ottoman Turks arrived in sixteenth century, and ruled until 1911 with the exception of the period from 1711 to 1835, when a local family of Ottoman notables, the Qaramanli, took control. Besides the main city of Tripoli, the Ottomans attempted to exercise direct rule over the interior – constituting the first attempt to dominate the tribes of the hinterland.

European imperialism began when Italy fought a brief war with the Ottoman Empire in 1911, and Italian troops landed in Tripoli and Benghazi. The Italian conquest faced opposition from the powerful Sanusiyyah movement, led at the time by Muhammad Idris al-Mahdi al-Sanusi, the grandson of the founder. The Sanusiyyah was a Muslim reformist movement that began in 1837, and later ascended to political prominence as it sought to curb Ottoman power. The Sanusiyyah skirmished with Italian, French, and British forces across North Africa. In Libya during World War One, the movement began a long campaign of guerilla warfare against the Italian administration which would not fully end until 1932, when Italian forces finally subdued most armed factions, including the famed resistance fighter and Senusi leader Omar al-Mukhtar. Al-Mukhtar is still venerated today as a symbol of anti-colonial nationalism in Libya, and across the Arab world.

In 1934, Italy officially adopted the name "Libya" to refer to its colony consisting of Cyrenaica, Tripolitania, and Fezzan. World War Two interrupted Italy's plans for further colonization. By the end of 1942, when British and French forces had swept the Italians out of Libya, the North African campaigns had devastated the country. Between 1943 and 1947, the British established a caretaker military administration in Tripolitania and Cyrenaica, and the French set up one in Fezzan, until the final status of the territories was settled in the Italian Peace Treaty of 1947. The United Nations eventually determined that Libya should become an independent state no later than January 1, 1952. That resolution gave approximately two years to prepare for independence. British and French administrations continued during much of the period. Eventually, Libya was established as a federal kingdom in which substantial autonomy was given to each of the three component units. Chosen as monarch was the chief of the Sanusiyyah, Muhammad Idris, who began his reign as King Idris on December 24, 1951.

From monarchy to the Qaddafi era

The 1951 constitution established the United Kingdom of Libya as a federal constitutional monarchy. Islam was declared the religion of the state and Arabic the official language. In practice, the regime was authoritarian in nature. Executive power was granted to the king, whereas legislative power was shared by the king and a bicameral parliament, the lower house of which was elected. The federal government exercised legislative and executive powers as described in detail in the constitution. In areas not solely under federal purview there were provisions for joint powers between the federal and provincial governments. Such a system was a necessary compromise, allowing for a common authority while preserving some autonomy for Cyrenaica, Fezzan, and Tripolitania (the latter of which was most urbanized, and contained more than half the national population).

Changes unfolded, however. The federal structure disappeared in 1963, when a new constitution established a unitary system and country's name was changed to the Kingdom of Libya, with Idris remaining an increasingly powerful monarch. The discovery of oil by Western prospecting firms in the late 1950s and the rise of Egyptian president Gamal Abdel Nasser as a charismatic figure in the Arab world transformed the Libyan political scene. As King Idris grew more disconnected from daily governance, opposition to the monarchy increased in many quarters – particularly among educated young urbanites attracted to Arab Nationalism, and who saw the government's pro-Western foreign policy as problematic.

On September 1, 1969, a military coup overthrew the Idris government while the ailing king was out of the country. In the first few weeks afterwards, a number of moderate civilians and army officers were appointed to the government, but the real power rested in the hands of the officers responsible for the takeover. They announced that revolution had come to Libya. They formed a Revolutionary Command Council (RCC), which was headed by a young army officer named Muammar al-Qaddafi. Al-Qaddafi advocated radical economic, social, and political change, and at first attempted to emulate Nasser of Egypt in his anti-Western rhetoric and proclamation for pan-Arab unity. In the mid-1970s, however, Qaddafi moved away from Nasserism and invented his own brand of socialism, which he called "natural socialism." He enunciated its principles in his *Green Book*, published in three volumes between 1976 and 1978. Therein he preached complete egalitarianism and the abolition of wage labor and private ownership of land. Trade was exploitative and nonproductive. He called for support of the Palestinian cause and the creation of a powerful coalition of Arab states to fight Israel.

In domestic terms, the post-coup decades of Libyan politics grew increasingly repressive as the regime became more personalistic, centered upon the figure of Qaddafi and his personal cliques rather than any major institution, party, council, or organizing principle. Until 1977, government activities were managed by a cabinet appointed by the RCC. After an attempted coup against Qaddafi by RCC members in 1975, the RCC was reduced from its original 12 members to five. In 1977, the General People's Congress – the 2,700-person national legislative body of Qaddafi, which met periodically for symbolic purposes and to burnish his autocracy – changed the country's name to the Socialist People's Libyan Arab Jamahiriya. The regime proclaimed the establishment of people's power, abolishing the RCC as the supreme authority but naming the five remaining RCC officers as members of the Congress's secretariat. The cabinet became the General People's Congress Committee.

All these institutional reconfigurations obscured the underlying structure of power, which remained extremely concentrated within Qaddafi and his circle. Qaddafi's family was deeply involved in affairs of the state. Mutassim, for instance, would ultimately serve as his national security adviser, while Western-educated Saif became prominent in diplomatic and policymaking circles. Other members of the family reaped wealth from the state's oil coffers and selective investments made to the state-led economy, which unlike most other Arab countries never entertained the painful transition to market-oriented economics after the oil price crash of the mid-1980s. The only constant was Qaddafi's varying mistrust in potential threats within the Libyan state apparatus, which resulted in frequent shuffles, purges, and fractures.

Opposition to the regime, however, did exist. On an everyday level, dissent was nonexistent: the regime's intelligence and security services ensured that visible outbursts of mobilization and criticism were harshly eliminated. However, there were reports of mutinies in the military starting in the 1980s, though the reaction was always swift and deadly. In the case of a 1993 mutiny, Qaddafi ordered Libyan Air Force planes to bomb rebellious military units. The best-known organization opposing the regime was the National Front for the Salvation of Libya (NFSL). In the 1990s, Islamists became another major opposition force in Libya. Some had roots in older movements, such as the *Ikhwan* (Muslim Brotherhood) of Egypt. Other Islamists began springing up, including militant cells. One, the Libyan Islamic Fighting Group, even made attempts on Qaddafi's life before its bloody suppression. In sum, as might be expected in a highly coercive and personalized dictatorship, most Libyans by the eve of the Arab Spring obeyed the regime – not necessarily out of loyalty, but due to the fear, repression, and uncertainty engendered by the agents of an increasingly disconnected strongman.

Libya's second revolution, 2011–2014

Libya was the third country, after Tunisia and Egypt, to experience an uprising during the 2011–12 Arab Spring. On February 15, 2011, the first demonstrations began in the eastern city of Benghazi, where hundreds of protesters gathered in front of a police station. Two days later, thousands of demonstrators began protesting peacefully throughout eastern Libya. Security forces responded with live ammunition; about a dozen people were killed. Rather than ending the protests, the government's actions created more anger and led to the takeover of Benghazi by protesters on February 20. Army units defected to join the rebels. As the takeover of Benghazi was unfolding, a small group, including former justice minister Mustafa 'Abd al-Jalil, human rights lawyer 'Abd al-Hafiz Ghoga, and Mahmoud Jibril, a Libyan professor teaching in the United States, formed the National Transitional Council (NTC), claiming that they represented the Libyan people. The NTC succeeded in convincing European powers and eventually the United States to recognize it as the legitimate interim government. The NTC served as a provisional government over the next year.

On March 17, the United Nations Security Council approved Resolution 1973, which imposed a no-fly zone over Libya to prevent Qaddafi's forces from bombing civilians and authorized international military action to protect civilians. Two days later, NATO military operations against Qaddafi's forces began. Qatar and the United Arab Emirates were the only two members of the Arab League to participate, providing Western forces with logistical support. These actions were welcomed by the largely unarmed and untrained Libyan rebels, which faced off against Qaddafi's substantial forces, among them elements of the Libyan military as well as various militias and paramilitary groups, including African mercenaries.

The fighting in Libya lasted eight months. After conquering the eastern cities such as Benghazi, the rebels began moving westward and were joined by others, including Islamists, who also wanted to overthrow Qaddafi. Throughout August, these forces fought in and around Tripoli, which fell by the end of the month. His ground forces and heavy units depleted by fighting or destroyed by the NATO air campaign, Qaddafi went into hiding; some of his family fled to Algiers, though others were killed or captured by rebels. The loyalist stronghold of Sirte represented the last gasp for regime loyalists, and fell after more than two months of fighting in October 2011. Qaddafi was captured and killed, ending his 42-year rule in Libya. A month later, his son and heir apparent, Saif, was also detained and imprisoned.

Following the promulgation of the Interim Constitutional Declaration in August 2011, a document that would essentially serve as the new national constitution, a new electoral law was drafted in January 2012 determining that the General National Congress (GNC) would be composed of 200 seats: 120 constituency seats for independent candidates and 80 seats for parties based on proportional representation. It thus ensured that members of tribes and ethnic minorities, as well as regional representatives, could be candidates without being required to run on party lists. Originally, the GNC was supposed to act as a constituent assembly, but, bowing to federalist pressures, the NTC amended the Constitutional Declaration so the new GNC would appoint a 60-member committee that would draft the constitution. A few days before the October 2012 elections, the declaration was further amended to provide that the 60-member committees be chosen through national elections.

On July 7, 2012, more than 2.7 million Libyans, an estimated 80 percent of eligible voters, went to the polls in the first fully free and fair election in national history. More than 3,000 candidates ran for office, including 600 women. The largely secular National Forces Alliance led by Mahmoud Jibril won 39 out of the 80 party seats, while the Justice and Construction Party, the Muslim Brotherhood's party, won 17. Once seated, the GNC assumed formal powers of government, and the NTC dissolved itself in August 2012 to institutionalize the shift. The successful election dimmed in importance, however, in the months following. The GNC was not a coherent and unified body; it was rife with powerful personalities, each of which gave their backing to competing militias, blocs, and tribes. With insecurity spreading, the NTC, and later the GNC, put many of these armed groups on the government payroll. This hybrid security system was characterized by loose collaboration between weak, official forces – the army and police, representing remnants of the old regime and newly recruited members – and stronger, unofficial armed groups, which enjoyed the backing of traditional tribal or religious notables. Armed groups in the two main cities of Tripoli and Benghazi often took on a predatory role, pressuring the country's elected bodies to pursue certain political or ideological agendas.

For months, assassinations and abductions obstructed political progress, especially in Benghazi, where Islamist and non-Islamist militias vied for control of the city. A high point of tension was reached in September 2012, when radicalized Islamists, including the Salafi militia group Ansar al-Shari'a, led protesters to attack the American consulate in Benghazi and set it on fire, killing Ambassador Christopher Stevens and three other Americans. In October

2013, militias went so far as to kidnap Prime Minister Ali Zeidan; though he was released shortly thereafter, this event inflicted a heavy blow on the credibility of the Libyan government. By the winter of 2014, militias from the western cities of Zintan and Misrata had split Tripoli and the surrounding region, seizing control over airports, ministries, and other key sites. The episodic clashes that shook this precarious equilibrium further polarized the GNC, signaling the collapse of central authority and the fierce competition of power that lay ahead.

Civil conflict and state fragmentation

In May 2014, a former Libyan military officer who had returned to participate in the initial uprising, Khalifa Haftar, launched Operation Dignity. Haftar had come to command the Libyan National Army, which began in 2011 as the reconstituted national military under the NTC but later became beholden to Haftar's interests. Operation Dignity involved a major offensive by the LNA and its allies, including militia brigades from Zintan and tribal groupings, against various opponents, including radical Islamists and adversarial militia brigades from Misrata; as Haftar attacked the GNC in Tripoli, the GNC responded by calling for its own militias, resulting in a standoff. Astonishingly, authorities were still able to hold national elections in June 2014 to replace the GNC with a nationally elected parliament, the 200-member House of Representatives (HOR). The elections resulted in a heavy defeat for the Islamists; however, out of an eligible population of four million voters, only 1.5 million registered to vote, and of these fewer than half actually went to the polls.

Despite the successful contest, power and authority continued to splinter along provincial, tribal, and religious lines. The 2011 Interim Constitutional Declaration continued to operate beyond its two-year remit, as a permanent constitution had yet to be drafted. In June 2014, various Islamists and Misrata militia units launched Operation Libya Dawn as a response to Haftar's earlier campaign, taking control of Tripoli and the international airport. By the end of July 2014, they had reinstated the old GNC as the true legislative assembly (and thus contended the HOR was no longer legitimate), and established a new government in Tripoli that styled itself as the National Salvation Government. Following the Libya Dawn campaign, the newly elected HOR was forced to flee the capital and find refuge in the eastern city of Tobruk. The HOR, unlike its rival in Tripoli, enjoyed international recognition. It soon appointed a government located in the city of Al-Bayda. These events pitting the old GNC and its western backers against the now eastern-based HOR and its affiliated forces further divided the country, marking the beginning of Libya's ongoing civil strife.

In an attempt to reconcile the splintered country, the United Nations appointed Spanish diplomat Bernardino León as special representative. A national dialogue was held in multiple cities, from Libya to Switzerland to Morocco, until in October 2015 both sides announced a proposal to share power in a Government of National Accord (GNA), tasked with reestablishing security and rebuilding its political institutions and economic infrastructure. Most participants signed the agreement, with the exception of some representatives of the Tripoli-based GNC. A new institution, the Presidential Council (PC), was created as the functional government ordained by the GNC and internationally recognized by the United Nations, United States, and other major global actors. It would also incorporate members from the eastern forces and HOR. Fayed al-Sarraj was chosen as chairman of the PC, and thus effectively President of Libya, and also Prime Minister of the GNA, and so head of its government. Despite grumbling, the agreement marked a major step forward in attempting to resolve the Libyan crisis.

However, despite its installation in December 2015, the new GNA turned out to be too weak and incapable of dealing with the armed militias and terrorist groups that entrenched themselves in the country. Al-Sarraj quickly found that despite the national dialogue, the GNA was unable to formulate a common platform that all competing groups, in particular the HOR, could embrace. The HOR rejected the proposed governments of al-Sarraj, who also escaped several assassination attempts. Thus began another period of infighting and discord, with political authority cleaved due to the peculiar bifurcation of political institutions. The GNA and al-Sarraj were based in Tripoli and were recognized internationally as the executive branch and government of Libya. The HOR, the internationally recognized elected legislature of Libya, was located in Tobruk, east of Tripoli. The HOR was, and remains, backed by Haftar and his LNA as the rightful governing body of the country. Finally, as a third powerbroker, the old GNC still commanded its supporters, including powerful Misrata-based militias, but had been displaced in Tripoli by 2017. It still sought to challenge its HOR foes, but many of its politicians had since defected to back the GNA and al-Sarraj.

This alphabet soup of competition, with a Byzantine array of militia units and tribal paramilitaries backing each side, foreclosed any meaningful state unity. It also heralded increasingly brutal internecine violence through civil war, with the eastern HOR-affiliated faction becoming militarily dominant.

In June 2017, Haftar declared victory in Benghazi against armed extremist groups that had gained a foothold in the city; in May 2018, the LNA finalized the liberation of Derna, a northeastern city under Islamist control that had been under siege by his forces since May 2014. Afterwards, Haftar reached out to cull more southern allies and gain control over Libya's largest oil fields, exploiting the neglect shown to the region by the Tripoli-based GNA. In April 2019, having already declared the GNA null and the national dialogue inactive, Haftar and his LNA began a military offensive to conquer Tripoli, thereby seeking to depose al-Sarraj and the PC despite its international recognition. That campaign raged throughout the summer, despite pleas for mediation and ceasefire from many outside actors. Within Libya, legal observers accused the LNA and its militia allies of committing war crimes, particularly against civilians caught in the middle of the increasingly brutal civil conflict.

The Islamic State of Iraq and Syria (ISIS) exploited this instability after the Arab Spring, filling the vacuum in many areas of the collapsed state to garner support and establish a presence. It was followed by other Salafi militias and armed groups, including Ansar al-Shari'a, which until its 2017 disbanding would become notorious for its role in the September 2012 attacks on the US Consulate in Benghazi. The placement of ISIS's main stronghold, Sirte, was no coincidence: it is the home region of Qaddafi, which he openly favored during his rule, and the city geographically falls between the eastern and western regions. ISIS solidified its territorial control in Sirte throughout 2015. In 2016, the United States launched an air campaign in conjunction with ground forces, nominally aligned with the GNA and mostly from Misrata, and drove ISIS units out of Sirte. In 2017, however, ISIS forces had reconstituted themselves, beginning a new series of terrorist attacks, including brazen strikes on the election headquarters, the National Oil Corporation, and the Foreign Ministry building in Tripoli. Though estimated to widely vary in number, from a few hundred to a few thousand, ISIS militants are difficult to track given their dispersion across the central desert regions, and they have grown adept on exploiting the latent insecurity resulting from the absence of central political authority.

SOCIAL AND ECONOMIC ENVIRONMENT

Libya constitutes the eastern part of the Maghrib (Map 6.1). It is situated in North Africa, bordered by the Mediterranean Sea in the north, Egypt and Sudan in the east, Chad and Niger in the south, and Algeria and Tunisia in

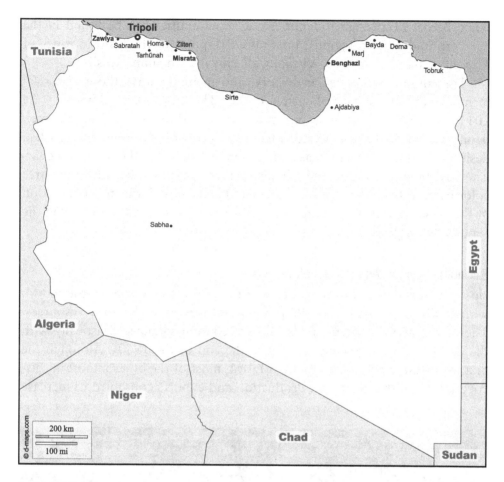

MAP 6.1
State of Libya. Major cities shown.

Source: D-Maps.

the west. It has an area of just under 1.8 million square kilometers (685,000 square miles), more than 90 percent of which is desert. There are no natural rivers. It has a small population for such a large territory, with less than 6.5 million in 2019; 90 percent live in less than 10 percent of the total area, primarily along the Mediterranean coast. About 70 percent of the population is urban, concentrated in the two largest cities, Benghazi and Tripoli. Almost all Libyans are Arab, and many descend from tribal confederations, practicing nomadic and semi-nomadic lifestyles under the unforgivingly arid environment. African ethnicity exists in the south (the historic region of Fezzan), while Berber (Tamazight) identities and communities can be found in the northern and eastern regions, in what correspond to the historic zones of Tripolitania and Cyrenaica. Virtually all Libyans are Sunni Muslims.

The country is steeped in history, and in many ways those historical memories inflect the pace of current events. The Libyan flag adopted by the 2011 constitutional process, for instance, replaced the much-despised green banner brandished by the Qaddafi regime in favor of restoring the 1951 flag designed for Libya when it was a kingdom. The new flag (Photo 6.1) is characterized by a white star and Islamic crescent against a backdrop of three color bands – from the top, red, black, and green – with the medium section of the crescent and star juxtaposed against the black band representing the Senussi dynasty's emblem.

Economy, resources, and development

Upon independence, Libya was one of the poorest countries in the world, with an illiteracy rate of over 90 percent and very limited natural resources. The nature and prospects of the Libyan economy changed drastically with the discovery of petroleum reserves at the end of the 1950s. Although the first major oil finds were in western Libya, most of the other important discoveries lay in the northeast. Production and exports continued to increase

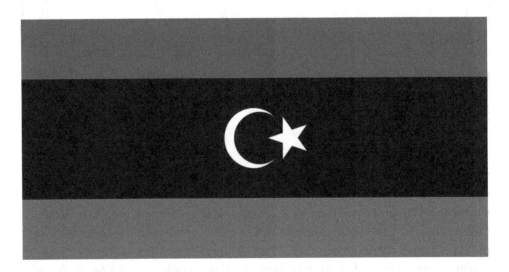

PHOTO 6.1
Flag of Libya (since 2011)

Source: Pixabay.

rapidly over the next decade, rising from 6 million barrels in 1961 to 1.2 billion in 1970, transforming Libya into a rentier state and making hydrocarbon production the centerpiece of its fiscal well-being – a pattern that continues today. As of 2019, hydrocarbon rents composed more than one-third of Libya's GDP, although as discussed earlier, it was not used uniformly by a single political authority. Apart from oil, Libya had a handful of other established industries prior to its civil conflicts, including iron and steel production, petrochemicals, and some textiles.

Libya also has natural gas resources, although these are of lesser importance than its crude oil reserves. The Western Libyan Gas Project (WLGP), which came online in 2004, made it possible to transfer natural gas to Europe via a 520-kilometer underwater pipeline called the Green Stream. In 2005, 10 billion cubic meters of gas were produced (up from 7 billion the previous year); 8 billion were sold to Europe, and 2 billion were consumed domestically. The WLGP is a fifty-fifty joint venture between Italy's Ente Nazionale Idrocarburi (ENI) and Libya's National Oil Company. As of 2015, Libya had 52.8 trillion cubic feet of proven natural gas reserves.

Libya's major economic activity before the discovery of petroleum had been agriculture. However, only 1.2 percent of Libya's land is arable, and of that, less than 1 percent is irrigated, and prior to the Arab Spring economists estimated the agriculture sector to contribute less than 7 percent of the GDP. The country does not produce enough to feed its own population and has long needed to import most of its food. Similarly, water is scarce, and the supply is very irregular in areas where rainfall is its main source. In 1984, a massive water pipeline project, the Great Manmade River (GMMR), was inaugurated at the Sarir Oasis. One of the largest civil engineering projects in the world, by early 2011, the GMMR was supplying 6.5 million cubic meters of freshwater per day to the major population centers on the Mediterranean coast. Some of this water infrastructure was damaged during the 2011 uprising and rebellion, but today – perhaps out of universal need – continues to operate unabated, providing nearly three-quarters of all freshwater used in Libya.

If and when a unitary and consolidated political government emerges in Libya, stimulating economic growth remains an urgent priority. Unemployment exceeds 17 percent, although instability and strife in many areas make this World Bank estimate somewhat unreliable. More certain is the youth unemployment rate, which at nearly 42 percent is among the highest in the MENA. Contributing factors include not only endemic fighting, which has destroyed the economy in some areas and reduced productivity in others, but also the misshapen economic structures upon which the country operated when Qaddafi fell. Economic development under Qaddafi ranged from inefficient to irrational. At first, the government's role in the economy became predominant. The state not only took majority control of the oil companies operating in its territory but also nationalized the local assets of some companies, such as Shell in 1974. By the end of 1970, the number of commercial banks had been reduced to five. Large- and medium-sized industries with foreign owners – primarily Italians, who owned 75–80 percent of all industrial plants in Libya – were also taken over by the state.

Thereafter, government efforts failed to facilitate the development of an entrepreneurial middle class. Libyan businessmen with government contracts invested their huge profits abroad. Qaddafi's response was his *Green Book* and aggressive programs to redistribute wealth and collectivize many economic assets starting in the late 1970s. Workers were encouraged to take over a large number of commercial and industrial enterprises. A 1978 law decreed that each Libyan should own his home and encouraged tenants to take immediate possession of their rented houses. Furthermore, all foreign trade was to be conducted by the state. With no meaningful private sector, Libya's economy suffered in the 1980s when Qaddafi's support of terrorism pitted Libya against the United States and other Western countries, resulting in major economic sanctions against Libyan oil exports and preventing many goods, in particular new technologies, from entering Libya. These embargoes and freezes, coupled with the 1986 oil price collapse, threw the state-driven economy into depression, as the cash-strapped government proved unable to generate the employment and goods necessary to keep pace with popular demand. In 1992, the economy stumbled further as the United Nations Security Council imposed economic and travel sanctions for Libya's role in the 1988 bombing of Pan Am flight 103.

These sanctions were suspended in 1999, after two bombing suspects were turned into a Scottish court. Only after Libya officially accepted responsibility for the bombing and agreed to pay $2.7 billion in compensation to the families of the victims did the Security Council vote to lift the sanctions in September 2003. Afterwards, Libyan officials flirted with foreign investors and set into motion different programs and initiatives that, at least to Western observers, suggested one of the most closed Arab economies was opening itself to global competition and market transactions. This process was embryonic and uncertain, however, when the Arab Spring occurred. The years during and after the uprising exposed the economy's addiction to oil. In 2011, Libya's GDP contracted by 60 percent due to instability disrupting oil production. When Libyan oil production returned to 1.4 million barrels per day in 2012, followed by a gradual increase in oil prices, the economy rapidly improved; at least in urban areas like Tripoli, middle-class Libyans saw increased subsidies and wages, more jobs, and new commerce. Political infighting again hampered responsible policymaking and more importantly oil production, however, and the GDP contracted by 24 percent in 2014. Since then, there has been no sustainable pattern or trend in Libyan economics, but the following do not bode well for future growth: first, extreme reliance upon stable oil exports; second, the sensitivity of hydrocarbon infrastructures (such as production facilities and pipelines) to militant attacks; and third, the refusal of different political centers to pursue common developmental policies.

In social terms, Libyans have suffered from the past decade of instability and strife. Still, there persists a high literacy rate, at 91 percent; this partly stems from historical legacy. After the 1969 revolution, the RCC initiated compulsory and free elementary education. The program was successful and by 2010, the percentage of the population over fifteen that could read had risen to 89.2 percent. Similarly, major efforts by the Libyan regime under Qaddafi to modernize the country resulted in rising health standards and well-being. The number of medical doctors rose to 1.29 per 1,000 people in 2008, which compared favorably with industrialized countries such as the United Kingdom (1.66/1,000) and Singapore (1.40/1,000).

POLITICAL STRUCTURES

Libya's political institutions and dynamics have been in constant evolution since 2011, characterized by competing claims of power. One of the least controversial political structures was the NTC, which during its brief tenure from March 2011 through August 2012 was accepted by a plurality of Libyan rebel groups and competing armed blocs; it helped that for some of this time, Libyans were generally united alongside the international community in efforts to upend the Qaddafi regime. However, internal bickering weakened the council over time, until its dissolution in August 2012. The NTC transferred power at that point to Libya's first parliamentary body, the General National Congress (GNC), which was elected in July 2012. New elections in June 2014 replaced the GNC with the House of Representatives (HOR), which later fled east to Tobruk due to continued fighting.

As the winners of internationally monitored free and fair elections, the HOR and the government it appointed were recognized by most global actors as Libya's sovereign political authority. However, Operation Libya Dawn resulted in the reconstitution of some GNC elements into the National Salvation Government, setting up the country's implicit west-east cleavage. The later creation of the Government of National Accord, or GNA (and its Presidential Council, led by President and Prime Minister al-Sarraj) after the 2015 national dialogue, based in Tripoli and recognized internationally as the national executive body, further aggravated acrimony. The government created by the national agreement through the GNA is a cabinet chaired by the PC head. There also exists a High Council of State (HCS), an advisory body also created by the 2015 agreement and charged with bridging the gap between the GNA and HOR.

As of 2019, the GNA and HOR remain at odds with one another. This political rift in Libya has paralyzed most government institutions. For instance, although the Central Bank, the National Oil Company, and the Libyan Investment Authority do their best to distribute funds and resources equitably across the country, reporting to two governments makes neutrality a significant challenge. The Supreme Court was considered pro-GNC after issuing a November 2014 ruling that declared the HOR's electoral victory unconstitutional, but regardless the judiciary became paralyzed in the years following, as threats and insecurity prevented many courts and legal offices from properly functioning. Indeed, the Constitutional Drafting Assembly (CDA), elected in February 2014 and charged with creating a permanent constitution, is the only democratic body not contested by the two sides – perhaps only because of the institution's lack of progress since its inauguration in April 2014.

Despite the difficulties in meeting and operating in such a fractious environment, the CDA licensed a draft version of a new constitution in July 2017. Talks are still ongoing on the possibility of holding a constitutional referendum before the proposed 2019 national elections, which were initially envisaged to incorporate both a parliamentary round and a presidential contest. Municipal elections in 20 localities were held in March and April 2019; though only a small number of the over hundred municipalities, a 38 percent participation rate and some surprising results showed Libyans were still willing to participate in democratic processes. However, as General Haftar's military campaign to take Tripoli instigated widespread resistance and civil conflict through late 2019, the prospects for the country to hold new elections and ratify its nascent constitutional framework dimmed.

Insecurity has worsened in the post-Arab Spring decade; there is nothing approximating a Weberian state in Libya, whereby a single central political authority possesses a monopoly over the legitimate use of coercion. Instead, many residents in cities rely upon a kaleidoscope of armed militias, each claiming a tribal, provincial, or ideological origin, to guard neighborhoods, prisons, migrant centers, and critical infrastructure including the airport. Unregulated, militias also engage in illicit financial operations, including trafficking and foreign currency sales. The paradox is that while many are essentially thugs entrenched in criminal and illicit activity, they deliver essential crime fighting and counterterrorism operations that the government is too weak to provide. Moreover, the coalition of militias and their respective territorial controls often shifts. In Tripoli, for instance, there exist four main militias: Rada Special Deterrence Force, Nawasi Brigade, Abu Salim Brigade, and Tripoli Revolutionaries Brigade (TRB) – each group having no more than a few hundred fighters.

At one point, the LNA was considered the closest equivalent to a national military. The LNA consists of a navy, air force, and regular army totaling 20,000 to 25,000 fighters and an additional 30,000 supporting fighters from localized militias. The air fleet was furnished by Egypt and UAE during 2014–15, bypassing UN efforts to reduce the arms flowing into Libya. As of 2019, the LNA has proven moderately successful in capturing new territory, albeit not without significant failures and oversteps.

POLITICAL DYNAMICS

As discussed thus far, at the level of elites and institutions, the post-Arab Spring period of Libya has been typified by negotiations and compromises followed by breakdown and conflict, all of which has destroyed much of state authority. Within society, however, there exist multiple vectors and forces operative on the political arena, and which may propel further change.

First, the role of civil society and non-governmental organizations (NGOs) as democratic advocates in Libya has, historically, been limited. NGOs did exist under the previous regime; however, all of them were functioning under the umbrella of the government. The fall of the Qaddafi regime resulted in an efflorescence of new civic groups and NGOs, from human rights entities to service providers. While many struggle for lack of funding and leadership today, they play an indelible role in facilitating the political transition. For instance, after 2011, new organizations focused on new issues such as elections, minority rights, legal justice, security services, youth, and women's issues. Various civil organizations demonstrated their capacity to increase demands for greater transparency and accountability in governmental institutions, such as political monitoring teams that attended ministerial meetings in Tripoli and reported back the flow of political discussions to a wider audience.

In 2012, the Ministry of Culture established the Civil Society Commission to help register and regulate this new sector of voluntarism and associational life, but here factionalism has also undermined operations. The GNA-HOR split resulted in the commission itself dividing into two commissions, with the Tripoli-based branch eventually being seen as the more credible and objective body that could review, vet, and authorize new NGOs. Libyan activists pushed back on requests made by the commission for local civic groups to gain prior authorization for certain activities, and to fully report their membership and partnering organizations. At the same time, Libyan civil society groups were victimized by violence as well. For instance, a number of young Libyan activists have suffered abduction or murder since 2014, such as Abdelmoez Banoon, Jabir Zain, and other known bloggers, writers, and organizers who ran afoul of armed enemies by virtue of their criticism.

Second, Libya has a robust and visible tribal structure, especially in the eastern and southern regions, where imagined kinship and geographic origin shapes the perception of many social relations. After the Qaddafi regime fell, tribal communities contributed a combination of militia units and notable leadership in many areas, although this has also manifested in some areas in heightened conflict due to longstanding tribal rivalries and feuds. This speaks to the enduring nature of tribalism. Qaddafi sought to reduce tribal pluralism with his ideological rhetoric, but in other ways amplified it by drawing upon some tribal forces far more than others in his constant bid to seek the most loyal segments of Libyan society. Today, while tribal affiliations have enabled many areas to reduce crime, maintain order, and govern efficiently, they have also fueled the worsening divide. The LNA, for instance, exploits tribal alliances in its bid to increase its operational capacity; this was instrumental in its victory over Islamist groups in Benghazi.

Third, women's rights represent another area of potential political change. Libyan women participated in the Libyan uprising in large numbers, and their role in driving forward many demonstrations and protests were instrumental in sustaining the momentum of revolution. Women's informal networks also strategized and reported on ongoing events, capitalizing on newfound opportunities for leadership through social media. In addition, they were pivotal in maintaining contacts with the foreign press. A 2013 poll by the International Foundation for Electoral Systems (IFES) showed that 77 percent of Libyan women were interested in the political situation of their country, and that 66 percent had participated in the 2012 elections. However, the degradation of law and order, and prevalence of male-dominated militia groups, have more recently undercut the work of women within civil society and politics. Threats of abduction, rape, and murder have limited the contributions of many; indeed, prominent female voices have been killed, including the journalist Naseeb Miloud Karfana and the former HOR member Fariha al-Berkawi.

Moreover, despite constitutional requirements for women to be represented at parity with men in general elections (which enabled female candidates to secure 30 of the GNC's 200 seats in 2012), Libyan women have been underrepresented in most other government bodies. This suggests persistence of the patriarchy. The NTC, for instance, initially only included two women. Social requirements likewise have further stifled women's rights since the revolution. In Tripoli, Islamic authorities issued rulings in 2013 that called for Libyan women to wear the *niqab* (veil) more frequently and to have a male companion when traveling abroad. In 2017, the LNA issued a travel ban on women under the age of 60, justifying the move as necessary to prevent international espionage. Nonetheless, social life shows significant variance, with women enjoying far more personal freedoms and social autonomy in metropolitan cities like Tripoli and Benghazi than in rural areas that are perceived as more tribalized and conservative. The final draft of the constitutional framework shared in 2017 will help settle some of these issues, although women's rights activism will likely be a recurrent theme in Libyan civil society assuming security returns to the country.

Fourth, Libyan youth represent a huge social force that is nearly universally literate but also largely jobless, with youth unemployment reaching 42 percent in 2019. Most of the politicians involved in key governing bodies on all sides, from the GNC to HOR, are far older than the average Libyan, and some youth activists within civil society have cynically noted that one of the commonalities shared by the Tripoli and Tobruk governments has been their disdain for youth opinions. Many economists and observers have identified a range of programs necessary for national implementation to take advantage of this demographic dividend, including improving schools, opening vocational training programs, maintaining decrepit universities, and otherwise luring youth away from militia involvement and extremist group recruitment, especially by Salafi networks like ISIS. The 2015 World Values Survey shockingly revealed that close to 21 percent of Libyan youth carried firearms.

Fifth, minority groups in Libya – long relegated to the periphery by Qaddafi – have become vocal once more. The Tamazight, including the Tuareg living in the south, as well as the non-Berber Tubu nomads, all established self-governing councils during the Arab Spring. Their demands vary, but among the most visible issues made at Libyan policymakers since 2011–12 has been Tamazight petitioning for official recognition of their language. Obstinate refusal on this linguistic issue resulted in all three minority groups withholding their representatives from participating in the Constitutional Drafting Assembly's work, and thus the constitution drafting process. In the midst of the political conflict, dire security situation and duplication of government institutions, the minority groups have not succeeded in advocating for their rights. This has opened the door for considerable manipulation. Under Qaddafi, for instance, the Tuareg and Tubu communities were largely ignored, as they seldom fit the dominant narrative of Libya as an Arab nation. By contrast, the LNA in its military expansion struck coalitional bargains with both these groups with the promise of future recognition, among other concessions.

FOREIGN POLICY

Libyan foreign policy has somewhat normalized after decades of increasing isolation under Qaddafi. Initially, monarchist Libya under King Idris hewed closely to British and American support, with treaties allowing both countries to establish military bases in return for security guarantees and some development aid. Western firms, in particular Esso – the predecessor to Exxon and later ExxonMobil – discovered and established the oil industry in the late 1950s. Qaddafi, upon his ascent, reversed this course. To legitimize its power, the RCC prioritized removing Libya's foreign bases so as to claim it was liberating Libya from Western imperialism. Agreements were reached between the RCC and the United States and British governments to quickly evacuate the former's Wheelus base, and then British bases at Tobruk and al-Adam.

Qaddafi focused much of his energies on pan-Arab unity during his early years, during a period of Arab Nationalist adherence. Indeed, Libya's relations with its neighbors under Qaddafi were characterized by seven attempts at unity. The Tripoli Charter of December 1969 was the first of these – in this case with Egypt and Sudan. Subsequent proposals at unification occurred in 1971, with Egypt and Syria to create the United Arab Republic, and again in 1974, with Tunisia to create the Arab Islamic Republic. Both merger plans failed in the face of significant domestic and regional opposition. Libya was also party to the failed Arab Maghrib Union project in 1989, which was meant to foster economic integration on the model of the European community.

That pan-Arab symbolism came accompanied by enduring hostility against Israel and support for the Palestinian cause. Qaddafi condemned Zionism as aggressive nationalism and supported the more radical leftist groups among the Palestinians, such as the Popular Front for the Liberation of Palestine. After the Camp David agreement of 1978 cemented peace between Egypt and Israel, Libya became a leader of the "rejection front" – Arab states that denounced any political settlement with Israel. Libya provided Jordan, for instance, with significant foreign aid after 1978 to deter the Hashemite Kingdom from seeking its own separate peace and ensure regional unity against Israel. After the second Palestinian intifada began in the fall of 2000, Qaddafi's regime again became very vocal in its criticism of Israel and, by corollary, American policy in the region. The Libyan stance on Israel has changed little under the post-revolution governments. While the GNA and HOR have not issued statements on Israel that approach the vehement hostility evoked by Qaddafi, and both also have embraced the goal of Palestinian statehood, their long-term strategy remains uncertain.

Of all MENA countries, however, Egypt occupies the central place in Libya's foreign policy outlook. Libyan-Egyptian relations were close at times but turbulent during other moments. After early closeness with Nasser during the first year of the Libyan revolution, relations deteriorated progressively under Anwar Sadat, culminating in Egypt's bombing of Libya in 1977. In the 1980s, relations with the regime of Hosni Mubarak improved markedly. Tens of thousands of Egyptians sought employment in Libya, and a large number of joint infrastructural, industrial, and agricultural projects were set up between the two countries. Mubarak and Qaddafi shared intelligence on radical Islamists on both sides of the border, and Mubarak personally interceded on Libya's behalf for the lifting of UN sanctions. Today, the HOR-affiliated government in Tobruk maintains close official ties with the Egyptian government and President Abdel Fattah al-Sisi. Egypt – whose Western desert shares a seven-hundred-mile border with Libya – has an incentive to ensure the policing of extremist activity on the frontier. In fact, by targeting most Islamists as enemies, Haftar arguably mirrored Sisi's blanket approach to rejecting all religious opposition to political authority. From May 2014, Egypt also conducted airstrikes in Libya's east and south in support of the LNA.

While Libya's place in the Arab world has yet to be fully recalibrated given its ongoing strife, one interesting point of conjecture is whether a future Libyan state will orient itself as much south towards Africa as it does towards the Arab countries. Qaddafi showed special affinity to sub-Saharan Africa, and supported Muslims there politically, financially, and culturally. In kind, the Organization of African Unity (OAU) passed a resolution in June 1998 declaring that its member states would no longer recognize the UN embargo on flights to and from Libya or United Nations sanctions against Libya unless the United States and United Kingdom agreed to try the Libyan bombing suspects in a neutral country. The OAU's actions and Nelson Mandela's support for Libya were critical in the final negotiations to hold the Lockerbie trial at The Hague. In the late 1990s, Qaddafi even declared that a "United States of Africa" should be formed to replace the OAU; in February 2009, he was elected chairman of the OAU's successor, the African Union, at a closed session in Ethiopia. During the uprising against Qaddafi, many African states tried to mediate between the parties to prevent the collapse of his regime. These attempts failed, mostly because of the reluctance of the revolutionary governments in Benghazi to trust non-Western interlocutors as a neutral mediator.

Libya's relations with the United States deteriorated rapidly until the Arab Spring thrust Western interests back into the country's political innards. Until the 1973 Arab-Israeli War, Qaddafi had been merely critical of American policies. After the war, Sadat moved closer to the West and to the United States in the prelude to the Camp David peace accords. Perceiving a threat to Libya's security in this shift, Qaddafi then moved Libya closer to the Soviet bloc, a strategy that either caused or facilitated increased support to various terrorist groups around the world. In December 1979, the American Embassy in Tripoli was sacked and burned. The Reagan administration then chose Qaddafi as the principal target of its antiterrorist policy. As the Libyan government also pursued a crash program to develop nuclear capabilities, the United States and its allies responded with further economic and political measures to isolate the country regionally and internationally.

These efforts culminated in the American bombing of Tripoli in 1986 in retaliation for a terrorist bombing initially blamed on Libya, but later traced to the radical Palestinian Abu Nidal organization. In 1991, the United States and the United Kingdom formally charged Libya with the bombing of Pan Am flight 103 over Lockerbie, Scotland, while France issued arrest warrants for four Libyans accused of participating in a 1988 bombing of a French airliner over Niger. The resulting sanctions further detached Libya from the international system, earning the country the moniker of being a "rogue state" for many Western analysts.

The 2000s saw a thawing of this diplomatic quarantine, starting with the Libyan decision in 1999 to turn over several men accused of the Lockerbie bombing to The Hague and agreements to pay restitution to the victims' families. The terrorist attacks of 9/11 in the United States also jarred the Qaddafi regime, not least because it heralded a more aggressive and interventionist American policy that would level its enemies, from the Taliban in Afghanistan to fellow dictator Saddam Hussein in Iraq, with military firepower. Perhaps for that reason, in December 2003, the Libyan government announced it would end all programs aimed at developing weapons of mass destruction. In the following month, it ratified the Comprehensive Nuclear Test Ban Treaty and allowed a compliance-monitoring team to be posted in its territory. In response to these initiatives, the US administration lifted its travel ban and unilateral trade and investment sanctions. It also unblocked Libya's frozen assets, encouraged people-to-people exchanges in education and health, and in 2006 restored full diplomatic relations with Libya. In 2007, Libya was elected to the UN Security Council; it even assumed the presidency of the council for a month in January 2008.

The Arab Spring transformed Libya's relations with the West, which sided early on with the opposition. France and the United States, for example, quickly recognized the NTC as the legitimate interim government of Libya. The subsequent NATO air campaign beginning in March 2011 drew enthusiastic participation from both the Obama administration and major European Union governments. The extended military strikes, intended firstly to protect civilians but expanded silently later on to destroy all of Qaddafi's coercive capacity, were vital in ensuring the end of the regime and victory for Libyan rebels. Since then, Western allies have supported reconciliation between the rival factions in Libyan politics. The 2015 national dialogue effort, for instance, was not only a United Nations initiative but also consistently backed by all Western powers. The European Union has had a more proximate strategic reason to stabilize Libya: the country is not only a source of illegal migration and potential security risks as a corridor for radical Islamist terrorism, but it is also a major provider of oil and gas. Most Libyan crude oil exports head to the EU, with Italy, Germany, and France typically serving as the key buyers. The worsening civil conflict throughout 2019 alarmed many EU governments, which have sought to end the violent rivalry between the LNA and GNA through diplomatic efforts.

FUTURE PROSPECTS

The political dynamics coupled with the current social and economic developments suggest Libya stands at a critical juncture. With no viable central government extant given the tenacious clashes today between different factions, but with the country's stability extremely important to outside interests, several scenarios could emerge. A first scenario sees the simple continuation of the current situation. No political side wins the upper hand, but low-level violence and ongoing insecurity slowly undermines the bonds that kept the society relatively united. A progressive erosion of national values and ties, in favor of local tribal and factional realities fueled by militia supremacy, would mean Libya is a state on paper only – but not quite a collapsed state so fully dissolved that it creates massive refugee exoduses.

The second scenario envisions the success of the UN-led negotiations and the reconciliation between the GNA government and the HOR-LNR side. This could be sanctioned by an agreement that sees a new government formed by technocrats under the leadership of al-Sarraj work to stabilize the country, while the armed forces under the command of Haftar and a military council formed by high officers from the various regions of Libya work to bring order to the country and build a new security apparatus that could demobilize the militias and restore security everywhere. The third scenario is that the HOR-LNR faction simply conquers the rest of the country, bringing Haftar to power as the national leader and removing the GNA from existence. Whether such a government forged in civil war will be democratic, or at least as open to pluralism as the early transitional phase, is open to question.

FURTHER READING

Excellent primers into Libyan political development are Dirk Vandewalle's *Libya since Independence: Oil and State-Building* (Cornell University Press, 1998) and the more recent *History of Modern Libya* (Cambridge University Press, 2012). Ronald Bruce St. John, *Libya: Continuity and Change* (Routledge, 2015) is also a readable introduction.

Recent books that focus on the 2011 uprising and the complicated politics since include Lindsey Hilsum, *Sandstorm: Libya in the Time of Revolution* (Penguin Press, 2012); Jason Pack, *The 2011 Libyan Uprisings and the Struggle for the Post-Qadhafi Future* (Palgrave Macmillan, 2013); Ethan Chorin, *Exit Gaddafi: The Hidden History of the Libyan Revolution* (Saqi, 2012); and Peter Cole and Brian McQuinn, *The Libyan Revolution and its Aftermath* (Oxford University Press, 2015). The most recent and well-reviewed studies of Libya's conflicts and disintegration since Qaddafi include Frederic Wehrey, *The Burning Shores: Inside the Battle for the New Libya* (Farrar, Straus and Giroux, 2018) and Ulf Laessing, *Understanding Libya since Gaddafi* (Hurst, 2019).

Deeper historical works include John Wright's *Libya* (Praeger, 1969), which focuses on the period from 1911 to 1951. Wright's latest iteration, *A History of Libya* (Columbia University Press, 2012), covers the time afterwards. E. E. Evans-Pritchard's *The Sanusi of Cyrenaica* (Oxford University Press, 1949) provides an important study of Libya's main religious order and its role in the country's development, as does Nicola Ziadeh's *Sanusiyyahh: A Study of a Revivalist Movement in Islam* (Brill, 1968). Henry Serrano Villard, the first US minister to Libya after independence, gives a general overview of the monarchical period in *Libya: The New Arab Kingdom of North Africa* (Cornell University Press, 1956). The UN commissioner in Libya, Adrian Pelt, describes the transformation of Libya from an Italian colony to an independent state in *Libyan Independence and the United Nations: A Case of Planned Decolonization* (Yale University Press, 1970). Lisa Anderson covers the social and political history of Libya for a century and a half in *The State and Social Transformation in Tunisia and Libya, 1830–1980* (Princeton University Press, 1986). Majid Khadduri, *Modern Libya: A Study in Political Development* (Johns Hopkins University Press, 1963), discusses the period following the end of World War Two to the granting of independence in detail. Another informative historical take on identity formation in colonial Libya is Anna Baldinetti, *The Origins of the Libyan Nation* (Routledge, 2013).

Studies of Libya's political, social, and economic system since 1969 include J. A. Allan, *Libya since Independence: Economic and Social Development* (Croom Helm, 1982); Omar L. Fathaly and Monte Palmer, *Political Development and Social Change in Libya* (Lexington Books, 1979); John K. Cooley, *Libyan Sandstorm* (Holt, Rinehart and Winston, 1982); Marius Deeb and Mary-Jane Deeb, *Libya since the Revolution: Aspects of Social and Political Development* (Praeger, 1982); E. George H. Joffe and Keith Stanley McLachlan, *Social and Economic Development of Libya* (MENAS Press, 1982).

The following works are more focused on Qaddafi's regime and its authoritarian strategies of control and governance: Lillian Craig Harris, *Qadhafi's Revolution and the Modern State* (Westview/Croom Helm, 1986); Jonathan Bearman, *Qadhafi's Libya* (Zed Books, 1986); John Anthony Allan, *Libya: The Experience of Oil* (Westview Press, 1981); Ruth First, *Libya: The Elusive Revolution* (Penguin Books, 1974); Mirella Bianco, *Gadafi: Voice from the Desert* (Longman, 1975); David Blundy and Andrew Lycett, *Qaddafi and the Libyan Revolution* (Little, Brown, and Co.,1987); Edward Haley, *Qadhafi and the United States since 1969* (Praeger, 1984); Mansoor El-Kikhia, *Libya's Qaddafi: The Politics of Contradiction* (University Press of Florida, 1997); and Luiz Martinez, *The Libyan Paradox* (Hurst, 2006). A comprehensive tracing of Qaddafi's political career rests in Alison Pargeter, *Libya: The Rise and Fall of Qaddafi* (Yale University Press, 2012).

Mostly dedicated to a sophisticated analysis of Libya's historical foreign policy and regional role is Mary-Jane Deeb's *Libya's Foreign Policy in North Africa* (Westview Press, 1991). An excellent discussion of Qaddafi's foreign relations approach is presented by Ronald Bruce St. John, *Qaddafi's World Design: Libyan Foreign Policy, 1969–1987* (Saqi, 1987). René Lemarchand, *The Green and the Black: Qadhafi's Policies in Africa* (Indiana University Press, 1988) is a more specific discussion of Qaddafi's policies in Africa. Studies of Libya's global strategy during the Qaddafi years include Yahudit Ronen, *Qaddafi's Libya in World Politics* (Lynne Rienner Publishers, 2008), and Tim Niblock, *"Pariah States" and Sanctions in the Middle East: Iraq, Libya, Sudan* (Lynne Rienner Publishers, 2001). More recently, Christopher S. Chivvis, *Toppling Qaddafi: Libya and the Limits of Liberal Intervention* (Cambridge University Press, 2014) and Florence Gaub and Rob Weighill's *The Cauldron: NATO's Campaign in Libya* (Oxford University Press, 2018), are very well-researched and documented narrations of the international community's actions to help rebels in toppling the Qaddafi regime.

Online sources

Like other countries shaken by the Arab Spring, the downfall of a creaky dictatorship carved out space for a media renaissance. An avalanche of new publications and creativity emerged after 2011 in Libya, albeit of varying quality and (like its politics) increasingly fragmented nature. Useful websites covering the latest news and angles include the following: The Libya Herald (www.libyaherald.com/); Libya Al-Mostakbal (www.libya-al-mostakbal.org); Libya 218 (www.218tv.net/); Libyan Express (www.libyanexpress.com/); The Libya Times (www.libyatimes.net/); and Libyan Arab National Agency (www.lana-news.ly/eng). Increasingly, media providers have become aligned with different political figures and blocs. For instance, a pro-Haftar website is Libya Address (www.addresslibya.com/en/), while a supportive publication for some Islamists is Libya Observer (www.libyaobserver.ly/).

Official institutions and observing organizations also maintain many useful websites. See, for instance, Libya's High National Elections Commission (http://hnec.ly/?lang=en); the United Nations Support Mission in Libya (https://unsmil.unmissions.org/); and the United Nations Development Programme's Libya portal (www.ly.undp.org/). Libya Monitor provides a steady fount of business-related and financial information (www.libya-monitor.com/). The Carnegie Endowment for International Peace also has a useful portal with country-level analyses (https://carnegieendowment.org/regions/147).

Please note that URLs may change far more quickly than books can be printed; so if these exact URLs do not work, simply search Google or another engine by the titles of these websites and online resources.

Arab Republic of Egypt

Kira Jumet

INTRODUCTION

A convenient starting point for Egyptian politics is the early twentieth century, as Ottoman rule gave way to British domination. Decades later, a group of military officers staged a coup d'état ousting the Egyptian king, and eventually the British, transforming the political system from a monarchy to an authoritarian semi-presidential republic. From 1952 until 2011, Egypt was ruled by four men consecutively of military background, and following the 2011 uprising, a military junta oversaw the state during the transitional period until 2012, when Egypt's first civilian president was elected to power. In 2014, Egypt returned to military rule when General Abdel Fattah al-Sisi was elected president, following his coup against the elected government led by the Muslim Brotherhood the previous year.

Since then, Egyptian politics has become less pluralistic and more repressive, as a rejuvenated military dictatorship has consolidated power. However, though democratization efforts have failed in the short term, it is undeniable that the 2011 uprising, contextualized as part of the Arab Spring, changed the course of Egyptian politics. With a large youthful population and a constrained economy having created educational and unemployment bottlenecks, the societal landscape may well give rise to future transformational moments of contestation and contentiousness.

Box 7.1 provides vital data for this country.

BOX 7.1 VITAL DATA – ARAB REPUBLIC OF EGYPT

Capital	Cairo
Regime type	Authoritarian (presidential republic)
Head of state	President Abdel Fattah al-Sisi (since 2014)
Head of government	Prime Minister Mustafa Madbouly (since 2018)
Legislative institution	Unicameral parliament, with 596 elected seats (*Majlis al-Nuwaab*, or House of Representatives); an upper chamber will be restored in 2020
Female quota	No
Percentage of seats held by women	14.9%
Major political parties (share of seats in most recent general elections, 2015)	Free Egyptians Party (10.9%), Nation's Future (8.9%), New Wafd (6%), Homeland Defenders (3%), Republican People's Party (2.2%), Conference (2%), Al-Nour (1.8%)
Population	97,553,151
Major ethnic groups	Arab (99%), other (1%)
Major religious groups	Muslim (90%), Christian, mostly Coptic (9.5%), other (0.5%)
GDP per capita	$2,573 ($13,367 at Purchasing Power Parity)
Unemployment rate	11.4%
Youth unemployment rate	32.6%
Major economic industries	Textiles, chemicals (e.g., fertilizers), agricultural produce, petroleum, construction, metals, tourism
Military spending as % GDP	1.8%

HISTORICAL BACKGROUND

Modern Egypt emerged out of the Ottoman Empire. From 1805 to 1848, Ottoman governor Muhammad Ali Pasha administered Egypt as an independent state, devoted his efforts to modernizing the country and upgrading its army and bureaucracy. Because Egypt was a rural country with comparative advantages in cotton and other agricultural production, the economy developed as a raw producer for European markets. His descendants ruled as monarchs, and shared his goal of modernizing Egypt, but did not have the revenue to cover the costs. Successive leaders relied on credit lines from Europe as they pursued grandiose development projects, such as the Suez Canal, and these projects eventually bankrupted the country. The British entered the fold in 1882, using its financial and commercial resources to subordinate the monarchy. The weak extant parliament served as a popular buffer, but also let some elites espouse dissent.

World War One brought down the Ottoman Empire, but Britain continued to support Egypt's monarchy. The regional explosion of Arab Nationalism catalyzed new political parties and anti-colonial sentiments in Cairo, such as the Wafd Party. Parliament began to exert more influence, as elections became the chief means for the population to resist British colonialism and chide the weak king. The British granted Egypt formal independence in 1922, and the political system that emerged during the so-called liberal era (1923–39) was multifaceted. The monarch occasionally conspired with parliament against the British, but he also needed British support to stay in power. Mass movements, such as the Muslim Brotherhood and the Wafd Party, developed paramilitary wings to counterbalance one another. The rate of political assassinations rose, but no relief was possible in an unstable system that blended imperialism, weak executive rule, and an underdeveloped economy controlled by a wealthy elite. By 1952, less than 1 percent of the population owned more than 50 percent of the land, and 44 percent of the people in rural areas were landless – economic inequality that neither monarchy nor British advisers addressed.

As Egypt's domestic conditions deteriorated, world powers recognized the newly established State of Israel in 1948. Many in Egypt, and the Arab world, were concerned that the Israeli state had come at the expense of the Palestinian people. Egypt's army was routed in the resulting war, as were most other Arab armies save the Jordanians. The Egyptian population was disappointed by the military defeat, but those sent to fight in the 1948 war were even more discontented with their country's feckless leadership, lack of economic development, and the concession to continued foreign meddling in its affairs. In July 1952, military officers sympathetic to the anti-colonial resonance and proud message of Arab Nationalism, known as the Free Officers, orchestrated a coup and abolished the 150-year-old monarchy. With King Farouk exiled, the young officers now commanded the state and inherited the legacy of its colonial problems.

Nasserism and state-building
Initially, the military's intervention had ambivalent support from the population. Mohamed Naguib served as the republic's first president, but was

replaced by another officer, Gamal Abdel Nasser, who would become the keystone to the new political order. Experience under the monarchy fueled the officers' desire for a country with greater autonomy and genuine independence, in both economic and diplomatic terms. Yet their opinions for reaching their objective differed. The Free Officers fragmented into two groups centered on Naguib and Nasser. The former favored party and parliamentary politics; the latter preferred militarized control and a stronger political hand. After a struggle between the rival camps, Naguib finally resigned and spent the rest of his life under house arrest or away from public life. Nasser officially became president in 1956, although he informally ruled Egypt from 1954.

Nasser created a repressive authoritarian state whose elaborate security offices penetrated society in ways that demanded obedience for the "sake of a better Egypt." The Muslim Brotherhood, communists, and other political formations with mobilizational potential to resist suffered violent crackdowns. He disbanded parliament and reined in civil society organizations, and his ruling party, the Arab Socialist Union (ASU), became the chief vehicle of political life; in this new single-party state, it was impossible to advance politically or professionally without joining the ASU. Adopting a model of corporatism, Nasser created state-controlled associations to monopolize all activities in key political and economic sectors, such as youth and women's organizations. The state-controlled Egyptian Trade Union Federation (ETUF) emerged to encompass wage-earners and organized labor. Indeed, the only institution that Nasser left somewhat unfettered was the one from which he recruited his most trusted allies – the military. The state also regulated religious discourse by assuming control over Al-Azhar University, the famous center of Sunni Islamic learning; Al-Azhar's Islamic *'ulama* (jurists and experts) became mouthpieces for the tamed and instrumentalized Islam favored by Nasser.

Advocating an ideology of Arab Nationalism and pan-Arabist thought targeting the poor and middle-class alike, and desiring to use the machinery of the rapidly expanding state to fulfill social and economic objectives, Nasser's regime drew polarizing opinions across the Arab world. He issued fiery invectives against Israel, and also doubled down on industrialization to pursue massive state-led developmental programs, from infrastructural projects such as the Aswan High Dam to economic nationalization of foreign assets. As in other late-developing countries in the MENA, the public sector and especially government institutions became major employers for the growing population, while briskly expanding educational opportunities kept pace with urbanization. In July 1956, Nasser demonstrated his nationalist commitments by appropriating the Suez Canal from its British-French management firm; as the canal had been treated as a semi-autonomous British zone even after Egypt's 1922 independence, this bold claim of Egyptian ownership won rapturous applause from the public.

The move offended Western sensibilities, and led Britain, France, and Israel to invade Egypt in a war that was eventually ended through American and Soviet mediation. Nasser and his supporters had now captured the heights of Arab discourse through assertive resistance to foreign hegemony – supplemented, quietly, by securing significant military and diplomatic backing from the Soviet Union. Thereafter, the Arab world experienced a mini-Cold War of its own, as Nasser led an informal coalition of so-called radical republics including Syria and Iraq after 1958, while more conservative and mostly monarchist states like Saudi Arabia and Jordan remained more tightly wedded to Western patronage and protection. The experiment reached its nadir in 1967, when despite Nasser's bombastic promises of victory, Egyptian forces and other Arab armies were destroyed by Israel during the Arab-Israeli conflict in June, alongside the collective losses of the Gaza Strip and West Bank to Israeli occupation. Despite scaling back on his pan-Arabist fervor, Nasser remained popular among many Egyptians until his death by heart attack in 1970.

Autocratic reorientations, Sadat to Nasser

After Nasser, Vice President and fellow Free Officer Anwar Sadat came to power, but he lacked the charisma and anti-colonial credentials of Nasser's near-mythical career. To consolidate his presidency, Sadat reconstituted the political establishment, leading to a professionalization of the military and security apparatus and creating a political field that was far more personalized than Nasser's party-based political structures had been. Realizing that he might become a tool in the hands of the party and the military, Sadat launched a so-called corrective revolution; he arrested powerful politicians and rotated the military's high brass frequently. He dismembered Nasser's ASU in 1976 and in 1978 created a new ruling party, the National Democratic Party (NDP). In addition, he cautiously allowed other parties to be established, such as the Ahrar (Liberal) Party, so long as its leadership remained loyal to him. He also surprised many by relaxing the repression unleashed upon the Muslim Brotherhood by Nasser; some Brotherhood leaders were released from prison, and the Islamist movement was allowed to reconstitute itself, albeit under tight legal and policing constraints.

Like Nasser, however, Sadat was fond of unveiling grand initiatives framed as transformations of Egyptians state and society. He promulgated a new constitution in 1971 and expelled Soviet advisers from Egypt in 1972. He launched a war against Israel in 1973 – another Arab-Israeli conflict that, despite being a military defeat, became a diplomatic victory. He liberalized the economy starting in 1974 in modest ways, signaling that state-led development and government planning may have run its course, and favoring instead a tentative economic policy of *infitah* (opening) through selective market-based reforms. He reopened the Suez Canal in 1975, and visited Jerusalem in 1977; the latter began a diplomatic process with Israel and the United States culminating in the 1978 Camp David negotiations and the 1979 Israeli-Egyptian peace treaty. In the process, Sadat realigned Egypt with the United States and away from the Soviet camp, although this also resulted in Egypt's expulsion from the Arab League and shunning by most fellow Arab leaders. It was readmitted into the League a decade later, in 1989.

Such intrepid autocratic maneuvers bewildered Egypt's political establishment, and instigated public discontent that occasionally defied state repression. For instance, the bread riots of 1977, like others in the Arab world, symbolized public rejection of *infitah*, as hundreds of thousands protested the rising price of bread due to fiscal austerity measures implanted by the World Bank and International Monetary Fund. The peace treaty with Israel especially inflamed popular sentiments, particularly among conservative groups and Islamist activists who saw such a move as capitulation. Weeks after a customary security roundup of dissenters, Islamist army officers assassinated the president during a military parade in October 1981.

Vice President Hosni Mubarak swiftly became the republic's fourth president. After the tumult of the Sadat years, Egypt settled in for a long period of political stagnation. No one could have predicted that Mubarak, an air force officer from a rural background, would go on to become Egypt's longest-serving leader since Muhammad Ali. For nearly 30 years, Mubarak fought to maintain the strong presidential system he had inherited. If there was any notable trend, it could be found in Mubarak's fixation on strengthening the presidency vis-à-vis other potentially autonomous political groups – whether they were part of the opposition or the ruling coalition. His risk-averse style made politics predictable, despite changes in the political landscape. During Mubarak's time in office, more opposition parties emerged, elections became more frequent and more contested, a violent insurgency erupted during the 1990s, and the country existed on the brink of serious economic crisis.

However, Mubarak, the ruling party, and Egypt's primary external patron – the United States – remained unshakable features of politics in Egypt until the Arab Spring.

During the 1980s, Mubarak, who has inherited not just the presidency but also the NDP as his ruling party, oversaw a controlled opening of the political scene, as the regime allowed legal parties such as the Wafd and Liberal parties to contest seats; the Muslim Brotherhood, though still formally outlawed, also began running candidates as independents, and gained representation. However, the Egyptian state excelled in manipulating and constricting electoral participation to prevent opposition from ever gaining too much ground; parliamentary elections in 1984, 1987, 1990, 1995, and 2000 became depressingly predictable. While the 2005 parliamentary elections resulted in large wins for members of the Muslim Brotherhood running as independents, the 2010 contest was the most rigged in Mubarak's tenure as changing rules and swift detentions decimated the opposition playing field. In any case, Mubarak never governed with a parliament that did not have his NDP wielding a supermajority of at least 74 percent.

The domestic security services, operating out of the Interior Ministry, took on a more prominent role as well, with multiple overlapping state security, civil policing, criminal investigations, and civilian monitoring organs. The entire repressive apparatus became bloated, both in personnel and budgets. According to one estimate, the Interior Ministry employed more than 1.5 million people by 2009, a number comparable to the East German Stasi secret police before 1989. The imposition of such stifling coercion to control public opinion is important because Mubarak's NDP never became a party capable of winning grassroots support by developing a platform or issuing policies that attracted everyday people. The party existed as a vehicle to provide patronage in the form of services, jobs, or favors to local strongmen and the citizenry. Indeed, the NDP, which had over two million members by the end of Mubarak's presidency, was an ineffective political wasteland dominated by corrupt personalities rather than institutionalized rules of conduct. Egyptians joked that the NDP was "three lies in three words," as it was neither national, nor democratic, nor a party.

At the same time, Mubarak also directed the country through many potentially destabilizing moments, such as near-bankruptcy in 1990, a violent Salafi insurgency in the 1990s, and – at least in the eyes of security officials – the ever-present threat of the Muslim Brotherhood, which flourished in many urban quarters to provide education, health care, and other state-like goods that the increasingly decrepit Egyptian ministries and government administration could no longer furnish. Activists in civil society began to increasingly mobilize in the 2000s around human rights issues, which the regime suppressed; but they also directed their anger against the United States and the West during periods of regional crisis, such as the Second Intifada in the Palestinian territories in 2000 and later the 2003 Iraq War.

Within the opaque world of Mubarak and his political elite, the Egyptian regime by the late 2000s appeared to be preparing for a hereditary succession. After Syria's Bashar al-Asad succeeded his father in 2000, many commentators speculated that Mubarak's younger son, Gamal, had presidential ambitions. Gamal Mubarak's meteoric rise within the NDP was mirrored by a concomitant shift in policy emphasis by state technocrats in implementing more neoliberal economic policies and embracing market-oriented globalization measures – a position that won Egypt applause by both foreign investors and the International Monetary Fund, which had sponsored structural adjustment programs for the past two decades. Prime Minister Ahmed Nazif after 2004 oversaw the single greatest expansion of neoliberal economic policies, which achieved rapid gains on some metrics (such as more trade and privatization) but also producing rising income inequality and labor unrest. Egypt experienced massive industrial strikes, with over two million workers participating in over 2,100 strikes between 2006 and 2009 alone, most of which were not sanctioned by the official ETUF.

Revolution, democracy, and coup

By January 2011, Egypt was simmering politically. Nearly a decade of crushing neoliberal economic reforms, corruption, and repression led to new protest movements, from the preexisting April 6 Youth Movement and to the new We Are All Khalid Said Facebook group. Inspired by the Tunisian example, Egyptian youth activists – not, pointedly, leaders of the Brotherhood or established legal opposition parties – called for national protests against Mubarak on the national police holiday just days after Ben Ali's deposal. Mubarak's seemingly durable presidency collapsed in just 18 days. In the initial unrest, spontaneous yet organized crowds braved countless canisters of tear gas, buckshot pellets, and water cannons before overwhelming the riot police. Mobilization spread across the country as police stations, where egregious acts of torture and brutality had often occurred, were ransacked. The NDP's national headquarters and several provincial party offices were set ablaze.

After the uprising's fourth day, the army moved tanks and armored personnel carriers into the capital's streets, but military leaders refrained from any interference. Instead, after three speeches by Mubarak failed to empty occupied squares in Cairo and other urban areas, the military issued its first communiqué, recognizing the "legitimate demands" of the protesters. A group of approximately 20 senior generals formed the Supreme Council of Armed Forces (SCAF), and on February 11, 2011, after Vice President Omar Suleiman announced Mubarak's resignation, the SCAF assumed power until June 2012, when Egypt held its first post-uprising presidential elections.

The honeymoon period was short-lived. Revolutionary protesters aimed to ensure that a full democratic transition took place and that presidential elections would be held in a timely manner. However, in the post-Mubarak era, the governing SCAF's primary concern was protecting the military's economic interests and preventing any radical change that would upend its preferred state structures. The generals promised to return to their barracks as soon as a new president was elected, but by the end of 2011, presidential elections still had not taken place despite promises for a new constitution, parliament, and set of laws. As activists feared, the SCAF's delay of the transition allowed old elites from the Mubarak regime to regroup, resulting in renewed protests. The SCAF, along with the security forces, responded with violence; one notable instance the October 2011 Maspero Massacre, when Coptic Christian and some Muslim protesters mobilizing against sectarian violence were killed by security forces. In this manner, the year of the SCAF rule was marred by cycles of contention between revolutionaries and conservative generals. Interestingly, the SCAF implicitly partnered with the Muslim Brotherhood during this time period; though the Brotherhood did not lead the January uprising, it threw its popular weight behind the transition, but hedged all bets by reaching out to military officials.

When parliamentary elections did transpire in the most democratic legislative contest in Egyptian history, Islamists emerged victorious. The multi-round process from November 2011 to January 2012 resulted in the Brotherhood and its allies winning 45 percent of the 508 seats, while the more conservative Salafi Nour bloc won a further 25 percent. Revolutionary candidates affiliated with the youth groups and protest movements during the initial uprising only managed to secure 9 seats, a sign of their poor organization and disarray after Mubarak's toppling. After a June 2012 Supreme Constitutional Court (SCC) decision allowed the SCAF to dissolve that parliament, the Brotherhood watched its candidate, Mohamed Morsi, win the presidency with 52 percent of the vote in the June 2012 presidential elections – the freest also in Egyptian history.

The transition thus far had produced astounding changes, not just in political life where uncertainty reigned but also in everyday social routines and public discussion. Egypt went from having a rubber-stamp parliament and rigged elections, where only around 15 percent of the population voted, to making generational gains in the arts, political creativity, and electoral lawmaking. The Muslim Brotherhood transformed from holding illegal status to winning the biggest bloc in parliament and securing the presidency of the most populous country in the Arab world and MENA region. Morsi's presidency, however, over the next year was typified by growing social tensions and economic degradation. Religion proved to be a major bifurcating point of controversy, as many Egyptians grew suspicious of the Brotherhood and Islamist ideology generally; inversely, many in the Brotherhood saw their group as unfairly maligned, and adopted a siege mentality after having just won democratic elections. Qatar aided the Morsi government, but other countries in the region did not because of their opposition to the Brotherhood and fears that Islamist-led democratization would spread across the region.

The Egyptian state dithered, as many bureaucrats refused to follow Morsi's directives and policies; in response, Morsi and his advisers legislated unilateral declarations to centralize more presidential authority, which further seeded mistrust and suspicions among secular Egyptians about an impending theocracy. Morsi's November 2012 constitutional declaration, for instance, resulted in a rushed referendum on a questionable constitution created by an Islamist-dominated committee that marginalized other voices from Egyptian society, and was met by mass protests from youth activists who called for Morsi to step down. In July 2013, Morsi was ousted in a coup overseen by SCAF member and Defense Minister Abdel Fattah al-Sisi, and putatively supported by a hitherto unknown popular movement called Tamarrud (rebellion) that claimed to have gathered 22 million signatures, but whose origins remain hotly contested today. More certain was that many Egyptians had indeed grown exhausted with the cycles of political disputes, tit-for-tat protests between Islamists and anti-Islamists, and the declining economic situation as manifest in fuel shortages, insecurity, and worsening unemployment.

General Sisi's coup heralded the return of the generals and authoritarian rule, ending Egypt's brief flirtation with democracy. It also inaugurated a bloody fate for the Brotherhood, as Sisi called for a popular mandate to lead a war on terrorism. The Muslim Brothers were the central target of that campaign. Well over a thousand Brotherhood supporters were killed in the six weeks following the coup. Human Rights Watch documented that more than eight hundred people were murdered by security forces during the dispersal of their occupation of Raba'a al-Adawiyya Square in Cairo on August 14, 2013, making this the largest state massacre of its own population since China's Tiananmen Square in 1989. The rest of the Brotherhood's core leaders and activists were arrested (including Morsi), or else driven into exile.

Since then, Egyptian politics has returned to authoritarianism, but with some tragic twists. Sisi won the May 2014 presidential elections with an absurdly high 96.9 percent of the popular vote, and his April 2018 re-election bid with the same landslide margin of victory. Both contests took place in a context of worsening repression that exceeds even the Mubarak period, when the Brotherhood was somewhat tolerated and a façade of institutional pluralism was flaunted for Western observers. Since 2014, the Egyptian government has promulgated an armada of new laws that have suffocated civil society, reduced party diversity, deterred local dissent, suppressed student mobilization, and rolled back virtually all the gains made since the revolution. In the April 2018 elections, for instance, the only other candidate was a Sisi supporter, as all oppositionists ceased campaigning in the months prior under intimidation and violent threats. Unlike Mubarak, Sisi has not maintained even the rhetorical need for a ruling party. Further highlighting worsening repression, in June 2019 former President Morsi suddenly died while on trial. Like many other Muslim Brotherhood leaders who had served in the post-revolutionary government, Morsi had been imprisoned on dubious charges since the July 2013 coup. His passing signified the intentions of the Sisi dictatorship to eradicate all traces of Egypt's brief democratic breakthrough.

Two clear winners seem to be firstly technocrats, whom the Sisi regime has selectively backed in advancing a costly vision of economic revamping through high-tech modernization and private-sector growth, albeit with financial resources that Egypt does not possess and institutional mechanisms that the state-led economy has never possessed. The other is the military, which remains an entrenched actor with a vast sector of economic assets, financial accounts, and political supporters. So long as Sisi retains military backing, much as past autocrats did, his rule will be assured, at least from elite competition. Meanwhile, Egyptian society ranks as the largest Arab national population, with its nearly 100 million people suffering decades of underdevelopment and broken political promises.

SOCIAL AND ECONOMIC ENVIRONMENT

Egypt is located in the northeast corner of the African continent, at the crossroads of the Maghrib and Mashriq. Its neighbors are Libya, Israel, Palestine, Jordan, Saudi Arabia, and Sudan (Map 7.1). Its populational centerpiece is Cairo, a massive urban area encompassing nearly 20 million people. The city is well-known not only for its political centrality to Egypt but also for its storied history and ancient lineage, having been the seat of numerous dynasties and empires. Its architecture is a hodgepodge of old and new, with major monuments – like the Great Mosque of Muhammad Ali Pasha, an Ottoman-era construction – punctuating many areas (Photo 7.1).

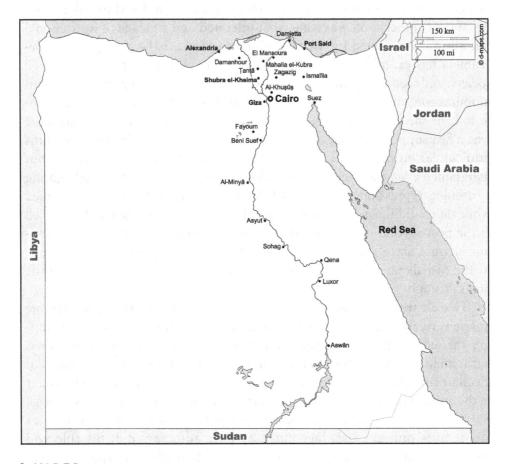

MAP 7.1
Arab Republic of Egypt. Major water bodies, rivers, and cities shown.

Source: D-Maps.

PHOTO 7.1
Great Mosque of Muhammad Ali Pasha in Cairo

Source: Pixabay. Public domain.

The Mediterranean lies to its north, and the Red Sea to its east. The world's longest river, the Nile, finishes its nearly 6,000-mile journey by emptying into the Mediterranean through Egypt. The Nile creates some of the most nutrient-rich soil in the world, and 95 percent of the country's approximately 100 million people live along its narrow banks. Egypt also hosts the Suez Canal, which remains strategically important because it connects the Mediterranean Sea and the Red Sea, thereby offering European ships a direct route to the Indian Ocean. The government charges a hefty toll on every ship transiting through the canal; in 2018, Egypt raised a record $5.6 billion in tolls and fees. In 2014, President Sisi initiated the Suez Canal Corridor Area Project, which would expand the zone and make it even more financially lucrative. On the other side of the canal is the sparsely populated Sinai Peninsula.

Population and social trends

Egypt has a fairly homogenous population. Most citizens identify themselves as distinctly Egyptian, although there are Bedouin communities in areas such as Sinai which are less attached to a particularly national Egyptian identity. Almost all Egyptians speak Arabic, with small dialectical differences between Cairo and the rest of the country. Near the Libyan border resides Egypt's very small Tamazight (Berber) population. Around 90 percent of Egyptians adhere to Sunni Islam, while the other 10 percent comprise mostly Christian denominations, of which the largest is the Coptic Church. There are a handful of other tiny sectarian minorities, including the Baha'i.

Like other large MENA countries, Egypt's demography also exhibits a youth bulge. Nearly 34 percent of Egyptians are under the age of 15, and well over half under the age of 30. Egyptian youth literacy exceeds 88 percent, but youth unemployment is nearly 33 percent – far higher than the nominal 11.4 percent overall jobless rate reported last in 2018. Indeed, analysts believe Egypt's youth population was particularly disgruntled prior to the 2011 revolution due to economic deprivation; relatively well-educated but unable to find viable jobs in either the small private sector or else swollen public sector, Egyptian teenagers and millennials often suffer worse prospects for mobility than their parents. For young Egyptian men, who are unable to marry until they first gain employment and secondly have funds to purchase a home, such "waithood," as sociologists term it, can be extremely burdensome.

Egyptian women have also played a prominent role in the country's political scene, from Huda Sha'arawi, an Egyptian feminist from the early twentieth century, to Maya Morsi, a political scientist and current president of the country's National Council for Women. During the January revolution, many female activists helped mobilize protesters by posting videos and messages on social media, acting as street coordinators, and pioneering new forms of contentious resistance. Thereafter, women played a significant role in the revolutionary process, visibility that in turn rendered them a target of violence and sexual assault from multiple perpetrators, including security forces. During 2011 under the SCAF, for instance, the Egyptian military arrested many female protesters and subjected them to humiliating virginity tests. This underscores a deeper problem of patriarchy and gender norms, as most Egyptian women report being subjected to sexual harassment at some point in their lives.

Despite the atmosphere of political repression under the Sisi regime, Egyptian women today remain active in battling sexual harassment and transforming gender inequities through new activist networks, online reporting forums, moral shaming platforms, and direct political action. Among the recent innovations are HARASSmap, which allows Egyptian women to report sexual harassment hotspots in real-time, and Operation Anti-Sexual Harassment, a new activist group that monitored major protests and religious festivals. While women do hold positions of political prominence, as they comprise about 15 percent of the current parliament, state protections still fall short. Unlike some other MENA countries, there is no national female quota to guarantee women representation in parliament, for instance.

For many Egyptians, political participation has been conditioned by the authoritarian state structure since 1952. While ruling parties have come and gone, and civil society suffered cycles of mild toleration followed by draconian restrictions, the trajectory of Islamism is useful to understanding everyday approaches to politics. Islamism, as defined by the Muslim Brotherhood, was revived during Sadat's presidency. Encouraged by Sadat to counterbalance residual Nasserist elements, Islamists penetrated many quasi-state institutions and many sectors of civil society, resulting in highly polarizing reactions: some Egyptians became ardent supporters of this new current promising social and political renewal through religion, while others rejected Islamist ideology and spoke darkly of their theocratic aspirations. Islamist or otherwise, though, Egyptians have been unable to halt the drift of the political system towards more closed forms of authoritarianism since the July 2013 military coup. In February 2019, President Sisi floated a proposal to extend presidential term limits and thus extend his power; he may theoretically remain leader until 2034.

Economic conditions

Egypt's economic conditions today represent the product of many decades of state-led economic planning that only began to change course late in its developmental arc. Its origins begin with Nasser and the Free Officers, who inherited an underdeveloped, agrarian economy in 1952 that had been structured to serve Europe's markets. Given this narrow foundation, Nasser initiated pumped funds into new programs to achieve the dual goals of industrializing Egypt and consolidating the Free Officers' regime. Nasser accomplished his objectives through state intervention and economic populism, which gained support from segments of the population that benefited from the policies. Indeed, Egypt epitomized the authoritarian social contract residing at the heart of the post-colonial MENA political economy, in which nondemocratic rulers provided material benefits and security in return for political obedience and support.

Thus in the 1950s, the Egyptian state began to nationalize privately owned assets, which it then redistributed across society. The state undertook land reform, seizing land from large agriculturalists and giving small lots to peasant farmers. It also seized factories to eliminate uncontrollable political rivals. These assets gave the state considerable revenue, which it used to provide social benefits such as universal health care, university education, and guaranteed state employment for graduates. The benefits by the 1960s were apparent: the population became healthier, schools and universities were packed, and public-sector employment ballooned as joblessness plummeted. Despite the regime's repressive tendencies, many Egyptians experienced unprecedented upward social mobility. In the process, the Egyptian state fused political and economic considerations into one indistinguishable entity.

By the end of the 1960s, however, the internal tensions and contradictions of Nasser's state-led model had produced a large national debt, a chronic imbalance of loan payments, and a capital-accumulation crisis. Attacking the owners of capital raised public cheers, but it also suppressed domestic businesses and deterred foreign investment. Though it could draw upon two sources of rentier income – Suez Canal revenues, and modest offshore crude oil fields in the Gulf of Suez – the government was hard-pressed to keep pace with a growing population and the ceiling of growth that inevitably came to inefficient state-owned industries in sectors like textiles and steel. In addition, Egypt's ongoing conflict with Israel and Nasser's bid to lead the Arab world meant the government was also undertaking substantial military expenditures.

For his part, Sadat drastically altered Egypt's economic policies and ushered in a post-populist era, but his macroeconomic policies were no more effective than Nasser's. Rather than focus on domestic considerations or painful economic reforms, Sadat used Egypt's economy as a geostrategic tool to elevate his presidency on the international stage, for instance securing billions of dollars of guaranteed American foreign aid every year following the Camp David peace accords. Sadat's tepid economic liberalization under the moniker of *infitah* resulted in significant societal pushback, as in the 1977 bread riots, but also gained support in the United States and Western backers eager to break the Soviet near-monopoly on selling arms to Egypt and its sprawling military. Foreign debt grew sharply through the 1970s, as the retraction of some state protections exposed local industries to an onslaught of foreign commodities. Crony capitalists grew wealthy while the poorer segments of society grew more impoverished. The cost of living increased, currency lost some of its value, and the service sector outgrew the industrial sector. Egypt became for the first time a net importer of grain.

Mubarak's economic policies did more than Sadat in reconfiguring the pillars of national productivity, but were still plagued by corruption and cronyism. Repeated loans from the International Monetary Fund came with varying austerity conditions that the Mubarak government freely rejected when its tenets, from downsizing the public sector with its massive payrolls to cutting more food and fuel subsidies, would have been too politically costly. On the other hand, the government during the 1990s also enacted plainly neoliberal economic reforms to improve overall competitiveness, such as reversing outdated land tenant laws, restricting union activity and labor rights, and privatizing some public companies. Egypt's textile industry lost nearly half its jobs as a result, and economic growth was uneven. In the 2000s, Gamal Mubarak and his generation of technocrats went further in implementing market-oriented initiatives by selectively funneling capital to export-oriented sectors while largely neglecting labor-intensive ones, all in the hope of generating rapid overall growth.

There was some success; Egypt regularly produced a 7 percent annual growth rate and was routinely named as one of the World Bank's top reformers from 2005 to 2010. Yet as in other countries, trickle-down economics did not produce a rising tide of prosperity for all, as unemployment and poverty remained unmanageable and income inequality grew. The wave of labor unrest and worker strikes in the late 2000s reflected the inability of either the government or firms to make their wages keep pace with inflation and rising living costs. The situation was not helped by the revolution, as major economic activity stopped for several months in 2011. The economy contracted by 4.2 percent during the first quarter off that year, and Egypt experienced its highest level of unemployment in over a decade.

Since then, the Egyptian government under Morsi and then Sisi has exhibited a common problem: it simply has insufficient revenue to execute its bombastic programs to create jobs, stimulate the private sector, encourage new industry, reduce widespread poverty, and upgrade deteriorating infrastructure. One in three Egyptian youths remain unemployed. One saving grace has been a steady flow of foreign aid from Egypt's primary allies in the MENA; Saudi Arabia, Kuwait, and the United Arab Emirates have contributed unprecedented dollops of aid. Indeed, from 2011 through 2019, economists estimate that the Gulf kingdoms have provided $92 billion in various support mechanisms, from cash grants and investment guarantees to free oil and other assistance – the greatest one-way flow of rentier resources in regional history.

Today, the Egyptian economy suffers from several structural problems. One is inefficiency and competitiveness, the legacy of state-led development. The agricultural sector, for instance, still contributes nearly 12 percent of the GDP, but uneven technology and increasing drought means that the country is still reliant on importing its food supply, while only its cotton production remains globally competitive. The second is the military, which has not only colossal political influence but also retains financial and economic assets, including companies and real estate, which cannot be touched in any transformational program. Third, crony capitalism still abounds; between Mubarak and Sisi, business moguls and investors who have contributed their resources and loyalties to the presidential circle have secured outlandish contracts and licenses to operate. Official support for more grassroots entrepreneurship and small-scale economic enterprises languishes, with little credit available from most banks.

Finally, popular demands for economic justice and new opportunities run counter to government accession to neoliberal policies. In November 2016, the regime shocked many by allowing the national currency, the Egyptian pound, to float freely in a bid to improve its trade imbalance, reduce cash shortages, and lure foreign investment. In the short term, such a monetary maneuver eliminated a core plank of the state-led development model and increased the cost of all imported goods, thereby also fueling some inflation and hoarding. The regime has also cut subsidies to energy and consumables, precluding popular protests only with promises to restore them or else warning dissenters of dire consequences. Yet Sisi has also attracted global attention for extravagant plans for industrial and urban megaprojects, from the expansion of the Suez Canal to a proposed new capital city – endeavors requiring mammoth funding that must come from either foreign investments or else the government's cash-strapped treasury.

POLITICAL STRUCTURES

After the 1952 military takeover, Egypt's new elites reshaped the state's political structure. Although constitutions and laws dictated how state institutions should operate, the reality was often quite different in practice. Nevertheless, authoritarian governance did operate in distinctive, predictable ways. Nasser, Sadat, and Mubarak maintained and expanded presidential authority vis-à-vis other institutions, which ensured that the president had autonomy to act while the parliament and judiciary were constrained. The Egyptian political system was not without institutionalized competition or debate, but various organs – legislative bodies, courts, councils, advisers, and committees – were only allowed to contest each other in limited ways. Formal institutions that have existed since 1952 generally cannot act without the president's blessing. Today, for instance, the Egyptian government is formally headed by a prime minister, Mustafa Madbouly, who has only marginal autonomy and largely serves to carry out presidential imperatives.

Prior to the January 2011 revolution, the Egyptian legislature functioned as a bicameral entity split between an elected lower house, the People's Assembly, and a semi-appointed upper house, the Shura Council. However, the legislature always has had circumscribed authority, and was dominated by the ruling NDP under Sadat and Mubarak. The parliament was dismissed during the revolution, and so the 2011–12 elections were supposed to signal a fresh start for a more pluralized elected body. It was in that assembly that the Brotherhood won nearly 38 percent of the ballots cast. The new parliament, in turn, appointed a 100-member Constituent Assembly to draft a new constitution, which produced a controversial document in late 2012; the constitution was superseded by the 2014 constitution, which was drafted under the Sisi regime in fall 2013. Both are based somewhat on the 1971 constitution, but the 2014 version gives more substantial authority and autonomy to the military. The 2014 constitution notably abolished the Shura Council, turning parliament into a unicameral body. However, a 2019 constitutional referendum successfully restored the Shura Council, which will operate once more after the 2020 general elections. Regardless of these changes, the Egyptian parliament in its current form has little policymaking prerogatives; the presidential office commands the regime and state.

Egypt's judiciary has been the state institution that has given rise to considerable and often unpredictable contestation between different ideas since the 1950s. Courts established in the colonial era became the sites where people challenged colonial authorities. In the process, Egyptians gained legal training and judges became professionalized. Nasser largely left the judiciary to its own devices, but in 1969, not long before his death, he purged the judiciary of political opposition. When Sadat committed himself to the rule of law, he brought experienced judges back to the bench. The judiciary's independence thus became a sticking point for Mubarak. He abided by all SCC rulings, as the SCC was the only institution that ruled on constitutional issues, but he was selective in implementation of rulings from the state administrative and high courts. Mubarak also relied on martial law regulations to try opponents and override legal protections with specially designated courts. He occasionally used military trials for civilians.

With respect to opposition politics, no organized movement was ever capable of toppling Egypt's autocratic regimes after the 1950s. The Egyptian revolution in 2011 succeeded not due to any organized civil society group or elite-led movement, but rather due to spontaneous and sustained protests by youth activists. This was much like the bread riots of the late Sadat period, in which social unrest and political rage manifest not through organized civic channels but rather popular expressions of rebellion, against which the state had little response apart from repression. That said, legal opposition parties, civil society organizations, and the region's largest Islamist movement have always set Egypt's political and social arena apart from other MENA countries.

Egypt's largest Islamist group, the Muslim Brotherhood, is the oldest such movement in the Arab world. Founded in 1928 by Hassan al-Banna, the Brotherhood began as a religious and social movement as influenced by the ideas of Islamic reformers, such as Jamal al-Din al-Afghani and Mohammed 'Abduh. The Muslim Brotherhood repudiated Western influence in the region and the dominance of European colonial powers. Sensing a threat to its power, in 1948 the monarchist state ordered the group's dissolution. In retaliation, later that year members of the Brotherhood assassinated the prime minister; in 1949, the government responded by assassinating al-Banna. Since then, Egyptian leaders have fluctuated between repressing and accommodating the Brotherhood. Nasser's suppression contrasted with Sadat's opening and Mubarak's wary toleration; Sisi's crackdown has returned the cycle to its original position. By the 1980s, the Muslim Brotherhood had emerged as the largest challenger to the Egyptian regime, wielding an impressive base of disciplined cadres, national activists, financial networks, and a spiritual leadership. The group's appeal stemmed from its messaging, its provision of social services to both the poor and middle classes, and the weaknesses of existing secular and liberal political parties.

Yet the Brotherhood never convinced most Egyptians to allay their suspicions about its long-term intensions regarding the nature of Egyptian political order and the role of religion in politics and society. The ideological adamancy and independent appeal of Islamism differed greatly from the tamer face of official Islam, as espoused by Al-Azhar University and government ministries who sought to control religious discourse. Morsi's unspectacular year as president, which apart from secularist opposition was distinguished by many unsuccessful economic proposals, did not help matters. Following the July 2013 coup, much of the Brotherhood was dismantled. Sisi's regime confiscated the group's assets and labeled the organization as terrorist. Today its leadership is either imprisoned or living in exile abroad, and it is difficult to imagine when or whether it would be able to reconstitute its pre-coup form.

Given that the modern Egyptian republic was established by a coup in 1952, it is unsurprising that the armed forces still constitute the regime's spine. During Nasser's presidency, over a third of all cabinet ministers were from the military. This number decreased to 20 percent under Sadat and 8 percent under Mubarak. However, military officers under Mubarak remained the key appointees in crucial provinces, and the armed forces gained monopolistic market shares in some sectors of the economy. While the military's companies were initially dominant in the public sector, they can now be found in the private sector and in public-private joint ventures; at times they act as local representatives for foreign investors. The military's companies produce everything from staples, such as olive oil and bread, to heavy industrial items, such as tanks. The military also remains in charge of the petrochemical sector, and is Egypt's largest landowner.

The 2011 uprising provided the military with the opportunity to intervene and eliminate its political and economic competitors, such as Gamal Mubarak's technocrats, some of whom were rumored to openly question the wisdom of allowing the military to retain its inefficient and uncompetitive industrial enterprises. The uprising also allowed the SCAF to influence the terms and sequence of the transition. The 2013 military coup and Sisi's subsequent election permitted the military to maintain its interests and consolidate its position vis-à-vis civilian institutions.

POLITICAL DYNAMICS

Egypt's central political dynamics are products of how its presidents and ruling regimes have designed and manipulated the political arena, with some of the most important relationships – such as advising and consultative roles, and the distribution of patronage to supporters – hidden behind the scenes. Historically, from the 1950s to the current day, one general pattern remains constant: when the state loosens political restrictions, cooperation between the citizens and polity improves. When state elites enforce illiberal policies or tighten the reins on organizational and political activities, opposition fragmentation occurs in parallel to increased state repression of civil society.

These autocratic practices have never eradicated political contestation or opposition challenges, even today, but they have often atomized society. What is unprecedented today is the degree to which repressive institutions have utilized new technologies, such as Internet monitoring tools and sophisticated legal tactics, to surveil social media, track down critics, penetrate civic circles, intimidate political dissidents, and cow opponents into quietism.

Egypt has held regular elections since the days of Sadat, though none until the Arab Spring passed basic democratic thresholds for being free, fair, and competitive. Rather, elections have helped expose minor currents in opposition movements while revealing the extent to which dominant parties have successfully reached out to their clients and supporters. Under Mubarak, elections proliferated. Parliamentary elections occurred in 1984, 1987, 1990, 1995, 2000, 2005, and 2010. Mubarak was also subject to popular referenda in 1981, 1987, 1993, and 1999, before competing in a multicandidate direct election in 2005. Based upon its patronage networks and a coherent elite base, the NDP won 87 percent of seats in the 1984 parliamentary election and 79 percent in the 1987 election. As Mubarak became more powerful, the NDP's parliamentary majority increased to 90 percent in 1990 and 95 percent in 1995. When the SCC in 2000 ruled that judicial supervision of elections was constitutionally mandated, the NDP's majority slipped to 88 percent. In 2005, the Muslim Brotherhood shocked the establishment by winning 20 percent of the seats in parliament, though this was due mainly to miscalculations by the NDP. The final parliamentary election under Mubarak, in 2010, was the most flagrantly rigged and returned a 94 percent NDP majority.

Elections during 2011–12 were vastly different, as they allowed Egyptians to cast ballots in far more democratic environs. Following Mubarak's overthrow, between February 2011 and Morsi's election in June 2012, Egyptians had numerous opportunities to vote, from constitutional referenda to legislative and executive elections. For the first time, there was not a dominant ruling party. As a consequence, elections were more representative, despite the organizational advantages of the Muslim Brotherhood and state-affiliated politicians. Turnout proved to be high, signifying a higher degree of citizen buy-in. The first post-revolutionary parliamentary elections in 2011 witnessed a nearly 55 percent turnout rate, whereas human rights monitors estimated actual turnout for the fraudulent 2010 contest was a paltry 10–15 percent. The high turnout trend was repeated during the presidential elections of June 2012, when over 52 percent turned out in what was a close second-round vote between Ahmed Shafiq, a former military officer linked to the previous regime, and Mohamed Morsi of the Muslim Brotherhood. Morsi won just over 51 percent of the valid ballots cast. However, under the Sisi regime, both parliamentary and presidential elections have reverted to being empty spectacles, with some modest competition between elites but little real hope for democratic opposition to make inroads. Sisi's margins of victory in 2014 and 2018, around 97 percent, indicate this hollowness.

Within civil society, Egypt has enjoyed a long tradition of voluntary organizations stretching back to the Ottoman period. While Egypt is the largest Arab country, it also has the most robust tradition of civil society organizations. Between 1923 and 1952, Egyptian activists in all fields – workers, students, women, liberals, and nationalists – created new groups and clubs devoted to their interests. Nasser rolled back this pluralism under his autocratic fist, with Law 32 of 1964 designed to constrict all non-state entities. State-controlled organizations like ETUF emerged to take control of entire societal sectors, such as workers and students. Egyptian civil society made something of a comeback in the 1980s and 1990s however, as Mubarak relaxed some restrictions. The Brotherhood was responsible for some new initiatives, but in other areas professional syndicates and civic associations, such as the Egyptian Engineers' Syndicate, became leading incubators for democratic politics by entertaining vibrant internal debate and questioning regime decisions. Over 14,000 civil society organizations reportedly operated in Egypt during the 2000s, despite Mubarak's passing of Law 84 of 2002, which made organizational registration more difficult and gave the state authority over all foreign funding.

Another dynamic that has been explosive at times is the growing sectarian dimension of Egyptian politics. While Egypt is relatively an ethnically homogenous country with a majority Muslim population, up to 10 percent of the population is Christian, most of whom are Copts. The Coptic Church has traditionally avoided conflict with the state, but sectarian clashes have increased since the revolution despite memorable displays of Christian-Muslim unity during the January protests, and exhortations from Al-Azhar's Islamic authorities for intercommunal peace. In some neighborhoods, rumors and feuds have led to deadly clashes, the destruction of churches, and damage to property. The October 2011 Maspero Massacre is one of the deadliest examples. Rather than systematically promoting or eliminating discrimination, the state haphazardly encourages it by not using the legal system to punish criminal behavior, and instead promoting reconciliation through informal means.

Terrorism plays an important role in shaping public perceptions of political performance; in the 1990s, for instance, the Mubarak regime used a violent Islamist insurgency to win support for harsh security measures. Egypt under Sisi has merited considerable attention from Salafi groups and violent extremists. In the 2010s, Egypt suffered a number of attacks on tourist resorts, churches, buses, planes, and military checkpoints that have killed hundreds of civilians and troops. The Islamic State of Iraq and Syria (ISIS) claimed responsibility for several such strikes after 2012, and its local recruitment networks helped thousands of young Egyptians travel to Syria and become radicalized. Egyptian army units continue to hunt and battle Salafi militants in remote areas.

FOREIGN POLICY

Egypt is the largest Arab country by population and has long occupied a central place in terms of international powers desiring good relations with the Arab world. Moreover, the Suez Canal provides the shortest distance for shipping goods and commodities between Asia and Europe, which makes the country's stability a high priority for all regional powers and the West. The American military has used the canal for its various wars in Iraq over the past several decades.

During the Cold War, Egypt under Nasser tried to remain nonaligned, and Nasser's strategy was to play one superpower against the other. Essentially, whichever power attached the fewest strings to its diplomatic support and aid could rely on Egypt's friendship. The Soviets proved to be far more amenable to Nasser's insistence on non-conditionality. Thus, the Soviet Union provided extensive assistance in constructing the Aswan High Dam, as well as arms and military experts, in exchange for military cooperation. Under Nasser and Sadat, Egypt needed such foreign assistance because of its ongoing conflicts with Israel, with conflicts in 1948, 1956, and 1967 punctuating its wartime footing.

Nasser also used pan-Arabism to project Egyptian power in the region. The Arab League, designed to be an instrument for regional unity, was symbolically founded in 1945 in Cairo, and during the Nasserist era was frequently used by Egypt to issue strong statements and initiatives regarding Israel and the West. On a discursive level, Nasser's speeches, which invoked themes of Arab independence, pride, and unity, resonated deeply in a region whose inhabitants believed they lived in a colonial playground. The leaders of the other Arab republics, such as Iraq, Syria, Tunisia, Algeria, and Libya, emulated such imagery. In fact, in 1958 Syrian leaders successfully appealed to Nasser to merge Syria and Egypt into what was the first formal attempt at a pan-Arab state, the United Arab Republic; however, internal squabbles and disagreements over confederal division scuttled the short-lived experiment in 1961. Nasser's advocacy of a nonaligned pan-Arabism also shaped Egypt's openness to receiving and interaction with revolutionary movements in other developing countries; for instance, he firmly backed Che Guevara's militancy in Latin America.

When Sadat became president in 1970, a pan-Arab foreign policy was no longer possible. This also marked the slow decline of the Arab League as a vessel of Arab diplomatic cohesion. Still reeling from the humiliating 1967 defeat by Israel, Nasser had begun the process of dismantling Arabism as the pillar of Egypt's foreign policy. Sadat chose to shift to an "Egypt First" posture, and tried approaching both the United States and Israel about regaining Egypt's occupied Sinai lands. Unsuccessful, Sadat drove forward the 1973 war as his opening salvo, followed by post-war negotiations and an about-face that resulted in the 1979 peace treaty with Israel. Through that, Egypt regained the Sinai Peninsula, as well as annual American commitments of over two billion dollars in combined economic and military aid. That aid faucet continues to flow today, uninterrupted even during the tumult of the past decade. Since Camp David through 2018, in fact, the United States delivered well over $80 billion in foreign assistance to Cairo, making Egypt the second highest recipient of American aid monies in the world after Israel.

Egypt's realignment to become an American client during the 1970s fundamentally changed the balance of power in the MENA. It gave the United States three core allies: Saudi Arabia with its oil, Israel with its military, and Egypt with its large population and strategic location. If pan-Arabism's demise was not already apparent, the peace treaty with Israel became its death knell, not least as it resulted in Egypt's expulsion from the Arab League. Yet while the United States may have bought Egypt's president, but it did not own Egyptians – a state of affairs that continued under Mubarak and remains today under President Sisi. Egypt's regimes since Mubarak have remained resolutely pro-American, even as most Egyptians in public opinion surveys express anti-American attitudes. Egypt's participation with the United States during the global war on terror as part of the international renditions and torture program remains a sore point of contention.

Inversely, despite reports of undeniable human rights abuses and crackdowns on American-funded civil society organizations, the United States has almost never conditionalized its support and foreign aid upon Egyptian political reform, remaining a staunch backer. In fact, President Barack Obama chose Cairo as the city in which to deliver a major speech to the Arab world in 2009, and his administration waited considerably until choosing to back the incipient revolution in 2011; it did not call for Mubarak's ousting until virtually the end of the protest wave. It likewise supported the SCAF-led transition and accepted President Morsi's election, given that even an Islamist government was unwilling to overturn the key geopolitical tenets of American grand strategy, including peaceful ties with Israel and ongoing strategic collaboration. While the Obama administration briefly froze aid following the August 2013 massacre in Raba'a Square in Cairo, it did not take long for relations to resume as normal. The Trump administration, for its part, has exhibited even less interest in human rights and democratic reform issues, simply perpetuating the Egyptian-American alliance.

Part of Egypt's pragmatically pro-Western strategy in recent years has been orientation towards the Gulf, in particular Saudi Arabia, which remains a vital aid donor and has eclipsed Egypt as the most geopolitically influential Arab state. Aligning itself with its foreign patrons, the Sisi regime has heartily backed Saudi-led initiatives against Iran, and backed the so-called "deal of the century" strongly pushed by the United States under the Trump administration. That shift in alliance-making has resulted in some strange confrontations, such as the Sisi regime participating in the June 2017 economic blockade of Qatar, which had previously broken ranks in the Gulf kingdoms to support the Muslim Brotherhood-led government of President Morsi. One analyst estimates that Qatar provided $8 billion in emergency funding to the Morsi government during 2012–13. Yet in the week following the July 2013 coup, signifying a shared enmity to the Muslim Brotherhood and democracy, Saudi Arabia, Kuwait, and the UAE provided $12 billion of their own funding. Egypt also championed the Saudi-led intervention and war in Yemen after 2015. Tethered increasingly to the West and the Gulf, the Sisi regime has marked its geopolitical lines in the regional sands.

FUTURE PROSPECTS

The Arab Spring brought both change and continuity to Egypt. The dramatic revolution and upsurge in contentious politics nearly a decade ago contrasts starkly with images of repressive authoritarianism that characterizes the Egyptian state today. Yet if there is one major weakness, it is the economy. Sisi has yet to bring economic prosperity despite continuing support from Gulf aid donors and multilateral financial institutions. Fiscal austerity, widespread unemployment, youth immobility, and structurally constrained growth require the attention of the government in the coming years, not least because the same problems that existed before the Arab Spring are still present now. Too many Egyptians do not feel fulfilled and satisfied by the institutional rules and material opportunities presented by the current political order; and in the face of repression, the only option is to rebel.

Even if the Sisi regime can resolve its most pressing problems of underdevelopment and job creation, the potentiality also persists of new social mobilization. As the Arab Spring indicated, even extensive repression and fear cannot fully eliminate pockets of dissent and subversion, and social media alongside new strategies of organization have made today's youth activists adept at their craft. Protests have not been curbed fully, an example of which was the 2016 demonstration against the government's decision to gift the Egyptian islands of Tiran and Sanafir in the Red Sea to Saudi Arabia. The maintenance of autocratic supremacy may prove increasingly difficult, especially if the next elections prove no more competitive than the last farcical exercises.

FURTHER READING

An excellent reader into modern Egypt is Bruce K. Rutherford and Jeannie Sowers, *Modern Egypt: What Everyone Needs to Know* (Oxford University Press, 2018). Another accessible introduction is Tarek Osman, *Egypt on the Brink: From Nasser to the Muslim Brotherhood* (Yale University Press, 2013).

More intricate histories of modern Egypt and its colonial state formation include Jacques Berque, *Egypt: Imperialism and Revolution* (Praeger, 1972); Afaf Lutfi Sayyid-Marsot, *A History of Egypt: From the Arab Conquest to the Present*, 2nd ed. (Cambridge University Press, 2007); Joel Beinin and Zachary Lockman, *Workers on the Nile: Nationalism, Communism, Islam and the Egyptian Working Class, 1882–1954* (Princeton University Press, 1988); Khaled Fahmy, *All the Pasha's Men: Mehmed Ali, His Army, and the Making of Modern Egypt* (Cambridge University Press, 1998); Timothy Mitchell, *Colonizing Egypt* (University of California Press, 1991); and Ahmed Abdalla, *The Student Movement and National Politics in Egypt, 1923–1973* (American University in Cairo Press, 2009).

On state formation and the post-1952 developments from Nasser to Mubarak, scholars have produced a veritable library of historical and political analysis. The most notable entries are: Raymond Baker, *Egypt's Uncertain Revolution under Nasser and Sadat* (Harvard University Press, 1978); John Waterbury, *The Egypt of Nasser and Sadat: The Political Economy of Two Regimes* (Princeton University Press, 1983); Raymond Hinnebusch, *Egyptian Politics under Sadat: The Post-Populist Development of an Authoritarian-Modernizing State* (Cambridge University Press, 1985); Joel Gordon, *Nasser's Blessed Movement: Egypt's Free Officers and the July Revolution* (Oxford University Press, 1992); Robert Springborg, *Mubarak's Egypt: Fragmentation of the Political Order* (Westview Press, 1989); Maye Kassem, *Egyptian Politics: The Dynamics of Authoritarian Rule* (Lynne Rienner Publishers, 2004); Bruce Rutherford, *Egypt after Mubarak: Liberalism, Islam, and Democracy* (Princeton

University Press, 2008); Tamir Moustafa, *The Struggle for Constitutional Power: Law, Politics, and Economic Development in Egypt* (Cambridge University Press, 2009); Joshua Stacher, *Adaptable Autocrats: Regime Power in Egypt and Syria* (Stanford University Press, 2012); and Yoram Meital, *Revolutionary Justice: Special Courts and the Formation of Republican Egypt* (Oxford University Press, 2017). On the US-Egyptian relationship, see Jason Brownlee, *Democracy Prevention: The Politics of the US-Egyptian Alliance* (Cambridge University Press, 2012).

The Arab Spring and Egyptian revolution have created a cottage industry of literature seeking to explain why popular mobilization succeeded, and how the transition devolved into military authoritarianism. Among the best works are Steven A. Cook, *The Struggle for Egypt: From Nasser to Tahrir Square* (Oxford University Press, 2011); Jeannie Sowers and Chris Toensing, eds., *The Journey to Tahrir: Revolution, Protest, and Social Change in Egypt* (Verso, 2012); Hazem Kandil, *Soldiers, Spies, and Statesmen: Egypt's Road to Revolt* (Verso, 2012); Nadina Sika, *Youth Activism and Contentious Politics in Egypt: Dynamics of Continuity and Change* (Cambridge University Press, 2017); Neil Ketchley, *Egypt in a Time of Revolt: Contentious Politics and the Arab Spring* (Cambridge University Press, 2017); Nermin Allam, *Women and the Egyptian Revolution: Engagement and Activism during the 2011 Arab Uprisings* (Cambridge University Press, 2018); and Kira D. Jumet, *Contesting the Repressive State: Why Ordinary Egyptians Protested during the Arab Spring* (Oxford University Press, 2017); H.A. Hellyer, *A Revolution Undone: Egypt's Road beyond Revolt* (Oxford University Press, 2017); and M. Cherif Bassiouni, *Chronicles of the Egyptian Revolution and Its Aftermath, 2011–2016* (Cambridge University Press, 2017).

The Egyptian economy and the politics of its underdevelopment have amassed many excellent studies. Analyses of its structural deficits include Khalid Ikram, *The Political Economy of Reforms in Egypt: Issues and Policymaking since 1952* (American University of Cairo Press, 2018) and Naiem Sherbiny and Omaima Hatem, *State and Entrepreneurs in Egypt: Economic Development since 1805* (Palgrave Macmillan, 2015). Recent studies on specific aspects of Egyptian financing, debt, migration, and reform include Robert Vitalis, *When Capitalists Collide: Business Conflict and the End of Empire in Egypt* (University of California Press, 1995); Timothy Mitchell, *Rule of Experts: Egypt, Techno-Politics, Modernity* (University of California Press, 2002); Samer Soliman, *The Autumn of Dictatorship: Fiscal Crisis and Political Change in Egypt* (Stanford University Press, 2011); Gerasimous Tsourapas, *The Politics of Migration in Modern Egypt: Strategies for Regime Survival in Autocracies* (Cambridge University Press, 2019); and Jessica Barnes, *Cultivating the Nile: The Everyday Politics of Water in Egypt* (Duke University Press, 2014).

The many issues in Egyptian society touched upon here – women, religion, youth, sect – have given rise to a plush repertoire of scholarly research. While too numerous to exhaustively preview, a few relevant themes emerge. There are firstly many sharp studies of informal politics and culture; including: Diane Singerman, *Avenues of Participation: Family, Politics, and Networks in Urban Quarters of Cairo* (Princeton University Press, 1996); Jessica Winegar, *Creative Reckonings: The Politics of Art and Culture in Contemporary Egypt* (Stanford University Press, 2006); and Samer Shehata, *Shop Floor Culture and Politics in Egypt* (State University of New York Press, 2009). Labor politics and workers' issues are explored in Dina Bishara, *Contesting Authoritarianism: Labor Challenges to the State in Egypt* (Cambridge University Press, 2018).

A comparative survey of Egyptian laws and religion is found in Yuksel Zezgin, *Human Rights under State-Enforced Religious Family Laws in Israel, Egypt, and India* (Cambridge University Press, 2013). A brilliant study of Christian Coptic politics rests in Laure Guirguis, *Copts and the Security State: Violence, Coercion, and Sectarianism in Contemporary Egypt* (Stanford University Press, 2017).

On the Muslim Brotherhood, see Richard Mitchell, *The Society of Muslim Brothers* (Oxford University Press, 1969); Carrie Wickham, *Mobilizing Islam* (Princeton University Press, 2002) and *The Muslim Brotherhood: Evolution of an Islamist Movement* (Princeton University Press, 2013); and Martyn Frampton, *The Muslim Brotherhood and the West: A History of Enmity and Engagement* (Harvard University Press, 2018). Another look on how and why Islamism shapes political preferences in Egypt can be found in Tarek Masoud, *Counting Islam: Religion, Class, and Elections in Egypt* (Cambridge University Press, 2014), while the origins and effects of its political advantages are engaged in Steven Brooke, *Winning Hearts and Votes: Social Services and the Islamist Political Advantage* (Cornell University Press, 2019). A more anthropological perspective on Islamist social life is Mona Atia, *Building a House in Heaven: Pious Neoliberalism and Islamic Charity in Egypt* (University of Minnesota Press, 2013).

Online sources

Useful websites on Egypt proliferate for news and analysis, and exist almost entirely outside the country given the climate of media repression and informational control currently in place. Typical English-language media are pro-government, such as *Daily News* (www.dailynewsegypt.com/). One occasional exception is *Al-Ahram*, which toes the official line but also often questions it (http://english.ahram.org.eg/Index.aspx). The best independent platforms are Mada Masr (www.madamasr.com), Jadaliyya's Egypt site (www.jadaliyya.com/Country/39), Human Rights Watch's Egypt page (www.hrw.org/middle-east/n-africa/egypt), Freedom House's Egyptian portal (https://freedomhouse.org/country/egypt), Al-Monitor's Egypt Pulse (www.al-monitor.com/pulse/egypt-pulse), Middle East Eye's Egypt portal (www.middleeasteye.net/countries/egypt), and finally the International Crisis Group's country portal (www.crisisgroup.org/middle-east-north-africa/north-africa/egypt).

The World Bank's Egypt section bursts with data and reports on the economy (www.worldbank.org/en/country/egypt). Social news and happenings are reported in the journalist-driven Egyptian Streets (https://egyptianstreets.com/). The HARASSmap initiative against sexual harassment discussed in this chapter is easily accessible online (https://harassmap.org/en). The International Center for Non-for-Profit Law also closely monitors associational life and protests in Egypt (www.icnl.org/research/monitor/egypt.html). The Arabist began as an Egyptian blog before branching out to cover the Arab world, but still has extremely relevant and incisive content (https://arabist.net/).

Please note that URLs may change far more quickly than books can be printed; so if these exact URLs do not work, simply search Google or another engine by the titles of these websites and online resources.

Near East

Israel, Palestine, Syria, Lebanon,
Jordan, Iraq, and Turkey

State of Israel

Mira Sucharov and Hamed Mousavi

INTRODUCTION

Founded in 1948, the State of Israel is a product of Zionism, the Jewish national movement that was formed in the late nineteenth century to establish a sovereign state in the land of ancient Israel, commonly known as Palestine. While some Jews have always resided in the area, Jews lived and flourished in diaspora communities from the time of the Babylonian conquest and exile in 586 BC. After waves of Roman and then Christian suppression of Jewish life in Palestine (such as the capture of Jerusalem and destruction of the Jewish Temple in 70 AD), an overwhelming majority of Jews lived outside the area by the beginning of the Middle Ages. And while many Jews longed to return to Palestine over the centuries, Zionism took shape only at the end of the nineteenth century in response to social and political forces in Europe at the time, including the "push factor" of anti-Semitism and the "pull factor" of modern nationalism.

By the mid-eighteenth century, there were between 2.5 and 3 million Jews worldwide and only 5,000 in Palestine, which had a population of 250,000–300,000 people, mostly Sunni Muslim Arabs. In the course of establishing the State of Israel in 1948, roughly 750,000 Arab Palestinians were exiled as refugees and their property was expropriated or destroyed. The crux of these two events – the establishment of a Jewish state after centuries of Jewish exile and suffering, and the tragedy of Palestinian exile and dispossession that resulted, and which Palestinians refer to as *al-nakba*, or catastrophe – has formed the crux of the Israeli-Palestinian conflict. While it is near impossible to separate discussion of modern Israel from the Palestinian context, this chapter will lay out the array of social and political forces shaping politics in Israel today, including the state's relationships with its own Palestinian citizens, with Palestinians living under Israeli occupation in the West Bank, and with the surrounding Arab states.

Box 8.1 provides vital data for this country. Note that Israel held general elections in September 2019, as this book went to press. The Blue and White Party narrowly defeated the Likud, putting the position of Prime Minister up for grabs.

BOX 8.1 VITAL DATA – STATE OF ISRAEL

Capital	Jerusalem
Regime type	Democratic (parliamentary republic)
Head of state	President Reuben Rivlin (since 2014)
Head of government	Prime Minister Benjamin Netanyahu (since 2009, but may change after September 2019 elections)
Legislative institution	Unicameral parliament, with 120 elected seats (Knesset)
Female quota	No
Percentage of seats held by women	24.2%
Major political parties (share of seats in most recent general elections, 2019)	Blue and White (27.5%), Likud (25.8%), Arab Joint List (10.8%), Shas (7.5%), Yisrael Beiteinu (6.7%), United Torah Judaism (6.7%), United Right (5.8%)
Population	8,713,300
Major ethnic groups	Jewish (74.4%), Arab (20.9%), other (4.7%)
Major religious groups	Jewish (74.4%), Muslim (17.7%), Christian (2%), Druze (1.6%), other (4.3%)
GDP per capita	$41,644 ($37,972 at Purchasing Power Parity)
Unemployment rate	4%
Youth unemployment rate	6.9%
Major economic industries	High-technology products (e.g., aviation, software, electronics), military arms, mining (potash and phosphates), cement, food processing, chemicals, plastics, textiles, tourism
Military spending as % GDP	4.7%

HISTORICAL BACKGROUND

In 1897, Theodor Herzl, a Viennese Jewish journalist who had proposed establishing a Jewish state in his book *Der Judenstaat* (*The Jewish State*), organized a conference in Basel, Switzerland, proposing "to create for the Jewish people a home in Palestine secured by public law." The Zionist movement reflected in that sentiment had made important gains by World War One. The war forced the Ottoman Empire, which had ruled the traditional area of Palestine since the sixteenth century, to relinquish the territory. Moreover, with the help of Chaim Weizmann, a prominent Zionist leader and chemist who had contributed to the British war effort, the Zionist movement secured the 1917 Balfour Declaration from the British Government. This document was ambiguous. On one hand, it stated that "His Majesty's Government view with favour the establishment in Palestine of a national home for the Jewish people." On the other hand, it was not clear whether this "national home" was to be an actual sovereign state. Still, the Yishuv (the extant Jewish community in Palestine) viewed the Declaration as an achievement.

Following World War One, the League of Nations allocated the Palestine mandate to Great Britain, which controlled the area from 1920 to May 1948, when Britain relinquished its hold on the area. Yishuv leaders followed suit by declaring an independent State of Israel following the United Nations General Assembly proposal to divide the land into an Arab and a Jewish state. During the mandate period, the British mandatory government had entrusted the Yishuv with the responsibility for Jewish communal affairs – but not with foreign policy or defense. The Yishuv also controlled the clandestine recruitment and military training of Jewish youth in the Haganah (the proto-military force, whose name means "defense"), which after independence formed the core of the IDF (Israel Defense Forces). The Yishuv soon came to be dominated by the Labor Zionist movement led by David Ben-Gurion, which synthesized Jewish nationalism with socialist goals by arguing that the creation of a Jewish working class was essential to establishing a national home. Several of the semi-governmental organizations that were created during this time – including the General Federation of Labor (Histadrut), founded in 1920, and the Jewish Agency – also continued to play important roles after Israel's independence.

By the 1930s, Labor Zionists not only controlled the Yishuv government but were also a major force in the World Zionist Organization and the Jewish Agency. The Histadrut and Haganah, both dominated by Labor, were the most important sources of the movement's power within the Yishuv. The Histadrut soon extended its activities to meet the political, educational, cultural, social, and economic needs of the Jewish population. As a result, it became a state-building institution, through which the Labor movement was able to create a centralized quasi-government structure during the British mandate. Through its commitment to create a new Jewish identity based on Labor Zionist principles, the Haganah also helped maintain the predominance of the Labor Zionist movement in the Yishuv.

The Labor Zionists, however, were not without competitors. In the 1920s with the founding of the Revisionist Zionist Alliance and the "Betar" youth movement by Ze'ev Jabotinsky, a secular right-wing movement was established that grew into a major political force within the Zionist enterprise. In line with Labor Zionism, the revisionists also sought to establish an independent Jewish state in Palestine. Where they differed from their ideological rival was in their absolute emphasis on the scope of territorial claims and the need for absolute militarism in order to achieve them. Based on such a worldview, the Irgun, the revisionists' main military organization, carried out numerous terrorist operations against Palestinian civilians. In 1946, the Irgun also bombed the British administrative headquarters at the King David Hotel, killing 91 people. Less than two years earlier, Lehi, a breakaway Irgun group, had assassinated Lord Moyne, British minister of state in the Middle East, in Cairo.

The Labor rivalry with the Revisionists culminated in the Altalena Affair in June 1948, during which Ben-Gurion demanded that the cargo of a ship carrying arms by the Irgun be handed over to the newly established IDF. When the Irgun, led by Menachim Begin, refused, Ben-Gurion ordered the IDF to shell the ship, killing 16 Irgun fighters and three IDF soldiers. Though now confined to the political arena, the Labor-Revisionist rivalry has continued until today. The Altalena affair was not solely the result of the Labor-Revisionist rivalry; it also resulted from the newly established state emphasizing its monopoly on violence. Ben-Gurion had adopted the principle of *mamlachtiut* (statism), an approach emphasizing the importance of the nation and the state over civil society and the priority of political power over social action. The centralization of power by the Labor movement and its organizations such as the Histadrut should be seen in line with the principle of mamlachtiut. With the founding of the State of Israel in 1948, the Labor movement in accordance with the concept of mamlachtiut gave up control of its schools, the Haganah, and some of the functions and organizations of the Histadrut.

Throughout the mandate period, the Jewish and Arab communities of Palestine were in conflict. The peak of these clashes came with the 1936–39 Palestinian uprising, which demanded Palestinian independence and an end to Jewish immigration. The uprising was forcefully suppressed by the British and the Haganah; ten percent of the Palestinian adult male population was either killed, wounded, imprisoned, or exiled. British policy vacillated, but now restrictions on Jewish immigration became a central element of the British response. Unable to find a solution, the British eventually turned the problem of the mandate over to the United Nations.

The UN Special Committee on Palestine recommended that the mandate be terminated; however, the committee was divided over the future of the territory. The majority proposal recommended partition into a Jewish and an Arab state linked by an economic union, with Jerusalem to be an international enclave. The minority opinion recommended that Palestine become a single federal state, with Jerusalem as the capital and with Jews and Arabs enjoying autonomy in their respective areas. On November 29, 1947, the UN General Assembly adopted its Partition Plan. The Zionists reluctantly accepted the decision as the best practical outcome. The Palestinians and the Arab states rejected it, believing its acceptance would legitimize the Zionist cause. Moreover, even though the Jewish population was less than half of that of the Palestinian Arabs, the plan allotted 55 percent of land for a Jewish state.

The situation in Palestine deteriorated rapidly into violence. The British high commissioner departed, and on May 14, 1948, Israel declared independence. Armies of the Arab states entered Palestine and engaged in open warfare with the recently established IDF. The 1948 war was a turning point for Zionism not only because it secured the newly created State of Israel but also because the war helped shape a new "Jewish warrior" identity that was utilized by the Labor movement to assimilate recent immigrants into the new Israeli nation. Israel increased the territory it controlled from the 55 percent specified in the Partition Plan to 78 percent of Palestine. On the Palestinian side, the war not only led to the expulsion of about 750,000 Palestinians from their homes but also dashed their efforts to create an independent state. The conflict ended when the United Nations secured armistice agreements in spring 1949, but no general peace settlement was achieved. In December 1949, the United Nations General Assembly passed Resolution 194, which stated, "Refugees wishing to return to their homes and live at peace with their neighbors should be permitted to do so at the earliest practicable date."

Arab-Israeli conflict: from the Six-Day War to the Israeli-PLO War

The first half of Israel's history was dominated by Arab-Israeli wars: six between 1948 and 1982 inclusive, not including the War of Attrition (1969–70). The 1967 war, known by Israelis and some scholars as the Six-Day War, involved a preemptive attack by Israel to stave off the perceived threat of an Arab invasion. The results of Israel's victory significantly changed the state's political and strategic landscape, as Israel went on to take the Sinai Peninsula and the Gaza Strip from Egypt, the West Bank and East Jerusalem from Jordan, and the Golan Heights from Syria. Israel now, however, had a large Palestinian population in the West Bank and Gaza Strip under occupation. While Israel asserted that it would not withdraw from the occupied territories until negotiations with the Arab states led to permanent and secure peace, the war did little to change Arab opinion. This had been clearly articulated three years earlier in the Palestine National Covenant of 1964, which called the creation of Israel "null and void," and in the "three no's" resolution – "no peace with Israel, no recognition of Israel, no negotiations with it" – of the Arab League summit meeting in Khartoum in September 1967.

The Six-Day War had far-reaching consequences. On the one hand, the area under Israeli control tripled. On the other, Israel faced international pressure to withdraw. In November 1967, the United Nations Security Council unanimously adopted resolution 242 demanding a "withdrawal of Israel armed forces from territories occupied in the recent conflict." The war also led to important developments within Israeli politics. The Revisionist movement's "Greater Israel" idea, which called for the settlement and annexation of the newly occupied territories, gained popularity. This development, coupled with the turmoil of the 1973 Yom Kippur War, set in motion forces that created a political earthquake (*mahapach*) that led to the Likud Party's defeat of Labor in the 1977 Knesset (parliamentary) elections, putting an end to the Labor Party's long domination of Israeli politics. The 1967 war also shaped the religious Zionist movement, transforming it to a messianic movement that became increasingly influential. This ideological transformation also meant the convergence of the policy orientation of religious Zionists with that of secular revisionists in the post-1967 period, in which both groups advocated for Jewish settlement of the newly occupied territories, particularly the West Bank.

The occupation, now having stretched on for over five decades, has put a strain on Israeli democracy. Critics contend that Israel's rule of around 2.8 million disenfranchised West Bank Palestinians compromises its democracy. Staunch Israel advocates argue that Palestinians do not represent a credible "partner for peace," and that Israel should not be punished in the court of public opinion for its part in a two-way conflict. Finally, some – namely, those comprising the core of the settler movement – argue that Israel has a God-given claim to the entire West Bank, which the settler movement (and Israel's government) calls "Judea and Samaria." Still, early attempts to reduce tensions with the Arab world were made. A visit by Egyptian President Anwar Sadat to Jerusalem in 1977 sparked negotiations that culminated in the 1978 Camp David agreement and Israeli-Egyptian peace treaty of 1979. However, this has been a "cold" peace in which long-standing mistrust has not been replaced by friendly relations. The upheaval in Egyptian politics since the 2011 Arab Spring has made Israel even more wary of its southern neighbor.

By the early 1980s, the political scene in Israel was deeply divided between left and right. In the 1981 Knesset election, electorate awarded neither bloc a majority of seats. Yitzhak Navon, the Israeli president at the time, a mostly ceremonial job whose role includes selecting the elected official most likely to be able to form a government, granted the mandate to form the new government to Begin, who succeeded in forming a Likud-led coalition. The election also continued to highlight the ethnic issue in Israeli politics: Likud secured the majority (probably some 70 percent) of the Mizrahi Jewish vote. That year, Israel extended Israeli law to the Golan Heights, effectively annexing it.

Egyptian-Israeli peace was soon overshadowed by the Israeli-PLO War in Lebanon. Israel's border with Lebanon had been unstable for several years due to attacks and counterattacks by the IDF and the PLO operating in south Lebanon. On June 6, 1982, Israel launched a major military offensive to assure security for northern Israel and "destroy the PLO infrastructure." Moreover, religious Zionists, the strongest advocates of the war, believed that southern Lebanon was part of the "Jewish homeland." The operation's political objectives were more controversial, as the Israeli government decided to back Lebanon's Christians in their civil war against other mostly Muslim sects. Yet the 1982 invasion resulted in a large number of casualties, and as the war dragged on, Israelis protested. Never before had the government fought a "war of choice," which is the term Prime Minister Begin used to describe the war, in contrast to the "wars of no alternative," which Israelis had believed themselves to be fighting since 1948.

The results of the war were ambiguous. The PLO's military infrastructure in Lebanon was destroyed and the northern border became more secure, although Israeli troops who remained in Lebanon became targets. The political achievements were less tangible. Despite some losses in credibility, the PLO remained the primary representative of the Palestinians, and

Yasir Arafat, now operating from Tunis, soon rebounded to his preeminent position in Palestinian politics. Yet more troubling, the IDF had supplied flares for the horrendous massacre of Palestinian civilians in the Sabra and Shatila refugee camps (carried out by the Christian Phalangist militia) during the war, leading Israelis to demand through mass protests that their government be investigated. The Kahan Commission found Israel to be indirectly responsible for the events at Sabra and Shatila and Defense Minister Ariel Sharon personally responsible for "not taking appropriate measures to prevent bloodshed." While Israel withdrew from Lebanon in 1985, it continued to occupy a strip of land in southern Lebanon, representing about 10 percent of the country's territory, until May 2000. The war also resulted in the establishment that year of the Shi'a Islamist group Hizbullah, which gradually became one of Israel's fiercest foes.

The 1984 elections saw a new rival to the Likud Party in the form of the Sephardi ultra-Orthodox Shas Party. In these elections, the Labor alignment secured 44 seats, and Likud secured 41. Shas earned four. The new government inaugurated an experiment in Israeli politics: a "national unity agreement" in which power was shared between the two major parties with a rotation of their leaders, Shimon Peres and Yitzhak Shamir, in the positions of prime minister and foreign minister.

1987–2006: the first intifada and the second intifada

Five years after the Lebanon war, the first *intifada*, or Palestinian uprising, began when Palestinians in the Gaza Strip and West Bank began protesting against Israeli occupation in December 1987. The initial effect of the intifada on Israel was to reinforce the sharp public cleavages between those who believed the Palestinian issue had to be resolved through territorial compromise and those who believed Israel could have both peace and land. By forcing Israelis into more jarring awareness of the plight of Palestinians, the intifada was instrumental in leading Israel to pursue peace with the PLO in the form of the 1993 Oslo Agreement. Falling during the Palestinian uprising, the 1988 elections were inconclusive. Likud emerged with only a slight edge over Labor. The Mizrahi community continued to vote for Likud in greater numbers than for Labor, although support for Likud was weakening in the face of Shas and other religious parties. These elections saw another "national unity" government emerge, with Shamir at the helm through the government's tenure.

After the 1991 Gulf War, which included Iraqi Scud missile attacks on Israel, Arab-Israeli peace talks commenced at the 1991 Madrid Conference, hosted by the United States and the Soviet Union. As the war concluded, US President George H.W. Bush announced that "the time had come to put an end to the Arab-Israeli conflict." The conference did not achieve a substantive breakthrough, although it broke the procedural and psychological barriers to direct bilateral negotiations between Israel and its neighbors. The Madrid meetings were followed by a series of bilateral and multilateral talks that ended in late 1993 and early 1994. In the bilateral discussions with Syria, the core issue was the fate of the Golan Heights. In the Israeli-Palestinian discussions, the disagreement centered on the Palestinian desire for an independent state in the West Bank and Gaza Strip. The Oslo talks held secretly in 1993 – resulting in the Oslo Agreement of September of that year – would prove to be more fruitful.

Meanwhile, in January 1992, with the intifada dragging on, the right-wing Tehiya and Moledet Parties, which together held five Knesset seats, resigned from the government. They opposed Shamir's willingness to discuss an interim agreement on Palestinian self-rule. In the subsequent June elections, Labor, led by Yitzhak Rabin, was the victor, ending a decade and a half of Likud rule. Rabin moved quickly to forge a coalition that included the left-wing Zionist Meretz Party and the dovish Shas Party. This generated initial euphoria among many in the peace camp; external observers were hopeful that the peace process might be reinvigorated. Indeed, secret negotiations between Israel and the PLO began in Oslo, Norway in the spring of 1993 and led to an exchange of mutual recognition in September 1993 and to the signing of a Declaration of Principles on the White House lawn.

The Oslo Accords proved a crucial and historic breakthrough. After the initial agreement, additional implementing pacts were signed in Paris and Cairo in spring 1994; and Oslo II, also known as the Taba Agreement, was signed in September 1995. In October 1994, Israel and Jordan also signed a formal peace treaty, ushering in an era of peace and normalization of relations between those two states. Some movement also took place in Israel's negotiations with Syria, but these talks suffered a huge blow when Rabin was assassinated in November 1995 by Yigal Amir, a right-wing religious Zionist Israeli. In the months leading up to the assassination, the Revisionist and religious Zionist movements had led a vicious campaign of character assassination against Rabin and had warned about the consequences of the negotiations.

The 1996 elections were held under altered electoral processes that allowed Israelis to vote both for Knesset members and the prime minister. Shimon Peres, now Labor Party leader, campaigned on the themes of continuity and expansion of the peace process, against the background of suicide bombings by Palestinian radicals seeking to "spoil" the peace process. Likud's Benjamin Netanyahu, who was less enthusiastic about negotiations, narrowly defeated Peres and declared that he would never accept a Palestinian state. Negotiations with the Palestinians moved slowly, but did achieve the 1997 Hebron Agreement and the 1998 Wye River Memorandum. In 1999, Ehud Barak – former IDF chief of staff and newly-chosen leader of the One Israel bloc, comprising Labor and two smaller parties – was elected prime minister, defeating Netanyahu in the direct election. However, One Israel was able to obtain only 26 seats, requiring a broad and disparate coalition. Some progress was made further. For instance, Ehud Barak transferred some control in the West Bank to the Palestinian Authority, and also hinted that he might return nearly all of the Golan Heights to Syria in exchange for peace. But negotiations held in Shepherdstown, West Virginia, and Geneva, Switzerland, in early 2000 failed to produce an agreement. In May 2000, however, Barak had fulfilled his pledge to withdraw Israeli forces unilaterally from Lebanon to the internationally accepted border.

After June 2000, Barak's coalition unraveled. Barak soon called for a new, special direct election of the prime minister. This time he faced Ariel Sharon, who had replaced Netanyahu as Likud leader. The 2001 election occurred against the backdrop of the Second Intifada. While the earlier intifada was less violent and confined to the occupied territories, the new uprising was more violent and targeted Israelis in Tel Aviv and beyond. It also came on the heels of the failed Camp David II peace negotiations, in which US President Bill Clinton, Barak, and Arafat had sought comprehensive peace. Despite intensive efforts and some areas of accord, these latest efforts failed. As the Second Intifada wore on, 141 suicide bombings by Palestinians occurred between 2000 and 2005, and many Israelis became deeply cynical. The result was the election of a series of hawkish governments. On the Palestinian side, the intifada was devastating, with 4,228 Palestinians, including 855 children, dying between 2000 and 2007, largely as a result of harsh IDF tactics.

Sharon, who made clear in the 2001 election campaign that the security of Israelis was his government's paramount concern and that he considered the Oslo process dead, enjoyed a resounding victory over Barak. Sharon's government was broad-based and included Likud, Labor, and Shas. For the first time, the government also included an Israeli Arab (that is, a Palestinian citizen of Israel) minister. Yet the coalition government collapsed in October 2002, when Labor ministers resigned in a dispute over reallocating funding to West Bank and Gaza settlements. In 2002, under the direction of Sharon,

Israel began construction on a controversial seven-hundred-kilometer security barrier around the West Bank. However, rather than running along the Green Line (the 1949 armistice line separating Israel from the West Bank), 85 percent of this barrier fell inside the West Bank, leaving at least 11,000 Palestinians living between the wall and the West Bank. In addition to hindering Palestinians' freedom of movement, some farmers have been cut off from their land, leading to accusations of apartheid.

The 2003 elections resulted in another victory for Sharon, with Labor suffering its worst defeat up to that point. On December 18, 2003, Sharon announced that Israel would take unilateral steps to ensure the country's security given what he saw as the absence of a Palestinian "partner for peace." Yet an increasing number of Israeli elites began to be critical of the occupation: as Sharon observed in 2003, "You may not like the word, but what's happening is occupation. This is a terrible thing for Israel, for the Palestinians, and for the Israeli economy." With Gaza proving to be a liability, and with much less at stake symbolically than the West Bank, Israel could afford to withdraw its Gaza settlers. The last months of 2004 and the first months of 2005 therefore focused on the Gaza disengagement plan, which called for withdrawing all of Israel's ground troops and dismantling Gaza's settlements, affecting 7,000 settlers, and four small, isolated settlements in the northern West Bank.

However, Israel's disengagement from Gaza in August 2005 proved a controversial measure. After the 2006 Palestinian elections brought to power Hamas, after which Hamas took over the Gaza Strip in 2007, leaving the West Bank to be ruled by the Palestinian Authority (and still under overall IDF military control), Israel also put into place a naval, air, and land blockade. In the years since, Israel's control of Gaza's borders and the IDF's three major incursions into the area (2008–9, 2012 and 2014) have been used by Hamas and other Gaza-based groups to justify escalating missile attacks as well as digging tunnels into Israel, instigating reciprocal Israeli strikes and measures in cycles of asymmetrical violence that continue to this day.

The death of Palestinian Authority President Yasir Arafat on November 11, 2004, shook Palestinian politics. On January 9, 2005, Palestinians elected Mahmoud Abbas (also known as Abu Mazen) to succeed him. Even with Arafat's death and the opportunity presented by his disengagement proposal, however, Sharon resigned from his fractious Likud in November 2005 and created a new centrist party, Kadima, which he would lead in the 2006 Knesset elections. Sharon took with him a number of Likud ministers and members of the Knesset (MKs) and was joined by some Labor Party members and other elites. Within Labor, Amir Peretz, a Mizrahi Israeli and head of the Histadrut, defeated Shimon Peres for leadership of the party in November 2005; Peres subsequently joined Kadima. Before the March 2006 Knesset elections could take place however, Sharon suffered a major stroke in January and fell into a coma. His incapacitation, followed by the Palestinian parliamentary elections of January 25, 2006, which brought Hamas to the forefront of the Palestinian governing structure, posed a major challenge.

Political change, 2006–present

In early April 2006, the Kadima-led governing coalition deemed comatose Sharon unable to discharge the duties of office. They chose Ehud Olmert to serve as interim premier. The 2006 election marked the beginning of a new period in Israel's political life, although it should be noted that voter turnout was only 63.2 percent – low by Israeli standards. Kadima won 29 seats, and its new leader, Ehud Olmert, was tasked with forming the new government. Labor was the second largest party, winning 19 seats. Likud, which had dominated Israeli politics for more than a quarter century, shrank in size and influence. On May 4, 2006, the Knesset approved Israel's thirty-first government, headed by Ehud Olmert.

Olmert preferred negotiations with the Palestinians, but only with a Palestinian Authority that upheld all previous agreements, respected Israel's border security, and "fought terrorism." Olmert also noted that major settlement blocs in the West Bank would remain part of Israel. His tenure in office was beset by crises from the outset. In June 2006, Hamas captured Gilad Shalit, an Israeli soldier. In July, Hizbullah initiated a cross-border raid from Lebanon into Israel, killing several Israeli soldiers and capturing two others. The Hizbullah raid was followed by an Israeli invasion of southern Lebanon that lasted 34 days. These crises underscored for many Israelis the inexperience of the prime minister and Defense Minister Peretz. Similar to the wars of 1973 and 1982, which ended without clear or overwhelming success, there developed after the 2006 Lebanon war a series of conflicting opinions. Observers noted not only the substantial attacks on Israeli territory, with more than 3,000 missiles fired by Hizbullah into northern Israeli cities and towns, but also the number of Israeli soldiers wounded and killed and the substantial attacks on, and damage suffered by, Lebanese civilians.

After allegations of financial corruption, Olmert announced he would resign as prime minister following the Kadima Party's primary election in

September 2008. Unable to form a new coalition, the new Kadima leader, Tzipi Livni, recommended to Israel's president that new elections be held, and an election date was set for February 10, 2009. Under Israeli law, Olmert and the incumbent government remained in office, pending the formation of a viable successor government. In this caretaker capacity, the Olmert-led government prosecuted Operation Cast Lead, the 23-day IDF operation against Hamas in the Gaza Strip from December 27, 2008 to January 18, 2009. The efficient operation enjoyed public support. Nevertheless, with 1400 Palestinian casualties and only 13 Israeli dead, world opinion turned against Israel. The UN-sponsored Goldstone Report, released in 2009, accused both Israel and Hamas of war crimes.

The run-up to the 2009 elections focused almost exclusively on security and peace issues. Following Ariel Sharon's dramatic departure, Benjamin Netanyahu had been chosen again to lead the Likud Party. Livni's Kadima Party won 28 seats, one more than Netanyahu's Likud. The right-wing Russian Yisrael Beiteinu Party rose to third place with 15 seats, pushing a controversial agenda that called on Israeli Arabs to take a voluntary "loyalty oath" to the Jewish state, while Labor took 13 seats and Shas won 11. After consulting with the parties, President Peres invited Netanyahu to form the coalition, despite Likud's one-seat loss to Kadima.

However, two issues challenged Netanyahu's government on the domestic front. First was the 2011 tent protests, where hundreds of thousands of Israelis took to the streets to protest social justice and cost-of-living issues, particularly those related to affordable housing. The government appointed a committee headed by economist Manuel Trajtenberg to address the protestors' grievances, but by Trajtenberg's own admission, the tax reforms adopted by the government would not satisfy the protestors' demands. The protests even featured two self-immolations in a tragic repeat of what had sparked the Tunisian revolution a half-year earlier. Prime Minister Netanyahu expressed regret for these events but remained committed to unfettered free-market principles. Two of the protest leaders, Stav Shafir and Itzik Shmuli, were elected to the Knesset in 2013 and in 2015, where they still serve.

Second was the challenge of addressing the inequality inherent in the official exemption of Haredi (ultra-Orthodox Jews, namely those who adhere strictly to Jewish law and reject much of modern culture) men from military service, which had been given legal expression in 2002 through the Tal Law. On February 12, 2012, Israel's High Court of Justice ruled against the constitutionality of the Tal Law and its exemption allowance. Netanyahu pledged that his government would formulate new legislation that would guarantee "a more equal sharing of the burden." However, he ultimately shocked observers by striking a deal to bring the Kadima Party into the government. Passing legislation to integrate Haredim into the IDF was a key element of the Likud-Kadima coalition agreement. However, little progress was made, and Kadima quit the coalition in July 2012. More recent legislation has taken the teeth out of the proposals to expand the draft, given that Haredi evaders will not face criminal sanction.

Political life afterwards featured two constants: Netanyahu's leadership as prime minister, and an increasing shift to the right concomitant with the worsening state of Palestinian relations. In January 2012, as Israel and Hamas were again clashing in Gaza, veteran journalist and media personality Yair Lapid announced his intention to create a new centrist political party. Early surveys suggested that Lapid's Yesh Atid ("there is a future") Party could garner votes from center-left and center-right secular parties in the election for the nineteenth Knesset, scheduled for no later than spring 2013. MK and former IDF Chief of Staff Shaul Mofaz had previously ousted Tzipi Livni as leader of the Kadima Party in a party primary on March 27, 2012. Nonetheless, in the 2013 elections, Israelis awarded the Likud/Yisrael Beiteinu alliance the victory. Netanyahu formed a government with the centrist Yesh Atid, orthodox Jewish Home, and liberal Hatnuah parties. In July 2014, his government launched another major military operation in the Gaza Strip that provoked international controversy, given the vast disparity in the number of deaths – with 66 soldiers and five civilians killed on the Israeli side and more than 2,100 killed on the Palestinian side, of whom 1,473 were civilians, including 501 children, according to the United Nation's Office for the Coordination of Humanitarian Affairs.

The results of the 2015 elections took observers by surprise, as polling had suggested a comeback for the left in the form of an alliance between Labor and Hatnuah called the Zionist Union and led by Isaac Herzog and Tzipi Livni. Instead, with 30 seats for Likud and only 24 for the Zionist Union, Netanyahu stayed on as prime minister. He succeeded in forming a coalition with Jewish Home, United Torah Judaism, Shas, and Kulanu, the new centrist kingmaking party led by Moshe Kahlon. The Arab Joint List Party made significant gains. Netanyahu drew international criticism after he declared his opposition to a Palestinian state, a statement he reversed following the elections. He was subsequently accused of racism and bigotry as he tried to galvanize his base by announcing that Arab voters were "coming out in droves." Netanyahu was also dogged by accusations of corruption, with State Prosecutor Shai Nitzan later recommending indicting Netanyahu for bribery.

At the end of 2018, Netanyahu's coalition fell apart, with the Yisrael Beiteinu party withdrawing and the ultra-Orthodox threatening to quit over the Haredi military draft issue. As a result, in December Netanyahu dissolved the Knesset and called snap elections for April 2019. Those elections brought to bear another surprising result: Likud and a new centrist-liberal bloc, Blue and White, each took 35 seats, with no other party obtaining more than eight. Counting Yesh Atid among its constituent parties, Blue and White, led by former IDF Chief of Staff Benjamin Gantz, campaigned on anti-corruption and, among other issues, a promise to reconsider the Palestinian peace process, though under very strict conditions. However, Netanyahu failed to form a governing coalition in the aftermath due to irreconcilable conflicts, among them the exemption status of Haredi Israelis from military conscription. Another round of snap elections was therefore scheduled for September 2019 – the shortest time ever between elections in Israeli history. Those elections returned stunning results. The Blue and White (33 seats) narrowly defeated the Likud (31 seats), while the Arab Joint List came third with 13 seats. This suggested the era of Netanyahu's dominance was drawing near.

SOCIAL AND ECONOMIC ENVIRONMENT

Israel is bordered by the Mediterranean Sea to the west; the West Bank, the Jordan River, and the country of Jordan to the east; Lebanon to the north; and Egypt to the south (Map 8.1). Israel's area is approximately 20,770 square kilometers, which does not include the occupied West Bank (about 5,879 square kilometers), and the Golan Heights (about 1,150 square kilometers). It has a Mediterranean climate with long dry summers and a rainy winter that lasts from November to May. While Israel is a relatively small country, its geography is quite diverse, with mountains in the north and desert in the south. The Negev Desert, which occupies the southern half of Israel, is hot and sparsely inhabited. The Tel Aviv metropolitan area (Gush Dan), with a population of nearly 4 million people, is the country's economic hub. The government, however, has claimed Jerusalem as the capital for generations, despite the controversy this entails for Palestinians as well as the international community. Jerusalem contains the Temple Mount, an ancient hill that is the holiest site for Judaism and the third holiest site for Islam; it is often identifiable by its Dome of the Rock (Photo 8.1).

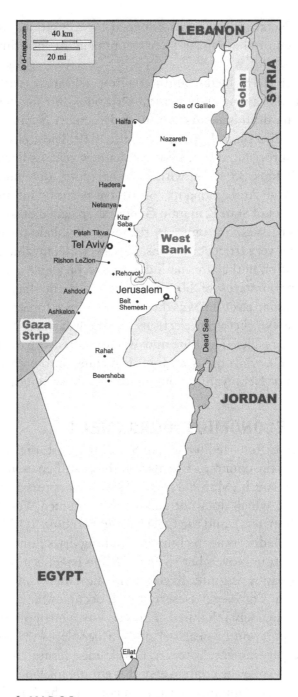

MAP 8.1
State of Israel. Major water bodies, territories, and major cities shown.

Source: D-Maps.

PHOTO 8.1
Jerusalem from the Temple Mount.

Source: Pixabay. Public domain

Culture and society

Israel's primary self-identified purpose is to maintain itself as a Jewish and democratic state. These twin aims are sometimes in tension. As the Jewish state, it seeks to serve as a refuge for world Jewry through an open immigration policy toward Jews, embodied in the Law of Return. Israel's Law of Return has not been without its critics, namely Palestinian refugees who wish to return to what is now Israel and demand a right of return under UN Resolution 194, which specifies that refugees seeking to return to their homes should be permitted to do so. As for mass immigration, though absorption of immigrants is not without its challenges, immigration serves Israel's needs by providing the human capital necessary for Israel's security and development and for maintaining Israel's Jewish demographic character.

The early Zionist immigrants to Palestine laid the foundations for a predominantly European culture in Palestine, influenced by Central and Eastern European political movements. Ashkenazi (Jews from central and eastern

Europe) immigrants developed the Yishuv structures of land settlement, trade unions, political parties, and educational institutions in preparation for building a democratic state. Later immigrants, both Sephardi Jews from North Africa, Turkey, and the Balkans – descendants of Jews expelled from Spain in the late fifteenth-century – and other Jews hailing from countries in the Middle East and North Africa known by the umbrella term Mizrahi (or Eastern Jews), who arrived in the 1950s and 1960s, sometimes faced challenges breaking into existing power structures.[1] The Mizrahi-Ashkenazi divide has long simmered in the background of Israeli nation-building. While the 1977 election, in which Likud unseated Labor for the first time, hinged largely on Menachem Begin's attempt to champion the rights of the Mizrahi population, it wasn't until 2012 that a major political party, in this case Kadima, was headed by someone of Mizrahi descent: Shaul Mofaz. Today, the divide is decreasing in salience as Israelis marry freely across Ashkenazi-Mizrahi lines, but many Ashkenazi Jews' sense of ethnic superiority coupled with latent racism that haunts the society remains a shadow.

Two later groups, post-Soviet immigrants and those from Ethiopia, have presented new cultural challenges and opportunities for Israel. The story of the Russian *aliyah* (immigration to Israel) was a momentous one: one million arrivals in 1990 streamed into Israel after the fall of the Soviet Union, where many had been persecuted. Russian *olim* (meaning those who immigrated) have tended to be secular and hold right-wing attitudes on Arab-Israeli issues. This influx has affected some of the religious-political debates. Some Russians are not considered Jewish according to *halacha* (Jewish law), and currently over 6,000 are barred from marrying due to this. There is no mechanism for marrying across religious identities in Israel. This policy touches on an ongoing debate about conversion processes and the broader "Who is a Jew?" question. Quick to rise to political prominence among the Russian immigrants were Natan Sharansky, who currently serves as head of the Jewish Agency, and Avigdor Lieberman, head of the right-wing party Yisrael Beiteinu.

The Ethiopian *aliyah* – which came in two waves, 1985 and 1991 – have been less successful than that of the Russian influx, partly due to the lower levels of literacy and job readiness, and partly due to racism. Compulsory military service has helped these communities integrate. A more recent population tension comes from the approximately 60,000 asylum seekers primarily from Eritrea and Sudan whose asylum claims are, for the most part, not heard by the Israeli government, which fears "demographic" challenges from this non-Jewish population. This is also an ongoing policy debate in Israel.

Other important social issues in Israeli society are the tensions between religion and state and between the Jewish character of the state and the country's Palestinian citizens. First, there is the issue of whether the Jewish people, and hence the majority of Israelis, should be considered a nation or a religion (they are generally understood to be both). Second, for those who wish to convert to Judaism to ease immigration access, there is disagreement among Israeli authorities over the proper conversion process – an issue that came into sharper relief with the influx of Jews from the Soviet Union, many of whom were not deemed Jewish according to Orthodox religious law. Third, Orthodox hegemony in civil matters sometimes makes non-Orthodox Jews, such as Conservative Jews and Reform Jews – never mind the many secular Jews – feel marginalized.

Underscoring all of this is the fact that in matters of personal status, religious laws affect how the state treats marriage, divorce, death, and other matters. Israeli citizens have no recourse to civil channels. These matters are strictly the purview of each citizen's particular religious authority, which means that Orthodox Judaism, embodied in the Rabbinate, has an outsized influence in matters of day-to-day life for Israel's Jewish citizens. Israel's non-Jewish citizens have their own religious authorities governing personal status matters. In the case of Judaism, only Orthodox rabbis and synagogues are supported by the state, with other denominations – Conservative (roughly 4 percent of Israeli Jews according to a 2013 study) and Reform (3 percent of Israeli Jews, according to the same study) – clamoring for recognition. Complicating this is the fact Israeli society has largely been secular for most of its history; today, 40 percent of Israeli Jews consider themselves "secular," 18 percent consider themselves Orthodox or Haredi (ultra-Orthodox), and 23 percent consider themselves largely "traditional."

When Israel was founded, Prime Minister David Ben-Gurion reached an arrangement with the Haredi – then numbering only a few hundred – allowing them to study Jewish texts (Torah and Talmud) instead of serving in the military. The agreement also promised them modest financial compensation, and most opted not to work. Over the years and owing to higher birth-rates, the Haredi population grew exponentially, now comprising roughly 10 percent of the population. Low levels of secular knowledge and high poverty rates plague the community.

In recent years there has been particular tension around the status of women in the context of religious elements of society, with some ultra-Orthodox men harassing women they deem inappropriately dressed, as well as some attacks and arrests of women who seek to don ritual garb at the Kotel (Western Wall) in Jerusalem, garb traditionally reserved for men. LGBTQ life, on the other hand, is generally free and unrestricted, and Israel's military has long welcomed gay and lesbian members. However, without any channels for civil marriage and with personal status issues under the domain of Muslim, Christian, and Orthodox Jewish religious authorities, there is no same-sex marriage, though since 2006 the government has recognized same-sex marriages conducted abroad.

Around 92 percent of the population lives in urban areas. However, since the country's electoral system is based on a national proportional representation in which the entire country is a single district, the urban-rural divide characterizing other political systems is largely absent. Nevertheless, not all rural populations enjoy equal rights. Around 160,000 Bedouins, nomadic Arabs, live in the Negev area, in dozens of towns and villages that are not recognized by the state. In some cases, these villages are even off the electricity grid and the government routinely demolishes their unlicensed structures, forcing the displacement of their inhabitants.

Some 21 percent of Israeli citizens are Palestinian – Arabs who have lived in Israel/Palestine since before 1948, as well as their offspring. Palestinian citizens of Israel (sometimes known as Arab Israelis or Israeli Arabs) face various challenges. From 1949 until 1966, the Palestinians suffered under an oppressive martial law, whereby they were granted citizenship but forbidden to travel into or out of security areas without permission. Although Palestinian citizens vote, sit in the Knesset, serve in government offices, and have their own Arabic-language school system (alongside the various Hebrew-language school systems in Israel: state, state-religious, and Haredi), they face state-sponsored discrimination as well as informal prejudice. There are significant funding differentials between the Arab and Jewish school sectors, building permits are difficult to obtain in Arab towns, and infrastructure in the Arab sector is generally less well funded than in the Jewish sector. Compounding the systemic discrimination is the fact that Palestinian citizens generally do not serve in the IDF (with the exception of Arab Druze, who comprise 8 percent of the Palestinian citizen population). Indeed, the 2 percent of Israelis who are Christians, and the nearly 18 percent who are Muslim, mostly do not serve, although some Bedouin volunteer. All of this is backgrounded by the Arab-Israeli tension over the West Bank occupation, the siege of Gaza, and memory of the Nakba.

In the spring of 1976, Israel's Arabs participated in their first general protest. But it was not until the Second Intifada that concerted activism among Palestinian citizens of Israel took shape. In October 2000, at the beginning of the uprising, Arab Israelis demonstrated in support of the Palestinians in the West Bank and Gaza and expressed long-standing grievances. 12 Palestinian citizens of Israel (and one resident of the Gaza Strip) were killed in clashes with police. A government-appointed commission of inquiry concluded that specific circumstances, combined with a long-standing grievance in Israel's Arab community concerning unfair treatment and discrimination, had triggered the riots.

In February 2006, Israel's High Court of Justice held that Israel's Arab citizens must not be discriminated against in resource allocation and that racism and other forms of discrimination must be avoided. The court noted that although Israel is defined as a Jewish and democratic state, any favorable bias in education budgets for Jewish communities must be rejected outright. However, budget parity still has not been achieved, and high-profile, symbolic moments of identity tension rear their head from time to time. Later on, the 2015 elections represented a watershed for Arab participation. Following a 2014 law that raised the entry threshold from 2 percent to 3.25 percent, four Arab parties merged into a political alliance known as the Joint List, headed by the charismatic Ayman Odeh, and won 13 seats (10.6 percent of the vote) to become the third largest party in the Knesset. Odeh's inaugural Knesset speech was dubbed by some observers as the Martin Luther King Jr. speech for the rights of Palestinian citizens of Israel. Nevertheless, the Palestinians have had difficulty translating their Knesset share into political influence; Arab parties have never been included in a government coalition in Israeli history.

Economic conditions

Israel's economy has grown substantially. In its early decades, it was characterized by a somewhat state-led developmental trajectory, burdened by low natural resources, massive immigration, universal conscription, and regional tension, including the constraining fact that it could not trade with almost any of its Arab neighbors. It is now a diversified, high-tech economy adhering closely to market-based principles favoring openness and globalization. By GDP, it is the fourth largest economy in the MENA after Turkey, Saudi Arabia, and Iran, and it has the highest GDP per capita of any non-rentier country in the region – as of 2019, nearly $42,000. The Israeli people live in one of the healthiest countries in the world, and the government provides extensive social services for its population. Per capita, there are more technology startups in Israel, attracting significant amounts of venture capital investment. For much of the past decade, unemployment has been among the lowest in the MENA, measuring just 4 percent in 2018 and youth jobless-ness under 7 percent. At the same time, Israel's massive growth has led to troubling wealth gaps between the rich and poor. The 2011 popular protest movement over social justice issues such as housing and living costs attests to this.

Currently, Israel's most productive economic sectors include high-tech products, such as software and electronics, as well as textiles, machinery, chemicals, mining of potash and phosphates, and food products. It has a profitable agricultural export portfolio despite its small size, and key goods include citrus, cotton, vegetables, and dairy. Military arms represent a vital industry; Israel regularly ranks among the world's top ten arms exporters. Israel's dearth of energy resources has made it almost completely dependent on foreign supplies of oil, coal, and natural gas. Since the 1980s, Israel's oil imports have contributed significantly to its large balance-of-payments defi-cit. However, two natural gas fields discovered off Israel's coast in 2009–10, with estimated reserves of 18.9 trillion cubic meters of gas, elicited commer-cial interest and development. In 2017, Israel began exporting natural gas to neighboring Jordan.

Economic development can be traced to an investment program financed from outside sources, including US loans and grants, the sale of Israel bonds, investments, and German reparations and restitution payments. At the same time, charitable contributions from the global Jewish community have helped reduce the government's burdens in social welfare, thereby permit-ting the use of domestic funds for development projects. During its political domination from before independence to 1977, the Labor Party pursued socialist economic policies in a mixed economy. The government played a central economic role, aided by the Jewish Agency, the United Israel Appeal, the Jewish National Fund, and the Histadrut labor federation. When the more capitalist Likud Party came to power in 1977, free-market practices intensified. Hyperinflation in the mid-1980s was arrested by an aggressive stabilization program, but the economy was negatively affected by the Pal-estinian intifada starting in December 1987, the mass immigration of Soviet Jews beginning in 1989, and the crisis resulting from the Iraqi invasion of Kuwait in 1990 and the ensuing Gulf War of 1991.

In the early 1990s, Israel's high-tech sector took off. There was a large influx of well-educated immigrants, and prospects for regional peace seemed to improve. These factors combined to create strong economic performance, which slowed only in the second half of the decade. The economy recovered in late 1999 due to industrial exports in high-tech sectors. Israel had also adopted important structural reforms, including privatization of core industries and reduced controls on foreign companies operating in Israel. At the same time, the country made progress toward a more open, competitive, market-oriented economy, although public spending remained a significant proportion of GDP and top marginal income tax rates remained high.

The outbreak of the second Palestinian intifada in September 2000 plunged Israel's economy into a recession. GDP shrank for two years, unemployment reached 11 percent, and tourism all but disappeared. A growing government budget deficit resulted in cuts in social welfare benefits. As before, however, conditions began to improve as the uprising was contained. By 2004, Israel's economy had returned to robust expansion, and emerged largely unscathed from the global financial crisis that began in 2008. Starting in 2011, Israel's economic growth began to slow, but overall its growth rate for the 2010s is almost identical to its 2000s pace – averaging 3.6 percent annual GDP growth. With few exceptions, the government under Netanyahu remains committed to market-oriented principles.

POLITICAL STRUCTURES

Instead of a constitution, Israel has a series of Basic Laws covering areas including the judiciary, the parliament, and basic human rights embodied in the 1992 Basic Law called Human Dignity and Liberty. Israel's self-definition as a Jewish state is perhaps the most significant area of consensus among the Jewish population, and the most notable area of tension between Jewish and non-Jewish citizens. Accordingly, those disavowing Zionism tend to be marginalized by state structures. In July 2018, the Knesset passed the controversial "Jewish Nation-State Law" which states: "The fulfillment of the right of national self-determination in the State of Israel is unique to the Jewish people." The law also demoted Arabic as an official language, leaving Hebrew the only official language. Critics have argued that the law openly discriminates against non-Jews, further marginalizing the 20 percent of citizens who are Palestinian. After the law passed, the leader of the Arab Joint List, Ayman Odeh, said that Israel "has passed a law of Jewish supremacy and told us that we will always be second-class citizens."

Israel has a parliamentary political system in which the government (cabinet) and parliament (Knesset) are the dominant institutions, headed by the prime minister. The president, essentially a ceremonial figure, is elected by the Knesset for a seven-year term and may not be reelected. The president is generally a figure of considerable stature enjoying popular support. Until 2000, all presidents completed their terms or died in office. Israel's current president is Reuven (Ruby) Rivlin, who took the post in 2014. The president participates in the formation of the government and receives its resignation. Although traditionally the leader of the largest party in the Knesset is chosen to form the government as prime minister, the president can use their discretion to select the person they deem most capable of creating a viable coalition.

In 1992 the Knesset decided to introduce direct election for the prime minister, in the hope of strengthening the prime minister's popular mandate. Ultimately, the reform did not work as hoped, leading to even more intense coalition politics. Voters now had the opportunity to support small parties as well as secure their choice for prime minister from one of the larger parties. After three elections (1996, 1999, and 2001), the practice was abandoned.

The prime minister is the most powerful political figure. Only one successful Knesset vote of no confidence has caused the ouster of a government, in 1990 when the government of Yitzhak Shamir fell. Despite the no-confidence vote, however, Shamir was able to form a new coalition after Labor leader Shimon Peres failed to secure the support of the religious parties. A government may also be dissolved by the ending of the Knesset's tenure, by its own resignation, or by the resignation of the prime minister.

The Knesset is a unicameral body of 120 members elected by national, general, secret, direct, equal, and proportional suffrage for a term not to exceed four years. Voters cast their ballots for parties rather than for individual candidates, and each party presents voters with a list of up to 120 candidates. Parties must receive a minimum of 3.25% of the popular vote to obtain a seat. Divided into numerous legislative committees, the Knesset approves the budget and taxation policy, elects the president, and participates in the appointment of judges.

The Supreme Court of Israel is unique insofar as all citizens have the right to direct appeal via the High Court. The Supreme Court does not formally have the power of judicial review of Knesset legislation, but it has the authority to invalidate administrative actions and declare statutes to be contrary to the Basic Laws. The court's growing activism in this regard has provoked criticism from all points on the ideological spectrum – sometimes earning scorn from conservative Israelis for recognizing anti-Arab discrimination and other times earning derision from global monitors for not fully ruling on the legality of Israeli actions in the West Bank.

POLITICAL DYNAMICS

Political participation is extensive, and parties play a central role in political life. Voter turnout is solid, never dropping below 63 percent. The 2015 elections saw a turnout of 72 percent, while the April 2019 elections saw turnout slightly diminish to 68.4 percent. Palestinian citizens of Israel tend to vote in lower numbers than Jews, though the 2015 elections saw a substantial increase in Palestinian turnout. Political diversity is apparent in the existence of multiple parties contesting Knesset elections and in the coalition governments that have been characteristic of Israel since its independence. However, Palestinian parties have never been invited into a coalition, which has severely curtailed their ability to influence policy.

Individuals or groups of individuals, no matter how prominent, generally have not fared well when divested of the support of the established parties. In the several instances in which there has been notable success – such as that of the Democratic Movement for Change in 1977 and the Centre Party in 1999 – change has been ephemeral. That said, in recent years individuals, such as Yair Lapid (Yesh Atid) and Moshe Kahlon (Kulanu), have shown impressive results at the polls.

The multiplicity of parties, the diversity of views they represent, and the proportional-representation electoral system have prevented any one party from winning a majority of Knesset seats in any of the 20 elections that have occurred between 1949 and 2015. This means that coalition governments have been the norm. Prior to the national unity government formed in 1984, only twice had a coalition government been truly broad-based, and those were established in times of national crisis: the provisional government formed at independence, and the national unity government formed in the lead-up to the 1967 war. The 1984 national unity government was unique in that it was based on a principle of power-sharing between Labor and Likud, the two major political blocs. This experiment was repeated after the 1988 election and lasted until spring 1990.

The requirements of coalition government have limited the prime minister's ability to control the cabinet and its actions. In addition, the prime minister does not appoint ministers in the traditional sense; he or she reaches accord with the other parties in the coalition, and together they select the individuals who will hold cabinet seats and share in the cabinet's collective responsibility for governing. The fragile nature of many coalition governments in Israel has increased the influence of junior coalition partners, which traditionally had been the religious parties, but more recently have included the rising centrist parties as well. Such a system could also increase the role and influence in policymaking of Arab parties, but since they have never been considered appropriate coalition partners and have never been invited to a governing coalition, they are underrepresented in policymaking.

As noted earlier, in the aftermath of the 1967 war, a messianic religious Zionist movement obsessed with settling and annexing the newly occupied territories, particularly the West Bank that was home to a large Palestinian population, began to emerge. Beginning in the mid-1970s, the religious Zionists initiated a settler movement to achieve this very aim. The settler movement acquired its ideology from the works of Rabbi Abraham Yitzhak Kook who was the Ashkenazi chief rabbi of Palestine from 1921 until his death in 1935. Kook believed that Zionism was not a mundane, earthly, and secular enterprise, but a movement ordained by God. He famously proclaimed that the only nationalism is that of the Torah and that "Zionism is a heavenly matter." More importantly, he explained that the settlement of the land by Jews would hasten the coming of the messiah and, as a result, that the enemies of Israel were in fact the enemies of God, trying to impede the "Lord's divine plans." The settler movement of the 1970s, led by the late rabbi's son, Rabbi Zvi Kook, quickly began to initiate settlement construction, aided in some cases by the government and defying both international law and some domestic criticism.

As the decade progressed, debate emerged over territorial compromise, especially in the West Bank. While the Likud Party and the religious Zionists opposed relinquishing any territory, the governments led by the Labor Party between 1967 and 1977 generally tried to limit Jewish settlements in the West Bank to those that could serve a security function. By contrast, Menachem Begin's Likud-led government, elected in 1977, viewed Jewish settlements as a natural right. Israel under Begin was following Jabotinsky's revisionist vision of a Jewish state in all of "Greater Israel" – the area spanning from the Jordan River to the Mediterranean Sea, at times also including the Sinai Desert and the Golan Heights. As a result, Israel refused to negotiate with the PLO and opposed establishing an independent Palestinian state in the West Bank and Gaza.

While the Likud was the main political force behind settlement activities, the actual settling of the territories was done by the religious Zionists, who created the Gush Emunim movement in 1974 to coordinate and organize settlement activities. The Gush was eventually eclipsed and effectively replaced by the Yesha Council in the late 1980s. The religious Zionist movement has also been very effective in Israeli party politics. The National Religious Party (NRP) represented the movement until 2008, when it joined smaller right-wing groups to form the Jewish Home Party. Israel's extreme multi-partyism has made religious Zionist and ultra-Orthodox parties kingmakers in Israeli domestic politics and has heavily influenced the state's worldview and its foreign policy direction.

It is also important to point out that, aside from using political avenues, religious settlers have also used violence to achieve their objectives. For example, in the past decade, the radical fringe of the Israeli settler movement has played a violent game of cat and mouse with the government, a game also known as "price tag" attacks because settlers retaliate with violence against Palestinians for government policies they oppose. For instance, if a West Bank settlement outpost – the small percentage of settlements deemed illegal even under Israeli law – is ordered moved, settlers might torch a mosque, destroy part of a Palestinian olive grove, or, less often, attack individual Palestinians. While the target may be the government, the victims are the Palestinians and their property. Sometimes these vigilantes actually spray paint the words *tag mechir* (price tag) on the walls of a firebombed building.

The issue of what to do with the occupied territories has gradually become a central point of contestation between "left" and "right" in Israel and between settlers and non-settlers. These labels of course are fluid in a way that ethnicity or religion is not. Nevertheless, the Israeli political spectrum is mostly fashioned along what are known as "security" issues, which means that left-right distinctions generally refer to one's position on solving the Palestinian (and broader Arab) issue. That said, the last decade has seen a rise in the salience of economic issues defining politics, especially since the 2011 tent protests.

The distinction between settlers and non-settlers also is fluid, given that Israelis can, and do, move in and out of the West Bank for various personal reasons. On top of this, there is great variation within the settler population itself, with some settlers motivated by religious or nationalist ideology and others motivated by economic concerns. By dint of living farther from the economic core of the country and benefiting from various government incentives, Israelis generally live more cheaply in the West Bank than in the country's geographic core. Though the settlement project has been promoted by both Labor- and Likud-led governments, parties on the right generally are more sympathetic to settler concerns.

Settlement expansion and the continuation of the occupation of lands captured in the 1967 war have not only affected Israel's foreign relations but have also affected internal politics and society. According to the Israeli Peace Now organization, the number of Israeli settlers in the West Bank has gone up from around 94,000 in 1991 when the Madrid Peace Conference was held to over 413,000 today, not including 214,000 in East Jerusalem. The continuous growth of Israeli settlements in the occupied territories has severely impeded the peace process and undermined the likelihood of a "two-state solution." This had led to the rise of debates regarding the prospects of a "one-state Solution" where Israel, the Gaza Strip and the West Bank would be joined in a single state where every inhabitant would have equal rights regardless of ethnicity. Such a solution however goes counter to most readings of Zionism, and more recently the Israeli Nation-State Law.

Another important actor in the political dynamics of Israel is the military. Israel lacks a strong civilian control over the military. Moreover, not only is the military semi-independent but it also strongly influences policymaking in the Jewish state in areas that are supposedly under the jurisdiction of the civilian sector. Not only does the IDF influence the civilian sector via policy recommendations and the provision of intelligence, but it also plays a central role in shaping Israeli public opinion, culture, and society for a singular reason: military service is an important requisite for positions of power and importance.

In the early days of the state, serving in the military helped integrate new Jewish immigrants into society. Israel's universal dual-gender conscription and frequent wars have also made the military an important avenue for national identity. Today, military service remains the rite of passage to adulthood for many, making the issue of service exemption for Haredi provocative on both political and symbolic grounds. Many university students begin their studies after serving in the military and remain likely to be called for reserve duty into their late thirties and forties. Thus, the IDF is an important player in the shaping of both public policy and public opinion, not least because so many prominent Israeli statesmen were also well-known soldiers. The rise of the new Blue and White party during both 2019 elections, for instance, partly reflected the ability of its leader, Benny Gantz, to capitalize on his IDF service and leadership as chief of staff. Inversely, the IDF remains an institutional barrier to socioeconomic access for Palestinian citizens, who, as a rule, are not served with draft notices. However, some Arab citizens, namely Bedouin and Druze, choose to volunteer.

FOREIGN POLICY

Israel spends a major portion of its budget on defense and defense-related items, with military spending typically representing up to 5 percent of GDP. It has, by regional standards, a sizeable standing army and reserve force widely considered of high quality and capability. It also possesses nuclear weapons, though it is highly secretive about its capabilities.

Israeli foreign policy has centered around peace processes with surrounding Arab states and the Palestinians – the success and intensity of which depend on the ruling government and the national mood of the day. The peace process with the Palestinians remains halting, and in the last few years, frozen entirely. Israel enjoys formal peace treaties with Egypt and Jordan, but it is unlikely that peace will break out between Israel and its other neighbors anytime soon. Against this has been the contested matter of Israel's territorial depth. Those on Israel's right wing favor keeping the West Bank, either by annexation or through maintaining the occupation that dates from the 1967 war and that was supposed to be temporary. Those on the left are troubled by Israeli human rights violations toward Palestinians in the West Bank and want Israel to withdraw from the territory in return for Israeli-Palestinian peace. While the Palestinians have never had the power to pose an existential threat to Israel, the rise of Hamas in the Gaza Strip has made Israelis feel more threatened. Although in its new charter, Hamas has implicitly accepted the 1967 borders as the basis for the creation of a Palestinian state and peace with Israel.

Tensions between Israel and Gaza have included several major military conflicts with Hamas as well as the involvement of international activists. In 2010, the Netanyahu government faced overwhelming international condemnation over the deaths of nine Turkish human rights activists when IDF troops boarded the passenger ship *Mavi Marmara*, part of a flotilla of activists who had attempted to break the IDF naval blockade of Hamas-controlled Gaza. A UN investigation charged that excessive force had been used by the IDF, even as it raised serious questions about "the conduct, true nature and objectives of the flotilla organizers." The incident caused tension in Israel's strategic relationship with Turkey, which demanded a formal apology from Israel for the activists' deaths; Netanyahu proffered such an apology in 2013 under American pressure. The ongoing blockade of Gaza has nonetheless triggered ongoing cycles of Hamas rocket attacks and Israeli punishment. In March 2018, Palestinians in Gaza launched a major wave of protests demanding their right of return; the IDF's violent responses, resulting in hundreds of deaths and thousands of injuries, was condemned by the UN. Low-level protests and Israeli countermeasures continued throughout the year.

In September 2010, Netanyahu agreed to resume long-stalled direct talks with the Palestinians, while also emphasizing the need for the Palestinians to recognize Israel as a Jewish state. This was a new demand that some critics argued was a way to sidestep the actual work that would have to go into negotiating a mutually acceptable solution to the Palestinian refugee issue. During this time, the Palestinian Authority turned to the United Nations to attempt to gain recognition for a Palestinian state. In November 2012, Abbas succeeded in achieving a more limited gain: the UN General Assembly granted Palestine "non-member state" status. In September 2015, the Palestinian flag was raised outside the UN headquarters in New York for the first time in history. During the same month, Abbas accused Israel of not committing to the Oslo Peace Accords and declared that as a result the Palestinian Authority was no longer bound by the Oslo agreements.

Despite the time and resources historically devoted to Israeli-Palestinian relations, Israel sees Iran as its most urgent threat. In a major foreign policy speech on June 14, 2009, Netanyahu described "the nexus between radical Islam and nuclear weapons" centered in Iran as "the greatest danger confronting Israel, the Middle East, the entire world and human race." The debate within Israel's security and intelligence community has focused on whether diplomacy and sanctions can deter Iran from acquiring a nuclear weapon and whether Israel could afford to go to war alone – without the support of at least one great power – to ensure Iran remains weapon free. In July 2015, the P5+1 countries (United States, Britain, France, Russia, China, and Germany) succeeded in reaching a negotiated deal with Iran that placed limitations on Iran's nuclear program while lifting sanctions on the country. Netanyahu opposed the deal, and common enmity to Iran drew Israel closer to Saudi Arabia. Years later, the Trump administration gave cover to scuttle it. With the lobbying of Israel and Saudi Arabia, the latter of which also sought to contain and suffocate Iran, the US officially withdrew from the nuclear deal in May 2018. The move exacerbated tensions between not only Iran and the US, but also between Iran and Israel, who have been engaged in tit-for-tat attacks in southwest Syria.

Syria represents another conundrum. When civil war consumed its northeastern neighbor after 2011, Israeli policymakers were divided. Some sought to maintain the Asad regime, arguing that the alternative would be either chaos or else a triumphant Islamic State of Iraq and Syria (ISIS), which would greatly undermine Israeli security. Others argued that as the 2006 war in Lebanon showed, an empowered Asad regime – helped by Iran and bolstered by Hizbullah – presented the real long-term danger. The Israeli government maintained official neutrality, but implicitly supported international efforts to contain ISIS, while denouncing excessive Iranian and Hizbullah mobilization in Syria.

Regarding Egypt, Israel became concerned in 2012 when Mohamed Morsi, the Muslim Brotherhood's candidate, was elected as the country's new president, bringing into question whether Egypt would continue to abide by the 1979 Egypt-Israel Peace Treaty. These concerns were alleviated when the new government vowed to respect previous agreements. After Morsi was overthrown by General Abdel Fattah al-Sisi in a 2013 military coup d'état, relations began to improve. Under Sisi, Egypt's approach has been much more in line with Israeli state preferences, enforcing a joint siege over Gaza as well as combating Hamas.

Since 1948, the persistent Arab-Israeli conflict has required positive relationships with states farther afield, especially in Europe, Africa, and Latin America, as well as with the superpowers during the Cold War and the United States since that time. Israel has had an ambivalent view of the United Nations, however. On one hand, it owes its sovereign existence in large part to the General Assembly's vote in favor of partition in 1947. On the other hand, by the mid-1970s, the General Assembly seemed more hostile to Israel's existence, largely owing to the changing composition of its membership in the postcolonial era. The 1975 "Zionism is racism" resolution, repealed in 1991, is an example of this. Nor has Israel deemed the United Nations sympathetic to its interests in recent years, as the General Assembly voted to grant the Palestinians non-member state status in 2012.

Israel's regional isolation continued to dissolve as the 1991 Madrid Peace Conference and subsequent negotiations involved a large number of other powers. The collapse of the Soviet Union led to the restoration of Israel's relations with many communist states that previously had been hostile. All of these developments contributed to an improved international position for Israel in the 1990s, but the failure of the Oslo process and the Palestinians' and Arab states' resort to the United Nations altered the status quo once again.

Israel has sought to maintain positive relations with countries in Europe, as with Australia, Canada, Japan, and South Korea because of their political influence, economic significance, and military assistance. A tacit alliance with France was supplemented by links with Great Britain and Germany, and over time Israel has established economic links with the European Economic Community, the European Union, and the Organization for Economic Cooperation and Development, albeit with limitations, and with various European states on a bilateral level. Germany, through its moral and material reparations for World War Two crimes, was an indispensable factor in Israel's economic development beginning in the 1950s, and France proved a valuable supplier of military aid until the 1967 war, assisting Israel to launch its nuclear weapons program. During the 2010s, Netanyahu sought increasingly closer relations with Victor Orban, far-right prime minister of Hungary, and other European leaders perceived as right-wing populists, a move critics say undermines Israel's democratic principles.

The emergence of the new states of Africa and Asia in the 1950s and 1960s led Israel to pursue a policy in keeping with Afro-Asian aspirations for economic development and modernization. In an effort to befriend these states and secure their support, Israel's multifaceted program focused on technical assistance, exchange and training programs, loans, joint economic enterprises, and trade. Support from the developing world helped to prevent the United Nations from adopting anti-Israel measures after the 1967 war, and in the early 1970s a committee of African presidents worked to promote Arab-Israeli negotiations, without success. The nadir of the policy was reached at the time of the 1973 war, when virtually all of the African states with which Israel had established ties broke off relations. For some Israelis these defections reflected a policy failure, although some African states have reestablished close links and some have sustained informal but significant ties despite official policies. By the 1970s, Israel had also developed friendly relations with South Africa's apartheid regime, being one of the only Western states not to participate in sanctions against the country.

Israel was among the first countries in the world to recognize the People's Republic of China in January 1950, but official relations were established with the start of the Oslo process. Since then, substantial links have been created in the areas of trade, aviation, culture, and scientific cooperation. Numerous reciprocal visits have taken place, and there has been progress in arms sales. India recognized Israel on September 18, 1950, and Israel soon opened a consulate in Bombay (now Mumbai), though its functions and jurisdiction were extremely limited. It wasn't until January 1992 that the two countries established full diplomatic relations. Since the 1990s, India and Israel have developed increasingly strong commercial and military ties. India has also become an increasingly popular tourist destination for young Israelis.

Until the 1990s, Israel, like all other states, had to operate within the confines of the Cold War, though Israel arguably had a more intricate task to manage than many other countries. The two superpowers, the Soviet Union and the United States, both were home to large segments of the world's Jewish population, and Zionism and the "ingathering of the exiles" require Israel to be concerned with the well-being of Jewish communities elsewhere. The Soviet Union had voted for the UN Partition Plan of 1947, accorded *de jure* recognition to Israel shortly after its independence, supported its applications for UN membership, and provided moral, political, and material support in Israel's early years. However, Soviet-Israeli relations deteriorated rapidly between 1949 and 1953. Soviet military and economic assistance to the Arab world, the Soviet Bloc's rupture of relations with Israel in 1967, and the continuation of that break led Israel farther into the Western camp, although it continued to seek the restoration of ties with the Soviet Union and its allies and to promote the well-being and emigration of Soviet Jews.

After the 1967 war, the Soviet Union attempted to become a more significant participant in the Arab-Israeli peace process but made limited progress until the Gorbachev era, when more liberal approaches to foreign policy permitted the relationship between Israel and the USSR to improve. Consular contacts and exchanges took place, Soviet Jewish emigration increased substantially, and several Eastern European states restored diplomatic relations with Israel. On October 18, 1991, the Soviet Union and Israel reestablished full diplomatic relations. From the early 1990s, some one million citizens of the former Soviet Union immigrated to Israel, and there was significant growth in bilateral relations with Russia and several former Soviet republics in the cultural and commercial domains. Nevertheless, Israel remains skeptical about Russia's ambitions in the Middle East, such as those reflected in President Vladimir Putin's support for Bashar al-Asad's regime in Syria's civil war and Moscow's refusal to participate in robust sanctions against Iran.

US-Israeli ties are a source of both pride and controversy. Once a power providing limited direct support for Israel, the United States has become a crucial supporter of Israel. The United States signed a free trade agreement with Israel in 1985 and now provides major political, diplomatic, moral, strategic, and economic support, including over $3 billion in military aid annually. The most recent US-Israel agreement, signed by President Obama in 2016, was for $38 billion over the next decade.

During the first decades after Israel's independence, the US-Israel relationship was grounded primarily in humanitarian concerns, religious and historical links, and moral-emotional-political ties rather than strategic-military ties. The United States declared an arms embargo on Israel (and the Arab states) in December 1947; there was practically no US military aid or sales and no formal or informal military cooperation between the two states for many years. Extensive US-Israel military and strategic cooperation began only in the 1970s. The current US understanding of Israel as a strategic asset was more an outcome of the developing relationship than a foundation for its establishment. After the 1967 war, the United States gradually became

Israel's principal arms supplier and committed itself to maintaining Israel's qualitative military advantage over its adversaries. Arms transfers became an important US tool for reassuring Israel and sometimes modifying its policies. Israel's special relationship with the United States in the twenty-first century, which is manifest in political-diplomatic support and military and economic assistance, has been the subject of some controversy. Some scholars and public commentators, especially John Mearsheimer and Stephen Walt, have argued that US policy toward Israel is the result of a well-funded and well-organized "Israel lobby." Others point to the intrinsic strategic interests shared by Israel and the United States.

The US commitment to Israel has taken the form of presidential statements reaffirming US interest in supporting Israel's political independence and territorial integrity. The United States has used its veto power 44 times in defense of Israel in the United Nations Security Council. It is also the source of Israel's sophisticated military hardware, and it is integral to the Arab-Israeli peace process. During the Obama administration, the relationship was tested when the US routinely criticized settlement expansion in the occupied territories as hampering the peace process and the possible establishment of a Palestinian state. Disagreements between the US and Israel reached a peak in December 2016 when the US declined to veto a UN Security Council Resolution which declared the settlements in the occupied territories including East Jerusalem to be illegal, which Netanyahu with American support called "shameful."

In Trump, Netanyahu found an ally who has been much more sympathetic to the policies of his right-wing coalition. In February 2017, President Trump announced during Netanyahu's first visit that the US would no longer require the creation of a sovereign Palestinian state as part of a lasting peace agreement. In December 2017, the US ordered the relocation of the US embassy from Tel Aviv to Jerusalem, despite considerable international criticism. The controversial move reversed decades of official US policy, whereby successive US presidents had signed a presidential waiver to delay the move, effectively keeping to the status quo so as not to upset the delicate balance of competing religious and national claims to the city. The move has further complicated peace talks between the Israelis and the Palestinians.

FUTURE PROSPECTS

Israel's position in the Middle East will remain complex, and full of contradictions. The country strives to maintain its democratic identity amidst a vibrant tradition of parliamentary governance dating back to its founding, although not all citizens believe they are fairly represented and ideological diversity has declined in recent years. The economy remains prosperous, driven by technology, tourism, investment, and defense; but complaints from urbanites about rising living costs continue to grow. The political arena is dynamic and unpredictable, and as both 2019 elections showed, the dominance of Netanyahu and his Likud has crested. Yet it remains to be seen how different future governments will be.

Israel maintains a strong position materially in geopolitics, thanks in large part to the United States. However, worsening relations with the Palestinian Authority, due to the inability to find viable solutions over issues of land and settlement in the West Bank, ongoing and bloody conflicts with Hamas, and its ongoing occupation and settlements continue to hamper Israel's international standing. Until Israel uses its formidable power to negotiate towards some permanent solution – whether a two-state solution or via a democratic, single state or some other confederated arrangement – global opinion will shift away from the state. The current boycott, divestment and sanctions movement against Israel's treatment of Palestinians has succeeded in placing human rights in the spotlight while presenting Israel with a new international challenge.

NOTE

1 This chapter uses the term Mizrahi Jews to denote non-Ashkenazi Jews primarily from the MENA region.

FURTHER READING

On Israel's history, see Zeev Sternhell, *The Founding Myths of Israel: Nationalism, Socialism, and the Making of the Jewish State* (Princeton University Press, 1998); Joel S. Migdal, *Through the Lens of Israel: Explorations in State and Society* (State University of New York Press, 2001); Howard M. Sachar, *A History of Israel: From the Rise of Zionism to Our Time*, 3rd ed. (Knopf, 2007); Colin Schindler, *A History of Modern Israel* (Cambridge University Press, 2008); Anita Shapira, *Israel: A History* (Brandeis University Press, 2014); and Daniel Gordis, *Israel: A Concise History of a Nation* *Reborn* (Ecco, 2017). The mandate period is discussed in Dan Horowitz and Moshe Lissak, *Origins of the Israeli Polity: Palestine Under the Mandate*, trans. Charles Hoffman (University of Chicago Press, 1978); Howard Greenfeld, *A Promise Fulfilled: Theodor Herzl, Chaim Weizmann, David Ben-Gurion, and the Creation of the State of Israel* (HarperCollins, 2005); and Liora R. Halperin, *Babel in Zion: Jews, Nationalism and Language Diversity in Palestine, 1920–1948* (Yale University Press, 2014).

On contemporary Israeli politics, see Bernard Reich and David H. Goldberg,

Historical Dictionary of Israel, 2nd ed. (Scarecrow Press, 2008); Barry Rubin, Israel: An Introduction (Yale University Press, 2012); Alan Dowty, The Jewish State: A Century Later (University of California Press, 2001); Robert O. Freedman, ed., Contemporary Israel: Domestic Politics, Foreign Policy, and Security Challenges (Routledge, 2009); Colin Shindler, The Rise of the Israeli Right: From Odessa to Hebron (Cambridge University Press, 2015); Gregory S. Mahler, Politics and Government in Israel: The Maturation of a Modern State, 3rd ed. (Rowman & Littlefield, 2016); and Brent Sasley and Harold Waller, Israel: Governing a Complex Society (Oxford University Press, 2016). Studies of Israel's parliament and prime ministers include Samuel Sager, The Parliamentary System of Israel (Syracuse University Press, 1985); Yael S. Aronoff, The Political Psychology of Israeli Prime Ministers: When Hard-Liners Opt for Peace (Cambridge University Press, 2014); and Guy Ziv, When Hawks Become Doves: Shimon Peres and Foreign Policy Change in Israel (State University of New York Press, 2014). Political parties are the focus of Peter Y. Medding, Mapai in Israel: Political Organization and Government in a New Society (Cambridge University Press, 1972); Jonathan Mendilow, Ideology, Party Change, and Electoral Campaigns in Israel, 1965–2001 (State University of New York Press, 2003); and Reuven Hazan and Gideon Rahat, Democracy Within Parties: Candidate Selection Methods and their Political Consequences (Oxford University Press, 2010).

The Arab-Israeli and Israeli-Palestinian conflict could fill libraries. The most informative primers and introductions include: Mark Tessler, A History of the Israeli-Palestinian Conflict, 2nd ed. (Indiana University Press, 2009); Charles D. Smith, Palestine and the Arab-Israeli Conflict: A History with Documents, 9th ed. (St. Martin's, 2016); Alan Dowty, Israel/Palestine, 4th ed. (Polity Press, 2017); and Dov Waxman, The Israeli-Palestinian Conflict: What Everyone Needs to Know (Oxford University Press, 2019).

More in-depth analyses of the conflict include the following critical approaches: Gershon Shafir, Land, Labor and the Origins of the Israeli-Palestinian Conflict, 1882–1914 (University of California Press, 1996); Mira Sucharov, The International Self: Psychoanalysis and the Search for Israeli-Palestinian Peace (State University of New York Press, 2005); Dov Waxman, The Pursuit of Peace and the Crisis of Israeli Identity (Palgrave Macmillan, 2006); Ilan Pappé, The Ethnic Cleansing of Palestine (Oneworld Publications, 2007); Benny Morris, 1948: A History of the First Arab-Israeli War (Yale University Press, 2008); Itamar Rabinovich, The Lingering Conflict (Brookings Institution Press, 2011); Mark LeVine and Mathias Mossberg, eds., One Land, Two States: Israel and Palestine as Parallel States (University of California Press, 2014); and Aaron J. Hahn Tapper and Mira Sucharov, Social Justice and Israel/Palestine: Foundational and Contemporary Debates (University of Toronto Press, 2019). On Zionism, see Peter Beinart, The Crisis of Zionism (Times Books, 2012) and Gershom Gorenberg, The Unmaking of Israel (Harper, 2012).

Social issues are richly researched, including topics of national identity, minority rights, cultural change, and gender. For a sample of this interdisciplinary field, see Myron J. Aronoff, Israeli Visions and Divisions: Cultural Change and Political Conflict (Transaction, 1989); Dan Horowitz and Moshe Lissak, Trouble in Utopia: The Overburdened Polity of Israel (State University of New York Press, 1989); Yaron Ezrahi, Rubber Bullets: Power and Conscience in Modern Israel (University of California Press, 1997); Daniel Gavron, The Kibbutz: Awakening from Utopia

(Rowman and Littlefield, 2000); and Lihi Ben Shitrit, *Righteous Transgressions: Women's Activism on the Israeli and Palestinian Religious Right* (Princeton University Press, 2016).

Palestinian Arabs within Israel are explored in Sammy Smooha in his two-volume *Arabs and Jews in Israel* (Westview Press, 1992), Ian Lustick, *Arabs in the Jewish State* (University of Texas Press, 1980), As'ad Ghanem, *The Palestinian-Arab Minority in Israel, 1948–2000* (State University of New York Press, 2001); Laurence Louer, *To Be an Arab in Israel* (Columbia University Press, 2007); Hillel Frisch, *Israel's Security and Its Arab Citizens* (Cambridge University Press, 2011); Oded Haklai, *Palestinian Ethnonationalism in Israel* (University of Pennsylvania Press, 2011); and Shira Robinson, *Citizen Strangers: Palestinians and the Birth of Israel's Liberal Settler State* (Stanford University Press, 2013).

Studies of Israel's economy include Dan Senor and Saul Singer, *Start-Up Nation: The Story of Israel's Economic Miracle* (Council on Foreign Relations, 2009); and Paul Rivlin, *The Israeli Economy from the Foundation of the State through the 21st Century* (Cambridge University Press, 2011).

Works on Israel's military include Yigal Allon, *The Making of Israel's Army* (Bantam, 1971); Ze'ev Schiff, *A History of the Israeli Army: 1874 to the Present* (Macmillan, 1985); Avner Cohen, *Israel and the Bomb* (Columbia University Press, 1998); Edna Lomsky-Feder and Eyal Ben-Ari, eds., *The Military and Militarism in Israel Society* (State University of New York Press, 1999); Baruch Kimmerling, *The Invention and Decline of Israeliness: State, Society, and the Military* (University of California Press, 2001); Yoram Peri, *Generals in the Cabinet Room: How the Military Shapes Israeli Policy* (United States Institute of Peace, 2006); Gabriel Sheffer and Oren Barak, *Israel's Security Networks:*

A Theoretical and Comparative Perspective (Cambridge University Press, 2013); and James Eastwood, *Ethics as a Weapon of War: Militarism and Morality in Israel* (Cambridge University Press, 2017).

On Israel's foreign policy and national security framework, see Zeev Maoz, *Defending the Holy Land: A Critical Analysis of Israel's Security and Foreign Policy* (University of Michigan Press, 2006); Avi Shlaim, *The Iron Wall: Israel and the Arab World* (W.W. Norton, 2014); Raffaella Del Sarto, *Israel Under Siege: The Politics of Insecurity and the Rise of the Israeli Neo-Revisionist Right* (Georgetown University Press, 2017); and Charles Freilich, *Israeli National Security: A New Strategy for an Era of Change* (Oxford University Press, 2018). The 18-volume *Israel's Foreign Relations, Selected Documents, 1947-2001* (Jerusalem: Ministry of Foreign Affairs, 1976-2002) provides the major documents of Israel's foreign policy from its inception through 1999. This documentary analysis is extended in Itamar Rabinovich and Jehuda Reinharz, *Israel in the Middle East*, 2nd ed. (Brandeis University Press, 2007).

The US-Israel relationship is dissected in Abraham Ben-Zvi, *Decade of Transition: Eisenhower, Kennedy, and the Origins of the American-Israeli Alliance* (Columbia University Press, 1998); Michael Oren, *Power, Faith and Fantasy: America in the Middle East, 1776 to the Present* (W.W. Norton, 2008); Aaron David Miller, *The Much Too Promised Land: America's Elusive Search for Arab-Israeli Peace* (Random House, 2008); John J. Mearsheimer and Stephen M. Walt, *The Israel Lobby and U.S. Foreign Policy* (Farrar, Straus and Giroux, 2008); Robert O. Freedman, *Israel and the United States: Six Decades of US-Israeli Relations* (Routledge, 2012); and Dov Waxman, *Trouble in the Tribe: The American Jewish Conflict Over Israel* (Princeton University Press, 2016).

Online sources

Much information about Israeli politics and policies can be found online, such as on the websites for the Israeli government (www.gov.il), the Knesset (www.knesset.gov.il), Ministry of Foreign Affairs (www.mfa.gov.il), Ministry of Defense (www.mod.gov.il), and the Central Bureau of Statistics (www.cbs.gov.il). The latter presents reliable fiscal data, including budget expenditures and revenues, for many decades. The Israel Democracy Institute's Peace Index runs monthly surveys on public sentiments in Israel regarding the Palestinian conflict (https://en.idi.org.il/centers/1159/1520). The Schusterman Center at Brandeis University contains a wide variety of online essays, syllabi, images, and resources devoted to Israeli studies (https://israelresources.brandeis.edu/).

The Israeli media scene is likewise vibrant, and spans the political spectrum. A sampling includes the left-wing *Ha'aretz* (www.haaretz.com), the right-wing *Jerusalem Post* (www.jpost.com), and the eclectic online news portals *Yediot Ahronot* (www.ynetnews.com) and *Times of Israel* (www.timesofisrael.com). Business and economic news are covered rigorously in *Globes* (https://en.globes.co.il/en/).

Please note that URLs may change far more quickly than books can be printed; so if these exact URLs do not work, simply search Google or another engine by the titles of these websites and online resources.

Palestine

Glenn E. Robinson

INTRODUCTION

Palestinians are descendants of peoples who settled this Eastern Mediterranean territory over the centuries, including the Jewish tribes that populated the area 2,000 years ago. Palestinians today seek to create a viable and independent state in the West Bank, Gaza Strip, and East Jerusalem, all lands conquered by Israel in the 1967 Arab-Israeli War. The Palestine Liberation Organization (PLO) declared an independent state of Palestine in 1988, with little success. In November 2012, the United Nations General Assembly voted overwhelmingly to recognize Palestine as a non-voting state, giving it the same status that the Vatican currently enjoys. At present, 71 percent of the UN's 193 member states formally recognize the state of Palestine.

In spite of this, Palestine does not yet control its own territory, which is still under occupation by Israel. Palestine's internationally recognized government, the Palestinian Authority (PA), exercises partial control (but not sovereignty) over about 40 percent of the West Bank, with its rival Hamas, the Palestinian Islamist group, running the smaller Gaza Strip. In both, Israel continues to exercise effective control, and regularly intervenes militarily to assert overarching sovereign power. Thus, Palestine as a state is currently more aspiration than reality, possessing some elements of statehood but lacking actual sovereign control over its territory. In recent years, the slow demise of the Oslo peace framework, and increasing Western futility to the issue, has made Palestinian statehood even less likely.

Box 9.1 provides vital data for Palestine.

BOX 9.1 VITAL DATA – PALESTINE

Capital	East Jerusalem (proclaimed); Ramallah (administrative center)
Regime type	Hybrid (semi-presidential republic)
Head of state	President Mahmoud Abbas (since 2005)
Head of government	Prime Minister Muhammad Shtayyeh (since 2019)
Legislative institution	Unicameral parliament, with 132 elected seats (*al-Majlis al-Tashri`i al-Filastini*, or Palestinian Legislative Council)
Female quota	Yes: parties must have a minimum (but not equal) proportion of women to men on candidate lists for those seats contested through proportional representation
Percentage of seats held by women	12.9%
Major political parties (share of seats in most recent general elections, 2006)	Hamas (56%), Fatah (41.7%), Popular Front for the Liberation of Palestine (2.3%)
Population	4,684,777
Major ethnic and religious groups (Gaza Strip)	Palestinian Arab (99%); Muslim (98.5%)
Major ethnic and religious groups (West Bank)	Palestinian Arab (72%), Israeli Jewish (28%); Muslim (70%), Jewish (28%), Christian and other (2%)
GDP per capita	$3,095 ($4,896 at Purchasing Power Parity)
Unemployment rate	30.2%
Youth unemployment rate	46.9%
Major economic industries	Agricultural produce, textiles, quarrying, crafts
Military spending as % GDP	N/A

HISTORICAL BACKGROUND

It was Roman rulers who coined the name "Palestine," drawing on Greek and possibly Semitic sources, after taking control in 63 BC. As the Roman Empire collapsed in the fourth century AD, control passed to the Byzantine, or Eastern Roman, Empire, which ruled from a distance until the Muslim conquest by tribes from the Arabian Peninsula in 634 AD. The conquest of Palestine marked the beginning of nearly 1,300 years of continuous Islamic rule, interrupted only by the European Crusades, primarily in the twelfth century AD. Saladin famously recaptured Jerusalem from the Crusaders in 1187.

The Ottoman Empire ruled Palestine for four centuries, from 1516 to 1920. During Ottoman rule, Arabs – both Muslim and Christian – remained the large majority in Palestine, although a small community of religious Jews existed as well, primarily in the cities of Hebron, Jerusalem, Tiberias, and Safad. However, in the latter part of the nineteenth century, Jewish immigration to Palestine from Europe increased, largely under the political banner of Zionism (Jewish nationalism). By 1914, the Jewish community in Palestine comprised 11 percent of the total population (75,000 of 690,000), a visible change from 1880, when Jews had made up about 6 percent of the population (35,000 out of 485,000).

With the defeat of the Ottoman Empire in World War One, Great Britain took control of Palestine. British leaders had already made conflicting promises to both Arabs and Jews, as evidenced by the controversial and ambiguous 1917 Balfour Declaration, which pledged support for a Jewish "national home" in Palestine without defining what this meant. As the chapter on Israel in this volume notes, the British Mandate period was marked by instability and conflict between two communities, Jewish and Arab, that each sought to claim the territory as their own. Palestinian nationalist forces resisted both British imperial rule and Zionist expansionism, resulting in the 1936–1939 Palestinian uprising. In 1947, the British announced the Mandate's end, turning the issue over to the United Nations. In November 1947, the United Nations General Assembly approved a partition plan that created a Jewish state with 55 percent of the territory, even though Jewish landholdings comprised less than 7 percent of the total land surface of Palestine, and most of the rest to Arab residents. Deprived of the best agricultural land and seaports, that Palestinian state would retain Galilee, the central mountains (now the West Bank), and the Gaza coast. The UN would administer Jerusalem as an international zone in this controversial Partition Plan, which was publicly rejected by the Arab states and their allies as an unjust outcome.

In 1948, the newly declared state of Israel decisively won the first Arab-Israeli War, which began as a communal war against Palestinian Arabs, and later became a state-to-state war against various Arab militaries. Motives for the 1948 war were mixed; for example, Egypt sought to not only attack Israel but also check Jordanian ambitions in the area, despite that both fought on the same side. In any case, the war saw not just the creation of the new state of Israel in 78 percent of Mandatory Palestine, but also the creation of over 700,000 Palestinian refugees, and simmering resentment of Israel in neighboring Arab states.

Fragmentation and exile: 1948–1967

Palestinians who were displaced during the war from lands both assigned to Israel by the UN and conquered by Israel during the war became permanent refugees on June 16, 1948, when Israel's new government took the decision not to allow them to return to their homes. Israel's "Plan Dalet" was designed to force many Palestinians from their homes during the war, which is why historians sometimes refer to it as a case of "ethnic cleansing" of Palestinians. Of the original 1.2 million Palestinian Arabs, nearly three-quarters of a million became refugees, dispersed to Egypt, Jordan, Lebanon, and Syria. Of those 500,000 who remained in place, 150,000 were in Israel (primarily in the Galilee region), with the remainder in the West Bank (annexed by Jordan) and Gaza Strip (administered by Egypt).

Palestinian society was changed profoundly by this trauma, which Palestinians call *al-nakba* (the disaster). Their society had previously been highly stratified and largely rural, with a powerful notable social class, a small middle class, and a large peasantry. In the wake of the war, Palestinian peasants were forced into wage labor; the elite lost the land that underpinned their power; and merchants lost their livelihoods. In time, dispersal would transform Palestinians into a mobile but highly insecure people among whom educational attainment and political activism ranked high as criteria for social standing, but physical dispersion made it difficult to reestablish a coherent political center. Palestinian political aims evolved significantly. At first Palestinians were determined to regain all of Palestine, but an increasing number conceded that territorial partition was the most they could achieve. That is, with their crushing defeat, Palestinians began to accept what they had rejected in 1947: two states for two peoples, Israel and Palestine, between the River Jordan and the Mediterranean Sea.

The Palestine Liberation Organization and the Palestinian Diaspora: 1967–1993

The 1967 Arab-Israeli War, referred to in Palestinian memory as *al-naksa* (setback or defeat) given the loss of the West Bank and Gaza, cleaved the Palestinian community in two: half now lived inside the boundaries of old Mandatory Palestine under Israeli rule, and half continued to live in the diaspora outside Mandatory Palestine, with the largest communities in Jordan, Lebanon, and Syria. (In Jordan, many had become Jordanian citizens, while others retained their refugee status.) The Palestine Liberation Organization (PLO) was created in 1964 by the Arab League as a diaspora organization representing the national aspirations of all these different Palestinian populations. The organization's charter called for the elimination of Israel, creation of a secular Palestinian state in its place, and return to Europe of Jews who had migrated under the banner of Zionism. It was a maximalist document that reflected Palestinian thinking of the time but which would evolve substantially in future decades.

The 1967 disaster provided the opportunity for Palestinian guerrilla groups to take control of the PLO and transform it into an autonomous umbrella organization. As an umbrella organization, the PLO contained many competing groups. The largest was the secular Fatah, led by Yasir Arafat, which espoused a Palestinian nationalist ideology, and which would dominate the PLO – and thus the visible face of Palestinian leadership – in future decades. The Popular Front for the Liberation of Palestine (PFLP), founded by George Habash, and the Democratic Front for the Liberation of Palestine (DFLP), led by Nayif Hawatmeh, were important factions that represented a leftist Arab nationalism. The PFLP gained international notoriety in 1970 with its spree of civilian-aircraft hijackings, which were intended to launch a broader Arab revolution.

The PLO began to flex its muscle by creating "states within states" in order to wage armed struggle against Israel. The PLO first did this in Jordan, which so threatened the Hashemite monarchy that it precipitated a civil conflict, which the Jordanian regime won in 1970. The PLO moved to Lebanon, entangling itself in internecine conflicts that ultimately catalyzed Lebanon's long civil war in 1975. The Lebanon-Israel border, never peaceful, became noticeably more violent in the ensuing years, as Israel sought to destroy the PLO and the PLO sought to inflict casualties on Israel. In the aftermath of Israel's 1982 invasion of Lebanon, the PLO was compelled to relocate to Tunisia, far away from historic Palestine and the largest populations of Palestinians in Lebanon, Jordan, and to a lesser extent Syria. At the same time, in the aftermath of the 1973 Arab-Israeli War, the PLO began to formally take steps to adopt a two-state solution as its favored approach instead of the maximalist position found in its 1964 Charter. Early steps in this transformation included the PLO's 1974 resolution to create a "national authority" in any part of liberated Palestine, and Yasir Arafat's famous 1974 speech at the UN in New York laying out the choice between war (the gun) and peace (the olive branch).

The 1979 peace treaty between Israel and Egypt dramatically altered the geostrategic landscape for the Palestinians. It removed Egypt from the Arab-Israeli conflict implicating Palestinian statehood, while inversely it enabled successive Israeli governments to leverage its peace treaty to vastly increase its colonization of the West Bank with Jewish settlements without fears of attack on Israel's western flank. Indeed, Palestinian national aspirations dwindled during the 1980s, as the PLO languished in its new headquarters in Tunis and the Soviet Union, its superpower patron, weakened. What rescued Palestinian national aspirations were two events. First, Palestinians living inside the occupied territories launched an uprising (*intifada*) against Israel in late 1987. The intifada showed that Palestinians inside the West Bank and Gaza were able to actively resist Israel's occupation and confiscation of Palestinian lands, even in the face of a badly weakened PLO out in the diaspora. Second, the PLO's support for Iraq's invasion of Kuwait in 1990 caused a chain reaction that further weakened the PLO both internationally and regionally, compelling its leadership to entertain a permanent peace with Israel in a process culminating in the Oslo Accords.

Social change in the West Bank and Gaza, 1967–1993

After the 1967 War, developments in the occupied West Bank and Gaza Strip were markedly different from the Palestinian diaspora. As the PLO gradually moved toward mainstream nationalism and accommodation with its Arab hosts, the "inside" Palestinians became increasingly radicalized and mobilized. In particular, three structural changes helped to transform Palestinian society: the opening of Israeli labor markets to Palestinians, the extensive confiscation of Palestinian lands by the Israeli government, and the establishment and expansion of the Palestinian university system.

First, after the 1967 War, Israel opened its domestic labor market to Palestinians from the occupied territories. Palestinians were recruited to do the unskilled or semiskilled jobs that Israelis often refused to do themselves – primarily in the agricultural and construction sectors – and this pool of cheap labor was a boon to Israeli businesses, which grew rapidly in the late 1960s and early 1970s. These jobs appealed because they paid relatively well and because there was an endemic shortage of local jobs. By the 1980s, over 120,000 Palestinians – 40 percent of the Palestinian labor force – worked in Israel daily. As much as 70 percent of the Gazan labor force worked in Israel or in Israeli settlements. The result was the virtual disappearance of the Palestinian peasantry and the destruction of many patron-client networks, especially in the West Bank, seriously undermining one of the pillars of social power for the Palestinian elite.

A second change was massive Israeli confiscation of land. In the wake of the 1967 War, Israel tripled the size of the municipal boundaries of Jerusalem and then annexed the lands within those boundaries. Large sections of this land were unilaterally declared state lands and taken by Israel, often for Jewish settlements. Other lands in East Jerusalem, the eastern sector of the city traditionally linked to Palestinian residents, were confiscated on "security grounds," while still other parcels were awarded to Israelis who had claims dating to before 1948. Palestinian claims on land parcels in West Jerusalem, also dating to the pre-1948 period, were not similarly recognized. Confiscation in the West Bank was even more extensive, as private property was also confiscated outright. On the eve of the Palestinian intifada in 1987, over half the West Bank and one-third of the Gaza Strip had been confiscated or otherwise made off-limits to Palestinians. Such confiscations attacked a second pillar of Palestinian elite power – control over land – further undermining the legitimacy of traditional Palestinian notables and local leaders.

The third change was the creation and expansion of a Palestinian university system. Prior to 1972, higher education was a privilege reserved for the Palestinian elite, as only those families could afford to send their children abroad for university. In 1972, the first full-fledged Palestinian university, Birzeit, was established. In subsequent years, universities were established in Bethlehem, Hebron, Gaza, Jerusalem, and Nablus. In the decade preceding the intifada, the Palestinian university-student population grew from a few thousand to between 15,000 and 20,000 annually. The effect was significant, as tens of thousands of Palestinians, most from the refugee camps, went through the university system and its concomitant political socialization. From this student population, a new Palestinian elite emerged in the 1970s and 1980s – one that was larger, more diffuse, from lower social strata, more pluralized, and less urban. As a result, Palestinian politics became more confrontational with Israel. During this period Palestinians built or expanded many labor unions, student blocs, and women's, agricultural-relief, medical-relief, and voluntary-works committees, creating a vibrant civil society.

Two international events helped spur the mobilization campaign. First, the Egypt-Israel Peace Treaty of 1979 shifted the regional balance of power dramatically in Israel's favor, forcing Palestinians to recognize that any positive solution to their dilemma would be a long way off. Thus, their primary objective was to make the West Bank and Gaza difficult for the Israelis to rule and absorb. Second, Israel's 1982 invasion of Lebanon had the unintended consequence of invigorating the emerging elite in the West Bank and Gaza and making it clear that they could no longer rely on the "outside" PLO for salvation; it would have to be accomplished by those Palestinians still living in the occupied territories. While this new elite was widely affiliated with the major factions of the PLO – Fatah, PFLP, DFLP, and the Palestinian Communist Party – it was significant that the political initiative clearly lay with those on the "inside."

Two intifadas and Oslo: 1987–2006

In December 1987, a mass uprising against Israeli occupation began. The intifada was spontaneous. It was not an armed uprising, nor was it particularly violent. Demonstrations, marches, and rallies were employed, especially in the first six months. However, the intifada was primarily about mass organized disengagement. In political terms, Palestinians denied Israeli authority on any number of issues and created alternative authoritative bodies to govern Palestinian society. The principal locus of authority for over two years was the Unified National Leadership of the Uprising (UNLU), an ever-changing body of local PLO activists who published periodic leaflets directing the intifada. Alternative Palestinian structures of authority sprang up everywhere as popular and neighborhood committees, which provided social services to meet needs generated by the intifada, including distributing food during curfews, organizing education, planting local food gardens, and organizing guard duty to watch for settler attacks. Palestinians boycotted Israeli-made goods, withheld taxes, and defected from some workplaces. Overall, the uprising was a vehicle of individual and communal empowerment, whereby, at least for a time, Palestinians believed they could actually roll back the occupation.

After an initial period of confusion, Israel responded to the intifada harshly, using, in the words of then-Defense Minister Yitzhak Rabin, "force, might, beatings" to crush it. Well over 1,000 Palestinians were killed by Israeli forces, with many thousands more injured, and tens of thousands were imprisoned, many without charge or trial. Most important was the strategy of collective punishment, whereby many were punished through house demolitions, curfews, destruction of crops, and similar means for the actions of a few. However, the intifada did bring some lasting change with the emergence of a powerful Islamist alternative to the PLO: Hamas, which espoused, and continues to espouse, a more radical and less compromising platform than the PLO, including ardent refusal to recognize Israel. More subtly, the intifada saw the internal weakening of the old Palestinian elite and the emergence of a new brand of activist leaders in the West Bank and Gaza, who prized local accountability and desired political pluralism.

In the aftermath of the 1991 Gulf War, the United States launched a major effort to resolve the Arab-Israeli conflict. In October 1991, the Madrid Conference convened with American, Arab, European, Israeli, Palestinian, and Russian participation. It led to a series of bilateral negotiations in Washington, which made little progress. The return to power of Yitzhak Rabin and the Labor Party in the 1992 Israeli elections, combined with a keen PLO interest in moving toward a peace agreement (and thus extracting itself from the political grave it had dug by backing Iraq in the 1990–1991 Gulf War), provided the basis for diplomatic progress. Secret negotiations begun in Oslo in January 1993 between PLO officials and two Israeli academics linked to the dovish Labor politician Yossi Beilin, which ultimately led to a breakthrough agreement between Israel and the PLO that was signed on the White House lawn in September 1993.

In addition to producing letters of mutual recognition, the 1993 Oslo Accord (formally known as the Declaration of Principles) established the principles upon which the interim period was to be based, and identified the key issues that the parties would need to resolve in a timely manner in order to enter into a final-status agreement. Indeed, the interim period was supposed to have ended in May 1999. The 1993 accord was followed by the Gaza-Jericho Agreement of 1994 that established the Palestinian Authority (PA) in the Gaza Strip and the West Bank city of Jericho. A full interim agreement was signed in September 1995. A subsequent agreement that expanded the territory under PA control was signed at Wye River, Maryland, in 1998.

The Oslo peace process essentially ended in the summer of 2000. US President Bill Clinton convened a summit meeting at Camp David in July to negotiate a final-status agreement between Israel and the PLO, but both the Israeli and Palestinian teams failed to reach mutual understanding. Israel offered to return all of Gaza and a large portion of the West Bank to Palestinian control but refused to engage the refugee issue and insisted on control over most of East Jerusalem. For their part, Palestinians noted that Israel's proposal for the West Bank left Palestinians with three unconnected cantons surrounded by Israeli territory. Each side came away from Camp David convinced that the other was not interested in a real peace agreement.

One way to understand the failure of Israeli-Palestinian negotiations without simply blaming one side or the other is to understand the different starting points used by each side. Put simply, the Palestinians negotiate as if the conflict began in 1948, while the Israelis negotiate as if the conflict began in 1967. For Palestinians, resolving *al-nabka,* their stinging defeat in 1948, means focusing centrally on the status of refugees – the Right of Return established by the UN in Resolution 194 – and on the overall distribution of land to the two states from the entirety of British Mandatory Palestine. Palestinians view their acceptance of Israel in 78 percent of historic Palestine as a major concession that has never been replicated by Israel. Conversely, when Israel effectively dates the conflict to 1967, neither the Palestinian refugee issue from 1948 nor Israel in its pre-1967 boundaries is relevant. Rather, the key issue for Israel is how much land conquered in 1967 should be given over to Palestinian control.

Understanding the failure of negotiations through the prism of 1948 versus 1967 helps make sense of the divergent understandings at Camp David in 2000 and since then in multiple failed talks. For example, Israelis view the offer to provide Palestinians with about 90 percent of the West Bank as exceptionally generous, while Palestinians view it as an act of bad faith: Israelis already have 78 percent of Palestine. The same logic applies to the issue of refugees: Israelis view pushing this issue too hard as an act of bad faith designed to delegitimize the Jewish state, while Palestinians view a serious reckoning with their Right of Return to be essential to the whole peace process. Arafat himself was a refugee.

The 2000s saw the slow death of the Oslo commitment to a two-state solution through mutual compromise. On September 28, 2000, Ariel Sharon, then fighting for leadership of the Likud Party, made a provocative visit to Jerusalem's Haram al-Sharif, which Muslims regard as the third holiest site in Islam, and which Jews regard as the Temple Mount, the site of the Temple of Solomon. Scuffles and rock throwing by Palestinians degenerated the next day into large demonstrations and clashes with Israeli police. A Second Intifada, also known as al-Aqsa Intifada, had begun. By contrast to the previous intifada, the uprising that began in 2000 was much more violent. Palestinians used small arms and suicide bombings. While more Israelis died as a result, far more Palestinians were also killed from IDF strikes, assaults, and reoccupation; from 2000 to 2007, 4,228 Palestinians lost their lives, including 855 children. The greatest casualty, however, was the peace camp in Israel, as Jewish Israelis soured on the prospect for a two-state solution – and indicated so in elections, as the right-wing Likud began to dominate Israeli politics, as Ariel Sharon became Israel's new prime minister in March 2001.

Last-ditch efforts by the Clinton administration at peacemaking in December 2000 and January 2001 failed, as the IDF reoccupied much of the West Bank by April 2003. Palestinian infighting also increased; both Hamas (never a part of the PLO) and the PFLP (a key constituent of the PLO) openly criticized Yasir Arafat for falling into a trap by agreeing to what would become a never-ending interim period with no Palestinian state ever resulting. Perceptions that the PLO leadership under Arafat was failing Palestinian aspirations helped increase support Hamas and its more militant stance. Arafat himself fell ill in October 2004, under Israeli siege in his headquarters in Ramallah, and died in November 2004. Mahmoud Abbas (Abu Mazen) was elected as the new Palestinian president in early 2005. Abbas has remained president ever since, even though his legal mandate as president expired in 2009 upon completion of his elected four-year term of office. Under Palestinian law, the president is limited to two four-year terms, thus even with re-election (which did not happen), Abbas's term of office could not legally extend beyond 2014. Abbas' persistent grip on power is the latest reason why the PA, though designed with electoral procedures and rules, has never sustained its democratic intentions.

The breakdown of the Oslo peace process led to two major Israeli moves. First, Israel began construction of a large barrier near its border with the West Bank. While its architect, Ariel Sharon, maintained that the wall was a security barrier, not a political line, in practice 85 percent of the wall cut into the Green Line (the pre-1967 demarcating boundary), effectively annexing parts of the West Bank to Israel while creating a "no man's land" separating thousands of Palestinians from their property. It also further restricted Palestinian movements, choking the last remnants of the once-vibrant flow of Palestinian workers who commuted to Israel. With much of it consisting of multilayered fences, concrete walls, and watchtowers, the securitizing structure is an austere reminder about Israel's ironclad control over the border (Photo 9.1).

Israel's second step was to withdraw from Gaza in the summer of 2005. The withdrawal was seen by Sharon as an effective means to prevent a larger peace process from unfolding, which would put pressure on Israel to quit the West Bank. An unofficial 2003 peace plan ("the Geneva Accord") that involved many former high ranking members of Israel's government, as well as top PA representatives, was gaining a great deal of support, much to the consternation of Israel's governing Likud Party. The Bush administration's "Road Map" for peace was a similar two-state solution backed by the quartet of the UN, US, European Union, and Russia.

PHOTO 9.1
Section of West Bank Barrier near Bethlehem

Source: Pixabay. Public domain.

Thus, refocusing attention on Gaza would put momentum for a serious and broader political process with the Palestinians in "formaldehyde" (to use the colorful words of Dov Weisglass, a top Sharon advisor). For its part, Hamas claimed (wrongly) that its violence, not the PA's negotiation strategy, had compelled Israel's withdrawal, which boosted Hamas' political fortunes. The chaos left behind in the wake of Israel's unilateral withdrawal indeed reduced international pressure on Israel to withdraw from the West Bank; critics have argued that Israel in essence swapped its nearly 10,000 settlers in Gaza for the hundreds of thousands more in the West Bank. Moreover, the withdrawal did not end the legal occupation status of Gaza, as Israel retained effective control over Gaza's land and sea borders and over its skies. Only Gaza's short southwestern border with Egypt near Rafah remained outside of direct Israeli control, and in subsequent years served as a lifeline as Israel imposed blockades over all other entry points.

Fragmentation, conflict, and despair: 2006–2019

Palestinian frustration with the lack of progress toward ending the occupation, and with worsening corruption and abuses of power by PA leaders, led directly to the success of Hamas in the 2006 parliamentary elections. In terms of votes, Hamas won 44 percent of the national vote to Fatah's 41 percent, but because of an unusual electoral law was able to parlay that plurality into a 74–45 seat differential – a commanding majority in the Palestinian Legislative Council, the functional legislative component of the Palestinian Authority. Hamas' victory led to a halt to any political process, and though Fatah's Mahmoud Abbas remained president of the PA, Israel froze relations with it. The United States and Europe also isolated the PA and withheld aid commitments as punishment.

Fatah did not take easily to the end of its years of one-party rule and the benefits and privileges that went along with this. Fatah conspired to take back what it viewed as its rightful role, instigating significant social turmoil as a result. This, combined with the general breakdown of Palestinian institutions of law and order during the Second Intifada, led to widespread lawlessness and factional violence in 2006 and early 2007. By June 2007, the Hamas government feared that Fatah was planning a coup to take back power. Hamas launched a preemptive putsch in its heartland, the Gaza Strip, routing Fatah in four days of heavy fighting and taking full control there. Fatah responded by dismissing the Hamas government and appointing a new government. Palestine was now effectively divided between a Hamas-controlled Gaza Strip and a Fatah-controlled West Bank.

Hamas' seizure of Gaza immediately led to an Israeli siege, wrecking an already fragile economy. Hamas' putsch in Gaza also sparked cross-border violence between Israel and Gaza. Israel was determined to undermine Hamas, and Hamas was determined to keep its place as the leading force of Palestinian resistance against Israel. The end result was periodic but bloody conflict, with significant clashes in Gaza in 2008–2009, 2012, and 2014. Violence also erupted in 2018 when Gaza's "great march of return" along its border with Israel sparked the killing of scores of protestors by Israeli snipers. Each occasion for conflict had its own spark, but the unifying theme in each was Israel's attempt to hit Gaza hard enough to precipitate the collapse of Hamas. Public opinion polls showed the opposite outcome, with Palestinians blaming Israel for the damage and supporting Hamas as much as they had before each round of battle. These rounds of conflict left about 4,000 Palestinians and nearly 100 Israelis dead, and caused extensive physical damage to the Gaza Strip's already strained infrastructure.

For its part, the United States proved increasingly incapable of guiding the process. The Obama administration worked hard to revive direct Israeli-Palestinian talks, which became a priority for Secretary of State John Kerry. However, the Israel government was dominated by the Likud Party for all eight years of the Obama White House; capitalizing on the ideological shift favoring right-wing politics in the Israeli electorate, Prime Minister Benjamin Netanyahu consistently thwarted all efforts to revive the two-state negotiation track under Oslo. The Trump administration, which came to office in January 2017, showed little interest in rejuvenating the peace process. In February 2017, the White House announced during Netanyahu's first visit that it would no longer stipulate the creation of a sovereign Palestinian state as part of a lasting peace agreement. The following December, the US formally recognized Jerusalem as Israel's capital and ordered the relocation of its embassy there from Tel Aviv, despite widespread protests in the Palestinian territories and several Arab countries. Hot-button issues, such as the 400,000 Israeli settlers in the West Bank, received virtually no attention, as American policymakers seemed content to allow the peace process and two-state solution to finally expire.

Over the 2010s, the Palestinian response has been adaptation in this time of despair. Rather than engaging in fruitless direct negotiations with a right-wing Israeli government backed by unwavering American support, Palestinians sought to internationalize the conflict in ways that would bring significant pressure to bear on the realities of the occupation. At the governmental level, Palestinians began to insist on international recognition of statehood and in 2012 successfully applied to the United Nations for recognition as a non-voting member state. The state of Palestine then set out to achieve recognition from individual states around the world, with 137 states so far granting recognition. Palestine also began joining scores of UN bodies, including the International Criminal Court, whereby Palestine could seek to charge Israeli officials with war crimes as a means to further pressure Israel.

For their part, Palestinian activists pushed for various boycotts and sanctions against Israel, invoking the memory of the anti-apartheid campaign against South Africa in the 1980s. EU countries began to respond favorably, shying away from some exports produced in Israeli settlements. An initiative launched by Palestinian civil society known as the Boycott, Divestment, and Sanctions (BDS) campaign gained considerable grassroots support around the globe, with advocacy rising after each asymmetrical conflict that maimed far more Palestinians than Israelis, such as the 2014 Gaza war and the 2018 Gaza border protests. Indeed, the BDS Movement was seen as sufficiently threatening to Israeli interests that both the Knesset and the American Congress passed laws trying to undermine it. US legislation at both the national and state levels has sought to criminalize support for economic boycotts of Israel, which critics suggest (correctly) violates free speech rights. In late 2018, the US closed the PLO Embassy in Washington, DC, arguing that it had not done enough to foster peace, and for the same reason cut funding to the UN Relief and Works Agency for Palestine Refugees (UNRWA) – the key international development actor providing education, healthcare, housing, and social services to Palestinian refugees, and their descendants, from the 1948 and 1967 wars.

As the 2010s close, the outlook on Palestinian statehood as defined by a sovereign regime, territorial control, and peaceful coexistence with Israel looks dire. Talk of yet another attempt, a so-called "deal of the century" backed by Israel, the US, and Saudi Arabia, was greeted throughout 2018–2019 with exasperation by many Palestinians. The plan putatively called for the Palestinian capital to be not East Jerusalem, but the village of Abu Dis located outside the city; for Israeli settlers in the West Bank to have complete rights to remain there; and for a future settlement date to create a Palestinian state to be pushed off indefinitely, thereby ossifying the status quo. The controversy this instigated suggested that neither the PA's formal efforts to internationalize the conflict, nor the unofficial civil society efforts to promote economic boycotts, were likely to generate significant pressure on Israel as long as the United States shielded Israel from their negative impacts.

SOCIAL AND ECONOMIC ENVIRONMENT

The West Bank (including East Jerusalem) and Gaza Strip constitute about 23 percent of historical Palestine and are separated by the state of Israel. Gaza is a small, urbanized, and densely populated area along the Mediterranean Sea, largely inhabited by refugees from the 1948 war and their families (Map 9.1). It possesses Palestine's largest city, Gaza City, with over a half-million inhabitants. Poverty rates are very high and have been exacerbated by frequent closures of the border with Israel, preventing Palestinians from working as day laborers in Israel. Unemployment is extensive and endemic, and childhood malnutrition has periodically occurred. Saltwater intrusion into Gaza's aquifer has polluted freshwater supplies, threatening public health. Gaza's only river, which flows from the Hebron hills in the West Bank out to the Mediterranean through Wadi Gaza, is seasonal and badly polluted. In terms of human misery, Gaza is one of the most desperate places on earth.

By contrast, the West Bank (Map 9.2) is larger and less densely populated, with somewhat better health and employment prospects for its residents.

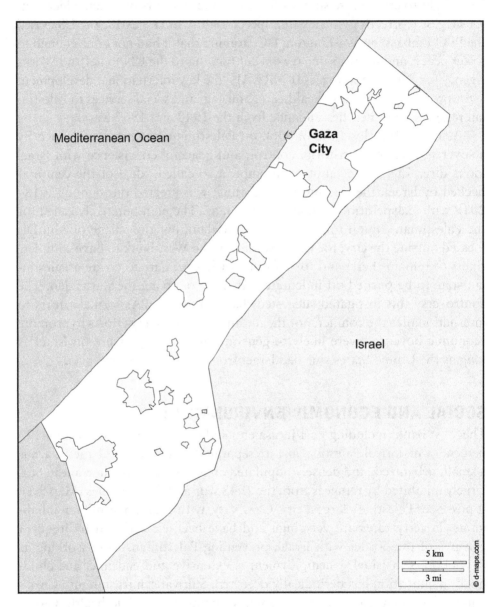

Mediterranean Ocean

Gaza
City

Israel

5 km

3 mi

© d-maps.com

MAP 9.1
Palestine – Gaza Strip. Major residential zones shown.

Source: D-Maps.

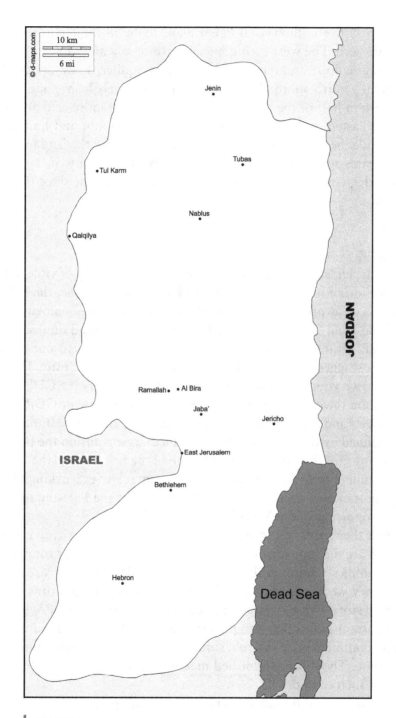

MAP 9.2
Palestine – West Bank. Major water bodies and cities shown.

Source: D-Maps.

Of the nearly five million total Palestinians living in the territories, 60 percent reside here. The west-facing hills receive significant winter rains, which promote agriculture and replenish the western aquifer, a key source of freshwater. A hilly north-south spine separates the relatively lush, populated areas in the western half of the West Bank from the much more arid and sparsely populated eastern half. These hills drop off into the hot and humid Jordan Valley. While the valley is below sea level, it is served by the Jordan River and thus generates agricultural production. The West Bank city of Ramallah has served as the temporary administrative capital of Palestine since the creation of the PA.

A struggling economy

Given its dependence upon Israeli openness, the frequency of violent conflict, the dispersion of its labor force, and lack of industrial base, the Palestinian economy is unsurprisingly stagnant and struggling. Stone quarrying, agriculture, textiles, and crafts are among the few productive (and tiny) sectors. The World Bank estimates the territories to suffer a 30.2 percent unemployment rate and a staggering 46.9 percent youth unemployment rate. That nearly one out of two young Palestinians is jobless explains why the GDP per capita is among the lowest in the region; why the economy is, in GDP, the absolute smallest; and why economic growth has been dormant. In the 2000s, a decade defined by the Second Intifada and lethargic gains on the peace front, the economy grew by just 1.7 percent. One of the few lifelines that many Palestinian families have is remittance income from relatives working abroad. In 2018, remittances constituted nearly 15 percent of the Palestinian GDP, the highest proportion in the MENA.

Across the territories, important social and demographic divisions exist. At the top are the remnants of Palestine's old class of elites, prominent landowning families whose wealth and property holdings today are a fraction of what they were a century ago. Palestine's merchant class runs the gamut from small store owners to wealthier businessmen. Under the PA, individuals with important political ties to power often have been rewarded with lucrative state contracts or monopolies that have generated significant wealth in a short time. The more established merchant community often feels resentment over such corruption.

The professional middle class rose to political prominence in the 1980s. Usually from modest origins, members of this socioeconomic group used university education as their stepping-stone to relative success. While Israeli confiscation policies did the most to undermine the notable elite in Palestine, the professional middle class had no love for what it collectively viewed as a regressive force in Palestinian society. In many cases, members of declining notable families dropped out and joined the professional middle class.

These old and new elites sit atop large blue-collar and agricultural working classes. Until recent decades, the peasantry had constituted the largest class in Palestine. Today, peasants and poor farmers remain, but their numbers are dwindling. Most Palestinian peasants became wage laborers following the 1967 War; throughout the 1970s and 1980s, the Israeli construction, service, and agricultural sectors became dependent on Palestinian wage laborers, who themselves preferred to leave their small farms in order to earn better wages in Israel. Before Israel's closure policy began in 1993, 40 percent of the Palestinian labor force worked in Israel, almost all as unskilled or semiskilled laborers. As Israel gradually closed its labor market to Palestinians, these workers rarely returned to agriculture. Many became unemployed.

Another important social cleavage exists between 1948 refugees and non-refugees. Generally, refugees have the lower social status. A similar cleavage exists between the West Bank and Gazan populations. Given its poverty and abundance of refugees, the Gaza Strip tends to be perceived as inferior by those in the West Bank. When the Palestinian Authority was first established in Gaza and then spread in 1995 to most West Bank cities, some West Bankers spoke openly of the *ihtilal ghazawi* (Gazan occupation). While that resentment was mostly transitory, there is no question that the physical separation of the two geographic parts of Palestine, as well as Israel's reluctance to allow Palestinians to travel between them, will keep these two islands moving on different social trajectories.

A demographic cleavage of diminishing importance is the one between Muslim and Christian Palestinians. Historically, Christians made up about ten percent of the total Palestinian population. However, given their privileged relations with European colonizers, Arab Christians have had much higher rates of emigration than their Muslim brethren. For example, while they are a small minority throughout the Arab world, Arab Christians make up about half of all Arabs who have immigrated to the United States. By 2019, Christians accounted for well under two percent of the Palestinian population in Palestine, and were concentrated in just a handful of locales (East Jerusalem, Ramallah, Bethlehem, Bayt Jala, and Bayt Sahur). Even though the institutions of state are secular, the rise of Hamas in recent decades has further pressured the Palestinian Christian population. The gradual decline of Christian communities has been replicated elsewhere in the Middle East, including Iraq, Lebanon, Syria, and Egypt.

Also of political importance, albeit diminishing over time, is the cleavage between "insiders" and "outsiders." The signing of the Oslo Accords in 1993 opened the door for some 100,000 Palestinians associated with Yasir Arafat's Fatah movement to move to the West Bank and Gaza. While most were rank-and-file members of police and security forces and their families, they also included the political elite that came to dominate Palestinian politics after Oslo. They were sometimes called "Tunisians" by local Palestinians, since so many came from the old PLO headquarters in Tunisia. The efforts of this outside elite to consolidate power were a defining element of Palestinian politics after Oslo.

Palestinian social demography is a complex web of relations and divisions, and a myriad of other social cleavages that cannot be discussed in detail here, such as relations between urban and rural Palestinians and between tribalized and non-tribalized Palestinians. But the dominant factor by far is Israel. More than any other force, Israel controls the facts on the ground in the West Bank and Gaza. Its government, and the IDF, decides if the borders are opened or closed; whether goods and services can move between towns or be exported or imported; whether Palestinians can come or go, or even travel internally; and whether settlements get built and more land gets confiscated. In short, since 1967, there is simply no important sector of Palestinian life that has not been directly affected by Israel.

POLITICAL STRUCTURES

The Palestinian Authority was initially constructed as a democratic polity resembling a semi-presidential republic. Its dominant institution was to be its parliament, known as the Palestinian Legislative Council (PLC). The executive branch under the *ra'is* (president) was designed to have complementary powers at best. An independent judiciary, harking to the days of British rule, was to play an important role in asserting the rule of law in Palestine. However, over time, the executive branch came to dominate both the parliament and the judiciary. The abuses of power associated with this office, as well as worsening corruption, Israeli interventions, and paralyzed governance in many areas, is the reason why this entity has never truly actualized its democratic blueprint. Neither, however, does it resemble the unambiguous dictatorships of other Arab countries, such as Egypt and Syria; this is not a government that flattens its society with repression so much as a government that simply cannot govern.

The dominant actor in the executive branch is the president, and there have only been two presidents in the history of the PA and the state of Palestine: Yasir Arafat (1996–2004) and Mahmoud Abbas (2005–present). The president runs the executive branch of government, which includes both civilian ministries and policing forces. To insulate himself from elite competitors and internal threats, Arafat created multiple and overlapping security institutions that often competed for funds and sowed corruption. Under Abbas, there has been significant reform and professionalization of Palestinian security forces, which work cooperatively with Israeli forces. Local governments, such as municipalities, also fall under the jurisdiction of the executive branch, specifically the Ministry of Local Government. Negotiations are in the domain of the PLO (as the designated Palestinian party that signed on to the Oslo Accords), but as a practical matter also fall in the jurisdiction of the president.

Under international pressure, the PA created a post of prime minister in 2003 in an attempt to strip Yasir Arafat of some authority. In reality, the prime minister holds only as much power as the president allows. Abbas was the first PA prime minister. The takeover of Gaza in 2007 created dual prime ministers: Isma'il Haniya was recognized as the legitimate PA prime minister by Hamas based on the 2006 elections, while Abbas as new PA president appointed Salam Fayyad as prime minister. The dueling prime ministerships in Gaza and the West Bank was not replicated at the presidential level as Hamas did not appoint or recognize a rival to Abbas, although Hamas has openly questioned the legitimacy of Abbas' presidency after his term of office expired. Haniya served as the prime minister in Gaza until promoted to head the Hamas political bureau, while Fayyad and Rami Hamdullah served in the same position in the West Bank.

Palestine's parliament, the PLC, was designed to be the primary source of authority in the PA, but has exercised little real authority in the face of the executive branch. There have been only two parliamentary elections, in 1996 and 2006. The latter was internationally monitored, and certified by Western observers to be free and fair – indeed, at the time some of the most competitive and democratic elections ever held in an Arab setting. Following the 2007 split between Hamas and Fatah, the PLC has ceased to function, with many of its Hamas members arrested by Israel. The unicameral body currently has 132 seats, and is led by a Speaker. In lieu of a parliament to pass laws, President Abbas has ruled by executive decree.

Unlike the parliament, the judicial branch of government continues to function in Palestine, although it has faced serious challenges in providing for the rule of law. The initial challenge was to merge the two distinct legal traditions. At the time of the signing of the Oslo Accords, Gaza's judicial tradition was a holdover from the British Mandate, with the traditions of British common law very much in ascendance. Neither Egyptian rule in Gaza (1948–1967) nor Israeli rule after 1967 fundamentally altered that British common law system, although the courts themselves were badly neglected. By contrast, the West Bank practiced French law, a reflection of the European conventions used in Jordan following Jordan's annexation of the West Bank. Merging these two distinct systems was a significant challenge, and the end product largely followed the West Bank's lead. Early high court rulings that went against the wishes of the executive branch prompted Yasir Arafat to try to stack the courts with his own loyalists. While this was not entirely successful, it is clear that the judiciary does not play its designated role as an equal branch of government providing a powerful check on executive power. As well, Israel destroyed much of the physical infrastructure of the judicial branch during the Second Intifada.

POLITICAL DYNAMICS

The PA's devolution into a hybrid marked by interrupted governance and authoritarian habits, as in the centralization and personalization of power, have been fueled by several dynamics: elite conflict, economic underdevelopment, and Israeli hegemony.

Elite conflict

The Oslo elite (e.g., the "Tunisians" or old guard) consisted of top PLO officials and their networks of supporters who returned to the West Bank and Gaza Strip when the PA was established in 1994. They were represented most dramatically by the late Yasir Arafat but also included cabinet ministers, high ministry officials, most top leaders of the security and police forces, and leading businessmen. Some of the most recognizable names of the Oslo elite are Mahmoud Abbas (Abu Mazen), Ahmad Qurei' (Abu 'Ala), and Nabil Sha'th. The second elite cohort consisted of native-born Palestinians in the West Bank and Gaza who were educated in Palestinian universities and Israeli prisons. These cadres were more numerous but less wealthy than their Oslo counterparts. They have variously been called the new elite, the intifada elite, and the young guard. The new elite and its heirs led both the first intifada (1987–1993) and second (2000–2004). Activist Marwan Barghouti, serving a life sentence in Israel for militant actions taken during the Second Intifada, is the most prominent of the new elite, which also includes Hamas leaders.

Both elite groups have strong national and family ties with each other; however, they are sociologically and philosophically quite distinct. These are not differences in policies as much as differences in how politics gets organized and practiced. In a simple sense, the Oslo elite represents more traditional politics, and the new elite holds more modern political sensibilities. These differences stem in part from diverse life experiences, but they also have a tactical political component. When Arafat and the Oslo elite returned from Tunisia, their primary political task was to consolidate their power, and to do that they needed to undermine the new elite. Only the new elite had the proven mobilization skills to thwart the Oslo project from within Palestinian society if it so chose.

The PA – an institution primarily of the Oslo elite – had some success in co-opting members of the new elite and intimidating others. The institutional home of the new elite consisted primarily of the organizations of Palestinian civil society. Indeed, the formation of civil society in modern Palestine was largely a result of the efforts of the new elite in the post-1979 period. In fact, the domination of civil society organizations by the new elite has been the underlying reason for the persistent PA attacks on its own civil society since 1994. To weaken the new elite, the PA engaged in a *politics of antithesis*, or the implementation of rules of politics at odds with the strengths of the new elite. For instance, the PA emphasized personalism, and a cult of personality around Arafat. Thus, one's office generally said much less about one's actual power than personal ties to Arafat and his lieutenants. By contrast, the new elite practiced diffused grassroots authority under Israeli occupation; it was against its democratic sensitivities that the PA exceeded its remit.

The al-Aqsa Intifada, the internal reform movement, and especially Arafat's death in November 2004 called into question how long the Oslo elite would be the dominant power in Palestine. The Oslo elite bet its political future in Palestine on the success of the Oslo peace process. The failure of that process in Palestinian eyes discredited this elite, opening the door for its rivals to reassume power within Palestinian society. Hamas' electoral victory in the 2006 parliamentary elections was further evidence of the weakening of the Oslo elite in the post-Arafat period. By clinging to power long after his term as president expired, Mahmoud Abbas protects the privileges of the Oslo elite.

The tension between these two elite groups is best seen as an evolving dynamic. From the establishment of the PA until the Second Intifada and concomitant reform movement, the cleavage between the groups was sharp and formed the decisive component of internal Palestinian politics. The Oslo elite, however, was predominant. The reform movement born of the al-Aqsa Intifada heralded a second stage in the evolution of this elite conflict. The reemergence of the new elite in this period was demonstrated in part by the new prominence of reformers in Palestinian government and the new political alliances that sprang out of the changed circumstances. The sharp and decisive distinction between the Oslo and new elites blurred as the latter reemerged on the political scene, most dramatically with the Hamas victory in 2006. Given the demographic weight of the new elite and the population it represents, the third stage in this evolving dynamic will likely see the consolidation of power by the new elite and the absorption of the remnants of the Oslo elite, likely with the passing of Mahmoud Abbas.

As the new elite consolidates power, cleavages will likely emerge. The most obvious is the already extant ideological cleavage between the Islamists of Hamas and the nationalists of Fatah. The cadres leading these movements are sociologically identical in terms of their class origins and educational backgrounds, but they are ideologically divided. It is useful to remember that Fatah itself emerged from the Muslim Brotherhood organization in Gaza in the 1950s, long before Hamas and Fatah cadres worked together periodically during the al-Aqsa Intifada. They have regularly shared cultural and ideological frames and symbols, with Hamas openly promoting Palestinian nationalism and Fatah embracing Islamic symbols. The emergence of the al-Aqsa Martyrs Brigade (*Kita'ib Shuhada' al-Aqsa*) out of alienated Fatah cadres is a case in point – its very name combines words that have nationalist and Islamic connotations.

Political economy

A second contributing factor to PA authoritarianism and corruption was the political economy established after Oslo, one quite similar to that of the oil-rich states of the Arabian Gulf. The Palestinian Authority can be considered a distributive, or rentier, state because a large majority of its budgetary revenues come from direct payments from international sources.

The most important payment has been the transfer by Israel to the PA of various taxes collected by Israel on Palestinian goods, services, and labor. But these transfers have proved unstable, as Israel has cut them off whenever the PA took actions that displeased the Israeli state. While tax revenues have varied in size from year to year, they have typically comprised over two-thirds of total PA revenues. In addition, foreign aid donors have contributed billions more to the PA treasury, although rarely in a consistent or predictable manner. Foreign aid is integral to Palestinians, such as through UNRWA's work among refugees; in the Gaza Strip, for instance, UNRWA administers services to 1.3 million, and enrolls a quarter-million children in its schools. However, other aid packages have taken the form of direct grants to the PA's budget, or else support for specific projects. Taken together, these two sources of PA funds typically generated more than 80 percent of PA annual revenues, on par with the percentage of budgetary revenues from oil in rentier states.

The taxes that Israel collects for the PA do legitimately belong to the Palestinian government. But the fact that they are collected by another state and transferred as a lump sum to the PA treasury has important political consequences. The PA's foreign aid reliance likewise creates fiscal pathologies that reward overspending and undermine accountability, similar to Jordan. All these direct payments create and sustain a top-heavy, centralized political structure. Creating a democracy out of a consolidated distributive political economy is extremely difficult.

Imbalance of power

A third factor contributing to authoritarianism in the PA was the vast imbalance of power between Israel and the Palestinians. The negotiating process accurately reflected this imbalance of power to Israel's advantage, including Oslo's focus on interim measures only, the absence of powerful policy levers for keeping Israeli withdrawal from Palestinian territory on schedule, the doubling of the number of Jewish settlers in the West Bank during the peace negotiations of the 1990s (a number that by 2019 had more than quadrupled from 1991 levels), and Israel having veto power on key issues, such as Jerusalem and refugees, which ultimately scuttled negotiations.

As the weaker party, the PA could accept or reject Israeli offers, but had little leverage to compel different terms. This often meant that the PA had little choice but to accept terms and conditions deeply unpopular within Palestinian society. Massive settlement expansion and regular Israeli closures of Palestinian areas while negotiations were ongoing were the most important exemplars of PA impotence vis-à-vis Israel in the eyes of most Palestinians. The imbalance of power meant the PA was forced to accept highly unpopular terms and realities. In turn, the PA had to crack down on the growing public dissent that resulted. Even if Arafat and the PA had been inclined to embrace democracy, the fact that elections would have empowered rejectionist elements – from the Islamist Hamas to the democratic mainstream – deterred the Oslo elite from conducting them. After Arafat's death, that basic logic continued under Abbas. For this reason, both parliamentary and municipal elections were only sporadically held, with office holders staying in their positions for years after their terms had expired.

Hamas rule in Gaza

Fatah's clumsy rule and corruption helped Hamas win the January 2006 PLC elections, after it had boycotted the 1996 contest. Hamas ran a disciplined election, never offering more candidates than available seats. Fatah-oriented candidates, however, ran in far greater numbers, thereby splitting their votes. As a result, Hamas was able to parlay a small 44 to 41 percent popular vote margin into a substantial parliamentary majority. This triumph also reflected its growing popularity due to its dogged policy of armed resistance to Israel's occupation. Fatah had chosen to negotiate, and it failed; Hamas promised armed resistance. After the elections, Israel, the United States, and Europe all tried to isolate Hamas, refusing to work with a group they classified as a terrorist organization. The bulk of Fatah's leaders favored isolating Hamas as well in order to win back power by any means necessary. Israel ceased transferring taxes and duties owed to the PA once Hamas controlled the purse strings and subsequently imprisoned without charge dozens of Hamas parliamentarians, cabinet ministers, and high officials. Resentment between Hamas and Fatah led to street clashes throughout 2006 and early 2007.

Matters came to a head in June 2007, following the publication of leaked documents that suggested an impending coup attempt by Fatah. Hamas struck first, routing Fatah forces in Gaza and consolidating its rule. PA president Abbas then dismissed the Hamas government and installed a new government under Prime Minister Salam Fayyad. However, Fayyad's government had effective control over only parts of the West Bank and no control in Gaza. The West Bank and Gaza were now formally split, with Fatah ruling the former and Hamas the latter.

Hamas' rule in Gaza had mixed results. On the positive side, Hamas was given credit for bringing the era of near anarchy to a close and establishing a degree of law and order. As part of this effort, Hamas took on clan militias in Gaza that were operating outside the law, often protecting lucrative black-market enterprises, including large-scale tunnel operations linking Gaza to Egypt. On the negative side, Hamas was largely intolerant of challenges to its rule and ideology, continuing its proxy war with Fatah. The international isolation of Gaza under Hamas rule, including Israel's tight siege, brought even more misery to Gaza, although the Palestinian population largely blamed others, not Hamas, for this condition. Various attempts to end Israel's blockade of Gaza, most notably by Turkish and international activists aboard the *Mavi Marmara* in 2010, have not succeeded. Israeli attacks on Gaza in 2008, 2012, and 2014 wreaked significant destruction but failed to change the political situation. Many analysts predict another Gaza war in the next few years.

FOREIGN POLICY

While not a sovereign state, the Palestinian Authority had an active foreign policy during the Oslo period of limited autonomy, and particularly during its drive for international recognition of statehood beginning in 2012. Formally, the PA was merely an interim government, and Palestinian foreign policy was conducted by the PLO. In actual fact, the two organizations merged to the point of being indistinguishable.

The PA had different audiences for its foreign policy. The United States was a key partner, as only the United States had the leverage over Israel essential to achieve Palestinian goals. Most Palestinians have despaired of Washington ever putting enough pressure on Tel Aviv to effectuate a two-state solution, an alienation that increased considerably with the Trump presidency. The European Union was also an important foreign policy partner because it contributed the most aid to the PA and because it was thought that European powers, especially Britain, could influence Washington on key issues. The Arab states constituted a third target audience because they could help deliver regional support and legitimacy to the Oslo process and Palestinian goals of sovereignty. Finally, there was Israel, the foreign power that held control over all Palestinian lands and must be convinced to relinquish that control. While some Palestinian leaders recognized that it was critical to try to win over domestic Israeli opinion, the PA never was adept at it. Any gains and inroads the Palestinians had made were lost entirely with the Second Intifada. Even after Arafat's death in 2004, there was a widespread belief in Israel that there was no suitable Palestinian partner for peace. As Israel has continued to shift to the right politically over the past two decades, the number of Israelis interested in a serious two-state solution has continued to decline.

From its inception, the PA had three primary foreign policy goals. First, it needed financial resources. The PA had as a core function a patronage role of distributing jobs and resources to key supporters and constituencies. It remains the largest single employer (by far) in the occupied territories, with about 20 percent of Palestinian households relying on such government jobs. Organizational survival was essential, and foreign aid was critical to this. The PA was generally successful in meeting this objective; indeed, in most years, it typically followed only Israel in receiving the most foreign aid per capita of any polity in the world, even excluding the humanitarian funding given to UNRWA. Between 1994 and 2003, the PA received nearly $4.5 billion in foreign aid from all global donors.

A second foreign policy objective was to ensure that the interim period generated the maximum degree of Palestinian sovereignty over the occupied territories. The PA needed to sell the Oslo peace process to a skeptical national constituency and set the stage for final-status negotiations. On this foreign policy objective, the PA failed. At its peak, the PA had full control over less than 20 percent of the West Bank ("Area A" in the lexicon of the Oslo Accords); Israel maintained full control over 60 percent of the West Bank ("Area C"), with the remainder being jointly administered ("Area B"). The PA had no control over East Jerusalem at any point. As for Gaza, the PA controlled about two-thirds of the Gaza Strip until 2005, when Israel unilaterally withdrew from the remainder. Even after the withdrawal, however, Israel still fully controlled the land and sea borders of Gaza and the airspace above it. The only exception was Gaza's land border with Egypt. As for the West Bank, the number of Jewish settlers in the West Bank doubled during the Oslo peace process in the 1990s, and doubled again after it failed; over 400,000 Israelis now reside there.

A third foreign policy objective for the PA was to gain tangible American support for a good final-status agreement, a quest that, to date, has failed. Winning over the United States when it came to key Palestinian positions was considered central to the overall strategy of securing a legitimate Palestinian state, at least until 2012. However, the US administration under Bill Clinton during the key period of the 1990s rejected the Right of Return for Palestinian refugees, insisted on significant Israeli sovereignty in East Jerusalem, never pushed Israel to cease its colonization of the West Bank, and advocated Israeli annexation of parts of the West Bank. The US administration of George W. Bush further distanced itself from Palestinian interests by allowing the Sharon government to implement unilateral measures in the occupied territories that were designed to prevent the emergence of a viable Palestinian state. The Obama administration genuinely pushed for a two-state solution and pressured the Israeli government of Benjamin Netanyahu to restrict the flood of settlers moving to the West Bank under Israeli government encouragement, but to no avail. Obama's failure to change the basic dynamic of the conflict led his administration to deemphasize the issue. The Trump administration fully backed the Netanyahu government; among its controversial measures since 2017 has been moving the US Embassy to Jerusalem, shuttering the PLO Embassy in Washington, DC, and ending its 70-year commitment to fund UNRWA despite the humanitarian consequences.

The Arab Spring further complicated PA foreign policy. While the far-reaching reforms demanded in a number of Arab countries through popular uprisings were not matched inside the West Bank and Gaza, the Arab Spring was nevertheless a setback for the Palestinians. Arab attention turned dramatically toward other issues in the region, from the civil war in Syria and the empowerment of ISIS, to the simmering regional rivalry between Saudi Arabia and Iran; international actors prioritized regional stability, the containment of extremism, and long-term geopolitical interests over the mundanely perennial problem of Palestinian statehood. Indeed, Saudi Arabia and Israel's shared interest in combating Iran and its spreading influence proved conducive to the latter's goal of further encaging the Palestinian leadership by pushing forward the "deal of the century." More than ever, Israel can impose unfavorable conditions upon the Palestinians without fearing major consequences from the Arab world – not only due to American support, but now also because of convergent interests against Iran.

FUTURE PROSPECTS

The future is bleak for the Palestinians for a simple reason: they do not control their own fate vis-à-vis Israel. The fragmentation of Palestine between Hamas rule in Gaza and Fatah rule in the West Bank complicates their prospects. Palestinians cannot speak with a unified voice in such a situation. Arguably, the historical period when a Palestinian state could be constructed has passed, while the occupation has grown more and more entrenched: more settlements, more checkpoints, more land confiscations, more segregated roads, more fragmentation of Palestinian communities. Internationalizing the conflict through the United Nations and through BDS and other boycott attempts may constitute a last gasp for Palestinian independence.

If creating a viable Palestinian state in the West Bank and Gaza is no longer possible, what does the future of Palestine look like? The most likely outcome is no solution at all, but rather just a continuation of the status quo. As long as the US protects Israel from international sanctions, then Israel can live with the minor inconveniences of BDS and periodic criticism. A second option is the ethnic cleansing of Palestinians from the West Bank, either through a long, slow, grinding process, or perhaps in a single lightening event, such as demanding they relocate to Jordan. Meanwhile, the reality on the ground increasingly appears by default to be one of a single, binational state in the whole of old Palestine. While this third outcome sounds lovely in theory, it will be a long time, if ever, before Palestinians enjoy equal rights with Jews in *Eretz Israel*, from the river to the sea.

FURTHER READING

The Palestine problem has been studied exhaustively from different political and analytical perspectives. The best start-to-finish narratives of Palestinian history and the conflict with Israel include Baruch Kimmerling and Joel S. Migdal, *The Palestinian People: A History* (Harvard University Press, 2003); Benny Morris, *Righteous Victims: A History of the Zionist-Arab Conflict, 1881–1999* (Knopf, 1999); Ilan Pappé, *A History of Modern Palestine: One Land, Two Peoples* (Cambridge University Press, 2004) and *The Biggest Prison on Earth: A History of the Occupied Territories* (Oneworld Publications, 2017); Mark Tessler, *A History of the Israeli-Palestinian Conflict*, 2nd ed. (Indiana University Press, 2009); Itamar Rabinovich, *The Lingering Conflict* (Brookings Institution Press, 2011); Mark LeVine and Mathias Mossberg, eds., *One Land, Two States: Israel and Palestine as Parallel States* (University of California Press, 2014); Charles D. Smith, *Palestine and the Arab-Israeli Conflict: A History with Documents*, 9th ed. (St. Martin's, 2016); Alan Dowty, *Israel/Palestine*, 4th ed. (Polity Press, 2017); and Dov Waxman, *The Israeli-Palestinian Conflict: What Everyone Needs to Know* (Oxford University Press, 2019).

Historical works on the Palestinian Mandate abound. Among the few studies of pre-twentieth-century Palestine, Beshara Doumani's *Rediscovering Palestine: Merchants and Peasants in Jabal Nablus, 1700–1900* (University of California Press, 1995) is outstanding for its insight into the political economy of an important town. Gershon Shafir emphasizes the centrality of land to the conflict in *Land, Labor and the Origins of the Israeli-Palestinian Conflict, 1882–1914* (Cambridge University Press, 1989). Also excellent is Alexander Scholch, *Palestine in Transformation, 1856–1882: Studies in Social, Economic and Political Development* (Institute for Palestine Studies, 1993). Salim Tamari examines the last years of Ottoman Palestine in *The Great War and the Remaking of Palestine* (University of California Press, 2017), while Daphna Sharfman does likewise in World War Two in *Palestine in the Second World War: Strategic Plans and Political Dilemmas, The Emergence of a New Middle East* (Sussex Academic Press, 2014). The best detailed treatment of the British Mandate period is Tom Segev, *One Palestine, Complete: Jews and Arabs under the British Mandate* (Henry Holt, 2000). A specialized study into law and gender during the Mandate years is Elizabeth Brownson, *Palestinian Women and Muslim Family Law in the Mandate Period* (Syracuse University Press, 2019), while economics is the focus of Sherene Seikaly, *Men of Capital: Scarcity and Economy in Mandate Palestine* (Stanford University Press, 2015).

Our understanding of the events surrounding the 1948 war have been revolutionized by the work of Israeli scholars who gained access to critical documents once the Israeli and British 30 year classification rules expired. Among many excellent books that shed light on 1948 are Benny Morris, *The Birth of the Palestinian Refugee Problem Revisited* (Cambridge University Press, 2004), *1948 and After* (Clarendon, 1990), and *1948: A History of the First Arab-Israeli War* (Yale University Press, 2008); Avi Shlaim, *Collusion across the Jordan: King Abdullah, the Zionist Movement, and the Partition of Palestine* (Columbia University Press, 1988); Ilan Pappé, *The Making of the Arab-Israeli Conflict, 1947–1951* (IB Tauris, 1992) and *The Ethnic Cleansing of Palestine* (Oneworld Publications, 2007); Zeev Sternhell, *The Founding Myths of Israel* (Princeton University Press, 1998); and Eugene Rogan and Avi Shlaim, *The War for Palestine: Rewriting the History of 1948* (Cambridge University Press, 2001). For an excellent depiction of the city of Jerusalem during the 1948 war, see Salim Tamari, ed., *Jerusalem, 1948: The Arab Neighbourhoods and Their Fate in the War* (Institute of Jerusalem Studies and Badil Resource Center, 1999). The Jordanian dimension of the Palestine problem is analyzed in Shaul Mishal, *West Bank/East Bank: The Palestinians in Jordan, 1949–1957* (Yale University Press, 1978).

Books on conditions and political struggles in the occupied territories prior to the First Intifada include George Emile Bisharat, *Palestinian Lawyers and Israeli Rule: Law and Disorder in the West Bank* (University of Texas Press, 1989); and Rita Giacaman, *Life and Health in Three Palestinian Villages* (Ithaca Press, 1988). A personal account of growing up under occupation can be found in Palestinian lawyer Raja Shehadeh's *Strangers in the House: Coming of Age in Occupied Palestine* (Penguin, 2003). Moshe Ma'oz, *Palestinian Leadership on the West Bank: The Changing Role of the Mayors under Jordan and Israel* (Frank Cass, 1984) offers insights into local Palestinian politics. Sara Roy's *The Gaza Strip: The Political Economy of De-development* (Institute for Palestine Studies, 1995) provides a comprehensive analysis of Israeli policies that stifled Gaza's economy, helping lead to the first intifada. Raja Shehadeh writes a penetrating critique of how law was used as a tool of occupation, not justice, in *Occupier's Law* (Institute for Palestine Studies, 1988).

The First Intifada spawned many books, including my own *Building a Palestinian State: The Incomplete Revolution* (Indiana University Press, 1997). While my book covers both the uprising and its political aftermath, other books focus solely on the intifada itself, including Zachary Lockman and Joel Beinin, eds., *Intifada* (South End Press, 1989); Jamal R. Nassar and Roger Heacock, eds., *Intifada* (Praeger, 1990); Zeev Schiff and Ehud Ya'ari, *Intifada* (Simon and Schuster, 1990); and F. Robert Hunter, *The Palestinian Uprising* (University of California Press, 1993). Helen Winternitz illustrates the impact of the uprising on a West Bank village in *A Season of Stones: Living in a Palestinian Village* (New Atlantic Monthly Press, 1991).

Life and politics in the Palestinian exile has generated interesting works. Yezid Sayigh has written the most detailed history of the PLO, titled *Armed Struggle and the Search for State* (Clarendon, 1997). Salah Khalaf (Abu Iyad), in *My Home, My Land* (Times Books, 1981), describes his key role in the establishment and growth of the PLO. Rashid Khalidi details the PLO's withdrawal from Beirut in *Under Siege: PLO Decisionmaking During the 1982 War* (Columbia University Press, 1986). Laurie Brand considers the circumstances facing Palestinians in exile in *Palestinians in the Arab World: Institution Building and the Search for State* (Columbia University Press, 1988). Salma K. Jayyusi's comprehensive *Anthology of Modern Palestinian Literature* (Columbia University Press, 1992) captures the spirit of Palestinians living in exile and under Israeli rule. The radicalization of Palestinians in Lebanon is considered in Bernard Rougier, *Everyday Jihad: The Rise of Militant Islam among Palestinians in Lebanon* (Harvard University Press, 2007).

The rise to prominence of Hamas has generated excellent works: Ziad Abu-Amr, *Islamic Fundamentalism in the West Bank and Gaza* (Indiana University Press, 1994); Khaled Hroub, *Hamas: Political Thought and Practice* (Institute for Palestine Studies, 2000); Shaul Mishal and Avraham Sela, *The Palestinian Hamas: Vision, Violence and Coexistence* (Columbia University Press, 2000); and Sara Roy, *Hamas and Civil Society in Gaza* (Princeton University Press, 2013). For understanding Hamas through the analytical lens of social movement theory, see Glenn E. Robinson, "Hamas as Social Movement," in Quintan Wiktorowicz, ed., *Islamic Activism* (Indiana University Press, 2003).

After the mid-1990s, a plethora of studies explore the two-state solution scenario. To envisage how to make that outcome after a rocky decade of the Oslo process, the RAND Corporation prepared a two-volume set on the requirements for creating a successful Palestinian state: the Palestinian State Study Team, *Building a Successful Palestinian State* (RAND, 2007); and Doug Suisman, Glenn E. Robinson, C. Ross Anthony, and Michael Schoenbaum, *The Arc: A Formal Structure for a Palestinian State* (RAND, 2005). The author of

this chapter (Glenn A. Robinson) was a principal leader of this RAND effort.

Studies of Palestinian politics and problems during the Oslo process include Joel Beinin and Rebecca L. Stein, eds., *The Struggle for Sovereignty: Palestine and Israel, 1993–2005* (Stanford University Press, 2006); and Amira Hess, *Drinking the Sea at Gaza* (Owl Books, 2000). Edward W. Said penned a scathing critique of the underlying principles and implementation of the Oslo Accords in *The End of the Peace Process: Oslo and After* (Pantheon, 2000). See also Glenn Robinson, "Authoritarianism with a Palestinian Face," *Current History* 97 (1998): 13–18 and "The Politics of Legal Reform in Palestine," *Journal of Palestine Studies* 27, 1 (1997): 51–60.

The Second Intifada also resulted in a number of mostly pessimistic books, including Roane Carey, ed., *The New Intifada* (Verso, 2001). Raja Shehadeh, *When the Birds Stopped Singing: Life in Ramallah under Siege* (Steerforth, 2003); Baruch Kimmerling, *Politicide* (Verso, 2006); and Rashid Khalidi, *The Iron Cage: The Story of the Palestinian Struggle for Statehood* (Beacon Press, 2007). A creative critique of Israeli occupation can be found in Jess Bier, *Mapping Israel, Mapping Palestine: How Occupied Landscapes Shape Scientific Knowledge* (MIT Press, 2017).

Today, for a good treatment of the possible futures of this conflict, see Jamie Stern-Weiner, ed., *Moment of Truth: Tackling Israel-Palestine's Toughest Questions* (OR Books, 2018), and Glenn A. Robinson, "The Death of the Two State Solution and the Revival of Palestinian Municipalities" in Robert O. Freedman, ed., *Israel under Netanyahu* (forthcoming, 2019–20).

Online sources

The online world presents a rich labyrinth of information regarding Palestine and Palestinian politics. Official sources with data, documentation, histories, and statements from the Palestinian Authority include the PLO Negotiations Affairs Department (www.nad.ps), the Palestinian Central Bureau of Statistics (www.pcbs.gov.ps), and United Nations Relief and Works Agency (www.unrwa.org).

Civil society groups are engaged by the Palestinian Non-Governmental Organizations Network (www.pngo.net). For survey data on Palestinian public opinion, see Palestinian Center for Policy and Survey Research (www.pcpsr.org). The Institute for Palestine Studies also hosts an array of research materials (www.palestine-studies.org/). Foundations and peace monitors include the Foundation for Middle East Peace (www.fmep.org), Badil Resource Center (www.badil.org), Palestinian Initiative for the Promotion of Global Dialogue and Democracy (www.miftah.org), Jerusalem Media and Communications Center (www.jmcc.org), and the Palestine Center of the Jerusalem Fund (www.thejerusalemfund.org). Online daily news sources in English that cover Palestinian issues include Beirut's *Daily Star* (www.dailystar.com.lb); Amman's *Jordan Times* (www.jordantimes.com); Tel Aviv's *Ha'aretz* (www.haaretz.com); and Doha's *Al-Jazeera* (www.aljazeera.com/topics/country/palestine.html). In addition, excellent Palestinian coverage with on-ground sources comes from *Palestine News Network* (http://english.pnn.ps/) and *Palestine Chronicle* (www.palestinechronicle.com).

Please note that URLs may change far more quickly than books can be printed; so if these exact URLs do not work, simply search Google or another engine by the titles of these websites and online resources.

Syrian Arab Republic

Thomas Pierret

INTRODUCTION

Syria's modern history is a tale of continuity and upheavals at once. By 2011, the country had been ruled by the same party, the Ba'th, and the same family, the Asads, for more than four decades. Yet, this period was far from stable as the country witnessed a socialist "revolution from above," internal coups and factional struggles, multiple crackdowns against the opposition, local uprisings and a nationwide Islamist insurgency (1979–82), in addition to direct military confrontations and proxy wars with all of the country's neighbors and the United States.

The devastating civil war that followed the 2011 uprising was the most significant break in Syrian history since independence. Although the regime was still in place at the end of the decade, the country had changed beyond recognition. Above a quarter of its pre-war population were now refugees abroad, while its economy had made a giant leap backwards as a result of large-scale destruction of infrastructure. Once a major player in Middle Eastern politics, Syria had turned into the region's battlefield, before non-state actors – the rebels, the Islamic State, and the Kurdish YPG, then foreign states, carved out zones of influence. By early 2019, Syria was best described as the juxtaposition of three protectorates – a Russian-Iranian one, a Turkish one, and a US one – than as a sovereign state.

Box 10.1 provides vital data for this country.

BOX 10.1 VITAL DATA – SYRIAN ARAB REPUBLIC

Capital	Damascus
Regime type	Authoritarian (presidential republic)
Head of state	President Bashar al-Asad (since 2000)
Head of government	Prime Minister Imad Khamis (since 2016)
Legislative institution	Unicameral parliament, with 250 elected seats (*Majlis al-Sha'b*, or People's Assembly)
Female quota	No
Percentage of seats held by women	13.2%
Major political parties (share of seats in most recent general elections, 2016)	National Progressive Front [Ba'th Party and allies] (80%); until 2011, no other parties permitted
Population	18,269,868
Major ethnic groups	Arab (80%), Kurdish (10%), Turkoman (4%), Assyrian (3%), Circassians (1%), Armenian (1%), Other (1%)
Major religious groups	Sunni Muslim (80%), Alawite Muslim (10%), Christian (5%), Druze (3%), Other (2%)
GDP per capita	N/A
Unemployment rate	50% (2015)
Youth unemployment rate	N/A
Major economic industries	Petroleum, textiles, food processing, tobacco, mining, cement, machinery
Military spending as % GDP	4.1% (2011)

HISTORICAL BACKGROUND

From 661 AD, Damascus was the center of the Umayyad Caliphate. Subsequently, Syria (known then as the broader *Bilad al-Sham*) became part of successive Islamic empires ruled from Baghdad or Cairo and, after the Ottoman conquest in the sixteenth century, from Istanbul. As Ottoman power began to decline in the eighteenth century, a new class emerged in Syria of urban notables who functioned as intermediaries with Ottoman officials and who would remain political players in Syria well into the twentieth century. In the second half of the 1800s, European encroachment in the Levant sparked the *nahda*, or Arab cultural renaissance that spawned nationalist reactions to Ottoman imperialism.

From World War One to the rise of the Ba'th party

The Ottoman Empire's decision to join the Central Powers in World War One was met with British support for an Arab revolt led from the Hijaz by Sharif Hussein and his son Faysal. The revolt began in 1916 in return for vague British promises of Arab independence, but London made contrary promises to its French allies in the Sykes-Picot Agreement. Consequently, the Syrian kingdom ruled by Faysal following the 1918 Ottoman withdrawal was occupied by French troops two years later. The League of Nations granted France and Britain Mandates over the Levant. The resulting arbitrary borders around Syria cut off the country from mercantile and cultural links in neighboring areas: Damascus was isolated from what is now Lebanon, Palestine, and Jordan; Aleppo's northern hinterland (Antep) and closest access to the sea (Sanjak of Alexandretta, or Hatay) became part of the future Republic of Turkey; in the east, the tribes of the Euphrates were separated from their Iraqi kin.

Inside Syria, French divide-and-rule policies translated into the establishment of five semi-autonomous provinces: Alexandretta (before its cession to Turkey in 1939) was carved out for the Turks; the remainder of the coast for Alawites; the southern region of Suwayda for the Druze; and the rest of the country was divided between the predominantly Sunni states of Damascus and Aleppo. This division along sectarian or ethnic lines gave particular salience to the concepts of "minorities" and "majorities" that were emerging in the context of nation/state-building and representative politics. Although the major anti-French rebellion that began in 1925 was defeated, unrest convinced Paris to rule indirectly through a parliamentary Syrian republic. In 1936, the Franco-Syrian Treaty recognized the country's independence and re-unification, but it was only after World War Two, in 1946, that the last French soldiers withdrew under British pressure.

After independence, Syria's parliamentary system was dominated by politicians who, like President Shukri al-Quwwatli, hailed from the elite landowning and merchant families that had held local power under the Ottomans and gained nationalist legitimacy from their struggle against the French. These notables coalesced into the rival National Party in Damascus and People's Party in Aleppo. However, this older generation came to be regarded by the younger generation as corrupt and unable to deliver on matters of social progress. Humiliating defeat in the 1948 Arab-Israeli War struck a first blow to the elite. The following year, a series of three successive military coups brought to power Colonel Adib al-Shishakli, who ruled in an increasingly autocratic manner until another putsch restored the parliamentary system in 1954.

In the 1950s, new political forces were rising that distinguished themselves from the elite parties by their middle-class leadership, radical ideology, and ambitions to mobilize the masses. Among them was the fascist-leaning Syrian Social National Party (SSNP), which advocated the union of Syria and its neighbors into a modern version of *bilad al-sham*, or Greater Syria. The SSNP was banned in 1955 for ordering a political assassination, but it survived and later reappeared as a regime ally under Bashar al-Asad. On the radical Left, the Communist Party's popularity benefited the Soviet Union's denunciation of Western imperialism. Yet, the most successful of the new political forces was the Ba'th Party, a pan-Arab group established in 1947 by Damascene schoolteachers Michel Aflaq and Salah al-Din al-Bitar. Their alliance with the agrarian MP Akram al-Hawrani provided the party with a socialist ideology and close ties with the Syrian military, which would soon become the final political arbiter in the country. The Ba'th steadily increased its share of seats in parliament and influenced the country's foreign policy, a trend that culminated in 1958 when Syria merged with Gamal Abdel Nasser's Egypt to form the United Arab Republic (UAR). However, Cairo's centralist, authoritarian, and socialist policies alienated both Ba'th leaders and traditional elites, pushing Syria to secede from the UAR in 1961.

After one last parliamentary interlude, the Ba'th came to power through a military coup on March 8, 1963. Built on a narrow base, the regime faced opposition across the whole spectrum of political society, from Nasserites to Islamists to liberals. In order to break out of its isolation, the Ba'th carried out a "revolution from above" that broke the economic hold of the oligarchy through nationalizations, won the support of peasants with land reform, and created a public sector employing major segments of the middle and working classes.

Within the regime, civilian party members were subjugated by their military counterparts, who were themselves divided by power struggles over ideology and personal ambition. Since sectarian affiliations played a prominent role in the construction of rival coalitions, Alawite officers emerged as the strongest contenders. Like members of other rural minorities, the Alawites used military careers as a means of social advancement, but they were more numerous than the Druze and Isma'ili. They were also more cohesive than their Sunni counterparts, who were divided along class and regional lines.

In 1966, intra-Ba'th struggle brought to power the party's radical leftist wing led by Alawite General Salah Jadid, whose stridently anti-Israeli stance backlashed as Syria lost the Golan Heights during the 1967 Six-Day war. Three years later, Jadid was toppled by his Minister of Defense Hafiz al-Asad, who carried out a "Corrective Movement" by placating the Sunni bourgeoisie through limited economic and political liberalization, as well as by toning down the regime's secularist ambitions. External resources provided by the Soviet Union and Arab Gulf monarchies allowed for the expansion of the state bureaucracy, the army, and security apparatus (*mukhabarat*). Asad's appointment of relatives and largely Alawite personal followers to key positions resulted in the construction of a "presidential monarchy" that concentrated power in the president's own hands. Decent military showing in the 1973 Arab-Israeli War provided the legitimacy to entrench his leadership.

Despite such initially favorable circumstances, Asad soon faced a formidable challenge from religious opposition. Rooted in the traditional urban middle class and at ease in the defunct parliamentary system, the now-outlawed Muslim Brotherhood were radically at odds with the country's new rulers because of their authoritarian, secularist, and socialist policies. A brief Islamist-led uprising was crushed by the army in Hama in 1964, and in 1973 Islamists orchestrated riots against a proposed secular constitution. In 1979, the proto-jihadi Fighting Vanguard launched an armed insurgency that dragged more mainstream Islamic groups like the Muslim Brotherhood into a deadly confrontation with the regime. The revolt ended in 1982, when regime forces killed tens of thousands in Hama. Afterwards, Islamist networks were eradicated through mass executions, internment in the infamous Palmyra prison, and exile. In parallel, Asad channeled the discourse of official Islam through conservative but politically submissive 'ulama like Grand Mufti Ahmad Kaftaro and Sa'id Ramadan al-Buti.

Presidential succession, stalled democratization, and "authoritarian upgrading"

The Islamist insurgency further entrenched the personalization of power, a trend illustrated by the state-organized cult of the Asads. Because Hafiz's brother Rif'at was exiled following a coup attempt in 1984, state propaganda prepared Syrians for the ascent to power of the president's eldest son Basil then, after his death in a car accident in 1994, of his ophthalmologist brother

Bashar. The latter was 34 when he succeeded his father to the presidency in 2000, thereby turning Syria into a *jumlukiyya,* an Arabic portmanteau for "republic" and "monarchy." The advent of a young leader portrayed as a modernizer raised expectations among the remainders of the domestic opposition, which set up forums and released petitions asking for reforms. By early 2001, however, this "Damascus Spring" ended with the arrest of the MP Riyad Seif, who had denounced the awarding of a mobile-telecommunications monopoly to Asad's cousin and crony, Rami Makhlouf.

In the middle of the decade, domestic dissent surged in a more forceful way as the US occupation of Iraq made the regime appear vulnerable. The jihadi networks that emerged across the country to send fighters across the border were neutralized, from the time being, through a combination of benign neglect, deflection toward Lebanon, and selective repression. In Kurdish-majority regions, however, several hundreds were killed in 2004 in the suppression of riots inspired by the post-Saddam emancipation of Iraqi Kurds. (On the eve of the Ba'th coup of 1963, part of the Kurdish population had been deprived of Syrian citizenship, and in the following decade, Arabization policies meant the creation of an "Arab belt" along the Turkish border through the settlement of Bedouin tribes. In the 1980s, Hafiz al-Asad had neutralized Kurdish dissent by allying with the anti-Turkish Kurdistan Workers' Party [PKK], but the alliance unraveled following the 1998 reconciliation between Syria and Turkey).

In 2005, the regime was further shaken by a combination of Western pressures over Syrian military presence in Lebanon, and internal factional struggles. A feud between the Asad clan, on the one hand, and a nexus composed of Vice-President 'Abd al-Halim Khaddam, interior minister Ghazi Kana'an, and Lebanese Prime Minister Rafik Hariri, on the other hand, came to an end as Hariri was assassinated, Kana'an committed suicide, and Khaddam fled to France. Following the killing of Hariri, Western pressures and mass protests in Beirut known as the "Cedar Revolution" forced Syrian troops out of Lebanon, while the UN investigation into the Hariri case alluded to the responsibility of the Syrian regime. Seizing the opportunity, the exiled Muslim Brotherhood joined forces with domestic opponents within the Damascus Declaration for Democratic Change. Yet, the regime dodged the bullet by arresting dissidents and bombarding the population with nationalist, anti-Western propaganda.

Politically, the regime's neoliberal economic reforms entailed a rollback in the populist social contract, thereby debilitating the regime's former cross-sectarian base, reinforcing its sectarian-family nature, and limiting its vote-getting capacity. Peasants simultaneously suffered from a reduction in state support for the agricultural sector, and from the terrible drought of 2007–9. Poor neighborhoods around the cities burgeoned with an influx of drought victims and Iraqi refugees. In addition, urban real-estate speculation unleashed by the influx of Gulf capital, together with an end to rent controls, drove the cost of housing beyond the means of the middle class. The conspicuous consumption of the new urban rich alienated working-class families in the suburbs, and free trade agreements ending tariff protection devastated small businesses. In addition, Bashar debilitated the party apparatus and the worker and peasant unions. Rural discontent was further fueled by attempts to crack down on smuggling networks that provided revenues to communities living along the borders of the country.

Alternative constituencies cultivated by the regime as part of its policy of "authoritarian upgrading" only partly made up for the estrangement of the working class. These new constituencies include reformist technocrats, the bourgeoisie, and formerly hostile Islamic circles like Shaykh Usama al-Rifa'i's Zayd movement. Sunni 'ulama and their businessmen allies were allowed to set up schools and well-funded charities that filled part of the void left by a shrinking welfare state. In long-marginalized Aleppo, the regime's relationship with the interlocked business and religious elites greatly improved as a result of economic openness to Turkey. Yet, the honeymoon with the Sunni 'ulama was short-lived, as the latter's empowerment unnerved the regime, which by 2008 curtailed both the influence of religious scholars in the charitable sector and expressions of religious identity in the public sphere.

The Arab Spring and civil war, 2011–2019

Inspired by the Tunisian, Egyptian, and Libyan revolutions, the Syrian uprising spread from the southern city of Der'a from March 2011 onwards. While demonstrators at first called for political reform, demands radicalized under the brutality of state repression. Two weeks into the uprising, Asad gave a defiant speech and branded the protest movement as a foreign conspiracy. More than ever, the minority character of the regime made it too risky to appease the opposition through democratic concessions. It also made Syria different from Tunisia and Egypt, whose respective dictators had fallen in a matter of weeks after they were abandoned by the military elite. Asad could rely on a cohesive Alawite military elite wedded to the ruling clan and ready to defeat the Sunni-dominated revolt by any means. Even before the uprising turned into civil war, thousands of demonstrators were killed, and dozens of thousands were arrested, at least 15,000 of whom eventually died in custody.

Still, the uprising continued as grievances fueled a plurality of the population. The protests initially spread in rural provinces (Der'a and Idlib), suburbs of Damascus (Duma, Daraya), mixed Sunni-Alawite areas (Homs, Banias, Latakia), and for obvious historical reasons, Hama. Tellingly, three of the uprising's first hotbeds (Banias, Der'a and Rastan near Homs) were the birthplaces of the foremost Sunni partners of Hafez Al-Asad (respectively Khaddam, Faruq al-Shara and Mustafa Tlass), all of which had been marginalized under Bashar.

Demonstrations occasionally took place in central Damascus, but the protest movement failed to establish a durable foothold in the capital. This resulted from a concentration of state coercion, but also weaker grassroots support. Although networks of activists included a significant middle-class, trans-sectarian contingent from the capital, they often lacked support from their social milieu. Many religious minorities (in particular Alawite and Christians) opposed the uprising out of fear of a takeover by the Sunni majority; others believed the revolution would come only at the price of great violence. The regime played on these sectarian and class fears by portraying protesters as Salafi extremists and peasant riffraff.

Peaceful protests continued to spread and culminated with the mass demonstrations that filled Hama's Orontes Square in July 2011. As regime tanks spread out, demonstrations decreased while the militarization of the uprising accelerated. Some Sunni officers had started to defect in June and, over the summer, proclaimed the establishment of a "Free Syrian Army" (FSA), then a mere label for autonomous local units. Although small in numbers and poorly equipped, military defectors and civilian volunteers grew increasingly successful in the last months of 2011. The regime lacked manpower to pacify rebel strongholds; it did not trust its Sunni soldiers and was over reliant on Alawite-heavy units. During the first two years of the uprising, a mere third of the army's order of battle was deployed in combat operations. In parallel, defections and losses gradually deprived the military of more than half of its 300,000 men. As a means to compensate the regime increased its firepower throughout 2012 by resorting to artillery, aircrafts, ballistic missiles, and chemical weapons. The spring of 2012 also witnessed massacres of hundreds of Sunni civilians at the hands of pro-regime paramilitaries on the fringes of the Alawite heartlands, most famously in al-Hula near Homs.

Military escalation did not prevent the spread of the insurgency, which by the end of the winter started to receive logistical support from Saudi

Arabia, Qatar, and Turkey. In July 2012, the regime seemed on the verge of collapse when rebels seized most of the province of Aleppo, including half of its capital, as well as the main border crossings with Turkey and Iraq. Vast parts of the country were now administered by an archipelago of self-standing courts, committees, and local councils run by insurgent groups and civilians. In the north, the regime abandoned most of Kurdish-majority areas to the Democratic Union Party, or PYD (PKK's Syrian branch), which established the so-called Autonomous Administration of Rojava and battled anti-Asad insurgents over oil fields and border crossings. At the same time, the ruling elite was shaken by a bomb attack that killed four high-ranking officials, including Asad's brother-in-law Asef Shawkat, and by the defection of the incumbent prime minister Riyad Hijab. Concomitant rebel incursions into central Damascus were quickly repelled. By the end of the year, however, insurgents had regained strength and were closing in on Damascus, even cutting off the city from the international airport for a few days.

In 2013, the regime forces turned the tide and stabilized their defense lines, secured strategic roads along the Damascus-Aleppo axis, and gradually encircled the rebels in Aleppo and the suburbs of Damascus. The following year, the insurgents were expelled from most of the province of Homs and Qalamun mountains, north of Damascus. The cause of this success was twofold. First, manpower shortage was alleviated by focusing on the protection of select strategic positions, by recruiting civilian fighters (mostly among religious minorities and loyal Sunni tribes) within the newly created National Defense Forces (NDF) and other paramilitary units, and by inviting in foreign Shi'a militias recruited by Iran's Revolutionary Guards Corps (IRGC) in Lebanon (Hizbullah), Iraq, and Afghanistan. Second, the lack of international reaction left Asad unhindered in implementing a strategy aimed at emptying rebel-held areas and forcing them into submission through the targeting of civilians with makeshift barrel-bombs, the destruction of vital infrastructures, and forced starvation. By 2014, an estimated half of the population had been forced to leave their homes.

On the opposition side, long-standing exiles, such as the Muslim Brotherhood, and recent fugitives set up the Syrian National Council in Istanbul in 2011. The following year, Western and Saudi concerns about Islamist influence within the council led to its integration into a broader Syrian National Coalition. Originally chaired by moderate Islamist Moaz al-Khatib, the Coalition became the chief representative of the Syrian opposition for the international community. In 2013, it established an Interim Government based in Gaziantep, Turkey. The Coalition had stronger ties with civilian activists and rebel groups inside Syria than Western common wisdom held, but it lacked the means to establish authority over them. Moreover, it suffered from factional struggles heightened by rivalries between its Saudi and Qatari patrons.

By mid-2012, two partly overlapping strands had emerged among rebel factions. On one side were "nationalist" groups run by defected officers such as General Salim Idriss, the head of the FSA's Supreme Military Council established at the same time as the Syrian National Coalition. Although ostensibly supportive of the Council, state sponsors undermined its authority by dealing directly with their favorite member factions. On the other side were Islamist groups led by civilians, many of whom were released from the Seydnaya prison by the regime in the months following the 2011 uprising. Due to their leaders' background of militant or religious activism, Islamist factions often displayed better organization than their nationalist counterparts. Islamist rebels ranged from moderates linked to the Muslim Brotherhood, like the Sham Legion, to hardline, transnational jihadis like the Nusra Front. In order to bolster their credibility in the eyes of foreign states and private financiers from the Gulf, mainstream Islamist factions formed rival coalitions such as the Salafi-dominated Islamic Front (2013–14), whose leading components were the Idlib-centered Ahrar al-Sham Movement and Damascus-based Army of Islam.

In 2013, the insurgency underwent a process of radicalization as a result of several factors. First was disappointment with the West, as hopes for a Libya-style intervention waned. Second was the turn of some insurgents towards banditry, which discredited moderate factions. Third was the intervention of the Lebanese Hizbullah in the battle of al-Qusayr (Homs), which vindicated the Islamists' framing of the conflict as a Sunni-Shi'a struggle. Fourth was the arrival of thousands of Sunni foreign fighters, thanks to the collapse of state authority in northern Syria, and lax border control by Turkey. Fifth was the Islamist overbidding sparked by the rise of the Islamic State in Iraq and Syria (ISIS), which emerged after a failed attempt at merging the Islamic State in Iraq with the Nusra Front, its Syrian franchise that ultimately established itself as a rival organization loyal to Ayman al-Zawahiri, the leader of Al-Qa'ida.

In early 2014, ISIS's repeated aggressions against other rebels sparked a counter-attack that forced the group to abandon western Syria. In the east, however, ISIS gained exclusive control of most of the Euphrates and Khabur valleys after ruthlessly suppressing local resistances, notably by decimating the Shu'aytat tribe. In June, after its seizure of western Iraq and proclamation of the Caliphate under the authority of its leader Abu Bakr al-Baghdadi,

ISIS, now renamed simply the Islamic State, established its de facto capital in Raqqa. Although chiefly detrimental to the rebels at the onset, the rise of ISIS eventually weakened the regime as well: indirectly, because Iran-backed Iraqi militias were repatriated home to counter Baghdadi's group, thereby aggravating the regime's manpower shortage; directly, because in the spring of 2015, ISIS's capture of the gas-rich region of Palmyra in the central desert coincided with simultaneous rebel advances in Western Syria. Ahrar al-Sham and the Nusra Front allied in a *jaysh al-fath* (Army of Conquest) that seized Idlib and Jisr al-Shughur before threatening the Alawites' heartlands, while in the province of Der'a, the FSA-banner Southern Front captured the regime's last border crossing with Jordan.

The critical juncture came in late 2015. By summer 2015, regime setbacks translated into internal instability, as factional struggles revived, while Alawites demonstrated against the unbearable human cost of the regime's war effort for their community. Asad, however, avoided defeat thanks to the dispatch of around 50 Russian aircraft to the coastal airbase of Hmeimim in September 2015. As ISIS weakened in Iraq, Iran was also able to send back its local affiliates to Syria. Within a few months, the combination of Russian airpower and Iranian foot soldiers reversed the course of the war. By March 2016, the rebels were expelled from the coastal mountains. At the end of the year, they left the eastern neighborhoods of Aleppo; pro-regime troops then filled the void left in the central desert by ISIS following the latter's debilitation by the US-led coalition, and fully recaptured Deir ez-Zor city in December 2017.

From 2018 onwards, the Asad regime, empowered by its international support, moved to increasingly eliminate the last major resistance and erase any global doubt of its staying power. In the first half of the year, regime forces dealt the rebels a fatal blow by retaking the suburbs of Damascus, the southern provinces of Der'a and Qunaytra, and the northern countryside of Homs. In all cases, evacuation deals were given to rebel fighters who refused "reconciliation" (that is, switching sides) and to civilians who feared for their lives under Asad's restored rule. Through early 2019, the only parts of the country that were still escaping Damascus' authority owed their situation to foreign protection. In September 2014, the US-led international coalition had started providing air support to People's Protection Units (YPG), which served as the Kurdish PYD's armed branch. The campaign foiled ISIS's assault on the town of Kobane on the Turkish border. From its Kurdish-majority strongholds in the north, the YPG subsequently expanded southward, seizing Raqqa in October 2017.

Otherwise, throughout 2019, the Asad regime finalized its triumph in the civil war, insofar that defeat was defined as its deposal. The conquest of the entire eastern bank of the Euphrates was complete with ISIS's final defeat in Baghuz in March 2019. As large Arab communities (and to a lesser extent Turkomans and Assyrians) fell under the control of the Kurdish movement, the latter restyled itself in a multi-ethnic fashion: the YPG led a military coalition called "Syrian Democratic Forces" (SDF) fashioned in 2015, while its autonomous administration was renamed the Democratic Federation of Northern Syria the following year. Finally, the northwestern part of the country became a Turkish zone of influence. It chiefly consisted of two areas directly controlled by Ankara's army since their capture from ISIS in early 2017, in the case of al-Bab, and from the YPG a year later, for Afrin. In the meantime, Turkey established military outposts around the remaining rebel stronghold of Idlib to protect it from regime ground assaults. Nonetheless, Syrian government forces continued advancing upon the last militant pockets around Idlib in the summer and fall of 2019. Fears of Turkish invasion abated slightly when the US and Turkey agreed to create a demilitarized buffer zone in the area, but tensions remain high as the increasingly confident Asad regime has flexed its muscle over the devastated country.

SOCIAL AND ECONOMIC ENVIRONMENT

The eastern four-fifths of Syria constitute a large, mostly semiarid desert plain – in essence the northern extension of the Arabian Desert. Consequently, nearly 80 percent of all Syrians live in the western 20 percent of the country, with the majority of inhabitants residing in a north-south line of cities – Aleppo, Hama, Homs, Damascus – that separates the more fertile western areas of the country from the semiarid and desert plain (Map 10.1). Rainfall is seasonal, most of it coming in the winter months and falling in the northern and westernmost parts of the country. By 2011, the population of Syria numbered a little over 22 million, 35 percent of which were below the age of 14. Almost half of the population was living in the two metropolitan provinces of Damascus and Aleppo.

However, the war brought about cataclysmic demographic change. Half a million Syrians died in the conflict, and life expectancy fell down by 20 years (to an estimated 55.7 years) at the height of the war. At least 12 million people (about 55 percent of the population) were displaced, nearly half of which sought refuge abroad, mostly in Turkey, which hosted over three

MAP 10.1

Syrian Arab Republic. Major water bodies, rivers, and cities shown.

Source: D-Maps.

million Syrians, and in Lebanon, Jordan, and Germany. As of 2019, the population residing inside Syria had fallen well below 20 million.

Ethnic and religious groups

Available data on the ethnic and sectarian complexion of Syrian society are mere estimates given the ban on the collection of such data. Yet statistics released by the Syrian government before 2011 suggest significantly different birth rates among religious sects. Indeed, the population of the predominantly Sunni provinces was increasing up to twice as quickly as populations of provinces that were home to large non-Sunni communities (Latakia, Tartus, Suwayda). Overlooking this trend often resulted in overestimating the proportion of religious minorities in the Syrian population. Demographic imbalance between sects was probably a crucial factor in the regime's ability to play on the fears of minorities.

Arabic is the most widely spoken and the only official language in the Syrian Arab Republic. The Kurds, who make up between 8 and 15 percent of the population, are concentrated along the Turkish border and in Damascus and Aleppo. Small ethnic minorities include the Turkomans, Circassians, Armenians, and Assyrians. Sunni Muslims (including Kurds) probably account for 80 percent of the population. Arab Bedouin tribes, mostly sedentarized under the Ba'th, account for an estimated 15 percent of the population and are particularly widespread in the Euphrates valley. Before the 2011 uprising, the vast majority of Sunni Muslims subscribed to a traditionalist, often Sufi-leaning brand of Islam, as both quietist and militant Salafis were ruthlessly suppressed. The rise of Salafi rebel factions throughout the civil war was not so much a function of a broad, preexisting social base but rather a consequence of superior organization.

Alawites constitute the second largest religious group at about 10 percent of the population. Alawitism is an offshoot of Shi'a Islam that is considered heretical by Sunni Muslims, and even by many Shi'a Muslims. Alawites were marginalized for centuries before becoming the ruling elite under the Ba'th. They originated in the Latakia mountains, but in the twentieth century many of them migrated to the cities of the coast, Homs and Damascus. Other non-Sunni Muslim minorities include the Druze at 3 percent (mostly in the southwestern province of Suwayda), and small communities of Isma'ili (mostly in Hama) and mainstream Twelver Shi'a. Christians are divided among almost two dozen denominations, the largest of which is Greek Orthodox. Due to low birth and high emigration rates, Christian Syrians came to compose no more than 5 percent of the population by 2011. The formerly several-thousand-strong Jewish community mostly vanished after it left the country in the 1990s.

Women

The Ba'th Party has long adopted the selective advancement of women as part of its authoritarian platform. Like all other "popular organizations," the Syrian General Union of Women is entirely subordinate to the regime. At the top of the state hierarchy, women like Vice-President for Cultural Affairs Najah al-'Attar and Bashar's media adviser Buthayna Sha'ban have played a role of representation rather than of decision. State feminism in Syria has at times taken radical forms, as illustrated by the forced unveiling of Damascene women in the early 1980s. Subsequently, however, the regime was forced to show increasing tolerance towards female Islamic garments as they spread even among Sunni elites.

Pre-war Syria was characterized by regional disparities in terms of female human development, most significantly between Sunni-majority, heavily rural and tribal governorates (Aleppo, Raqqa, Deir ez-Zor), on the one hand, and Alawite, Druze, or heavily urbanized governorates (Latakia, Tartus, Suwayda, and Damascus), on the other hand: female literacy ranged from 50 to 90 percent, and the share of women in the non-agricultural workforce ranged from 3 to 30 percent. Nationwide proportion of endogamous marriages (i.e. marrying among paternal cousins) was 40 percent. So-called "honor killings" of women existed among all sects, and women's rights associations faced significant social backlash in their call for stricter penalties against perpetrators.

The war adversely impacted women's status and rights in several ways. Many were raped by regime forces. The loss of male relatives, the destruction of properties, and displacement increased economic precariousness, depriving girls from education opportunities and favoring early marriage. Within Syria, the lack of men as a result of death, imprisonment, conscription, and migration entailed increased rates of polygamy and prolonged female celibacy. War also forced women to endorse new roles. The regime and the YPG recruited female fighters, in order to fill their ranks but also to score points among international audiences (the YPG's feminist ideology also provided for a formal ban on polygamy, and the appointment of male-female duumvirates to front political and military positions). In regime-held areas, where job opportunities were more numerous and more or less conservative, women increasingly made up for the lack of male workforce in cafés, restaurants, and retail stores. In the diaspora, particularly in Western countries, an unprecedently high rate of Syrian women were enabled to ask for divorce because of loosening family structures, and the availability of alternative income.

Economic development

By 2011, agriculture accounted for a greater share of the GDP in Syria (about 18 percent) than in any other Middle Eastern country. Yet, of Syria's 71,504 square miles (185,170 square kilometers), arable land amounts to only about one-quarter of the total, the rest consisting of a semiarid steppe and desert. In the late 1980s, the government invested heavily in irrigation systems to achieve self-sufficiency and to alleviate a severe fiscal crisis by acquiring hard currency through export, notably cotton.

After it seized power, the Ba'th postulated a vision for modernization not unlike the state-led development strategies elsewhere in the MENA. State intervention was necessary to push forward industrialization and create a more equitable distribution of national wealth, which was monopolized by the landed oligarchy. As a consequence, the 1963–66 period was characterized by nationalizations of banks and large industry and a land reform that limited the size of the great estates and redistributed the surplus to landless peasants. Statist economics, however, also resulted in a bloated, inefficient public sector used as a source of patronage to ensure regime survival. Arbitrary implementation of laws on "economic crimes" allowed for keeping in check the remaining private sector. After a modest *infitah* (opening) in the early 1970s, economic liberalization began after severe fiscal crisis faced by the country in 1986, as Syria was battered by the region-wide economic recession after the oil price collapse. Indeed, GDP growth bottomed out in the 1980s, averaging just 2.8 percent after experiencing nearly 9 percent throughout all the 1970s. Investment Law No. 10 of 1991 aimed to boost the private sector, but market-oriented reforms were shallow so as to not undermine the public-sector patronage system. Further measures were suspended until the conclusion of ongoing peace talks with Israel.

The economic challenges facing the country when Bashar al-Asad came to power in 2000 were manifold. Syria had not managed to advance beyond the group of lower-middle-income countries, with per capita incomes (at Purchasing Power Parity) measuring only $5,100 by 2011. The country also needed to rapidly expand its labor market to absorb a projected annual labor force increase of 4 percent, due to high population growth and a youth bulge in which nearly two-thirds of the population fell under the age of 30. The hydrocarbon industry was not the answer. Syria began exporting from its modest oil fields in the 1980s, but production fell from a million barrels per day to 385,000 by 2011 from a lack of new discoveries. Gas production essentially catered for domestic consumption.

At the Ba'th Party Regional Congress in June 2005, President Asad proposed the adoption of a "social market economy" combining market economy with social safety nets. Syrian officials wanted to emulate the Chinese model – economic liberalization under continued authoritarian rule. Private banks and a stock market were approved, holding companies were established by crony businessmen, and tariffs with Turkey and the Arab countries were slashed. More structural reform, however, was retarded by the fear, which eventually materialized, that the income inequalities associated with liberalization would engender political instability.

The civil war that followed the 2011 uprising destroyed the Syrian economy. By 2018, one-third of all housing in Syria had been obliterated. The war cost an estimated \$400 billion in damage, and reduced the GDP by more than 70 percent. Trade flows with neighbors were decimated as borders closed. The national currency, the Syrian pound, depreciated to one-tenth of its pre-war value, and an estimated two-thirds of the population plunged into extreme poverty. The World Bank estimated unemployment at 50 percent in 2015. Food production decreased, while industries like manufacturing, textiles, and oil production collapsed or became subsumed by ISIS and then the SDF. The Syrian regime managed to avert financial collapse thanks to aid from Iran, and for the macabre reason that it simply spent less on services since it lost so much territory. Inversely, a war economy flourished, one where profiteering, smuggling, and brokerage benefited many armed groups and actors.

By 2019, the regime's apparent military victory had not brought much economic relief besides reopening border crossings with Iraq and Jordan, resulting in a trickle of more trade. A severe fuel shortage hit the country as a result of new American sanctions deterring transport and insurance companies from getting involved in Iranian oil shipments to Syria. Beyond the latter, and lines of credit, Iran contributed little to reconstruction, as it was merely competing with Russia for the control of the country's most lucrative economic sectors, that is, the hydrocarbon industry, phosphate mines, and mobile phone networks. Tehran's investments in real estate were dictated by a drive to enshrine its influence in Damascus, and Moscow's were non-existent.

POLITICAL STRUCTURES

Despite formal similarities, Syria's political system is not a single-party regime nor a military dictatorship, because neither the Ba'th Party nor the army possess any power of their own. In fact, all institutions are subordinate to the ruling family through informal networks based on kinship and (Alawite) sect. The Asad family's control over the military is best illustrated by the unwritten rule according to which the brother of the president (Rifa't under Hafiz; Maher under Bashar) is the most powerful figure in the military. Other presidents' relatives and numerous Alawites were appointed to key positions in the military and the *mukhabarat*. Atef Najib, the local head of intelligence whose ruthless behavior sparked the 2011 uprising in Der'a, was a cousin of Bashar al-Asad. After 2011, the symbiosis between the ruling family and coercive institutions constituted a major obstacle to political transition, because transition would precisely have required a dissociation of these institutions from the ruling family.

During his reign, Hafiz al-Asad concentrated personal power in a "presidential monarchy." Unopposed referenda were held at the end of each renewable seven-year presidential term until Bashar al-Asad won the first pseudo-pluralistic election in 2014. After 2000, extensive presidential prerogatives in matters of appointment and public policy were key to Bashar's ability to overcome resistance to his personal leadership and economic reforms from among state elites. Prime Ministers came and went; while technically heads of government, in practice the presidential office wielded supremacy. Even before the Syrian civil war, visitors to the country saw media campaigns glorifying Bashar's leadership and exalting him as the nation's conscience in a personalization not often seen outside the Arab monarchies (Photo 10.1).

PHOTO 10.1
Damascus Street Poster with President Bashar al-Asad: "We Are All With You"

Source: Photo by watchsmart, Flickr.

The president's coercive power relies, first, on the heads of the four main intelligence agencies (Military Intelligence, Airforce Intelligence, State Security, Political Security) and the National Security Bureau that coordinates between them. Endowed with extralegal power, the dreaded *mukhabarat* (intelligence services) surveil, and suppress, possible threats from external enemies, domestic opposition, the army, bureaucracy, and each other. They vet candidates for office and promotion, and act as powerful brokers whose support ambitious politicians and prominent businessmen seek. They control large parts of society via networks of informers and the dispensing of semi-illicit privileges. After 2011, their influence further increased as they were tasked with recruiting paramilitaries such as the Tiger Forces.

The military, the Syrian Arab Army (SAA), was called upon in order to quell the most significant threats to the regime, such as the Hama uprising in 1964, the 1979–82 insurgency, and of course the 2011 revolt. To ensure the army's loyalty in such situations, and to shield himself from military coups, Hafiz al-Asad adopted a two-pronged strategy. First, sectarian stacking brought the proportion of Alawites within the officer corps above 80 percent. Second, because the rank-and-file still predominantly consisted of Sunni conscripts, Hafiz al-Asad created praetorian units such as the Republican Guard and Rif'at al-Asad's Defense Companies which, after their commander's coup attempt, were turned into the Fourth Armored Division (led during the civil war by Bashar's own brother Mahir). Recruited from the Alawite population and, to a lesser degree, loyal (Sunni) Bedouin clans, these were endowed with the most advanced equipment. During the civil war, losses and defections deprived the SAA of half of its manpower, but they were partly compensated by extending the duration of conscription, by entrusting the SAA with the chaperoning of paramilitaries, and later in the conflict, by absorbing a number of defeated rebels who were spared prosecution.

The Ba'th is a pillar of the regime – not as a power center of its own, but as an instrument of control and patronage. The party lost its autonomy since the late 1970s in terms of retaining internal control and filtering out the political field; it thereafter became a tool of the president. Although the party's Regional Congress is supposed to be held every fourth year, Hafiz al-Asad ceased to convene it in 1985, and Bashar did it only once to eliminate rivals. The Ba'th's top body is the 14-members Central Command (Regional Command until 2018), which is roughly divided between senior military commanders, senior cabinet ministers, and top party officials. It is theoretically answerable to the 80-members Central Committee, a body comprising senior elites – party functionaries, ministers, generals, security chiefs, governors, heads of syndicates, and university presidents. By 2011, the Ba'th had over 11,000 cells grouped into 154 subbranches at the district or town level, which were combined into 18 branches in the provinces and major institutions such as the military, bureaucracy, and universities. Before the war, active membership numbered nearly one million, for a total of 3.5 million registered members.

The party controlled "popular organizations" such as sector-specific unions (for workers, peasants, professionals, students, etc.) and youth movements that initially gave the regime new roots in society and bridged sectarian and urban-rural gaps. The party's debilitation in the 2000s, when it was an obstacle to economic reforms, helps account for the anti-regime mobilization of 2011. Der'a, the birthplace of the uprising, had long been a Ba'th stronghold. The party suffered devastating blows during the civil war, losing perhaps half of its membership as vast swathes of the country fell to the rebels. Yet, the Ba'th remained relevant as a pool of regime loyalists, who set up their own paramilitary group, the Ba'th Battalions. In the 2018 local elections, the Ba'th was rewarded with an increase in its share of town councilors.

Civilian executive power is represented by the Council of Ministers and the province governors, all of which are appointed by the president. The parliament (People's Assembly) merely responds to government initiatives. Deputies act as brokers between officials and their constituents – notably those seeking favors. Two-thirds of seats are reserved for candidates appointed by the National Progressive Front, an alliance of the Ba'th Party and ten small leftist and nationalist parties, while the rest is left for "independent" candidates who stem mostly from the urban bourgeoisie. The bureaucracy plays a key redistributive role through the payment of salaries and provision of services. During the civil war, some civil servants living in rebel-held areas kept on receiving their pay as part of the regime's quest for loyalty.

The judiciary is politicized through party control of appointments. The legal process suffers from corruption and fails to guarantee civil liberties and property rights. Redress of grievances typically rests on access to informal clientelist connections with the *mukhabarat*. The rule of law has been further undermined by extra-constitutional measures such the emergency law promulgated in 1963. The latter was formally lifted in April 2011, yet this did not prevent the regime from perpetrating the worst human rights violations in Syria's modern history.

At the close of 2019, the very few regions in Syria still escaping Damascus' authority were subjected to three types of governing structures.

The US-protected Autonomous Administration of North and East Syria was ethnically and religiously pluralistic, but real power was monopolized by the Kurdish PYD and, behind it, its military branch, the YPG. In the northern countryside of Aleppo, Turkish authorities governed through a combination of direct rule and administration by local councils. As for Idlib, it was predominantly administered by the Syrian Salvation Government, a civilian front for Hay'at Tahrir al-Sham (the ex-Nusra Front, which had broken ties with Al-Qa'ida in 2016 before militarily subduing rival rebel factions like Ahrar al-Sham). However, despite enjoying Turkish support, this militant organization and other local rebels have been battered by Syrian government campaigns to retake Idlib, and the future of this region remains unclear.

POLITICAL DYNAMICS

Syria's politics is presently dominated by three Rs: reconquest, restoration, and reconstruction. Reconquest concerns the regions that continue to escape regime control. The Turkish-controlled north seems off-limits given Ankara's rampant annexation of a region it considers as a forward defense line against the PKK. Damascus' ambitions thus focus on the province of Idlib, which lies on strategic highways linking Aleppo to Damascus and the coast, is only protected by small Turkish military outposts, and is dominated by an internationally blacklisted jihadi organization, Hay'at Tahrir al-Sham. Although the 2018 Russian-Turkish Sochi agreement provides a framework for a compromise through partial demilitarization of the frontline and the reopening of highways to civilian traffic, it is vulnerable to spoiler moves from the Syrian regime and ultra-jihadi factions like the Al-Qa'ida-affiliated Hurras al-Din.

East of the Euphrates, the fate of the YPG's autonomous administration is largely dependent on US determination to extend their military protection past the defeat of ISIS. President Trump's announcement of a full withdrawal in December 2018 generated considerable anxiety among YPG leaders. In case the US were to implement that decision, and in order to shield itself from a consequent Turkish military assault, the Kurdish group approached the regime to negotiate the contours of a deal that would bring back eastern oil resources and Arab-majority regions under Damascus' control in exchange for a modicum of local autonomy in Kurdish-majority areas.

Political restoration has most obviously taken place in the regions that were retaken from the rebels since 2016. Following systematic looting, it has consisted in arrests and occasional assassinations, conscription of fighting-age men, re-erection of statues of Hafiz al-Asad, and the dissolution of opposition-era local councils in favor of municipalities "elected" in 2018. At a psychological level, the return of the regime has translated into the rebuilding of the "wall of fear" that revolutionaries had broken in 2011. The southern province of Der'a is a particular case in that respect, because the surrender agreements brokered by Russia in 2018 provided for the non-entry of regime soldiers into certain towns or neighborhoods, and the maintaining of former rebel units as law enforcement forces there. This scheme temporarily preserved some breathing space for anti-regime activism as illustrated by small demonstrations in early 2019.

The reassertion of the regime's authority has not only targeted former opponents, but also pro-regime militias. Some of them had acquired considerable autonomy when the regime was at its weakest, that is, before the Russian intervention, as they funded themselves through predatory and criminal activities such as ransoming, tolling, and trafficking. Russia, in particular, has pushed for the absorption of paramilitaries into the SAA's order of battle through the creation of the Fifth Corps, which was Moscow's primary tool to co-opt "reconciled" rebels. In Der'a, the Fifth Corps has competed for the loyalty of former insurgents with Mahir al-Asad's Fourth Division. The latter is backed by Iran and has formally integrated foreign IRGC affiliates whose withdrawal from Syria is requested by Israel and the US. Rather than a consolidation of the SAA, thus, the regularization of paramilitaries seems to translate into further "militia-fication" and fragmentation of the country's military.

Although reconstruction is principally an economic issue, it has obvious political aspects. First, a property law issued in 2018 (Decree No. 10) suggested that the regime was willing to use so-called "urban renewal" to seize real estate in former rebel neighborhoods, turn them into upscale developments, and permanently prevent the return of property owners. The thirty-day limit given to the latter to prove ownership was extended to one year under pressure from the Lebanese government, which was concerned that the law would hinder the return of Syrian refugees to their country. Yet, public threats against refugees by Syrian officials indicated that the regime would continue to seek ways to indefinitely keep what it sees as troublemaker-communities out of the country.

Reconstruction is also political to the extent that its funding depends on the regime's ability to normalize relations with the international community. Asad's main sponsors, Iran and Russia, do not have the necessary financial means. China does, but resource-poor, war-stricken Syria offers few prospects of return on investment for a country whose Middle Eastern policies remain dictated by economic, as opposed to strategic, considerations. As a result, the regime eyes capital from two groups of countries with which it has a fraught relationship during the war, namely, Gulf monarchies and Western states. Among Gulf monarchies, the drive for normalization with Asad was spearheaded by the United Arab Emirates, which had never completely cut ties to Damascus. In 2018, Abu Dhabi facilitated the regime's southern offensive by pressuring its chief rebel client in the region, Shabab al-Sunna's Ahmad al-'Awde, to sign a reconciliation deal with Russia. In December of that year, the UAE was the first Gulf country to reopen its embassy in Damascus, followed by Bahrain. Yet, follow-up investments in the Syrian economy were deterred by threats of US sanctions, and Saudi Arabia still seemed reluctant to follow suit due to its anxiety towards Iran's influence in Syria.

This context explains why, in spite of the regime's vengeful rhetoric towards the Western countries that supported the opposition, Russia lobbied the same countries for normalization with Damascus. The European Union should fund Syria's reconstruction, Moscow argued, because it is the only means, if not to allow for the return of most refugees, at least to prevent further outflows of population from Syria. Yet, even though some EU members seem open to a rapprochement with the Asad regime, France, Germany, and the UK see major obstacles to it. First, they have conditioned the granting of reconstruction funds on significant progress in the UN-led peace process, which the regime strongly opposes. Second, in the name of human rights violations committed by the regime, the Syrian opposition has lobbied Western governments for reinforcement of economic sanctions against the regime and its economic partners, and filed criminal complaint against high-ranking Syrian officials with Western courts (in 2018, a German judge issued an arrest warrant against Major General Jamil Hassan, the powerful head of the Airforce Intelligence).

FOREIGN POLICY

After independence, Syria's pluralistic polity allowed for competing foreign influences such as that of pro-Western Iraq, then under its Hashemite monarchy, which sought to bring the Arabs into the anti-Soviet Baghdad Pact. Arab Nationalist Egypt, which advocated Cold War neutrality, also had its pull, as Syrian political elites tried to bolster their legitimacy by appealing to Nasser's pan-Arab ideals. This trend was best illustrated by the 1958 merger with Egypt, creating the UAR, as well as the regime's firebrand posture toward Israel on the eve of the 1967 Arab-Israeli War. The Syrian army was poorly prepared for the latter and lost the Golan Heights and Mount Hermon, two strategic locations only a short distance from Damascus. Ideology also drove a failed Syrian military intervention in support of the Palestine Liberation Organization against the Jordanian army in 1970. The further consolidation of Ba'th rule under Hafiz al-Asad allowed the regime to strike a balance between rejectionist policies aimed at maintaining nationalist legitimacy and a realist, Syrian-centered approach sometimes at odds with popular sentiments.

The Hafiz era

After Asad came to power in 1970, Syria's foreign policy was revised to prepare for war against Israel: it maintained close ties with the Soviet Union to secure state-of-the-art weapons, reconciled with the oil-rich conservative Arab Gulf monarchies to obtain financing, and struck a strategic alliance with Anwar Sadat's Egypt, the most militarily powerful of the Arab states. In 1973, Egypt and Syria launched a surprise attack on the Israel-occupied Golan Heights and Sinai Peninsula, thereby initiating the war known as the October War in Syria and the Yom Kippur War in Israel. Despite spectacular initial advances that were hailed as "victories" in Damascus and Cairo, Arab armies were eventually defeated. However, their brief show of force as well as the Arab oil embargo gave Syria and Egypt enhanced political leverage. In 1974, US Secretary of State Henry Kissinger's mediation led to a disengagement agreement, according to which Israel evacuated a small portion of the Golan Heights.

The Syrian-Egyptian alliance subsequently came to an end as Sadat engaged in the negotiations that eventually led to the 1979 peace treaty between Egypt and Israel. As Cairo withdrew from the Arab-Israeli conflict, both Syria and Israel redirected their attention towards the civil war that began in Lebanon in 1975. The following year, Asad ordered an unpopular military intervention against the Palestine Liberation Organization (PLO) to prevent its victory over the right-wing Maronite Christians militias, before switching sides in 1978 as Israel moved against the PLO in South Lebanon and allied with the Maronites. By inserting itself as the civil war's arbiter, Syria achieved several objectives: first, it secured direct influence over a country whose independence had always been contested by Syrian ruling elites – it would take until 2009 for Damascus to open an embassy in Beirut; second, it acquired forward defense bases against the Israeli army; third, Lebanon's open, comparatively prosperous economy provided Syrian officers with countless opportunities of personal enrichment.

In 1982, Beirut fell into Israel's orbit as the Israeli military besieged the city and expelled the PLO after a brief confrontation with Syrian troops. Thereafter, Syria backed various Lebanese proxies, including what was to become Hizbullah, against the Israelis and the American-French contingent that was deployed to support the government of President Amin Gemayel. Following the Western withdrawal in 1984, Syria forced Gemayel to renege on the Lebanese-Israeli accord signed the year before. Asad's drive for hegemony in Lebanon also translated into a second war against PLO leader Yasir Arafat.

In parallel, Syria compensated for the loss of Egypt's alliance by establishing a long-term strategic partnership with Iran, which had turned into a fierce enemy of Israel after the Islamic revolution. Asad and the new Iranian regime had another common enemy, namely, Saddam Hussein's Iraq. In 1980, Damascus condemned the latter's attack against Iran while in return, Tehran unexpectedly supported Asad against the Islamists who were trying to carry out their own Islamic revolution in Syria. Syria also benefited from the military effectiveness of the Iran-sponsored Hizbullah that fought the Israeli occupation of southern Lebanon until 2000.

After the Iran-Iraq War ended in 1988, a vengeful Saddam Hussein supported Syria's chief opponent in Lebanon, General Michel Aoun. By joining the US-led military coalition in response to Iraq's invasion of Kuwait in 1990, Asad obtained American support to destroy this one last obstacle to "Pax Syriana" in Lebanon. Standing with Saudi Arabia against Iraq enabled Syria to break out of Arab isolation due to its alignment with Iran: economically, the resumption of subsidies from the Gulf oil states brought much-needed relief to a country that had refused to seek loans from the International Monetary Fund after the 1986 fiscal crisis. Ultimately, however, Syria's decision to join the anti-Iraq coalition was shaped by the weakening of the Soviet ally, which left the US as the sole superpower. Syria's submission to the new world order resulted in two rounds (1995, 1999) of bilateral negotiations with Israel over the Golan, which Israel had unilaterally annexed in 1981. The two sides came very close to a settlement, but the talks hit a snag over Israel's demands to keep its surveillance station on Mount Hermon as well as 5 percent of the Golan's territory adjoining Lake Tiberias.

Foreign policy under Bashar al-Asad

Following the collapse of Syria's peace negotiations with Israel, another strategic challenge emerged in 2000 with Israel's withdrawal from southern

Lebanon. For a growing number of Lebanese, this development removed the main justification for Syrian military presence in the country. Moreover, Israel now directly targeted Syrian military positions in Lebanon in response to Hizbullah's attacks on the Shebaa Farms, a hamlet which the Iran-backed militia described as Lebanese territory still occupied by Israel, whereas the latter claimed it as part of what it considered as the formerly Syrian Golan.

The 9/11 attacks initially had an ambivalent impact on bilateral relations with the United States. On the one hand, Syria objected when some of its allies – which it regarded as national liberation movements (e.g., Hamas and Hizbullah) – were included among the targets of the global war on terror. On the other hand, Damascus provided Washington with intelligence in the struggle against Al-Qa'ida within the wider global war on terror.

A more dramatic deterioration of US-Syrian relations occurred when Syria opposed the 2003 US invasion of Iraq, most spectacularly by allowing volunteer fighters to move across Syria's border into Iraq and giving refuge to Iraqi Ba'th officials. Whereas in 1991 Syria could justify its participation in the Kuwait war on the basis that the operation's goals were limited to restoring Kuwaiti sovereignty, Bashar was wary of another American war aimed at toppling another Ba'th regime. Moreover, relations with Saddam Hussein had improved with the 2001 reopening of the oil pipeline between the two states, which gained the Syrian treasury a badly needed billion-dollar annual windfall and enabled Iraq to evade UN sanctions. Finally, Syrian public opinion was extremely inflamed against the invasion.

Fears that the US would attack Syria following their triumph over Saddam Hussein were rapidly dissipated by growing American difficulties in the face of the Iraqi insurgency, which Damascus continued to support, though more discreetly than before the fall of Baghdad. However, the deterioration of Syria's strategic position resulted in the first Israeli airstrikes inside Syrian territory since the 1973 war: in 2003 against a Palestinian military facility, and in 2007 against a secret nuclear plant under construction near Deir ez-Zor. The George W. Bush administration presented Damascus with a list of non-negotiable demands that threatened Syria's regional influence, including ending support for Palestinian militants and Hizbullah, withdrawing from Lebanon, and cooperating with the occupation of Iraq. The cost of defiance was the Syria Accountability Act, a set of sanctions that discouraged Western companies from doing business with Syria and consequently pushed Syria to strengthen ties with Turkey and the Gulf.

In 2004, the United States and France challenged Syria's role in Lebanon through UN Security Council Resolution 1559 that called for Syria to withdraw its military forces from that country. Paris joined Washington's anti-Syrian strategy because it was siding with pro-Saudi Lebanese Prime Minister Rafik Hariri in his bid to prevent the widely unpopular extension of the tenure of pro-Syrian president Émile Lahoud. Asad was all the more suspicious of Hariri that, in addition to his ties to the West, the Lebanese politician was close to two major rivals of the ruling family within the regime, namely, Vice-President 'Abd al-Halim Khaddam and minister of Interior Ghazi Kana'an.

In February 2005, the assassination of Hariri in a massive car bombing sparked the Cedar Revolution, a large-scale anti-Syrian protest movement led by the main Sunni, Maronite Christian, and Druze political forces which, combined with covert Western military threats, forced Syria to withdraw. However, Damascus later managed to reconstitute its influence in Lebanon thanks to its Shi'a allies Hizbullah and Amal, and, owing to intra-Maronite rivalries, its former enemy Michel Aoun. Syria's standing in Lebanon was further consolidated by two developments: the July 2006 war, that saw Hizbullah withstand a month-long Israeli military offensive thanks in part to Syrian logistical support; the May 2008 seizure of West Beirut by pro-Syrian militias following brief clashes with their pro-Western rivals, and subsequent formation of a national unity government in which Hizbullah held veto power.

Syria's struggle with the Saudi-backed Hariri family over Lebanon shattered the partnership Syria had established with the kingdom after the Kuwait war, and Damascus's relations with Egypt and Jordan – Riyadh's key Arab partners – suffered accordingly. Meanwhile, the deepening of the long-standing strategic alliance between Syria, Iran, and Hizbullah formed the backbone of the so-called "resistance axis," formalized in 2006 by a Syrian-Iranian mutual defense pact. A portion of the Syrian Sunni opinion resented this alliance, because of Iran's support for the regime during the 1979–82 insurgency, and because of suspected Shi'a proselytising efforts emanating from holy sites such as the shrine of Sayyida Zaynab near Damascus, which had been rebuilt in a Persian architectural style and attracted a growing number of foreign Shi'a pilgrims and religious students.

It remains to be said that regional alignments after the invasion of Iraq were not necessarily determined by sectarian affinities. First, the "axis of resistance" also included the Palestinian Hamas, which gave the Syrian regime significant nationalist legitimacy, in particular during the Gaza war of late 2008. Second, although not a member of the axis, Qatar was close to it and provided sympathetic media coverage through its widely popular information channel Al-Jazeera. Third, both Syria and Iran reconciled with Turkey following the advent of the Justice and Development Party (AKP).

In the 1990s Syria had supported the Kurdistan Workers' Party (PKK) against Turkey to pressure Ankara into giving it a greater share of Euphrates River water controlled upstream by new Turkish dams. Turkey and Israel also had cooperated closely to oppose Syria and Iran. Military threats by Turkey in 1998 led to the signature of the Adana agreement that formalized Syria's abandon of its support for the PKK. The empowerment of Iraqi Kurds following the fall of Saddam Hussein in 2003 gradually drove Ankara, Damascus, and Tehran closer over the shared threat of Kurdish separatism. Turkey refused US demands to isolate Syria and even tried to broker Syria-Israel peace negotiations in defiance of the United States. Although military cooperation between the two countries remained minimal, Syria's exchanges with the rapidly expanding Turkish economy largely overshadowed those with Iran.

In 2008, US commandos carried out an unprecedented cross-border attack against jihadi militants using the province of Deir ez-Zor as a safe haven for their operations in Iraq. By that time, however, relations with the West had already started to improve. Asad was invited in Paris to celebrate Bastille Day beside President Nicolas Sarkozy, and in 2009, the better-meaning Barack Obama succeeded George W. Bush as US president. Thus, despite ongoing tensions with the Saudi-led bloc, Asad had few dedicated foreign enemies by 2011. The uprising, however, reshuffled the cards and unleashed a struggle for Syria.

An internationalized civil war

Although Asad portrayed hostile foreign powers as a driving force behind the uprising, in reality, it was the deterioration of the situation on the ground that led foreign states to adopt an increasingly tough stance towards the regime. Turkey and Qatar initially used their close ties to Damascus to try brokering a deal with the opposition, but they eventually broke with the regime over the August 2011 military crackdown. Saudi Arabia was equally slow to turn against Asad, as its hostility to revolutionary change across the region temporarily trumped its animosity toward the regime. Riyadh waited until early 2012 to formally voice (through an Arab League resolution) its desire to see the Syrian president step down. The UAE, although a member of the anti-Asad Friends of Syria Group established at the same time, never completely forsook "authoritarian solidarity" with Asad and kept on hosting relatives and assets of regime officials.

Although quantitatively significant, foreign logistical support for the rebels was late, gradual, limited, and reactive rather than proactive. It only materialized one year into the uprising, after the deadly siege of Homs in February 2012 which sparked such a moral shock among public opinions across the region that not responding would have put the domestic legitimacy of Gulf monarchies at risk. By backing select FSA factions, Saudi Arabia, the UAE and Jordan also aimed to counter the rise of (notably Islamist) groups supported by Turkey and Qatar. Guided missiles, which the rebels badly needed against the regime's armors, were only supplied in significant numbers as of mid-2013, in reaction to an Iranian military intervention which, by that time, had already turned the tide of the conflict. As for the provision of surface-to-air missiles by Qatar, they were rapidly interrupted by the US out of proliferation concerns.

The US organized and monitored arms deliveries initiated by regional states through its CIA-run, covert Timber Sycamore operation, whose multinational "Military Operation Centers" based in Turkey and Jordan vetted recipient factions on an ideological basis, that is, to the exclusion of Islamists. Obama signed off on Timber Sycamore but he never supported forcible regime-change in Syria. Unlike in Cairo or Tunis, Washington had no long-standing partners among the Syrian military that could supervise a transition while preserving US interests – in 2011, it had taken Obama five months to call for Asad to step down, as opposed to two weeks for Egyptian president Hosni Mubarak. Subsequently, the rise of jihadi insurgents convinced the White House that military stalemate was preferable to outright rebel victory. Direct military action against Asad was further inhibited by Obama's concern not to jeopardize the secret negotiations that eventually led to the 2015 Iran nuclear deal.

Rather than a drive for regime change or the "responsibility to protect" (civilians), thus, direct US intervention in Syria was eventually sparked by two issues that had dominated Washington's post-Cold War security agenda in the Middle East, namely, weapons of mass destruction and jihadi terrorism. In August 2013, one year after Obama had warned that the use of chemical weapons was a "red line," he reluctantly threatened military retaliation against the regime following a sarin nerve agent attack that killed about a thousand people in the suburbs of Damascus. However, the UK Parliament opposed participation in the operation, giving Washington the opportunity to abandon the planned airstrikes in favor of a Russian initiative to dismantle the Syrian chemical arsenal by way of the Organization for the Prohibition of Chemical Weapons. Yet, the regime remained able to use sarin stockpiles it had hidden from international inspectors as well as dual-use (i.e. non-prohibited) chlorine. In 2017 and 2018, smaller-scale chemical attacks in Idlib and the eastern suburbs of Damascus prompted the Trump administration to launch limited missile strikes against regime military facilities.

As for game-changing action by the US, it was reserved for the struggle against jihadis. In September 2014, airstrikes against ISIS were extended from Iraq to Syria, where they also occasionally targeted the Nusra Front and its allies. Additionally, a Pentagon-run training program was established to support the SDF and rebel factions operating against ISIS from the northern countryside of Aleppo and the desert base of al-Tanaf on the Jordanian border. Partners on the ground were supplemented with small contingents of Western special forces and artillery units, which at their 2018 peak included 2,000 US soldiers. Within the EU, the United Kingdom and, especially, France, were Asad's most dedicated enemies but were unable to play more than a support role for US operations. Europe's most potent weapon against the regime was economy, in the form of a ban on Syrian oil imports and targeted sanctions against regime officials.

Western policies contrasted with those of Israel, which focused on the growing military footprint of Iran in Syria. From 2013 on, the Israeli air force carried out dozens of attacks on facilities run by the IRGC and/or suspected of sheltering advanced weaponry destined for Hizbullah. To keep loyalists away from the Golan ceasefire line, Israel also provided fire and logistical support to a handful of FSA factions in the area. Israel's policy was little affected by the Russian intervention: owing to a tacit understanding with Moscow, bombing raids even intensified and led to major incidents in 2018 as Syrian air defense successively shot down an Israeli fighter jet and, by mistake, a Russian reconnaissance aircraft.

Among regime allies, Iran was the most unhesitant in bolstering Asad's hand. Tehran immediately gave Damascus several billion dollars a year in economic aid. From 2012 onwards, Iranian military advisers supervised the dispatch of tens of thousands of Shi'a foreign fighters recruited among IRGC affiliates from Lebanon (Hizbullah), Iraq (notably Asa'ib Ahl al-Haqq), and Afghanistan (Fatimid Brigade). The scale of Iranian support to the regime was function of the latter's importance as the strategic depth of Hizbullah, hence as the key to the Islamic Republic's military relevance in the Arab-Israeli conflict. Iran's involvement in the Syrian war provided it with the opportunity to entrench itself further in the country, by securing direct control over strategic military facilities, and by establishing a "Syrian Hizbullah" consisting of a network of local Twelver Shi'a militias responding directly to the IRGC's orders.

Russia's approach to the conflict was initially more careful. By 2012, Moscow was granting Asad economic assistance and vetoing even verbal condemnations of the regime by the UN Security Council, but the 2015 military intervention finally came as the result of unanticipated developments: Obama's climb-down on the 2013 chemical attack, the Ukraine crisis the following year, and finally the regime's disarray in mid-2015. Putin had no vital interest to defend in Syria at the start of the war: the country was a loyal, but insolvent customer of Russia's military industry, and the military facility leased by Moscow in the port of Tartus since the 1970s was a modest technical support point for medium-sized vessels. Russia's eventual decision to step into the conflict is thus better understood as an example of "offensive realism," in the sense that Russia filled a void left by Obama's hands-off approach to the conflict in order to retrieve a major role in Middle Eastern, and by extension, global politics.

Russia's new status as a regional hegemon was illustrated by the realignments that ensued from its intervention. Jordan promptly ceased to support anti-regime operations by Southern Front rebels. Saudi Arabia and the UAE all the more easily lost interest in the rebel cause since they were now mostly absorbed by their own campaign in Yemen.

Turkey initially counter-escalated, even shooting down a Russian bomber over its border, but concerns over territorial gains by the US-backed YPG later convinced Ankara to mend fences with Moscow. In the summer of 2016, the YPG captured Manbij from IS, thereby contravening Turkey's demand to the US that the Western bank of the Euphrates be cleared by Ankara's Syrian rebel allies. In response, Turkey's Euphrates Shield operation targeted adjacent IS-controlled areas, and achieved its main objective with the conquest of al-Bab in February 2017. Russian acquiescence allowed for subsequent Turkish operations against the YPG-held, Kurdish-majority region of Afrin, and the deployment of a Turkish peacekeeping force around Idlib as a part of stabilization efforts that culminated with the signature of the Sochi agreement between Putin and Erdogan in September 2018.

US reaction to the Russian intervention was somewhat confused, due to conflicting views between government agencies. On the one hand, both the Obama and Trump administration kept on prioritizing the anti-IS campaign and deterrence against the use of chemical weapons by the regime. Accordingly, Washington implemented deconfliction measures with Russia and even discussed military cooperation with Moscow against jihadi groups in 2016. On the other hand, the CIA escalated support for select rebel units until Timber Sycamore was suddenly put to an end by Trump in July 2017; in December 2018, Trump's announcement of an impending US withdrawal from Syria generated considerable backlash from military and diplomatic circles, to the extent that full withdrawal was at least temporarily postponed.

As the conflict seemed to be winding down, multilateral diplomatic efforts carried on. Following the dispatch of Arab League observers during the winter of 2011–12, a joint mission of the United Nations and Arab League had been established under the aegis of former UN secretary-general Kofi Annan. Annan deployed unarmed observers inside Syria and organized the June 2012 Geneva I conference, whose communiqué called for establishing a transitional governing body with full executive powers. However, this statement did not translate into actual pressure on the regime because Russia refused to interpret it as a call for Asad's resignation. The Annan mission collapsed a few weeks later, as spectacular rebel advances suggested that the regime might not survive into the next year. Diplomatic efforts were only revived after the agreement on Syrian chemical weapons, which paved the way for the January 2014 Geneva II conference held under the supervision of Annan's successor, Akhdar Brahimi. Whereas Geneva I was attended only by non-Syrian state parties, Geneva II witnessed the first direct negotiations between regime officials and the Syrian National Coalition. Talks rapidly stalled as the regime rejected the opposition's and Brahimi's request for power-sharing.

The failure of Geneva II sparked the replacement of Brahimi by Staffan de Mistura, who downplayed talk of transition and encouraged local ceasefires. The latter being favored by the regime, they were unsurprisingly rejected by the opposition. Following the Russian intervention, diplomatic initiatives resumed along two main patterns. First, the revived Geneva process (no less than six additional rounds of talks took place in 2016 and 2017) reflected the new military balance: at meetings held in Riyadh, the Syrian National Coalition was forced to form a High Negotiation Committee in partnership with dovish and even Russian-sponsored rivals; content-wise, discussions (headed by de Mistura's successor, Geir Pedersen, as of 2019) shifted from transition towards constitutional reform. Second, Russia initiated parallel ceasefire schemes designed to assist in the loyalist camp's war effort. For instance, a cessation of hostilities agreement negotiated with the US in 2016 allowed the regime to retake Palmyra from ISIS. In 2017, four de-escalation zones were agreed upon (as part of the Astana process, a parallel and less credible peace track led by Russia, Iran, and Turkey) – only to be retaken (except for Idlib) by pro-regime forces the following year. In essence, as the 2010s wound down, international negotiations and peace engagements all but cemented the permanence of Asad's regime.

FUTURE PROSPECTS

As of 2019, Idlib and eastern Syria remain contested, and Syria is not whole again. The Asad regime is likely to stay, but now rules over a shattered land. The country's economy will long remain plagued by the consequences of the civil war, all the more so if foreign funding for reconstruction is minimal. The lack of opportunities will provide few incentives for refugees to return. Scarce resources will be predominantly distributed among loyalist constituencies that expect long-term rewards for their sacrifices during the war. Combined with the regime's abysmal legitimacy among the communities suffered its brutal counter-insurgency campaign, this situation will preclude even modest political liberalization in the medium term. Syria's Sunni question, itself a consequence of Alawite domination over the state, will reemerge sooner or later. The huge Syrian diaspora will play a pivotal role, and refugee populations abroad may well resemble the historic plight of the Palestinians. Some refugees live in miserable conditions, but others have mobilized considerable resources against the Syrian regime.

Tensions among foreign tutelary powers are also likely to define Syria's politics for the foreseeable future. Russia, Iran, and Turkey do not have uniform interests in Syria apart from their preference for Asad's rule over a more radical alternative. Even as the US fades into the backdrop, with ISIS contained and the Trump administration espousing an anti-interventionist agenda, these other regional interests will continue to overlap and conflict. Issues like the division of Syria's meager economic resources, the sponsoring of rival military and paramilitary factions, and the contrast between Russia's willingness to appease Israel versus Iran's eagerness to perpetuate confrontation with Israel will come to the forefront of the geopolitical game.

FURTHER READING

For overviews of modern Syrian history that provide clear introductions to the country, see John McHugo, *Syria: A Recent History* (Saqi Books, 2014); James Reilly, *Fragile Nation, Shattered Land: The* *Modern History of Syria* (Lynne Rienner, 2019); and David W. Lesch, *Syria: A Modern History* (Polity, 2019).

Historically, rich studies tackle different periods of the Syrian state. On the post-independence era, see Kevin Martin, *Syria's Democratic Years: Citizens, Experts, and Media in the 1950s* (Indiana University Press, 2015). On the Baʻth era in general, see Hanna Batatu, *Syria's Peasantry, the Descendants of Its Lesser Rural Notables, and Their Politics* (Princeton University Press, 1999); Raymond Hinnebusch, *Syria: Revolution from Above* (Routledge, 2001); Nikolaos Van Dam, *The Struggle for Power in Syria: Politics and Society under Asad and the Baʻth Party* (IB Tauris, 2011); and Fred Lawson, *Global Security Watch – Syria* (Praeger, 2013). On Hafiz al-Asad's rule in particular, see Patrick Seale, *Asad of Syria: The Struggle for the Middle East* (IB Tauris, 1988); for an updated retrospective, Eyal Zisser, *Asad's Legacy: Syria in Transition* (New York University Press, 2001).

On Bashar al-Asad's rule, including the institutional dynamics of the regime, see Carsten Wieland, *Syria, A Decade of Lost Chances: Repression and Revolution from Damascus Spring to Arab Spring* (Cune, 2012); Steven Heydemann and Reinoud Leenders, *Middle East Authoritarianisms. Governance, Contestation and Regime Resilience in Syria and Iran* (Stanford University Press, 2013); Raymond Hinnebusch, Tina Zintl, Christa Salamandra, and Leif Stenberg, eds., *Syria from Reform to Revolt* (Syracuse University Press, 2015); and Esther Meininghaus, *Creating Consent in Baʻthist Syria: Women and Welfare in a Totalitarian State* (IB Tauris, 2016). Overall political domination under the Asads is the focus of Lisa Wedeen, *Ambiguities of Domination: Politics, Rhetoric, and Symbols in Contemporary Syria* (University of Chicago Press, 1999), as well as Salwa Ismail, *The Rule of Violence: Subjectivity, Memory, and Government in Syria* (Cambridge University Press, 2018).

On political economy, including how development and modernization have been tethered to political stability, see Volker Perthes, *The Political Economy of Syria under Asad* (IB Tauris, 1995); Bassam Haddad, *Business Networks in Syria: The Political Economy of Authoritarian Resilience* (Stanford University Press, 2012); and Linda Matar, *The Political Economy of Investment in Syria* (Palgrave Macmillan, 2016).

On political Islam, see Raphaël Lefèvre, *Ashes of Hama: The Muslim Brotherhood in Syria* (Hurst, 2013); Thomas Pierret, *Religion and State in Syria* (Cambridge University Press, 2013); and Naomi Ramirez Diaz, *The Muslim Brotherhood in Syria* (Routledge, 2018). On minorities, see Leon T. Goldsmith, *Cycle of Fear: Syria's Alawites in War and Peace* (Hurst, 2015); Michael Kerr and Craig Larkin, *The Alawis of Syria* (Hurst, 2015); Harriet Allsopp, *The Kurds of Syria* (IB Tauris, 2014); Michael Gunter, *Out of Nowhere: The Kurds of Syria in Peace and War* (Hurst, 2014); and Haian Dukhan, *State and Tribes in Syria* (Routledge, 2018).

For general accounts and analysis of the 2011 uprising and subsequent civil war, an astonishing library has been borne in the last few years alone. For a sample: Robin Yassin-Kassab and Leila al-Shami, *Burning Country: Syrians in Revolution and War* (Pluto Press, 2016); Yassin Al Haj Saleh, *The Impossible Revolution: Making Sense of the Syrian Tragedy* (London: Hurst, 2017); Charles Lister, *The Syrian Jihad: Al-Qaida, the Islamic State and the Evolution of an Insurgency* (Hurst, 2017); William Harris, *Quicksilver War: Syria, Iraq and the Spiral of Conflict* (Hurst, 2018); Adam Baczko, Gilles Dorronsoro, and Arthur Quesnay, *Civil War in Syria: Mobilization and Competing Social Orders* (Cambridge University Press, 2018); Raymond Hinnebusch and Omar Imady, *The Syrian Uprising: Domestic Origins and Early Trajectory* (Routledge, 2018); and Samer Abboud, *Syria* (Polity, 2018).

On particular aspects and participants in the conflict, see Friederike Stolleis, ed.,

Playing the Sectarian Card: Identities and Affiliations of Local Communities in Syria (Friedrich Ebert Stiftung, 2015); Christopher Phillips, *The Battle for Syria: International Rivalry in the New Middle East* (Yale University Press, 2016); Aron Lund, *Into the Tunnels. The Rise and Fall of Syria's Rebel Enclave in the Eastern Ghouta* (The Century Foundation, 2016); Sam Heller, *Keeping the Light On in Idlib: Local Governance, Services, and the Competition for Legitimacy among Islamist Armed Groups* (The Century Foundation, 2016).

On the Islamic State of Iraq and Syria, see William McCants, *The ISIS Apocalypse: The History, Strategy, and Doomsday Vision of the Islamic State* (St Martin's Press, 2015); Michael Weiss and Hassan Hassan, *ISIS: Inside the Army of Terror* (Regan Arts, 2016); Fawaz Gerges, *ISIS: A History* (Princeton University Press, 2016); and Simon Mabon and Stephen Royle, *The Origins of ISIS: The Collapse of Nations and Revolution in the Middle East* (IB Tauris, 2016).

On displacement and refugees, see Sarah Deardorff Miller, *Political and Humanitarian Responses to Syrian Displacement* (Routledge, 2017), and Dawn Chatty, *Syria: The Making and Unmaking of a Refugee State* (Oxford University Press, 2018). For first-hand (and wrenching) accounts of the conflict, see Jonathan Littell, *Syrian Notebooks: Inside the Homs uprising January 16-February 2, 2012* (Verso, 2015); Samar Yazbak, *The Crossing: My Journey to the Shattered Heart of Syria* (Rider, 2016); Wendy Pearlman, *We Crossed a Bridge and It Trembled: Voices from Syria* (Custom House, 2017); Marwan Hisham and Molly Crabapple, *Brothers of the Gun: A Memoir of the Syrian War* (One World, 2018); and Rania Abouzeid, *No Turning Back: Life, Loss, and Hope in Wartime Syria* (Norton & Company, 2018).

For general overviews of, and bibliography on, Syrian foreign policy, see Bente Scheller, *The Wisdom of Syria's Waiting Game: Syrian Foreign Policy under the Asads* (Hurst, 2013); Emma Jorum, *Beyond Syria's Borders: A History of Territorial Disputes in the Middle East* (IB Tauris, 2015). Additional case studies include Ghada Hashem Talhami, *Syria and the Palestinians: The Clash of Nationalisms* (University Press of Florida, 2001); Sonoko Sunayama, *Syria and Saudi Arabia: Collaboration and Conflicts in the Oil Era* (IB Tauris, 2007); Nikolaj Kozanov, *Russia and the Syrian Conflict: Moscow's Domestic, Regional and Strategic Interests* (Gerlach Press, 2016); and J. K. Gani, *The Role of Ideology in Syrian-US Relations: Conflict and Cooperation* (Palgrave Macmillan, 2014).

Online sources

The Syrian civil war catapulted the country into the global limelight, resulting in a proliferation of online sources and research platforms. Not all are reliable, but these are good sources for analysis and developments on the war and Syrian politics: Al-Jumhuriya (www.aljumhuriya.net/en); Syria Deeply (www.newsdeeply.com/syria); and the Carnegie Endowment for International Peace's Syria portal (https://carnegie-mec.org/diwan/issue/1558?lang=en). Two blog-like portals for opinions and briefings include websites of Aymenn Jawad Al-Tamimi (www.aymennjawad.org) and Joshua Landis *Syria Comment* (www.joshualandis.com/blog/).

For data on the humanitarian and military aspects of the situation in Syria, see the International Displacement Monitoring Centre's page on Syria (www.internal-displacement.org/countries/syria); the Syria Human Rights Observatory (www.syriahr.com/en/); the Syria Civil War Map website, which tracked the ebb and flow of the conflict (https://syriancivilwarmap.com/); the Middle East Directions Programme (http://middleeastdirections.eu/); and Human Rights Watch's Syria country portal (www.hrw.org/middle-east/n-africa/syria). Al-Monitor's Syria Pulse also provides decent coverage of these issues (www.al-monitor.com/pulse/syria-pulse).

Please note that URLs may change far more quickly than books can be printed; so if these exact URLs do not work, simply search Google or another engine by the titles of these websites and online resources.

Republic of Lebanon

Imad Salamey

INTRODUCTION

Lebanon is a state without a nation, characterized by an unwavering quarrel over its national character and political direction. The result is a protracted identity crisis that has fragmented its society along uncompromising camps contesting every aspect of nationhood. The country is the product of 18 recognized sects. Despite its small size, it has attracted exceptional international attention prompting frequent foreign interventions. Contestation among regional and international powers has in turn interlocked communities and political groups in a bitter struggle. Internally, a consociational system allocating political resources and political offices along confessional lines attempts to distribute ministerial portfolios, parliamentary seats, and key civilian and military posts to all these competing groups.

This delicate balancing act is the product of regional trauma, as the country's politics has proven a magnet to regional conflicts. At various historic junctures, violence racked its social fabric and global and regional powers intervened to reconstruct its political institutions, from the 1958 American intervention to the brutal civil war that began in 1975, which ended only through acts of great political will and international mediation. The consociational system of governance that prevails today seeks to accommodate communal interests and prevent domination by any one actor, which perhaps explains why the country remained quieter than its neighbors during the Arab Spring. Understanding the historical evolution of this unique system of accommodationist politics amidst changing geopolitical winds is the focus of this chapter.

Box 11.1 provides vital data for this country.

BOX 11.1 VITAL DATA – REPUBLIC OF LEBANON

Capital	Beirut
Regime type	Hybrid (semi-presidential republic)
Head of state	President Michel Aoun (since 2016)
Head of government	Prime Minister Saad Hariri (since 2016)
Legislative institution	Unicameral parliament, with 128 elected seats (*Majlis al-Nuwaab*, or Chamber of Deputies)
Female quota	No
Percentage of seats held by women	4.7%
Major political parties or coalitions (share of seats in most recent general elections, 2018)	March 8 Alliance [Free Patriotic Movement, Amal, Hizbullah, and others] (56.3%), March 14 Alliance [Future Movement, Lebanese Forces, Progressive Socialist Forces, and others] (36.7%)
Population	6,082,357
Major ethnic groups	Arab (95%), Armenian (4%), other (1%)
Major religious groups	Sunni Muslim (28.5%), Shi'a Muslim (28.5%), Christian (35%), Druze (5%), other (3%)
GDP per capita	$9,257 ($14,684 at Purchasing Power Parity)
Unemployment rate	6.2%
Youth unemployment rate	17.4%
Major economic industries	Finance, tourism, real estate and construction, food processing, textiles, cement, chemicals, metals
Military spending as % GDP	4.5%

HISTORICAL BACKGROUND

Lebanon's commercial self-image, sense of history, and even genetic markers trace back to the Phoenician traders who gave the world its first alphabet from the coast of Mount Lebanon more than three thousand years ago. However, modern Lebanon's character as a conglomeration of sectarian communities began with the Islamic conquest of the Roman Levant between 636 and 640 AD. The area around Mount Lebanon, the country's central mountainous range parallel to the Mediterranean coast, witnessed an influx of (Sunni) Muslim Arabs in the seventh and eighth centuries.

Simultaneously, Mount Lebanon continued to host a substantial Christian population. In the late seventh century, a new Christian sect penetrated the area – the Maronites, who originated around the monastery of Maro in the Orontes valley.

The Muslims of Lebanon diversified as 'Abbasid power contracted after the mid-ninth century. Twelver Shi'a dominated the hills south of Sidon and much of the Beqa'a Valley, the fertile strip running in parallel to Mount Lebanon in the east. In contrast, more mystical Isma'ili Muslims gained sympathizers in the southern Beqa'a and near Beirut. When the Isma'ili Fatimid Caliph al-Hakim died in Egypt in 1021, a call went out to his followers to give him allegiance as a manifestation of the divine on earth. The Tanukh chiefs of Mount Lebanon took up the call, thus establishing the Druze sect. In 1516 came the Ottoman conquest of the Mashriq, resulting in the selective empowerment of local leaders and sects. Through the eighteenth and early nineteenth centuries, sectarian relations between Druze, Sunni, Shi'a, and Maronite Christians tipped and tilted continuously. By mid-nineteenth century, Druze fear of Maronite advances interacted with Maronite peasant ferment to plunge Mount Lebanon into 20 years of turbulence, ending only with European intervention on behalf of the Maronites, with Mount Lebanon retaining a Christian majority.

Regnant tensions persisted for decades. At the same time, contacts between Lebanon and the West intensified afterwards, as foreign missionaries spearheaded an educational florescence. Presbyterians from the United States founded the Syrian Protestant College in 1866, later renamed American University of Beirut, and French Jesuits established Saint Joseph University in 1875. Economically, Beirut profited from European trade with the Syrian interior. After 1880, and the subsequent decline of local silk agriculture and industry, mass migration of poor Maronites and Christians headed toward the New World countries.

State formation in the twentieth century

World War One terminated Ottoman rule. An Anglo-French agreement allocated Mount Lebanon and its surroundings to the French, who in 1920 created the political entity of Greater Lebanon – the modern Lebanese territorial state – under a mandate from the League of Nations. In consultation with the Maronite Patriarch, this area incorporated Beirut, Tripoli, Sidon, southern Lebanon, the Beqa'a Valley, and the Akkar region in the north. The expansion added sizable Sunnis and Shi'a citizens to the new state. Christians maintained a slight majority, which was recorded in the 1932 census – the last census conducted in Lebanon.

France designed a sectarian power-sharing system. Administrative rule was guided by Lebanon's first constitution of 1926, which provided for the election of its parliament and president. Local contentions with the French authority only mounted as a new political generation of Lebanese sought national independence, particularly in Muslim communities. Hopes to end French rule emerged after the British army seized Lebanon in 1941 and ended the Vichy government's authority. After 1943, communal elites continued to share power, but the monopoly held over the presidency by Maronites was resented by Sunnis and Shiʻa as the demographic balance shifted in favor of Muslims. In the late 1940s, President Bechara al-Khoury and Sunni Prime Minister Riyadh al-Solh concretized the 1943 National Pact, in which communal leaders agreed to a 6:5 Christian edge in allocation of parliamentary and top state posts. A brief breakdown occurred in 1958, when (Christian) President Camille Chamoun feared the pull of Egyptian President Gamal Abdel Nasser's Arab Nationalism on Lebanon's Sunni Muslims. After fighting broke out, the US intervened in July under its Eisenhower Doctrine in order to prevent pro-Nasserist forces from toppling the pro-Western government.

The 1960s saw destabilizing developments in terms of relations between the major sectarian communities. Urbanization brought poorer Christians and Shiʻa from the countryside to the booming metropolis of Beirut. The 1960s also saw the Shiʻa arrival in modern politics, at first under the moderate leadership of Musa Sadr. The June 1967 Arab-Israeli War introduced additional critical factors. The defeat of the Arab states ended the quiescence of Lebanon's Palestinian Arabs, who had come to the country as refugees after the 1948 war. The Palestinian Liberation Organization (PLO) and growing militancy on part of Palestinian nationalists began to inflame sentiments in Lebanon's sizable Palestinian refugee camps. Many local Lebanese joined leftist Palestinian-Lebanese armed groups, with Israel as the target. Notably, internal communalism became entangled with the Palestinian issue: Lebanese Sunni and Druze leaders believed siding with Palestinian leaders would compel the Maronite Christians to share more power.

The 1969 Cairo Accord expressed the growing frailty of the Lebanese state, as it allowed the PLO and other Palestinian groups – including guerillas, militants, and insurgents – to operate freely in the country. Lebanese militias and armed movements aligned with them enjoyed, by extension, similar autonomy. Christians responded belligerently. Noting the paralysis of the Lebanese armed forces in favor of the increasing power of non-state armed groups, the Maronites' own paramilitary force, the Phalange, and other Christian units built up sizable weaponry arsenals. After its expulsion from Jordan in 1970, the PLO relocated to Lebanon entirely, turning the country into the new frontline of the wider Arab-Israeli conflict and the Palestinian struggle. At the same time, Hafiz al-Asad's takeover of Syria began a trend of Syrian interference in Lebanese politics, particularly under President Suleiman Frangieh.

Civil war, 1975–1990

By the mid-1970s, the elements for internecine conflict were set. Different sects and communities had given rise to parochial parties and militias; the government and its armed forces were unable to maintain order; and the Palestinian factor and regional geopolitics transformed the balance of internal power. In early 1975, fighting exploded between the Christian-led Lebanese Front and Palestinian militants in Beirut, resulting in different areas becoming armed cantons. Despite Christian fears of Syrian designs on Lebanon, President Frangieh invited Syrian military intervention to forestall PLO advances. Syrian forces, with US and Israeli acquiescence, deployed through most of Lebanon to contain Palestinian militancy. In 1978, however, Christian militias turned to Israel instead. The Lebanese army split along religious affiliations, and northern Maronites loyal to the pro-Syrian Frangieh clan splintered from other Christians.

In March 1978, Israel invaded southern Lebanon to eliminate its Palestinian foes and establish a security zone. In response, the PLO under Yasir Arafat strengthened Palestinian positions in western Beirut and the south, using Lebanese allies to loosen Syria's grip. The Christian militias in eastern Beirut and its hinterland coalesced into a super-militia, the Lebanese Forces (LF), under the charismatic Bashir Gemayel, while the Syrians consolidated their presence in the Beqa'a Valley and northern Lebanon. Meanwhile, the disappearance of Shi'a leader Musa Sadr on a visit to Libya, popular frustrations with Palestinian activities, and the 1979 Iranian revolution led to defiance within the Shi'a community. The country seemed to be disintegrating, with a battered Lebanese government only barely operating as different communal forces competed in a free-for-all with their respective foreign patrons.

Israel's invasion into Beirut in 1982, ostensibly to eliminate the PLO once and for all, transformed the Lebanese scene. Israel expelled Arafat and the PLO and reduced Palestinian militancy in Lebanon, and also dealt a military blow to Syria. Reeling, the Syrian regime saw Bashir Gemayel's September

1982 election as president with Sunni and Shi'a support as intolerable. Bashir was assassinated before his inauguration, an act that catalyzed violent reprisals from the LF. One result was the infamous massacres in the Sabra and Shatila Palestinian refugee camps, with Israeli assistance. Another was the conflict's internationalization. The Lebanese parliament elected Bashir's older brother, Amin, to the presidency, and Amin turned to the United States, which mobilized a multinational force staffed mainly by NATO countries to buttress the flailing government. Opposed to this move was the Shi'a Amal group, founded by Musa Sadr in 1974 and today led by Shi'a politician Nabih Berri.

When Israel left Beirut in 1983, Druze forces under leadership of Walid Jumblatt attacked the Christian militias. Alongside most Muslim groups, they opposed the US intervention and its backing of President Amin Gemayel; so, too, was the Syrian government and its Soviet backers, alarmed at the Western military buildup. On October 23, 1983, Shi'a suicide truck bombers killed 241 American and 60 French soldiers in their Beirut military compound, eventually resulting in the US-led multinational force pulling out. In February 1984, Shi'a militias overran western Beirut, the Lebanese army remained fractured, and Gemayel's authority shrank to the Christian heartland of Mount Lebanon. Another destabilizing factor was the rise of Hizbullah (Arabic for Party of God), a Shi'a Islamist movement that was backed by Iran, targeted Israel, and, like Islamists elsewhere, called for an Islamic political order.

Through the late 1980s, the civil war became even more complicated as multiple axes of conflict and communal contestation ravaged society. The Syrian regime supported the Shi'a Amal movement in its sieges of Palestinian camps, but Hizbullah soon eclipsed Amal and began a campaign of terrorism that contributed to a climate of anarchy engulfing much of Beirut. Syrian aspirations to dominate Lebanon in this period of weakness were impeded by Iraq's regime of Saddam Hussein, which shipped arms to the Lebanese military and the LF – thereby implicitly backing the Christian presidency and militias – partly as revenge for Syrian backing of Iran during the Iran-Iraq War. In 1988, President Gemayel's crisis-wracked presidency ended, but at the last moment he appointed the Lebanese military chief and Maronite, Michel Aoun, as acting prime minister along with a military cabinet made up of four Muslim and four Christian army generals. The Muslim generals refused to take their post, however, and the outgoing Prime Minister Salim Hoss, a Sunni, refused to exit. Lebanon now had two governments, a confusing situation as Aoun (with Iraqi backing) launched attacks on Syrian forces.

With many sides exhausted and foreign patronage drying up, the possibility of peace emerged after these years of bloodshed. The US and Arab states promoted the Ta'if peace talks in October 1989, which tentatively ended all fighting in return for constitutional amendments, presidential elections, and some Syrian assistance. Yet instability lurked; the newly elected President René Mu'awadh was assassinated just 17 days into his tenure, while Aoun and the LF militias continued their armed campaign. With American complicity, however, the Syrian army overran Aoun's forces in October 1990, partly given the need to employ Syria in the international coalition against Iraq during the Gulf War. With Syria now the suzerain power, Lebanon had peace.

Reemergence and reformulation, 1991–2011

By 1991, all the militias except Hizbullah disbanded, and the Lebanese army reconfigured itself to integrate sectarian brigades under its new Maronite commander, General Émile Lahoud. Shi'a Islamists released American hostages, and Palestinian militants in Sidon and Tyre were limited to the refugee camps. Peace settled over the country, apart from Hizbullah's contest with Israel. The post-Ta'if governments, however, featured many politicians and leaders who were on the Syrian payroll; inversely, the LF and other Christian parties were marginalized or exiled. From 1992 on, the Syrians operated through a Lebanese government lead by the troika of (Maronite) President Ilyas Hrawi, (Sunni) Prime Minister Rafik Hariri, and (Shi'a) Speaker of Parliament Nabih Berri. Syrian military units remained stationed in the country, and in 1998 General Lahoud was elevated into the presidency. Lahoud and his Syrian allies worked against Hariri, who had garnered growing Saudi support and began acting more independently. Distrust intensified when Bashar al-Asad took over as Syrian president in 2000, as his regime actively sought to undermine Hariri and support Hizbullah, led by Secretary-General Hassan Nasrallah. Syria and Hizbullah also stirred fresh border tensions with Israel, which continued to occupy a security zone in the south to considerable international controversy.

By the time the US invaded Iraq in 2003, Hariri was moving more intensively against Syrian dominance. His political base exploited increasing American and French opposition to the undeniable grip the Syrian regime held over Lebanon, which opened the door to Iranian influence and increased power for Hizbullah – classified as a terrorist actor by most Western government. In September 2004, the US and France mobilized the United Nations

Security Council to pass Resolution 1559, which ordered the Syrian army out of Lebanon and demanded the dissolution of remaining militias including Hizbullah. On February 14, 2005, Hariri and 22 others were assassinated in a massive explosion in central Beirut, an event that triggered a massive outpouring of frustration and sympathy by not just Hariri's supporters but other Lebanese who had grown tired of Syrian hegemony.

Tensions rose as Syrian supporters also came out in force. On March 8, 2005, Hizbullah and its allies organized a pro-Syria demonstration in Beirut that mobilized hundreds of thousands of supporters. On March 14, a counter-protest held by a coalition of other parties, including Christians, Druze, and Sunni Muslims, attracted a larger crowd in demanding the end of Syrian influence. These two iconic events are seared into Lebanese political memory in a period of time often called the Cedar Revolution given the enormous expression of popular sentiment and public activism. Today, these two competing protest fronts also align with the prevailing parliamentary coalitions that somewhat still adhere to their composition and ideals – the March 8 Alliance and the March 14 Alliance.

In April 2005, under international pressure, the Asad regime bowed to these demands, thereby ending three decades of Syrian military presence. The UN Security Council also established an independent investigation commission into the murder of Hariri, with the resulting findings suggesting that Syrian and Hizbullah agents were involved. Other changes were apace. Michel Aoun, freshly returned from his Syrian-imposed exile, controversially broke from the March 14 coalition, led by Rafik Hariri's son, Saad. The March 14 alliance still took a majority (72 out of 128 seats) in the May-June parliamentary elections, but Aoun, allied contingently now with the Amal-Hizbullah March 8 front, was able to rally their minority (25 seats) to block the government on many initiatives. The summer 2006 war between Hizbullah and Israel waged in the south temporarily took attention away from domestic politics, but for many Lebanese it also bolstered Hizbullah's prestige given its success in resisting Israeli incursions.

Domestic political instability loomed, however. The March 14-oriented government, led by Prime Minister Fouad Siniora, prevailed during a period of assassinations against the coalition's leaders and activists. Protests and sit-ins exposed worsening polarization, amplified by the fact that when President Lahoud's term ended in 2007, the divided parliament could not secure a two-third quorum necessary to elect a new President. Siniora served as interim president, but competing protests between the March 8 and March 14 factions and a military takeover brought the entire political landscape to a halt. The standoff ended only after a comprehensive agreement brokered in Doha, Qatar, reached a solution with the agreement that the new president would be Lebanese army chief Michel Suleiman, and his government would give the March 8 groups strong representation. However, the June 2009 elections did not bring much change to the equation, as the March 14 alliance took 71 seats and the March 8 (and Aoun) alliance won 57.

Thereafter, the premiership fell to Saad Hariri, who for better or for worse became a conduit for increased Saudi influence. Saudi efforts did partly normalize relations between Hariri and Syria, but the March 8-March 14 cleavage continued to escalate and freeze many policymaking domains. The Hariri-led government collapsed in 2011, and the Druze faction under Walid Jumblatt's direction likewise defected from the March 14 coalition. The new premier, Najib Mikati, gave the March 8 groups more influence, including Hizbullah.

Lebanon and the Syrian conflict, 2011–2018

During the Arab Spring Lebanon was never a candidate for an upheaval such as those that toppled the autocrats of Tunisia and Egypt in early 2011, because the country already featured the pluralism that the crowds in Tunis and Cairo sought. Its consociational system of confessionalism and lack of a sectarian majority failed to grant any single national group sufficient power to topple the system – or, conversely, the power of dictatorship. Nonetheless, the country swiftly became hostage to the conflict in neighboring Syria, beginning March 2011. Confessional groups, mainly Sunni and Shi'a, took on opposite positions in supporting or opposing the Asad's regime, deepening the split between the March 8 and March 14 coalitions. Tripoli, the second largest and mostly Sunni city, was a bellwether of Lebanese Sunni sentiment as Syria descended into civil war. Long-standing hostility between the city's Sunni Lebanese and Alawites, the Shi'a minority from which the ruling Asad family and elites of Syria hail, ignited clashes that caused 125 deaths between mid-2011 and late 2013. Sectarian tensions worsened as the army killed a prominent Sunni religious figure in May 2012, causing suspicion of Hizbullah intervention, and bombings of two Sunni mosques in Tripoli in August 2013 killed 47 worshippers.

Thus, Shi'a-Sunni relations, already fraught, plumbed to new depths as the Syrian crisis proceeded, reducing security in Lebanon. The decisive development was Hizbullah's military deployment to Syria by early 2013 to support the Asad regime; under Iranian steerage, its expeditionary force swiftly expanded to over five thousand and played key roles in winning battles and territories for Asad, albeit at a cost of at least a thousand fighters by 2015. Lebanese Sunni militants responded by also sending mobilized units to Syria, some in collaboration with jihadi groups like al-Nusra Front. Attacks on Hizbullah and the Iranian Embassy in Beirut occurred. At the same time, Syrian rebels themselves often crossed the border into Lebanon, sometimes fighting Hizbullah units maintaining border security and other times clashing with the Lebanese military, resulting in the deaths of dozens. In 2017, Hizbullah and the army fought together to expel Syrian rebel groups from the Lebanese border in a rare show of cooperation.

Paralleling the sectarian tensions, a swelling tide of Syrian refugees, overwhelmingly Sunni in faith, entered Lebanon from mid-2011. Their numbers mounted from 160,000 in late 2012 to a peak of 1.5 million by early 2015, equivalent to one-third of Lebanon's own population. Their potentially permanent residence threatened to reconfigure the national demography; both Shi'a and Christian voices noted that their respective denominations would become dwarfed by a massive new Sunni majority. Because Lebanon refused to grant refugee status or administer formal camps to the newcomers, refugees huddled in informal and often miserable settlements, resulting in humanitarian problems and increased local tensions.

Yet despite all these challenges, by the mid-2010s it became apparent that Lebanese groups and elites had little appetite for the kind of sustained conflict and violence experienced in the 1975–90 civil war. The Syrian civil conflict, in many ways, reminded Lebanese observers of the horrors of unending internal violence. This did not translate into political stability, though. The scheduled 2013 general elections raised controversy and were eventually cancelled, as Hizbullah wished to change the electoral law and dissolve internal security institutions within the Lebanese state, which were well-known to be headed by March 14 members. Lebanon entered a new presidential vacuum in May 2014 after Suleiman's term expired. The March 8 and March 14 coalitions compromised on Tammam Salam, an urbane Sunni elite, as prime minister; Salam was able to form a national unity government in February 2014. However, by now Iran and Saudi Arabia had also emerged as the clear foreign patrons for the March 8 and March 14 coalitions, respectively. The Lebanese state gave this type of paralyzed politics and piecemeal progress a name – *idarat al-'azma* (administration of crisis).

After more gridlock and wrangling, Michel Aoun re-emerged as the compromise candidate to become the next president, though not without a complicated backstory involving mistrust and deals with Samir Geagea, head of the LF, opposition from Hariri and Berri, and the brief entry of Suleiman Frangieh, Jr., son of the former president. The eventual government featured Hariri returning as prime minister under President Aoun. The national unity government created in late 2016 was beset by many challenges, among them finding ways to end parliament's prolongation of terms and drafting an updated electoral law. More than 18 proposed amendments were presented, each articulating a unique calculus for prevailing parties. The version chosen in the end sought to reduce sectarian fragmentation by adopting proportional representation allocated to small districts, and creating pre-printed ballots to prevent communal vote-buying.

The elections held in May 2018 were the first in nearly a decade, and put Hariri and his March 14 camp in the minority. Reflecting perhaps their growing demographic strength as expressed in a proportional electoral system, March 8 groups won more than 56 percent of parliament's seats, while the March 14 coalition was reduced to just over a third. Saad Hariri remained prime minister, but his leadership was overshadowed by his curious (and controversial) sojourn in Saudi Arabia in November 2017, when he tendered his resignation – but weeks later rescinded it. The move was widely reported as the product of Saudi pressure during a scheduled visit to remove Hizbullah from the government and reduce Iranian influence in the region, even at the cost of Lebanese political instability. With an increasing number of Lebanese citizens chafing under the constant predicaments and breakdowns that have wracked their politics over the past decade, it remains to be seen as the 2010s close whether pragmatism and compromise can result in a more successful period of cross-sectarian governance.

SOCIAL AND ECONOMIC ENVIRONMENT

Lebanon maintains its population of over six million within a small area (Map 11.1). Most of the territory is relatively high-altitude. There are four major geographical regions: a coastal plain, Mount Lebanon, the Beqa'a Valley, and the Anti-Lebanon Mountains. The coastal plain varies in width from about eight miles (12 kilometers) in the north to almost nothing in some places. Most of the country's major towns are on this plain, including the three largest: Beirut, Tripoli, and Sidon. Mount Lebanon, from the Akkar in the north to the Barouk range and the hills of Jabal 'Amil in the south, rises abruptly from the plain. The highest peaks of the coastal massif are inland from Tripoli and Beirut, within 15 miles (about 20 kilometers) of the

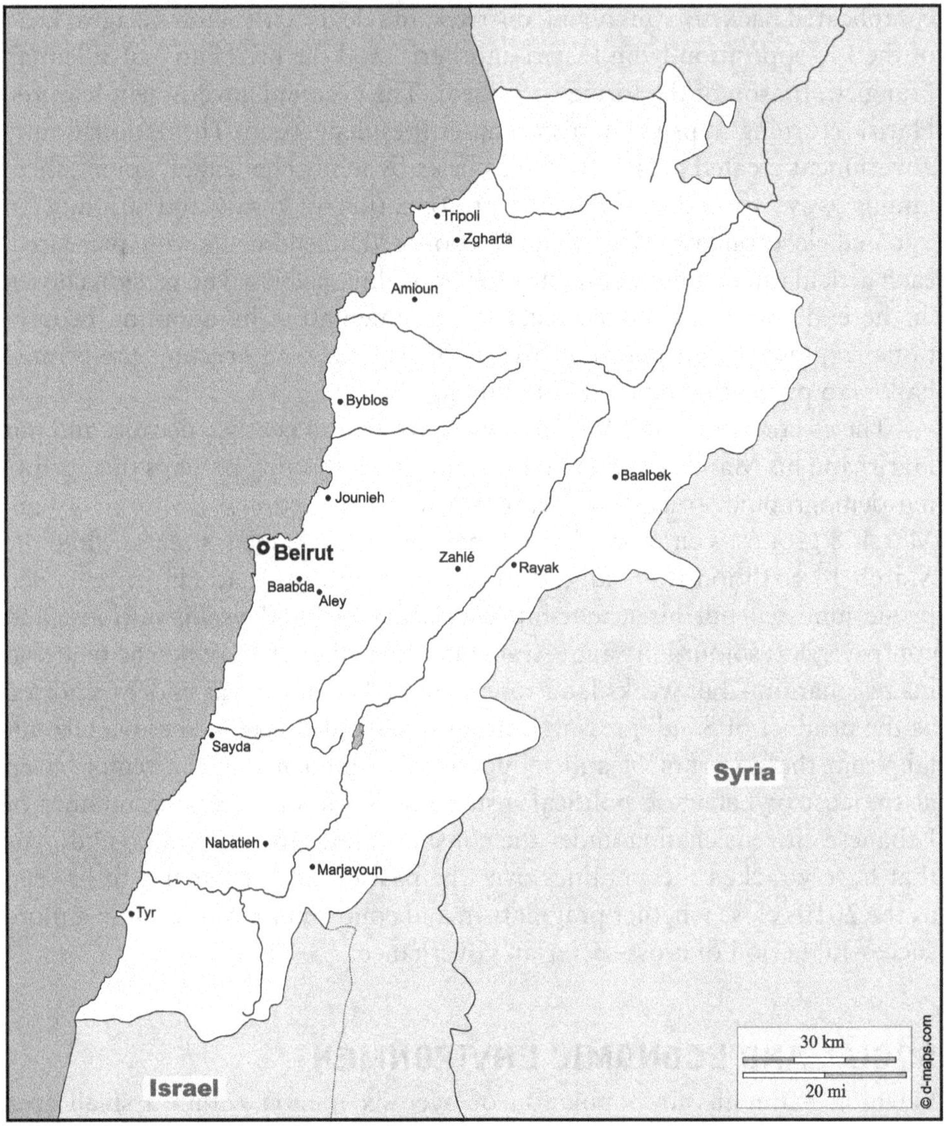

MAP 11.1
Republic of Lebanon. Major rivers and cities shown.

Source: D-Maps.

coast. These stand between 8,000 and 10,000 feet (2,500 and 3,000 meters). The population is concentrated in coastal urban centers; half of the country lives in Beirut and its suburbs, followed by the cities of Tripoli, Sidon (also known locally as Sayda), and Jouneih.

The fertile Beqaʻa Valley lies between Mount Lebanon and the Anti-Lebanon Mountain Range. Much of the valley floor is about 3,000 feet above sea level, bounded by fault lines that express Lebanon's vulnerability to earthquakes. It is widest north of Baalbek, where it gives rise to the Orontes River, which flows north into Syria. In most of the valley, however, the Litani River is the main water source. The Litani flows southward, turning toward the Mediterranean about 12 miles (20 kilometers) north of the Israeli border. To the east, the Anti-Lebanon Mountains lie partly in Lebanon and partly in Syria; the boundary between the two countries is not well demarcated. At 9,232 feet (2,900 meters), Mount Hermon on the Syrian-Lebanese-Israeli border is the second highest peak. Mount Lebanon receives the most reliable rainfall in the Levant. Lebanon is the only Arab country self-sufficient in water resources, though its pollution problems are severe.

The communal fabric: ethnicity, religion, sect

Lebanon represents a unique coalescence of Christian, Muslim, and other communities at the boundaries of East and West. Its mountains have been a refuge for minorities, and its large Christian population and central coastal position in the Levant have made it a gateway for European penetration since the seventeenth century. Most Lebanese identify with their system of government and hold strong affiliation to the country territorial configuration, yet communal interpretations shape national allegiance. Most Maronites emphasize that ties with the West differentiate Lebanon from the Islamic neighborhood, Sunnis see Lebanon as a distinctive component of a wider Arab and mainly Sunni environment, and Shiʻa view Lebanon as a vehicle for their own community, with Iranian as well as Arab ties. About 95 percent of Lebanese use Arabic as their mother tongue, though some speak another language at home. The differences among the confessional groups, however, remain great. In Lebanon, religion is more than a belief system; it is a major element in family and self-identity.

Christians and Muslims comprised roughly equivalent portions of the population through the late Ottoman period until the mid-twentieth century. Maronite dynamism maintained the Christian share, despite emigration westwards after 1860. Between the 1920s and the 1990s, however, higher Muslim population growth and continued Christian emigration caused a substantial shift. Surveys and estimates indicate that by the 1990s Christians made up less than 40 percent of resident Lebanese. At the same time, strong differentiation between Sunni and Shi'a Muslims meant that Lebanon remained a country without a majority community. Shi'a, trailing Maronites and Sunni Muslims in the 1932 census, had become approximately equal to the Sunni community by the 1980s. Today, this would leave Shi'a and Sunnis each at perhaps 28 percent of the population, Christians between 35 and 38 percent, with Maronites making up about half of the Christian proportion. The Druze represent about 5 percent. Lebanon's present population of over 6 million, excluding Palestinian refugees, encompasses roughly 1.7 million Shi'a, 1.7 million Sunnis, and 1.2 million Maronites; in comprehensive terms, there are about 3.6 million Muslims and 2.4 million Christians. All estimates are speculative, however, given the lack of any real census.

The Palestinian refugee population – dating back to the major Palestinian influx of 1948 and 1949, accompanying the creation of Israel – presents other debatable data. There are perhaps 200,000 Palestinians in Lebanon, half of them living in squalid refugee camps alongside the main coastal cities. Shi'a and Christians, in particular, oppose permanent Palestinian settlement because of its anticipated effects on communal balances in favor of Sunnis.

Lebanon has 18 recognized sectarian communities defined largely by religion. The main groups are the three "great" communities, each above 20 percent of the population: Maronite Christians and Sunni and Shi'a Muslims. Four other non-Muslim communities are also guaranteed ministerial positions in Lebanese governments – Druze, Orthodox Christians, Greek Catholics, and Armenians. To a greater degree than the smaller Christian sects, Maronites are extensively represented among poorer and lower-middle-class Lebanese. Yet they also have a powerful political, professional, and commercial elite, and they remain the bulk of the population in most of eastern Beirut and the northern half of Mount Lebanon. Maronites have long looked toward Western nations as protectors, and their Lebanese nationalism was often perceived by Muslim Lebanese as contrasting with Arab Nationalism or denying Lebanon's Arab affiliation.

Orthodox Christians constitute the second-largest Christian community. Traditionally, they are more urbanized than the Maronites and also not exclusive to Lebanon as Orthodox communities can be found in other Mashriq countries. Not inhabiting a compact territory like the Maronites, they are more used to being a minority, have had more interaction with Sunni Muslims, and are more comfortable with Arab identity than are many Maronites. Since the 1960s, however, the powerful Islamic emphasis in Arab Nationalism has led most Lebanese Orthodox to gravitate toward

Maronite Christian politics while still presenting themselves as more open to other Arabs. Away from Beirut and Tripoli, Orthodox Christians inhabit the Koura district, parts of the Matn above Beirut, and Marjayoun in the South.

Smaller Christian groups include the Greek Catholics, whose residency originates from the eighteenth century, when a number of Orthodox Christians in Ottoman Syria went into communion with Rome. They live mainly in eastern Beirut and the Beqa'a Valley town of Zahle, with a scattering of villages in less defensible locations than the Maronite heartland. They have tended to follow the Maronite political lead. Another are Armenians, who number about 200,000 and live overwhelmingly in eastern Beirut and Beqa'a Valley. As non-Arabs, they are distinct from other Christians and Lebanese, and they maintain their ethnic identity and language. They came to Lebanon during and after World War One as refugees from Turkey. Armenians have kept their distance from Lebanese political factions, supported forces in power, and looked for freedom to manage their own community.

Until the 1980s, the Maronite political advantage in post-Ottoman Lebanon and Muslim resentment of it obscured the divide between the Sunni and Shi'a communities. Sunni politicians utilized a double-edge strategy: they partnered with Maronite leaders to command Lebanon in the 1943 National Pact, and they championed Muslim demands for adjustment, seeking to contain radical elements. This worked as long as they could direct their own community and Shi'a remained rural, quiescent, and aligned with their traditional chiefs. The Sunni position, however, foundered in the late twentieth century when leftist and Palestinian groups attracted Sunni loyalty and Shi'a urbanized and mobilized in greater numbers. Sunnis differ from both Maronites and Shi'a in their long-standing urban concentration in Beirut, Tripoli, and Sidon.

By contrast, the Shi'a remained economically and politically marginalized until recently. For most, migration in the 1960s and 1970s from southern Lebanon and the Beqa'a to the southern neighborhoods of Beirut (labeled as "belts of misery") – from the periphery of the country to the periphery of the capital – simply meant exchanging rural for urban poverty. Young Shi'a created their own militant organizations. In the 1980s, they also acquired foreign patrons in the form of the only two Shi'a governments in the MENA, the new Islamic Republic of Iran and Syria, which enabled them to match the Western-Maronite and Arab-Sunni sponsorships. The 1989 Ta'if Agreement gave Shi'a parity with Sunnis in parliament and increased the powers of the Shi'a speaker of the house. In the 1990s, Syrian hegemony over Lebanon provided an opportunity for Shi'a to project their political and economic power, while Iran pumped money into the religious wing of the community.

Critically, in contrast to other Lebanese militias of the 1975–90 period, which were disbanded in 1991, Hizbullah retained and enhanced its armed wing. Hizbullah's justification was resistance to Israeli occupation of Lebanese land, and the movement took credit for Israel's unilateral withdrawal and the collapse of Israel's ally, the South Lebanese Army, in May 2000. These events consolidated Hizbullah's standing as Lebanon's most effective political movement after 1990, with social service provisions (such as education and healthcare) for Shi'a neighborhoods and unrivaled Syrian-Iranian foreign backing. In the 2000, 2005, and 2009 parliamentary elections, Hizbullah and the more moderate Amal movement commanded the Shi'a population of southern Lebanon, the northern Beqa'a Valley, and the southern suburbs of Beirut.

Suspended between the Muslims and Christians, the Druze community stands in a peculiar position. The Druze faith derives from Islam but merges many aspects of non-Abrahamic mysticism. Estrangement from the Maronites led Druze leaders, above all Kamal Jumblatt, to embark upon highly pragmatic and contingent strategies that saw, at various times, the Druze ally with Sunni Muslims, leftists, Palestinians, and Christians. Since Lebanon's independence, the Druze have often felt challenged by the two larger communities, the Maronites and Shi'a; indeed, the rise of Hizbullah and Shi'a political power has mainly provoked Druze anxiety. Limited Druze numbers are to a degree offset by the community's strategic location in the Shouf hills above Beirut, straddling the main road from Beirut to Damascus, and on the slopes of Mount Hermon, between southern Lebanon and the Beqa'a Valley.

In addition to religion, extended families and villages also play a role in giving sectarian communities their historical identity. Because one does not normally marry outside one's religion, family and religious identification are mutually reinforcing. The family was long the vehicle of political advancement, plugging into wider clan and patronage networks. Family associations have also provided support functions elsewhere performed by the state. Nonetheless, the war years after 1975 saw a weakening of the family in political affairs, with financial resources, sectarian parties, and obeisance to Syria and the security apparatus becoming better promotion routes by the 1990s.

Economic conditions

Lebanese society is famous for its entrepreneurial talent. It has produced the Arab world's oldest global diaspora, and unique among the MENA, largely eschewed the state-led developmental strategies embraced in the post-World War Two era in favor of more freewheeling commerce driven by trade and services.

After independence and before 1975, the Lebanese enhanced their regional economic role. The creation of Israel cut economic ties between the Arab world and most of the former British Mandate for Palestine, leaving a gap that the Lebanese filled. For example, Tripoli replaced Haifa as a terminal for the Iraq petroleum pipeline. More generally, overland transport and communications that might have traversed the southern Levant were funneled into Beirut, and international corporations and banks established regional headquarters in the Lebanese capital. The Lebanese also took advantage of the growing wealth of the region's oil rentier states. Beirut supplied entertainment, investment opportunities, and a transit point for goods and services. With Arabs from the prospering Gulf kingdoms flocking to Beirut and Mount Lebanon each summer, the Lebanese provided their guests with recreation, banking arrangements, and European-style shopping. Lebanon's schools and universities educated children of Arab elites.

In the decade before the collapse into chaos in 1975, Lebanon experienced rapid industrial growth. In the 1960s, a manufacturing belt had begun to grow in the poorer suburbs of Beirut, mostly small enterprises producing light consumer goods, textiles, and processed foods. The agricultural sector gradually declined, though many people continued to earn incomes from their small landholdings or tenant farms. Apples, citrus fruits, olives, olive oil, and grapes – a diversity of crops made possible by Lebanon's varied topography – remain export items. Remittances from Lebanese emigrants, including workers in the oil-producing states, and hard currency from Lebanon's service sector were profuse, a pattern that continues today. In 2018, for instance, remittances from Lebanese working abroad composed over 13 percent of the GDP, the second highest figure in the MENA after Palestine.

The civil war punctured Lebanon's economic ascent as a regional commercial hub and destroyed water, communications, and power infrastructure. By the World Bank's measure, the economy exhibited an incredible -42.5 percent rate of decline across the 1980s. The Lebanese economy since then has reflected its post-war recovery. Rafik Hariri, who prior to his political career was an extraordinarily successful businessman, had amassed a fortune in Saudi Arabia. His government undertook ambitious reconstruction, but the cost far exceeded Lebanon's capacity to pay; in addition, Syrian meddling, corruption, and political uncertainty contributed to a tepid response from potential investors. As a result, the Lebanese government borrowed money at inflated interest rates, principally from domestic banks. When Hariri came to office, the public debt was about $900 million; in 1998, it reached $18 billion, and at its 2018 peak ballooned to nearly $80 billion – 150 percent of GDP, one of the worst debt-to-GDP ratios in the world. Debt servicing (that is, paying the interest) alone ate up half the national budget after the mid-1990s. Despite liberal government deficit spending, economic growth was only modest, unemployment was substantial, income gaps stretched, and the middle class saw its economic status erode.

Still, the Lebanese economy recovered partly, with growth in real estate, construction, finances, and services driving much of the post-war trajectory. The GDP grew by nearly 10 percent annually across the 1990s. The year 2005 marked a faltering point; Hariri's assassination, plus billions in damage from the 2006 conflict with Israel, scared many prospective investors and traders away. The departure of the Syrian military, however, and international favor for the government of Hariri's adviser, Fouad Siniora, lured more capital back. Indeed, Lebanon sailed through the 2008–9 global recession unscathed. Its banks had avoided risky financial instruments; regional backers of Shi'a and Sunni factions, principally Iran and Saudi Arabia, directed money into the country; and tourism boomed, as wealthy Arab visitors from the Gulf flocked to the country.

The Arab Spring hurt the Lebanese economy due to disruptions of trade, tourism, and the costs of additional security and refugee absorption. From 2011–18, the GDP featured a lethargic growth rate of just 1.7 percent, and by 2018 youth unemployment reached 17.4 percent – nearly three times the overall adult jobless rate. Meanwhile, underlying fiscal imbalances remain. Government spending barely covers debt servicing, public salaries, and the state electricity company – an exemplar of profligate public business. Despite the influx of Syrian refugees, there remain few resources for patching up infrastructure like decrepit Internet provision, while the national electricity company, Electricité du Liban, has a paltry budget and little regulatory power. This has resulted, in many urban areas, in a familiar sight in crowded streets – patchworks of electrical wires between buildings and homes that transmit, steal, splice, and transfer power, created by citizens and brokers who have long since stopped relying upon the national utilities grid (Photo 11.1).

PHOTO 11.1
Patchwork Electricity Wiring in Urban Beirut

Source: Pixabay. Public domain.

Officials have suggested the economy can be buoyed by new sectors, such as promising offshore hydrocarbon prospects and high-tech services, but international companies have remained cautious. Nonetheless, the banking system has managed some of its debt load, gold and foreign currency reserves have remained stable, and remittances from expatriate Lebanese continue to flow in. The economy, in sum, is weathering a mighty regional storm, but equitable development and future prosperity remain far off.

POLITICAL STRUCTURES

The 1926 constitution and the 1943 National Pact, later modified by the 1989 Ta'if Agreement, constitute the tenants of Lebanon's modern governing structure. The structure of Lebanese politics has been called *consociational*, meaning a regime that institutionalized power-sharing between conflicting groups that are not individually strong enough to rule alone, but are so wracked with contestation that they abide by regular consultation to maintain institutional order. For instance, since 1943, the president, chosen by parliamentary vote for a single six-year term, has been a Maronite. The president customarily nominates a Sunni Muslim as prime minister on the basis of mandatory consultation with the parliamentary deputies, and in turn the prime minister forms a cabinet-based government that is ideally half-Christian and half-Muslim/Druze. The speaker of parliament is Shi'a, and his deputy is an Orthodox Christian. Ministerial portfolios are allocated according to confessional shares, as are many other positions in the executive, legislative, and judicial branches. The army commander and the head of the national bank are customarily Maronites, and there is a religious balance among security service chiefs.

Lebanon's unicameral parliament, the Chamber of Deputies, elaborates the sectarian political system. Parliamentary seats are distributed along confessional and geographical quotas. Each of the 15 electoral districts (26 prior to the 2017 electoral law change) is allocated a fixed number of seats based on religious affiliation and communal size. The latter has often broached controversy for obvious reasons: there has not been a census since 1932, so the allocation of seats for different sects is based not upon known demographic breakdowns but guesswork and political considerations. In the 2018 elections under the new law, Lebanese citizens vote in a hybrid system in which they cast two ballots: one for a single party-based list of candidates, and the second for their preferred candidate on that list. Despite the fuzziness of numbers, in many areas religious sects concentrate to justify constituency-based allocation. The areas of Tripoli and Sidon are overwhelmingly Sunni; Zgharta, Kisrawan, and Jbail are similarly Maronite; Tyre, Nabatiyah, and Baalbek have Shi'a majorities; and Koura is predominantly Orthodox. Even in areas of mixed population, villages tend to belong primarily to a single religious group. In Beirut, many Christians, Sunnis, and Shi'a live in separate neighborhoods.

Lebanon's constitution has remained one of the oldest liberal texts that guarantees economic freedom and civil rights. Beirut remains a regional publishing center, noted for the vigor of its print media. Nevertheless, from 1990 to 2005, Syria-dominated Lebanon went through a period of constricted public freedoms. Senior politicians and the security agencies interfered in elections within the union movement and professional organizations. Business and banking associations resisted coordination during this period, preserving effective electoral practices, and the basic culture of political pluralism provided the platform for a powerful rebound of civil society. Indeed, the hybridity of Lebanon's political regime embodies not just the consociational nature of its confessional politics, which prevents democratic competition across sectarian lines (though for the overarching reason of preserving peace); it also stems from the frequent nature of foreign interventions – Israeli, Syrian, Western – that have amplified domestic abuses of power and contravened constitutional protections of basic rights.

As for the country's military, Lebanon moved from a small Maronite-dominated army, largely neutral in political affairs until the 1960s, to a larger force incorporating militia personnel in the 1990s, with a more representative officer corps. Under Syrian hegemony after 1990, the army command of General Émile Lahoud, military intelligence, and the public security directorate were politicized in favor of Syria. The restructured army brigades, however, maintained popular legitimacy and respect as an apolitical armed force.

Finally, Lebanese judicial institutions are pluralistic. They apply civil, Islamic, and Christian laws. Ordinary courts have civil and criminal, civil chambers, with appellate structure divided along three levels – first instance, appeal, and cassation, all administered by a Supreme Judicial Council under the Ministry of Justice. There are also administrative, state, and constitutional councils as well as a full-fledged military court system. Legal personnel are competent, but political pressure has subverted the legal authorities and undermined the independence of the judiciary. Beyond the state, each sectarian community has its own religious institutions, with personal-status issues (e.g., marriage, divorce, custody, and inheritance) subject to religious codes – not civil law. Such institutions – for example, the Maronite Church and patriarchate, the office of the Sunni chief mufti, and the Higher Shi'a Islamic Council – control extensive property and their own courts. Spiritual leaders can have significant political influence.

POLITICAL DYNAMICS

Lebanese politics exemplifies confessional consociationalism – confessional, because the basis of power-sharing is upon religiously-based confessional groups, and consociational, because power-sharing is inscribed as the goal of political institutions rather than unfettered democratic competition. Apart from the rigidity of sectarian quotas, though, the most prominent defect of confessional consociationalism is the discouragement of national or secular parties. National coalitions often present incoherent assemblies of parliamentarians, denying them the formation of ideological parties with coherent programs. The frequent movement of parties in and out of the March 14 coalition is testament to this. Historically, ideological parties, like the

Communists, Syrian Social Nationalists, and Ba'th, have seldom succeeded. The only two breaking his mold combined ideology with strong family leadership. The Progressive Socialist Party of the Jumblatt clan brought together leftists with a traditional Druze following; and the Phalange as led by the Gemayel family combined Maronite pride with Lebanese nationalism.

As a result, Lebanese parliaments are highly fragmented. Prior to the civil war, for instance, typically at least a dozen parties would squabble in the chamber, split across varying parliamentary blocs. Presidents and prime ministers were chosen without partisan support, and thus were unable to establish a strong command of government. Governance depended on unstable coalitions, and presidents fell back on familiar tools of manipulation, bribery, and threats. Nonetheless, the majority of Lebanese kept allegiance to local chiefs as long as their basic concerns were satisfied – security, plus a share of government largesse – were accommodated.

Much of today's political fragmentation reflects the changes to the system made from the Ta'if peace deal. In those meetings, 62 of 73 surviving members of the 1972 Lebanese parliament, the last elected before the war years, convened in Ta'if, Saudi Arabia, from September 30 to October 22, 1989, to adjust the constitution to reconcile Muslim grievances with Christian fears. They modified the balance of power while perpetuating most of the 1926 constitution and the National Pact. Among the shifts was reducing the executive power of the presidency in favor of the cabinet-based government, thereby tilting power modestly from the Maronites to Sunni Muslims; and second, it also gave more prerogatives to parliament and its Shi'a speaker. For example, the president could no longer veto legislation; he could only require it to be presented a second time. The Ta'if process also changed parliament's composition, altering the ratio of Christian to non-Christian deputies from 6:5 to one of parity, in addition to equality between Sunnis and Shi'a. The number of deputies was increased from 99 to 128 in 1992. The 64 Christian seats became allocated as follows: 34 to Maronites, 14 to Orthodox, 8 to Greek Catholics, 6 to Armenians, 1 to a Protestant, and 1 to other Christians. The 64 non-Christian seats were to include 27 Sunnis, 27 Shi'a, 8 Druze, and 2 Alawites.

These mathematical allocations hold today, but the long-term effect has been to sharpen sectarianism. What has changed is that confessional rivalries have shifted since the 1990s from Christian/Muslim friction to Sunni/Shi'a competition, with a shared understanding that the Shi'a – exemplified by Hizbullah – now desire not only an equitable voice but often more influence than the other groups, by virtue of their rapid ascent. Further, the notion of a regime defined by competition within (rather than across) communal groups, and where power and resources are distributed based upon fixed understandings, remains inextricable from Lebanese political relations. Amplifying all of this has been foreign interferences and sponsorship of favored groups. Today, for instance, March 8 is associated with Iranian support, by virtue of its Hizbullah composition; March 14 is associated with its pro-Western orientation.

The emancipation of women has yet to significantly affect these dynamics. Women received the vote in 1953, and the army opened the gate to female officers in 1992. Female literacy in Lebanon is nearly 92 percent. Yet the number of women in parliament is miserably low: 6 out of 128 deputies after the 2018 elections, down from 7 in 2005. In 2009, two female parliamentarians, Nayla Tueni (Orthodox) and Bahiya Hariri (Sunni), owed their prominence to being, respectively, the daughter and sister of murdered male politicians. Sethrida Geagea (Maronite) is the wife of politician Samir Geagea. Three belonged to the March 14 bloc, and one, Gilberte Zouein (Maronite), to Michel Aoun's group. In the 2018 election, Paula Yacoubian, backed by civil society groups, broke traditional party dominance and won an Armenian allocated parliamentary seat. Female participation in the legal profession, by contrast, is impressive. In late 2009 Amal Haddad became president of the Beirut Bar Association, and Joyce Thabit became the Lebanese deputy prosecutor for the special international tribunal for the Hariri murder case. The number of female judges has come to exceed those of male counterparts.

Lebanese civil society, meanwhile, is vibrant. Youth activism is robust and ongoing, with a culture of protest and public expression unrivaled in the Mashriq. Today, for instance, activists continue to clamor around amending the electoral system to ensure higher participation, as turnout from the 2018 election barely reached 50 percent. Others advocate for a gender quota, much as Jordan and other Arab countries have. Still others desire to reduce sectarian stratification, with young educated Lebanese the least likely to adhere to strict religious and communal boundaries. Administrative decentralization is another reform demand that promises local empowerment away from the control and watchful eyes of sectarian elites. Uniquely, environmental management and consumer protection have become a major concern since 2015. That year, youth activists and grassroots networks began a series of street demonstrations, the You Stink movement, protesting the pileup of garbage in Beirut due to the closure of nearby landfills and the mismanagement of local authorities.

FOREIGN POLICY

Lebanon is located at the outskirts of the Arab world, culturally and politically serving as an exchange outpost between the West and the East. The external associations of each of Lebanon's three dominant communities – the Maronites with France and the West, the Sunnis with major Arab states, and the Shiʻa with Syria and Iran – compound the strategic significance of this country. Geopolitically, Lebanon further stands between historic rivals, Syria and Israel, while historically enabling armed Palestinian and Shiʻa Islamist groups to attack Israel. The variety of Lebanon's external connections and its strategic relevance to great powers have increased the stakes in the country's political alignment.

In the mid-twentieth century, from the 1940s to the 1960s and within the constraints of its Western-Arab and Muslim-Christian dualities, Lebanon had played an active role in international affairs. It was a founding member of both the United Nations and the Arab League, for instance. At the same time, accommodating different regional spheres of influence, Lebanon typically took a neutral position to many regional conflicts. Deviation from this approach has invariably brought trouble, because of strong opposition from one or more of the country's major communities or an external power exercising its power through its Lebanese sympathizers.

For instance, in the 1950s, President Chamoun's relations with the West were suspect to many Muslims, and Egypt's influence on Sunni Muslims was in turn suspect to most Christians. After 1967, regime compromises with the Palestinians led Christians to arm themselves, and Maronite relations with Israel and Iraq later contributed to Syria's determination to manipulate its local allies to achieve hegemony. After 1985, Hizbullah's ties to revolutionary Iran stimulated a variety of counter-pressures on Lebanon from the US, Israel, and Saudi Arabia. After 2000, the mounting Christian, Sunni, and Druze alienation from Syria was bound to bring a day of reckoning. The reckoning came in 2005, but Syria and Iran were able to operate through the Shiʻa to encourage a schism over the convergence of the majority in the new Lebanese government. Today, foreign sponsorship continues to influence internal happenings. Saad Hariri's dramatic 2017 entanglements with Saudi Arabia, long seen as a backer of the Sunni Muslim groups in the March 14 coalition, riveted Lebanese politics but also exposed the domestic consequences of such external support.

As regards to Arab-Israeli affairs, Lebanese governments paid lip service to anti-Israeli stances through the 1950s and 1960s but had little taste for activism. Israeli transgressions into Lebanese territory from the 1970s on, however, hardened Lebanese attitudes. Even many Christians viewed Israel as partly responsible for Lebanon's Palestinian problem, for the 1983–84 Christian massacres in the Shouf hills, and for Shi'a radicalism. In the 1990s, many Lebanese wanted calm on their southern border and resented being coerced by Damascus into serving as Syria's surrogate front line, but they felt little impetus toward an Israeli-Lebanese peace treaty. Syrian pressure to ensure that Lebanon did not emulate the PLO and Jordan in making a separate deal with the Israelis was unnecessary. In 2006, Walid Jumblatt spoke for the non-Shi'a majority when he favored Lebanese army deployment along the border and Hizbullah disarmament, with application of the 1949 Lebanese-Israeli armistice agreement, not a formal peace, as long as conditions did not permit a general Arab-Israeli settlement.

The Syrian shadow has hung over much of Lebanon's foreign relations since the civil war. Lebanon could pass as a proper territorial state from independence in 1943 until the early 1970s. Thereafter, for one-third of a century, the procession of sectarian cantons, foreign occupations, and Syrian hegemony meant that Lebanon was simply a territorial shell within which the Lebanese regime was a subordinate actor. The Lebanese state reasserted itself in 2005, but its authority remained partial, dependent on backing from the international community. Syria's grudging military evacuation enabled Lebanon to restore state command of the north and the Beqa'a Valley, but Syrian aid to various parties continued. So too did the lure of its support, as evidenced by the reconciliation visit of Michel Aoun to Syria in December 2008 – the same country that forced him out of politics earlier.

Nonetheless, Lebanese foreign policy began to exhibit its own independent tendencies after 2005 under the leadership of Prime Minister Fouad Siniora. The Hariri assassination and the 2006 Israeli-Hizbullah armed conflict led to a level of United Nations intervention in the country unique in the world: the UN assassination inquiry and the special tribunal, the enlarged UN Interim Force in Lebanon, the UN Border Assessment Team, and special UN envoys to report on implementation of Security Council Resolutions 1559 and 1701, all in addition to the older UN Truce Supervision Organization for the 1949 armistice and the UN Relief and Works Organization for the Palestinian refugees. Further, until 2011 and despite opposition from Shi'a who were suspicious of US support for Israel, Prime Ministers Siniora and Saad Hariri made efforts to cement relations with the United States, which increased aid to the Lebanese army. Lebanon's new majority also had to cope after May 2007 with French President Nicolas Sarkozy's flirtation with Damascus, as well as with uncertain support from Saudi Arabia and

Egypt, while Iran and Syria underwrote the opposition. Siniora nonetheless scored impressive promises of more international aid and developmental assistance.

The Arab Spring threw Lebanon's foreign outlook into uncertainty, as Hizbullah's deployment to Syria and Iran's increasing regional interventionism clashed with the Western-leaning, Saudi-supported stance of the March 14 coalition. Indeed, Saudi Arabia and France worked to bolster the Lebanese army so as to keep it away from Hizbullah and Iranian influence with the offer of major military investment. Joint fear of the Islamic State of Iraq and Syria facilitated this in the mid-2010s. Against this, the July 2015 Iranian nuclear agreement with the United States and other major powers softened Iran's dealings with Lebanon, only to retrench once the Trump administration withdrew from the agreement in 2018. Lebanese foreign policy, as the 2010s close, remains typified by a pragmatic streak when it can afford to be independent – and by multiple and overlapping tilts to different foreign sponsors when it cannot.

FUTURE PROSPECTS

The domestic efforts required to preserve Lebanon's pluralistic politics are Sisyphean tasks. Yet despite its vulnerability, Lebanon remains an exceptional state. Consider the Arab Spring: it now appears far more resilient and prosperous than neighboring Syria, its former dominator. Its government is often fragile, but its sheer persistence shows how far the country has come since its ruination by 15 years of civil war. Thanks to its consociationalism that has equipped the political system with an elaborate mechanism to mitigate disagreements, Lebanon's hybrid political apparatus has not devolved into sustained violence. Communal decentralization and relative autonomy, despite its splintering and fragmenting momentum, has insured relative protectionism and preservation; thus easing the tension and preventing the type of fears that have overwhelmed societies under autocratic rules.

Lebanon, however, remains subject to a volatile environment. Surrounding conflicts and their repercussions on internal fragmentation are constant concerns. Accommodating and negotiating the return of refugees to their respective countries is another monumental challenge. Economic inequalities and gender disparities, especially in politics, require urgent attention. Political and administrative reforms to control spending, reduce corruption, and attract investments remain on the agenda, but fractious political coalitions often mean discussions of laws are postponed to future dates, or else subsumed in the deeper discourse of confessional rivalries. Overcoming these stakes is not easy to achieve, but Lebanese ingenuity and resilience to recurring crises inspire hopes that the country can rise up to the challenge.

FURTHER READING

For Lebanon's history, the best starting point remains Kamal Salibi, who offers surveys grounded in Arabic sources, including *The Modern History of Lebanon* (Praeger, 1965) and *A House of Many Mansions: The History of Lebanon Reconsidered* (IB Tauris, 1988). Updated historical primers include William Harris, *Lebanon: A History, 600–2011* (Oxford University Press, 2014) and Fawaz Traboulsi, *A History of Modern Lebanon*, 2nd ed. (Pluto Press, 2012). Another introductory reader is Andrew Arsan's *Lebanon: A Country in Fragments* (Hurst, 2018).

Different phases of early modern Lebanese history have attracted excellent work. Cesar Farah's *The Politics of Interventionism in Ottoman Lebanon, 1830–1861* (IB Tauris, 2000) and Leila Fawaz's *An Occasion for War: Civil Conflict in Lebanon and Damascus, 1860* (IB Tauris, 1994) dissect the mid-nineteenth-century turmoil. Engin Akarli's *The Long Peace: Ottoman Lebanon, 1861–1920* (University of California Press, 1993) analyzes the autonomous province of Mount Lebanon. Lebanon's transition to independence after 1943 has also received careful attention. Kais Firro and Raghid al-Solh investigate ideological underpinnings in *Inventing Lebanon: Nationalism and the State under the Mandate* (IB Tauris, 2003) and *Lebanon and Arabism: National Identity and State Formation* (IB Tauris, 2004), respectively. These supplement Meir Zamir's two-volume study, *The Formation of Modern Lebanon* (Croom Helm, 1985) and *Lebanon's Quest: The Road to Statehood, 1926–39* (IB Tauris, 1997).

Treatment of Lebanon's political progression through the 1950s and 1960s toward breakdown in the mid-1970s is haphazard. Samir Khalaf clarifies Lebanese integration of representative politics with sectarian influences in *Lebanon's Predicament* (Columbia University Press, 1987), and Wade Goria reviews political personalities in *Sovereignty and Leadership in Lebanon, 1943–76* (Ithaca Press, 1986). Studies of the Khoury and Chamoun presidencies (1943–1958) include Eyal Zisser's *Lebanon: The Challenge of Independence* (IB Tauris, 2000)and Caroline Attié's *Struggle in the Levant: Lebanon in the 1950s* (IB Tauris, 2004). Nasser Kalawoun discusses Lebanon's interaction with Gamal Abdel Nasser in *The Struggle for Lebanon: A Modern History of Lebanese-Egyptian Relations* (IB Tauris, 2000). The best analysis of Lebanon's difficulties after the 1967 Arab-Israeli War is Farid el-Khazen's *The Breakdown of the State in Lebanon, 1967–1976* (Harvard University Press, 2000). Irene Gendzier's *Notes from the Minefield: United States Intervention in Lebanon, 1945–1958* (Columbia University Press, 1997) is a classic on the unique role played by the US during the post-war decades, especially the 1950s. An equally critical take is James Stocker, *Spheres of Intervention: US Foreign Policy and the Collapse of Lebanon, 1967–1976* (Cornell University Press, 2016).

Much has been written about civil war and its aftermath. Early analyses include Samir Kassir's *La guere du Liban: De la dissension nationale au conflit régional, 1975–1982* (Karthala, 1994) and Itamar

Rabinovich's *The War for Lebanon, 1970–1983* (Cornell University Press, 1984). Theodor Hanf's *Co-existence in Wartime Lebanon: Death of a State and Birth of a Nation* (IB Tauris, 1993) provides an encyclopedic overview. William Harris's *New Face of Lebanon* (Markus Wiener, 2006) and Elie Salem's *Violence and Diplomacy in Lebanon: The Troubled Years, 1982–1988* (IB Tauris, 1995) concentrate on the 1980s.

Analysis of post-1990 trends proliferates. Barry Rubin, ed., *Lebanon: Liberation, Conflict, and Crisis* (Palgrave Macmillan, 2009) and Are Knudsen and Michael Kerr, eds., *Lebanon after the Cedar Revolution* (Oxford University Press, 2014) contribute multifaceted surveys. Rola el-Husseini's *Pax Syriana: Elite Politics in Postwar Lebanon* (Syracuse University Press, 2012) portrays Lebanon under the Asads. Nicholas Blanford gives the Hariri story in *Killing Mr. Lebanon: The Assassination of Rafik Hariri and Its Impact on the Middle East* (IB Tauris, 2006). Oren Barak assesses the military in *The Lebanese Army: A National Institution in a Divided Society* (State University of New York Press, 2009). Michael Young's *The Ghosts of Martyr's Square: An Eyewitness Account of Lebanon's Life Struggle* (Simon and Schuster, 2010) is a rewarding read.

For issues of economic development, consult Caroline Gate's *The Merchant Republic of Lebanon: Rise of an Open Economy* (IB Tauris, 1998) and Michael Johnson's *All Honourable Men: The Social Origins of War in Lebanon* (IB Tauris, 2001). Kamal Dib examines the social-economic interface in his *Warlords and Merchants: The Lebanese Business and Political Establishment* (Ithaca Press, 2004), while Latif Abul Husn's *The Lebanese Conflict: Looking Inward* (Lynne Rienner, 1998) interprets communal interactions. A sweeping study comparing many decades is Toufic Gaspard's *A Political Economy of Lebanon, 1948–2002: A Political Economy of Lebanon* (Brill, 2003).

Lebanon's post-war development is problematized in Reinoud Leenders' *Spoils of Truce: Corruption and State-Building in Postwar Lebanon* (Cornell University Press, 2012). Another critique lies in Hannes Baumann, *Citizen Hariri: Lebanon's Neoliberal Reconstruction* (Oxford University Press, 2017).

The emergence of the Shi'a is covered in Majid Halawi's *A Lebanon Defied: Musa al-Sadr and the Shi'a Community* (Westview Press, 1992), and Augustus Richard Norton's *Amal and the Shi'a: Struggle for the Soul of Lebanon* (University of Texas Press, 1987). Roshanack Shaery-Eisenlohr, *Shi'ite Lebanon: Transnational Religion and the Making of National Identities* (Columbia University Press, 2008), interprets Shi'a outlooks. An incisive anthropological take on Shi'a identity is Lara Deeb and Mona Harb, *Leisurely Islam: Negotiating Geography and Morality in Shi'ite South Beirut* (Princeton University Press, 2013).

Hizbullah occupies many rigorous works, among them Nizar Hamzeh's *In the Path of Hizbullah* (Syracuse University Press, 2004); Augustus Richard Norton, *Hezbollah: A Short History* (Princeton University Press, 2007); Nicholas Blanford's *Warriors of God: Inside Hizbullah's Thirty-Year Struggle against Israel* (Random House, 2011); Joseph Daher, *Hezbollah: The Political Economy of Lebanon's Party of God* (Pluto Press, 2016); and Aurélie Daher, *Hezbollah: Mobilization and Power* (Oxford University Press, 2019).

On the Druze, Robert Brenton Bett's *The Druze* (Yale University Press, 1988) and Fuad Khuri's *Being a Druze* (Druze Heritage Foundation, 2004) deserve note. In contrast, the Maronite and Sunni communities have not received adequate attention in English-language literature since Michael Johnson's *Class and Client in Beirut: The Sunni Muslim Community and the Lebanese State, 1840–1985* (Ithaca Press, 1986).

Online sources

United Nations programs and agencies provide continuous monitoring and analysis reporting of Lebanon, particularly with respect to refugees and humanitarian responses, labor conditions, human rights, elections, security, and development. For relevant websites, consult the UN High Commissioner for Refugees (www.unhcr.org/lebanon.html); UN Development Programme (www.lb.undp.org/content/lebanon/en/home.html); UN Interim Force in Lebanon (https://unifil.unmissions.org/); UN World Food Programme (www1.wfp.org/countries/lebanon); and UN Relief and Works Agency for Palestine Refugees (www.unrwa.org/where-we-work/lebanon).

The Lebanese media sphere is vibrant, vociferous, and reflective of sectarian politics. For current affairs in English, consult the *Daily Star* (www.dailystar.com.lb). *Al-Akhbar* is widely read but has been described as pro-Hizbullah (www.al-akhbar.com/). Naharnet remains one of the most popular online news portals, and provides exhaustive English-language coverage (www.naharnet.com/). Independent stories, analysis, and commentaries can also be found from the writers of *Ya Libnan* (http://yalibnan.com/). Lebanese civil society is similarly active and productive; an excellent organizational directory is located here (www.daleel-madani.org/civil-society-directory). An excellent database of articles and reports covering Lebanese affairs is the Lebanon News and Reports Index (https://ulib.aub.edu.lb/lnri/). The academic Moise Khayrallah Center for Lebanese Diaspora Studies also displays cultural histories about the vast global diaspora (https://lebanesestudies.ncsu.edu/).

Please note that URLs may change far more quickly than books can be printed; so if these exact URLs do not work, simply search Google or another engine by the titles of these websites and online resources.

Hashemite Kingdom of Jordan

André Bank

INTRODUCTION

For almost a hundred years by now, the state of Jordan has defied predictions of its imminent demise. The country was established as the British Mandate of Transjordan in 1921 and evolved into its current form as the Hashemite Kingdom of Jordan after World War Two. Throughout its history, Hashemite rule over Jordan has been challenged, both from without and within. Externally, Jordan's location at the "heart" of the Middle East has been both a blessing and a curse: being surrounded by the larger and more powerful neighbors of Syria, Iraq, Saudi Arabia, and Israel/Palestine meant that Jordan has often felt under pressure from abroad, necessitating an active involvement in regional politics. Even though these external balancing acts did not always prevent Jordan from becoming an arena of regional struggles, they still often shielded the Hashemite monarchy, in particular from negative fallouts of the Arab-Israeli conflict. At the same time, Jordan's crucial geostrategic location has regularly provided the monarchy with massive financial and military support from major powers, first from Great Britain and since the Cold War from the United States, Europe, and the oil-rich Gulf monarchies. This external support has been decisive for the economic survival of the resource-poor kingdom.

Internally, the Hashemite monarchy has been challenged by different opposition. From the 1950s to the 1990s, it was urban-based, leftist, or Islamist Jordanians – often of Palestinian origin – who protested their status as second-class citizens. Since the beginning of the twenty-first century and especially during the Arab Spring, new social opposition, such as the *hirak* (movements), emerged from among the country's more rural communities of East Bank tribes, the traditional backbone of the regime. To counter these domestic challenges, the Hashemite monarchy has relied on its loyal security agencies as well as on selective cooptation and cosmetic reforms. Performing these multiple, external, and internal balancing acts has been of central importance. In an otherwise often volatile Middle East, the Hashemite Kingdom has by now become, perhaps curiously, one of the most stable countries in the entire region.

Box 12.1 provides vital data for this country.

BOX 12.1 VITAL DATA – HASHEMITE KINGDOM OF JORDAN

Capital	Amman
Regime type	Authoritarian (monarchy)
Head of state	King Abdullah II (since 1999)
Head of government	Prime Minister Omar Razzaz (since 2018)
Legislative institution	Bicameral parliament, with elected 130-seat lower house (*Majlis al-Nuwaab*, or House of Representatives)
Female quota	Yes: women can run for any seat, but 15 are reserved for female candidates exclusively through a national proportional representation system
Percentage of seats held by women	15.4%
Major political parties (share of seats in most recent general elections, 2016)	Islamic Action Front (7.7%), Islamic Centrist (3.8%), Zamzam (3.8%), National Current (3.1%)
Population	9,702,353
Major ethnic groups	Arab (97.5%), other (2.5%)
Major religious groups	Muslim (97.2%), Christian (2.2%), other (0.6%)
GDP per capita	$4,278 ($9,433 at Purchasing Power Parity)
Unemployment rate	18.6%
Youth unemployment rate	37.2%
Major economic industries	Mining (primarily potash and phosphates), textiles, fertilizer, cement, pharmaceuticals, food processing
Military spending as % GDP	4.8%

HISTORICAL BACKGROUND

Of all the peoples of antiquity, the Nabataeans were most likely the direct ancestors of modern Jordanians. Shortly after 800 BC, the Aramaic-speaking inhabitants of Petra created their kingdom along the key north-south trading routes, maintaining their independence until they were conquered by the Romans under Pompey in 64 BC. In socio-cultural terms, the Islamic conquest of the area had the greatest impact. The Battle of Yarmouk in 636 AD expelled the Byzantine Christians and laid the groundwork for the establishment of Islam as the religious and cultural foundation for the majority of the people. At various times the area was ruled from Damascus, Baghdad, Cairo, Jerusalem, and Istanbul. Under Ottoman rule, southern Jordan was governed as part of the Hijaz, while the north was included in the Damascus governorate.

The Kingdom of Jordan is thus one of the many successor states of the Ottoman Empire. The Hashemite family, namely the dynastic predecessors of the ruling monarchy today, fought with the British in the Great Arab Revolt in 1915–16 against the Ottoman Empire. But shortly after World War One ended in 1918, they were defeated and expelled from the western Hijaz region of Saudi Arabia by the rival House of Saud. While the Saudi conquest ultimately carved out the modern Kingdom of Saudi Arabia, the loss of the Hijaz meant the Hashemite clan could no longer claim protectorship over Mecca and Medina, the two holiest cities of Islam – a position it had held for some time under Ottoman suzerainty. In the post-war period, the British government decided to install two brothers of the family, Abdullah and Faysal, respectively, in their mandates of Jordan and Iraq. The British thus established new borders and new dynasties for both countries. While the Hashemite monarchy in Iraq was overthrown and eliminated in a bloody coup in Baghdad in 1958, the Hashemite monarchy in Jordan has survived until today.

The emergence of modern Jordan

Like many other post-colonial states in the Middle East, the Hashemite Kingdom of Jordan has largely artificial boundaries, drawn by European imperial powers. In the aftermath of World War One, Britain and France divided the territories of the former Ottoman Empire between themselves. As part of the 1916 Sykes-Picot agreement, the territory that is modern Jordan came under British tutelage. In 1921, having secured the League of Nations' official mandate for the territories of Palestine, Transjordan, and Iraq, the British government created the Emirate of Transjordan through an agreement with its new ruler, Emir Abdullah (later King Abdullah I) of the Hashemite family. Given their Hijaz origins in the Arabian Peninsula, the Hashemite monarchs in Jordan have since emphasized their Arab heritage and Islamic lineage, especially direct family descent from the Prophet Muhammad – a credential only shared in the Arab world by the Alaouite monarchy of Morocco.

Hence the colonial birth of Jordan transpired in 1921. Establishing a governmental system for the new Emirate of Transjordan took much time and effort on the part of the British. Being politically severed from Syria, with whose government its people had been traditionally associated, Jordan lacked a national identity and had practically no industrial base. The few Arab administrators in Jordan had fled from the French in Damascus and were generally more concerned with reasserting Arab control in Syria than with making Jordan an independent, self-sufficient state. Less than three percent of the land was under cultivation. With virtually no other economic assets in the country, the new government was heavily dependent on British financial support.

With the assistance of a small group of British officials, Jordan under Emir Abdullah made slow progress toward more comprehensive independence. At first, the administration was simple, and Abdullah ruled with the advice of a small executive council staffed mostly by advisors and officers that had served his Hashemite family during World War One. British officials handled defense, foreign affairs, and finance. Relations with the local tribal communities, which practiced varying forms of peasant agriculture and nomadic herding, were initially tense. The social hierarchies and traditions of these Transjordanian tribes were different from the Hijazi expectations of the new monarchy, and local *shaykhs* (chieftains) chafed at the imposition of a foreign king. Conflicts erupted early on over the collection of taxes, land reforms, and other administrative issues. They soothed over time, as the Jordanian regime learned to incorporate key shaykhs, pacify others with payments, selectively crush those that resisted (with British firepower), and generally work to legitimate its rule. Over time, the Hashemite kingship became inculcated with the wider political ecology of tribalism, such that in future decades the ruler would be seen as *shaykh al-mashayikh* – the paramount chieftain.

The British remained the supreme hand, however. A major step toward more substantial independence came with a new treaty in 1928 that gave greater authority to the emir. However, the British retained the right to oversee finances and foreign policy, and British officers still controlled the

Jordanian army, the Arab Legion. The Organic Law of 1928 made the first move toward a representative government by providing for a legislative council to replace the old executive council. In 1946, Jordan and Britain reached a new agreement whereby a constitution replaced the Organic Law of 1928, and Abdullah was recognized as king of Jordan. Two years later, the British government agreed to continue paying a subsidy in return for British access to two military bases, while its officers still led the Arab Legion.

During the 1930s and 1940s, the rising crisis in Palestine became the dominant concern of the fledgling state. Abdullah's policy toward Palestine differed from that of other Arab states as he met secretly with Zionist leaders in an attempt to work out some modus vivendi with the Jews in Palestine. Nevertheless, when Israel declared independence in May 1948, the Jordanian Arab Legion occupied areas of Palestine adjacent to Jordan that had been allocated to the Arabs in the United Nations Partition Plan of November 1947. Abdullah's forces were the most successful of the Arab armies. When the fighting halted, the Arab Legion held 20 percent of the total Palestinian territory, including East Jerusalem.

On April 24, 1950, Abdullah unilaterally annexed the portion of Palestine called the West Bank, the territory west of the Jordan River. The 1948 Arab-Israeli War had also resulted in a massive Palestinian refugee influx to Jordan, among other surrounding countries. By the early 1950s, then, Jordan's demography was transformed completely. Prior to the war, Jordan counted no more than 380,000 mostly tribal residents in its territory on the east bank of the Jordan River; now, it accommodated the 450,000 Palestinians living in the West Bank, and an additional 350,000 refugees who had entered from both sides of the kingdom. The annexation was not popular regionally. When most Arabs joined the Palestinians in believing that Abdullah had betrayed them by annexing part of Palestine, Jordan became a pariah among the Arab states, with only the fellow Hashemite regime in Iraq offering support. At the same time, Abdullah alone among the Arab rulers extended full citizenship rights to the Palestinians living in the Hashemite-controlled territories east and west of the Jordan River, although many refugees refused the offer, fearing that Jordanian citizenship would foreclose their future return to an independent Palestine. Nevertheless, many Palestinians were frustrated by what they perceived to be his self-serving action and betrayal of their desire to obtain Palestinian national rights. As King Abdullah was leaving the al-Aqsa Mosque in Jerusalem on July 20, 1951, he was assassinated by a Palestinian nationalist.

Jordan under King Hussein: 1950s–1990s

After his death, Abdullah was succeeded by his eldest son, Talal, under whom a new constitution was promulgated in January 1952. Talal, however, had a long history of mental illness and abdicated in favor of his son Hussein, who was still a minor. A regency council of three was formed to govern for several months until the young Hussein reached majority and officially assumed the throne in May 1953. King Hussein ruled Jordan until his death in 1999 and therefore became one of the longest-serving monarchs of the twentieth century. The king had served for so long, in fact, that his imprint remains indelibly marked on the evolution of Jordan as a modern state. Hussein consolidated the Hashemite regime and defended it against internal and external challenges, neither of which were in short supply. With almost 46 years in office, at the start of the twenty-first century, most Jordanians knew only one monarch as architect of the kingdom's domestic and foreign policy, and modern builder of the Jordanian state. Indeed, only at the close of the 2010s has a generation of Jordanian millennials come of age who have no living memory of Hussein's leadership.

By the mid-1950s, Arab Nationalism surged in its popularity across the Arab world, driven by Nasser's charisma and Egyptian foreign policy. Jordan was not alone in seeing many of its educated professionals, including military officers, show sympathy to an ideology that lambasted Western hegemony and called for Arab unity. In 1957, King Hussein avoided a conspiracy by Arab Nationalists in the Jordanian army. The middle part of the decade was also typified by popular protests, driven by a variety of factors: energized Palestinian organizers in Amman and the West Bank; the growth of leftist political parties rising elsewhere in the Arab world, particularly the Ba'th, communists, and Arab Nationalists; urbanization and the emergence of more students, teachers, and activists; and ferocious public sentiment aligned against the pro-Western orientation of the Hashemite monarchy. The latter came to light during the Baghdad Pact crisis of 1956, when the British sought to create a anti-Soviet military alliance linking Jordan to Iraq, Turkey, Pakistan, and Iran. The secretive nature of these dealings resulted not only in the regime turning down the Pact, but also forced Hussein to dismiss the long-serving British commander of the Arab Legion, General John Bagot Glubb (known locally as Glubb Pasha) and make other concessions to an angry public.

Demonstrating its porousness to regional influences and geopolitical dynamics, the Jordanian opposition had become emboldened by 1957, resulting in a showdown that sprung between monarchy and dissenters.

Hussein thwarted attempts by conspiring army officers to overturn the monarchy in April of that year, while his royal advisors also cracked down hard on the popular leftist and Arab Nationalist parties that had won the October 1956 elections. The post-1957 years featured repression and clampdown, as military purges, a ban on all party activities, and censorship enabled the young monarch and his defenders to reset the political system and restore centralized autocratic order. The US was instrumental in this consolidation, as the Eisenhower administration began furnishing Jordan with significant economic and military aid as part of its grand strategy in the region to secure the loyalties of client states. The patronage and partnership forged in those years is the basis of Jordan's continued pro-American stance today.

In the 1960s, Jordan's political system continued to deal with domestic sentiments that swirled in favor of Nasser and his exhortations against the conservative, pro-Western monarchies of the region. The 1958 Iraqi coup and revolution was traumatizing; not only did it result in the slaughter of fellow Hashemites, it also extinguished a bulwark of the wider Hashemite vision of an Arab world led by them rather than Nasser. Once the guardians of Mecca and Medina, the Hashemite family was now reduced to governing an irregularly shaped hinterland on the Jordan River's east bank. The June 1967 Arab-Israeli War presents another dire threat. That military disaster carried profound social, economic, and political implications, as Jordan lost control of the entire West Bank to Israeli forces, including East Jerusalem and its holy places. The latter was a major loss symbolically, because since 1948, the Hashemite monarchy had retooled itself as the Islamic custodian of the Jerusalem holy sites, referring to the al-Aqsa religious compound – the third holiest site in Islam, after Mecca and Medina. That symbolic pan-Islamic claim of custodianship persists to this day, indicating the importance placed upon it by Jordanian royals.

Following the 1967 debacle, Jordan's size was thus forcibly reduced by almost half. Further, though the war cleaved the West Bank from Jordan, it also resulted in hundreds of thousands of Palestinians fleeing across the Jordan River. Thus, the kingdom remained a Palestinian-majority country only decades after the monarchy had anchored itself as a new regime amongst a mostly tribal, non-Palestinian populace. The changing demographics and regional tensions soon exploded within the kingdom, as the frontline state became ground zero for the armed struggle waged by the Palestinian Liberation Organization (PLO). The PLO's increasing autonomy within Jordan tested the patience of many royalists and security officials, particularly as they took control over some Palestinian neighborhoods and refugee camps – thereby creating a "state within a state." Critically, not all Palestinians in Jordan supported the new guerillas and militants, who had arrived in Jordan after the 1967 disaster, but enough did to give the PLO a local social base. Tensions between the regime and PLO exploded in the Black September civil war of 1970, when King Hussein's regular army and its supporters, among them the moderate Islamists of the Muslim Brotherhood (MB), forced the PLO to depart. However, the scars of that bitter conflict remained for many decades and still form part of the collective memory today; among the legacies is ingrained suspicion by many Jordanians of non-Palestinian origins – Transjordanians, or East Bankers – of the political loyalties of Palestinians.

Jordan largely managed to avoid the 1973 Arab-Israeli War, with the regime arguing that another wartime loss would spell the end of Jordan entirely. The kingdom also remained outside the post-war peace process between Egypt and Israel. Hussein was a masterful diplomat, and managed to secure Jordan billions of dollars in promised pan-Arab aid after 1974 and 1978 in return for Jordanian recognition of the PLO as the rightful representatives of the Palestinian people, and to join the Arab line in rejecting Israel (and thus castigate Egypt for its Camp David peace talks with Israel). At the same time, regional tensions threatened once again, this time to the east of Jordan. The 1979 Iranian Revolution and the 1980–88 Iran-Iraq War created a new set of challenging circumstances for Jordan, as the conflict's externalities and the oil price collapse threw Jordan into an economic tailspin. As the war dragged on, Jordan increased its support for Iraq, a policy that coincided with the Arab Gulf states and the US as the latter aimed at balancing the revolutionary regime in Tehran. Jordan provided Iraq with a safe port, strategic depth, and a good trading partner. But if Iraq was Jordan's strongest regional ally in the 1980s, by the onset of the 1990s it was threatening to become an enormous liability.

Jordan's most serious international challenge since the Black September conflict resulted from the August 2, 1990, Iraqi invasion and occupation of Kuwait. The overwhelming majority of Jordanians supported Iraq against the allied coalition, and King Hussein concurred in a decision that shocked Western capitals; Algeria, Yemen, and the PLO were the only other Arab actors to back Iraq over Kuwait. Foreign assistance from the US, other Western allies, and the Gulf rentier kingdoms all but evaporated. The Gulf states also began expelling 300,000 Jordanians working there as political punishment, which would be a further blow to the Jordanian economy after the war given the vital remittances sent back by those expatriates.

In the immediate aftermath of the war, Jordan rehabilitated its regional image while struggling to deal with its worst economic crisis since the 1967 Arab-Israeli War. Financial collapse in the late 1980s, emergency loans by the International Monetary Fund, and required fiscal austerity including the rollback of subsidies to consumer goods like fuel caused social unrest. In spring 1989, major riots erupted against the curtailment of fuel subsidies; another round in 1996 railed against the cutback of bread subsidies. What was particularly worrisome was that such uprisings came not from Palestinians, who were largely urbanized and comprised the kingdom's middle-class, but rather from rural tribal communities long considered the bedrock of Hashemite support. Though anti-austerity demonstrations were contained through security measures, the monarchy understood after the Gulf War that its financial hands were tied: stripped of remittances, buffeted by war, lacking strong industries, and now starved of foreign aid, the kingdom needed to secure its economic fortunes abroad.

And so it did. The Hashemite regime played on Jordan's vital role in any Arab-Israeli peace settlement by enthusiastically accepting terms for multilateral negotiations to begin in Madrid in 1991. Jordanians and Palestinians initially formed a joint delegation to the peace talks before eventually shifting to distinct negotiating teams in Palestinian-Israeli and Jordanian-Israeli tracks. After Israel and the PLO reached a breakthrough in the Oslo Peace Accords in 1993, the Jordanians pushed for a full and formal peace treaty with Israel. Jordan and Israel made their peace official in 1994, and Jordan was able to utilize the peace process to reestablish its warm ties with the US and European states. By the late 1990s, Jordan had also restored diplomatic relations and was receiving some assistance from most of the Arab Gulf monarchies, including Kuwait and Saudi Arabia.

Jordan under King Abdullah: 1990s–present

In February 1999, King Hussein of Jordan passed away from cancer. He was succeeded by his oldest son, King Abdullah II, born in 1962. This royal succession marked the last in a series of dramatic transformations in Jordanian politics during the last decade of the twentieth century. These included, first, a process of limited political liberalization, with the holding of full parliamentary elections in 1989 (the first in decades), the end of censorship and martial law, and the promise of future democratic reforms. Though some of these pledges were broken, and indeed the idea of constitutional monarchism proved anathema to many royalists, the strategy of liberalizing politics was necessary to counterbalance the social and economic pain of ongoing restructuring efforts by the International Monetary Fund and World Bank, which substantially reshaped the country's political economy. The return of parliamentary life and the renaissance of civil society were welcome; though the legislature was largely powerless, the proliferation of new social movements and advocacy groups showed considerable pluralism among the citizenry. Jordanians prized the newfound ability to voice many concerns and interests to their government without overt fear of repression. Another transformation was the aforementioned signing of the peace treaty with Israel in 1994. The latter was, however, not followed by substantially improving bilateral relations due to the rise of a right-wing, anti-peace government in Israel. The next source of change was the neoliberal economic program endorsed by Abdullah and his favored cohort of technocrats, who sought to undo some areas of state-led economics through privatization, free trade, investments, and other market-oriented reforms. That tilt towards technocratic politics drew criticism from tribal communities, including rural shaykhs and Transjordanian intellectuals, who compared Abdullah's bias towards globalization in stark contrast to his father's more traditional bias towards social protection and patronage, even though the latter was a major reason why the Jordanian treasury had become aid-dependent and constantly teetered on bankruptcy.

The 2000s were marked by more domestic shuffling and geopolitical crisis, recurrent themes in Jordanian history. The US invasion of Iraq in 2003 could have been catastrophic; Jordanians were already seething from the Second Intifada, and the peace treaty with Israel had come under fire. With the destruction of the Iraqi state, Jordan lost a major trade market as well as subsidized oil supplies. However, Abdullah maneuvered Jordan to support the American operation, and also ensured the Jordanian military and intelligence services cooperated handily with US forces in its worldwide anti-terrorist campaign. In return, Jordan received unprecedented volumes of foreign aid, albeit also at a time when worries about anti-American sentiment convinced the regime to shutter parliament for two years and stifle many forms of civic life. The promise of returning to the issue of democratic reforms was especially contentious when the regime dealt with the Muslim Brotherhood, with its vociferous popular base, anti-Israeli stance, and demand for more political devolution. The influx of over a half-million Iraqi refugees in the late 2000s due to the insurgency and violence there caused additional economic strain.

In 2011–12, the Arab Spring hit Jordan in two ways. First, the Arab Spring also spawned a Jordanian Spring. During 2011–12 a plethora of groups – Islamists, leftists, students, youth, and civil society actors like the professional unions – mobilized thousands of peaceful demonstrations demanding, among other reforms, a crackdown on endemic corruption, more equitable economic policies, and democratic rights. In June 2011, King Abdullah surprised many by promising a constitutional monarchy in the future on a nationally televised speech, but cynics doubted his intentions. Years later, they have been proven right. Protests then, and since, highlight growing disillusionment about the Jordanian political order, especially from tribal areas. The most notable development has been the rise of young tribal protesters calling themselves *hirak* (Arabic for movement), who have decried the regime's neoliberal economic bent and railed against perceived corruption. Spreading like wildfire, such spontaneous hirak activist networks caused problems for intelligence and security officials not accustomed to policing tribal communities for dissent, as opposed to the more familiar Muslim Brotherhood, civil society organizations, professional syndicates, and other established opposition. At the same time, unlike neighboring Syria, Jordanian police and gendarmerie have tolerated popular demonstrations so long as they remain peaceful; when violent riots break out, as in a November 2012 wave of agitation against fuel subsidy cuts, they intervene in kind.

The second impact came with the Syrian civil war, which unleashed the specter of the Islamic State of Iraq and Syria (ISIS). Thousands of young Jordanians left to join the jihadi movement. Before it closed its borders, further, Jordan received nearly a million Syrian refugees, resulting in enormous material costs in terms of accommodation and security. With the international coalition against ISIS using Jordanian facilities, the regime at times adopted a wartime footing, believing such extremism constituted a grave danger. Jordan also contributed directly to the campaign, though at cost: the execution of the Jordanian pilot Mu'ath al-Kasasbah, who was killed in early 2015 after his plane crashed in ISIS territory, shocked the public.

The responses from above to contain both threats fall in line with Jordanian actions in the past. The Hashemite regime leaned heavily onto its Western partners, including the US, in securing more foreign aid, obtaining guarantees of protection, and navigating the maze of regional diplomacy. That strategy continues today, but it has not been easy. Under the Trump administration, for instance, the US began marginalizing Jordanian positions about the Palestinian-Israeli peace process, about which the regime has always advocated for a two-state solution, in favor of its own "deal of the century" formulated with Israeli and Saudi input. That Jordan remains a Palestinian-majority kingdom means that any long-term resolution to the Palestinian issue will immediately affect its political stability.

Domestically, as its geopolitical footing has slipped the regime has tightened its grip on power. Though Jordan did not revert back to the darker days of state repression prior to the 1990s, when political prisoners numbered in the hundreds and censorship was rife, the regime did roll back many earlier allowances for pluralism and freedom. Among the controversies since the Arab Spring, for instance, has been a stifling new Anti-Terror Law, the extension of press laws to online media, selective intimidation and arrests of critics, the targeting of journalists, meddling to fracture the Muslim Brotherhood, the detention of tribal leaders, and other forms of de-liberalization. Parliamentary elections have occurred on a stuttering basis, but the toothless nature of the legislature and its constant bickering meant that for most Jordanians seeking political change, the primary venue of advocacy remained the street.

SOCIAL AND ECONOMIC ENVIRONMENT

The Hashemite Kingdom of Jordan sits on part of the north Arabian plateau, which Jordan shares with Syria, Iraq, and Saudi Arabia (Map 12.1). No natural frontiers exist between Jordan and its Arab neighbors. The western border of Jordan is the Great Rift Valley, through which the Jordan River flows. From an average altitude of 600 to 900 meters (2,000 to 3,000 feet) on the plateau, the landscape plummets to well below sea level in the valley. The Great Rift Valley also includes the Dead Sea and the Gulf of Aqaba to the south. Jordan's only coastline is a 12-mile stretch on the Red Sea and includes the port of Aqaba. Beyond the Great Rift Valley to the west lie Israel and the West Bank highlands. More than four-fifths of Jordan is desert or semi-desert, receiving less than four inches of rain annually. Jordan's population is concentrated in the western part of the kingdom where rainfall, averaging about 12 to 16 inches annually, permits some farming. All of Jordan's major cities – Amman, Irbid, and Zarqa – are concentrated in this area.

Social patterns

Most Jordanians are of Arab heritage and are commonly divided into two principal groups: Palestinian Jordanians and East Bank Jordanians, also called Transjordanians. Palestinian Jordanians trace their roots to west of the

MAP 12.1
Hashemite Kingdom of Jordan. Major water bodies and cities shown. There are no major inland rivers.

Source: D-Maps.

Jordan River, in historic Palestine. Most arrived in Jordan in several waves of refugees during and after the 1948 and 1967 Arab-Israeli wars. East Bankers trace their lineage to east of the Jordan River, and many have roots in the tribes and clans that originally allied with the Hashemites to create the modern Jordanian state. Since 1948, Jordan alone among the Arab states has given full citizenship to Palestinians. With the important exception of many of the hundreds of thousands of Palestinians who arrived in Jordan in 1967 and who have been affiliated with anti-Hashemite, left-leaning Palestinian organizations, no official distinction is made between Palestinian and East Bank Jordanians, and all Jordanians share the same legal rights. Grievances remain, however, particularly among less well-to-do Palestinians, who often feel that theirs is a secondary status in Jordanian society. Generally speaking, East Bank Jordanians dominate much of the government, public sector industry, and the military and other state security organs, while Palestinians are better represented in private sector businesses and in the various professions. For many in the regime, the East Bank tribes remain the rock upon which the Hashemite monarchy was built – which hence makes tribal protests and riots extremely alarming for palace watchers.

Most Jordanians are Sunni Muslims, although a small Christian minority also exists. Many East Bank Jordanians are members of one of several hundred Arab tribes, though the majority belong to just a handful of the largest confederations, including the Bani Hassan, Bani Sakhr, Abbadi, and Huwaytat. Contrary to popular belief, most tribes in the area were not Bedouin (i.e., nomadic) prior to the twentieth century. However, Bedouin values and traditions continue to have an important influence in society. In Jordan, more than any other state in the Mashriq, tribal elements provide a disproportionate number of recruits for the military and are guaranteed representation in parliament.

Two minority groups – Christians and Circassians – have also provided backing for the Hashemites. Jordan's Christian population of 2–3 percent is mainly urban and has lived in the area for centuries. Predominantly Greek Orthodox and Greek Catholic, most are descendants of very early converts to Christianity, whereas others allegedly descend from the Crusaders. The Circassians settled in Jordan in the last decades of the nineteenth century. They were part of the approximately one million Muslims who fled the Caucasus region when the Russians captured it from the Ottoman. The Circassians are Sunni Muslims who have traditionally been loyal to the monarchy and have held senior government positions. They are particularly well represented in the security services, military, and police, as well as the personal honor guard for the king, and are guaranteed representation in parliament.

The Jordanian population historically has also encompassed an enormous proportion of refugees and expatriates. First, there has been a large and diverse group of foreign guest workers residing in Jordan, including a few hundred thousand Egyptians, Sudanese, and Yemenis who typically work in construction, agriculture, and basic services. Tens of thousands, or perhaps more, also come from South and Southeast Asia to work in industrial and domestic service positions. Second, the recent wars in the Middle East have led hundreds of thousands of Iraqis after the 2003 Iraq War and even more Syrians post-2011 to flee to Jordan. Most of the more than half-million Iraqis have since returned, but most of the nearly million Syrian refugees that came to Jordan in 2012 remain as of 2019, as insecurity, fear, and hardship faced back in Syria discourage any mass return despite the Jordanian-Syrian border partly reopening in late 2018.

In terms of gender dynamics, it is little surprising that in socially conservative Jordan, the upper echelons of the political, military and also business elites are almost exclusively dominated by men. While female Jordanians have served as, inter alia, ministers, ambassadors, parliamentarians, and oppositionists in the country, they have clearly remained a striking minority, very rarely making it to the key decision-making posts. Female quotas in parliament have been in place for years, however, which ensures a minimal number of women are visible in the legislature. The problem with gender disparities percolates downwards to everyday social life. Jordanian women are highly educated, with a 97.4 percent literacy rate in 2018 – the highest in the entire region, including Israel. Yet only a third attend college or university, and only 15 percent of all women enter the labor market to seek jobs in a striking absence that hints at strong social norms and pressures for women to marry rather than become financially independent. The same overall marginalization goes for younger Jordanians, unless they have direct "*wasta*," i.e. personal connections, to older members of elite networks. For some liberal Jordanians, the current Queen Rania, who has a Palestinian elite family background, has been considered a role model. More conservative Jordanians, especially the rural East Bank tribes, have regularly criticized her for being too Westernized or profligate in her spending.

Economic constraints

The Jordanian economy has been historically constrained by three factors: land, energy, and tribe. In terms of land, the lack of arable estates and difficulty of sustained large-scale farming has made Jordan dependent upon trade partners for food. Irrigated agriculture does exist, particularly in the fertile Jordan Valley, but agriculture today represents only four percent of the GDP. Energy has been a complicating restriction. Jordan possesses no oil or gas of its own, and it has relied upon the hydrocarbon rentier kingdoms in several ways – for foreign aid, for remittances from Jordanians working in those states, and for cheap oil and gas. When energy prices fluctuate or geopolitical shocks affect the wealthiest rentier kingdoms like Saudi Arabia and Kuwait, Jordan suffers immensely, as the 1980s and 1990s demonstrated. Energy imports remain a point of vulnerability in financial and political perspective. In 2015, the kingdom opened its first liquefied natural gas terminal in the Red Sea port city of Aqaba, but plans to purchase gas supplies from Israel has met fierce popular resistance. Late 2018, Jordan moved back to importing Egyptian liquid gas which, since January 2019, has covered around half of the kingdom's total energy needs despite the potential that sabotage to Egypt's Sinai pipeline could disrupt this flow, as happened in 2011.

Finally, social demands for protection, patronage, and welfarism have long constrained the Jordanian state. The compact between monarchy and tribes from the 1920s onwards was a version of the authoritarian social contract seen elsewhere – loyalty and obeisance in return for security and prosperity. In past eras, when aid monies flowed in and capital was abundant, the government could employ East Bank Jordanians in its swollen public sector, security services, and military, and provide for a range of expensive provisions like cheap bread, fuel, water, electricity, and housing. When fiscal crises hit, as in the late 1980s when the national debt was twice the GDP, the regime must cut back due to the conditions made by emergency lenders – but counter-cyclically, demands for services intensify from tribal constituencies. It does not help, as well, that aid dependency as a form of rentierism since the 1920s and 1930s has sabotaged the incentive to develop a well-honed taxation system. The tradition of low taxes, or rampant tax evasion, became politicized in summer 2018 when mass protests over a new stringent tax law endorsed by the International Monetary Fund forced King Abdullah to reshuffle the government.

Jordan's economy today reflects these constraints. Early decades of state-led development created brisk growth, with an astonishing 15.2 percent annualized GDP expansion rate in the 1970s. The energy crisis, regional conflicts, and refugee crises of future decades leveled the economic arena, however. During 2011–18, the economy grew by an average of just 2.5 percent annually, with job creation lagging behind the booming population of youths seeking employment. Today, the economy is still dominated by services, from retail and banking to government and administration. Its primary industry and still lead export income earner is potash and phosphate production. Pharmaceuticals have been a notable breakthrough sector since the 1990s, with Jordan now producing a considerable amount of generic medication for global sales.

Apart from traditional industries like cement, transportation, and food processing, the textile sector comprises the second largest source of exports. Jordan produces clothing for many well-known retail brands in the West, a trend that began in the late 1990s with the introduction of the Qualifying Industrial Zones – joint investment projects with Israel where locally produced goods, such as garments, enjoyed free trade conduits to the US. Since the 2000 free trade agreement with the US, Jordanian textile production has vamped up considerably, with major labels like Victoria's Secret and Gap setting up shop. Indeed, free trade has been a major priority of Jordan under King Abdullah, alongside maximizing trade ties with Arab countries, particularly the Gulf kingdoms. Jordan joined the World Trade Organization in 2000 and committed itself to more open trade flows with the European Union. Today, it continues to proudly host the World Economic Forum (WEF), an annual gathering of some of the world's most influential business and political leaders in its Dead Sea resort area. Here, Jordan portrays itself as a veritable oasis of moderation and stability, one filled with promises of high-tech growth and youth creativity in stark contrast to other Mashriq countries that have become synonymous with conflict and turmoil.

However, the lack of major industries and fiscal difficulties prompting frequent foreign aid bailouts and loans has proven crippling to Jordan's ability to generate sufficient jobs. IMF and World Bank interventions in 1989, 1996, 2012 and, most recently, 2018 have come with austerity conditions that retrench public spending, which deprives the Jordanian state of its political tools of creating easy government jobs and social services to mollify its restive tribal constituencies. Yet the lethargic private sector, with only a few productive industries, cannot pick up the slack. Further, geopolitical shocks, such as neighboring wars, disrupt the few other conduits of productivity, such as tourism, trade, and investments. The end result is an economy in crisis two decades into the new century. Poverty in Jordan approached 15 percent in 2015, the last recorded measurement. Unemployment has crept up in recent years, hitting nearly 19 percent as of 2019. Youth joblessness exceeded 37 percent in the same year, the second highest figure in the Arab world behind only Palestine. Impoverishment has disproportionately hurt poorer Jordanians, including both Palestinian Jordanians living in urban areas and refugee camps as well as East Bank tribes, the latter of which often compare the affluence of Amman's richest western neighborhoods with the destitution of rural areas. Most alarming, joblessness endures despite most women never entering the labor market, and with hundreds of thousands of

Jordanians again now living abroad and remitting their incomes back home, thanks to smooth relations with most Gulf kingdoms.

Employment is also a sensitive issue given the Syrian refugee crisis since 2012. In 2016, the "Jordan Compact," an international agreement to provide Jordan more foreign aid in order to create economic opportunities for its refugee communities, purported to give Syrians up to 200,000 legal work permits. Until then, most, much like the Iraqi refugees of the late 2000s, had worked illegally in informal and insecure settings. However, by January 2018, only around 80,000 work permits had been provided in total; and given that some temporary or sector-specific permits had been given to the same person, it is fair to assume that only between 35,000 and 45,000 Syrians had actually benefited from legal access to the Jordanian labor market. There have actually been few incentives for Syrians to apply for legal work permits in sectors in which low wages and minimal protection is provided, such as basic factory and food service jobs, while many Jordanians questioned the wisdom of creating Syrian employment when jobs for Jordanians seemed to be scarce.

POLITICAL STRUCTURES

On paper, the Hashemite Kingdom of Jordan is a constitutional monarchy with a bicameral parliament. The latter consists of an elected lower house (*Majlis al-Nuwaab*) with 130 deputies, and an appointed upper house with 65 senators (*Majlis al-'Ayan*). In practice, political decision-making is determined by the king, who commands wide-ranging competencies: as the most important person of the state's executive, he is not subject to a system of checks and balances. He can act and decide fully independently, only influenced by his close advisors, whom he regularly rotates. The Jordanian monarchy is steeped in Hashemite symbolism and Sharifian legacy, much of it a deliberate strategy of the crown desiring a broad regional audience and attempting to burnish its famous historical credentials. The national flag of Jordan, indeed, is based on the original Hashemite flag of the 1916 Great Arab Revolt (Photo 12.1); the star and red chevron represent the Hashemite dynasty, whereas the three descending color bands – black, white, and green – symbolize the 'Abbasid, Umayyad, and Fatimid Caliphates of old.

Both symbolically and institutionally, then, the king is the centerpiece of the state. He can appoint and depose the government, including the prime minister; parliament has little say in the creation of the cabinet. Indeed, the prime minister and cabinet often simply implement the policy priorities set at

PHOTO 12.1
Flag of the Hashemite Kingdom of Jordan

Source: Pixabay. Public domain.

a higher level, meaning inside the bureaucracy of the royal palace or among the king and his advisors. In the case that the prime minister or individual ministers have been criticized by the larger public or by specific influential elites, the king typically sacks the respective persons – a safety valve policy to protect the monarch from direct criticism. Against this backdrop, it is not uncommon that the Jordanian king regularly replaces the cabinet, including the prime minister. On average, historically, governments only last roughly 17 months before their dismissal. Relatedly, the Jordanian king can dissolve parliament and then govern via decrees. The latter was very common under King Hussein (1953–99). His son and successor, King Abdullah II, has also used this prerogative, for instance from November 2001 to June 2003 and from November 2009 to November 2010. Beyond these *de jure* competencies, the Jordanian king's *de facto* political power is even more extensive since he controls a wide-ranging patronage network through his administration, the royal court (*diwan*) which includes, among others, Transjordanian tribal notables and Palestinian-Jordanian business elites.

The monarchical regime is protected by powerful institutions of coercion. The king commands the Jordanian Armed Forces, which has arguably the best reputation of any institution in Jordanian society, particularly among tribal Jordanians who see the institution as their own. Beyond this, the monarch controls the security agencies, including the General Intelligence Directorate (*mukhabarat*), which has become a central decision-making body while also possessing vast authority to monitor society and crush any threat. Finally, the Public Security Directorate is tasked with the maintenance of domestic public order; this is the civil police and gendarmerie (*darak*). These security agencies can just as easily root out hard security risks, such as jihadi terrorism, as they can intimidate and spy upon citizens. Indeed, only rarely do terrorist networks successfully launch major attacks in the kingdom; recent examples include the November 2005 hotel bombings, and a small string of attacks linked to ISIS throughout 2016.

Alongside the powerful monarchy, the parliament barely possesses any independent control or law-making functions. Instead of drafting laws, setting the budget, and creating foreign policy initiatives, the Lower House's task is to support, to complement and, only in exceptional cases, to reject the decisions made by the royally-appointed government. These clearly limited competencies of Jordan's Lower House do not automatically mean that parliamentary elections are only a pseudo-democratic reform theater aimed at appeasing their own population or at pleasing the country's Western donors. Rather, there actually exists a strong competition for seats to the Jordanian parliament. Typically, however, this competition is less about programmatic-ideological differences between the candidates and more often about which elites, from tribal shaykhs to business moguls, can obtain patronage opportunities and state resources. For some legislators, access to those resources – e.g., funneling development spending to their districts, thereby creating easy jobs – is the primary goal; such members have been called "service" deputies given their apolitical stances on other issues.

This has had two effects. First, voters remain cynical, the electoral process is vulnerable to vote-buying, and parliament is a highly contentious and mistrusted institution among the Jordanian public. The 2016 elections featured turnout that barely exceeded 37 percent; though this reflected a larger pool of newly registered voters, the absolute number of voters has never matched the optimistic projections of government officials hoping to convince the international community that Jordan is democratizing. Moreover, some past elections exhibited extreme irregularities that suggested fraudulence, such as the 2007 contest, which decimated opposition (and especially Islamist) representation through suspected tampering by the security services.

The second effect is that parties do not play an important role. Most parliamentarians gain office as independents. The return of party life in the 1990s after decades of prohibition failed to spark much interest. Though many have ideological platforms, such as leftist and Arab Nationalist currents, they have few members and often squabble amongst each other. For instance, the leftist and Arab Nationalist parties supported the Asad regime during the Syrian civil war, whereas other opposition parties sided with the Syrian opposition. The only enduring and relevant opposition party has been the Islamic Action Front (IAF), the party connected with the Jordanian Muslim Brotherhood which has existed as a social movement in the country since the 1940s. Even though the Brotherhood was officially forbidden in 2015, the IAF was allowed to run in the last parliamentary elections of 2016. Working in a coalition called *Islah* (reform) with allied Christian parties, the IAF's group took 15 seats out of the 115 contested seats that lay outside the female quota. The IAF constituted ten of those seats, thereby becoming (as has been common in the last 30 years) the most represented party in a vapid Lower House. Currently, as of 2019, there are 47 registered political parties, most of which have never – and will likely never – win seats.

Jordan is divided into 12 governorates (*muhafazah*). Each province is administered by a governor appointed by the king; Jordanian security and civil institutions have been present all across the territory. Historically, power has been centralized in the capital, with little empowerment of the governorates. But with the decentralization law, ratified in 2015, the regime at least formally presented a reform which suggested some more devolution of powers to municipalities, including regional elections. While the latter have taken place in 2017, a more substantial devolution of competencies to the local level has not taken place yet.

There are three sources of Jordanian law: European codes, *shari'a* (Islamic law), and local tradition. The Jordanian constitution and the Court Establishment Act of 1951 mandate a judiciary to reflect these sources of law. Three categories of courts are outlined in the constitution: regular civil courts, religious courts, and special courts. The civil courts system, which is heavily based on Western law, has jurisdiction in all cases not specifically granted to the others. The religious court system has responsibility for personal status and communal endowment. Shari'a courts have responsibility for Muslims, whereas the various Christian sects have their own councils.

The special courts have responsibility for tribal questions and land issues. The king retains the right to appoint and dismiss judges and pardon offenders. On the local level, especially in the rural south, tribal dispute settlement mechanisms still play a role.

POLITICAL DYNAMICS

Since his ascension to the throne in February 1999, King Abdullah II has decisively shaped political dynamics. Contrary to his father Hussein, whose primary focus had been on foreign and regional policy, Abdullah has put a relatively strong emphasis on domestic politics, especially in the initial years of his rule in the 2000s. He favors a gradual, back-and-forth approach, shifting between political restrictions and more openness. The field of electoral politics is a good example in this basic toleration of pluralism, and the trappings of political competition, though without all the substance. Parliamentary elections have regularly taken place in Jordan during Abdullah's two decades as king, i.e. in 2003 (after two years' delay), 2007, 2010, 2013, and 2016. The same goes for municipal elections, which took place in 2003, 2007, 2013, and 2017.

Yet despite such regular contestation, major decisions cannot be carried out at any level without the assent of royal autocracy. Indeed, the five parliamentary elections in the last two decades have not at all altered the relationship of pro-government versus opposition deputies; the former continue to make up around two-thirds to three-fourths of members of parliament. Even when considering that Jordan's Lower House has little authority to initiate legislation, these figures remain striking. They underline a major problem in electoral life: district constituencies are gerrymandered to the benefit of more rural communities outside of the urban, Palestinian-dominated centers of Amman, Irbid and Zarqa, thereby allowing for relatively more conservative, East Bank Jordanian deputies to enter the Lower House. Such malapportionment, in which a far lower ratio of voters-to-seats exists in the tribal areas than in dense urban zones, reflects the long legacy of Black September and the anti-Palestinian bias of many officials.

Civil society and social pressures

Jordanian media include a plethora of independent newspapers, magazines, and tabloids. But laws affecting the press and publications, including the ominous Anti-Terror Law, include ambiguous regulations preventing journalists from harming state security. Since what might be read as "harming" is unclear, journalists in Jordan often practice self-censorship to avoid running afoul of the mukhabarat. Similarly, Jordanian civil society has grown to encompass thousands of societies and associations created for a variety of purposes, such as educational, cultural, professional, environmental, and, of course, political. But here, too, the glass appears to be both half-full and half-empty. There is clearly no shortage of civil society organizations in Jordan, but the whole purpose of civil society is to be independent of the state, while many organizations are registered with and closely monitored by officials.

Identity issues are seldom discussed publicly but remain the elephant in the room, as well. Violence in Palestine, for example, typically revives questions within the kingdom about the nature of Jordan-ness: Who exactly is a Jordanian? If a Palestinian state were to be established, would Palestinians in Jordan be loyal to that state or to Jordan? The latter question is asked by powerful, conservative East Bank elites, partly to sow doubts among others about the loyalty of Jordanians of Palestinian origin, despite that many have lived in the kingdom for generations and have little intention of leaving. Even economic liberalization carries ethnic implications. As the state slowly privatizes various industries, the historically Palestinian-dominant private sector grows while the East Bank Jordanian dominance of the public sector is under threat. For its part, the monarchy insists on its stated policy of "Jordan first," arguing that any emphasis on a Jordanian-Palestinian rift is outdated, divisive, and even unpatriotic. King Abdullah and his wife, Queen Rania (who is of Palestinian origin), both argue that intra-ethnic divisions are part of Jordan's past, not its future.

Driving much visible change in politics has been the Jordanian street since the Arab Spring, with a regular pattern of protests and social mobilization characterizing the relationship between Jordanian citizens and their state. In Jordan, the controversial parliamentary elections of November 2010 began the current period of heightened activism. Criticizing vote-rigging at the polls, violent clashes erupted in rural tribal areas. By mid-January 2011, "street politics" in Jordan shifted increasingly to the cities of Amman and Zarqa, inspired by revolutionary developments in Egypt. It was only then that the Muslim Brotherhood, which had advocated a constitutional monarchy with a real division of powers, gathered momentum. The regime permitted the demonstrations – typically on Fridays, after prayer time – to take place, but under a massive police and secret service presence. Its accompanying cooptation strategy raised public sector wages and rescinded announced subsidy cuts.

This began a series of peaceful protests, authoritarian responses, and counter-protests that consumed much of 2011–12. Concessions made, such as when the king replaced the unpopular prime minister Samir Rifa'i with tribal stalwart Marouf Bakhit, failed to quell popular fervor regarding economic hardships (including unemployment) and demand for political reform. Much of the new grassroots opposition was young, peaceful, daring, and above all Transjordanian. To be sure, after the 2011–12 crescendo of Jordanian activism that tracked closely with the Arab Spring, youth-driven mobilization quieted down due to sheer protest fatigue, fear of chaos due to the Syrian civil war, and regime pushback in the form of manipulation and repression. The latter involved not just arresting leading hirak activists and political critics, particularly when they crossed "red lines," such as openly questioning the legitimacy of the Hashemite monarchy and calling for King Abdullah to step down; they also involved legally expanding the domain of formal coercion. These include the expansion of press and publication guidelines to regulate online content, including social media; expanded powers to detain journalists indefinitely; the closure of some websites; a revised 2014 Anti-Terror Law that criminalized an impossibly broad range of speech and activities; and financial and legal pressures imposed upon familiar foes, like the Muslim Brotherhood. Yet protests continue, as in the May/June 2018 anti-tax law demonstrations, which forced King Abdullah to sack his government and appoint a young popular premier, Omar Razzaz, to appease public anger.

Islamism

Jordan has a large Islamist sector, which historically has been politically subordinate to the monarchy and therefore legal. Indeed, the Muslim Brotherhood branch in Jordan supported the Hashemites during key political crises, such as the troubles of the mid-1950s and the 1970 Black September civil war. In the 1990s, however, political liberalization and parliamentary elections gave the Brotherhood more visibility as a divergent voice. The Brotherhood helped lead civil society opposition against the 1994 peace treaty with Israel, and has also sought to push the government away from its traditionally pro-Western orientation. The Brotherhood's political party, the Islamic Action Front, leveraged its disciplined cadres and superior organization to become the most consistent party in parliament, thereby raising the ire of many officials. Over time, its membership also became increasingly Palestinian, which resulted in a stance sympathetic to Hamas and ardently opposed to Israeli diplomacy despite the monarchy's need to maintain close ties with Israel, and thus also the West. During the Arab Spring, the Brotherhood also led a series of large, but peaceful and self-contained, demonstrations in Amman demanding democratic reform and anti-corruption measures.

At the same time, the rise of more conservative or extreme variants of Islamism elsewhere has forced the Brotherhood to maintain a moderate stance regarding political change. Jordan also has a strong Salafi community; and although most are "quietist" in preferring education and religious activities to Islamize the kingdom, a minority subscribe to jihadi goals. Several thousand Jordanians joined ISIS. While the government intensified its efforts to regulate and monitor Islamic discourse, the Brotherhood consistently decried ISIS, and maintains a wary distance from Salafi networks.

The Brotherhood has been weakened somewhat due to more recent political manipulations. In 2015, as other Islamists suffered crackdowns in Egypt and Saudi Arabia, the government succeeded in exploiting an internal division within the group's leadership between hardline voices and a more reformist wing. It facilitated the reformist wing's defection to create a new Muslim Brotherhood-styled organization, which quickly gained official recognition by a regime eager to see more tempered expressions of Islamist sentiment. The remainder of the Brotherhood organization lost its license as a charitable entity, and therefore also lost access to much of its financial assets. Seeking to recalibrate itself, this more traditional Brotherhood base officially severed ties with the Egyptian Muslim Brotherhood, technically its "parent" entity, in 2016, while continuing to support and operate its successful IAF party. It remains to be seen whether this bifurcation in the Islamist community will result in stronger, weaker, or simply different political mobilizations of Islamist activists in the future.

FOREIGN POLICY

From the foundation of the Hashemite state onward, Jordan maintained close strategic ties to Britain and later the United States and the Arab Gulf states. After the onset of the Cold War, Jordan established stronger and stronger links to the United States, as Western powers came to view Jordan as a conservative bulwark against communism and radical pan-Arabism as well as a potentially moderating element in the Arab-Israeli conflict. From the beginning, then, Jordan has held close ties to the US and European powers, relying heavily on foreign aid from these countries to remain financially viable. In the post-Cold War era, these powers considered Jordan as a moderating influence against regional states and threats deemed radical – Al-Qa'ida, Iran, Syria, and essentially any actor that did not conform to the regional order desired by the West.

Jordan's centrality in Middle East politics and geography has also carried with it real strategic vulnerability. Given its location, Jordan from the outset was deeply involved in the various dimensions of the Palestinian-Israeli and broader Arab-Israeli conflicts, be it in 1948, 1956, 1967 or (less so) in 1973. It was also strongly affected by the more recent wars in neighboring Lebanon 1975–90, Iraq since 1980 and in particular post-2003, and Syria after 2011. Jordan under both the late King Hussein and currently under King Abdullah II has attempted to stay out of a direct involvement in these wars, aiming to prevent negative fallout in terms of regime security while securing outside security and economic assistance to neutralize the collateral damage in the form of refugee influxes, lost trade and investment, and the necessity of tightening border security.

Critically, foreign policy in Jordan is a conduit of regime survival because it secures not just military support but also economic aid. In every single year since its inception, the government budget has required considerable infusions of grants and loans from strategic donors in order to close its spending gap, particularly on the military and public salaries – a problem also stemming from its notoriously weak domestic taxation scheme, which leaves the state short on internal revenues. As a small and relatively poor state, Jordan relies on external sources of aid and oil, as well as access to foreign labor markets. Tourism and foreign investment are cornerstones of King Abdullah's approach to national development, both requiring domestic and regional stability. As a result, Abdullah has actively pursued a regional role as diplomatic facilitator, mediator, or even peacemaker. For instance, despite its small size, Jordan sends soldiers on UN peacekeeping operations throughout the world.

With his immediate neighbors, King Abdullah has maintained the kingdom's peace treaty with Israel while pressing for a peace settlement between Israel and the Palestinians. Arguing that the Palestinian issue has remained the single most destabilizing issue in Middle East politics, the Jordanian government consistently offers its good offices in relations between the United States, Israel, and the Palestinian Authority. But with periodic Palestinian uprisings and Israel attacks since the late 1990s, the intra-Palestinian split between a West Bank-dominated Fatah and a Gaza Strip-ruled Hamas since 2007, and the continued Israeli settlements in the West Bank and East Jerusalem, Jordan's moderating position has been more and more difficult to maintain. The fact that a majority of Jordan's citizenship population is Palestinian means that official regime policies of pragmatism often diverge sharply from the intense preferences of the public to punish Israel. The last several years have seen Jordan's position in this regard take a turn for the worse. The right-wing Israeli government under Prime Minister Benjamin Netanyahu has not only kept Jordan at arm's length, but the Trump administration's proposed "deal of the century" froze Jordan out of almost all backroom planning. The moving of the US embassy to Jerusalem from Tel Aviv, the halting of American foreign aid to Palestinian institutions, and fears that an even more radical solution – asking Palestinians everywhere to simply relocate to Jordan as their alternative homeland – have forced the monarchy to launch a diplomatic blitz, but to no avail.

In other areas, despite the intensity of regional insecurity, Jordan for the most part has remained stable and secure within its borders, while the regime continues to emphasize economic development, trade, investment, and an active tourism industry as the ultimate keys to Jordan's present and future. These priorities, in turn, have led the monarchy to pursue warm relations with economically influential states, from the Arab Gulf monarchies to the EU and the US. At the start of the Arab Spring in 2011, Jordan received an invitation to join the Gulf Cooperation Council (GCC), the alliance of the Arabian Gulf monarchies of Bahrain, Kuwait, Oman, Qatar, Saudi Arabia, and the United Arab Emirates. (While Jordan is not a Gulf state, or an oil power for that matter, it is a Sunni Arab monarchy with extensive linkage to Western powers – and in that sense fits the GCC mold.) The enthusiasm was not shared by all states in the GCC, however, and soon the offer came into a permanent state of indecision due to disagreements within the Gulf bloc. But Jordanian-GCC ties increased nonetheless, and Jordan has become reliant on occasional large financial grants from individual GCC states to meet its budgets, keep its economy afloat, and deal with its rising refugee crisis. Saudi Arabia and Kuwait, for instance, sent Jordan several billion dollars of financial support after the 2011–12 protests to bolster its flailing finances.

This warming of Jordan-GCC relations came to a partial halt after the mid-2010s with the intra-GCC split between Saudi Arabia and the UAE on the one hand and Qatar on the other hand. The swift rise of Muhammad bin Salman in the Saudi monarchical system has had strong implications for neighboring Jordan. Saudi Arabia's aggressive foreign policy behavior in the MENA post-2015, such as its brutal military intervention in Yemen, the full blockade of Qatar, vehement desire for war against Iran, and the neglect of Palestinian people, has pressured Jordan to adopt the Saudi platform under threat of withholding future economic aid. Yet doing so would force Jordan to surrender its more traditional role of serving as a moderate regional state – one that follows the American lead on regional geopolitics but without stirring the pot with controversial measures.

FUTURE PROSPECTS

Under King Abdullah II, as under King Hussein before him, Jordan has presented itself as a source of regional moderation and stability in an otherwise turbulent Middle East. Yet the country also remains vulnerable to crises erupting in its immediate neighborhood – from Israel-Palestine to Iraq to Syria – as well as to internal tensions as regime and opposition struggle over the question of domestic reform. In the short term, Jordan is likely to remain stable given the lack of a credible political alternative to ruling monarchism, the loyalty of the security agencies, fracturing of the Muslim Brotherhood, national attention focused upon nearby regional crises, and ongoing channels of international aid and assistance. It benefits from a "regional politics of comparing" – meaning, while Jordan today might not be exemplary in terms of democratic and socially inclusionary reforms, its regime can still convey the image that Jordanians still live better lives than most Syrians or Palestinians, and enjoy more freedoms than in Egypt or Saudi Arabia.

Yet trouble lurks. The regime's crisis management strategies for its contentious society driven by young citizens chafing under joblessness and political closure have been a combination of neglect, repression, and cooptation. These strategies do not guarantee long-term survival, particularly as East Bank families, including tribal factions and communities, continue criticizing King Abdullah. Neither does Jordan's new uncertainty help matters regarding Gulf pressures, Israeli intransigence, and the Palestinian cause under changing American presidential administrations. Against this background, it can be expected that the Hashemite regime will have to continue pursuing the multiple balancing acts that have already characterized its history in the last almost hundred years.

FURTHER READING

There are excellent general histories of Jordan that serve as primers. Two are Philip Robins, *A History of Jordan* (Cambridge University Press, 2004); and Kamal Salibi, *The Modern History of Jordan* (IB Tauris, 1998).

Historical works on Jordan since are divided into different periods. The best study on the period immediately before the foundation of the Jordanian state is by Eugene L. Rogan, *Frontiers of the State in the Late Ottoman Empire: Transjordan, 1850– 1921* (Cambridge University Press, 1999). The early decades from the 1920s through 1940s are detailed in Maan Abu Nowar's *Trilogy: The History of the Hashemite*

Kingdom of Jordan: The Creation and Development of Transjordan, 1920–1929 (Ithaca, 1989); *The Development of Trans-Jordan 1929–1939: A History of the Hashemite Kingdom of Jordan* (Ithaca, 2006); and *The Struggle for Independence 1939–1947: A History of the Hashemite Kingdom of Jordan* (Ithaca, 2001). Mary C. Wilson's *King Abdullah, Britain and the Making of Jordan* (Cambridge University Press, 1987) remains the gold standard in analyzing the diplomatic machinations and elite politics during the colonial period of Jordan. Closely following that is Nasser Aruri's *Jordan: A Study in Political Development, 1921–1965* (Martinus Nijhoff, 1972). Social histories of Jordanian state formation that consider the pivotal role of tribalism include Yoav Alon, *The Making of Jordan: Tribes, Colonialism, and the Modern State* (IB Tauris, 2007), and Tariq Tell, *The Social and Economic Origins of Monarchy in Jordan* (Palgrave Macmillan, 2013).

From the 1950s onwards, Jordan's political and social trajectory is well-mapped. Robert Satloff's *From Abdullah to Hussein: Jordan in Transition* (Oxford University Press, 1993) traces out the conflicts and unrest of the 1940s through 1950s. Opposition and protest politics take center stage in Betty Anderson, *Nationalist Voices in Jordan: The Street and the State* (University of Texas, 2005). Military and security concerns also tell the story of Jordanian survival during the Cold War; see, for instance, Lawrence Tal, *Politics, the Military, and National Security in Jordan: 1955–1967* (Palgrave Macmillan, 2002); Samir Mutawi, *Jordan in the 1967 War* (Cambridge University Press, 1987); and Uriel Dann, *King Hussein and the Challenge of Arab Radicalism* (Oxford University Press, 1991).

Jordanian identity and social issues constitute important topics. On the construction of Jordanian national identity, see Joseph Massad, *Colonial Effects: The Making of National Identity in Jordan* (Columbia University Press, 2001). Women and gender in Jordan is a topic finally making inroads after decades of neglect. A sample of work includes Amira Sonbol, *Women of the Jordan: Islam, Labor, and the Law* (Syracuse University Press, 2003); Julia Droeber, *Dreaming of Change: Young Middle-Class Women and Social Transformation in Jordan* (Brill, 2005), and Afaf Jabiri, *Gendered Politics and Law in Jordan: Guardianship over Women* (Palgrave Macmillan, 2016). The intersection of religion, class, and economic status is explored in Sarah Tobin, *Everyday Piety: Islam and Economy in Jordan* (Cornell University Press, 2016). Perspectives that incorporate the regional system into the quest for Jordanian identity are provided by Marc Lynch, *State Interests and Public Spheres: The International Politics of Jordan's Identity* (Columbia University Press, 1999) and André Bank and Morten Valbjørn, "Bringing the Arab Regional Level Back in … Jordan in the New Arab Cold War," *Middle East Critique* 19, 3 (2010): 303–319.

The Palestinian question looms large. An historical overview can be found in Clinton Bailey, *Jordan's Palestinian Challenge, 1948–1983: A Political History* (Westview, 1984). Engaging essays can also be found in Joseph Nevo and Ilan Pappé, eds., *Jordan in the Middle East: The Making of a Pivotal State: 1984–1988* (Cass, 1994). A more challenging discussion about the Palestinian question after the 1988 disengagement with the West Bank can be found in Mustafa Hamarneh, Rosemary Hollis, and Khalil Shikaki, *Jordanian-Palestinian Relations: Where to?* (Royal Institute of International Affairs, 1997). A critical approach that explores the historical origins of discrimination against Palestinians is by Adnan Abu Odeh, *Jordanians, Palestinians, and the Hashemite Kingdom in the Middle East Peace Process* (United States Institute of Peace, 1999). Luigi Achilli, *Palestinian Refugees and Identity: Nationalism, Politics and the Everyday*

(IB Tauris, 2015) and Louisa Gandolfo, *Palestinians in Jordan: The Politics of Identity* (IB Tauris, 2012) are excellent interrogations of Palestinian identity. The Israeli-Jordanian dynamic occupies Dona Stewart, *Good Neighbourly Relations: Jordan, Israel, and the 1994–2004 Peace Process* (IB Tauris, 2012).

Work on Jordan's development and political economy abounds. Classic Cold War-era perspectives emphasizing aid dependency and rentierism are Bichara Khader and Adnan Badran, eds., *The Economic Development of Jordan* (Croom Helm, 1987), and Rodney Wilson, ed., *Politics and Economy in Jordan* (Routledge, 1991). The transition after the 1980s to market-oriented neoliberalism is covered in Timothy Piro, *The Political Economy of Market Reform in Jordan* (Rowman & Littlefield, 1998) and Warwick Knowles, *Jordan since 1989: A Study in Political Economy* (IB Tauris, 2005). Consequent struggles to Jordanian well-being are described in Anne Marie Baylouny, *Privatizing Welfare in the Middle East: Kin Mutual Aid Associations in Jordan and Lebanon* (Indiana University Press, 2010), and Pete Moore, *Doing Business in the Middle East: Politics and Economic Crises in Jordan and Kuwait* (Cambridge University Press, 2004), the latter of which also illuminates the important ties between business leaders and the Jordanian state apparatus. An exhaustive exploration of Jordan's most pressing problems in terms of unemployment, demographics, and hardship is found in Ragui Assaad, ed., *The Jordanian Labor Market in the New Millennium* (Oxford University Press, 2014). The economics of the refugee question is taken up by Katharina Lenner and Lewis Turner, "Making refugees work? The Politics of Integrating Syrian Refugees into the Labor Market in Jordan," *Middle East Critique* 28, 1 (2019): 1–31.

Studies of Jordanian politics since the 1990s have been directed by several core questions. One is Islamism. On Islamists in Jordan, see Jillian M. Schwedler, *Faith in Moderation: Islamist Parties in Jordan and Yemen* (Cambridge University Press, 2006); Janine A. Clark, *Islam, Charity, and Activism: Middle Class Networks and Social Welfare in Egypt, Jordan, and Yemen* (Indiana University Press, 2004); and Quintan Wiktorowicz, *The Management of Islamic Activism: Salafis, the Muslim Brotherhood, and State Power in Jordan* (State University of New York Press, 2000). Joas Wagemakers, *Salafism in Jordan: Political Islam in a Quietist Community* (Cambridge University Press, 2016) is the best take on the Salafi community.

A second question has been that of political reform. Here, works tend to emphasize the promise of liberal opening in the 1990s followed by the authoritarian closure and stabilization since then. See, for instance, Curtis R. Ryan, *Jordan in Transition: From Hussein to Abdullah* (Lynne Rienner, 2002); George Joffé, ed., *Jordan in Transition: 1990–2000* (Hurst, 2002); André Bank and Oliver Schlumberger, "Jordan: Between Regime Survival and Economic Reform," in Volker Perthes, ed., *Arab Elites: Negotiating the Politics of Change* (Lynne Rienner, 2004); Ellen Lust-Okar, "Elections under Authoritarianism: Preliminary Lessons from Jordan," *Democratization* 13, 3 (2006): 456–471; and Sean Yom, "Jordan: Ten More Years of Autocracy," *Journal of Democracy* 20, 4 (2009): 151–166.

A third, albeit smaller issue has been local politics and the question of decentralization in Jordan. The landmark study on this has been by Janine A. Clark, *Local Politics in Jordan and Morocco: Strategies of Centralization and Decentralization* (Columbia University Press, 2018); Malika Bouziane has looked at dynamics in the tribal area of Ma'an: "Negotiating (Informal) Institutional Change: Understanding Local Politics in Jordan," in Malika Bouziane, Cilja Harders, and

Anja Hoffman, eds., *Local Politics and Contemporary Transformations in the Arab World* (Palgrave Macmillan, 2013). Grace Elliott, Matt Ciesielski, Rebecca Birkholz examine the effects of the 2015 Decentralization Law in "Centralized Decentralization: Subnational Governance in Jordan," *Middle East Policy* 25, 4 (2018): 130–145.

On Jordan's international relations and foreign policy, scholarship thrives. An early study is Mohammad Ibrahim Faddah, *The Middle East in Transition: A Study of Jordan's Foreign Policy* (Asia Publishing House, 1974). Archive-driven approaches exploring Jordan's reliance upon British and American support are Miriam Joyce's *Anglo-American Support for Jordan: The Career of King Hussein* (Palgrave Macmillan, 2008) and Clea Lutz Hupp, *The United States and Jordan: Middle East Diplomacy during the Cold War* (IB Tauris, 2014). Notable studies that chart Jordan's foreign relations from the 1970s onwards include the classical study by Laurie A. Brand, *Jordan's Inter-Arab Relations: The Political Economy of Alliance Making* (Columbia University Press, 1995) and Curtis R. Ryan, *Inter-Arab Alliances: Regime Security and Jordanian Foreign Policy* (University Press of Florida, 2009). Anne Mariel Zimmermann's *US Assistance, Development, and Hierarchy in the Middle East: Aid for Allies* (Palgrave Macmillan, 2017) creatively explores the domestic implications of US aid. Sean Yom's *From Resilience to Revolution: How Foreign Interventions Destabilize the Middle East* (Columbia University Press, 2016) likewise engages this question, and finds that too much outside support can have ambivalent effects in dependent states like Jordan.

The Arab Spring and its effects on mobilization, politics, and stability in Jordan has catalyzed a new cottage industry of analysis. Studies of new opposition movements include Sean Yom, "The New Landscape of Jordanian Politics: Social Opposition, Fiscal Crisis, and the Arab Spring," *British Journal of Middle East Studies* 42, 3 (2015): 284–300 and "Tribal Politics in Contemporary Jordan: The Case of the Hirak Movement," *Middle East Journal* 68, 1 (2014): 229–247. Sara Ababneh focuses on gender dynamics in "Troubling the Political: Women in the Jordanian Day-Waged Labor Movement," *International Journal of Middle East Studies* 48, 1 (2016): 87–112; Jillian Schwedler studies the spatial dynamics of protest in "The Political Geography of Protests in Neoliberal Jordan," *Middle East Critique* 21, 3 (2012): 259–270. Curtis R. Ryan provides a book-length overview over most of the aforementioned trends in Jordan post-2011: *Jordan and the Arab Spring: Regime Survival and Politics beyond the State* (Columbia University Press, 2018). Inversely, authoritarian responses to popular mobilization have led many studies, among them: Maria Josua, "Co-Optation Reconsidered: Authoritarian Regime Legitimation Strategies in the Jordanian Arab Spring," *Middle East Law and Governance* 8, 1 (2016): 32–56; Dana M. Moss, "Repression, Response, and Contained Escalation under 'Liberalized' Authoritarianism in Jordan," *Mobilization: An International Quarterly* 19, 3 (2014): 261–286; Benjamin Schütze "Marketing Parliament: The Constitutive Effect at Parliamentary Strengthening in Jordan," *Cooperation and Conflict* 53, 2 (2018): 237–258.

Online sources

Jordan has a large and active space for Internet research. The first stop for political data is the Phoenix Center's Guide to

Jordanian Politics (www.jordanpolitics.org/en/home), which maps out the cabinet and parliamentary composition. The government has pushed many institutions online. E-government websites include the official portal (https://jordan.gov.jo/), where some ministries and councils maintain decent websites; the Department of Statistics, which provides quantitative data on every aspect of the country (http://dosweb.dos.gov.jo/); and parliament's page (www.parliament.jo/). Civil society organizations are mapped out as well here at the FES-Phoenix Center's guide (www.civilsociety-jo.net/en/home). Relevant laws affecting civic groups and associations are monitored at the ICNL page (www.icnl.org/research/monitor/jordan.html).

Many sources of news flourish online. For English-language daily reporting, see *Jordan Times* (www.jordantimes.com/); monthly stories are found in *Venture* (www.venturemagazine.me/tag/jordan/). The official news can be read at Petra News Agency (http://petra.gov.jo/). Similarly pro-government sentiments exist at Roya News (https://en.royanews.tv/). However, independent sources of critical analysis include the popular multimedia *7iber* (www.7iber.com), the Arabic-language *Raseef22* (https://raseef22.com/) and *Aramram* (www.aramram.com/), and AmmanNet, a community media organization (https://ammannet.net/). Middle East Eye's Jordan page also has many critical stories (www.middleeasteye.net/countries/jordan).

Please note that URLs may change far more quickly than books can be printed; so if these exact URLs do not work, simply search Google or another engine by the titles of these websites and online resources.

Republic of Iraq

Ariel I. Ahram

INTRODUCTION

Since the first modern government of Iraq was created by and under British mandate in 1920, observers inside and outside the country have argued over its imperial and colonial legacies, identity, and viability. Some saw Iraq as an artificial creation of European imperialism, arguing that Iraqis' primary identity was that of Arab or Kurd, Sunni or Shi'a, Christian or Jews – not as Iraqi. Others, though, see in Iraqi nationalism a real force of cohesion, born in response to Ottoman and British impositions and enduring across many of its institutional developments and political narratives.

Foreign occupations serve as critical junctures in Iraq's modern history: the Ottomans in the sixteenth century, the British twice in the twentieth century, and the Americans in the twenty-first century. Upon regaining sovereignty in 2005, Iraq had an opportunity to showcase its successful transition from dictatorship to democracy – an historical shift that sought to move beyond much of its authoritarian legacy, including the infamous tenure of Saddam Hussein. However, this transition has been characterized by persistent violence and the continued weakness of Iraqi state institutions overall, a problem amplified by the civil conflict involving the Islamic State of Iraq and Syria (ISIS), new demands from vocal groups in Iraqi society, and renewed political competition.

Box 13.1 provides vital data for this country.

BOX 13.1 VITAL DATA – REPUBLIC OF IRAQ

Capital	Baghdad
Regime type	Hybrid (parliamentary republic)
Head of state	President Barham Salih (since 2018)
Head of government	Prime Minister Adil 'Abd al-Mahdi (since 2018)
Legislative institution	Unicameral parliament, with 329 elected seats (*Majlis al-Nuwaab al-'Iraqi*, or Council of Representatives)
Female quota	Yes: women must constitute at least one-quarter of all winners in general elections, meaning no less than 82 (out of 329) seats
Percentage of seats held by women	25.2%
Major political parties (share of seats in most recent general elections, 2018)	Alliance Towards Reforms [Sa'irun] (16.4%), Conquest Alliance (14.6%), Victory Alliance (12.8%), Kurdistan Democratic Party (7.6%), State of Law Coalition (7.6%), National Coalition [Wataniyyah] (6.4%), National Wisdom Movement (5.8%)
Population	38,274,618
Major ethnic groups	Arab (75%), Kurdish (20%), other (5%)
Major religious groups	Sunni Muslim (33%), Shi'a Muslim (65%), Christian (1%), other (1%)
GDP per capita	$5,930 ($17,659 at Purchasing Power Parity)
Unemployment rate	7.9%
Youth unemployment rate	16.6%
Major economic industries	Petroleum, chemicals, textiles, construction, food processing, fertilizer, leather, metal processing
Military spending as % GDP	3.9%

HISTORICAL BACKGROUND

The state of Iraq rests in what had been known for millennia as Mesopotamia, between the Tigris and Euphrates rivers. Geography and access to water made it one the earliest cradles of civilizations. Cities appeared as early as 5,300 BC, deriving their economic wealth from their ability to harness the rivers for irrigation and commerce. Muslim armies from the Arabian

Peninsula defeated the Persian empire in 633 AD, conquering Iraq and establishing it as an important component of the Caliphate. Over the next decades, Iraqi cities became centers for supporters of Ali, the group known as Shi'a, who believed that as cousin and son-in-law of the Prophet, he (and his direct descendants) were the rightful successors to the position of leadership over the Muslim community. By insisting on Ali's sole right to rule, the Shi'a denied the legitimacy of the majority (Sunni). Ali's son Hussein led a revolt against the Umayyad Caliphate and was killed in the Battle of Karbala in 680 AD. Eventually this political and tribal dispute came to take on deeper theological and sectarian dimensions. While the vast majority of the Muslim world accepted the Sunni view, Shi'a Islam continued to be a considerable voice of dissent in Iraq and elsewhere. In the eighth century, the Abbasid Caliphate arose and established a new capital in Baghdad. Iraq became the center of a prosperous empire in which science, architecture, and literature flourished, a zenith in Islamic history. Between the thirteenth and fifteenth centuries, however, invasions by Mongol and Turkic raiders devastated the region.

By the 1500s, Iraq was a frontier on the seam between the ascendant Ottoman Empire and Iranian Safavid (and thus Shi'a) dynasty. The Ottomans and Safavid empires fought a number of wars for control over the region. The Ottomans distrusted the Shi'a population in Iraq, and Shi'a clerics proselytized among the Arab tribes of southern Iraq. Until the late eighteenth century, the Ottomans ruled through local intermediaries, particularly Sunni urban notables. In the late eighteenth century, the central Ottoman government began directly appointing governors of the Mosul, Baghdad, and Basra provinces, the three geographic divisions that today largely correspond to Iraq. The Ottomans also repaired irrigation systems, established railroads and telegraph lines, and improved riparian navigation, connecting Iraq to international markets. At the same time, while a handful of urban merchants, farmers, and tribal chieftains became rich, rural poverty in many cases worsened.

Colonialism and revolution, 1914–1958

The British takeover of Mesopotamia during World War One was singularly responsible for creating Iraq in its modern form. Britain had maintained an interest in Iraq as part of its defense of India, the crown jewel of its global empire. British forces invaded and occupied southern Iraq during the war. In 1920, the League of Nations awarded London a mandate to rule Iraq as a glorified protectorate and prepare it for independence. There was immediate resistance to British rule, as Sunni and Shi'a Arabs joined together in a massive revolt in 1920. The British responded with a combination of brutal aerial bombardment and efforts to co-opt selected tribal *sheikhs* (chieftains) through material gifts and political patronage. Then, and now, Sunni Muslims constituted only a minority of the population; Shi'a Muslims were far more numerous, while Kurdish communities represented the smallest part of this tripartite population.

In 1921, the British installed Faysal, scion of the prominent Hashemite clan of Mecca, as monarch in the new Kingdom of Iraq. Faysal, who had never before been to Iraq, walked a tightrope. On one hand, he understood the imperative to respond to British directives. British advisors oversaw all of Iraq's key ministries and set up bilateral treaties guaranteeing British access to Iraq. British air power became the anchor protecting the Iraqi state from restive tribes and foreign aggression. On the other hand, Faysal also worked with his close circle of advisors – mostly ex-Ottoman officers (the vast majority of whom were Sunni Arabs) loyal to his Hashemite family and desirous as well of Iraqi independence. Unsurprisingly, many segments of Iraqi society were dissatisfied with this newly grafted regime. Iraq's parliament was independent and worked at the mercy of the crown. The nationalists alternatively cooperated with and resisted the British. Shi'a leaders complained of their effective exclusion from political authority in the new state, and Kurdish leaders held out hope of gaining a state of their own.

Iraq was admitted to the League of Nations in 1932. Although technically sovereign, Iraq remained under Britain's indirect control. Independence in many ways heightened the tensions within the country. In 1933, the Iraqi army massacred the Assyrian Christians who had taken up arms demanding the right to self-government. Revolts broke out among Shi'a in the south in the mid-1930s, as religious leaders and tribal chiefs sought greater representation and more recognition of their religion and culture. Revolts in Kurdistan continued largely unabated. Ultimately, the government responded with a combination of blunt force and selective inducements to stem these attacks.

The increasing prominence of repression also brought about the increased influence of military officers, whose vision for Iraq was quite different from the pro-British monarchy. In 1936, the army staged the first of a number of coups aimed at replacing what was seen as a dysfunctional cabinet. During World War Two, a clique of nationalist officers and politicians backed a pro-Axis coup. Britain invaded and re-installed a reliably pro-British government. After World War Two, the monarchy remained reliant on Britain and, increasingly, the United States. Revenues from oil increased dramatically, giving the government new means to invest in dams, roads, health, and education. Benefiting from the expansion of rural education, more Shi'a and Kurds entered the political establishment.

Beneath the surface, however, discontent simmered. The political system remained effectively closed, despite pretenses of parliamentary democracy. Economic growth continued to be highly uneven, with land inequalities worsening. Peasants and formerly nomadic tribesmen fell into debt and became sharecroppers on the estates of wealthy landlords. Escaping rural poverty, Iraqis moved to Baghdad and other cities, often establishing demi-urban slums. Shi'a Iraqis especially flocked to the illegal Iraqi Communist Party (ICP), which promised to ameliorate the growing social and economic divide. By the 1950s, the ICP was the country's largest party. Other Iraqis looked to Arab nationalism, championed by Egyptian President Gamal Abdel Nasser. On July 14, 1958, troops under the command of Colonels 'Abd al-Karim Qasim and 'Abd al-Salam 'Arif stormed the royal palace, executed the royal family and the prime minister, and declared Iraq to be a republic.

Republican Iraq, 1958–2003

The overthrow of the monarchy ushered in another decade of political instability. Between 1958 and 1968 there were four changes of regime, several involving considerable bloodshed. The revolution placed the army in power. Colonel Qasim (1958–63) was the first leader of the republican regime. Unlike many others in the Sunni-dominated officer corps, Qasim was half-Shi'a and half-Kurdish (the latter a constituency generally considered to be left-leaning in politics). He introduced agrarian and social reforms, including capping the size of landholdings and rent, and giving women more rights. He signaled his support for creating a Kurdish autonomous region or even federation, reaching out to Mullah Mustafa Barzani, head of the Kurdish Democratic Party (KDP). He legalized the ICP and made overtures to the Soviet Union, breaking from Iraq's pro-Western stance. In 1961, he began the process of nationalizing the Iraqi oil industry from its British overseers.

Qasim's mercurial style of rule alienated many supporters and placed him on a collision course with his former co-conspirators. In February 1963, 'Arif and an eclectic coalition of opposition, including Nasserists, the Ba'th Party, and the Iraqi branch of the Muslim Brotherhood, moved against the regime. They dispatched of Qasim, as well as hundreds of other regime sympathizers including those associated with ICP or the Kurdish nationalists.

The new regime reflected the more nationalist leading of Iraq's Sunni Arabs. By November, 'Arif had fallen back upon his military roots and used the army to push aside the Ba'th Party. However, the humiliating defeat of the 1967 Arab-Israeli war undercut the army's prestige. On July 17, 1968, a new crop of Ba'th Party activists and elites seized power.

The Ba'th Party was founded in the 1940s by secular ideologies based on principles of Arab unity and vague theories of economic and social justice. Until the early 1960s, the party was tiny, counting only a few thousand members in Iraq, Syria, and other Arab countries. Importantly, though, the Ba'th ideology appeared to offer a chance to transcend ethnic, tribal, or sectarian ties – at least in theory. Upon assuming power in 1968, the party's composition and ideological orientation changed. Through the 1970s and 1980s, party membership became a key credential for education, employment, and promotion. Millions of Iraqis joined the party, less out of political conviction than a desire to get ahead. Party members, therefore, comprised the bulk of administrators and professionals in the country. They hailed from all different ethno-sectarian backgrounds and tended to be secular and nationalist in orientation. The Ba'th Party set up a parallel system of rule between the party and the regular organs of the state. A new constitution declared Iraq to be a socialist republic but made the state bureaucracy subservient to the party. The Ba'th apparatus, now in control over all major institutions, had the authority to promulgate laws, attend to defense and security, declare war, and approve the budget.

Even as it became a mass-based, ruling party, the true core of the Ba'th centered upon Saddam Hussein and a small clique of his close kinsmen from the mostly Sunni city of Tikrit. Saddam's cousin was the first president of the republic and chairman of the party, while Saddam was his deputy. By 1979, Saddam had pushed his uncle aside and assumed complete and personal control. Saddam made sure that the upper strata of the Ba'th Party, the officer corps, and the security and intelligence services, were dominated by trustworthy individuals. This meant people with tribal or familial connections to his Tikrit base, or elsewhere in the towns and villages of largely Sunni areas of central and western Iraq. Saddam was brutal toward any potential challengers, real or imagined. He manipulated clan relationships to ensure loyalty. He also continued the modernization push begun in past decades by post-monarchist regimes, with the common thread being the need to rapidly develop and industrialize Iraq. Oil revenues had funded ambitious programs, including electrification, agricultural reform, land redistribution, and new programs for rural education and health. Imbibing the need to become a major regional military power, the regime also embarked on a military-industrial program that included chemical and nuclear weapons, while the army expanded with the strict application of conscription.

One of the key regions of focus was Kurdistan. In the 1960s, the Ba'th was initially amenable to granting Kurds cultural and national rights within Iraq. However, the regime also believed that through modernization, it could win the loyalty of Iraq's Kurdish citizenry and defang its leftist opponents, including the remnants of the ICP and Arab Nationalists who desired Iraq to become subordinate to Nasser. The Ba'th negotiated with the KDP and in 1970 offered a plan for Kurdish autonomy. Implementation, however, was slow. The KDP suspected the Ba'th of prevaricating while Ba'th leaders accused the KDP of seeking outright secession. Negotiations broke down and Mustafa Barzani, still the leading Kurdish nationalist, launched a new revolt. The revolt collapsed, however, after Iraq came to an agreement with Iran in 1975. Barzani was forced into exile, and the Kurdish movement split between the Kurdish Democratic Party (KDP), eventually led by Barzani's son, Masoud, and the Patriotic Union of Kurdistan (PUK), led by Jalal Talabani. With the Kurds defeated, the Ba'th unilaterally launched its autonomous plan, creating a puppet legislature and executive council for the northern region. It also razed Kurdish villages along its borders with Turkey and Iran, forcibly resettled Kurds, and encouraged Arabs to settle in the north, especially in the oil-rich city of Kirkuk.

With no internal checks on his power, Saddam engaged in risky and destructive gambits. The first was the invasion of Iran in 1980. Saddam believed that new Islamic Republic of Iran would make territorial concessions, possibly even over Khuzestan, an oil-rich province inhabited largely by Arabs. But he was also fearful that its revolutionary vision of Shi'a Islamism would reach the Iraqi Shi'a. After initial advances, Iraq's army became bogged down. In 1982, Iraqi forces retreated back to the border as Iran continued to attack, declaring its intent to topple the Ba'th and calling upon Iraq's Shi'a majority to revolt. The Iranian regime helped exiled Iraqi Shi'a to set up the Supreme Council for Islamic Revolution in Iraq (SCIRI) to fight against the regime. The conflict settled into a long war of attrition, with the US, Arab Gulf states, and the Soviet Union backing Iraq financially, politically, and militarily. Despite expectations otherwise, most Iraqis, even the Shi'a, fought for their state over sectarian fraternity. Kurdistan was a partial exception, where rebels received support from Iranian forces; Saddam responded with unprecedented brutality, leveling villages with artillery, aerial bombardment, and poison gas. The war finally ended in July 1988, with an estimated

150,000 Iraqis dead and an additional 100,000 killed in Kurdistan. The Iraq oil industry was crippled and the country had taken massive loans from its Gulf neighbors, which threw the regime into debt. At the same time, Iraq had emerged from the war with its territory and its military intact.

Even as Iraq recovered from the Iran-Iraq war, Saddam launched another disastrous adventure in August 1990: the invasion and annexation of Kuwait. Saddam claimed Kuwait was naturally part of Iraq, cleaved away only by British imperialism, and that Kuwait had illegally siphoned from Iraq's oil fields. Once again, he miscalculated. The US organized a 30-nation coalition, including NATO members and other Arab states, to force Iraq out of Kuwait. After a devastating air campaign beginning on January 16, 1991, the ground assault routed the Iraqi army. More critically, in March, disgruntled Iraqi soldiers started a popular rebellion in Basra. Within days, most of the Shi'a-inhabited territory from the outskirts of Baghdad to Basra had come under rebel control. In the north, Kurdish factions launched a similar revolt, exploiting the breakdown of state power. By June, only Baghdad and the primarily Sunni areas of the west were in government hands. Many rebels counted on the US to protect them from Saddam's counterattack, but worries about the destabilizing impact of the rebellion resulted in little aid. The United Nations backed a no-fly zone in southern Iraq to prevent Iraqi forces from threatening Saudi Arabia and Kuwait, but with no ground intervention, the Iraqi military suppressed the Shi'a uprising in the south. When rebels retreated into the marshes along the Iran-Iraq border, Saddam systematically drained the waters and destroyed villages that had provided sanctuary to the rebels. In the north, Kurdish rebels were able to consolidate their gains. The coalition prohibited both aircraft and ground forces from flying north of the 36th parallel. Free of control from Baghdad, the Kurds operated a mostly autonomous government in the north.

After the catastrophe of 1991, Saddam focused on basic questions of regime survival. Iraq's state sovereignty was severely compromised. International inspectors mounted a highly intrusive regime of inspections intended to dismantle Iraq's chemical, biological, and nuclear weapons programs. The United States and its allies maintained the no-fly zones over both the north and south of the country, and economic sanctions remained in place. The sanctions compounded the economic devastation caused by the war and subsequent revolt. The government cut public subsidies and spending, and the country's once burgeoning middle class was virtually wiped out by high inflation and low salaries. Political repression intensified as well, as Saddam sought revenge on those he felt had betrayed him. He bloodily purged the party and army, and personalistically concentrated more power in his hands and family. While many Iraqis suffered economically, he struck new alliances with smugglers and co-opted Sunni tribal chiefs, who were granted a measure of autonomy in return for helping to maintain a semblance of order in the countryside. The regime also began to propagandize Islamic virtues as a source of identity.

Occupation and civil war, 2003–2011

The US invasion of Iraq in 2003 took an already frail state and tore it to tatters. The invasion was motivated by a number of factors. The most important were the unfounded concerns that Saddam still had caches of chemical or biological weapons, and actively assisted Al-Qa'ida. American policymakers also believed that removing Saddam would hasten a democratic cascade in the region and undercut the appeal of Islamic radicalism. Reliant on intelligence and counsel offered by Iraqi exile groups, the Bush administration believed it would be welcomed in Iraq as a liberator.

While the American military faced very little resistance in the initial phases of invasion, it soon found itself sinking into a quagmire. With the collapse of Saddam's regime, looters and saboteurs took to the street, and the US did not commit enough troops on the ground to preserve law and order. Orders to dismantle the Iraqi army and depose any government official with Ba'th party membership further broke down state capacity. The Coalition Provisional Authority (CPA), the interim government installed by the US, appointed a new governing council comprised largely of exiles to hopefully lead this transition, but it suffered a severe deficit of legitimacy. The governing council was organized along more or less explicitly sectarian terms designed to reflect Iraqi diversity, with 13 Shi'a, 5 Sunni, 5 Kurds, a Turkoman, and a Christian. The United States thus found itself in a marriage of convenience with Shi'a sectarian parties like SCIRI, which also maintained close ties to Iran. The two leading Kurdish parties, the KDP and PUK, were also prominent in the council.

While the transitional institutions of governance wrote a new constitution, civil war and state collapse loomed. While Shi'a and Kurdish political factions had come to Baghdad in triumph following Saddam's downfall, for Sunni Iraqis the situation was very different. The dismantling of the Iraqi army, the purging of Ba'th officials, and other measures meant to demonstrate a clean break from the Saddam era seemed punitive. In total, some 450,000 military and security personnel and 50,000 party members were put out of work – some of the best trained and most competent personnel within Iraq. Teachers, journalists, and doctors were dismissed, despite the fact that many had joined the party as a means for advancement, not out of loyalty to Saddam. The dissolution of the Iraqi army was especially damaging. Disgruntled officers and soldiers who returned to their homes without even a ceremonial dismissal or discharge formed a ready pool of recruits for the insurgency that would envelop Iraq in the coming years.

By the late summer of 2003, a full-blown insurgency had emerged in Sunni areas of the north and west. The insurgents targeted US forces and suspected Iraqi collaborators. On August 29, 2003, a suicide bomber killed a senior Shi'a cleric and head of the SCIRI, as well as 84 others, in Najaf. The Sunni insurgency integrated many disparate elements: ex-Ba'th Party members and Saddam loyalists, Islamist extremists, and tribal militants. Probably the most aggressive element within the insurgency was Al-Qa'ida in Iraq (AQI), a branch of the international terrorist organization led locally by a Jordanian national, Abu Musab al-Zarqawi. Unlike some of the nationalist Ba'th factions, AQI perceived the turmoil in Iraq through distinctly sectarian lenses, seeing especially Iraqi Shi'a as heretics. AQI's strategy, then, was not just to attack American military targets but also Shi'a with the aim of provoking a violent response that would incite a regional sectarian war in which Sunni Arabs would eventually prevail. AQI was responsible for horrific bombings of international organizations, attacks on Shi'a shrines and mosques, and assassinations of many local and tribal leaders. The political agenda of the insurgency masked a more banal criminal element. With the dissolution of the army and police, villages, towns, and neighborhoods needed protection, which armed groups could provide in return for "taxation."

Violence also touched the Shi'a-dominated south. Several of the Shi'a exile groups entered Iraq with their own militia forces, including the Iranian-backed Badr Brigade, the arm wing of SCIRI. Paralleling the breakdown in order in Sunni areas, other armed groups emerged organically in Shi'a areas. Some of these were little more than extortion rackets and many were aligned with tribal leaders or religious authorities. The most significant of these was Jaysh al-Mahdi (the Army of the Messiah, or JAM) under the leadership of Muqtada al-Sadr. Though a junior cleric, Sadr hailed from a distinguished religious family, as his father had led Iraq's Shi'a during the difficult 1990s and was later assassinated. Sadr presented a particular expression of Iraqi nationalism that appealed especially to younger and poorer Shi'a. The JAM used force against rivals, but also eventually found ways to reconcile with other Shi'a factions and even establish a modus vivendi with American forces. With the installation of the Shi'a-dominated government in December 2005, the Badr Brigade and JAM became virtual auxiliaries of the Ministry of Interior and police forces. The militias were involved in a campaign of illegal detention, torture, imprisonment, and assassination against suspected terrorists.

The US was disastrously unprepared for the responsibilities of occupying Iraq. With the state effectively fragmented, many civilians had little choice but to accept the protection of armed non-state actors linked to specific ethno-sectarian communities. American troops also leaned heavily upon heavy-handed tactics, including aerial bombardment and heavy weaponry, often resulting in significant collateral damage and further alienating Iraqis. Only in 2006 did the US begin to form a new counterinsurgency strategy by committing to a "surge" of troop deployments in critical areas, such as Baghdad and northern Iraq, and also reaching out to local communities to win their support. The most important of these latter efforts was the so-called Awakening movement that began in the Anbar region in western Iraq, which had been the deadliest province. US forces offered Sunni tribal sheikhs money and weaponry if they turned against the insurgent forces, as well as significant autonomy to rule their territories according to tribal custom, without interference from outside authorities. Though the insurgency was hence eventually contained by the late 2000s, civil violence was catastrophic. Iraqi Body Count, an NGO, estimated that more than 105,000 Iraqis were killed between 2003 and 2008. In addition, some 4,500 US, British, and allied troops were killed in action.

Iraq's democratic experiment came in the midst of this worsening violence. Not surprisingly, the elections in January 2005 for delegates to a constitutional assembly and in December 2005 for parliament – contests trumpeted internationally as the birth of Iraqi democracy – ran almost entirely along ethno-sectarian lines. Many Iraqis were wary of participating in an electoral process that might appear to legitimate the US invasion and occupation of Iraq. Yet Grand Ayatollah Ali Sistani, Iraq's pre-eminent Shi'a cleric, urged his followers to join in the electoral process and form a united political front. Iran, which had close ties to many Shi'a factions, also favored a unified Shi'a front. The United Iraqi Alliance (UIA) formed as a pan-Shi'a umbrella, consisting of the SCIRI (later renamed the Islamic Supreme Council of Iraq), Sadr's movement, Da'wa (Islamic Call), plus a number of smaller groups.

The UIA overwhelmingly won the January 2005 elections, taking 48 percent of the vote, giving it an untrammeled legislative majority. In December, in the mandatory new elections required by the ratification of the new constitution the previous October, the UIA list took 41 percent of the vote and 128 seats, still more than enough to form a majority coalition with the two largest Kurdish parties. By contrast, Iraq's Sunni Arab leaders had boycotted the January election, with little subsequent voice in drafting the constitution. The December 2005 elections featured some Sunni forces entering the political arena, but others remained adamantly opposed and supported the insurgency. As a result, the Sunni vote was divided. Some Sunnis supported parties like the Iraqi National List of Iyyad Allawi, a Shi'a Iraqi exile who had returned after the invasion with heavy American support but espoused a secular and unifying brand of Iraqi nationalism. Yet Allawi's coalition took only 25 seats in December out of the 230 up for contestation, reflecting that many Sunni Arabs instead gravitated to sectarian parties.

The electoral process, then, provided both a real democratic mandate and also deepened ethno-sectarian divisions. Iraq's first democratically elected prime minister was the UIA's Ibrahim al-Ja'afari, a leader of the Da'wa and another former exile. Al-Ja'afari was not only unable to stem the violence, but in many ways seemed to contribute to it. Individual ministries divided like spoils among the various UIA coalition parties. The ministry of interior was granted to SCIRI, which quickly went about installing its Badr Brigade militia as the country's security forces. The Badr, JAM and other pro-government militias help wage a "dirty war" against Sunnis. In May 2006, al-Ja'afari resigned in favor of Nouri al-Maliki, another Da'wa activist and exile. Maliki quickly began to consolidate control in his own hands. He personally assumed the portfolios for the defense and interior ministries, giving him direct control over Iraq's security and intelligence services. He created special brigades within the army as counterterrorism units, while the office of chief commander was moved to the prime minister's office and staffed with loyalists.

Maliki defined his premiership as necessary to ensure Iraq's security and stability. He turned on fellow Shi'a, using force against Sadr-associated militias in Baghdad and the south, but also sought to crush AQI and other Sunni insurgent groups. At the same time, Maliki's understanding of the rule of law was distinctly self-serving; corruption flourished as the government began to garner more oil revenues in its post-war recovery, while new anti-terrorism legislation was frequently turned against Sunni political rivals. Further, to the dismay of Kurds, Maliki had little regard for notions of federalism and power-sharing embedded in the 2005 constitution. Infighting caused the UIA alliance to splinter, with Maliki leading a reduced coalition called the State of Law (SoL). In the 2010 elections, Allawi's new political alliance, the Iraqi

National Movement, won a surprising but narrow victory in the popular vote, taking 24.7 percent of the vote and 91 parliamentary seats. Maliki's SoL was second with 24.2 percent and 89 seats. The closeness of the election precipitated nine months of political crisis, with Maliki using a number of constitutional and legal maneuvers to block Allawi from taking power. As it was, Maliki's SoL was better positioned to form a ruling coalition. With the support from the US and Iran, Maliki retained his premiership and effectively sidelined Allawi.

Meanwhile, the Kurdistan region was evolving to its own pace. The turmoil in southern and central Iraq contrasted with the relative peace and stability of the Kurdish north. The KDP and PUK had established a de facto government in Irbil in 1992, the Kurdish Regional Government (KRG); it had no formal legal standing, but still created its own parliament and national flag. It ran schools and organized security forces outside of Baghdad's control. While southern and central Iraq suffered sanctions, the Kurdistan region enjoyed some economic prosperity. Yet there were political divisions; for instance, right-leaning nationalists followed the KDP while more leftist-oriented, progressive figures joined the PUK. The KDP also drew most of its supporters from the more rural and mountainous northern and western areas of Kurdistan, while the PUK was centered in the more urbanized, less tribal, lowland areas of the east.

With Saddam's ouster, Kurdish leaders from both played a delicate role, with KDP's Barzani and PUK's Talabani serving initially in the US-backed governing council. The KDP and PUK, operating as a single block, also participated in the 2005 elections, while Kurdish *Peshmerga* (armed militia units) proved among the most competent elements in the Iraqi security forces. At the same time, Barzani demanded maximal autonomy for the KRG, suggesting that Kurdistan's attachment to Iraq was voluntary and contingent, despite pushback from Arab and minority Turkoman groups who accused the Kurds of trying to tip the demographic balance and Iraqi politicians who deemed these moves a prelude to secession. Sporadic violence erupted between various ethnic militias. The KRG also sought to have an independent conduit to Iraq's oil wealth, demanding the right to sell petroleum to outside buyers without permission from the central government in Baghdad. Over time, the KDP-PUK alliance would be strained as new Kurdish parties emerged in the northern political scene, but the one constant was the tug-of-war between Kurdish leaders desiring more autonomy and a Baghdad-based national government wary of secessionism and fragmentation.

ISIS and conflict, 2011–present

The outbreak of new protests linked to the 2011–12 Arab Spring belied the hope that Maliki's 2010 parliamentary victory heralded a turn toward "normal" democratic politics in Iraq. In Iraqi cities, citizens mobilized protests for the same issues found in other Arab countries – ending corruption, reducing repression, and demanding economic opportunities. While these were mostly peaceful, elsewhere the remnants of AQI were reconstituting themselves in western Iraq in the Anbar area to form the basis of the movement that would become the future Islamic State of Iraq and Syria (ISIS). They exploited local networks, including smuggling operations and extorting from local officials, to quickly aggregate resources to recruit new members, playing on the grievances of Sunni Iraqis who felt marginalized by the larger power struggles in Baghdad as played out by Shi'a groups, Sunni elites, and Kurdish parties.

The Syrian civil war gave these armed factions a safe haven, enabling the formal creation of ISIS in April 2013. ISIS became an existential threat to Iraq. Its leader, Abu Bakr al-Baghdadi, was a Sunni Iraqi who declared himself Caliph. While ISIS' core was made up of local Iraqi and Syrian fighters, ISIS also attracted foreign volunteers from across the world, including both Arab countries and the West. By early 2014, ISIS had come to control Anbar. By that summer, ISIS' forces, consisting of 30,000 fighters, launched a broad offensive. Infused with experienced former military and Ba'th officers, they overcame weak Iraqi military and security forces to take Tikrit and then Mosul, Iraq's second largest city. By the end of the year, ISIS controlled the upper reaches of both the Tigris and Euphrates rivers north of Baghdad and thus well into Iraq's central heartland. In areas of conquest, ISIS rule was horrific; local units massacred Shi'a, Yezidi Iraqis, and other communities they considered as infidel (*kafir*), while women were sold into sexual slavery. ISIS leaders took on state-like functions, operating their own courts, police, and tax collection, while oil smuggling provided a stream of outside income.

In Baghdad, Maliki's ruling coalition won a decisive electoral victory in April 2014, but struggled to develop a strategy against ISIS. The turning point occurred when Ayatollah Sistani called upon Shi'a volunteers to defend the country, effectively reviving pro-government militias like the Badr Brigade and JAM. These forces, organized as the Popular Mobilization Units (PMU), protected central and southern areas of Iraq with support from Iran. Meanwhile, Kurdish forces mobilized in the north to occupy positions abandoned by the Iraqi army, while the US offered air strikes and on-ground military assistance, though it remained wary about openly collaborating with Iran. In August 2014, Maliki stepped down from the premiership under pressure from the US, Iran, and many internal political factions; his replacement was another former Da'wa exile, Haydar al-'Abadi, who maneuvered his government closer to Iran and Russia while still accepting American assistance in the campaign against ISIS. On the ground, Iranian contributors, Kurdish units, and rejuvenated Iraqi forces began pushing back, resulting in slow and plodding battles that saw grotesque human rights violations on all sides. Still, Mosul was recaptured in July 2017, effectively ending ISIS' reign in Iraq.

Normal politics did not return, however. Corruption flourished under 'Abadi's leadership, and reconciliation between sectarian political forces did not occur despite collective relief that ISIS had been defeated. The May 2018 general elections hence were a popular referendum on the efficacy of Iraq's squabbling political elites. Though some expected PMU candidates to ascend, surprisingly the list put forth by the Sadrist movement, the Alliance Towards Reform (informally known in Arabic as *Sa'irun*) won a plurality of seats (54 out of 329), with the Iran-backed PMU list, the Conquest Alliance, finishing a close second. The Sadrist alliance mixed appeals to Iraqi nationalism with promises to crack down on corruption and reduce unemployment, which resonated among younger Shi'a Iraqis who had become disaffected by the remote struggles of Shi'a elite politicians.

The technocratic Adil 'Abd al-Mahdi became prime minister, but immediately struggled to deal with competing geopolitical pressures as American demands for scaling back Iranian influence squared off against Tehran's wishes for continued involvement. After decades of near-constant conflict and turmoil, the Iraqi economy and fractured society also required urgent attention in terms of restoring services, boosting growth, and securing popular trust in a country that had become accustomed to factionalism. Developments in the Kurdish north also worried Baghdad, as a victorious Barzani – building off his success in battling ISIS – conducted a referendum on Kurdish independence in September 2017, and claimed that 90 percent of voters favored secession. The Iraqi government responded by blockading Kurdistan, sending troops toward the disputed Kirkuk zone while cutting off its regional budget. Iran, Turkey, and the United States all voiced support for Iraq's territorial integrity and sent troops to secure the border, resulting in the forced stand-down of Peshmerga forces and ultimately the resignation of Barzani from the Kurdistan presidency.

SOCIAL AND ECONOMIC ENVIRONMENT

Iraq's nearly 40 million people live in a country spread out over nearly 169,000 square miles (437,072 square kilometers). It features four different geographic terrains – western desert, the mountainous highlands in the north, the fertile Tigris and Euphrates river basin in the center, and the flatlands extending from the central river basin to the Arabian Gulf. Its largest cities are Baghdad, the capital; Basra, in the south; and Mosul, Irbil, and Kirkuk in the north (Map 13.1). Basra is Iraq's primary port and oil hub,

MAP 13.1

Republic of Iraq. Major water bodies, rivers, and cities shown.

Source: D-Maps.

as it abuts the Gulf, while Irbil serves as the capital of the Kurdish Regional Government. Najaf is a significant southern city and a Shi'a religious center.

Social currents

Since the establishment of the Iraqi state in 1920, ethnic, sectarian, and tribal loyalties have all seemed to undermine the effort to build a coherent, unified national identity. Yet the salience of these cleavages has not been constant. Other notions of political belonging associated with class, gender, and alternative affiliations are also present and, in some instances, override these primordial ties. Common economic and political experiences historically have helped foster a sense of Iraqi national identity, although not always the one that the state itself wished to promote.

About three-quarters of Iraq's population is Arab, and Arabic is the language spoken virtually exclusively from southern Basra to the northern Mosul plains. Iraqi Arabs of the center and south are themselves divided along a major sectarian fault line – Sunni and Shi'a. Shi'a Arabs comprise the majority of the population (around 65 percent), and mostly inhabit the area from Baghdad south to the Shatt al-Arab, where the Euphrates and Tigris converge upon the Arabian Gulf. This is the most densely populated section of the country, and includes the cities of Najaf and Karbala. These hold important Shi'a shrines and seminaries, and are historically important to the wider Shi'a world. As the Shi'a of Iraq were systematically disenfranchised under the Ottoman rule and under the Sunni Arab autocracies that followed, the Shi'a south tended be more rural and agricultural, with lower levels of development. From the 1940s to the 1960s many Shi'as were drawn to the Iraqi Communist Party, which offered a voice of protest against inequality. In the 1960s and 1970s, new Islamist movements began to gain traction among the Shi'a, including the Da'wa movement of Ayatollah Muhammed Baqr al-Sadr, and the Supreme Council for the Islamic Revolution in Iraq (now known as the Islamic Supreme Council in Iraq, or ISCI). The impetus of Shi'a politics in Iraq has never been self-determination, like the Kurds, but for political representation commensurate with their status as the demographic majority.

Sunni Arabs constitute roughly 20 percent of the Iraqi population. For more than four hundred years of Ottoman, British, and Arab rule, they dominated the military and political life of the country. Under Saddam, they constituted a majority in the officer corps and the upper echelons of the Ba'th Party. They benefited disproportionately from modernization and education and, as a consequence, tended towards more secular attitudes. In the 1990s and especially after 2003, Islamism has become more prominent among Sunni Arabs, and on the radical side, Salafi-jihadi groups embracing violence have thrived among disenfranchised Sunni Arab communities.

Kurdish Iraqis are mostly Sunni but not Arab, and represent around 15–20 percent of the national population. State authorities have always had difficulty controlling the mountains of the Kurdistan region given the distance, clan politics, and collective identity of many Kurdish communities. A notable Kurdish minority is the Yazidi people, who do not follow an Abrahamic religion (and were mistreated harshly by ISIS for it). Under recent pressures from war, economic development, and land reform during the twentieth century, Kurdish society changed drastically. In the 1970s and 1980s Saddam forcibly resettled or destroyed many Kurdish communities and encouraged Arab transmigration to the north to shift the demographic balance. Since 2003, when such systematic persecution ended, Kurds have been moving into Kirkuk, Mosul, and other northern cities outside the KRG's zone of control. Though many Kurds are still engaged in agriculture, a strong urban, educated class has thus emerged, fueling the KDP, PUK, and other Kurdish parties.

Besides Shi'a Arab, Sunni Arab, and Kurds there are a number of smaller, politically consequential minority groups representing 5 percent of the national body. Turkomans are a Turkic people in the north who follow Sunni Islam and descend from Ottoman settlers. In the south, Persian (Iranian) speakers have historically had a strong presence in the seminary cities of Najaf and Karbala. Saddam expelled Iranian nationals in the 1970s and 1980s, but many have returned since 2003. Finally, Iraq has a variety of Christian sects, including Chaldeans, Assyrians, Armenians, and Greek Orthodox. The Sabaeans, a pre-Christian group, live in the south. Iraq had a large and flourishing Jewish community during the Ottoman and British mandatory era, but most emigrated to Israel by the 1950s.

Iraq's social structure

Traditionally, Iraqi society was characterized by a pronounced dichotomy between rural society, organized for the most part by tribes, and urban life. Since 1950, this gap has been greatly narrowed by mass urbanization, the spread of education and health services to rural areas, and the emergence of an educated middle class. In the 1950s, about 70 percent of the population lived in rural communities; by 2012, the proportion was reversed in favor of cities. Rural agricultural areas continue to remain much poorer than most cities, but conditions have improved since colonial times, when a few land-lords and tribal leaders controlled large portions of the farmland and peasants were virtual serfs. Successive land-reform measures eliminated most of this landlord class and gradually extended landownership to a class of small and middle-level farmers. Yet Saddam's skewed modernization programs, which favored industrial development and investment in Sunni Arab areas, and long years under economic sanctions and oil-for-food programs mismanaged by the Ba'th regime, had a devastating impact on life.

The expansion of education significantly affected Iraq's social structure. Elementary education was available to virtually all Iraqi children. High schools graduated students in the hundreds of thousands, colleges and universities in the tens of thousands. Over time, Iraq produced one of the Arab world's largest professional classes, including scientific and technocratic elites. Along with a middle class came an urban working class, particularly in the oil and industrial sectors located in Baghdad and Basra. Under the Ba'th, much of Iraq's urban classes worked, and still do, for the government as industrial employees, teachers, bureaucrats, and army officers.

Beginning in the 1990s and accelerating since 2003, religion has played a much more significant role in Iraqi society, especially in shaping governance, civil society, and education. In post-Saddam Iraq, clerics from both sects wield significant influence. In addition to religion, family, clan, and tribal ties have always been strong as well, particularly in the Kurdish north. As bureaucratic structures and civil society eroded under the impact of wars and sanctions, Iraqis' reliance on tribal and family ties grew stronger. Despite regime change and the introduction of democratic institutions and processes, political life and social security remain essentially tribal and family centered, resulting in patterns of kinship and patronage that are often at odds with liberal democratic norms.

Women and youth

In the 1970s and 1980s, the Ba'th government tried to portray itself as progressive on issues of women's rights in a familiar pattern seen elsewhere in the Arab world – state feminism in the service of authoritarianism. Iraqi women held a wider range of freedoms and opportunities than their counterparts in many other Arab countries, particularly the Gulf. They were entitled to education and to work outside the home; polygamy was banned in 1978. By the mid-1980s, about a third of all high school and 30 percent of university students were women. Yet at the same time, the Ba'th rulership (particularly during the Saddam period) remained animated by patriarchal norms as well. The regime forbade and dissolved marriages to Persians, and used sexual violence, including rape, as part of its effort to intimidate and subjugate suspected regime opponents.

The post-2003 era saw continued tensions between traditional and more progressive attitudes toward women. Thanks to the 2005 constitution and the female quota in parliament, at least one-quarter of legislative seats are required to be held by women, but most parties and government institutions feature few senior female politicians. In addition, reversing Ba'th-era policies, personal status laws in post-Saddam Iraq restrict women's inheritance and rights to child custody. Even more significantly, the breakdown in social order after the US invasion led to dramatic increases in rape and sexual assaults. Women were often forced to rely on male kin for protection and became even more sequestered in the home. ISIS also readily deployed sexual violence as part of its military strategy, as did its Iraqi opponents. Female literacy in Iraq today is just 76 percent, well below past levels, while just 13 percent of women enter the workforce.

Youth currents are evolving. As in many Arab countries, traditional modes of religious and tribal authority in Iraq favor elders over youth. The longevity of leadership and the rarity of retirement compounds this tendency. Many of Iraq's contemporary political leadership were born in the middle part of the twentieth century, and gained seniority quickly within the exiled political movements of the 1970s and 1980s. Upon coming to power after 2003, however, they crowded politics and created a logjam at the top of the political system. Iraq's prime ministers have been senior figures who came of political age decades ago, and wage nepotistic battles that often alienate young voters. The gerontocratic tendency is especially visible in Kurdistan, as the senior leadership of the KDP under Barzani and PUK under Talabani have been fixed in place for several decades.

This has made some young Iraqis a strong social base for political mobilization. For instance, the Sadrist movement gained significant electoral support by appealing to younger Iraqis, while in Kurdistan, new opposition parties and protest groups have emerged, fueled by young urbanized Kurdish activists. Overall, however, youth apathy is a major reason why turnout has declined in Iraqi elections; the 2018 general contest, for instance, featured just 44.5 percent turnout, well below the 60.5 percent figure in 2014. Compounding matters is economic difficulty. Youth unemployment in 2019 reached nearly 17 percent, more than double the national jobless rate of 7.9 percent, and young Iraqis were a major driver behind the 2011–12 protests during Iraq's version of the Arab Spring. Youth literacy runs about 81 percent today, on par with the adult literacy rate – among the lowest figures in the Arab world, and one that reflects nearly two decades of destruction to educational systems by war and violence.

Economic forces

Like Algeria, Libya, and the Gulf kingdoms, Iraq is a rentier state. Oil revenues have been the dominant feature in Iraq's economy since the 1950s. Iraq has at least 140 billion barrels of proven crude oil reserves, making it fifth in terms of global supply behind Venezuela, Saudi Arabia, Canada, and Iran. About 90 percent of the oil fields are located in the south, near Basra, and 10 percent in the north around Kirkuk and other Kurdish areas. After the nationalization of the British-run oil industry in the 1960s, Iraqi political rulers had the resources to foster and direct long-term development, such as irrigation systems to transform feudal agrarian lifestyles as well as create new schools, hospitals, and industries. Thus, hydrocarbon rents fueled state-led development. After the 1958 revolution, development planners adopted heavy industry, collective farming, and state management. Though publicly avowing socialist ideals, Saddam's regime partially loosened government controls and encouraged private investment in agriculture, commerce, and light industry. The conversion to a market economy was only partial, however, as it also refused to allow foreign private investment, preferring to hire foreign firms to undertake projects that were turned over to the government upon completion.

In the sanctions regime of the 1990s, oil revenues declined and the oil sector itself suffered from lack of investment, further compounding a drop in government revenue. After 2003, the oil sector recovered, though not consistently given the frequent interruptions of violence, insurgency, and civil war. As of 2019, hydrocarbon export revenues compose 38 percent of GDP, one of the highest ratios in the MENA. However, with wealth has come problems. Rent-seeking behavior abounds, as political factions vie to control resources and distribute revenues, mostly for their own benefit and that of their supporters. Corruption is pervasive in many government ministries. Another major stumbling block remains in the question of ownership of the oil itself. The 2005 constitution left control of already discovered and exploited resources in the hands of the federal government, while the provincial governments "own" all new and unexploited oil. Thus, the central government and the KRG have seen a protracted disagreement over control of the northern oil fields. Escalating oil production has intensified this dispute, as overall crude production doubled over the 2010s, reaching 4.5 million barrels per day in 2019 and giving the government a rare gift – a massive budget surplus. Partly due to this steady stream of income, the Iraqi economy has grown by an annual average rate of 6.2 percent between 2011 and 2018, an impressive figure given the carnage occurring in some areas.

While oil is certainly the most lucrative segment of Iraq's economy, other productive sectors exist, including textiles, construction, food processing, and light manufacturing. Agriculture composes less than 5 percent of GDP, but was the mainstay of local communities for millennia. In northern Iraq, there is enough rainfall to permit "wet" farming. In the arid south, agriculture has always depended on irrigation derived from the flows of the Tigris and Euphrates rivers. Through the 1950s, Iraq was able not only to feed itself but also to export wheat and barley, although most of the profits went to wealthy landlords rather than to cultivators. The political instability of the post-1958 era, as well as many ill-conceived and poorly executed land-redistribution schemas, damaged this once thriving sector. Water shortages constitute a major ecological threat, as the Tigris and Euphrates rivers and their tributaries emerge in the highlands of Turkey, Syria, and Iran before reaching Iraq. International tensions have arisen periodically over who has control and the right to use these waters. Drought, particularly in the late 2000s, further threatens agricultural productivity.

Most analysts conclude that Iraq's economic future depends on human, not natural (including oil), resources. In the 1950s to 1970s, Iraq had one of the best-educated populations in the Arab world. Standards of living, including crucial measures like infant mortality and life expectancy, improved dramatically. A middle class, mainly comprised of civil servants and others connected to government service, emerged, albeit tethered to the Ba'th Party. War, sanctions, and occupation badly degraded these accomplishments, however. The quality of public infrastructure, including schools, universities, hospitals, and sanitation and public health measures, declined dramatically starting in the 1990s. Iraq experienced a brain drain, as those with education and training emigrated, particularly during the post-2003 insurgency and civil conflict. Nearly two million Iraqis had fled the country by the late 2000s to neighboring countries, though some have since returned. Still, despite rampant corruption, mismanagement, and violence, a new class of young professionals has emerged, authoring creative trends and at the forefront of new media, civil society organizations, and activism. It remains to be seen if they can transform an elite-driven political system within a rentier economy.

POLITICAL STRUCTURES

Iraq's 2005 constitution contains many important tenets consistent with democratic values and practices. Drafted with heavy American input and creating a federal governmental system, it guarantees equality without regard to gender, sect, opinion, belief, nationality, religion, or origin. It also recognizes that Iraq is a country of many nationalities and guarantees that Iraqis can educate their children in their own language in state and private schools. Arabic and Kurdish hold special status as recognized languages. Institutionally, it specifies a separation of powers between the legislative, executive, and judicial branches. The parliament selects a prime minister to serve as head of the government and elects the president and two deputies from among its ranks to serve as heads of state, a largely ceremonial role. Equally important given Iraq's history of coups, military personnel are banned from political office and activity. The armed forces and intelligence services are under civilian control.

Iraq is defined as a federal state, and its provinces have significant authority to tax and administrate. The Kurdish Regional Government is granted even greater autonomy, and to date represents the most realistic option for Kurdish statehood across the MENA. The Kurdish government has retained the right to maintain the Peshmerga as its own military force (Photo 13.1). The Peshmerga (which in Kurdish translates, roughly, into "those who face death") were particularly effective in battle against ISIS, even employing female fighters, though they have also struggled with growing corruption and infighting.

The federal government in Baghdad has limited powers: it can promulgate foreign, diplomatic, economic, trade, and debt policies, but it does not have authority to tax. The management of the country's natural resources and distribution of its revenues fall under federal authority, but a distinction is made between "old" resources (already discovered and exploited), which come under federal authority, and "new" oil and gas resources, which are to come under provincial authority. By law, Iraqi provinces have the option to vote to merge and create a regional government comparable to the KRG. In practice, the federal authorities in Iraq, driven by the elite-based parties and movements, have tried to hamper efforts to exercise provincial autonomy, especially as it pertains to the largely Sunni provinces in the north.

Informal arrangements also help maintain ethno-sectarian power-sharing. Since 2005, every prime minister has been Shi'a, but a Sunni or a Kurd

PHOTO 13.1
Kurdish Peshmerga fighters in Northern Iraq.

Source: Photo by Kurdishstruggle, Flickr.

has been deputy prime minister; the president has been a Kurd, with a Shiʻa and Sunni Arab deputy; the speaker of the parliament has been a Sunni, with a Kurdish and Shiʻa Arab deputy. In addition, the Iraqi unicameral parliament also guarantees eight seats for minorities, including five for Christians. Such implicit consociationalism lightly mirrors the Lebanese model. This arrangement of deputies from different communities is likewise mirrored in most ministries, and it often requires delicate negotiations and tact. For instance, in 2010, a new electoral law increased the number of seats in parliament from its previous total of 275, allocated on the basis of the estimated number of voters in each province and abroad. However, a new census, necessary to determine the population in each province and mandated by the constitution, has been postponed until 2020, largely because political factions cannot agree on when or how this should be done.

Elections and parties

Iraq's democratic system, though imperfect, has been slowly moving on the trajectory for consolidation. Between 1932 and 2003, no ruler of Iraq left office without bloodshed. Since then, there have been three peaceful transitions of power, each abiding more or less to democratic principles of alternating parties through constitutional stricture.

The national elections that take place across the 18 governorates have used an open-list electoral ballot since 2009, meaning that voters choose a party but can rank their choices of candidates within that party's electoral slate. The 2005 election used a closed-list system in which voters chose only a party. This latter system placed inordinate amount of power in the party leaders, and the rule was changed following criticism from international electoral experts. The party system itself is fluid and fragmented; coalitions of different factions form, merge, dissolve, and change names quickly. Besides personality of their leaders, the parties are mainly characterized by their appeal to ethno-sectarian groups and by their attitudes on federalism. Alliances between parties form when regional-specific parties join with larger national parties on a common electoral list or in alliances. Once candidates from these parties are voted into office, further alliances result in the ruling majority coalition in parliament.

In Iraq's transitional year of 2005, political parties were largely a proxy for ethno-sectarian affiliation. Among Shi'a-dominated actors, fractiousness began after a brief period of initial unity. The UIA, formed at the behest of Grand Ayatollah Ali Sistani, basically represented all the Shi'a-affiliated parties and won both the 2005 elections. Sistani did not want the Shi'a to squander the opportunity to shape Iraqi politics, so he both urged the masses to participate and urged major Shi'a parties to form a unified front. Sistani's intervention was crucial to legitimizing the electoral process in Iraq, but also made electoral competition from the very start into a proxy for ethno-sectarian identities, amplified by a proliferation of new actors.

The UIA fractured in the late 2000s into its constituent Islamist networks, each with their own patrons, supporters, and personalities. By the 2018 elections, this had produced a confusing and sometimes overlapping constellation of forces. One major party is Da'wa, originally founded in 1970 as an underground Shi'a Islamist group. It drove the creation of the SoL coalition in 2009, helping that front garner 89 seats in the 2010 elections, but by 2018 it had split, with some staying with SoL and others driving forward the new Victory Alliance. Yet another is the ISCI (formerly SCIRI), which is rooted in southern Iraq and operates the Badr Brigade; it broke off from the SoL coalition in 2017, in favor of its successful Conquest Alliance for the 2018 elections. A third is the Sadrist movement. Led by Muqtada al-Sadr, and the progenitor of the JAM forces that clashed with occupying US troops and then ISIS, the Sadrists mobilize much popularity from poor disenfranchised youths in the south. In the 2018 general elections, it led its own alliance, Sa'irun (Alliance Towards Reform), that won the most seats – mostly due to their fierce criticism of corruption and economic conditions, but partly due to improbable alliances made with the non-Islamist ICP.

On the Sunni side, a visible force is the National Coalition, or Wataniyyah. Affiliated with former Prime Minister Iyyad Allawi, this gathering won the 2010 general elections but has since faded, despite securing support from many Sunni Arab groups. Those Sunni parties are small, and include Hiwar (Iraqi National Dialogue Front), the Muttahidun (United for Reform), the Iraqi Islamic Party (linked to the Muslim Brotherhood), several tribal-based factions, and the Iraqi Turkoman Front. Finally, similar to the breakdown of the UIA alliance, the unified Kurdish list that ran in 2005 has fractured, as the KDP and PUK competed for more power. In response to public discontent in Kurdish areas with their duopoly, new parties, like the Gorran (Change) Movement, have coalesced.

POLITICAL DYNAMICS

Iraq's political system is often classified as hybrid given its conflicting dynamics: while democratic in design and girded by an explicit constitutional framework, the frequency of violence and feckless pluralism have often hindered effective governance, protection, and participation for much of the populace.

Much like Libya, the future of Iraqi democracy turns on a more fundamental dimension – state capacity, defined as the ability of the central state apparatus to exert its writ across the national territory. Rulers like Saddam justified their authoritarian style precisely because of the need to build state capacity: only an autocrat could deal with the myriad challenges facing Iraq. The country, according to them, needed to raise an army to suppress sectarian tensions and combat regional rivals. It needed a bureaucracy to build roads, schools, hospitals, and other institutions necessary for economic growth. It had to overcome embedded tribal and ethno-sectarian divisions and cultivate a sense of Iraqi nationalism. Since 2003, though, Iraqis have wagered that an inclusive political system can solve the problems of state-building that its previous dictatorship left unresolved. However, the lack of state capacity continues to undercut the functioning of Iraqi democracy, particularly as security challenges from internal unrest and violence expose the vulnerability of many communities. In plain terms, there cannot be participatory elections and peaceful competition if voters cannot vote and institutions cannot function.

Since 2003, Iraq's security and military forces have struggled to overcome internal rivals. Pitted against the "official" coercive organs of the state, the various militias, brigades, and movements run by Sunni, Shi'a, Kurdish, and other sectarian actors have often proved to be superior in terms of commitment and strategy. Worsening matters, foreign powers have intervened, sponsoring armed groups as local proxies within Iraq. As a result, Iraqi leaders have resorted to extraordinary measures to maintain order, such as recruiting those same militias to defeat threats like ISIS, and resorting to dictatorial measures such as secret detention facilities and torture to quieten dissent. Just like Saddam, Iraqi leaders well into the 2010s have justified these tactics as necessary to preserve and enhance public order. But these measures not only weaken democracy, they also weaken the state; for instance, recruiting militias to fight insurgents has made the task of building an effective and professional army less urgent.

The tensions between state control and democracy are also evident in broader patterns of economic growth and development in Iraq. In a state lacking a strong bureaucratic culture or effective monitoring and oversight agencies, problems like corruption, bribery, and nepotism are pervasive. Petty bribes permeate everyday life, affecting how people get jobs and positions at universities, start businesses, and buy or sell property. At the higher echelons, Iraqi politicians are renowned for taking kickbacks and peddling influence, particularly within sectarian hierarchies in which notables (such as party leaders and clan notables) have no recourse outside their community. For that reason, Iraq has consistently been criticized by monitors such as Transparency International and the World Bank for its corruption. Many Iraqis now see these practices, broadly understood as part of the culture of *wasta* (favoritism or connection), as essential for their personal survival. That bribery allows a certain measure of commerce to occur dampens the need for political reform or building new forms of civic national identity.

One factor that could improve matters is civil society, but this arena remains fragile. Emerging from the degradation of the Saddam era in 2003, Iraq saw a veritable efflorescence of local non-governmental organizations. Between 8,000 and 12,000 were registered in the immediate post-2003 years, and some hoped that these NGOs would form the kernel for a strengthened Iraqi national identity and sense of civic pride. Many of these have ties to specific political actors or sectarian blocs, but also provide services, from humanitarian relief to loans and education. The larger national organizations, such as the Bar Association and student unions, also incubate internal politics that can express both the best (e.g., peaceful competition) and worst (e.g., violence) of post-war Iraq.

In sum, Iraq is caught in a vicious cycle typical in many developing societies. While nearly all aspire to create a high-capacity and democratic state in the long term, expediency and necessity dictate practices that undermine state capacity and short-circuit democracy. While its institutions and structures intend to produce a federal democracy, in practice something else has emerged – not quite authoritarian, often burdened with corruption and violence, and open-ended as to the future.

FOREIGN POLICY

The historical pathway of Iraq's foreign policy has been defined by a curious kind of inversion also found in other countries in strategic positions across the MENA. Political elites often needed support from outside powers to protect their position and counterbalance internal opposition. In turn, outside powers viewed Iraqi factions as proxies in their own bids for regional hegemony. Thus, when Iraq's monarchy aligned with Great Britain and the United States at the height of the Cold War, Iraqi opposition factions tended to favor the Soviet Union. After the 1958 overthrow, various Iraqi leaders began to tilt toward the Soviet Union while Kurdish factions built alliances with the US, Israel, and Iran.

The Saddam era saw multiple and bold foreign policy moves, as well as disastrous blunders. Iraqi foreign policy under Saddam expressed a wider ambition to lead the Arab world and to buck international opinion when necessary. Internal weaknesses involving latent ethnic and sectarian schisms were never far from regime considerations; indeed, the decisions to invade Iran in 1980 and Kuwait in 1991 were driven in part by fear that outside powers would exploit Iraq's societal differences to weaken or even dismember the country. At the same time, Saddam believed Iraq could endorse a grander vision of Arabism against Iran, Israel, and Turkey while securing more economic and territorial resources. During the 1990s, Iraq suffered the US-imposed label of being a "rogue" state, alongside Libya under Qaddafi, Iran, and, outside the MENA, Cuba and North Korea, due to the Iraqi regime's stubbornness regarding disarmament as well as ongoing human rights abuses. As a result, Iraqi foreign relations suffered greatly in the years prior to the 2003 invasion, as much of the West and other parts of the global system shunned Iraq (and, by mandatary sanctions, its oil exports).

The removal of Saddam and Ba'th rule precipitated a definitive reorientation in Iraq's foreign policy. The US had hoped that a democratic and secular Iraq would serve as a bulwark against Iran and catalyze political reform within the Arab world. Yet many of Iraq's neighbors were skeptical, and held conspiratorial perspectives on American motivations. Arab states, particularly Jordan, Egypt, and the Gulf kingdoms, were wary of removing an important pillar of the Arab state system – that is, a Sunni regime that flanked Iranian ambitions westward. Dominated by Shi'a and Kurdish forces, they feared that a post-Saddam Iraq would not even continue to consider itself an Arab state so much as a pro-Iranian Shi'a one, or perhaps multiple fragments of a formerly unified state wracked by discord and strife. Turkey, too, hesitated to support the US invasion for fear that Kurdish separatists in Iraq would embolden its own Kurdish militants. Iran likewise feared that the 2003 war was part of a grander strategy to encircle it, especially given that American forces were already operating in neighboring Afghanistan.

Once installed in power through electoral victories, Iraq's coalition governments – being dominated by various Shi'a parties and groups – indeed turned toward Tehran, resulting in a dramatic warming of relations and raising Western fears about the rise of a new Shi'a "crescent" that would encircle Sunni Arab allies like Jordan and Saudi Arabia. Iran's government had nurtured close ties with many Shi'a movements that emerged in the political arena, so such permeation was to be expected. At the same time, no Iraqi government or prime minister has espoused a foreign policy where Iraq serves as a glorified client state to a hegemonic Iran. Rather, they have sought to reverse Saddam's belligerent legacy and instead cultivate close financial, cultural, and diplomatic ties with its neighbor. In turn, that backing has netted Iraq considerable logistical and military support from Iran during its campaign against ISIS, which the US and Sunni Arab neighbors begrudgingly accepted given their preference for a pro-Iranian Iraqi state over one run by ISIS.

Yet for all its tilt towards Iran, Iraq remained dependent upon the US for various economic, military, and diplomatic resources after 2003, and particularly during the instability and civil conflict of the post-Arab Spring era. Through the early 2010s, Iraq remained one of the top recipients of American foreign aid, while its post-war years were characterized by welcome generosity by the World Bank and major economic powers in terms of debt cancellation and loan facilities to enable reconstruction. Further, though the US shuttered much of its formal military infrastructure in the country after

2011, when the Obama administration pulled out most American forces, US firepower in the form of air strikes and other interventions proved essential for the campaign against ISIS. As of 2019, thousands of US troops – primarily Special Forces units and other irregular operators – continued to operate in Iraqi territory, enjoying particularly cooperative receptions in the Kurdish north. Despite enmity from the Iraqi Sunni and Shi'a publics, and rhetoric showings of anti-Western sentiment periodically from the government, Iraqi policymakers are resigned to their continued reliance upon American interventionism given that the extant political structure was entirely birthed through a US-led war.

FUTURE PROSPECTS

Given its lack of state capacity, does Iraq have a future? Thus far, a number of factors have helped keep Iraq together, not least the interests of the international community in keeping Iraq intact. Whether its democratically designed (but often problematically executed) political system is one of them remains to be seen. The succession of authoritarian leadership in Iraq that lasted from its imperial conception until Saddam's ouster depended on overwhelming force to keep the state intact. Elections and political competition, however, have become typified by tenacious pluralism and endemic corruption cut along sectarian disputes – disharmony that has instigated periods of extreme violence, from the post-war insurgency to the rise of ISIS.

At the same time, slower-moving societal changes are also at play. Though no ethnic and sectarian group may have felt particular allegiance to Iraq in 1920, the country's inhabitants have been living as Iraqis for nearly a century now. They went to Iraqi schools, were conscripted into the Iraqi army, used Iraqi currency, and traveled on Iraqi passports. They suffered through wars and sanctions together. Some have argued that these collective experiences have built up a sense of national identity that supersedes parochial affiliation, notwithstanding the persistence of Kurdish demands for more autonomy in the northern region. Ultimately, much of Iraq's future depends on the interests and abilities of Iraqi politicians. For better or worse, they act as politicians do everywhere: they argue, complain, compromise, prevaricate, and try to avoid public scrutiny. Through this bluster, Iraqi politicians could well find circuitous and ingenious means to manage or resolve seemingly intractable conflicts, so long as they also maintain the necessary security and order to allow Iraqis to feel more closely connected to their state.

FURTHER READING

The most comprehensive studies of Iraq's modern history are found in Phebe Marr, *The Modern History of Iraq*, 4th ed. (Routledge, 2017); Charles Tripp, *A History of Iraq*, 3rd ed. (Cambridge University Press, 2007); and Adeed Dawisha, *Iraq: A Political History* (Princeton University Press, 2011).

For the period between the world wars, see Toby Dodge's study *Inventing Iraq: The Failure of Nation Building and a History Denied* (Columbia University Press, 2003); and Reeva S. Simon, *The Creation of Iraq, 1914–1921* (Columbia University Press, 2004). A sharply critical study of Iraq under the Ba'th is found in Marion Farouk-Sluglett and Peter Sluglett, *Iraq since 1958: From Revolution to Dictatorship* (IB Tauris, 2001). Kanan Makiya wrote two brilliant but polemical depictions of the Ba'th: *Republic of Fear* (University of California Press, 1989) and *Cruelty and Silence* (Norton, 1993). For a critique of this literature with the advantage of hindsight, see Achim Rohde, *State-Society Relations in Ba'thist Iraq: Facing Dictatorship* (Routledge, 2010).

A number of recent works have taken advantage of Ba'th archives made available after the 2003 war to gain unprecedented perspectives on the inner workings of Saddam's regime. These include Kevin Woods, David E. Palkki, and Mark Stout, eds., *The Saddam Tapes: The Inner Workings of a Tyrant's Regime, 1978–2001* (Cambridge University Press, 2011); Joseph Sassoon, *Saddam Hussein's Ba'th Party: Inside an Authoritarian Regime* (Cambridge University Press, 2011); Dina Rizk Khoury, *Iraq in Wartime: Soldiering, Martyrdom, and Remembrance* (Cambridge University Press, 2013); Amatzia Baram, *Saddam Husayn and Islam, 1968–2003: Ba'thi Iraq from Secularism to Faith* (Johns Hopkins University Press, 2014); Aaron Faust, *The Ba'thification of Iraq: Saddam Hussein's Totalitarianism* (University of Texas Press, 2015); and Lisa Blaydes, *State of Repression: Iraq under Saddam Hussein* (Princeton University Press, 2018).

On Iraq's social and political structure, nothing compares to Hanna Batatu's monumental *The Old Social Classes and the Revolutionary Movements of Iraq* (Princeton University Press, 1978). Elizabeth Fernea draws a compelling picture of life in a poor southern village in the 1950s in *Guests of the Sheikh* (Hale, 1968). Two noteworthy studies of the Kurds are David McDowall's *The Modern History of the Kurds* (IB Tauris, 1997); and Denise Natali, *Kurdish Quasi-State: Development and Dependency in Post-Gulf War Iraq* (Syracuse University Press, 2010). The historical evolution of the Shi'a communities of Iraq are best addressed in Yitzhak Nakash, *The Shi'a of Iraq* (Princeton University Press, 1994); and Faleh Jabar, *The Shi'a Movement in Iraq* (Saqi, 2003).

Iraq's numerous wars have spawned a large number of studies with different foci. On the Iran-Iraq war, the best are Shahram Chubin and Charles Tripp, *Iran and Iraq at War* (Westview Press, 1988); Dilip Hiro, *The Longest War: The Iran-Iraq Military Conflict* (Routledge, 1991); and Williamson Murray and Kevin Woods, *The Iran-Iraq War: A Military and Strategic History* (Cambridge University Press, 2014). On the Kuwait war and its aftermath, see Elaine Sciolino, *The Outlaw State: Saddam Hussein's Quest for Power and the Gulf Crisis* (John Wiley, 1991); Anthony Cordesman and Ahmed Hashim, *Sanctions and Beyond* (Westview, 1997); and Amatzia Baram, *Building toward Crisis: Saddam Husayn's Strategy for Survival* (Washington Institute for Near East Policy, 1998). Ibrahim al-Marashi and Sammy Salama, *Iraq's Armed Forces: An Analytical History* (Routledge, 2008) is a historical study of the Iraqi military's political role.

The 2003 war and its aftermath produced a flood of analysis. Probably the best journalistic treatments are Anthony Shadid, *Night Draws Near* (Henry Holt, 2005); Anne Garrels, *Naked in Baghdad* (Farrar, Straus and Giroux, 2003); George Packer, *The Assassins' Gate: America in Iraq* (Farrar, Strauss, and Giroux, 2005); and Rajiv Chandrasekaran, *Green Zone* (Vintage Books, 2010). Memoirs by CPA officials and military officials provide interesting – and often unflattering – assessments based on first-hand experience. See Paul Bremer, *My Year in Iraq: The Struggle to Build a Future of Hope* (Simon and Schuster, 2006); Peter Mansour, *Surge: My Journey with General David Petraeus and the Remaking of the Iraq War* (Yale University Press, 2014); Emma Sky, *The Unravelling: High Hopes and Missed Opportunities in Iraq* (Public Affairs, 2015); and Rory Stewart, *Prince of the Marshes* (Mariner Books, 2007). An academic perspective is Muhammad Idrees Ahmad, *The Road to Iraq: The Making of a Neoconservative War* (Edinburgh University Press, 2014). A critique of failed state-building and flawed strategies under US occupation come through in Michael MacDonald, *Overreach: Delusions of Regime Change in Iraq* (Harvard University Press, 2014).

Studies of Iraqi politics and events since 2003 are highly variable. The first account by an Iraqi written in English is Ali Allawi, *The Occupation of Iraq: Winning the War, Losing the Peace* (Yale University Press, 2007). The constitutional drafting process and electoral politicking are described in Haider Ala Hamoudi, *Negotiating in Civil Conflict: Constitutional Construction and Imperfect Bargaining in Iraq* (University of Chicago Press, 2014). On the challenge of counterinsurgency and analyses of armed militias, see Ahmed Hashim, *Iraq's Sunni Insurgency* (Routledge, 2013) and Nicholas Krohley, *The Death of the Mehdi Army: The Rise, Fall, and Revival of Iraq's Most Powerful Militia* (Oxford University Press, 2015). For the changing nature of sectarianism in Iraq, see Fanar Haddad, *Sectarianism in Iraq: Antagonistic Visions of Unity* (Oxford University Press, 2011); Eric Davis, *Memories of State: Politics, History, and Collective Identity in Modern Iraq* (University of California Press, 2005); and Caroline Marji Sayej, *Patriotic Ayatollahs: Nationalism in Post-Saddam Iraq* (Cornell University Press, 2018). The best accessible treatments of ISIS so far are William McCants, *The ISIS Apocalypse* (St. Martin's, 2015); and Charles Lister, *The Islamic State: A Short Introduction* (Brookings Institution, 2015).

Online sources

Much of Iraq's media sphere exists online, but much of it also follows sectarian and communal allegiances that make it difficult to sift through objective reportage. A generic source of English-language news is Iraqi News (www.iraqinews.com/). Al-Zaman has a popular readership, and is often considered the most independent by Iraqi readers (www.azzaman.com/). Voice of Iraq is an eclectic radio station (http://voiraq.com/). Regional outlets provide excellent country analyses, including Al-Jazeera (www.aljazeera.com/topics/country/iraq. html). A multilingual portal for political and social briefings is Niqash (www.niqash.org/).

Third parties, such as think tanks, have published many libraries of research online regarding Iraqi politics and happenings. One example is the Iraq country pages by the International Crisis Group (www.crisisgroup.org/middle-east-north-africa/gulf-and-arabian-peninsula/iraq), Chatham House (www.chathamhouse.org/research/regions/middle-east-and-north-africa/iraq), and Human Rights Watch (www.hrw.org/middle-east/n-africa/

iraq). Based in Baghdad, the Iraq Memory Foundation documents past abuses under Ba'th rule (www.iraqmemory.com/en). Finally, Iraqi blogs furnish unmediated views of political and social life inside the country. Examples include Musings on Iraq (http://musingsoniraq. blogspot.com) and Abbad Kadhim's blog (www.abbaskadhim.com).

Please note that URLs may change far more quickly than books can be printed; so if these exact URLs do not work, simply search Google or another engine by the titles of these websites and online resources.

Republic of Turkey

Kristin Fabbe

INTRODUCTION

Situated between Europe and Asia, Turkey occupies a critical geostrategic position in the world. This unique geography, no doubt, has much to do with the complexities and continuities that have characterized Turkey's political development. Turkey is anchored to Europe, both through a vast network of trade linkages, its membership of NATO, and its bid for European Union membership. So too is it enmeshed in the politics of the greater Middle East by virtue of its proximity to and involvement in the conflict zones in Syria and Iraq, as well as its dependence on Iranian energy resources. Striking this balance has proved challenging, and so too have the dynamics of Turkey's domestic politics, which are marked by a strong tradition of executive rule punctuated by fleeting stints of democratic deepening and political liberalization.

In the early 2000s, Turkey enjoyed rapid economic growth and became the poster child for how to successfully blend Islamist and democratic politics. In the last decade, however, much has changed. Both the outside world and many Turks themselves now question the robustness of the country's democratic institutions. The economy has also suffered immensely since 2017. The very forces that propelled Turkey's growth – foreign credit, government spending on infrastructure, and a construction boom – have now rendered its economy vulnerable to collapse. Furthermore, ongoing tensions regarding the country's Kurdish population, vicious intra-Islamist feuds, deepening political polarization and nationalism, and the influx of nearly four million Syria refugees have combined to pose very real threats to social cohesion. The coming years are likely to be difficult ones for Turkey, though historically the country has proved remarkably resilient despite frequent bouts of economic and political turmoil.

Box 14.1 provides vital data for this country.

BOX 14.1 VITAL DATA – REPUBLIC OF TURKEY

Capital	Ankara
Regime type	Democratic (presidential republic)
Head of state	President Recep Tayyip Erdoğan (since 2014)
Head of government	President Recep Tayyip Erdoğan (since 2018)
Legislative institution	Unicameral parliament, with 600 elected seats (*Türkiye Büyük Millet Meclisi*, or Grand National Assembly)
Female quota	No
Percentage of seats held by women	17.4%
Major political parties (share of seats in most recent general elections, 2018)	Justice and Development (49.2%), Republican People's Party (24.3%), People's Democratic Party (11.2%), National Action Party (8.2%), İyi (7.2%)
Population	80,745,020
Major ethnic groups	Turkish (70%), Kurdish (20%), Arab (5%), other (5%)
Major religious groups	Muslim (99%), Christian and other (1%)
GDP per capita	$9,346 ($27,956 at Purchasing Power Parity)
Unemployment rate	10.9%
Youth unemployment rate	20.5%
Major economic industries	Textiles, food processing, automobiles, mining, electronics, agriculture, tobacco, steel, petroleum, construction, lumber, paper
Military spending as % GDP	2.2%

HISTORICAL BACKGROUND

The origins of the Turkish people date to pre-Islamic Central Asia. Their conversion to Islam came in the ninth and tenth centuries as a result of territorial expansion by the Islamic Empire. Among the new Muslim-Turkic polities was the Seljuq dynasty, which grew from Persia. In 1071 the Seljuqs defeated the Byzantine armies in a historic battle, which opened the gates of Anatolia to the Turks. With their new capital in Konya, the Seljuqs established a great civilization. The Ottoman Empire emerged from the remains of the

Seljuqs after their demise, and continued the Turkish tradition of westward territorial expansion. After taking Constantinople (modern-day Istanbul) in 1453, Ottoman armies conquered the Balkans and most of eastern Europe, and by the mid-sixteenth century, they had reached the gates of Vienna. At its height, the empire encompassed vast amounts of territory, and served as the last Islamic Caliphate – thus making its ruler, the Sultan, the Caliph of the (Sunni) Muslim world, although over time such titular authority faded. At the start of the nineteenth century, the empire included much of North Africa (except Morocco), the Balkans, Anatolia, the Mashriq, and parts of the Arabian Peninsula.

A flair for bureaucratic organization distinguished the Ottomans. Initially, the armed forces dominated the government apparatus, but once the era of conquest ended, the problems of administering the huge Ottoman territories demanded increased attention. In response, the civilian hierarchy expanded in prestige, size, and complexity. Thus, it was as much a bureaucratic as a militaristic empire in which the state sought political legitimacy in the eyes of its subjects. At the same time, the Ottoman imperial system had enshrined collective privileges for religious groups through the *millet* system. Over the centuries, this system engendered deeply ingrained patterns of local-level rule and social organization, but such localization also helped awaken nationalist movements over time.

However, the effort to keep the Ottoman Empire competitive with its European rivals triggered severe internal conflict about how to reform. Modernizers in the nineteenth century saw the adoption of European technology, laws, and concepts as the way to cope with Western intrusions into Ottoman territories in North Africa and Europe, as in the Young Ottoman and Young Turk movements. Traditionalists advocated a return to religious purity and a rejection of Westernization as the recipe for staving off European imperialism. Ultimately, Ottoman reforms were cut short by the demise of the empire itself, as financial crises, domestic revolts, and geopolitical competition with Britain, France, and Russia weakened the Ottoman state. By the 1880s, European powers recognized the "sick man of Europe" was interminably declining, as its North African holdings in Tunisia and Egypt became lost to French and British intrusions. Self-determination movements elsewhere in Ottoman lands also weakened loyalties to the Caliphate.

Turkish nationalism did not fully emerge until the Ottoman Empire disintegrated, but the seeds were planted early on. After the 1908 Young Turk revolution, in which political reformists forced the Ottoman Sultan to establish a new constitutional order, economic nationalism appeared in reaction to financial controls imposed by European creditors. Yet not even the Young Turks' activists and officers ever abandoned their hope of maintaining the empire, especially its Arab and Islamic elements. What sealed the Ottoman fate was World War One, which wrested control of most territories outside Anatolia towards of British, French, and Italian rulership, followed by the 1919–23 Turkish War of Independence. There, the charismatic Mustafa Kemal Atatürk led nationalist forces to victory against Allied plans to partition the remains of the Ottoman state. He served as a critical rallying point against the invading Greeks, and convinced the Western powers to end their occupation. It was in the wake of this Kemalist victory, signified in the 1923 Treaty of Lausanne, that the Caliphate was abolished and the new Turkish Republic was born.

The Kemalist inception, 1924–1950s

Modern Turkey was built upon the political structures erected by the Young Turks' reforms. The Ottoman parliament restored in 1908 continued as the Grand National Assembly, and the Committee of Union and Progress served as the model for Atatürk's new political vehicle, the Republican People's Party (CHP). At the center of this new political order was Mustafa Kemal, who after reestablishing public order began the extensive, top-down modernization of Turkish society. He saw little need to retain any Arab dominions, but nonetheless insisted on keeping a Kurdish-inhabited segment of the Anatolian Peninsula and other minority-populated areas, which he considered essential for national coherence. He also disempowered traditional sources of religious authority, moved the capital to Ankara, and in 1924 ended the position of Caliph in a demonstration of national authority and state sovereignty. Signifying the republican intention to regulate and control Islamic discourse, the Ministry of Islamic Affairs and Religious Endowments was shuttered and replaced by a more politically subservient bureaucracy to administer religion, the *Diyanet* (Directorate of Religious Affairs).

Seeking to transform Turkey quickly and radically, Atatürk offered social and legal reforms that ran the gamut, from establishing modern dress codes to replacing the Arabic alphabet with the Latin. The Kemalist government abolished shari'a courts, forced religious schools to close their doors, and imposed a number of other decrees undermining autonomous sources of Islamic authority. Atatürk's Kemalist vision resonated with secular commitments, but it was also instrumentalist: the Turkish Republic would not prohibit religiosity, but rather harness it in extremely circumscribed ways. By the late 1920s, religious administrators and civil servants had a clear new mission: to transform the masses of loyal Turkish citizens through state-sponsored Turkification and nationalization initiatives. The state that emerged was a parliamentary republic in form, though an autocracy in practice. Atatürk used his Republican People's Party to dominate politics. Six fundamental pillars comprised the party's ideology: republicanism, populism, nationalism, laicism, statism, and reformism. Backed by a hand-picked parliamentary majority, Mustafa Kemal shut down rival political groups, starting with supporters of the Caliph in the 1923 elections and the Progressive Republican Party in 1925.

Mustafa Kemal's death in 1938 interrupted this process of state-building, but left behind a robust foundation. The government afterwards became even more authoritarian, lashing out at domestic minorities. Atatürk's successor, İsmet İnönü, sought to align the republic with the victors of World War Two and secure their support against the Soviet Union. Partly for this reason, he decided to liberalize the regime to gain favor with the West, allowing an opposition group against the CHP, the Democrat Party, to form in 1946. The Democrats won in 1950, capitalizing on widespread discontent generated by years of atrophying CHP rule. The Democrats had the support of rural areas as well as the private sector they had championed. By contrast, Kemalists remained ensconced in the civilian and military bureaucracy, suspicious of the Democrats' willingness to relax Atatürk's reforms. Military officers perceived themselves as losers in the new order, and some began as early as the mid-1950s to secretly agitate for a coup. The absence of a political tradition of tolerance engendered a climate of oppression, as the Democrats continued winning elections in 1953 and 1957.

Praetorianism and republicanism, 1950s–1980s

Upset with the Democrats, army officers executed a coup in 1960; they proceeded by banning the Democrat Party, executing three of its leaders, and introducing a new constitution. Within a year, they had transferred power to a new parliament that chose İnönü as prime minister, and he formed a series of weak and unstable coalitions. The year 1965 brought unexpected change when a new political group led by Süleyman Demirel, the Justice Party, successfully challenged İnönü and the Republicans by winning an overwhelming electoral victory in 1965 and again in 1969. However, political unrest again challenged the institutional equilibrium, with criticism emerging this time from a newcomer – Necmettin Erbakan, a politician who appealed to Islamic activists. Erbakan founded the National Order Party in 1970, an early expression of Islamism. Mounting student and labor disorder led the army in March 1971 to issue an extraordinary public demand for more effective rule. Otherwise, they warned, the armed forces would seize power.

This cemented a pattern of praetorian interventionism, ostensibly for the sake of safeguarding the Kemalist legacy and recalibrating state institutions: when social unrest, driven by leftist or right-wing mobilization and amplified by elite bickering, became too great, the military intervened to reset the political game. After the 1971 warning, thus, Demirel resigned, and parliament voted into power a series of technocratic cabinets under nonpartisan prime ministers. Under the military's tutelage, these governments imposed martial law, narrowed many constitutional protections, banned the Marxist party, and made widespread arrests to suppress terrorism. Intellectuals, journalists, and labor leaders filled the jails. Erbakan's National Order Party was also disbanded on the grounds that it violated Turkey's constitutional commitment to secularism. The 1973 elections exposed political shifts in the ideological spectrum, as the Justice Party's centrist-right base fragmented while the CHP, now led by Bülent Ecevit, won a plurality of seats. Erbakan's party regrouped as the National Salvation Party.

This began a series of coalition governments, with Ecevit and Demirel alternating as prime minister and each drawing upon the National Salvation Party as a critical swing vote. Ecevit's first coalition sent Turkish troops into Cyprus in July 1974, following a Greek-inspired *putsch* against President Makarios. But when Ecevit resigned, hoping to force early elections to cash in on the popularity of sending troops, he was outmaneuvered and blocked by Demirel. The 1977 elections failed to resolve the impasse, and rivalries between the CHP and Justice Party resulted in political paralysis. Worse, the economy trended downwards as foreign currency shortages, triple-digit inflation, rising unemployment, and import shortages roiled the citizenry. Violent clashes between leftist and right-wing student groups also flared. While financial support by the International Monetary Fund rescued Turkey's financial standing, a deadlocked parliament failed to elect a president. The major parties ignored repeated warnings from the military to cooperate; indeed, the National Salvation Party flouted constitutional provisions against exploiting religion, Kurdish unrest began to grow in the east, and no-confidence motions against cabinet ministers challenged the government's existence.

The military responded with a coup. It ousted the government in September 1980 and closed parliament. It ruled for several years via its National Security Council, during which period party propaganda was prohibited, old parties were abolished, and institutions such as universities and unions were fundamentally restructured. Military tribunals detained and tried hundreds of thousands of people; among them were Ecevit, Demirel, and Erbakan. A new constitution in 1982, quickly approved via referendum, invoked clearer rules and boundaries regarding the presidency and other political structures. This heralded the presidency of General Kenan Evren until 1989; during his tenure, many civil liberties remained suspended, while youth organizations and student groups were sternly disciplined to prevent future social violence.

Curiously, though, this period also allowed elements of Islamism to percolate into politics, as some military elites believed this could temper the radicalism of leftist and right-wing ideologies. This would have profound long-term consequences. In the 1980s, analysts estimate that 1500 new mosques were constructed annually, and religious organizations found themselves with newfound latitude to shape culture and education. Long-standing institutional arrangements around religion were expanded in ways that permanently enlarged the religious field, despite the ostensibly secular nature of the Turkish state and the military's prerogatives. The 1982 constitution, for instance, strengthened the Diyanet, tasking it with the goal of protecting "national solidarity and integrity" – a clause that implied Islamic ideals to lay close to the notion of Turkishness. Among the new religious voices that mobilized was the preacher Fethullah Gülen, who led his followers around a self-proclaimed Hizmet (Service) movement.

By the mid-1980s, political pluralism returned as a two-party system created by the military did not stand the test of popularity. After the 1983 elections, the old parties re-emerged under different names, with even Ecevit, Demirel, and Erbakan resurrecting their careers. What helped their rejuvenation was a new rule – a 10 percent electoral threshold, which prevented smaller parties from entering parliament and strengthened larger ones. In the 1987 elections, the most successful party was the new Motherland Party, led by the technocratic Turgut Özal, who had served as prime minister under Evren. Özal eventually became president, serving between 1989 and 1993. His tenure saw Kurdish unrest in the southeast, the increasing salience of Islamist politics, and mounting inflationary and budgetary pressures. Özal's neoliberal reforms deregulated the economy; marking the move away from state-led developmentalism, the government reduced trade barriers, initiated privatization, attracted foreign investment, and eliminated capital controls. A new class of wealth emerged around this market-oriented opening, and public investments resulted in upgraded transportation, communication, and infrastructure. On the downside, fiscal deficits mushroomed and public debt mounted.

To soothe social tensions, the Motherland-led government eased restrictions on the use of the Kurdish language, and prohibitions on the right to espouse class or religious ideologies were dropped from the penal code. The Kurdish issue was especially troublesome. The emergence of the Kurdish Workers' Party (PKK) in the mid-1980s, and its call for an uprising against a Turkish state that refused to entertain the possibility of Kurdish autonomy, resulted in armed clashes and terrorist attacks. In the 1991 elections, the Motherland Party came in second to Demirel's True Path Party, resulting in a new coalition that faced almost immediate challenges from the Kurdish insurrection and foreign pressures. The aftermath of the 1991 Gulf War inflamed Turkey's deepening Kurdish unrest. Forceful government retaliation, including thrusts into northern Iraq against PKK bases, led Kurdish politicians active in parliamentary politics to break away.

New directions, 1990s–2010s

Against this background, the unexpected death of President Özal in April 1993 brought about significant change: Demirel was elected president; he then named a newcomer, Tansu Çiller, as Turkey's first female prime minister. Çiller disappointed many, as she alienated key constituencies and allowed rampant corruption. By the time of the December 1995 elections, her popularity flailed alongside a newcomer – Refah (Welfare), led by a grizzled Erbakan and the successor to the National Salvation Party of the 1970s. Refah's appeal as untainted by corruption overcame voters' reluctance to support a religiously oriented party. It also capitalized on the slow-moving trend towards greater Islamic expression among the Turkish public, exploiting the contributions of Islamic charitable endowments (*vakıf*) and voluntary religious associations (*dernek*). The number of *vakıf*s doubled from less than 1,000 in the early 1980s to just under 2,000 by the early 1990s, while the number of religious associations likewise grew. Another plank of support came from Gülen and his spiritual movement, which had begun funding private schools, charitable foundations, and other social services to fill widening gaps in the state's developmental capabilities. The Gülenist movement would soon become multifaceted and enormous in scope, with members and sympathizers active across the business community, civil society, the armed forces, the judiciary, and other government offices.

Refah won the 1995 elections, winning 158 out of 550 contested seats. This created shock waves among the civilian and military elite, who saw the Kemalist vision of secular republicanism under attack. After some shuffling, Çiller and her True Path Party formed a coalition government with Refah that rewarded Erbakan with the premiership. Tension between the new government and the military quickly materialized. In February 1997, military generals issued an 18-point set of demands to preserve secularist institutions, posing a direct challenge to the policies espoused by Refah politicians. So began what some observers called Turkey's post-modern coup: the military, working in tandem with secular civilian partners, engineered the government's downfall in June 1997. Under the military's influence, the Constitutional Court banned Refah and Erbakan from politics. The party, however, reconstituted itself as the Virtue Party – a common resurrection strategy in Turkey where, in anticipation of party banning, shell parties are created to absorb members of parliament and activists.

After a brief premiership by Motherland's Mesut Yilmaz, Ecevit returned as prime minister in 1999. His fortunes received an unexpected boost that year when US officials handed PKK leader Abdullah Öcalan to Turkish authorities, after having tracked down his whereabouts in an extensive intelligence effort. Ecevit's reputation for probity and the capture of Öcalan catapulted his Democratic Left Party from fourth to first place in the 1999 elections, winning a plurality of the popular vote. Close behind was the right-wing National Action Party (MHP), which had its roots in the right-wing militant movements of the 1970s. The resulting coalition government appeared more serious than its predecessors about budgetary discipline and trying to meet the criteria for inclusion in the European Union, which appeared to be a major goal.

These promising developments were set back when Ecevit and the president, Ahmet Necdet Sezer, engaged in a heated public row over corruption. The February 2001 dispute occurred at a time when the banking sector was reeling from over a decade of poor management, regulatory liberalization, and risky arbitrage operations that permeated to infect other areas of economic productivity. In 2001, financial crisis hit as investors fled the country, the Turkish currency (lira) depreciated by half, inflation rose again, and credit disappeared. The World Bank and IMF lent funds once again, but this time with stricter structural adjustment policies. The resulting neoliberal economic reforms helped produce a gradual recovery, but not before unemployment increased and spending cuts exposed more Turkish communities to poverty.

The 2002 elections catalyzed the political trajectory upon which, as of 2019, Turkey still follows. In that year, the new Justice and Development Party (AKP) captured almost two-thirds of the seats in parliament, although it garnered only 34 percent of the vote. The AKP was an offshoot of

Erbakan's Virtue Party, formed by a breakaway faction led by Recep Tayyip Erdoğan, Abdullah Gül, and Bülent Arınç. Erdoğan, the former mayor of Istanbul, and Gül, the party leader, maneuvered the AKP initially towards a more conciliatory approach to the republican state's secularist traditions. They distanced themselves from – and even repudiated – Erbakan and his hardcore followers. Their success was electrifying to global watchers: an Islamist party, though a comparatively moderate one, had come to power on its own, would not need to rely upon partners to form a coalition government, and seemed to be under no military threat. Gül became prime minister, followed by Erdoğan in March 2003.

The Erdoğan government's first priority was to deepen the reforms needed to advance Turkey's EU candidacy. The AKP quickly introduced a series of reforms that began to curtail some of the military's praetorian powers. It continued neoliberal economic reforms, while relaxing political restrictions on the Kurdish minority and promising to crack down upon corruption. Erdoğan also engineered an about-face in Turkey's Cyprus policy. As a result, the EU in December 2004 announced that Turkey had become a candidate for membership and in October 2005 officially initiated accession negotiations. While some feared that the AKP harbored a hidden agenda, the business community – both domestic and international – had high hopes for this new era in Turkish politics.

The normalization of Islamism proceeded with rising political controversies, as the ruling party began to exercise its political muscle. The AK Party maintained close ties with the Gülenist movement, with each Islamist entity drawing upon the other to legitimize their standing. In the 2007 elections, the AKP retained its majority, winning 46.6 percent of the vote to the CHP's 20.9 percent and MHP's 14.3 percent. It was around that time that legal investigations began in what culminated in the "Ergenekon trials." Ergenekon is the name of an alleged secret organization with ultra-Kemalist leanings that was charged with inciting violence and plotting to overthrow civilian governments. After a supposed Ergenekon plot was divulged in 2007, over 500 people were detained and nearly 300 were charged with committing some crime in connection with the organization. Among the accused were top-ranking military generals, university professors, mobsters, editors, writers, and journalists. At one point, one-tenth of all active generals and admirals were in prison or awaiting trial.

That trial divided the Turkish public. Some welcomed the weakening of the army's praetorian instincts, and argued that true democracy could not coexist with a "deep state" that could rule Turkey from behind the scenes with support from the military. Critics of the trial believed that most of the charges were fabricated and that the AKP and its supporters were unjustly using the judiciary to silence opponents and cement party authority, not least to immunize itself from future coups. By 2010, the AKP managed to establish total civilian control over the military, in part through a popular referendum on a sweeping package of constitutional reforms. The package, which passed with 58 percent of the popular vote, included a measure to make the military answerable to civilian courts. The passage reform package was welcomed by Europe and other Western powers, who touted the reforms as the beginning of the end of military tutelage. Not long after, another round of high-level arrests shook the military establishment, with accusations that military elements had conspired to overthrow the AKP in 2002 in an operation called Sledgehammer. The chief of staff and the commanders of the army, navy, and air force all resigned in protest against the arrests; and though most officers were eventually exonerated because Erdoğan and the AKP decided to part ways with the Gülenist movement, whose judges led the investigation, the military became an emasculated force.

Erdoğan's premiership continued into the 2010s, as the AKP won the 2011 elections with nearly 50 percent of the national vote, and CHP and MHP again running a distant second and third, respectively. That sustained popularity stemmed not only from high turnout among pious voters and Islamist elements, but also from continued beliefs among many lower-income and middle-class citizens that the current government could maintain its steady economic hand while expanding social services through impressive new investments in infrastructure, education, and healthcare. This success was followed in August 2014 by the first direct presidential election, in which Erdoğan ran for and won the presidency with 52 percent of the vote. This victory was all the more remarkable given the Gezi Park protests that rocked Turkey in the summer of 2013, which had a distinctly anti-AKP bent as millions of Turkish youths rallied against the government.

These protests also spelled the end to the long-standing alliance between the AKP and the Gülenist movement. Although tensions between the AKP and Gülenists had been simmering for some time, the alliance ruptured when Erdoğan signaled his intention to force the closure of Gülenist-run schools. These schools were central to the movement's financing structure, the Gülenists claimed that the closures were an act of retaliation after the movement had criticized government suppression of the Gezi protesters. Corruption scandals with the AKP by 2013 were magnified by accusations that Gülenist judges were attempting to unseat the party; as president, Erdoğan dubbed the entire Gülenist movement as a terrorist organization, and began purging known Gülenists from state agencies while shutting down their media outlets. Indeed, Erdoğan's 2014 victory in the presidential elections cemented a troubling pattern of increasing political abuses, as critics of the AKP – Gülenist or otherwise – found themselves under intense judicial and financial scrutiny. Fines, prosecutions, and detentions became increasing threats to journalists, academics, activists, and other political voices, while at the electoral level political competition intensified as the CHP began rallying its Kemalist base.

The June 2015 elections produced a curious result made worse by overt manipulation. The CHP argued it was increasingly unable to challenge the AKP's domination of state institutions and unconstitutional behavior, in part because of its increasing grip over the media. Yet the AK Party won only 41 percent of the vote, partly because the pro-Kurdish People's Democracy Party (HDP) decided to run as a party – an earthquake of a decision, as it removed the conservative Kurdish electorate's support away from the AKP. As a result, the HDP, with 13 percent of the votes, crossed the 10 percent threshold necessary to win seats in parliament and won a total of 80 seats – a net gain of 60 compared to the previous elections. However, the resumption of hostilities with the PKK that summer and failure to form a government forced snap elections in November 2015, in which the AKP regained its majority. The previous month, the deadliest terrorist attacks in Turkish history occurred when suicide bombers with suspected ties to the Islamic State of Iraq and Syria (ISIS) killed over 100 at a peace rally in Ankara. Given the dark climate, opposition parties remained relatively docile, but alleged electoral fraud and other anti-democratic practices at Erdoğan and the AKP afterwards.

Politics has become increasingly polarized in the years since. In July 2016, Turkish domestic politics was upended when military conspirators attempted to overthrow the government in a chaotic set of events that initially saw the shutdown of state media, violent armed clashes between mutineers and loyalists, and finally street confrontations that eventually overwhelmed pro-coup soldiers. Hundreds died and thousands were injured in the clashes, which days later were pinned – by Erdoğan, at a press conference – upon the Gülenist movement and its infiltrators in the military. The government imposed emergency rule and organized a massive rally to shore up its popular base. This began a period of ratcheting illiberalism, as the Turkish government tenaciously pursued suspected Gülenist sympathizers and other oppositionists.

The 2018 round of Turkish elections consolidated the AKP's reign, making Western observers – former enthusiasts of the government – open critics of what it saw as a frail democracy backsliding into authoritarianism. Having passed constitutional amendments in 2017 turning the political system into a presidential one, Erdoğan won his presidential elections with 52.6 percent of the vote over Muharrem İnce, the CHP's candidate. Notable other candidates were Selahattin Demirtaş, the HDP's leader who had been detained in the post-coup crackdown on politicized charges, and thus ran from prison; and Meral Akşener, the female leader of the new İyi (Good) Party, which was established the year before as a right-leaning Kemalist party. For its part, the right-wing MHP struck an alliance with AKP. The parliamentary elections revealed similar results: AKP won over 295 of the 600 seats in the newly enlarged (but institutionally weakened) parliament, with CHP winning 146, the MHP 49, the İyi 43, and HDP 67.

As the 2010s closed, Turkish politics thus came to resemble – for better or for worse – a trend seen in some Western democracies. Elections had become extremely contentious, politics polarized by often poisonously divisive discourse, and the incumbent party increasingly willing to cut corners and employ all possible tactics to maintain its power of government.

SOCIAL AND ECONOMIC ENVIRONMENT

Turkey is a land of pronounced physical contrasts and sharp disparities. Extending 783,562 square kilometers (302,535 square miles) – 40 percent larger than France – it ranges from sea level to the 5,165-meter (16,945-foot) peak of Mount Ararat, which is higher than any European mountain. The western part of the country, bordering on the Aegean and Marmara Seas, is a region of developed communication and easy access to the inland plateau. Eastern Turkey, abutting the Caucasian republics, Iran, and Iraq, is mountainous, cut by rivers into more or less isolated valleys. The population is over 80 million, and is increasing at a rate of around 1.5 percent a year, the recent Syrian refugee influx notwithstanding. Major cities are spread across the land (Map 14.1). Istanbul, the former Ottoman capital, remains the largest city, with a rapidly growing population of over 15 million, while Ankara, the capital, reached 5.5 million in 2019. Other major cities include coastal İzmir and Adana; Bursa, another former Ottoman capital; the former Seljuq capital, Konya; and newly industrializing Anatolian cities like Denizli, Mersin, Kayseri, and Gaziantep.

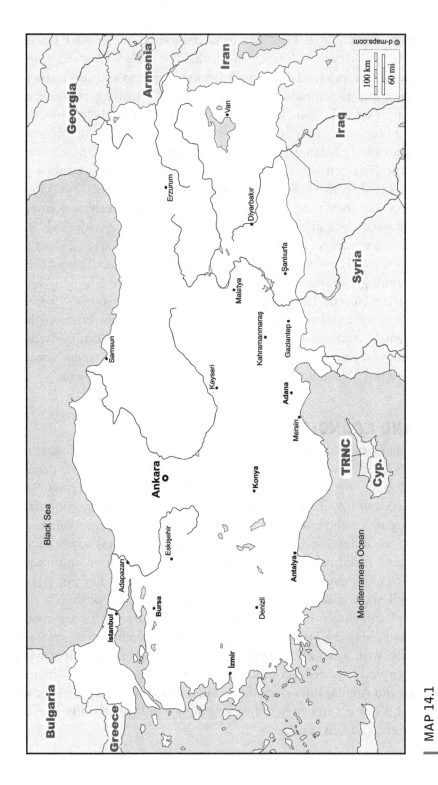

MAP 14.1

Republic of Turkey. Major water bodies, rivers, and cities shown.

Source: D-Maps.

With a 99 percent Muslim population, modern Turkey is far more homogeneous than the multiethnic, multireligious Ottoman Empire. Sunni Islam predominates, but the heterodox Alevi sect accounts for at least 15 to 20 percent of Muslims. Kurds constitute the most significant ethnic minority. Inspired by France, Turkey's official understanding of citizenship does not recognize ethnic minorities, which makes precise data on the size of this minority group also impossible to come by. Yet it is commonly estimated that about 20 percent of Turkey's population is of Kurdish origin. Kurds represent a clear majority in Turkey's southeast provinces and speak a distinct Indo-European language with several different dialects.

The complexities of Turkey's social and economic environment have been compounded by rapid urbanization. By 2018, some 75 percent of Turkish citizens lived in urban areas, up from just 40 percent in 1990. Over the last 30 years, the rapid influx of traditionally oriented, religiously observant rural dwellers has given many urban areas a bifurcated appearance, where the modern and traditional chaotically coexist. On the gender front, the picture is also quite mixed. Turkey has brought urban women into the mainstream of political, professional, and cultural life. The educational level of women has risen steadily, and the literacy rate of school-age girls is approaching that of boys: male literacy is around 98 percent, while female literacy is close to 94 percent. Although many social barriers still exist, females have not faced legal obstacles hindering employment opportunities since the 1930s. In the villages, however, the traditional male-dominated pattern of life persists, as it does to some extent in the urban communities where new migrants from the countryside have settled.

Salient issues of identity and minority status in Turkey are rooted in the country's difficult transition from a cosmopolitan Muslim empire to a sovereign nation-state that privileged Turkishness and Sunni Islam. The Kurdish population is a case in point. Turkey's transition to multi-party democracy during the Cold War significantly shaped the position of Kurdish identity politics in the political environment. As the nation was a NATO member with Soviet borders, left-right political divisions came to characterize Turkish politics. Generally speaking, political Islam became associated with the anti-communist right, while the Kurdish movement was part of the socialist Left. Kurdish dissent was therefore long expressed in terms of "class conflict" rather than ethnic grievances, which enabled Kurdish political assimilation within Turkey's leftist movements.

In the 1980s, however, the rise of the PKK and outright demands for Kurdish autonomy politicized the issue of national and subnational identities, while also securitizing numerous areas in southeastern Turkey, where the military waged counterinsurgent battles against Kurdish militants. Between 1984 and 1999, the Kurdish conflict caused some 35,000 deaths among insurgents, the local population, and security forces, costing the Turkish economy an estimated $120 billion and hindering the economic integration and development of many provinces in the southeast. The conflict abated after the 1990s, with Öcalan's capture, various ceasefires, and promises to establish more linguistic, cultural, and political rights for Kurds. Low-level violence and hostilities persist, however.

Complicating matters is that Turkey's Kurds have not remained geographically concentrated. Due to conflict-induced migration, over half of the Kurdish population came to inhabit the western and southern regions of the country. Istanbul, for instance, became home to the largest urban concentration of Kurds in the world. Further, most Kurds used to have tribal connections, but the influence of traditional leaders has been waning rapidly. These chiefs frequently also head branches of dervish orders (Nakshibandi and Kadiri) or belong to religious sects (such as the Nurcular). Especially in eastern Turkey, this social organization historically both perpetuated an identity separate from that of the rest of the Turkish population and divided the various tribes and clans into rival units.

The Alevi-Sunni cleavage remains one of the most important divisions in Turkish society. Under the Sunni supremacy of the Ottoman Empire, Alevis were a persecuted minority given their Shi'a proclivity and heterodox practice of Islam. The Ottomans' historic rivalry with the Shi'a Safavid Empire further complicated the status of Alevis and put in question their loyalty to the Sunni-led Ottoman government. Many Alevis therefore enthusiastically supported the modernizing reforms of Mustafa Kemal Atatürk that led to the weakening of the Sunni religious establishment in Turkey. Yet the peculiar nature of religion-state relations in Turkey, where the state recognizes, controls, and administers the Sunni branch as the only legitimate practice of Islam, is an ongoing source of disappointment. Equally problematic is the anti-Alevi societal and political bias in Turkey, based mainly on the grounds that Alevis do not attend mosques and have their own community centers and religious rituals. To this day intermarriage between Alevis and Sunnis remains quite exceptional.

Economic conditions

Economic development has been a major engine of political transformation. A number of prominent family business groups emerged in the early republican period with state support, when Turkey began state-led development strategies. From the 1950s, Turkey witnessed significant growth in agricultural productivity thanks to improved mechanization and large-scale irrigation. Yet state-led industrialization drives characterized most of the 1960s and early 1970s. Public investment in heavy industry and state-owned enterprises produced a robust manufacturing base that targeted the domestic market. Furthermore, it was during the 1960s that many of the largest multiactivity family firms transformed themselves into holding companies. The holding company structure, which is characterized by high levels of diversification across unrelated sectors and the flexibility to shift between importing and exporting strategies, was advantageous given the frequent shifts in government policy.

Turkey's economy grew briskly in the 1960s, averaging nearly 6 percent GDP growth per year. Yet there were clear limits to be felt by the 1970s. Turkey, unlike successful late-developing economies, never managed to fully switch from import-substitution to export-led growth. Businesses – big and small alike – remained heavily dependent on the state. Chambers of industry and commerce had become fora for political and economic debate in the multi-party era, yet they also hindered private-sector interests from collectively organizing around particular issues. In response, big business became disenchanted with the chambers' organizational structure, as larger firms struggled to exert their prerogatives in the face of resistance from each regional chamber's multitude of smaller firms. This resulted in some internal restructuring of the economy. The first voluntary big-business association, the Turkish Industrialists and Business Association (TIBA), was established in 1971, with the objective of strengthening the political clout of its members. TIBA developed a quasi-public function through which it could influence the country's economic orientation by interfacing directly with political officials. Although TIBA developed into (and still is) a significant actor in Turkish politics and economics, the state remains the most dominant force in terms of shaping the economy.

More so than the immoveable state, social unrest in the form of major labor disputes and commitments to economic populism – all escalated by fierce political battles and electoral dramas – drained Turkey's economic performance throughout the 1970s. At the end of the decade, the surge in oil prices, growing trade deficits, an overvalued currency, mass budget deficits, and high inflation shook the economy. Market dynamics and the private sector remained secondary forces to the public sector and state-owned firms, which dictated the rhythms of trade and so were unable to adapt to changing external conditions. To cope with these challenges and hasten integration and stability, Turkey began to entertain neoliberal reforms under IMF guidance in the early 1980s. Under Prime Minister Özal, the government dismantled subsidies on energy and other basic commodities and enacted policies to stimulate exports. Despite considerable structural reform, though, by the end of the decade Turkey was still unable to control its public debt. In the absence of strict fiscal and monetary restraint, Turkey also failed to deal with rampant inflation, which in real terms never sunk below 30 percent during the decade.

The 1990s represented a decade of difficult economic transition, as inflationary pressures and increased trade openness squeezed the traditional state-owned economy. GDP growth swung wildly; though it averaged over 4 percent during the 1980s, annual rates ranged from 10 percent in 1987 to virtually nothing two years later, when recession took hold. Tighter monetary controls and budget ceilings helped stabilize inflation, reduce capital flight, and achieve some financial liberalization, but it took much of the decade for industries and consumption habits to adapt. Much like the 1980s, the 1990s were characterized by macroeconomic volatility compounded by political uncertainties; years of economic rebound were counterbalanced by major fiscal crises in 1991, 1994, 1998, and 1999 – the latter partly reflecting the devastating earthquake that killed 17,000.

One stabilizing factor was the rise of new business actors, such as the Independent Industrialists' and Businessmen's Association (IIBA), which was established in 1990. Encompassing thousands of private-sector firms that sought to break the virtual monopolies held by major family-owned, state-supported corporations in many sectors, the IIBA included pious business networks sympathetic to Islamism. Alongside other new business groups, the IIBA helped improve access to finance and investment funding as well as in building a religiously sensitive consumer base and a competent labor force, all by leveraging trust-based networks built upon shared religious and culture values and institutions. A great many of the suggestions put forward in IIBA's 2002 annual report were reflected in the first economic strategy documents of the newly established moderate Islamist party, the AKP, reflecting the fusion of a winning political formula – a tamed Islamism with neoliberal economic tendencies.

In this context, Turkey's improved relations with the European Union after the 1999 Helsinki Summit provided much-needed external İncentives for further reforms. The EU's impact became particularly clear in the November 2002 elections when the AKP campaigned to further Turkey's future inclusion. Commensurate with the AKP's ascent, one particular Islamist movement, that of the aforementioned Fethullah Gülen, gathered momen-tum. Gülenists made great efforts to build up their support base by guiding their members to engage and invest in civic causes, such as building schools in Turkey and elsewhere. The Gülenist-associated Turkish Confederation of Businessmen and Industrialists also encompassed new firms and entrepre-neurs, boasting some 49,000 members by 2012. Though Gülen later fled to the US in 1999 under threats of prosecution, these overlapping networks of Gülenism were allied with the AKP and its social and business coalitions, which helped stabilize economic policymaking by the 2000s.

Indeed, during its first decade in power, the AKP remained strongly com-mitted to its reformist agenda. Structural changes, productivity growth, and a broadening base of economic activity all contributed to a climate of optimism. Between 2002–07 Turkey enjoyed five years of rapid economic growth, with GDP per capita increasing at almost 6 percent per annum. By 2005 the Turkish economy had stabilized, and inflation fell to levels that allowed lopping six zeros off the currency. From about 2007 onwards, how-ever, economic growth slowed significantly. This slowdown resulted, in part, from vagaries in the global business cycle. The European economic crisis cast a pall, but the Arab Spring had less of an impact upon productivity given the westward focus of Turkish exports and investment. In 2011, economic growth leapt by 11.1 percent; and through it slowed down, as of 2018 the GDP had expanded by an average annual rate of 6.6 percent for the decade. By 2019, the Turkish economy remained among the world's top twenty as measured by GDP size.

The later years of the 2010s, however, brought new challenges in the form of currency and debt crises. The former manifest in the plunging value of the Turkish lira concomitant with rising inflation, prompting some ana-lysts to call for another International Monetary Fund intervention. The lat-ter was expressed in increasingly large budget deficits and current account imbalances, as Turkish imports exceeded export revenues and Turkish banks turned to heavy borrowing to cover their spending. Indeed, the country had become heavily dependent on a steady flow of foreign loans to finance mas-sive investments in infrastructure and mega-projects, including housing, roads, bridges, and airports. Cronyism and favoritism also began to take root. Firms with government connections received a disproportionate amount of state contracts and privileged access to deals involving state-owned land.

Compounding matters has been politics, as the increasingly abusive tendencies of the AKP-led government and Erdoğan's unorthodox beliefs stripped the Central Bank of its independent authority. Erdoğan's decision to appoint his son-in-law to lead a newly combined ministry of treasury and finance in the summer of 2018 only further alienated many foreign creditors, while international rating agencies responded by downgrading Turkish sovereign debt further into junk territory. By 2019, the country's economic outlook had become bleak once more.

POLITICAL STRUCTURES

Turkey is a unitary republic with a presidential system. The 1982 constitution, as amended, centers on a 600-seat unicameral legislature, the Grand National Assembly. That constitution made cabinet ministers "jointly responsible" for the execution of the government's general policy and personally liable for their ministries' acts. The prime minister, who traditionally served as the top executive, headed the Council of Ministers. The president of the republic, long a ceremonial position, was elected by the Grand National Assembly for a seven-year term. However, as a result of constitutional amendments passed in 2016 and implemented soon after, Turkey became a presidential republic with no prime minister. The president serves as both head of state and head of government, and is elected directly by citizens for a five-year term, with a two-term limit. Parliamentarians serve for four-year terms, but the legislature now has less power at the expense of the enlarged executive powers of the presidency. The Turkish president can now appoint cabinet ministers directly (as well as dismiss them), in addition to top judges. The presidency also now reserves considerable independent authority to legislate issues through decree, and declare states of emergency.

One of the most important objectives of the 1982 constitution was to strongly reassert the authority of the state, partly as a reaction to the 1961 constitution, which was perceived as too liberal. Drafted after the 1980 military intervention, the 1982 constitution prioritized law and order and set up state security courts, where military judges served with civil judges. These courts were abolished in 2004 under the AKP's pro-EU democratization program, and underwent further reorganization after the 2016 amendments. Although superior administrative and military courts have final jurisdiction over cases within their competencies, the Turkish judicial system provides for the Constitutional Court to rule on the constitutionality of laws and decrees. The Constitutional Court functions as the supreme court of the land and therefore decides all cases relating to political parties. The Turkish judiciary remains highly vulnerable to executive influence, however, particularly given the new powers wielded by the president.

Understanding Turkey's evolving political structure requires a basic grasp of the republic's foundational principle. Unlike most other Western democracies, Turkey has an official state ideology. This ideology, Kemalism, is named after Mustafa Kemal Atatürk, the founding father of modern Turkey. Today, however, there is no consensus among Kemalists themselves on what Kemalism stands for in the twenty-first century. Historically the military has been the state's backbone, serving as the guardian of the republic's Kemalist legacy. During the Cold War, whenever the military intervened in the realm of politics, it justified all actions as necessary for maintaining stability of the republic. Yet unlike Latin American militaries, which tended to rule through *juntas* for long periods of time, the Turkish army never remained in power. To preserve its professionalism, it always returned to the barracks. None of the three major military interventions in Turkish politics (1960, 1971, and 1980) lasted more than three years.

In the post-Cold War era, the Kemalist military has viewed the primary threats to the republic to be Kurdish nationalism and political Islam. At the same time, the pattern of military interventions changed. Instead of directly overthrowing governments, the military used a variety of less blunt means to dislodge or pressure elected governments, sometimes through pronouncements, as in February 1997 and April 2007. The Ergenekon trials and consequent constitutional reforms, however, greatly eroded the power of the armed forces. Indeed, opponents of those reforms argued that those proposals to strengthen the control of the president and parliament over the appointment of judges and prosecutors reflected the AKP's desire to erode the separation of powers between the executive and the judiciary. The blowback from the subsequent controversy over the Sledgehammer operation further discredited the military, disrupting the chain of command and weakening the military's appetite for political intervention.

Turkey's political parties operate with relative efficiency in mobilizing voters. Participation in elections has generally been high, historically involving between 64 and 94 percent of eligible voters. As of 2019, the dominant party is the Islamist AKP, which has won a plurality in every election since 2002 under the leadership of Erdoğan (Photo 14.1). Although the AKP has suffered some defections since 2017, with both activists and elites alike becoming disgruntled with Erdoğan's domineering leadership, the party remains the largest in Turkish politics. Its primary opposition has been the leftist CHP, which strongly retains a Kemalist identity. Allied to the CHP is the center-right İyi Party, which entered the electoral scene in 2018 and siphoned off votes from the right-wing MHP, which allied itself with the

PHOTO 14.1
President Recep Tayyip Erdoğan of Turkey.

Source: Pixabay. Public domain.

AKP. The Kurdish HDP remains something of an enigmatic kingmaker. Though it has spent some years implicitly working with the AKP, partly due to Erdoğan's vague promises of enhancing Kurdish rights and representation, by the late 2010s the party forged a more independent path, even as its leader, Demirtaş, languished in jail on questionable charges.

POLITICAL DYNAMICS

Until recently political patterns in Turkey have shown remarkable continuity, despite frequent military interventions. On the one hand, that continuity reflects the longevity of political figures in Turkey, where tenures of 30 or even 40 years for major political leaders are not uncommon. On the other hand, voting blocs themselves have changed little in proportion over the years, which would give the right-of-center a marked edge were it not torn by intense personal rivalries at various junctures. Another major aspect of continuity, albeit one that has been eroded since the advent of the presidential system under Erdoğan, has been the commitment to elective parliamentary rule, which most political elements, including the military, have seen as the principal legitimizing political process.

Turkish voters do not cast ballots on a class basis. Rather, the ups and downs in party performance suggest that many Turkish voters – excluding the ideologically committed, who stand squarely at the base of their respective parties – seek successful leaders who keep their promises, bolster the economy, and avoid the appearance of corruption. The AKP government, which won elections in 2002, 2007, 2011, 2015, and 2018, is thus enigmatic; it confirmed this pattern early on, but through the 2010s bucked the trend given the increasing visibility of its corruption and illiberalism, with the latter especially manifest in its intolerance of criticism, stranglehold on media, and tenacious pursuit of opposition after the July 2016 coup. Both because of its mobilizational power and its political tactics, the AKP has proven exceptionally successful so far in maintaining its grasp on power. Its 2007 victory was particularly extraordinary, as it was the first time an incumbent government had increased its vote share since 1954, but its 2018 dual victories in the parliamentary vote and Erdoğan's presidential election revealed the difficulties that opposition parties have in contesting its hegemony. Critics note that those elections were the first to take place under a new presidential system of governance, approved by a slim majority in a 2017 constitutional referendum. Both the referendum and the elections took place under emergency rule and in a climate of extreme media censorship.

Three conclusions seem apparent in terms of Turkey's political dynamics as the 2010s close. First, though Turkey remains an electoral democracy – not even the AKP has ever refused to hold a national election, and its legitimacy requires victory at the ballot boxes – growing judicial, financial, and political abuses by government officials under its leadership are greatly reducing space for pluralism and civil society. During 2016–19, the government shut down some 800 companies, over 1,000 schools, and 1,400 civic associations. It jailed more than 70,000 people, terminated over 150,000 civil servants, dismissed thousands of military personnel, detained a number of opposition MPs, and further clamped down on independent media. Thus, despite what many have predicted, the Turkish democracy is not coming to an end because of a clash between Islam and secularism. Instead, the real conflict is between electoral democracy and liberalism. Erdoğan has tended to reduce democracy to elections, and his populist understanding of politics has come at the expense of individual rights and liberties, freedom of expression and association, an independent media, and separation between the legislative, executive, and judiciary powers.

Second, politics has become dangerously polarized. Voting tendencies and left-right divisions are not comparable to the 1970s, when endemic violence between ideological militants marred social life and destabilized coalitional governments in a cycle that ended only with military interventions. Yet the battle for votes has taken on something of an existential tone, with AKP activists often accusing critics of being threats and enemies of the Turkish state, and anti-AKP oppositionists accusing Erdoğan and his party of "Arabizing" the country and violating Atatürk's legacy by turning the country overtly Islamist. In many ways, political disputes implicate the nature of Turkish identity itself, and the battle over its interpretation.

Third and finally, despite the worryingly autocratic inclinations of the AKP, the uncertainty of every vote and vibrant opposition mobilization makes every election must-see drama – even at the local level. The AKP suffered shock municipal election defeats in March 2019, losing control of both Ankara and Istanbul, which placed its vast patronage machine at risk. Erdoğan was quick to blame the losses on electoral fraud, launching a string of legal challenges against the results. He also vowed to confront opponents within his own party. In early May 2019, the Supreme Elections Council announced that a new vote would take place for the Istanbul mayoralty due to suspected "irregularities" – a charge that international monitors decried as ludicrously false, and which AKP activists celebrated as defending democracy. The June 2019 electoral rerun, however, delivered a humiliating blow to Erdoğan. The AKP lost by an even greater margin than before to the same CHP opposition candidate who had won in May – Ekrem İmamoğlu, who swiftly began his Istanbul mayoralty immersed in rumors of a future presidential run.

Although Turkey's backsliding from previous democratic aspirations continues, a united opposition could well challenge Erdoğan in the 2022 parliamentary elections and the 2023 presidential elections. This assumes, of course, that such elections will be held and that they will be fairly contested.

FOREIGN POLICY

Under Mustafa Kemal, Turkey distanced itself from the Arab world; in fact, in 1926, after defeating a Kurdish insurrection, Atatürk agreed to cede the mostly Kurdish-inhabited region of Mosul to Iraq. Kemal's most famous adage about foreign relations, "peace at home, peace abroad," also implied a degree of isolationism. World War Two was a particularly trying time; bereft of its strong leader, who had passed away in 1938, Ankara was caught between the entreaties of the Allied and Axis powers. Its military weakness prevented it from entering the conflict, save during the last months of the war. With the Allied victory in 1945, Turkey hitched its future to an alliance with the United States and Europe. The Truman Doctrine – enunciated by the United States on March 12, 1947, to support Turkey and Greece in the face of continuing Soviet pressure – heralded the beginning of both countries' active participation in the Cold War.

The Turkish government did its utmost to convince the United States to accept it as a member of NATO, which it viewed as the ultimate shield against an aggressive Soviet Union. The ruling Democrat Party sent troops to fight in the Korean War as a means of proving its bona fides, and so in 1952 Turkey indeed entered the ranks of NATO membership. As the sole NATO member bordering the Soviet Union, Turkey became an important asset in the Western policy of containment. Military cooperation between the United States and Turkey enabled Ankara to revamp its creaky armed forces. And while discord was not entirely absent – for example, the Turks were astounded to learn at the conclusion of the 1962 Cuban Missile Crisis that the Kennedy administration had decided to remove nuclear-tipped Jupiter missiles from Turkey in exchange for the removal of Soviet missiles from Cuba – Turkey became firmly ensconced in the Western fold, making its foreign policy framework predictable.

The 1974 Cyprus crisis was a turning point. Turkey felt obliged to respond to a coup against the government of Archbishop Makarios in Cyprus by Greek Cypriot nationalist elements. Turkey landed troops on Cyprus, but facing strong international pressure, halted its military action within two days, having secured merely a foothold in the Kyrenia region, north of Nicosia. Fighting erupted again, and Turkey soon found itself largely isolated in the international community. The US imposed an embargo on all arms deliveries to Turkey, which lasted until September 1978. In retaliation, Turkey closed all US installations (except the vital NATO base in Incirlik) and abrogated the 1969 Defense Cooperation Agreement. The embargo left a deep imprint on Turkish politicians regarding the reliability of the United States. Nonetheless, the Carter administration lifted the arms embargo in September 1978, US facilities were reopened, and a new Cooperation on Defense and Economy Agreement was signed in March 1980.

Turkey assumed a new, and quite different, role in the post-Cold War era. For the US, Turkey represented a perfect foil for Iran's ambitions in Central

Asia – an area freed from direct Soviet control. Turkey's linguistic and cultural affinity toward Azerbaijan, Turkmenistan, Kazakhstan, and Uzbekistan, several of which had extensive energy reserves, was an asset. Turkish concerns and US support for non-Russian transportation routes led to construction of the Baku-Tbilisi-Ceyhan pipeline, which has been transporting Caspian Sea oil to Turkey's Mediterranean coast since 2006. Iraq's 1990 invasion of Kuwait further complicated Turkey's relations with its neighbors and the West. More than half a million Kurdish refugees streamed towards the Turkish border during the turmoil. Turkey, the United States, and Britain helped establish a no-fly zone over northern Iraq and pushed Iraqi troops back from the Kurdish regions, enabling the refugees to return. Iraqi Kurds, now protected by a US-UK air umbrella and no longer under the tutelage of Saddam Hussein, began to manage their own affairs. Because the air assets enforcing the no-fly zone were based at Incirlik, Turkey unwillingly became the midwife to an autonomous Kurdish entity in northern Iraq.

Operation Provide Comfort, as this endeavor was called, caused tensions between Turkey and the US. The conundrum for the Turkish government was that Iraqi Kurds – divided among themselves – were incapable of exercising complete authority over their territory and controlling the PKK, which the Turkish government saw as a dangerous threat to national security. The Turkish military, sometimes with the cooperation of the two Kurdish groups and sometimes on its own, conducted cross-border operations against PKK camps near the border in its efforts to end the Kurdish insurgency at home. Nonetheless, the US lobbied the EU to give Turkey a chance at membership, and in 1999 the EU decided to reverse its earlier rejection of Turkey's candidacy for EU membership.

By the early 2000s, however, Turkish foreign policy began to turn away from the West and become more oriented towards the MENA – if nothing else, due to the geopolitical exigencies of regional insecurity and threat. In the run-up to the 2003 war against Iraq, the US wooed the new AKP-led government to use Turkish territory for the operation. The government tentatively agreed, but the Turkish military refused to cooperate, fearing collateral damages and the overall cost. The Turkish parliament sealed matters when it denied permission for American access entirely. The invasion of Iraq went ahead without this northern front, though Ankara did allow US Special Forces and agents to infiltrate Iraq from its territory.

By now, the AKP government strongly believed, not without justification, that Turkey had traditionally punched well below its weight in terms of regional influence. The new plan for Turkish foreign policy with its neighbors was called "zero-problems." Turkey made significant strides to improve its relations with many of its neighbors, especially in the hitherto ignored Arab world. Turkish diplomacy, aided by an expanding transportation, educational, and trade ties, improved economic fortunes. This new MENA-oriented foreign policy encroached upon Western consensus on several occasions. For example, when the EU and the United States agreed on a strategy to force Syria's withdrawal from Lebanon in 2005, Turkey initiated a diplomatic campaign to reduce Syria's isolation. When they devised a strategy to isolate the Palestinian Islamist group Hamas, Turkey invited its exiled leader, Khalid Mash'al, to Ankara.

On other fronts, Turkish foreign policy has likewise run into challenges in its regional reorientation and domestic shifts. In April 2009, Turkey and Armenia agreed on a comprehensive framework for reconciliation – a long overdue move, given the latter's traumatic memories of what befell Ottoman Armenians during World War One. The first steps were to have been taken by late 2009, with the opening of the Turkish-Armenian border, the establishment of diplomatic relations, and the creation of bilateral commissions to address various issues. Yet soon after the agreement was made public, Turkey backtracked in the face of mounting nationalist reactions in both Turkey and Azerbaijan.

Nonetheless, Turkey was intent on projecting its influence and by 2008 it had successfully lobbied to win a seat on the UN Security Council for the first time since the early 1960s. Under Ahmet Davutoglu, who became foreign minister in 2009, Turkey further intensified its MENA strategy of carving out a space of influence, maintaining good relations with Arab neighbors, and maximizing its economic gains from regional networks. At first, Turkish-American relations appeared to have improved with the arrival of the Obama administration and the April 2009 presidential visit. The Arab Spring, however, complicated Turkey's security outlook. In Libya, Egypt, and Syria, Turkey's aims were frustrated and its diplomacy suffered significant setbacks, as the AK government had invested heavily in Libya's Muammar al-Qaddafi and Syria's Bashar al-Asad. By 2012, with the violence in Syria escalating, and Syrian refugees beginning to pour into Turkey, the government decided to become a frontline state against Asad – and later ISIS, which more than Asad explicitly targeted Turkey as an enemy. In Egypt too, Turkey's foreign policy stance backfired, as Erdoğan condemned the 2013 coup against another Islamist government, the Muslim Brotherhood presidency of President Mohamed Morsi. In the resulting repression, many members of the Brotherhood sought refuge in Turkey, creating ire with Gulf states like Saudi

Arabia and the UAE, which both designated the Brotherhood as a terrorist organization in 2014.

Turkish foreign policy navigated the Syrian challenge, but not without cost. Large numbers of jihadi volunteers crossed Turkey's permeable borders to fight in Syria or Iraq, while the country also absorbed several million Syrian refugees. The challenges associated with refugee integration have been difficult given the extant economic crisis and political tensions. The government has been slow to develop a long-term strategy for integrating Syrians into Turkey's economy, fearing a public backlash if it openly accepts refugees' permanent presence but is also unable to return them back to even a peaceful Syria under the renewed reign of the Asad regime. The other challenge with Syria is one of hard security and territory. Starting in August 2016, the Turkish military began occupying a strip of northern Syria as a buffer zone. Not far away, Syrian Kurdish militias with ties to the PKK waged a successful war against ISIS, helped by significant US military assistance. American support for this Kurdish campaign, and thus the potentiality of an autonomous Kurdish region there, unsettled many Turkish observers, who wished to weaken Kurdish militarization but without incurring excessive liabilities. At the same time, Turkey welcomed Russian and Iranian entry into the Syrian civil war to bolster Asad's regime against its opposition and ISIS, and participated in the Russian-led negotiations – one of two parallel tracks of peace talks – to end the conflict.

Suggesting a foreign policy that is increasingly confident and no longer US-centric, Turkish relations with Russia warmed considerably throughout the Syrian civil war, despite a brief crisis when Turkish fighter jets shot down a Russian warplane near the Syria-Turkey border in late 2015. Russia lifted most of the sanctions it had imposed on Turkey, relaunched joint energy projects, and agreed to Turkish purchases of Russian S-400 missile systems – a sensitive topic, as the advance weaponry poses a threat to the F-35 jet fighters the US wished to sell Turkey. The Obama and Trump administrations also repeatedly rebuffed President Erdoğan's requests to extradite Fethullah Gülen, while EU monitors levied intense criticism on the worsening state of human rights in Turkey, all but signaling the end of its potential accession.

FUTURE PROSPECTS

The combination of a majority government, consistent economic growth, and a determined effort to join the EU has provided Turkey with a degree of outward political stability unseen since the mid-1980s. That Turkey has held democratic elections for nearly two decades under the rule of an Islamist party that eschews violence and has always legitimated its rule in electoral majorities is also significant. However, upon a closer look, two decades of AKP governance has resulted in severe side-effects – among them new challenges in the form of currency and debt crises, increasingly widespread cronyism and corruption, extremely polarized political discourse, and multiplying abuses of power wielded by officials against opposition and critics. Erdoğan, the figure at the center of the AKP's rise, has little wish to leave the political limelight. The Kurdish crisis likewise continues without easy resolution, while the Syrian front and regional instability creates another source of territorial anxiety.

There are two pathways from here. One is the continued evolution of the "Turkish model," in which alternation of power occurs, executive overreach is retracted, and regular policymaking resolves its economic instability and backsliding into authoritarian hybridity. This would require concerted civic mobilization, opposition reformation, and perhaps international pressure. The other pathway is the continued aggregation and hegemony of Erdoğan and the AKP, which may next manifest through cancelled elections, outright fraudulence, unremitting coercion, and other signature tactics of unapologetic autocracies. In this future, the old type of Turkish governance, where military and bureaucratic elites often overrode the wishes of elected officials, would simply be replaced by another type of elective authoritarianism.

FURTHER READING

An accessible introduction to Turkey is Andrew Finkel, *Turkey: What Everyone Needs to Know* (Oxford University Press, 2012).

The historical emergence of Turkey commands a sizable library. Bernard Lewis's *The Emergence of Modern Turkey* (Oxford University Press, 1961) remains the classic volume on Turkey. Feroz Ahmad's *The Making of Modern Turkey* (Routledge, 1993) covers Turkish politics up to the 1990s. Erik J. Zurcher, *Turkey: A Modern History* (IB Tauris, 1994) gives a good overview. Stanford J. Shaw's two-volume *History of the Ottoman Empire and Modern Turkey* (Cambridge University Press, 1976–1977) contains a mine of data on the events it chronicles.

Andrew Mango, *Atatürk: The Biography of the Founder of Modern Turkey* (Overlook Press, 2000) gives a reliable account of Turkey's great leader as does Sukru Hanioglu, *Atatürk: An Intellectual Biography* (Princeton University Press, 2011). Banu Turanoglu, *The Formation of Turkish Republicanism* (Princeton University Press, 2017); Hale Yilmaz, *Becoming Turkish: Nationalist Reforms and Cultural Negotiations in Early Republican Turkey, 1923–1945* (Syracuse University Press, 2013); Soner Cagaptay, *Islam, Secularism and Nationalism in Modern Turkey: Who is a Turk?* (Routledge, 2006); and Carter Vaughn Findley, *Turkey, Islam, Nationalism and Modernity: A History 1789–2007* (Yale University

Press, 2010) also provide fantastic coverage of the late Ottoman and Republican period. For an excellent series of articles on Kemalist modernization, see Resat Kasaba and Sibel Bozdogan's *Rethinking Modernity and National Identity in Turkey* (University of Washington Press, 1997). A comparative take of Turkish with Japanese identity formation is given in Jennifer Dixon, *Dark Pasts: Changing the State's Story in Turkey and Japan* (Cornell University Press, 2018).

The political system engendered by the 1980s is analyzed in Ergun Ozbudun, *Contemporary Turkish Politics: Challenges to Democratic Consolidation* (Lynne Rienner Publishers, 2000). For an earlier view, see George S. Harris, *Turkey: Coping with Crisis* (Westview Press, 1985). Hugh Poulton's *Top Hat, Grey Wolf and Crescent: Turkish Nationalism and the Turkish Republic* (Hurst, 1997) is a detailed study of the nationalist roots of modern Turkey. For the evolution of political parties up to 1989, consult Metin Heper and Jacob M. Landau, eds., *Political Parties and Democracy in Turkey* (IB Tauris, 1991).

For recent developments in the AKP era, see Kaya Genc, *Under the Shadow: Rage and Revolution in Modern Turkey* (IB Tauris, 2016); Cihan Tugal, *The Fall of the Turkish Model: How the Arab Uprisings Brought down Islamic Liberalism* (Verso, 2016); and Soner Cagaptay, *The New Sultan: Erdoğan and the Crisis of Modern Turkey* (IB Tauris, 2017). For an analysis of the 2016 coup attempt, see Ates Altinordu, "A Midsummer Night's Coup: Performance and Power in Turkey's July 15 Coup Attempt" in Feride Cicekoglu and Omer Turan, eds., *The Dubious Case of a Failed Coup* (Palgrave Macmillan, 2019). An analytical exploration of the AKP's success is Toygar Sinan Baykan, *The Justice and Development Party in Turkey: Populism, Personalism, Organization* (Cambridge University Press, 2019). An overview of electoral dramas is

F. Michael Wuthrich, *National Elections in Turkey: People, Politics, and the Party System* (Syracuse: Syracuse University Press, 2015). Two recent and very accessible reads are Simon Waldman and Emre Caliskan, *The New Turkey and Its Discontents* (Oxford University Press, 2018), and Ilter Turan, *Turkey's Difficult Journey to Democracy: Two Steps Forward, One Step Back* (Oxford University Press, 2015).

Issues of culture, society, and minority rights deserve considerable attention. Peter A. Andrews, ed., *Ethnic Groups in the Republic of Turkey* (Ludwig Teichert Verlag, 1989) gives a magisterial treatment of Turkey's cultural geography. Women's issues are treated in Sirin Tekeli, ed., *Women in Modern Turkish Society: A Reader* (Zed, 1995). Lerna Ekmekcioglu, *Recovering Armenia: The Limits of Belonging in Post-Genocide Turkey* (Stanford University Press, 2016) offers a candid look at Turkey's difficult identity politics and minority issues as does Senem Aslan, *Nation Building in Turkey and Morocco* (Cambridge University Press, 2015).

The Kurdish challenge is covered in David McDowall, *A Modern History of the Kurds* (IB Tauris, 1996). Later investigations include Henri J. Barkey and Graham E. Fuller, *Turkey's Kurdish Question: An Example of a Trans-State Conflict* (Rowman and Littlefield, 1998), and Kemal Kirisçi and Gareth Winrow, *The Kurdish Question and Turkey* (Frank Cass, 1997). Later analyses include: Omer Taspinar, *Kurdish Nationalism and Political Islam in Turkey: Kemalist Identity in Transition* (Routledge, 2005); Henri J. Barkey, *Preventing Conflict over Kurdistan* (Carnegie Endowment for International Peace, 2009); Nicole Watts, *Activists in Office: Kurdish Politics and Protest in Turkey* (University of Washington Press, 2010); and Mustafa Gurbuz, *Rival Kurdish Movements in Turkey: Transforming Ethnic Conflict* (Amsterdam University

Press, 2016). An economic approach lays in Veli Yadirgi, *The Political Economy of the Kurds of Turkey: From the Ottoman Empire to the Turkish Republic* (Cambridge University Press, 2018).

On economic issues, the magisterial work by the most famous Turkish academic economist is Sevket Pamuk, *Uneven Centuries: Economic Development of Turkey since 1820* (Princeton University Press, 2018). Elsewhere, Z.Y. Herslag's *The Contemporary Turkish Economy* (Routledge, 1988) examines the Turkish economy through the post-1980 period of export orientation. Anne O. Krueger and Okan A. Aktan provide an analysis of Özal's reforms in the 1980s in *Swimming against the Tide: Turkish Trade Reform in the 1980s* (Institute for Contemporary Studies Press, 1992). Ayse Bugra and Osman Savaskan, *The New Capitalism in Turkey: The Relationship between Politics, Religion and Business* (Edward Elgar, 2014) offers a comprehensive overview of developments in the field of political-economy and state-business relations.

The role of the military in politics is well depicted by William M. Hale, *Turkish Politics and the Military* (Routledge, 1995). For an anthropological approach to civil society relations in Turkey, see Ayse Gül Altinay, *The Myth of the Military Nation: Militarism, Gender, and Education in Turkey* (Palgrave, 2004).

Turkish foreign policy is a topic of considerable scholarly interest. Amit Bein, *Kemalist Turkey and the Middle East: International Relations in the Interwar Period* (Cambridge University Press, 2017) provides an excellent revisionist history of Kemalist foreign policy. Linking foreign policy to state-building is Reem Abou-El-Fadl, *Foreign Policy as Nation Making: Turkey and Egypt in the Cold War* (Cambridge University Press, 2019). Philip Robins, *Suits and Uniforms: Turkish Foreign Policy since the Cold War* (University of Washington Press, 2003) is another comprehensive approach to Turkish foreign

policy. Alvin Z. Rubinstein and Oles M. Smolansky, eds., *Regional Power Rivalries in the New Eurasia: Russia, Turkey, and Iran* (ME Sharpe, 1995) covers the early stages of Turkey's relationship with the newly independent states of the former Soviet Union. A constructivist take on how Turkish identity conflicts play out in foreign policy comes from Lisel Hintz, *Identity Politics Inside Out: National Identity Contestation and Foreign Policy in Turkey* (Oxford University Press, 2018). Modern US-Turkish relations are laid out in Ekavi Athanassopoulou, *Strategic Relations between the US and Turkey, 1979–2000: Sleeping with a Tiger* (Routledge, 2014). The tortuous process of EU accession is laid out in Melek Saral, *Turkey's "Self" and "Other" Definitions in the Course of the EU Accession Process* (Amsterdam University Press, 2018). Finally, on the Cyprus issue, see Michael Emerson and Nathalie Tocci, *Cyprus as Lighthouse of the East Mediterranean: Shaping Re-unification and EU Accession Together* (Center for European Research, 2002).

Religion in Turkey is a dense, multifaceted subject. Richard Tapper, ed., *Islam in Modern Turkey: Religion, Politics, and Literature in a Secular State* (IB Tauris, 1991) gives the background to religious developments. A more specialized treatment can be found in Jenny White, *Islamist Mobilization in Turkey: A Study in Vernacular Politics* (University of Washington Press, 2002) and *Muslim Nationalism and the New Turks* (Princeton University Press, 2014). Comparisons of Israel and Turkey, and their treatment of religion as part of national identity, are found in Yusuf Sarfati, *Mobilizing Religion in Middle East Politics: A Comparative Study of Israel and Turkey* (Routledge, 2014), and Sultan Tepe, *Beyond Sacred and Secular: Politics of Religion in Israel and Turkey* (Stanford University Press, 2008).

More specialized takes on how Islam and religious discourse have been harnessed in politics include: Brian Silverstein, *Islam and Modernity in Turkey* (Palgrave Macmillan, 2011); Iren Ozgur, *Islamic Schools in Modern Turkey: Faith, Politics and Education* (Cambridge University Press, 2012); Ceren Lord, *Religious Politics in Turkey: From the Birth of the Republic to the AKP* (Cambridge University Press, 2018); and Kristin Fabbe, *Disciples of the State?: Religion and Statebuilding in the Former Ottoman World* (Cambridge University Press, 2019). On the Gülenist movement, see Berna Turam, *Between Islam and the State: The Politics of Engagement* (Stanford University Press, 2007) and Joshua Hendrick, *Gulen: The Ambiguous Politics of Market Islam in Turkey and the World* (New York University Press, 2013).

Online sources

Despite the closure of many Turkish media outlets, online sources provide penchant takes on the latest events there. Examples include Turkey Analyst (www.turkeyanalyst.org/), the Turkey portal of *Al-Monitor* (www.al-monitor.com/pulse/turkey-pulse) and the Turkish publication *Hurriyet Daily* (www.hurriyetdailynews.com/). Other sources of politics include the Turkish daily, *Daily Sabah*, despite its pro-AKP leanings (www.dailysabah.com/politics), and the television news channel CNNTurk (www.cnnturk.com/). Turkish foreign policy is explored in the online version of the journal *Insight Turkey* (www.insightturkey.com/).

The Institute for Turkish Studies has a wealth of online resources regarding the further study of Turkish politics and society (www.turkishstudies.org/). Economic data and studies on Turkey's financial issues are found on the World Bank's country site (www.worldbank.org/en/country/turkey/overview). The Turkey Project of the Brookings Institution likewise has a dense collection of briefings and reports (www.brookings.edu/project/the-turkey-project/). Finally, the Atlantic Council's Turkey webpage offers rolling coverage of economic, social, and energy-related affairs (www.atlanticcouncil.org/in-turkey).

Please note that URLs may change far more quickly than books can be printed; so if these exact URLs do not work, simply search Google or another engine by the titles of these websites and online resources.

The Gulf

Saudi Arabia, Iran, Kuwait, Bahrain, Qatar, UAE, Oman, and Yemen

Kingdom of Saudi Arabia

Sean Foley

INTRODUCTION

Although the history of modern Saudi Arabia officially begins with its unification in 1932, its story dates back to the early eighteenth century, when an impoverished principality in central Arabia began expanding outwards. Since the commercial production of large oil deposits began in the 1940s, the country has gradually emerged as one of the largest and wealthiest in the MENA. Because Islam's two holiest cities, Mecca and Medina, are situated within the kingdom, Saudi Arabia and its vision of Wahhabi Islam have also enjoyed wide influence throughout the Muslim world over the last century. Today, Saudi Arabia is a pillar of the world economy, not least because of its close strategic ties to the United States and the West.

However, times are changing as the Saudi monarchy shifts into a newer, younger, and more controversial leadership. Thanks to his ambitious plans to reform the kingdom's economy, the costly war in Yemen, and renewed crackdowns on dissent at home and abroad – all since 2015 – Saudi Crown Prince (and putatively, the next king) Muhammad bin Salman (MbS) has thrust the kingdom into geopolitical controversy regarding its future stability and regional leadership. Internally, it is evolving; although Saudi society is widely seen as rejecting any manifestation of the contemporary world – in the past, famously banning women from driving and providing scores of recruits to radical Islamist groups – it has successfully integrated many global practices and Western notions into its social routines. Equally importantly, the Saudi state has educated multiple generations of young people, with women now accounting for 60 percent of all college students. Over the past two decades, the country has also witnessed the rise of a vibrant artistic movement. Time will tell whether such shifts will cause earthquakes in politics, or simply slow, tectonic adaptations.

Box 15.1 provides vital data for this country.

HISTORICAL BACKGROUND

The founder of the Saudi dynasty was Muhammad ibn Saud (born 1703), who was emir of Dar'iyyah, a small oasis town in the central Najd, outside of what is today Riyadh. In 1744, he formed an alliance with Shaykh

BOX 15.1 VITAL DATA – KINGDOM OF SAUDI ARABIA

Capital	Riyadh
Regime type	Authoritarian (monarchy)
Head of state	King Salman bin 'Abd al-Aziz (since 2015)
Head of government	King Salman bin 'Abd al-Aziz (since 2015)
Legislative institution	Unicameral consultative assembly, with 150 appointed seats (*Majlis al-Shura*, or Consultative Assembly)
Female quota	Yes: one-fifth of all seats set aside for women
Percentage of seats held by women	20%
Major political parties (share of seats in most recent general elections)	None: no elections, and parties are prohibited
Population	32,938,213
Major ethnic groups	Arab (90%), other (10%)
Major religious groups	Sunni Muslim (80%), Shi'a Muslim (10%), other (10%)
GDP per capita	$23,566 ($55,944 at Purchasing Power Parity)
Unemployment rate	5.9%
Youth unemployment rate	25.8%
Major economic industries	Petroleum, petrochemicals, cement, fertilizer, plastics, construction
Military spending as % GDP	10.3%

Muhammad ibn 'Abd al-Wahhab, a Muslim cleric who had been exiled from a neighboring town because of his appeals for religious and social reform. The alliance, which proved so beneficial to both men that it has been maintained by their descendants, still serves as a foundation of the Saudi state.

The Wahhabi interpretation of Islam that followed was among the earliest expressions of what scholars today call Salafi thought, in that it called for Muslims to return to the most conservative, unabridged, and literal fundaments of their faith. Adaptations of Islamic values and beliefs to modern circumstances were to be rejected. Al-Wahhab anchored this view on two sources: the Hanbali school of Islamic jurisprudence, one of four recognized schools within Sunni Islam's expansive view of *shari'a* (Islamic law), and the writings of Taqi al-Din Ahmad ibn Taymiyyah, a thirteenth century Hanbali theologian who would also inspire some Islamists two centuries later. Saudis and others who adhere to this Wahhabi framework prefer to be called *muwahhidin* (unitarians or monotheists), expressing adherence to the central monotheistic doctrine of *tawhid*, rather than "Wahhabists," as that would imply worshipping a person or ideal rather than God. The descendants of al-Wahhab are among the most prestigious families in Saudi Arabia, and have contributed many religious leaders to the country.

Early conquests and state formation

By the end of the eighteenth century, the Saudi dynasty and its religious allies had, with relatively little notice by the outside world, conquered most of the central part of the Arabian Peninsula. But when in 1801 their forces sacked the Shi'a holy city of Karbala, in what is today southern Iraq, they drew the attention of the outside world. Convinced that pilgrimages to tombs of holy men constituted idolatry, the Saudis destroyed the tombs of a number of revered Shi'a "saints," including that of the grandson of the Prophet Muhammad, Hussein, whose tomb was venerated by Shi'a as a site for pilgrimage second in importance only to Mecca and Medina. In 1806, Saudi forces seized Mecca and Medina, and began pushing eastwards into what is now Oman and other parts of the Arabian Gulf littoral. In time, the Ottoman Empire pushed back, and in 1811 ordered its Egyptian viceroy, Muhammad Ali Pasha, to send an army to destroy the rising polity. They indeed destroyed many Saudi forces, who after years of abeyance re-emerged to recreate their conquest. Throughout the next decades, Saudi rulers moved to Riyadh as their authority waxed and waned, and conflicts sometimes cut short the tenures (and lives) of the family's anointed emirs. Ottoman forces frequently limited Saudi military gains, while local tribes also resisted. The fledgling Saudi state collapsed in 1887, after which another Arabian tribal leadership, the Rashid dynasty, seized Riyadh and forced the Saudi family into exile.

The fortunes of the House of Saud rose for a third and final time when 'Abd al-Aziz al-Saud, a young scion of the family who would later become known in the West as Ibn Saud, led a few dozen followers to recapture Riyadh in January 1902. From this start, 'Abd al-Aziz retook much of the territory of the old Saudi state, conquering other local tribal holdings and vanquishing the Rashid dynasty, among other rivals. Over the next decade, he and his allies won control of the southern region of the Najd over central communities like 'Unaiza and Buraydah, and the rich al-Ahsa oasis. Their dominance over the Qatif region, not far from al-Ahsa, also gave them authority over a large community of Shi'a. These eastern residents would form the basis of the future Saudi state's significant (and marginalized) Shi'a minority.

'Abd al-Aziz also struck an alliance with the Ikhwan (in Arabic, brothers; not to be confused with the Muslim Brotherhood, or *Ikhwan Muslimin*), fierce adherents to Wahhabi Islam who had fought alongside 'Abd al-Aziz for decades. Many of the Ikhwan were settled in hundreds of new settlements, where religious leaders taught them that farming, trade, and industry did not contravene religion – but drinking and smoking did. Under the careful watch of Saudi religious leaders, tribesmen could seemingly simultaneously enjoy the material benefits of settled life and use new technology, comfortable in the knowledge that they were doing both in a peaceful physical space in which the teachings of Islam were upheld.

At the start of World War One, the Ottoman Empire – just as it had been a century earlier – was a major regional power, albeit in its twilight. In the early months of the war, it sought the support of the major rulers in central Arabia. Yet the two most prominent Arab leaders, 'Abd al-Aziz as well as Sharif Hussein, whose Hashemite family had been granted by Ottoman authority custodianship over Mecca and thus ruled the Hijaz region in the western part of the Arabian Peninsula, chose the British. In the case of Sharif Hussein, the alliance followed a long series of secret negotiations with British officials for the creation of a new state in the Arab provinces of the Ottoman Empire. That revolt followed the suppression of Arab Nationalists in

Ottoman-held Damascus and the British setbacks in Gallipoli (in modern-day Turkey). Under the leadership of Emir Faisal, Sharif Hussein's son, the Arab forces steadily encroached northwards into the Ottoman-held Mashriq. In 1917, the British sent a mission to 'Abd al-Aziz to persuade him to cooperate with Sharif Hussein. While 'Abd al-Aziz declined, as he saw the Hijaz-based dynasty as his primary rival, he did befriend British officials, including Harry St. John Philby, who would later become a key adviser and confidante.

Following the end of the war and the collapse of Ottoman power in the Middle East and Gulf, 'Abd al-Aziz continued his conquests. His forces quickly defeated Sharif Hussein's army, only to be driven back by British forces. But after Hussein proclaimed himself the "King of the Arabs" and new Caliph for all the domain of Islam, while refusing to recognize London's post-war plans to carve out the Mashriq into a set of protectorates rather than facilitate the creation of a pan-Arab state as promised, the British abandoned him. That provided a critical opening for 'Abd al-Aziz, whose forces moved from the central Najd region into the western Hijaz area. They conquered the major commercial city of Jeddah and eventually all the Hijaz, thereby assuming control over Mecca and Medina. The newly unifying Saudi state now had its crown jewel, the two holiest cities in Islam, while continuing its pattern of eliminating tribal rivals and other armed resistance. Among the first imperatives passed after this conquest in 1926 was rehabilitating the Hajj pilgrimage, long a source of pride and commerce for Hijaz residents.

Meanwhile, the Ikhwan rebelled. They launched raids northwards into the British protectorates of Transjordan and Iraq, as well as nearby Kuwait. The Transjordanian and Iraqi incursions were especially controversial; both British Mandates were ruled by the sons of Sharif Hussein, thereby representing the continuity of the Hashemite dynasty after its deposal from the Hijaz by the Saudi leadership. This instigated British military retaliation into Saudi territory with airplanes and other modern weapons. The resulting conflict challenged the authority of 'Abd al-Aziz and his principal argument for settling the tribes – namely, to prevent them from raiding surrounding areas and thus creating a stably bounded and territorialized state. In this moment of crisis, 'Abd al-Aziz turned to Wahhabi *'ulama* (religious scholars and jurists) for support, invoking the alliance that had been the foundation of the first Saudi state. At a conference in Riyadh in 1928, they ruled decisively in his favor, stating that 'Abd al-Aziz, as leader of the Muslim community, had the sole prerogative to wage war. They confirmed that he was a pious

Muslim who faithfully adhered to Islamic principles. With the backing of the religious elites, he crushed the Ikhwan rebellion and disbanded their militias.

Two years later on September 23, 1932 the government changed the name of the Saudi state from the kingdom of Hijaz, the Najd, and Its Dependencies to the Kingdom of Saudi Arabia, with 'Abd al-Aziz adopting a new title, the King of Saudi Arabia. The modern Saudi state had come into existence with borders analogous to those of the first Saudi state more than a century earlier – a remarkable achievement for 'Abd al-Aziz, who only three decades earlier had only 40 warriors and few prospects for success.

Post-war developments: 1940s–1990

Despite this newfound period of stability, economic and social development in the kingdom lagged far behind that of its political administration until after World War Two. Oil, which had been discovered in sizable quantities in 1938, was finally developed into a viable national industry capable of transforming the kingdom's society in the 1950s. At that time, the discovery of offshore oil fields in addition to the Ghawar, still the world's largest conventional (i.e., onshore) field, signaled that the kingdom and its neighbors in the Gulf would become the center of the global hydrocarbon industry. When those discoveries were made, the country's leadership had passed from King 'Abd al-Aziz (after his death) to Saud, his eldest surviving son. Despite unparalleled revenues from the oil industry, the kingdom's treasury was often virtually empty given the tendency of the tiny government – dominated by the family, and lacking many institutional structures – to rampantly spend without any constraints or oversight.

Over time, however, partly due to Western advisers and partly due to the necessities of administering vast amounts of wealth as well as a sizable chunk of territory bordering many other countries, the Saudi government began developing the accoutrements of modern political order, among them appropriate ministries, offices, payrolls, accounts, and other bureaucratic features. In 1962, King Saud transferred government operations over to his half-brother Faisal. Two years later, Saud abdicated, living the rest of his life in exile until his death in Athens in 1969. King Faisal not only drew on years of experience in public life but also left a legacy that can still be felt in the kingdom in the twenty-first century. In 1919, as a 14-year-old teenager, Faisal represented his father on an official visit to Great Britain – an event portrayed in *Born a King* (2018), the first feature film to be screened in Saudi Arabia. There, Faisal was exposed to not only the diplomatic machinations of British imperialism but also the inherent weaknesses of the budding Saudi state if it could not resolve its domestic conflicts. Faisal later represented Saudi Arabia at the San Francisco conference that established the United Nations in 1945.[1] Faisal's mother hailed from the family of 'Abd al-Wahhab, and thus was dedicated to the preservation of a conservative Islamic way of life both in Saudi Arabia and the rest of the world.

King Faisal's tenure lasted until his assassination in 1975, but was marked by rapid political and social change in a way that laid the foundations for the kingdom today. He became the first Saudi ruler to adopt the title "Custodian of the Two Holy Mosques" (Mecca and Medina), a title formally used by the Ottomans when they ruled the Hijaz but which now has become an indelible part of the royal lexicon. He also strongly encouraged material and technological modernization, convincing many areas of society that radio, television, and other modern innovations were consistent with the country's cultural and Islamic traditions. Another contribution came in 1960, when the Saudi state created a host of state-funded primary, secondary, and technical schools for girls – a monumental change. Two years later women began to attend the kingdom's universities. By the twenty-first century, more women than men attended Saudi colleges and universities.

King Faisal's impact on foreign affairs was nearly as consequential as his impact on domestic life. When the Ministry of Foreign Affairs was created in 1930, he became the first foreign minister, a position he held for decades. During that time, he became one of the most widely traveled Saudi officials of his lifetime – a process aided by his command of multiple languages along with his vast array of foreign contacts and deep knowledge of global affairs. Those contacts proved especially useful as he negotiated the complicated politics of the Cold War, where his strident antipathy toward the Soviet Union and communism firmly aligned the country with the United States. While Faisal vehemently opposed Arab Nationalism, saw the Nasserist regime in Egypt as a threat, and believed the Arab republics' alignments with Soviet power was a mistake, he was willing to make common cause with Egypt, Syria, and other countries in support of the Palestinian cause, especially after the 1967 Arab-Israeli War. It should therefore come as no surprise that Faisal's most consequential foreign policy decision as king, the Arab oil embargo of the early 1970s, stood at the intersection of the Cold War and the Palestinian conflict.

In 1975, a deranged member of the Saudi royal family assassinated King Faisal, who was succeeded by his half-brother Khalid. During his reign, oil wealth flooded the treasury, allowing for another economic boom and fueling massive investments in housing, healthcare, education, infrastructure, communications, and urbanization. In 1979, armed militants declaring the House of Saud to be illegitimate seized the Grand Mosque in Mecca – Islam's singular holiest site – by force, demanding a variety of economic, political, religious, and social reforms. Among other things, they called on Saudis to return to Islam, abandon smoking, cease watching football (soccer), and refrain from other modern activities that had grown in popularity over the previous two decades. Though the uprising was forcefully suppressed, it nonetheless heralded the rise of the *Sahwa* (Awakening), a homegrown Islamic cultural and social movement that sought to realize a more pious society in the kingdom.

At the same time, it convinced the Saudi monarchy to give more authority and influence to the Wahhabi 'ulama who had long burnished the religious credentials of the ruling family, believing that stricter impositions of Wahhabi mores and norms from above would foreclose such radicalism in the future. The organ of the state empowered by this decision was the Committee for the Promotion of Virtue and Prevention of Vice, which deployed social enforcers (i.e., religious police) to ensure that appropriate religious dictates were observed. Among them was the wearing of the 'abaya (cloak) and hijab by women, to cover their bodies and hair; refraining from all drugs and alcohol; ensure gender separation in appropriate settings, and that women remain accompanied by a male guardian; and other practices that soon became synonymous with the stricter religiosity associated with Saudi Arabia in the Western imagination. Such limitations would only gradually begin to be lifted in the twenty-first century, under King Abdullah and then King Salman.

In 1982, King Khalid died of a heart attack and was succeeded by Fahd, another one of 'Abd al-Aziz's sons, who had considerable experience in government. This perpetuated the pattern of power transfer that would be tested later on – the throne passing between the sons of the kingdom's modern founder in a kind of lateral succession. At the same time, many of 'Abd al-Aziz's other sons retained important positions in government, partly to ensure the family's monopoly over state power and partly to also mollify jealous brothers, who would each rule over their own institutional and bureaucratic fiefdoms. Fahd's half-brother Abdullah became the heir apparent and first deputy prime minister, also retaining command of the Saudi National Guard, a position which he had held since 1962. Fahd's full brother Prince Sultan, the minister of defense, became the second deputy prime minister, while another full brother, Prince Salman, remained mayor of Riyadh, a position he had held since 1963. (Both Abdullah and Salman would ascend to the throne after Fahd.)

As king, Fahd continued modernizing the economy while overseeing an increasingly Islamic state and society consistent with the preferences of the Wahhabi 'ulama. Economic difficulties after the mid-1980s due to the global oil price collapse threw routines into a shock, delaying many projects. Still, King Fahd continued attempting to update the country's administration. For instance, in 1992, he promulgated a new Basic Law of Government designed to modernize the political process while also promulgating the Majlis al-Shura (consultative assembly), an advisory body of appointed elites who provided at least the façade of public participation in the political process. In foreign policy, King Fahd followed the lead of his predecessors, seeking close cooperation with the United States and other Western countries while working with Egypt and other "moderate" Arab states to address Middle East regional problems. In 1981, he even forwarded his own peace plan for the Arab-Israeli conflict modeled on past United Nations resolutions seeking to trade land for peace. While what came to be known as the Fahd Plan was largely ignored by the United States and Israel, Fahd's efforts to maintain close ties with the US – even after the fall of the Soviet Union and the end of the Cold War – bore fruit in 1990 after Iraq's invasion of Kuwait in 1990.

Modernity, succession, and controversy: 1990–present

The Gulf War was a watershed in Saudi domestic affairs and foreign policy. The Iraqi invasion of Kuwait threatened not only Saudi Arabia but also the rest of the oil-rich Arabian Peninsula. During the crisis, Fahd cooperated closely with US officials to assemble and pay for a military coalition led by the United States to protect the kingdom and eventually to drive Iraq out of Kuwait in 1991. That operation, which included stationing US troops within the kingdom, angered the generation of young Saudi volunteers who had fought the Soviet military in Afghanistan in the 1980s, a campaign justified and described by its underwriters in the Saudi government and elsewhere as a glorious jihad. King Fahd firmly rejected an offer made by one such Saudi volunteer from a well-known family, Osama bin Laden, to remove the Iraqis from Kuwait. Dejected by Fahd's rebuff, and insulted by the sight of American troops in the cradle of Islam, these veterans felt marginalized, returning to the religious vision that had given meaning to their lives as young men in the kingdom and had justified their crusade in Afghanistan. One of the principal organizations that these men joined was Bin Laden's Al-Qa'ida, a Salafi-jihadi organization that began staging terrorist attacks against Saudi and Western targets. By the middle of the 1990s, terrorism had emerged as the chief national security problem facing the country, with Al-Qaʻida becoming a major strategic liability for a monarchical regime that sought to maintain close Western guarantees of support and protection.

King Fahd, however, would not be the one to addresses these concerns, for he suffered a heart attack in 1995, passing over the reins of government to Crown Prince Abdullah, though he would not formally become king until 2005. It would be he who would be responsible for addressing two major terrorist incidents that would impact Saudi domestic and foreign policy. The first were the September 11, 2001 terrorist attacks in the US, in which 15 of the 19 hijackers were Saudis – and which brought worldwide attention to the kingdom's social and religious policies. The second was the May 2003 series of terrorist strikes on residential compounds in Riyadh, in which dozens of Western expatriates and Saudis were killed. Together, the terrorist attacks and the Western reaction to them, which included not only American interventionism in the MENA but also broad pressures imposed upon many Arab states to staunch violent extremism, compelled programmatic changes in Saudi policy. The government initiated an innovative (and in many ways successful) counterterrorism program, which blended the militaristic shutdown of terrorist cells with rehabilitating young recruits for re-entry into society.

When Abdullah officially became king in 2005, upon the death of Fahd, a major concern was growing popular pressure for more political participation and civil liberties. The success of universal education, more exposure to Western culture, and the demographic youth bulge revealed a growing society content to continually push against traditional restrictions. Adjusting to the challenges of the era, King Abdullah oversaw a series of reforms of the political process, judicial system, and educational sector. His reign also witnessed a cultural renaissance, with the emergence of a modern artistic movement across multiple genres – reviving a tradition that had, before the imposition of stricter religious enforcement in the post-1979 years, boasted cultural figures renowned throughout the Arab world, such as musician and singer Muhammad ʻAbdu. Benefiting from an upsurge in oil prices during the 2000s, Abdullah also invested generously in new educational institutions along with scholarship programs that sent tens of thousands of Saudi youths to study abroad, especially in the United States.

The Arab Spring of 2011–12 interrupted this rebound with a rude awakening. While there were some protests, involving not just young urban Saudi activists demanding democratic changes but also agitations from the marginalized Shiʻa communities of the Qatif region, where residents mobilized demonstrations for the release of political prisoners and for greater representation. While most such protests were suppressed harshly, with deaths interspersed with crackdowns against hundreds of young organizers and marchers, King Abdullah sought to quickly foreclose restiveness in the rest of the country through adroit redistribution of rentier wealth. His government ordered billions of dollars of public salary raises, infrastructural projects, and other investments. Quietly, as the Arab Spring roiled Tunisia, Egypt, Libya, and Yemen, the monarchy also began looking eastwards; with conservative royals believing the US had abandoned its autocratic allies during the revolutionary moment, a new belief held that Saudi Arabia could also better incorporate support from China and other rising Asian powers.

King Abdullah's death in January 2015 paved the way for Salman, his half-brother, to become King. Equally important was the rise of Salman's young son, Muhammad bin Salman (MbS), who became crown prince in 2017 after meteorically rising through the ranks of government offices, including becoming the youngest defense minister in the world in late 2015 at the age of 30. MbS's rise also signified a generational rupture: with the sons of the 'Abd al-Aziz virtually all deceased, the crown prince was positioned to be the first of the next generation of Saudi princes to become king.

The new regime caused considerable controversy. On the foreign relations side, it launched an aggressive military intervention in Yemen in 2015 against the Houthi rebel movement resulting in humanitarian crisis; led an economic blockade against Qatar in June 2017, in the culmination of its lopsided strategic rivalry with its fellow Gulf dynasty; and later in November that year, meddled in Lebanese politics by curiously detaining its Prime Minister, Saad Hariri, in the kingdom in order to force a resignation of his government. The latter reflected the kingdom's increasingly hardline stance against all forms of Islamist militancy that seemed to threaten its own religious credentials. Thus, not only did the Saudi monarchy welcome the Egyptian coup of July 2013, which ended both a Muslim Brotherhood government and a democratic experiment, but it also declared both the Brotherhood and Lebanese Hizbullah (the latter represented in the Lebanese government) to be terrorist organizations.

The most intense global criticism came, however, after the murder of Saudi journalist and critic Jamal Khashoggi in Turkey in fall 2018 by a team of Saudi assassins in an operation that captivated Western headlines for months. That murder came a year after MbS moved aggressively against senior princes in the family and various other business and political elites, imprisoning some and threatening others in a bid to simultaneously eliminate opposition while extracting significant sums of money. Such a clampdown came not long after MbS had rolled out Vision 2030, an ambitious economic modernization program that promised to halt Saudi Arabia's dependence on oil, develop new industries, liberalize the religious arena, and make the country the crown jewel of the MENA. At the same time, the young prince masterminded the visible relaxation of some of the stricter Wahhabi mandates; thus in 2018, women were permitted to drive, movie theaters opened for the first time since the 1970s, music concerts were planned and promoted, and the religious police saw much of their authority evaporate. Optimists suggested MbS was rolling back the post-1979 conservatism that stifled social life in the kingdom, while moving the country beyond its addiction to hydrocarbon rents. Critics pointed out the government's worsening repressive streak, including not just cracking down on alleged corruption but also arresting dissidents, activists, and youths on flimsy pretenses, resulting in even greater human rights abuses.

As the 2010s closed, the one constant seemed to be succession: so long as MbS remained crown prince, and with his ailing father (who turned 83 in 2019) still on the throne, the next kingship of Saudi Arabia would be one that portended dramatic – and perhaps unpredictable – change.

SOCIAL AND ECONOMIC ENVIRONMENT

Saudi Arabia occupies about 830,000 square miles (over two million square kilometers). It has taken many years for Saudi Arabia to demarcate its borders. In 1922, the Saudi-Kuwaiti Neutral Zone and the Saudi-Iraqi Neutral Zone were created to avoid tribal border hostilities. The first was abolished in 1966 and the second in 1975, and their territories were divided among the parties. The decades-old Buraymi Oasis territorial dispute among Saudi Arabia, Oman, and Abu Dhabi (the latter a part of the United Arab Emirates) was settled in 1974 when Saudi Arabia agreed to give up its claim to the oasis and adjacent territory in return for an outlet to the Gulf through Abu Dhabi. Since then, the kingdom has agreed in principle to demarcate the rest of its long border with Oman. In 2000, Saudi Arabia and Yemen signed a treaty on their international land and sea borders, ending a dispute that went back to the 1934 Saudi invasion of Yemen. After the summer 2017 diplomatic crisis and economic blockade with Qatar, the Saudi-Qatari border remains delineated but subject to transformation, due to a proposed canal project that would essentially cut off peninsular Qatar from the Arabian mainland and turn it into an island.

Although nearly all of Saudi Arabia is arid, only a part of it consists of real sand desert. There are three such deserts in the kingdom: the Great Nafud, located in the north (*nafud* is one of several Arabic words meaning desert); the Rub'a al-Khali, or Empty Quarter, which stretches along the entire southern frontier and is the largest contiguous sand desert in the world; and the Dahna, a narrow strip that forms a great arc from the Great Nafud westward and then south to the Rub'a al-Khali.

Nearly 84 percent of the Saudi population is urbanized, and the kingdom features a number of notable cities (Map 15.1). The largest include the capital of Riyadh, with nearly 6.5 million people; Jeddah, with nearly four million; the holy cities of Mecca and Medina, with nearly 1.9 and 1.3 million, respectively; and Ta'if, with over a million residents.

The kingdom is administratively divided into 13 regions, each containing a number of smaller governorates. Geographically and culturally, however, the kingdom is understood to comprise a handful of larger regions that have each held distinctive historical and social features, interlinked by preindustrial caravan routes, tribal nomadic movements, and patterns of conflict. Central Arabia, or the Najd (highlands), is predominantly an arid plateau interspersed with oases; it is both the geographical and the political heartland of the country. Many cities and towns are scattered throughout the Najd. The largest is Riyadh, which though a major metropolis now, was but a small oasis town in 1900 with just 7,500 residents. Just a few kilometers north, Dar'iyyah, the ancestral home of the Saudi clan, has become a suburb of the capital.

Western Saudi Arabia is divided into two areas, of which the Hijaz is most prominent. It contains Jeddah, the second-largest city and a major center of commerce. The Hijaz region also receives much economic and social traffic as a conduit for the Hajj pilgrimage to Mecca for Muslim travelers; performing the Hajj is among one of the pillars of Islamic piety. Including also the lesser pilgrimage, the Umrah, Mecca receives up to 11 million Muslim visitors a year. Physical infrastructure to accommodate the Hajj is extensive, including one of the largest commercial airports in the world at Jeddah, a modern hub on the Red Sea through which over 3 million people pass annually, and an expanding railway system. The Saudi government has also spent billions of dollars upgrading the Sacred Mosque in Mecca and the Prophet's Mosque in Medina, the two holiest sites in Islam. Mecca has already seen extraordinary commercial development; as Photo 15.1 shows, the view from the Ka'aba – the centerpiece of the Sacred

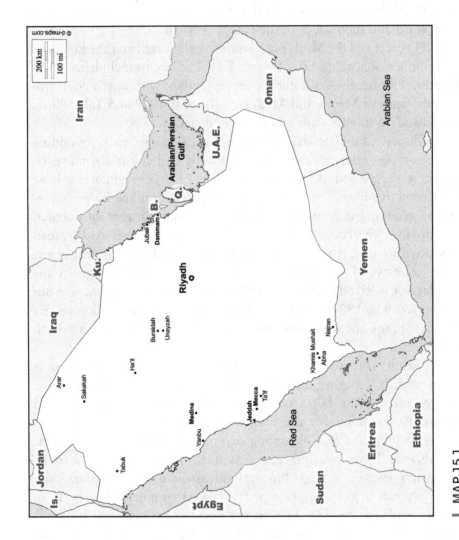

MAP 15.1
Kingdom of Saudi Arabia. Major water bodies and cities shown.

Source: D-Maps.

PHOTO 15.1
Upward View from the Sacred Mosque of Mecca.

Source: Pixabay. Public domain.

Mosque in Mecca – reveals a towering urban skyline (Photo 15.1). As part of its Vision 2030 program, the Saudi government hopes to attract more than 30 million visitors a year to this city.

Eastern Saudi Arabia is a mixture of old and new. It includes al-Hasa, the largest oasis in the world, and the Qatif region on the Gulf coast. The region has both the largest oil field in the world, the Ghawar, as well as the kingdom's greatest agglomeration of Shi'a residents. The presence of both makes stability and control over this area of immense political importance to the Saudi monarchy. The principal city is Dammam; once a small pearling and privateering port, it is now a major metropolis. South of Dammam is Dhahran, the location of the Saudi Aramco (the Saudi state oil company) along with King Fahd University of Petroleum and Minerals, one of the most prestigious universities in the kingdom.

There are many other sub-regions, urban systems, and economic zones too numerous to mention here, but overall the country shares one common physical trait – the harsh, hot climate typical of a desert area. Because of this climate and the desert terrain, a shortage of water has always been a major concern. In the interior, non-renewable aquifers are being tapped at an unprecedented rate, particularly as urbanization and population growth expand and as irrigated agricultural-development projects are created in the interior. To augment water supplies, the kingdom has created a massive desalination system. Despite the arid climate, sporadic rains do occur in Saudi Arabia, and there is occasional snow in the mountains. This water has to run off somewhere, and as a result, there is a drainage system of intersecting wadis, or dry riverbeds and valleys. After local, and occasionally heavy, rains, the wadis can become rushing torrents. In 2009 and 2011, Jeddah suffered from major floods.

There are variations that come with this ecological backdrop. In the interior, the lack of humidity causes daytime temperatures to rise sharply. In the summer, daytime readings can register over 130 degrees Fahrenheit (54 Celsius), then drop precipitously after the sun goes down, sometimes by as much as 70 degrees Fahrenheit (20 Celsius). In the winter, subfreezing temperatures are not uncommon. By contrast, the coastal areas both west and east – on the Red Sea, and the Arabian Gulf – combine heat and high humidity. The humidity usually keeps the temperature from exceeding 105 degrees Fahrenheit (40 Celsius) in the summer but likewise prevents it from dropping more than a few degrees at night. Winter temperatures are balmier and warmer at night than those in the interior, particularly the farther south one goes. The kingdom also has several mountainous ranges, including the Asir Mountains which run in the southwestern area parallel to the Red Sea; this terrain can receive significant rainfall of up to 20 inches annually, while also featuring much cooler weather.

Social currents

In 2018, Saudi Arabia had an estimated population of about 33 million people, of which roughly a third are expatriates (mostly foreign workers from other countries). Though the country's population is small in comparison to its oil wealth, it has experienced a population explosion in the past quarter century that has radically changed its demography. However, with a quarter of the population under 15, and more than half the national (non-foreign) population under 25, the kingdom is experiencing one of the more pronounced youth bulges in the Arab world. It has economic pressures accompanying that youthful trend, with youths presenting a 26 percent jobless rate as of 2019 – more than four times the overall adult unemployment rate. The fact that more than 80 percent of Saudis use the Internet, including most youths, magnifies the dilemma: those citizens more desirous of change, opportunity, and dignity are also most capable of communicating grievances, linking up with others, and expressing their ideas in innovative ways through social media and other technologies.

Today, virtually all Saudi citizens are Arab and Muslim, but not all Sunni. The Shi'a constitute around 10 percent of the country, with the rest of the Muslim population nominally belonging to the Sunni faith. Bloodlines, not geography, most often determine nationality, and being born in Saudi Arabia does not automatically entitle a person to citizenship. The extended family and tribes are the most important social institutions in Saudi Arabia. Not only is the Najd and the central part of the country the center of Saudi political power, but its tribal affiliations are among the most important on the Arabian Peninsula. Members of the leading tribal families of the Najd are at the top of the social order, and have retained that power as thousands of Saudis moved to Riyadh during the post-war period during a massive wave of urbanization – a process that changed a country in which a majority of the country lived in rural areas in 1970.

The western Hijazi population has been far more cosmopolitan than that of the central Najd because of centuries of immigration connected with the Hajj. The leading families of Jeddah historically constituted a powerful merchant class with often surprising cosmopolitan connections. It is not unusual to meet individuals in Jeddah who boast backgrounds as different as Bedouin, Indian, Kurdish, Sicilian, and Turkish. Visitors can still see that heritage in the signs in Malay and other languages in Jeddah, along with the cultural contributions those linkages have made to the kingdom. In 1925, for instance, Saudi authorities granted the request of Indonesians and Malaysians in Mecca to play the first football match in the country. Similarly, the eastern provinces, with their concentration of the oil industry, also have a polyglot population, and many families there have close ties in other Gulf states, including a large Shi'a community. Most Saudi Shi'a are members of the Twelver sect, although another group of Shi'a, concentrated in the Najran area near Yemen, follow the Isma'ili path.

In Saudi cultural terms, the distinction between nationals and foreigners is often construed in economic terms – the latter refers to non-Saudi residents in the kingdom to work in various occupations. However, in historical terms, the differences between native and non-native break down given the fuzzy, swirling movements of tribal confederations and clans prior to the modern era. Many of the old Sunni families of Kuwait and Bahrain, including their royal families, migrated from the Najd some three hundred years ago as members of much larger tribal groupings. Northern Saudis have close tribal ties to kin in Iraq, Jordan, and Syria. The tribal culture, hierarchies, and conventions of many Saudis are seen as possessing close affinities to those of neighboring Gulf kingdoms, namely Kuwait, Bahrain, Qatar, the UAE, and Oman; analysts frequently deem these six states as tribal dynasties. Within the Arabian Peninsula the creation of the Gulf Cooperation Council in 1981 was as much an expression of these common social and normative understandings of tribal identity as it was a security alliance against Iran.

The role of women in Saudi Arabia is a controversial topic. Women hold increasingly important positions, and gender disparities have gradually eroded in the last two decades – although they are still quite large. Women now have the right to drive, with the requirements for male guardianship reduced (but not eliminated); by royal decree, one-fifth of all seats on the advisory Majlis al-Shura are also reserved for women. Women have also been appointed ministers, and been elected to professional boards and business associations. Within the home, women also had influence within extended families through their spouses and male siblings. King 'Abd al-Aziz's closest political adviser was his blood sister Nura, and King Faisal's closest political adviser, particularly on women's affairs, was his wife Iffat.

At the same time, Saudi women have far weaker social rights and economic protections than men. While women may own properties and businesses, participate in professional life, open bank accounts, get an education, secure healthcare, and drive, enormous restrictions on their mobility remain in place. Male guardians still control whether they can travel, get married, and socialize in many ambits of public life. Partly due to social and familial expectations, only a quarter of Saudi women seek jobs despite comprising the majority of students at colleges and universities. Mandatory gender segregation holds in many workplaces, educational arenas, and public spaces. Divorce rights and child custody heavily favor men, and sexual violence against women has long drawn criticism from human rights monitors. How long such restrictions will remain in place remains to be seen, even given that much of the current male guardianship system as articulated by law has its roots not in classical Wahhabi practices, but rather in the post-1979 turn towards stricter Islamization.

Economic conditions

Despite the ambitious transformational goals laid out in Vision 2030, oil remains the backbone of the Saudi economy, accounting for most of its revenues and almost all of its export earnings. Saudi Arabia remains a close approximation to the theoretical concept of the rentier state, with virtually every aspect of its political development and financial wealth for the past 70 years tied to the sale of a single commodity – crude oil. The kingdom taxes little, sells oil and petrochemicals abroad, and seeks to provide to citizens as many economic and social goods as possible, from public employment in the bloated government sector to generous benefits in the form of accessible education, healthcare, and subsidized commodities. When rents flow inwards and the government is flush with cash, the formula works; when energy prices decline (as in the mid-1980s and the early 2010s), the monarchy is forced to rely upon its cash reserves in order to weather the inevitable storm of public grumbles, as the rentier social contract diminishes in scope.

It is difficult to imagine that, prior to World War Two, the country was one of the poorest in the world. Following the incorporation of the Hijaz into the Saudi realm in the 1920s, revenues generated from the annual Hajj pilgrimage became the major source of foreign currency earnings. When the global economic depression and political disorders leading to World War Two greatly reduced the number of Hajj pilgrims in the 1930s, the Saudi economy was devastated. The transition of the Saudi economy from subsistence to oil wealth began with Western firms prospecting for oil under permit from 'Abd al-Aziz, who in 1933, however, granted an oil concession to a US firm called Standard Oil of California. Resulting discoveries and corporate mergers produced a company called the California Arabian Standard Oil Company, which later became the Arabian American Oil Company – today's Aramco, the national oil firm.

The advent of World War Two prevented its export in significant quantities to international markets. Thus, Saudi Arabia did not begin the process of becoming a leading oil state until the late 1940s, and oil revenues began to fill state coffers in quantity only in the 1950s. In the 1960s, the kingdom joined the Organization of Petroleum Exporting Countries (OPEC) and quickly became the dominant member, given its enormous reserves and most of its production available for export. The original intent of OPEC was to pressure the foreign-owned oil companies to keep prices from collapsing in a buyers' market, but by the late 1960s, the United States, once the world's leading exporter, became a net importer, creating a new sellers' market. This resulted in a major oil shortage, exacerbated by the early 1970s Arab oil embargo. By that time, the oil-producing countries, including Saudi Arabia, were able to nationalize most foreign-owned production and hydrocarbon assets, thereby taking control of production and ownership of their energy reserves.

The high revenues of the 1970s enabled the Saudis to accelerate their economic and social welfare programs greatly; this was, in many ways, the heyday of the authoritarian bargain inherent to the logic of rentierism. The evolution from a traditional mercantile state to a major oil-producing state also wrought rapid changes to everyday practices. A vivid example is in the area of financial and fiscal transactions. Prior to the oil age, there were no commercial banks except foreign banks in the Hijaz, established to handle the Hajj trade. There was no paper currency, which the local population distrusted, and Aramco had to fly in planeloads of silver coins to meet its payroll and royalty payments. With Western assistance, however, the Saudi government created a monetary system and Central Bank, acculturated citizens to the notion of bills and currency, and thereby standardized transactions. The evolution of Islamic banking was another creative endeavor, for Islam proscribes charging interest. To avoid interest charges and payments, a banking system based on fees has been developed, and the kingdom is now one of the global centers of Islamic banking and finance.

The economy nonetheless rose and fell based upon oil prices. The high oil prices of the late 1970s led to increased worldwide energy efficiency and a drop demand, and in 1980 the market entered a glut from which it did not fully recover for two decades. The collapse of crude oil pricing six years later threw the economy into a tailspin: whereas the GDP increased by an incredible 14.2 percent annualized rate throughout the 1970s, during the 1980s it contracted, and in the 1990s only grew by 3.1 percent. Saudi oil production plummeted, and starved of revenue, the government quickly spent much of its cash reserves held abroad by its investment vehicles simply to maintain its existing infrastructural commitments and payrolls, as well as to escalate its military spending given the threats posed by the Iran-Iraq War in the Gulf. The 1990 Gulf War highlighted the inherent necessity for stronger armed forces to ensure national territorial security. The 1980s and 1990s, more than other Arab countries, represented lost decades of growth for Saudi Arabia's rentier engine.

The financial crises of that period instigated many planners to suggest that the Saudi economy should diversify beyond its hydrocarbon base. Indeed, the Sixth Development Plan (1995–2000) explicitly prioritized restructuring the economy, stressing privatization, free trade, liberalized investment, and human resources for the purpose of job creation through innovation. These themes have resonated in every major project, scheme, and framework rolled out by Saudi ministries and royal advisers – and the legions of Western consultants hired to analyze their feasibility – since then. Saudi Arabia joined the World Trade Organization in 2005, as part of this general strategy, while policymakers in the 2010s under MbS's guidance made lavish gestures to invite foreign investors to stake their capital inside the kingdom through updated banking institutions, liberalized property laws, and more lucrative commercial opportunities. Thus, Vision 2030 reflected the logical accumulation of nearly two decades of technocratic pressures to make the Saudi economy more robust and less oil-dependent. One of the few certainties the kingdom does possess is its massive sovereign wealth fund, the vehicle through which oil revenues have been deposited and invested for decades. As of 2019, Saudi Arabia's Public Investment Fund contains $320 billion – in essence, a gargantuan rainy day fund.

The problem of job creation, however, has become a major source of stress for Saudi planners. The rentier economy engendered by oil wealth meant that most Saudi citizens, for generations, saw public employment and other sequestered positions as logical occupations. Within the small private sector, and the semi-public sector, fields requiring different or lesser skills – teaching, construction, retail, transportation, domestic work, and the like – could simply be given to incoming foreign workers from other Arab countries and, later, South and Southeast Asian countries, whose residency in the kingdom was dependent exclusively upon their employability. Though the poor labor protections and sometimes grotesque abuses that befell expatriate workers would later garner harsh international rebukes, the real problem came in parallel systems of job-seeking that coalesced, with Saudis clinging to public-sector work and foreigners filling private-sector positions.

By the 2000s, the volatility of oil revenues and the explosion of youth job-seekers exposed the inability of the Saudi state to provide enough jobs to citizens. Efforts at "Saudization," in which officials encouraged Saudi citizens to replace foreigners in the private sector, failed, and by the 2010s, four-fifths of all non-government jobs were still filled by non-Saudi workers. The fact that most private-sector jobs remain in low-skilled fields, like construction, is a barrier, as few Saudis gravitate to such work. The more than quarter of Saudi youths currently unemployed hence expresses both a byproduct and the limitations of rentierism – something that Vision 2030 claims to rectify.

While the US has always supported Saudi efforts to diversify the basis of Saudi economic growth for the foreseeable future relies upon securing adequate revenues from its oil exports. This has intersected with American interests in a subtle but conflicting way. US oil production has surged since the early 2000s, with every presidential administration prioritizing energy independence. By late 2018, the US was producing more oil than either Russia or Saudi Arabia while exporting more oil than it imported for the first time since 1973. American hydrocarbon production, in other words, often contributes to the prolonged periods of depressed oil prices that harm the Saudi state's ability to maintain its rentierist economy.

POLITICAL STRUCTURES

Saudi Arabia's political system is based on the interpretation and application of divine guidelines from the Qur'an and other Islamic sources. The creation of modern Saudi political institutions starting in the 1950s was bred of necessity as the kingdom evolved from a traditional desert principality into a modern oil power. The Saudi monarchy is an authoritarian one, and royal succession is legitimized (in theory) through family consensus as well as consultation with religious leaders, technocrats, businessmen, and heads of important families not otherwise included in the palace. Until recently, consensus across the dynasty's multiple and often competing branches was thought to be the precondition for monarchical stability, but MbS' political consolidation through the repression and pursuit of other senior princes suggests a potentially dramatic transformation for how succession disputes may be handled in the future.

The monarchical structure is a powerfully autocratic one. The king is both the chief of state and head of government, and within the apparatus of the Saudi state, no institution is more powerful than the royal court. Executive and legislative powers are effectively fused when the king acts to impose major domestic and foreign policy decisions. However, Saudi Arabia is not an absolutist monarchy in the historic European sense; the doctrine of divine right would be considered heresy in Islam. Moreover, despite all the powers residing in the ruler, he cannot act in the face of a contravening consensus. Thus, historically, the Saudi king was not just chief of state and head of government, but also consensus-makers through the incorporation of consultations and voices from society, as well as from the rest of the family.

Like other non-democratic regimes, the Saudi monarchy also maintains a set of overlapping security institutions that, alongside its armed forces, maintains and projects royal authority. One is the General Intelligence Directorate, which has often played controversial roles in its past involvements with Western agencies, Cold War plots, and foreign interactions. The General Investigations Directorate deals with internal security issues, pursuing perceived threats that range from radical Islamists to critical writers and youth activists. The Saudi armed forces ostensibly exist to protect the kingdom's territories, but among its branches is the National Guard – a highly tribalized force that numbers 250,000, and whose role is to protect the royal family from any large-scale danger or mobilized threat. The other branches of the armed forces include a modestly sized army and an expensive air force. Saudi Arabia spends a substantial portion of its wealth for military purposes, including not just payroll but technologies, weaponry, and armaments; in 2018, the kingdom devoted more than 10 percent of GDP to defense expenditures.

Since the advent of oil wealth, the Saudi state has expanded to encompass a vast array of ministries, councils, organs, boards, and other structures. Despite the kingdom's reputation as an autocratic monarchy, there does exist an institutionalized, bureaucratized government. As the government expanded rapidly over the years, the sheer size and complexity of its operations made it impossible for the king to be personally involved in all but the most pressing issues. The Council of Ministers serves as the king's cabinet, which typically consists of the crown prince and senior ministers, with the most influential ones typically being the Ministers of Foreign Affairs, Defense, Interior, and Energy. The laws and bills it suggests must be ratified by royal decree, and the cabinet can be reshuffled upon the will of the king. This occurred, for instance, in April 2015, when King Salman replaced Crown Prince Muqrin (a sibling) with his son, MbS. While senior princes often fill the most important posts, the monarchy has also named technocrats (many young and Western-educated) to ministerial positions not connected with national security, such as those dealing with finance and social welfare. Such officials have considerable powers as principal advisers to the king in their areas of responsibility and as operational decision-makers.

Decision-making, thus, is a highly personalized affair involving multiple elites, institutions, and relationships. Missing is a legislature. Saudi Arabia lacks an independent national assembly. King Fahd decreed instead an entirely appointed Consultative Assembly in 1992 in order to further enhance consensus – not necessarily debate or opposition – regarding major policies. The assembly was inaugurated in December 1993 with 60 members;

it was expanded to 90 in 1997 and 150 in 2005. During the expansion, King Abdullah also sought greater input from elite citizens, such as by establishing a national dialogue organization. The newly enlarged assembly has met since then as a constant in political life. All members, including the 20 percent required to be women, are appointed by royal decree. Members are appointed for four-year terms and meet in closed sessions at least every two weeks, and include businesspersons, technocrats, officials, and ʻulama. Many are Western-educated, but apart from legitimizing monarchical policies, the body as a whole exerts little real authority within the royal system of decision-making.

Elections do occur, though, at the municipal level. In 2005, King Abdullah allowed half the members of the kingdom's 179 municipal councils to be chosen by popular vote. Among the main issues discussed by candidates were political reform, corruption, environmental issues, and public services in a rare showing of open debate. The second round of elections was postponed until September 2011, when 1,056 seats in 285 councils were elected. Women were not allowed to participate, but after considerable pressure, Abdullah promised them the right to vote and run for office. King Salman maintained these institutional promises. In December 2015, women participated in municipal elections in Saudi Arabia for the first time, with 20 women winning seats in local councils.

Judicially, Saudi Arabia has a well-developed legal system. As Article 1 of the Basic Law of Government, issued by King Fahd on March 1, 1992, states: "The Saudi Arabian kingdom is a sovereign Arab Islamic state with Islam as its religion; God's book and the Sunna [which together form the sources of Islamic law] are its constitution; Arabic is its language; and Riyadh is its capital." The Saudi legal system is based on Sunni interpretations of *shariʻa*, or Islamic law, principally but not exclusively, according to the Hanbali school of jurisprudence. Saudi courts are presided over by an Islamic judge, or *qadi*. Because Islamic law is considered to be divinely inspired, however, there is no legal precedent based on previous court decisions. Islamic law does provide for binding legal opinions, issued without a court case by a *mufti*, or Islamic legal expert.

Given the divine nature of Islamic law, legislative or statutory law is prohibited. There is, however, a means for regulating and adjudicating issues that did not exist during the time of Muhammad. Royal decrees issued by the king are used to provide regulatory and administrative rules, and special administrative tribunals and councils have been created to adjudicate disputes involving workers, commerce, and other pragmatic concerns.

POLITICAL DYNAMICS

The most critical element driving forward the political dynamics of Saudi Arabia are the relations that occur within the vast royal family, which remains the key political actor. Ties based on family, branch, generation, seniority, and siblinghood (particularly among siblings of the same mother) are very important. The ruling branch is tied to the surviving sons of King 'Abd al-Aziz. There are also collateral branches of the family, descended from brothers of former rulers. The two leading collateral branches are the Saud al-Kabir, who descend from an older brother of 'Abd al-Rahman ('Abd al-Aziz's father), and the Ibn Jaluwi, who descend from an uncle of 'Abd al-Rahman.

Among the sons (and grandsons) of 'Abd al-Aziz, seniority of birth has been important but not absolute in determining political influence. Historically, older princes not deemed capable of maintaining high government positions were excluded from the decision-making process except with regard to royal matters. Succession used to be determined by seniority among the sons of 'Abd al-Aziz, with the oldest son being nominated as king and then the next oldest installed as crown prince. However, Crown Princes Sultan and Nayif died unexpectedly in 2011 and 2012. King Abdullah and other senior members of the family then formed an Allegiance Council to determine the next crown prince; the chosen member was Prince Salman, who hence became king in 2015.

Succession within the family is pivotal to Saudi stability. The ascension of Salman to the throne brought the long-expected overhaul of the succession system, because it rotated MbS into the position of crown prince (displacing another son of 'Abd al-Aziz, Muqrin). For the first time, a grandson of the founder had been installed into a position to lead the kingdom. When he becomes king, Muhammad bin Salman will be the first monarch who is *not* a son of King 'Abd al-Aziz. Still, MbS retains a key connection with his grandfather – namely, a strong physical resemblance. That fact was illustrated by a brief video that went viral on Saudi social media in spring 2015, depicting the face of MbS transforming into the face of King 'Abd al-Aziz.

MbS' moves in 2017 to sideline other potential competitors in the royal family, including the well-reported drama of imprisoning many detained princes and elites at the Ritz-Carlton Hotel in Riyadh, are believed to have eliminated political challengers who may have chafed at the notion of King Salman's young son to have assumed so powerful a position. If the succession line holds and MbS ascends to the throne in the near future, then the Saudi regime will deal with several important political dynamics. One is retaining control over the decision-making process, with various ministers and princes responsible for an enormous range of developmental policies. Another is the religious establishment, particularly from the Wahhabi ʿulama. Even though MbS has consciously projected himself as a pious Muslim, his stated efforts to liberalize social life have faced resistance from reactionary voices. While the Wahhabi establishment's alliance with the House of Saud is in no danger of shattering, prioritizing liberal over conservative values in a kingdom that spawned Al-Qaʿida, and saw some 2,500 youths join the Islamic State of Iraq and Syria after 2012, will require carefully mediating between conflicting religious demands. The arrest of some well-known ʿulama starting in 2017 shows one strategic sidestep: by simply suppressing dissent from religious authorities, the regime can better control and regulate Islamic discourse, even if this also contravenes the preferences of its Wahhabi backers.

A third challenge rests from the Shiʿa minority. Tensions between the community and the government burst forth in the twenty-first century, fueled by sectarianism, conflict with Iran, and the overall climate of repression wrought by the Arab Spring. The 2016 execution of Shaykh Nimr, a Shiʿa cleric in the eastern province who levied criticism at the monarchy, inflamed local opinion while drawing criticism from international human rights monitors. Shiʿa grievances range from complaints about political underrepresentation, as there are few cabinet ministers, security officials, and other senior government posts filled by Saudis of Shiʿa faith, to the suppression of many Shiʿa rituals and practices, and ongoing discrimination in educational spheres and in the workplace.

Finally, Saudi human rights and women's rights activists will pose an ongoing challenge to how Saudi Arabia is perceived overseas – even if they do not fundamentally threaten the position of the monarchy at home. The murder of Khashoggi in fall 2018, well-publicized asylum cases of Saudi dissidents abroad, and continued scrutiny by Western critics suggest that reconciling social and economic reforms with the political requirements of maintaining autocratic control will remain a major challenge to the monarchy.

FOREIGN POLICY

Saudi foreign policies revolve around several interrelated major goals: preserving an Islamic way of life at home and abroad, protecting Saudi Arabia against external threats to national and regional security, maintaining a leadership role in the Arab world, and expanding its economic and financial networks into new arenas. To begin with, the Saudi monarchy has long taken pride that the kingdom is both the birthplace of Islam and the site of Mecca and Medina. As stewards of these two holy sites, Saudi kings have, for decades, assumed the massive financial and logistical responsibility for managing the annual pilgrimages to its holy sites. Beyond this, Saudi foreign relations also reflect a desire to maintain the country's unique cultural and religious heritage while defending its porous physical and sea borders from aggressive neighbors, which since the 1980s has invariably meant Iran (excepting the interlude of the Gulf War, when Iraq posed a direct coercive threat).

Until the 1990s, the Saudi central strategy was to avoid direct confrontation through the strategic use of the country's vast oil wealth along with a series of international alliances. For instance, it developed close ties with fellow Arab and Muslim states – often finding areas of common ground, even if they disagreed on regional or international issues. Saudi Arabia was hence not only a founding member of the United Nations, it also helped spearhead the Arab League, and in 1981 the Gulf Cooperation Council (GCC), which is headquartered in Riyadh. It is also a charter member of, and usually the prime mover in, the Organization of the Islamic Conference, whose secretariat is located in Jeddah. Expressing its pan-Islamic orientation, starting in the 1960s, the kingdom provided substantial assistance to Muslim charities and cultural institutions around the world, with much of its religious messaging and assistance being inflected by Wahhabi Islamic interpretations. Such foreign commitments resonated within the citizenry, particularly among Saudis who saw the kingdom's global image as one that needed to accord with its internal values.

Besides ties with Arab and Muslim nations, alliance politics with powerful partners sharing mutual interests has traditionally been the major focus of Saudi foreign security and economic policies. In the years leading up to World War One, King 'Abd al-Aziz relied on the British, the paramount power, for protection and economic assistance. Gradually, however, he turned to the United States, in part because he was convinced that it had no imperial designs on the region and also because his earliest experience with Americans in the oil industry was largely positive. Yet it was not until World War Two that the US established a resident diplomatic mission in the kingdom. Since then, the US-Saudi relationship emerged as an especially robust (if lopsided) one. At the heart of the relationship was a common interest in reliable supplies of oil flowing to the West along with close cooperation in regional security.

During the Cold War, Saudi Arabia usually played an important role in Western grand strategy in the MENA. The monarchy considered the Soviet bloc and its communist ideology to be an existential threat against the Islamic world; partly for that reason, the kingdom also opposed Arab Nationalists and republican leaders like Nasser of Egypt. Saudi Arabia participated in an ill-fated intervention in North Yemen in 1962, when its monarchy was overthrown by Arab Nationalists. US-Saudi relations, however, have not always been smooth. The most serious crisis was the 1973–74 oil embargo when Saudi Arabia and a coalition of Arab states cut oil sales to the United States and other states for their support of Israeli in the 1973 Arab-Israeli war. Such hiccups were eventually smoothed over, however, until the 9/11 terrorist attacks threw bilateral relations into another crisis, given that 15 of the 19 hijackers were Saudi. That began a gradual deterioration of US-Saudi relations that also dovetailed with a deeper transformation in Saudi Arabia's foreign policy – shifting from a moderate mediator to an aggressive intervener.

In regional terms, Saudi Arabia sought to position itself as a mediating power well into the 2000s. Following political examples and strategies that have evolved over centuries, the Saudi government used moderation, negotiation, reconciliation, and alliance-building in order to bring about the Ta'if accords that ended the Lebanese civil war in 1990, among other peace-making efforts. In 2002, the Saudi regime notably pushed forth a bold peace initiative between the Arab world and Israel, one that sought to provide statehood to the Palestinians and end all hostilities with Israel. Despite portraying Iran as a mortal danger to the Sunni monarchies of the Gulf, likewise, it never sought to use the GCC as an offensive weapon; rather, the GCC served to cement Saudi leadership in the Gulf region and enable greater coordination with its neighbors.

This moderate stance changed over time, morphing into a more aggressive interventionist position by the mid-2010s. This transformation began with the Iraq War, which deposed the Saddam regime. The attendant war on terrorism helped eviscerate Al-Qa'ida, which notably had attacked the Saudi monarchy as infidels; it also destroyed a major Sunni Arab power, which during the 1980s had helped contain Iran. The 1979 Iranian Revolution eventually brought to power an Islamic Republic that briefly sought to export its revolutionary ideology, principally to the Shi'a minorities living in abutting Gulf states like Saudi Arabia, where they might rebel against their monarchist authorities and emulate the Iranian model. Rising incidents of Shi'a terrorism in the 1980s in some Gulf kingdoms and the formation of the GCC in 1981 reflected increased caution, but the 1990s had brought the guarantee of American hegemony and military protection against Iran. The removal of the Saddam regime weakened a plank of this security guarantee.

In the 2011–12 Arab Spring, further, perceptions that the Obama administration had "abandoned" its Arab allies, such as Mubarak of Egypt, hammered home the fear that more than the Bush administration, the US had tired of interventionism in the MENA. In 2014, the decline of oil prices brought a period of fiscal hardship and more uncertainty, while US efforts to forge a nuclear deal with Iran in 2015 succeeded despite Saudi disapproval.

King Salman's enthronement in January 2015 thus quickly accelerated a foreign policy re-orientation. Whereas in the 1990s Saudi Arabia subsisted under the umbrella of American military hegemony, by the mid-2010s, a number of uncertainties clouded its global outlook. These were the volatility of rentier income; the Arab Spring's wave of regional unrest; and an unreliable American partner that, while still willing to sell enormous quantities of arms (the Obama administration provided a record $60 billion in weaponry sales to the kingdom, for instance), was increasingly diverging on the role of Iran, democracy, and openness in the MENA's geopolitics. King Salman and MbS thus positioned Saudi Arabia as a unilateral aggressor willing to attack perceived threats first.

The fruits of this new doctrine came quickly. Saudi Arabia had previously participated in the international coalition against ISIS, and strongly favored the end of the Asad regime given its support by Iran. In March 2015, however, the Saudi regime ordered the bombing of Yemen in a new military campaign that would drag on for years. The target was the Houthi movement, a Shi'a actor that received minor assistance from Iran but more importantly had toppled the post-revolutionary government of Yemen. The resulting conflict created humanitarian disasters while provoking intense global criticism. The Saudi government also took more hardline stances against Hizbullah and the Muslim Brotherhood, seeing both as threats for different reasons – the former due to its Iranian ties, and the latter due to its conflicting vision of Islamic legitimacy. Qatar's support for the Brotherhood escalated an already-simmering rivalry, and in summer 2017 the monarchy led its Arab allies to levy sanctions and other punitive measures against its peninsular neighbor, all but paralyzing the GCC. Harsher crackdowns against oppositionists, even those living abroad like Khashoggi, fell into this broader trend of unilaterally engaging perceived enemies and seeking to shape the regional climate.

The Trump administration's policies have thus been welcome by the Saudi monarchy, not least because of its muted criticism for human rights abuses. Plain intentions to renege on the nuclear deal with Iran, stated pledges to sell over $110 billion in new arms to the kingdom, and an overall geopolitical commitment to further defang the Iranian regime through more belligerent measures signified implicit acceptance of Saudi Arabia's more muscular position in the region. Aiding this rise was the destruction occurring elsewhere; for the first time in centuries, neither Cairo nor Damascus nor Baghdad were centers of Arab thought, decision-making, and power, due to the political instabilities, civil conflicts, and terrorism afflicting their countries. Riyadh, by the end of the 2010s, had risen as the most important Arab capital in the regional system.

FUTURE PROSPECTS

As Saudi Arabia enters the third decade of the twenty-first century, King Salman and Crown Prince Muhammad bin Salman continue to pursue an extremely active agenda for radical change at home and abroad – and for good reason. A growing youthful population remains hungry for jobs and education. Social liberalization has partly occurred, but Saudis also have exhibited a longstanding desire for more political voice and participation within a system that prizes hierarchy, monarchism, and authority. While the government has sought to diversify the country's economy in its Vision 2030 project, the kingdom remains a rentier state, with its financial fortunes beholden to energy prices worldwide.

Further complicating Saudi Arabia's future is its activist foreign policy in the MENA region, which may bring greater conflict with Iran. That policy is largely the product of the current king and Crown Prince, and therefore may well change should neither be in charge. This broaches upon the final factor shaping future stability. It is well-assumed that MbS will someday become king given the age of his father and the elimination of other competing princes, branches, and elites. Yet authoritarian systems incubate uncertainties as well, and opposition to MbS exists in many quarters, from the many dissidents and critics at home and abroad who have suffered regime backlash to members of the royal elite who may well seek to install a very different style of leadership as revenge. US backing will not insulate the monarchy from all these challenges, nor will seeking out new forms of assistance from non-Western global powers like Russia and China.

NOTE

1 In 2013, Saudi artist Shaweesh used a picture of Faisal signing the treaty founding the international organization as part of a collage entitled *Yoda*, which, remarkably, was mistakenly included in an official Saudi social studies textbook in 2017.

FURTHER READING

Definitive works on Saudi Arabia are few. For modern historical overviews, both Alexander Vassiliev's *The History of Saudi Arabia* (Saqi, 1998) and Madawi al-Rasheed's *A History of Saudi Arabia*, 2nd ed. (Cambridge University Press, 2010) are widely read. An accessible introduction as well is Karen Elliott House, *On Saudi Arabia: Its People, Past, Religion, Fault Lines – and Future* (Vintage, 2013). A recent text on today's fast-moving events under King Salmah is Madawi al-Rasheed, ed., *Salman's Legacy: The Dilemmas of a New Era in Saudi Arabia* (Oxford University Press, 2018). Another is Bernard Haykel, Thomas Hegghammer, and Stéphane Lacroix, eds., *Saudi Arabia in Transition: Insights on Social, Political, Economic and Religious Change* (Cambridge University Press, 2015).

Historically, studies also abound. R. Bayly Winder's *Saudi Arabia in the Nineteenth Century* (St. Martin's Press, 1985) is the standard work on the kingdom's earlier developments. Any of the several works by H. St. John B. Philby, though not scholarly, capture the feel of Saudi Arabia in the interwar and immediate post-World War Two period. Two of his books, *Arabian Jubilee* (Robert Hale, 1952) and *Saudi Arabia* (Ernest Benn, 1955), written to commemorate the fiftieth year of King 'Abd al-Aziz's reign, would be good places to begin. Another expose into the earliest construction of the Saudi state comes from J.E. Peterson, *Saudi Arabia under Ibn Saud: Economic and Financial Foundations of the State* (IB Tauris, 2018).

Readers interested in religion can begin with David E. Long's *The Hajj Today: A Survey of the Contemporary Makkah Pilgrimage* (State University of New York Press, 1979). Natana DeLong-Bas's extensive study on Wahhabism, *Wahhabi Islam* (Oxford University Press, 2004) is the benchmark on the topic. On the expression of radical Islamism, see Thomas Hegghammer, *Jihad in Saudi Arabia: Violence and Pan-Islamism since 1979* (Cambridge University Press, 2010). Nabil Mouline, *The Clerics of Islam: Religious Authority and State Power in Saudi Arabia* (Yale University Press, 2014) explores the origins and development of Wahhabism in political context. Raihan Ismail's *Saudi Clerics and Shi'a Islam* (Oxford University Press, 2016) explores how the country's Sunni clerics view Shi'a Islam. Another study explores the changing conceptions of modernism, including efforts to redefine conservativism and liberalize society, is Madawi Al-Rasheed, *Muted Modernists: The Struggle over Divine Politics in Saudi Arabia* (Oxford University Press, 2015). Stéphane Lacroix, *Awakening Islam: The Politics of Religious Dissent in Contemporary Saudi Arabia* (Harvard University Press, 2011) provides another incisive look into religious pluralism and opposition.

The impact of a changing society and an evolving youth culture are discussed in Pascal Menoret's ethnographic study of youth culture and urbanization, *Joyriding in Riyadh: Oil, Urbanism and Road Revolt* (Cambridge University Press, 2014). Toby Matthiesen has authored two widely-cited texts on the Arab Spring and the position of the Shi'a within it: *Sectarian Gulf: Bahrain, Saudi Arabia, and the Arab Spring that Wasn't* (Stanford University Press, 2013) and *The Other Saudis: Shiism, Dissent, and Sectarianism* (Cambridge University Press, 2014). An exploration of the intersection between jihadi ideals and cultural expression is Thomas Hegghammer, ed., *Jihadi Culture: The Arts and Social Practices of Militant Islamists* (Cambridge University Press, 2017). On gender, see Madawi Al-Rasheed, *A Most Masculine State: Gender, Politics and Religion in Saudi Arabia* (Cambridge University Press, 2013). A modern take on the country's artistic movement and cultural innovation is Sean Foley, *Changing Saudi Arabia: Arts, Culture, and Society in the kingdom* (Lynne Rienner, 2019).

There are a number of good studies on the development of the Saudi oil industry. Daniel Yergin's exhaustively researched best seller, *The Prize: The Epic Quest for Oil, Money and Power* (Simon and Schuster, 1990), is widely-cited. Another widely-cited text on the Saudi oil industry and the role of Americans in creating it is Robert Vitalis, *America's Kingdom: Mythmaking on the Saudi Oil Frontier* (Stanford University Press, 2007). A stylized narrative exists in Anthony Cave Brown, *Oil, God and Gold: The Story of Aramco and the Saudi Kings* (Houghton Mifflin, 1999). Toby Jones, *Desert Kingdom* (Harvard University Press, 2011) describes how oil and water forged modern Saudi Arabia, while Steffen Hertog sheds light on the political effects of oil wealth in *Princes, Brokers and Bureaucrats: Oil and the State in Saudi Arabia* (Cornell University Press, 2011).

Works on military and strategic issues, including foreign policy, are rife. Rachel Bronson's *Thicker than Oil: America's Uneasy Partnership with Saudi Arabia* (Oxford University Press, 2005) documents post-September 11 events well, while F. Gregory Gause's *The International Relations of the Persian Gulf* (Cambridge University Press, 2010) contextualizes Saudi Arabia within Western and Gulf geopolitics. One analytical survey of Saudi foreign policy is Neil Partrick, *Saudi Arabian Foreign Policy: Conflict and Cooperation* (IB Tauris, 2016). The US-Saudi relationship is unpacked in Bruce Riedel, *Kings and Presidents: Saudi Arabia and the United States since FDR* (Brookings, 2017). For those interested in China's growing relationship with Saudi Arabia, see Jonathan Fulton, *China's Relations with the Gulf Monarchies* (Routledge, 2019).

Online sources

Although the Internet was first introduced to Saudi Arabia in 1999, it has grown rapidly over the last two decades, reaching most of the population. Social media is widely used, especially YouTube, Twitter, and Instagram. Major English-language papers include *The Arab News* (www.arabnews.com/) and *Saudi Gazette* (http://saudigazette.com.sa/). Al-Arabiya is a Saudi-based pan-Arabic news channel, and a tenacious competitor to Qatar-based Al-Jazeera; its website has a wealth of stories (https://english.alarabiya.net/). Cultural expressions and entertainment are also rife online, particularly on YouTube and Twitter; the more daring and interesting media producers include Myrkott, Telfaz11, 8IES, and Uturn.

The Carnegie Endowment for International Peace also maintains a host of Saudi-related content (https://carnegieendowment.org/regions/211). The Middle East Institute's Saudi portal also presents briefings and analysis (www.mei.edu/regions/saudi-arabia). The International Center for Non-for-Profit Law monitors Saudi laws and restrictions, particularly regarding civic freedoms (www.icnl.org/research/monitor/saudiarabia.html). StepFeed also offers alternative takes on Saudi happenings from local youths, writers, and commentators (https://stepfeed.com/), while the online portal of *Arabian Business* investigates Saudi economic ventures and business developments (www.arabianbusiness.com/gcc/saudi-arabia).

Please note that URLs may change far more quickly than books can be printed; so if these exact URLs do not work, simply search Google or another engine by the titles of these websites and online resources.

Islamic Republic of Iran

Saeid Golkar

INTRODUCTION

Iran is a unique country in the Middle East and North Africa. Unlike many of the countries in this region, Iran was never colonized by a Western power. While the majority of people in the MENA speak Arabic, Persian is the official language of Iran. Unlike other Islamic countries, in which people follow the Sunni school of Islam, it is also the historical bastion for the Shi'a branch of Islam. Partly for that reason, Iran boasts a rich culture, renowned for its poetry, visual arts, and music. It is the birthplace of the Zoroastrian and Baha'i faiths. More recently, the 1979 revolution replaced an autocratic monarchy with today's Islamic Republic. All Iranian politics today stem from that moment of political reconfiguration.

As politics within Iran occurs within a framework of Islamism, moderates and radicals have alternated in power for decades, leaving the country unsettled and largely isolated in regional and global affairs. In recent years, Iran has dominated Western headlines given its oft-dramatic events, ranging from domestic protests and electoral uncertainties, and its cold relations with the US In July 2015, the Iranian government signed a nuclear agreement with the major powers that could have possibly inaugurated a new era of moderation, prosperity, and better relations with the West. Three years later, President Trump withdrew from the deal, and imposed a new round of sanctions in May 2018. This led to more enmity between Iran and the US, complicated by the multiple fronts of civil conflict and international interventions raging across the region.

Box 16.1 provides vital data for this country.

BOX 16.1   VITAL DATA – ISLAMIC REPUBLIC OF IRAN

Capital	Tehran
Regime type	Authoritarian (theocratic republic)
Head of state	Supreme Leader Ali Khamenei (since 1989)
Head of government	President Hassan Rouhani (since 2013)
Legislative institution	Unicameral parliament, with 290 elected seats (*Majles-e Shura-ye Eslami*, or Islamic Consultative Assembly)
Female quota	No
Percentage of seats held by women	5.9%
Major political parties or coalitions (share of seats in most recent general elections, 2016)	List of Hope (37.2%), Principlists' Grand Coalition (25.9%), People's Voice Coalition (4.5%)
Population	81,162,788
Major ethnic groups	Persian (62%), Azeri (16%), Kurdish (10%), Lur (6%), Arab (2%), Baloch (2%), Turkmen (1%), other (1%)
Major religious groups	Shi'a Muslim (90%), Sunni Muslim (9%), other (1%)
GDP per capita	$5,491 ($19,557 at Purchasing Power Parity)
Unemployment rate	12.1%
Youth unemployment rate	28.4%
Major economic industries	Petroleum, petrochemicals, gas, fertilizer, textiles, manufacturing, cement, food processing, agriculture
Military spending as % GDP	3.1%

HISTORICAL BACKGROUND

Iran's unique Persian identity dates back thousands of years. The ancestors of modern Iranians migrated to the Iranian plateau in the eleventh and tenth centuries BC, joining other ethnic groups that were already established. This pre-Islamic period shaped and influenced the collective identity of Iranians. Cyrus the Great united Iranian tribes and formed the first great

Persian domain, known as the Achaemenian Empire, in the sixth century BC. Another ancient imperial entity was the Parthian Empire, founded after the passing of Alexander the Great, which lasted until the third century AD. Its successor was the Sassanian Empire, which collapsed with the arrival of Arab armies and Islam in the seventh century.

Islamic Iran waxed and waned, ruled first as part of the wider Islamic Caliphate and then by more localized dynasties under which Persian poetry, art, and cities flourished. In 1251, Mongol invaders swept into the region from Central Asia, creating a major historical disjuncture. In 1501, the Safavid dynasty arose under *Shah* (king) Isma'il, who united territory roughly comprising Iran's current boundaries and made Shi'a Islam the state religion. The Safavid Empire conquered much of Central Asia and competed for regional power against the ascendant (and Sunni) Ottoman Empire, until it declined and collapsed in 1722. Decades later, the Qajar tribe took power, ensconcing themselves in Tehran and ruling over a recreated empire. Yet the Qajar monarchy was weak; Iran lost territory in the Caucasus and Central Asia to Russia, and became heavily indebted to European financiers and imperial powers, particularly Great Britain. Internally, it was wracked by social unrest from various minority groups, as well as urban activists and opposition; the latter's struggle culminated in the 1906 Constitutional Revolution, which created the *majles* (parliament).

The Pahlavi era, 1925–1978

The modern state of Iran began with the establishment of the Pahlavi dynasty in 1926. In 1921, General Reza Khan Pahlavi led a coup against the faltering Qajar government. During the next four years, he gradually consolidated power by eliminating his rivals, defeating tribal forces, and packing parliament with cronies. He was crowned Shah in April 1926, establishing the Pahlavi dynasty. Reza Shah was a modernizing despot, establishing the foundations of a modern economy and society but also harshly repressing political activity. Like his Turkish contemporary, Mustafa Kemal Ataturk, he did much to develop Iran's economy and society, building roads and railroads, a banking system, a professional civil service, educational institutions, and the country's first factories. Much of this was financed with proceeds from Iran's rapidly growing oil industry, which had been established in 1901 and was controlled by the British-owned Anglo-Iranian Oil Company. Reza Shah also forbad political parties and other civil society institutions, and undermined the Shi'a clergy and religious practice.

Britain and the Soviet Union jointly occupied Iran during World War Two to establish a supply route to Soviet forces, which were fighting desperately against German invaders in areas northwest of Iran. Reza Shah opposed the occupation and was therefore exiled and replaced with his 21-year-old son, Muhammad Reza Pahlavi. The young and weak monarch's accession enabled political activity to flourish, with various traditionalist, Islamist, nationalist, tribal, and leftist tendencies emerging. During the last year of the war, the Soviet Union and its allies in Iran's Communist Tudeh (Mass) Party encouraged Azeri and Kurdish separatist movements in northwestern Iran, producing an incipient crisis. These movements collapsed in 1946, however, as a result of domestic and foreign pressures.

Political activity continued to flourish in the late 1940s. Nationalist, leftist, and Islamist forces agitated against British influence in Iran, especially against British control over the oil industry. In 1949, a coalition of moderate nationalist parties and individuals created an umbrella organization called the National Front to promote nationalization of the oil industry. Many National Front leaders also wanted to establish democracy in Iran, which would entail wresting power from the pro-British traditional upper class, effectively weakening the monarchy. The National Front was led by Muhammad Mosaddeq, a venerable politician, who had long criticized Western policies, advocated oil nationalization, and opposed the Pahlavi monarchy.

As the oil nationalization movement grew in early 1951, and social pressures driven by urban opposition and party activists became insurmountable, the young Shah felt compelled to appoint Mosaddeq as prime minister. Mosaddeq then nationalized the oil industry, producing confrontation with Britain. The British organized a global embargo of Iranian oil exports and began covert efforts to undermine Mosaddeq. As the crisis persisted, Mosaddeq's coalition began to weaken, with key Islamist and nationalist allies joining the opposition. US officials feared Mosaddeq would become dependent on the Tudeh Party, thereby increasing Soviet influence in Iran. US and British officials began planning to overthrow Mosaddeq; the CIA then led a coup against him in August 1953, restoring the power of the Shah.

The 1953 coup marked a dramatic shift in Iran's political evolution, beginning a long period of political closure and authoritarian rule. The United States made extensive efforts to prop up the Shah's regime, giving it considerable economic and security assistance while also negotiating a 1954 agreement under which a consortium of foreign oil companies would purchase oil from Iran's new, state-owned oil production company. In addition, the CIA established a new domestic intelligence service, known by its acronym SAVAK, which became a key pillar of the renewed dictatorship. Domestic opposition suffered harsh repression.

By 1960, when political unrest had risen once again, US officials pressured the Shah to initiate liberalization measures. In 1962, the monarch announced a package of reforms, dubbed the White Revolution, which included a new land reform program, selective enfranchisement of women, and efforts to improve literacy and public health. These measures mollified many critics, and the land reform program weakened the conservative and powerful landowning class. However, many traditionalist Iranians were angered by the modernizing thrust of the White Revolution, and Ayatollah Ruhollah Khomeini and other Shi'a clerics organized a series of demonstrations in protest. Khomeini was arrested in June 1963, triggering enormous protests at which security forces viciously attacked the demonstrators, leaving hundreds dead and thousands injured. Khomeini was sent into exile in 1964 in a controversial turn of events. The Shi'a 'ulama (jurists) were not only religious authorities, but also constituted a major social force; their religious seminaries attracted tens of thousands of students, and their control over *waqf* properties (charitable endowments) gave them substantial resources. By clamping down on juristic dissent, the Shah was systematically eliminating religious opposition, after having defanged leftists and nationalists in the 1950s.

Iran's oil revenues grew rapidly in the early 1970s, producing economic growth that helped defuse unrest. Major investments saw the rapid expansion of urban infrastructure concomitant with more urbanization, particularly in Tehran; but migration from rural areas and unequal distribution of wealth also resulted in widening income gaps. Traditional classes such as the shopkeepers, craftsmen, and traders associated with the *bazaar* (the conventional marketplaces that anchored the urban economy) were displaced in favor of Western-inspired industrialization projects. For instance, the desire on part of many economic planners to rapidly modernize Iran through the familiar state-led strategy of import-substitution bore initial fruit with the creation of new industries, but it also required price controls that devastated many bazaar marketeers. Moreover, high inflation by the mid-1970s pummeled living standards after the previous decade of improvement. In rural areas untouched by oil-fueled industrialization, illiteracy and poverty stubbornly befell many peasants and farmers.

Politically, the 1970s represented the culmination of the Shah's coercive policies. In urban areas, students, workers, the pious, and bazaar merchants often had grievances with state policies, but the threat of coercion ensured their subordination to political dictates – for now. Parliament continued to operate, albeit with shallow state-controlled parties created by the monarchy to dominate the political arena; there was no meaningful pluralism, only competition among cronies and elites. SAVAK kept tight control over all opposition and dissidence. Viewed from afar, Iran appeared to be an "island of stability," as US President Jimmy Carter famously declared on New Year's Eve of 1977. Yet despite the appearance of calm, currents of pluralism and dissent existed during the 1970s. The three main groups who opposed the Shah and the Pahlavi monarchy were the Shi'a 'ulama; traditional nationalists, and militant Marxists. The weakest among these three opposition forces were the nationalist groups, including the aging National Front, and which would prove irrelevant in the coming years.

Dissenting religious clerics remained formidable. Among these 'ulama was Ayatollah Khomeini, who uniquely fused his juristic authority with Islamist ideals that demanded conservative adherence and the restoration of religious principles within the mechanisms of political governance. In that sense, Khomeini's beliefs represented an early expression of Shi'a Islamism, as distinct from the Sunni Islamism of other actors in the MENA, such as the Muslim Brotherhood. As an exile, Khomeini lived in the Shi'a holy city of Najaf, Iraq, from 1965 until 1978 and communicated with his network through emissaries who relayed messages and brought tapes of his fiery sermons into Iran. His writings provided a blueprint for the Islamic regime he hoped to establish in place of the Pahlavi monarchy, whose Shah was criticized as being too secular and pro-Western. Another major personality during the 1970s was the Islamist intellectual Ali Shari'ati, who developed a large following before his death in 1977.

On the Marxist and leftist front, several major guerilla organizations were established in the late 1960s and early 1970s by young Iranians who had become disillusioned with the moderate positions of the National Front and the weakness of the Tudeh Party, given the ease by which the Shah had wiped them aside. The most important were the Mojahedin-e Khalq (People's Warriors), which had a radical Islamic-leftist orientation, and the Marxist-Leninist Fedayan-e Khalq. These groups sent some members to Lebanon and elsewhere for guerrilla training, and maintained contact with Iranian student movements in the US and Europe. They launched a short-lived uprising in 1971, attacking police stations and attacking officials as well as American military and civilian advisers.

Revolution and Islamic reformation: 1978–1980s

By the mid-1970s, it was clear that the absence of political freedom and growing repression was alienating many Iranians, especially among urban classes. Inequality remained high, angering workers and youths. For his part, the Shah drew even closer to the US in the 1970s, buying vast quantities of arms, signing lucrative contracts with American corporations, and bringing tens of thousands of Americans to Iran to administer these projects. He embraced Western culture and deemphasized traditional Persian and Islamic values. He also maintained close relations with Israel. These trends angered not only traditionalist Iranians but also many modernists, who felt the Shah was compromising Iran's rich identity and creating an alarming gap between themselves and their more traditional countrymen. The monarchy's primary support base had dangerously narrowed, consisting primarily of secular, urbane, and well-off families who frequently contributed to the ranks of the business and political elites.

Economic crisis then unfolded. The mid-1970s oil boom produced rampant inflation, shortages, corruption, and extensive rural-urban migration that strained public services. The Shah responded with measures that further aggravated discontent, particularly among the bazaar traders; these included price controls, higher interest rates, an anti-profiteering campaign, and spending cuts. After the election of President Carter in 1979, US and European officials increasingly criticized human rights conditions in Iran, leading the Shah to temporarily relax some restrictions on opposition. Under these conditions, Iranian activists began to call for political reform, but the political system was still too hegemonic to allow for meaningful pluralism. In 1975, the monarchy had recalibrated the lethargic party system to create instead a single legal party, the Rastakhiz (Resurgence), which imposed compulsory membership, a large youth wing, forced mobilization, and requirements for political loyalty that seemed to borrow heavily from the dominant party tactics of other regional autocracies, such as the Ba'th republics of Syria or Iraq. It was the Rastakhiz that levied price controls and anti-profiteering penalties on the bazaar, whose merchants were vilified by officials despite their traditional importance.

While urban forces would drive the revolution, its seeds would come from more distant opposition. Ayatollah Khomeini's pupils organized large demonstrations in January 1978 in the city of Qom, a vital center for Shi'a learning and seminaries; in response, security forces pounced, killing seven and arresting scores. Following traditional Shi'a mourning practices, the Islamists organized more demonstrations 40 days later to commemorate those killed. Mobs attacked government buildings, theaters, and liquor stores and clashed with police, leaving nine dead and hundreds arrested. More violent demonstrations occurred at 40-day intervals in the following months. The Shah tried to end the chaos by replacing the prime minister, releasing hundreds of prisoners, and promising free elections. Moderate opposition leaders appealed for calm, but failed to stop the crisis. Labor unrest began to spread throughout the country, crippling the oil industry and public services. Islamist and leftist guerrillas increasingly attacked government targets as well, generating a cycle of continual protest and uprising.

Violent demonstrations swept Tehran in early November 1978, leading the Shah to appoint a military government and declare martial law. Despite the imposition of continued repression and violence, and SAVAK's best efforts, the opposition would not cease. The Shah finally persuaded National Front leader Shahpour Bakhtiar to form an interim government in hopes of assuaging the millions of demonstrating Iranians, but Bakhtiar did so only on condition that the Shah leave the country. Thus, the Shah left Iran on January 16, 1979, never to return, essentially ending 2,500 years of dynastic monarchism in Persia. Bakhtiar enacted a number of conciliatory measures such as lifting press restrictions, freeing all remaining political prisoners, disbanding SAVAK, but Khomeini responded by declaring his government illegal and appointing a Revolutionary Council. He returned to Tehran on February 1 to cheers.

Throughout 1979, Khomeini's acolytes and supporters not only sidelined Bakhtiar's brief leadership but also marginalized moderate voices in the new revolutionary government, which initially sought to incorporate a variety of Islamist and secularist voices but ultimately became beholden to the former. The regime that emerged was self-proclaimed as an Islamic Republic, and empowered many activists to undertake radical action, such as the storming of the US Embassy in November 1979, resulting in the infamous hostage crisis that ended only in 1981. Khomeini's supporters controlled the constitutional assembly, drafted a new constitution, and implanted within the emergent new political order the ideology of *velayat-e faqih*, which maintained that the 'ulama (and above all the highest-ranking jurist) should have guardianship and control over state decision-making. That ideological framework hence meant that Ayatollah Khomeini would serve as Supreme Leader with ultimate political and religious authority, but where in daily affairs a separate governmental system involving a presidency, various ministries and organs, and a parliament that could incubate meaningful debate would drive forward everyday decision-making.

What threw domestic events into turmoil was Iraq's invasion of Iran in September 1980, which sparked a bloody eight-year conflict. In some ways, the war consolidated the new Islamic Republic by compelling the nascent regime to mobilize for an existential struggle. Thus, Iran began a massive effort to mobilize resistance, producing an enormous outpouring of volunteers. At the same time, counterrevolutionary forces were liquidated. The leftist-Islamist Mojahedin-e Khalq guerilla group, for instance, had become disappointed with the new order, but their rallies and activism were quickly suppressed, resulting in a series of insurgent terrorist strikes against the government, followed by furious retaliations in the form of mass arrests and executions. A number of officials were assassinated, including both the shortly appointed new president and prime minister of the republic. In October 1981, Ali Khamenei, a radical cleric and ally of Khomeini, was elected president; he appointed Mir-Hossein Musavi, a lay Islamist, as prime minister. These men, together with Akbar Hashemi Rafsanjani, another influential colleague of Khomeini and recent appointee as speaker of parliament, worked to stabilize the political scene.

By the mid-1980s, this process was so successful that the core group of Shi'a revolutionaries – 'ulama, intellectuals, politicians, and activists – responsible for the new republic began feuding amongst themselves over practical issues, such as the redistribution of wealth, economic policymaking, and trade issues. In July 1988, the Iran-Iraq War ended, and a year later Ayatollah Khomeini died. He was succeeded by President Khamenei, who became the new Supreme Leader. Rafsanjani became the new president. At the same time, voters approved constitutional reforms aimed at reducing the gridlock that had paralyzed the political system. The most important was a measure to eliminate the position of prime minister and concentrate executive power in the presidency – all under the tutelage of the Supreme Leader, of course.

Recalibration and uncertainty, 1990s–present

President Rafsanjani assembled a government dominated by centrist technocrats. This was a shift from the first decade of the Islamic Republic, in which the political elite were mainly dominated by Shi'a 'ulama and revolutionary activists. Rafsanjani's highest priority was to revitalize the economy, which had deteriorated sharply as a result of the war, years of ideologically inspired policymaking, and the collapse of oil prices in 1986. The result was the marginalization of the last vestiges of leftist-Islamist thought, and the rise of a new bloc of political thinkers – the reformists – as embodied by the victory of Muhammad Khatami in the 1997 presidential elections. These reformists sought to break the political grip of conservatives and hardliners, defined by their zeal in ensuring revolutionary principles and ideological pursuits remained at the center of state policymaking. By contrast, reformists suggested adaptation and change, arguing that it was possible to retain the core principles of Shi'a Islamism while also relaxing social, economic, and political controls.

Thus, Khatami's administration pushed for political development (e.g., more liberalizing reform, relaxing restrictions on the media, loosening restrictions on civic activity); deeming this a threat, conservatives responded by assaulting and arresting reformist leaders, closing their newspapers, and deploying demagogic rhetoric. They closed a popular reformist newspaper in July 1999, triggering six days of severe student rioting that shook the regime's foundations. Khatami's reelection in 2001 suggested reformist thinking struck a chord among many Iranian voters, but conservatives aligned with the Supreme Leader and other traditionalist voices among the clerical establishment. The 9/11 terrorist attacks on the US, which made Iran part of the Bush administration's "axis of evil," further strengthened conservative rhetoric that too much laxity would destroy the fabric of the Islamic Republic.

Political fortunes swung the other way; conservative hardliners won the 2003 municipal council elections, the 2004 parliamentary elections, and the 2005 presidential elections, the latter of which catapulted a little-known lay person, Mahmoud Ahmadinejad, to the executive office. Ahmadinejad's election initiated a shift back toward the radicalism of the 1980s. During his first term, this manifested mainly in Iran's foreign policy – especially its pursuit of a nuclear program, which led the West to impose a series of harsh economic sanctions. After his inauguration, Ahmadinejad nominated a cabinet dominated by hardliners. During this period, Iranian political elites shifted in favor of the military-clergy alliance, in which the members of Islamic Revolutionary Guard Corps, the specialized branch of the military driven exclusively by religious ideology, began exerting more domestic influence over policymaking and social life. Ahmadinejad also began to implement the populist economics he had campaigned on, increasing public spending and pushing interest rates down significantly.

Ahmadinejad also brought cronyism and controversy, however. In the 2009 elections, Ahmadinejad won reelection in a controversial vote over his nearest contender, the reformist Mir-Hossein Mousavi, who had served as the last prime minister in the 1980s. Many citizens, however, accused the elections of being rigged, and so erupted in furious protests. The result was an unprecedented wave of demonstrations, marches, and strikes involving millions in the greatest expression of popular mobilization since the revolution. The regime responded to this Green Movement with mass repression, targeting many students, journalists, and intellectuals in a process that presaged the 2011–12 Arab Spring. Mousavi was placed under house arrest, and major reformist blocs, factions, and papers were outlawed. By 2011, thus, the political scene in Iran as expressed in the media, parliament, and other venues was reduced to conservative factions that aligned against or with Ahmadinejad, who also was rumored to be losing the support of the Supreme Leader after firing his foreign minister and intelligence minister.

With economic conditions deteriorating rapidly as a result of misguided policies and economic sanctions associated with the nuclear program, the June 2013 presidential elections presented an opportunity for more change. The winner was Hassan Rouhani, a moderate cleric who had been a protégé of Rafsanjani. This marked a political shift away from the previous conservative period, and a modest opening towards reformist ideas once again. The focus of Rouhani, however, was foreign policy rather than domestic political liberalization. He began negotiating a major agreement with the West under which most economic sanctions would be lifted in exchange for sharp limits on Iran's nuclear program. Iranian politics therefore remained stagnant, with the reformist faction fully contained, the press tightly controlled, and human rights conditions still poor. Domestic tensions remained high, with frequent outbursts of ethnic unrest, labor activism, and discontent among young people and the urban middle class.

Still, the historic nuclear deal, formally known as the Joint Comprehensive Plan of Action (JCPOA), which Iran signed with the 5+1 group (China, France, Germany, Russia, the United Kingdom and the United States) on July 14, 2015, was overwhelmingly welcomed by Iranian people as the beginning of potential normalization – that is, the reentry of Iran into a global system and the end of geopolitical isolation. The nuclear agreement temporarily boosted the Iranian economy, bolstered Rouhani's popularity, and strengthened the argument among reformists that pragmatic adaptation rather than hardline reactionary thought could best preserve Iranian prosperity. Moderates and reformists thus pulled out another promising victory in the 2016 parliamentary elections. Rouhani's reelection in 2017 confirmed this change in public sentiment, but hopes for cultural and societal pluralization ran into a dual challenge.

First, threatened by Rouhani's popularity, Ayatollah Khamenei and hardliners increasingly pressured Rouhani's administration through subtle means, such as rejecting the nomination of some ministers and maneuvering conservative deputies in the parliament to impeach others. Second, the Trump administration withdrew from the Iranian nuclear deal in 2018, which strengthened the conservative position that revolutionary adherence rather than outward engagement was still the winning hand. The imposition of more international sanctions pummeled an economy already buckling under chronic unemployment, financial mismanagement, widespread corruption, and social unrest. Several rounds of protests emerged throughout 2017–18 over bread-and-butter issues, such as poverty and food prices; unlike the Green Movement, these spread to rural areas and small towns rather than just the major cities. Like the Green Movement, such mobilization was harshly suppressed by security forces, leaving Iranian society squeezed between two increasingly embittered political poles.

SOCIAL AND ECONOMIC ENVIRONMENT

Iran is located in Southwest Asia, bounded to the north by the Caucasus region, the Caspian Sea, and the steppes of Central Asia; to the south by the Arabian (or Persian) Gulf; to the west by Turkey and Iraq; and to the east by Afghanistan and Pakistan (Map 16.1). It is divided by two major mountain ranges: the Zagros, running from the northwest to the southeast; and the Alborz, running from the northwest to the northeast, looping below the Caspian Sea. These natural borders have helped preserve Iran's unique identity through the ages. The largest cities are the capital of Tehran, with nearly nine million people, followed by Mashhad, Isfahan, Karaj, and Shiraz.

The central region of Iran, delineated by the Zagros and Alborz ranges, is a high, arid plateau. The eastern part of this plateau features two large, barren deserts. The remainder supports limited agricultural activity and includes Tehran, Isfahan, and Mashhad. North of the Alborz lies the lush Caspian coastal plain, where plentiful rains support the cultivation of rice and other crops. Across the Zagros to the southwest lies Khuzestan Province, a hot coastal plain that features Iran's only large river (the Karun), marshes, and most of the country's oil reserves. The Caspian and Gulf coastal regions support shipping, fishing, and tourism. Most of Iran's border areas are lightly populated and have rough terrain.

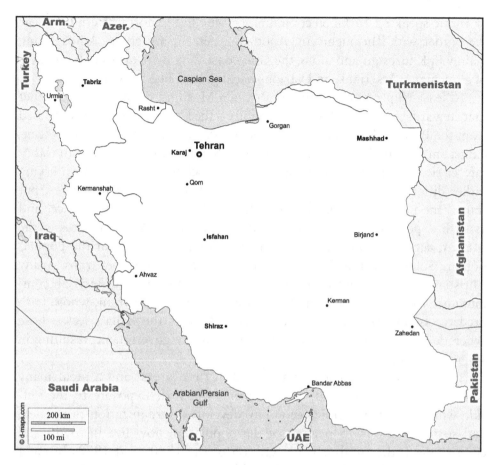

MAP 16.1
Islamic Republic of Iran. Major water bodies, rivers, and cities shown.

Source: D-Maps.

Society and trends

Iranian society is ethnically diverse. Persians are the largest ethnic group, comprising 62 percent of the population and dominating central Iran. Persians are an Indo-European people, and most speak Persian (also known as Farsi). Iran's small Lur and Baluch minorities also speak Iranian languages. Azeri Turks represent 16 percent of the population; they live mainly in the northwest and speak a variant of the Turkic language. Kurds compose 10 percent of the population and live in the mountainous northwest, adjacent to the Kurdish regions of Turkey and Iraq. Some 2 percent of the population consists of Turkic-speaking Turkmen communities, who live in northeastern Iran near the border with Turkmenistan. Another 2 percent are ethnic Arabs, living mainly in Khuzestan and along the Gulf coast. There are also small numbers of Armenians, Assyrians, and various tribal groups like the Qashqa'i.

At least 90 percent of Iranians are Shi'a Muslims, defined by their belief that stewardship of the Islamic community – the Caliph – should have passed from the Prophet Muhammad to his son-in-law, Ali, and Ali's male descendants. Shi'a Islam differs from the majority Sunni branch in having an elaborate clerical hierarchy, following a different school of law, and observing rather different practices. Iraq and Bahrain also have Shi'a majorities, but Iran is the undisputed spiritual and doctrinal center of Shi'a practice, and as such is perceived as a natural rival to large Sunni Muslim states in the MENA, such as Saudi Arabia and Egypt. About 9 percent of the population are Sunni Muslims, including Kurds, Balochis, and some Arabs. A tiny Christian minority mainly encompasses Iran's Armenian and Assyrian communities. An even smaller number of Iranians are Zoroastrian, whose faith predates Islam. Another notable minority faith is the Baha'i sect, whose syncretic belief system is considered heresy by the government, resulting in severe persecution.

Until the 1950s, most Iranians lived in rural areas, and a great many were landless peasants and small farmers with little exposure to the outside world. As Iran's rentier economy developed, urbanization proceeded, and so today about 75 percent of the population now live in towns and cities. Indeed, the rural-urban migration of the 1960s and 1970s brought large numbers of poorly educated, highly religious people into Tehran and other cities, providing the foot soldiers for the revolution. The country is also unique in the MENA in how economic development transformed urban society early on. Modern industrial plants began to emerge in Iran's cities and in the oil-producing areas of Khuzestan in the early twentieth century, creating an industrial working class unmatched by most Arab countries. In the same era, sharp increases in public-sector employment and services such as journalism and banking began to create a modern middle class, which differed from the traditional middle class mainly in its Western-style education and broader outlook. In the post-World War Two era, a modern upper class of businessmen and cronies of the royal court emerged, distinguished from the traditional upper class of wealthy landowners also by its Western education and cosmopolitan outlook.

Within cultural and religious discourse, there are several underlying trends that affect both social life and political developments. First, Shi'a

Islam's emphasis on martyrdom has been a recurring theme in Iran's modern history. Even before the upsurge of radical opposition in the 1970s, figures like Muhammad Mosaddeq were widely revered by secularists and Islamists alike for their willingness to make sacrifices for a just cause. Martyrdom and morality became central motifs in the discourse of the 1978–79 revolution and the Islamic regime it spawned, leading many to sacrifice their lives during the revolution and the Iran-Iraq War. Another recurring theme has been an emphasis on pluralism, reflecting not only the growing importance of the modern middle class but also Shi'a traditions that conventionally sought at least the appearance of inclusiveness and consensus-building among different clerical voices. Finally, family bonds remain strong and have a substantial impact on social and political organization. Politicians and clerics often rely heavily on their children, siblings, and old friends, who, in turn, benefit considerably from these connections. Civic and political factions can be highly personalized in this way, as many Iranians often judge public figures on the basis of family background and other personal connections. As a result, Iranian social relations can exhibit strong patrimonial and clannish tendencies, which in return undermines civil society institutions.

Economic conditions

Iran's economic history is a history of rentierism. Oil was first discovered in 1901 and became increasingly important in the 1920s and 1930s. Hydrocarbon revenue began to grow rapidly in the late 1950s, due to production increases and the better terms of the 1954 oil agreement. Oil prices then increased eightfold between 1970 and 1974, creating another huge increase. Iran's oil revenue financed much of the state's operating budget and a series of ambitious five-year development plans that greatly expanded Iran's economy. Real gross domestic product (GDP) grew by an annual average of 11.6 percent in the 1960s and 12 percent from 1970 to 1976, after which it stagnated and then fell sharply as the revolution unfolded. Through state-led developmental strategies, other new industries took root, such as steel, automobile manufacturing, and textiles.

The 1980s was a lost decade, however, much like other oil-exporting states due to the collapse of crude oil prices, compounded also by the cost of the war with Iraq and falling oil production. A sharp decline in oil revenue substantially reduced public investment, including the ability of the government to maintain its expenditures in areas where it counted the most – social services, public firms, and employment. The revolution and the war also reduced private investment, damaged infrastructure and production facilities, disrupted foreign borrowing and essential imports, and led many entrepreneurs and skilled workers to emigrate. Together with the high birth rate of the 1980s, these factors produced a 48 percent drop in Iran's real GDP per capita from its peak in 1976 to its 1988 level. Real GDP per capita did not return to its 1976 level until 2009.

Since the late 1980s, Iran's leaders have carried out a series of development plans whose main goal has been to stimulate economic growth and employment by liberalizing the economy and expanding non-oil industries. None of these plans have been very successful. The first development plan covered the period from 1989 to 1993 and was drawn up in consultation with the International Monetary Fund. It faced strong opposition from parliament, who feared neoliberal notions of privatization, subsidy cuts, exchange rate liberalization, and tight monetary policy would hurt the poor. Thus, most of the plan's key goals were never achieved. The second development plan (1994–99) had similar objectives – rein in spending, relax capital controls, and make state-owned companies more competitive through privatization in a slow shift to market-oriented economics. Again, opposition from the conservative-controlled parliament and lower oil prices prevented achievement of many of these objectives. The same fate held true for the third development plan, which ended in 2004. Despite these policy failures, the Iranian economy somewhat rebounded in the 1990s and 2000s, with GDP respectively growing throughout these decades at 4.6 and 5.3 percent, on average; however, job creation lagged behind population growth, and depressed oil prices squeeze state coffers perennially.

By contrast, the Ahmadinejad years were characterized by diametrically opposing strategies. President Ahmadinejad campaigned on an economic populist platform. He then implemented this platform once in office, sharply increasing public spending, pushing interest rates below the inflation rate, allowing consumer-goods subsidies to grow even further, and financing these efforts from Iran's rapidly growing oil windfall as energy prices rebounded in the late 2000s. These actions increased inflation, which spiked at 29 percent in 2008. As the election-related turmoil of 2009 subsided, Ahmadinejad and his opponents in parliament developed a plan to trim the vast array of subsidies on energy, food, and other products, worth an estimated $100 billion per year, and replace them with cash payments; but this swapped increasing inflation for fiscal deficits. At about the same time, the US and its allies greatly expanded their economic sanctions on Iran, hoping to stop its nuclear program.

The new economic sanctions, the subsidy-reduction plan, and Ahmadinejad's populist measures severely affected Iran's economy. By 2012, oil exports had fallen by more than 60 percent, the exchange rate plummeted by 70 percent, import shortages crippled the manufacturing sector, and inflation rose to 30 percent as almost no new net jobs were created from 2006 until 2011. These trends pushed Iran into a deep recession, with real GDP falling by a staggering rate of -6.8 percent in 2012. A modest recovery followed the JCPOA deal in 2015, but the restoration of sanctions in 2018 again hurt trade, commerce, and investments while pressuring the government again to balance its need for fiscal discipline with its redistributive commitments to ensure societal well-being. The decline of oil prices yet again after 2014 also squarely undercut long-term planning. By the late 2010s, it appeared that Iran would effectively exit the decade barely even, with its economy growing by just 2.2 percent on average for the 2011–18 period.

POLITICAL STRUCTURES

Iran's Islamic regime has an unusual mixture of authoritarian and pluralistic features, including a powerful repressive apparatus and institutions that ensure clerical control but also elections, and often-intense contestation among the diverse factions that support the regime. It has been simultaneously labeled as totalitarian, hybrid, and competitive authoritarian, by different scholars and based on varying criteria. For example, some have argued that Iran is a totalitarian regime given the pervasive way that social and moral behaviors are expected to conform to a revolutionary ideal. Others have suggested this is a hybrid regime, in which an electoral system coexists with a structure of tutelary guardianship. Perhaps the best way to capture its structure is that of a theocratic republic in which voters can select their president and parliament – but only among candidates that exhibit proper religious credentials, within elections that can be distorted or manipulated at will, and with the goal of producing a system of decision-making that must always abide by the preferences of unelected clerics who fuse political and religious power. In addition, there is no permissible area of public life that cannot conform to Shi'a Islamist principles, which configures (at least in theory) the underlying fabric of social relations and political interactions.

Iran's constitution anoints as the highest position the Supreme Leader, in accordance with the doctrine of *velayat-e faqih*, which permeates the foundations of Iran's political order. In this structure, the office of supreme leadership (*rahbar*) can only be occupied by the highest ranked Shi'a cleric whose knowledge of Islam, expertise in law, and immersion in religious practices makes him most qualified to oversee how a political community seeking salvation should structure its decisions, institutions, and policies. The Supreme Leader is thus the *marja-e taqlid* (source of emulation), whose authority cannot be contested by any elected official or even lesser cleric. Constitutionally, this empowers the Supreme Leader to not simply rule by decree, but set guidelines, supervise policy implementation, appoint the head of the judiciary, dismiss the president, and oversee the armed forces.

Working alongside the Supreme Leader is the Council of Guardians, the 12-member committee of experts charged with vetting all laws and supervising elections, including striking out any candidate who does not espouse the appropriate qualifications – a vagary that allows the council to greatly shape and manipulate the type of race preferred. Six of the Council are 'ulama appointed by the Supreme Leader, and the other six are lay members selected by parliament from a preselected slate of nominees. The Council does not initiate legislation so much as monitor debates and proceedings; it can veto any proposed legislation, without giving parliament any recourse. Finally, the Council oversees the selection of another body, the Assembly of Experts (Majles-e Khobregan), who advise the Supreme Leader and select his successor.

Apart from his obvious political authority, the Supreme Leader, and the religious-bureaucratic apparatus accompanying that position, wields impressive social and regulatory reach in several respects. First, most obviously, they regulate Friday prayer sermons, religious curricular, and other aspects of Islamic discourse. Second, they appoint the heads of Iran's major broadcast media, whose narrow programming disseminates conservative views and often portrays opposition and reformists as dangerous. Third, they also appoint the judiciary head, who in turn appoints prosecutors and judges staffing all levels of the court system. The legal system itself is specialized and well-developed. There are special courts for cases involving security matters, the press, and officials. There is even a special court for dealing with dissident clergy.

The Supreme Leader is also in control of the military and security apparatus, which consists of multiple organs. In addition to the regular armed forces, civil police, and intelligence institutions are specialized institutions designed to help the regime maintain maximum internal control while also projecting its interests outwards. One is the Revolutionary Guard Corps, which possesses about 125,000 troops and uniquely can deploy either within or outside the country at the behest of state interests. In the past, for instance, it has advised, trained, or fought in wars within Lebanon and more recently in Syria and Iraq, as part of efforts to eliminate the Islamic State of Iraq and Syria (ISIS). The Corps has been designated a terrorist organization by Bahrain, Saudi Arabia, and in 2019 the US; the latter raised many eyebrows, as it marked the first time the US has labeled a formal part of another sovereign state's armed forces as a terrorist actor.

Another is the Basij, a paramilitary force connected to the Revolutionary Guard Corps and staffed primarily by volunteers. The Basij famously deployed hundreds of thousands of youths as little more than cannon fodder during the Iran-Iraq War; after its reactivation in 1999, the regime utilized Basij militias both abroad but also domestically, such as in helping to contain the 2009 Green Movement protests. Over time, the Basij has thus also evolved into its own constituent social force, imposing political conservativism and ideological indoctrination upon members.

The electoral elements of the Islamic Republic are important to understanding its decision-making process. In addition to these aforementioned unelected bodies, the constitution also created a directly elected president and unicameral parliament, whose seats are allocated to Iran's provinces in proportion to population size. Five seats are reserved for Iran's Christian, Jewish, and Zoroastrian minorities. Elections are held every four years for parliament; municipal councils in cities and villages also abide by four-year electoral cycles. Presidential elections can be spirited, but with the caveat that candidates are vetted well in advance, and the conduct of elections is overseen by the Council of Guardians, much like parliamentary contests.

The constitution also allows for the establishment of political parties, provided they support the principles of the Islamic regime. This provision also was not implemented until the late 1990s, though several party-like organizations existed before then. Legislation authorizing the creation of parties was adopted in 1998, and many parties emerged in the following years. Several other Islamic modernist and secular nationalist parties were officially outlawed but allowed to operate within certain limits before the 2009 crackdown. None of these parties developed broad popular support, and today parliamentary elections feature not so much strong independent parties but rather broad coalitions and alliances of different groups, each typically centered upon a singular personality or idea. Several other civil society organizations emerged in the 1990s, including the Office for Consolidating Unity (Daftar-e Takhim-e Vahdat), which was a reformist student organization, and the Labor House (Khaneh-ye Kargar), which was a pro-reformist labor federation. Both were heavily suppressed and have become inactive. Various new professional, student, women's, and religious organizations emerged in the 1990s as well, which were then suppressed during Ahmadinejad's term and especially after 2009.

Another element of civil society is the news and entertainment media. Iran's newspapers were heavily restricted in the 1980s, providing one-sided news coverage and a narrow range of opinion. This changed in the early 1990s, when the Rafsanjani government allowed several independent newspapers and magazines to appear. The print media also flourished under Khatami before hardliners in the judiciary began a harsh crackdown after the 2000 elections, closing dozens of newspapers. Such censorship continues today, as Iran regularly ranks near the bottom for key press indices, such as the Reporters Without Borders' World Press Freedom Index, given its high rate of detaining journalists and closing outlets. At the same time, the country's media sphere is not wanting for lack of entries; in addition to around two million blogs, Iran has over 170 newspapers. The Iranian cinema scene is extremely vibrant, and subject somewhat less to government controls. Persian-language films have gained global renown over the past two decades for their creative subject matter and high production values.

POLITICAL DYNAMICS

Iran has changed substantially since the Islamic regime was established in 1979. The early 1980s was a time of revolutionary transformation, when the new leadership made a comprehensive effort to realign Iranian culture and society along its new vision of Shi'a Islamist political order by restructuring the country's laws and political institutions; using schools, religious institutions, and the media as instruments of indoctrination; and forcing Iranians to observe strict Islamic standards of dress and behavior. Islamization policies were meant to not only undo the perceived secularization of Iranian society and remove Western influences, but also by projecting the religious regulatory arm of the new state into both private and public life. Additionally, the radicals mobilized their supporters with inflammatory rhetoric and dramatic actions, like the US Embassy hostage crisis. They also attacked not only their political opponents but many apolitical, secular targets. Many Iranians supported the Islamic regime in this period, giving it a populist character; but many others opposed it, leaving society divided.

Much of the revolutionary fervor that animated this period dissipated by the late 1980s as a result of the war with Iraq, economic decline, and continuing repression. When Rafsanjani became president in 1989, he tried to reinvigorate popular support for the regime by revitalizing the economy and loosening cultural restrictions, while keeping the political system largely intact. To reconstruct Iran's economy, Rafsanjani primarily de-ideologized the machinery of government and lessened the ideological pressure on Iranian society by prioritizing technocratic expertise. During this time, the leaders of the various and newly streamlined bureaucratic and administrative actors began to emerge as powerful players in the new state. However, resistance and inertia blocked these initiatives, but the changes made to the political dynamics were indelible: now, policy debates could be waged on not just ideological grounds, but also on practical considerations about state interests, material cost, and institutional impact.

Thus, while the Supreme Leader, Council of Guardians, and other bulwarks of the Islamic Republic remained solidly in place during the 1990s, the discourse witnessed in the political arena during elections and within parliament took on a different tone. The expansion of the Iranian urban middle class in the 1990s, which drove forward a temporary expansion of critical media during the apex of reformist politics, gave birth to new questions about equitable development and effective governance. While conservative hardliners used their entrenched position to block changes advocated by President Khatami during his 1997–2004 administration, a lasting effect was increased polarization that sometimes took on generational overtones pitting youths against elders, and other times expressed itself in urban-rural cleavages, familial and class ties, and other non-religious affiliations. That cyclical discourse continues to drive the visible face of Iranian politics today, as it plays out in social discussions, election debates, and private circles. Ahmadinejad's administration escalated this climate of tension, with many youths expecting a political breakthrough in 2009 that never materialized.

The Green Movement exposed another reality of Iranian politics: the primary vector of change, apart from the fractiousness of clerical elites and political leaders, is youth. That protest wave captivated global headlines and shook the religious establishment, as young Iranians filled streets (Photo 16.1). Demographically, Iran is young. A quarter of the country is under the age of 15, and well over half is under the age of 30. This is the product not only of elevated birth rates and improved infant mortality, but also the slowness with which the Islamic Republic embraced family planning in the 1990s. Young Iranians, particularly students, have historically helped spearhead every popular uprising – from the 1906 Constitutional Revolution, to the leftist-nationalist opposition of the late 1940s, to the Iranian Revolution, and most recently the 2009 Green Movement. The number of university

PHOTO 16.1
Green Movement – youth protests in Iran, 2009.

Source: Photo by Hamed Saber, Flickr.

students has increased from 173,000 in 1978 to more than 4,300,000 in 2018, of which half are women; youth literacy exceeds 98 percent. Yet youth unemployment tops 28 percent, more than twice the national rate. Finally, Iranian youth are tech-savvy. They are avid users of social media like Instagram and Facebook despite government efforts to block access to these and other sites, like Twitter and YouTube.

In general, younger Iranians are better educated, more cosmopolitan, less committed to the Islamic regime, and more deeply affected by the economic stagnation and cultural restrictions than their elders. The generational divide is especially important, perhaps more so than in other MENA countries, because for decades the legitimacy of the Islamic Republic depended upon societal and political adherence to the vision of its ideological fathers. As citizens become increasingly detached from this revolutionary generation and turn instead towards more global, or even Western, forms of cultural expression, media, and norms, political battles may become more polarized.

Youths are more likely than not to favor reformist politicians (though many have also become apathetic and cynical); they are also more likely to favor leaving the country and emigrating to the West. As of the mid-2010s, in fact, Iran has the highest rate of the brain drain in the world, with more than 150,000 educated citizens migrating outwards annually as of the mid-2010s. At the same time, young Iranians have also culturally innovated in ways that exceed the expectations of older authorities. For instance, some analysts suggest that rising levels of Iranian nationalism among youth – centered upon Persian heritage and Iran's historical power, not upon religious doctrine – reflect an alternative source of identity to Islam.

President Rouhani's 2017 reelection indicates the sticky preferences of many younger Iranians towards reformist viewpoints that correlate, on some issues, with conventional views of liberalism and liberalization. For many voters, the seminal question was not so much the democratization of Iran, as that would involve a blanket transformation of the entire political structure and institutional dynamic installed with the revolution. Rather, it concerned the potentiality of gradual openings on a number of fronts where change was long debated, from basic political freedoms to the regulation of social behavior. The latter is especially contentious among some Iranian women, who see the actions of Iran's Guidance Patrols (e.g., the religious police) – for instance, ensuring women are properly veiled, or that gendered behaviors conform with traditional expectations – as overreaching.

The other pivotal factor that determines Iranian political change is the Supreme Leadership. Khamenei, as of 2019, is 80 years old, and according to some observers has fallen into ill health; he underwent surgery for prostate cancer in 2016. If he departs from power in the coming years, much will depend on who his successor is (as chosen by the Assembly of Experts) and whether his successor sees any utility in engaging reformist clerics and politicians. Succession may constitute momentum for rapid and dramatic change, particularly if a well-known cleric like Rouhani is chosen over more conservative options, such as Ebrahim Raisi, the current head of the judiciary.

FOREIGN POLICY

Before the 1979 revolution, Iran was closely allied with the United States, and the Shah's regime was regarded as a staunchly anti-Soviet pillar of Western strategy in the MENA. The various factions that seized power in 1979 generally opposed this orientation but held differing views on how Iran's foreign policy should be conducted. Consequently, disputes over foreign policy were a major focus of the power struggles that emerged after the revolution, and Iran's foreign policy has been closely intertwined with its domestic politics ever since. Iran's foreign policy in the post-revolutionary era has oscillated between prioritizing ideology versus pragmatic interests, with each side representing the conservative-reformist split. On one side, conservative hardliners have prioritized ideology, challenging the regional order of the MENA through confrontations with rival states (like Saudi Arabia) and global powers like the US. Moderates, or pragmatists, have preferred more engagement in the international arena, cooperation over conflict in the regional context, and see peaceful Western engagement as necessary.

Iran was highly confrontational during the first decade of the Islamic regime, as the hardline school guided its foreign relations. The central focus of Iran's confrontational foreign policy during this period was hostility toward the United States. This was manifested not only in the hostage crisis, but also in harsh anti-American rhetoric and indirect attacks on US targets, often through proxy terrorist groups. The US responded by backing Iraq in the Iran-Iraq War, attacking Iranian naval vessels during its naval intervention in the Gulf after 1986, and undertaking covert operations against Iran.

The secondary focus of Iranian foreign policy in the 1980s was exporting revolution. The Islamic Republic made extensive efforts to incite rebellion and resistance among Shi'a minorities in the Gulf kingdoms, particularly Saudi Arabia, Kuwait, and Bahrain. Iranian operatives repeatedly fomented unrest during the annual Hajj pilgrimage to Mecca in the mid-1980s, leaving hundreds dead and severely embarrassing the Saudi government. Such belligerency was the primary reason why the six Arab Gulf kingdoms created the Gulf Cooperation Council (GCC) in 1981, in hopes of creating a defensive shield against future Iranian intrusions. Iran also entered the Lebanese theater, where it assisted the radical Islamist group Hizbullah, while also funding Shi'a dissident networks in Iraq. In a broader sense, the latter phases of the Iran-Iraq War were interpreted as a revolutionary cause, as toppling Saddam's Sunni Arab regime would have marked a tremendous victory for the new Islamic Republic.

This confrontational posture, however, left Iran isolated and desperate to acquire arms and other assistance. This led Iran's leaders to establish close relationships with several unlikely countries, most importantly Syria under its Asad regime, but also Libya under Qaddafi's dictatorship and East Asian autocracies, such as China and North Korea. Practical considerations entered into the fold; Iran bought large quantities of arms from both Asian countries, despite that their communist regimes were avowedly atheistic. In the 1990s, Iran shifted away from such confrontational strategies in favor of more measured approaches. The July 1988 agreement to stop the war with Iraq ended its most ambitious effort to export revolution and produced optimism that its foreign policy would moderate. President Rafsanjani began to make overtures to the West, hoping this would facilitate his economic reforms. Most importantly, he indicated that Iran would seek the release of US and other hostages still being held in Lebanon by Hizbullah. (The last of the US hostages were released in 1992.) Iran also stayed out of the 1990–91 Gulf War, and reestablished diplomatic relations with Saudi Arabia and Morocco during this period.

However, normalization in the 1990s did not so much occur as merely become a diplomatic talking point, as many conservative voices within the Iranian state – particularly those linked to the Revolutionary Guard Corps and hardline clerics – sought to continually challenge international hierarchy. Iran maintained close connections with Hizballah, even as it attacked the Israeli Embassy and Jewish targets in Argentina in 1992 and 1994, respectively. It also developed links to Palestinian Hamas. More worrisome to the West, it worked to develop nuclear warheads, and the medium-range missiles to carry them. Western pressures and Khatami's rise in 1997 heralded a period where moderate reformists were able to briefly dictate the rhythms of foreign policy.

Though blocked by the Supreme Leader, President Khatami publicly announced his intentions of seeking some rapprochement with the US throughout 1997 and 1998. He was more successful with the European Union, as many EU countries reopened their embassies in Tehran by the end of the 1990s, while also agreeing to strengthen trade ties. While Iran improved relations with many Arab countries gradually (with Israel remaining an ardent foe), the US government was pleasantly surprised to find the Islamic Republic enthusiastically supportive of efforts to destroy the Taliban in Afghanistan after 9/11, given their jihadi-oriented, anti-Shi'a stance. Indeed, Iran nearly intervened in Afghanistan in 1998, but decided to continue to back anti-Taliban militias instead. Simultaneously, Khatami's government maintained cordial ties with Russia, which built nuclear power facilities and expanded trade and investment ties.

Still, Iranian linkages to radical elements in the MENA persisted. Iranian weaponry caches found their way to Hamas, and global criticism followed after Israel intercepted one such shipment. Being categorized as part of America's "axis of evil" or as a rogue state did not help Iran's international standing, and resulted in another bout of chilliness. The major crisis that shook this relationship, however, and whose legacies resonate today, began in 2002, when evidence emerged that Iran's nuclear program was more advanced than previously known and included activities apparently aimed at building nuclear weapons. Britain, France, and Germany began talks with Iran over the matter, and the EU suspended negotiations with Iran over trade and investment. Early European efforts to reach a compromise with Iran over the matter halted with Ahmadinejad's 2005 election, as it marked the return of an overtly hardline stance. In August of that year, Iran rejected a major European proposal on the nuclear dispute. In April 2006, Iran announced it had mastered the enrichment process, and by 2009 it had produced enough low-enriched uranium to make a single nuclear weapon, if enriched further. Iran deployed dozens of medium-range missiles capable of hitting Israel and southeastern Europe in this period, though these missiles did not have nuclear warheads. In 2006, the UN Security Council voted to impose a package of harsh economic sanctions on Iran aimed at stopping its nuclear program. It would vote to intensify and extend those sanctions repeatedly in the next few years.

Iran's foreign policy became more aggressive in other ways as well. While leaning still on non-Western powers like China and Russia, Ahmadinejad and other Iranian officials regularly denounced the United States and its allies, and Ahmadinejad made a series of statements calling for the destruction of Israel and expressing doubt about the Holocaust. Iran continued to give financial assistance and weapons to Hizbullah and radical Palestinians. More ominously, beginning in early 2007, US officials charged that Iran had been supplying improvised explosive devices and other assistance to insurgents in Iraq, resulting in the deaths of hundreds of US soldiers. US forces arrested several Iranian operatives inside Iraq. Iran indeed was deeply involved in Iraq in this period, both supporting the Shi'a-dominated new government of the country – which was paradoxically also backed by the US – as well as various Shi'a militias. By the late 2000s, Saudi Arabia and the other Gulf kingdoms, as well as Jordan and Egypt, began to speak ominously of Iran's regional ambitions to dominate the Arab world. Exploiting ambiguous phrases such as a rising "Shi'a Crescent," Sunni Arab leaders recognized the fall of Saddam's regime had removed a major firewall to Iranian aspirations to expand influence through Syria, Hizbullah, Hamas, and other proxy actors.

While a number of Arab countries desired increasingly aggressive efforts to contain or even attack Tehran, the US under the Obama administration attempted a different tack. US-Iranian tensions eased somewhat in 2008 and

2009, with diplomats holding bilateral talks for the first time in almost 30 years. These did not succeed; and so in June 2010, the US imposed new unilateral economic sanctions aimed at stopping Iran's nuclear program, while in January 2012 the EU voted to end all oil imports from Iran. Together with the UN sanctions of 2006–10, these actions severely disrupted Iran's economy. In addition, the US and/or Israel apparently carried out a series of deadly covert operations against Iran in this period, assassinating several nuclear scientists, launching cyberattacks against Iran's nuclear-enrichment facilities, and possibly carrying out sabotage attacks against Iranian oil facilities. Iran retaliated with a series of unsuccessful terrorist attacks against Israelis, a plot to assassinate the Saudi ambassador to the US, and cyberattacks on Saudi oil facilities.

By 2013, the prospects for better relations between Iran and the West seemed very remote. However, in March 2013, Iranian and US officials held secret talks in Oman about Iran's nuclear program. After Rouhani was elected president in June, high-level contact between Iranian and US officials paved the way for multilateral talks, which in turn produced an interim agreement in November 2013 and a final agreement in July 2015. In the resulting JCPOA framework, the UN, EU, and US agreed to remove most sanctions in return for strict limits on Iran's nuclear program. Despite strong opposition from conservatives in both Iran and the US, this agreement moved forward – only to be upended by the Trump administration's exit in 2018, which also bolstered the position of Iranian hardliners who proclaimed that the US could not be trusted to keep its commitments. Indeed, conservative elements of the Iranian state had sought to sabotage the deal from the start; for instance, on October 11, 2015, just days before the JCPOA was to enter implementation, Iranian armed forces tested a mid-range ballistic missile, arguing that this was integral to Iranian defense policy.

The oscillation between ideology and pragmatism – between confrontation and moderation – would also contribute to the worsening cold war between Iran and Saudi Arabia, which had the itinerant effect of overlaying many of the conflicts occurring in the region with a sectarian optic. While Iran was not affected directly by the popular uprisings of the Arab Spring, the GCC states accused Tehran of backing and assisting opposition protests among the Shi'a communities of Saudi Arabia and Bahrain. Several GCC summits throughout 2011–12 openly accused Iran of interfering in the domestic affairs of the kingdom. While Qatar, and to a lesser extent Oman and Kuwait, eventually backed off such bellicose rhetoric, Saudi beliefs that Iran had grander designs to dominate the region were confirmed in Syria. During the Syrian civil war, Iran and Hizbullah sent troops and arms to Asad's regime in its efforts to stabilize the regime from all threats, from secular opposition to ISIS militants. Whereas Hizbullah contributed ground units, Iran also delivered substantial financial and material support to the Syrian government. This, along with Russian military intervention and the wider global coalition against ISIS, helped ensure the survival of the Asad dictatorship. The Syrian conflict helped further Iranian-Russian ties; in November 2015, Russian President Vladimir Putin visited Iran for the first time in a decade and was received warmly by Ayatollah Khamenei.

In January 2016, Iranian protesters attacked the Saudi Embassy in Tehran in retaliation for the controversial execution of Sheikh Nimr, a Shi'a cleric in Saudi Arabia. This froze diplomatic relations between Iran and most of the GCC kingdoms, with ambassadors withdrawn and threats of open conflict invoked. The seizure of two small US naval boats by the naval units of the Revolutionary Guard Corps the same month further magnified geopolitical tensions. Though some analysts believed these actions reflected the natural outgrowth of the inevitable strategic rivalry between two large oil-rich countries with mutually incompatible political regimes in Saudi Arabia and Iran, others argued that sectarian strife was rearing its head; Iran was seeking to extend a Shi'a dominion over all the region, Saudi Arabia and its allies were seeking to defend Sunni Islam, and every national conflict was now a proxy battlefield. In various places, alarmists witnessed Iranian expansionism – Yemen, where modest Iranian support buttressed the Houthi rebel movement; in Lebanon, where Iran-supported Hizbullah was regularly participating in cabinet governments; in Syria, where the enduring Asad regime reminded the world of Iranian muscle; in Qatar, where the tiny gas-rich kingdoms defied the GCC consensus in maintaining relations with Tehran; and even in Israel, where Iran's nuclear capabilities would purportedly be utilized to attack first.

For its part, the Iranian government saw such arenas as flashpoints by which it could logically extend its geopolitical sphere of influence, much as Saudi Arabia or global powers might. Another interpretation is that hardline conservative voices indeed linked together disparate foreign policy entanglements in hopes of extending their revolutionary Shi'a crescent. Either way, blowback appeared in 2017 when rising terrorism from ISIS and other actors struck a number of Iranian targets, including the parliament building, a military parade, and various police and security installations. With 2019, it appeared that a new era of hostility and altercation had begun between Iran and its Arab and Western counterparts.

FUTURE PROSPECTS

Nearly four decades after the establishment of the Islamic Republic, the withdrawal of the JCPOA nuclear deal in 2018 marked the end of a hopeful period in Iranian politics and foreign policy. Many believed that opening would not only help reintegrate the country – long lampooned as a pariah state – back into the international system and global economy, but also consolidate the gains made by reformist voices within the restrictive boundaries of the domestic political system. Those advances had been made in a stuttering fashion since the 1990s, when more pluralistic interests began entering political discussions after the institutionalization of the revolution and implantation of Shi'a Islamism as the doctrine of the state. With the economy stagnant, the youth restless, and politics polarized, the prospects for drastic transformation are slim.

However, the country can also be arguably described as standing at a crossroads. The Supreme Leader, Ayatollah Khamenei, is aging, and his succession is uncertain, particularly behind the curtains of the opaque set of theocratic and juristic institutions installed to control state power. The potential for popular mobilization, driven by youths, is ever-present, with multiple triggers, from poor economic prospects to ineffective governance and corruption. On the domestic front, increased pressures from below may strengthen the hardline position and result in more repression of reformist media, activism, and political figures. However, it may also result in large-scale explosions of public expression, as in the 2009 Green Movement. Whether or not the regime could contain such an historic outpouring of societal frustration remains to be seen.

FURTHER READING

For sweeping surveys of Iranian history, see Abbas Amanat, *Iran: A Modern History* (Yale University Press, 2018); Homa Katouzian, *The Persians: Ancient, Mediaeval, and Modern Iran* (Yale University Press, 2009); Michael Axworthy, *A History of Iran: Empire of the Mind* (Penguin, 2010); and Ervand Abrahamian, *A History of Modern Iran*, 2nd ed. (Cambridge University Press, 2008). The twentieth century attracts particular attention in Ali Gheissari and Vali Nasr, *Democracy in Iran* (Oxford University Press, 2006); Fakhreddin Azimi, *The Quest for Democracy in Iran: A Century of Struggle against Authoritarian Rule* (Harvard University Press, 2008); and Ali Ansari's *Modern Iran since 1921: The Pahlavis and after* (Pearson, 2003) plus *Modern Iran: Reform and Revolution*, 2nd ed. (Routledge, 2007). A well-cited primer from one of the *doyen* of Iranian studies is Nikki Keddie, *Modern Iran: Roots and Results of Revolution* (Yale University Press, 2003).

Aspects of Iranian development, society, and politics prior to the revolution abound. On the 1906 Constitutional Revolution, see Janet Afary, *The Iranian Constitutional Revolution, 1906–1911* (Columbia University Press, 1996), and Vanessa Martin, *Iran between Islamic Nationalism and Secularism: The Constitutional Revolution of 1906* (IB Tauris, 2013). On the rise of the Pahlavi crown, see Sirus Ghani, *Iran and the Rise of Reza Shah* (IB Tauris, 1998); Stephanie Cronin, ed., *The Making of Modern Iran* (Routledge, 2003); and Touraj Atabaki and Erik Zürcher, *Men of Order: Authoritarian Modernization under Atatürk and Reza Shah* (IB Tauris, 2017). Events involving the 1950s are covered in: Richard Cottam, *Nationalism in Iran* (University of Pittsburgh Press, 1979); Mark Gasiorowski and Malcolm Byrne, eds., *Muhammad Mosaddeq and the 1953 Coup in Iran* (Syracuse University Press, 2004); and Stephen Kinzer, *All the Shah's Men: An American Coup and the Roots of Middle East Terror* (Wiley, 2008).

Other studies of pre-revolutionary Iran include Shahrough Akhavi, *Religion and Politics in Contemporary Iran* (State University of New York Press, 1980); Eric J. Hooglund, *Land and Revolution in Iran, 1960–1980* (University of Texas Press, 1982); and the comprehensive analysis by Ervand Abrahamian, *Iran Between Two Revolutions* (Princeton University Press, 1982). Nikki Keddie's eclectic collection, *Iran: Religion, Politics and Society: Collected Essays* (Routledge, 1980) is penetrating. Two excellent foreign policy studies of Iran during the Pahlavi years include Rouhollah K. Ramazani, *Iran's Foreign Policy, 1941–1973* (University Press of Virginia, 1975), and Roham Alvandi, *Nixon, Kissinger, and the Shah: The United States and Iran in the Cold War* (Oxford University Press, 2014). America's role in constructing Pahlavi dictatorship is examined in David R. Collier, *Democracy and the Nature of American Influence in Iran, 1941–1979* (Syracuse University Press, 2017), as well as Sean Yom, *From Resilience to Revolution:*

How Foreign Interventions Destabilize the Middle East (Columbia University Press, 2016). Finally, the last Shah has commanded something of a cottage industry; among the notable studies are Asadollah Alam, *The Shah and I* (IB Tauris, 1991); Mark Gasiorowski, *US Foreign Policy and the Shah* (Cornell University Press, 1991); and Abbas Milani, *The Shah* (Palgrave Macmillan, 2011).

The Iranian Revolution is one of the most well-studied modern political events in international affairs. Its most penetrating analyses include: Misagh Parsa, *Social Origins of the Iranian Revolution* (Rutgers University Press, 1989); Houchang E. Chehabi, *Iranian Politics and Religious Modernism* (Cornell University Press, 1990); Mansoor Moaddel, *Class, Politics, and Ideology in the Iranian Revolution* (Columbia University Press, 1993); and Charles Kurzman, *The Unthinkable Revolution in Iran* (Harvard University Press, 2004). Studies of the Shi'a Islamist ideology that underlay Ayatollah Khomeini's movement include: Roy Mottahadeh, *The Mantle of the Prophet: Religion and Politics in Iran* (Pantheon, 1986); Hamid Dabashi, *Theology of Discontent* (New York University Press, 1993); Mehrzad Boroujerdi, *Iranian Intellectuals and the West* (Syracuse University Press, 1996); Baqer Moin, *Khomeini: Life of the Ayatollah* (St. Martin's Press, 1999); Vanessa Martin, *Creating an Islamic State* (IB Tauris, 2000); Hamid Algar, *Roots of the Islamic Revolution in Iran* (IPI, 2001); and Michael M. J. Fischer, *Iran: From Religious Dispute to Revolution* (University of Wisconsin Press, 2003).

Post-revolutionary Iran during the 1980s, including its economic and political turmoil, have elicited deep shelves of work. The most enlightening reads about this decade of consolidation are: Shaul Bakhash, *The Reign of the Ayatollahs* (Basic Books, 1984); Said Amir Arjomand, *The Turban for the Crown* (Oxford University Press, 1988); Ali

Farazmand, *The State, Bureaucracy, and Revolution in Modern Iran: Agrarian Reforms and Regime Politics* (Praeger, 1989); Samih K. Farsoun and Mehrdad Mashayekhi, *Iran: Political Culture in the Islamic Republic* (Routledge, 1992); Anoushiravan Ehteshami, *After Khomeini* (Routledge, 1995); and Bahman Baktiari, *Parliamentary Politics in Revolutionary Iran* (University Press of Florida, 1996). Meanwhile, the role of religion in post-revolutionary Iran is thorny, bounded as much by interpretative battles as institutional struggles, but overviews of piety and religious discourse include Ervand Abrahamian, *Khomeinism* (University of California Press, 1993); Abbas Amanat, *Apocalyptic Islam and Iranian Shi'ism* (IB Tauris, 2009); and Richard Foltz, *The Religions of Iran: From Prehistory to the Present* (OneWorld, 2013).

Contemporary peeks at Iranian politics that extend into present decades, particularly cyclical clashes between reformists and conservatives, include Maziar Bahrooz, *Rebels with a Cause* (IB Tauris, 1999); Wilfried Buchta, *Who Rules Iran?* (Washington Institute for Near East Policy, 2000); Daniel Brumberg, *Reinventing Khomeini* (University of Chicago Press, 2001); Mehdi Moslem, *Factional Politics in Post-Khomeini Iran* (Syracuse University Press, 2002); Eric Hooglund, ed., *Twenty Years of Islamic Revolution* (Syracuse University Press, 2002); and Michael Axworthy, *Revolutionary Iran: A History of the Islamic Republic* (Oxford University Press, 2013). The struggle for democracy and plight of opposition are explored in Paul Aarts and Francesco Cavatorta, eds., *Civil Society in Syria and Iran: Activism in Authoritarian Contexts* (Lynne Rienner, 2012); Daniel Brumberg and Farideh Farhi, *Power and Change in Iran: Politics of Contention and Conciliation* (Indiana University Press, 2016); Misagh Parsa, *Democracy in Iran: Why It Failed and How It Might Succeed* (Harvard University Press, 2018); and

Ali Ansari, *Iran, Islam, and Democracy: The Politics of Managing Change*, 3rd ed. (Gingko, 2019). A useful overall guide is Mehrzad Boroujerdi and Kourosh Rahimkhani, *Postrevolutionary Iran: A Political Handbook* (Syracuse University Press, 2018).

Social issues, from gender to culture, are explored in: Samih K. Farsoun and Mehrdad Mashayekhi, *Iran: Political Culture in the Islamic Republic* (Routledge, 1992); Haleh Afshar, *Islam and Feminisms: An Iranian Case-Study* (St. Martin's Press, 1998); Fariba Adelkhah, *Being Modern in Iran* (Columbia University Press, 2000); Eliz Sanasarian, *Religious Minorities in Iran* (Cambridge University Press, 2000); Abbas Milani and Larry Diamond, eds., *Politics and Culture in Contemporary Iran: Challenging the Status Quo* (Lynne Rienner, 2015); and Rasmus Christian Elling, *Minorities in Iran: Nationalism and Ethnicity After Khomeini* (Palgrave Macmillan, 2016).

Studies of Iranian economic development in recent decades were spotty until better data allowed for rigorous evaluations. The best works on the economy of the Islamic Republic are Jahangir Amuzegar, *The Islamic Republic of Iran: Reflections on an Emerging Economy* (Routledge, 2014); Suzanne Maloney, *Iran's Political Economy since the Revolution* (NY: Cambridge University Press, 2015); and Farhad Gohardani and Zahra Tizro, *The Political Economy of Iran: Development, Revolution and Political Violence* (Palgrave Macmillan, 2019).

Analyses of post-revolutionary Iranian foreign policy, including entanglements with the US, include Shireen T. Hunter, *Iran's Foreign Policy in the Post-Soviet Era: Resisting the New International Order* (Praeger, 2010); David Crist, *The Twilight War: The Secret History of America's Thirty-Year Conflict with Iran* (Penguin, 2013); Alex Edwards, *Dual Containment Policy in the Persian Gulf: The USA, Iran, and Iraq, 1991–2000* (Palgrave

Macmillan, 2014); Robert Mason, *Foreign Policy in Iran and Saudi Arabia: Economics and Diplomacy in the Middle East* (IB Tauris, 2014); Pierre Razoux, *The Iran-Iraq War* (Belknap, 2015); and Sam Razavi and Thomas Juneau, *Iranian Foreign Policy since 2001* (Routledge, 2017).

On Iran's security forces and military strategy, see Steven R. Ward, *Immortal: A Military History of Iran and Its Armed Forces* (Georgetown University Press, 2009); Sepehr Zabir, *The Iranian Military in Revolution and War* (Routledge,

2011); Saeid Golkar, *Captive Society: The Basij Militia and Social Control in Iran* (Columbia University Press, 2015); Hesam Forozan, *The Military in Post-Revolutionary Iran: The Evolution and Roles of the Revolutionary Guards* (Routledge, 2015); Afshon Ostovar, *Vanguard of the Imam: Religion, Politics, and Iran's Revolutionary Guards* (Oxford University Press, 2016); and Bayram Sinkaya, *The Revolutionary Guards in Iranian Politics: Elites and Shifting Relations* (Routledge, 2017).

Online sources

Iran can strike observers as a surprisingly open country amenable to online research, despite its reputation for censorship. Useful websites that deliver news, analyses, and briefings include: Pars Times (www.parstimes.com), Payvand (http://payvand.com/), Iran Review (www.iranreview.org/), Iran Wire (https://iranwire.com/en), and the RadioFreeEurope/RadioLiberty Iran portal (www.rferl.org/Iran). Gooya also has a wealth of multimedia resources and news listings in Farsi and English (https://gooya.com/). Iran Human Rights Monitor tracks abuses of dissidents and oppositionists (https://iran-hrm.com/).

For economic data, the World Bank's Iranian Economic Monitor has plentiful reports and statistics (www.worldbank.org/en/country/iran/publication/iran-economic-monitor). Several think tanks maintain rich country pages on Iranian events

and foreign policy, including the RAND Corporation (www.rand.org/topics/iran.html), Chatham House (www.chathamhouse.org/research/regions/middle-east-and-north-africa/iran), and CSIS (www.csis.org/programs/burke-chair-strategy/iran). Several major university-based programs also dive into Iranian history and affairs; among them are Stanford's Program in Iranian Studies (https://iranian-studies.stanford.edu/) and Manchester's Nashriyah, a digital archive of Iranian historical periodicals, photographs, and documents (www.library.manchester.ac.uk/search-resources/manchester-digital-collections/digitisation-services/projects/nashriyah-digital-iranian-history/).

Please note that URLs may change far more quickly than books can be printed; so if these exact URLs do not work, simply search Google or another engine by the titles of these websites and online resources.

Gulf states
Kuwait, Bahrain, Qatar, United Arab Emirates, and Oman

Jill Crystal

INTRODUCTION

The five small kingdoms residing along the littoral shores of the Arabian (or Persian) Gulf – Kuwait, Bahrain, Qatar, United Arab Emirates, and Oman – have largely similar histories, cultures, and political systems. Alongside Saudi Arabia, they constitute the sub-region of the Khalij. Once British protectorates, they are today dynastic monarchies with fairly modest degrees of participatory politics, though with significant variation, ranging from Kuwait's liberalized parliamentarism to the more closed system of autocracy found in the UAE and Oman. Although shaken by the Arab Spring, they survived mostly unscathed (with the partial exception of Bahrain). All five states are dependent on oil and gas revenues; these are rentier states.

The Gulf states have often worked alongside one another, and are members (along with Saudi Arabia) of the Gulf Cooperation Council (GCC). Unity, however, has frayed since 2017 when Saudi Arabia, backed by the UAE and Bahrain, instituted a blockade against Qatar due to its increasingly independent foreign policy regarding Iran, the Muslim Brotherhood, and regional conflicts. While these rentier monarchies seek new strategies to retain power at home in an environment of increasing restiveness and sectarianism, their geopolitical outlook in navigating a Gulf region dominated by the much larger powers in Saudi Arabia and Iran, as well as American hegemony, has become increasingly uncertain.

Boxes 17.1–17.5 provide vital data on these five countries.

BOX 17.1   VITAL DATA – STATE OF KUWAIT

Capital	Kuwait City
Regime type	Authoritarian (monarchy)
Head of state	Emir Sabah al-Ahmad al-Jabir al-Sabah (since 2006)
Head of government	Prime Minister Jabir al-Mubarak al-Sabah (since 2011)
Legislative institution	Unicameral assembly, with 50 elected seats (*Majlis al-Umma*, or National Assembly)
Female quota	No
Percentage of seats held by women	3.1%
Major political parties or coalitions (share of seats in most recent general elections, 2016)	None: parties are prohibited
Population	4,136,528
Major ethnic groups	Arab (57.8%, of which one-half is Kuwaiti), Asian (40.3%), other (1.9%)
Major religious groups	Muslim (74.6%, of which one-third are Shi'a and two-thirds Sunni), Christian (18.2%), other (7.2%)
GDP per capita	$30,839 ($67,000 at Purchasing Power Parity)
Unemployment rate	2.1%
Youth unemployment rate	13.9%
Major economic industries	Petroleum, petrochemicals, cement, shipping, food processing, construction
Military spending as % GDP	5.8%

HISTORICAL BACKGROUND

Archaeological discoveries have revealed much about eastern Arabia's ancient past. Remains of the early Gulf trading culture of Dilmun, dating back to the fourth millennium BC, were discovered in 1953 outside Manama, Bahrain. Dilmun extended from Kuwait to Qatar, with a related culture dominating what are now the UAE and Oman. The fabled kingdom of Magan (or Makan), located in Oman, was a somewhat later culture whose wealth derived from control of copper sources. In about 4,000 BC, oasis date cultivation began

BOX 17.2   VITAL DATA – KINGDOM OF BAHRAIN

Capital	Manama
Regime type	Authoritarian (monarchy)
Head of state	King Hamad bin 'Isa al-Khalifah (since 1999)
Head of government	Prime Minister Khalifah bin Salman al-Khalifah (since 1971)
Legislative institution	Bicameral parliament, with elected 40-seat lower house (*Majlis al-Nuwaab,* or Council of Representatives)
Female quota	No
Percentage of seats held by women	15%
Major political parties or coalitions (share of seats in most recent general elections, 2018)	Parties are prohibited, but informal societies or blocs compete: Al-Asalah Islamic Society (7.5%), Progressive Forum (5%), National Unity Gathering (2.5%)
Population	1,492,584
Major ethnic groups	Arab (50.7%, of which 91% is Bahraini), Asian (45.5%), Other (3.8%)
Major religious groups	Shi'a Muslim (51.6%), Sunni Muslim (22%), Christian (9.3%), Other (17.1%)
GDP per capita	$25,851 ($50,057 at Purchasing Power Parity)
Unemployment rate	1.5%
Youth unemployment rate	5%
Major economic industries	Petroleum, refining, aluminum, iron and steel, fertilizers, banking and finance
Military spending as % GDP	4.1%

providing a vital food source. Beginning in about 3,000 BC, increasing climatic desiccation greatly reduced the population in the interior of the Arabian Peninsula. By 1,500 BC, the domesticated camel became indispensable to tribal nomadism among the Bedouin confederations and groups living in the desert interior.

By contrast, peoples living in coastal zones along the Arabian Gulf turned to the sea for their livelihood. Fishing, pearling, and maritime trade reached their apogee in the eighth and ninth centuries AD, and Arab seafarers in sailing ships created maritime trade networks reaching from East Africa to

BOX 17.3 VITAL DATA – STATE OF QATAR

Capital	Doha
Regime type	Authoritarian (monarchy)
Head of state	Emir Tamim bin Hamad al-Thani (since 2013)
Head of government	Prime Minister Abdullah bin Nasser al-Thani (since 2013)
Legislative institution	Unicameral assembly, with 45 seats of which 30 are to be elected at a future date (*Majlis al-Shura*, or Consultative Assembly)
Female quota	No
Percentage of seats held by women	8.9%
Major political parties or coalitions (share of seats in most recent general elections)	None: no elections, and parties are prohibited
Population	2,639,211
Major ethnic groups	Arab (28.7%, of which 45.9% is Qatari), Asian (60.5%), Other (10.8%)
Major religious groups	Muslim (67.7%), Christian (13.8%), Hindu (13.8%), Other (4.7%)
GDP per capita	$70,780 ($130,475 at Purchasing Power Parity)
Unemployment rate	0.1%
Youth unemployment rate	0.6%
Major economic industries	Natural gas, petroleum, ammonia, fertilizer, petrochemicals, banking and finance
Military spending as % GDP	2.5%

the coast of China. Arab maritime trade was superseded by Spanish and Portuguese shipping in the fifteenth and sixteenth centuries, but its transcontinental expansion helped to spread Islam to a truly global community. In the early seventeenth century, the Portuguese yielded maritime primacy to the Dutch and English, whose commercial ambitions were reflected in the English and Dutch East India Companies. The Dutch initially gained the upper hand over Britain, but by 1765 the British had become the dominant external regional power in the Arabian Gulf. To protect their commercial

BOX 17.4 VITAL DATA – UNITED ARAB EMIRATES

Capital	Abu Dhabi
Regime type	Authoritarian (federal monarchy)
Head of state	President Khalifah bin Zayed Al-Nahyan (since 2004) [also Emir of Abu Dhabi]
Head of government	Prime Minister/Vice President Muhammad bin Rashid al-Maktum (since 2006) [also Emir of Dubai]
Legislative institution	Unicameral assembly, with 40 seats of which 20 are indirectly elected (*Majlis al-Watani al-Ittihadi*, or Federal National Council)
Female quota	No
Percentage of seats held by women	17.5%
Major political parties or coalitions (share of seats in most recent elections)	None: no direct elections, and parties are prohibited
Population	9,400,145
Major ethnic groups	Arab (29%, of which 40% is Emirati), Asian (65%), Other (6%)
Major religious groups	Muslim (76%), Christian (9%), Other (15%)
GDP per capita	$41,711 ($69,382 at Purchasing Power Parity)
Unemployment rate	2.6%
Youth unemployment rate	7.8%
Major economic industries	Petroleum, petrochemicals, food processing, cement, aluminum, shipping, real estate, banking and finance
Military spending as % GDP	5.6%

interests, the British, like the Portuguese and Dutch, adopted a policy of indirect rule with minimal interference in local affairs. By the end of the eighteenth century, Napoleonic France had imperial designs on the Middle East. In response, Britain entered into a treaty with Oman in 1788, designed to deny France the Gulf and to protect Britain's lines of communication with its increasingly important Indian possessions.

Another threat presented itself in the form of piracy. Sailing from the shaykhdoms of Sharjah and Ras al-Khaymah, Arab privateers would strike

BOX 17.5 VITAL DATA – SULTANATE OF OMAN

Capital	Muscat
Regime type	Authoritarian (monarchy)
Head of state	Sultan Qabus bin Sa'id al-Sa'id (since 1970)
Head of government	Sultan Qabus bin Sa'id al-Sa'id (since 1972)
Legislative institution	Bicameral parliament, with elected 84-seat lower house (*Majlis al-Shura*, or Consultative Assembly)
Female quota	No
Percentage of seats held by women	1.2%
Major political parties or coalitions (share of seats in most recent general elections, 2015)	None: parties are prohibited
Population	4,636,262
Major ethnic groups	Arab (58%, of which 95% is Omani), Asian (40%), Other (2%)
Major religious groups	Muslim (85.9%), Christian (6.5%), Hindu (5.5%), Other (2.1%)
GDP per capita	$19,302 ($46,584 at Purchasing Power Parity)
Unemployment rate	3.1%
Youth unemployment rate	13.7%
Major economic industries	Petroleum, natural gas, construction, cement, copper, steel, chemicals
Military spending as % GDP	12.1%

at shipping, thereby threatening British trade routes to India. After heavy fighting, Anglo-Indian naval forces defeated the Arab privateer fleet based in Ras al-Khaymah in 1819 and signed a treaty with the local *shaykhs* (chieftains) that became the cornerstone of Britain's presence in the Gulf for the next 150 years.[1] This also cemented the importance of the Arabian Gulf: rather than possessing inherent importance, the Gulf was vital to servicing the real crown jewel of the British global dominion, British India. Although Arab privateering ended, tribal warfare continued to threaten stability. In 1835, Britain signed a second treaty prohibiting tribes under the rulers' jurisdiction from raids during the fishing and pearling seasons. In 1838 the ban was extended throughout the year, and in 1853 it was made permanent in the Treaty of Maritime Peace in Perpetuity.

These treaties formed the basis for British colonial rule in the Gulf. Subsequently, treaties of 1861 and 1880 committed Britain to protecting the Khalifah rulers of Bahrain, and by the early twentieth century, a British political agent (i.e., a diplomatic officer responsible for the area) resided in that shaykhdom. In 1892 Britain concluded "exclusive agreements" with the Trucial States (territories that would become the United Arab Emirates), assuming responsibility for their defense and foreign affairs. In 1899 a similar relationship, though not then made public, was established with Kuwait, and in 1916 another followed with Qatar. Oman remained outside this treaty system, but Britain retained a close relationship with the Bu Sa'id sultans of Muscat, who in the nineteenth century had lost effective control over Oman's interior.

In addition to taking direct control of these tribal principalities' external relations, Britain assumed some oversight over their domestic affairs. At the same time, much like its future blueprint of maintaining protectorates in the Mashriq, the British tendency in the Khalij was not so much direct rule and domination, but indirect influence. In the era before oil, the Gulf area was never seen as a viable site of colonial settlement, or even a territorial zone worthy of long-term military investment. Its importance lay simply in denying other global powers, from the Ottoman Empire to Russia and Germany, access to its maritime shipping and communication routes that ran through to British India. Thus, British diplomatic control was minimal in principalities that rarely intersected with British interests, such as Kuwait. In others, advice was freely proffered. Most rulers followed the advice; those who refused risked exile, ouster, or British naval bombardment.

The British hence left a lasting impact on the Gulf. The ruling families they supported remain in power today, as do the borders they established. The mere act of recognizing the legitimate rule of these families – the Sabah of Kuwait, Khalifah of Bahrain, Thani of Qatar, Bu Sa'id of Muscat/Oman, and the smaller dynasties of the Trucial States – was monumental. By signing treaties with these shaykhs, the British halted what was, until then, the slow process of tribal conflict and contestation that created and destroyed new rulerships in an evolutionary dynamic facilitated by the lack of permanent state boundaries and the nomadism of Bedouin fighters. (Thus much like the French in Morocco, and the British also in Jordan, Western mediation gave rise to powerful monarchism in the Gulf.) Indeed, some states, such as Qatar, which Saudi Arabia would surely have swallowed, owe their existence to the British presence. Britain also introduced and developed administrative and legal practices, including Western-style legal codes alongside Islamic law (*shari'a*). It also launched modest economic and social-development schemes. Another consequence of the British imperium in the Gulf was the establishment of English as the area's de facto second language.

British strategic interests in protecting maritime routes in the Gulf ceased with the independence of India and Pakistan in 1947. Without its crown jewel in South Asia, British imperium had little need of maintaining hegemony over the area except for the lingering purpose of denying access in the Cold War to the Soviet Union, and thus protecting the valuable oil fields of eastern Arabia. Yet fiscal crises and domestic troubles forced Britain to pull back from most of its global holdings in a familiar pattern of post-World War Two colonial decline. By the 1960s, the Gulf was all that remained of London's once-mighty space of control in the MENA. Britain granted full independence to Kuwait in 1961, and in 1968 it announced its intention to withdraw completely from the Gulf. In 1971 Britain terminated its defense treaty relationships with Bahrain, Qatar, and the Trucial States. Bahrain and Qatar became independent states, but the Trucial States eventually federated to form the United Arab Emirates. This territorial layout of the Gulf would stay unchanged in future decades (Map 17.1).

The 1970s brought both fears and fortunes. The fortunes came in the form of the rapid rise in oil revenues due to the Arab oil embargo in the wake of the 1967 and 1973 Arab-Israeli Wars. While the 1950s had created modest streams of income due to the energy needs of rebuilding Europe and Japan, the sheer volume of oil rents flooding state treasuries a decade later overwhelmed the administrations of most of these principalities, forcing them by the 1970s to quickly develop the bureaucratic institutions and mechanisms of governance required to provide social services, regulate economic policy, and centralize political order beyond the highly personalistic model of tribal dynasticism that had previously operated. Economic growth was rapid, with the Gulf kingdoms exhibiting incredible rates of expansion even by MENA standards; in the 1970s, for instance, the UAE's GDP grew by an annualized average rate of 12.6 percent, while Bahrain's grew at 11.4 percent and Oman's at 13.9 percent. While this decade would result in each of these rentier monarchies resorting to their own unique tactics to preserve power, ward off dissent, and deal with the demands of urbanizing societies, in terms of foreign relations the Gulf kingdoms generally shied away from aggression and militarism, believing that moderation and neutrality best ensured their future prosperity.

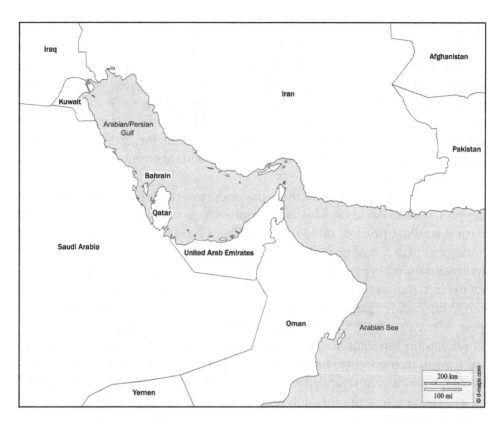

MAP 17.1
Gulf States: Kuwait, Bahrain, Qatar, United Arab Emirates and Oman. Major
water bodies and cities shown.

Source: D-Maps.

Affluence and state-building, however, were met by fear, which arose
as a result of the 1979 revolution in Shi'a Iran followed by the Iran-Iraq
War (1980–88). The revolution created, in due time, an Islamic Republic whose ideological intention of exporting its revolutionary creed and
sponsoring Shi'a-inspired uprisings threatened the domestic security of
all the Gulf states, but particularly Bahrain, where a Sunni minority rules
a Shi'a majority, and Kuwait and Saudi Arabia, with their sizable Shi'a
minorities. One response in 1981 came when Saudi Arabia and the five
littoral kingdoms founded the Gulf Cooperation Council (GCC). Discussions about creating such an organization to enhance regional security
had occurred since the British departure, but were never realized, largely
because of pressures from Iran (under the Pahlavi monarchy) and Iraq

(under its Ba'th regime) to be included. The Iran-Iraq War provided both a new incentive to create this security alliance, and the opportunity to exclude both warring states in a small but new effort to institutionalize the cultural, economic, and geographic ties of the Khalij. More pragmatically, all the Gulf states save Saudi Arabia were tiny in size, with small populations and even smaller militaries; survival in the face of foreign threats and internal unrest required band-wagoning with their larger Saudi neighbor, and pooling their collective resources to formulate common stances, policies, and strategies.

During the Iran-Iraq War, thus, the leaders of the GCC states threw their support behind Saddam Hussein, despite the economic crisis that ensued with the falling price of oil. Much like Saudi Arabia, the 1980s represented a major slowdown of growth as well as fiscal emergencies, as lower levels of hydrocarbon rents plus increased spending on security pushed many governments into dangerous territory. Kuwait, for example, saw its GDP shrink in the 1980s, while Qatar's crawled along at an average rate of 1.8 percent per year. War came in 1987, when Iran initiated attacks on Kuwaiti oil tankers in retaliation for Iraqi assaults on Iran's tankers and loading facilities. This led Kuwait to request US naval escorts and the reflagging of some of its tankers. This was a dramatic departure from Kuwait's and its neighbors' policy of maintaining security through non-military means, backed by an over-the-horizon US military presence. This was also a factor leading to Iraq's invasion of Kuwait in August 1990. The Kuwaiti royal family escaped into exile, but the Kuwaitis suffered through a brutal Iraqi occupation until February 1991, when the allied coalition of military forces led by the US drove Iraq out of Kuwait in Operation Desert Storm, drawing the Gulf states closer to the West in security cooperation. By the mid-1990s, GCC states had contracted for $36 billion in arms purchases from the US, a third of all American weaponry sales worldwide.

The Gulf War also had domestic reverberations, accelerating a nascent political-liberalization process across the Gulf. Following the war, these states created or expanded elected or partially-elected bodies that took various forms – assemblies, councils, forums – but which all were supposed to embody the greater participation of popular citizenries into decision-making. In Kuwait, where parliament had significantly greater power, the emir agreed to reopen the parliament he had suspended in 1986, holding elections in 1992. In Qatar, Crown Prince Hamad overthrew his father, Khalifah Thani, in a bloodless coup in 1995, and in the following years wrote a new constitution and held limited elections. In Bahrain, a government crack-down on Shi'a in the mid-1990s ended with another generational leadership change, as Hamad bin Isa Khalifah became emir after his father's death in 1999. He took modest and halting steps to liberalize Bahrain's political system, reinstating an assembly dissolved since 1975. In Oman, Sultan Qabus presided over a gradual liberalization, creating a new Consultative Assembly. In practice, these were not so much legislatures as political symbols; only in Kuwait did parliament historically wield substantive powers. Still, these domestic recalibrations suggested familiar problems: with oil prices low and citizenries restive, political adaptation was necessary.

The Al-Qa'ida attacks of September 11, 2001, in America deepened the US military presence in the Gulf, leading to two wars, first in Afghanistan and then in Iraq from 2003 to 2011. The Iraq War exacerbated growing tension between the GCC leaders and Iran, and the destruction of Saddam's dictatorship removed a major Sunni Arab regime from the region's geo-political chessboard. Now, some Gulf rulers feared, Iran could extend its "Shi'a Crescent" across the waterway and deep into the Mashriq and Arabian Peninsula, while also inciting unrest among the Shi'a living under these Sunni monarchies. The climate of hyperbolic sectarianism and the new cold war against Iran went hand-in-hand with domestic political retrenchment in these authoritarian monarchies. The regional political liberalization of the 1990s stalled, as royal autocrats instead insisted upon the maintenance of order in the face of new threats. For instance, in Bahrain, increasingly strident grievances led the main opposition, al-Wifaq, to boycott the 2002 elections. In Kuwait, confrontations between the government and its parliamentary opposition resulted in frequent gridlock. Qatar and the UAE gave little space for even literary and academic criticism of their ruling families, and the notion of direct elections where legal parties could mobilize voters and win seats in legislative bodies with meaningful power remained pure fantasy. Only in Oman did political liberalization continue to expand, albeit slowly and under a Sultan who still acted as supreme executive and legislative head.

The 2011–12 Arab Spring presented the next earthquake shaking these regimes. Overall, the Gulf monarchies proved more resilient than the region's single-party regimes, due to several factors: greater rentier wealth and their ability to spend it in politically-targeted ways, such as creating jobs and services for aggrieved citizens; well-established succession mechanisms, which helped erase doubt about who and why power would be transferred; and their unflagging support by the West and especially the US. By this time, the US was maintaining a vast armada of forces stationed in major installations – an army base in Kuwait, a naval fleet stationed at Bahrain, an air force command in Qatar, and port facilities in the UAE – and so had little appetite for revolution on the frontlines of containing Iran. Bahrain was the notable exception, as a mass revolutionary outbreak there nearly deposed the Khalifah monarchy until three forces converged to restore authoritarianism – a military intervention by Saudi Arabia and the UAE, the decision to engage in mass repression by the monarchy, and the refusal of Western powers to involve themselves in such internal turmoil. Elsewhere the GCC states generally sided with international opinion, for instance desiring the destruction of the Islamic State of Iraq and Syria (ISIS), although differences emerged. For instance, whereas the Qatari leadership supported the brief ascent of the Muslim Brotherhood in Egyptian politics during 2012–13, Bahrain and the UAE sided with Saudi Arabia in labeling the Brotherhood as a terrorist organization.

Today, the five dynasties ruling over Kuwait, Bahrain, Qatar, the UAE, and Oman are the same ones recognized by British imperialism centuries ago. Much has changed since then, above all their extreme ascension as prosperous rentier economies with tiny affluent citizenries that benefit from the gift of black gold (and in Qatar, natural gas). High living standards today contrast with the poverty and hardship that characterized the pre-oil era; the Gulf kingdoms feature the lowest infant mortality rates, highest life expectancy rates, and also among the highest adult literacy rates in the MENA. Prior to World War Two, starvation and death haunted many communities on the Gulf, whereas today the quality of life for national citizens has catapulted these five states to a position among the world's top-third (and the MENA's highest achievers) in terms of the Human Development Index. Other changes are less propitious. Internal rivalries have also worsened, with the Saudi-Qatari split resulting in an economic blockade of the latter in summer 2017 in an ongoing rift that has paralyzed the GCC. The massive presence of foreign workers and non-nationals in most of the kingdoms also creates unique political and social problems.

However, other traits remain the same. These are highly urbanized countries, with the proportion of national populations living in urban areas ranging from Oman's 83.6 percent to Kuwait and Qatar's nearly 100 percent. Their youths are highly adept at social media, mobile technologies, and online innovation; virtually everyone in these states now uses the Internet – a far cry from just two decades ago. They lean heavily upon the West in securing outside protection and military guarantees against regional threats, which for most kingdoms today means Iran. Both Bahrain and Kuwait are classified by the US as major non-NATO allies, for instance, which allow them to secure assistance and arms unavailable to many other clients. They also tend to spend heavily upon their security and defense needs, while until recently refusing to entertain the complexities of domestic taxation in order to supplement their oil revenues.

At the same time, these remain authoritarian monarchies. Political parties are prohibited in all Gulf states. National politics remain deeply reflective of the personalities and peculiarities of each ruling family, and its titular head. These regimes generally do not hesitate to levy repression when domestic opposition seems to imperil the status quo. They have also innovated their methods of coercion over time to adapt to new circumstances. For instance, most Gulf kingdoms upgraded their anti-terror laws after the Arab Spring to criminalize a wider range of speech, including social media, while also introducing a new form of punishment to permanently defang citizens – revocation of nationality, rendering their targets stateless.

As the following case studies show, the five Gulf kingdoms compare and contrast along all these axes of variation, while dealing with unique challenges for the future.

STATE OF KUWAIT

Kuwait's over four million residents live in a city-state bordering Iraq and Saudi Arabia, with a history shaped by the desert and sea (Map 17.2). It was settled in the late seventeenth and early eighteenth centuries when tribes from the central Arabian Unayzah confederation migrated toward the coast. The Bani 'Utub, as they came to call themselves, settled first in Bahrain and then Kuwait. Kuwait's climate could sustain little agriculture, so the settlers turned to the sea, developing an economy based on pearling, fishing, and long-distance trade. The tribal structures from their desert past remained largely intact, and Kuwait's ruling elite mainly consisted of descendants of the original Sunni settlers from the Arabian Desert. According to Kuwait's founding myth, these leading families chose one family from among them to rule, the Sabah. With time, other groups settled in Kuwait, forming a social hierarchy atop which remained the now urban descendants of these original Sunni families. As the economy shifted from the desert to the sea, the Bani 'Utub became a merchant elite. When oil was discovered and oil revenues overwhelmed other sources of income, the original economic basis of their wealth vanished, but the entrenched hierarchies remained.

Social and economic environment

In the early twentieth century, Persian Shi'a communities migrated to Kuwait, joining Arab Shi'a originally from Bahrain, Iraq, or Saudi Arabia's Eastern Province. These Shi'a formed the next rung in Kuwait's social hierarchy and constitute about one-fourth of Kuwait's population. In the late twentieth century, Arab Bedouins from the surrounding areas settled on the outskirts of the capital. Those who received citizenship formed the next rung down and now constitute just under half of Kuwait's citizens. In parliamentary elections, their tribal candidates win many seats, primarily in the outer districts.

With the discovery of oil in commercial quantities in 1938, Kuwait's social structure again changed. As in other GCC states, oil revenues changed the political dynamics of Kuwait by freeing rulers of their financial dependence on the merchants. Oil wealth also brought an influx of expatriate workers who now constitute over half of Kuwait's population. Originally, many were Palestinians who attained high positions in both the public and private sectors. After the Gulf War, however, most Palestinians were expelled from Kuwait due to their perceived support for Iraq. Today, most expatriate workers come from South Asia and Southeast Asia, alongside an older community of non-Kuwaiti Arab workers; together, these non-nationals represent the majority of the population. As a group, expatriate workers form an underclass beneath the Kuwaitis. A hierarchical division of social prestige also exists within the expatriate community, with Western and Arab expatriates at the apex, and Asians at the bottom.

A separate group of stateless residents called *bidun* (from the Arabic *bidun jinsiyyah*, meaning "without nationality") constitutes another element of Kuwaiti society. The bidun comprise an umbrella category of stateless people, many long-term Kuwaiti residents. Many are from the Shammar and Anayzah tribes, which extend into Iraq (as well as Saudi Arabia and Syria).

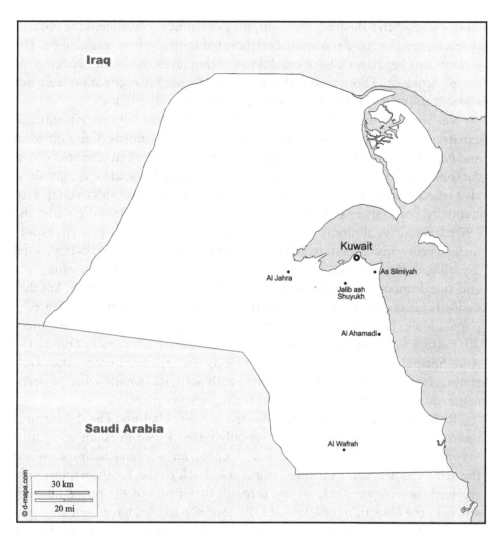

MAP 17.2
State of Kuwait. Major cities shown.

Source: D-Maps.

Some have lived in Kuwait for generations, but their ancestors never registered for citizenship when the Nationality Law was introduced in 1959.
Others came to Kuwait in the late twentieth century, with the ruler's encouragement, typically to join the police or military. In the decades before the
Iraqi invasion, some received nationality; the rest were slowly stripped of

many rights. After the Iraqi invasion, the government considered the bidun a suspect group because some had collaborated with the Iraqi authorities. The government began an all-out crackdown, firing *en masse* bidun working for the government. Those who had fled Kuwait during the occupation were not allowed to return; those still in Kuwait remain in bidun limbo.

The sharpest social divisions in Kuwait remain those between citizens and expatriates, Sunnis and Shi'a, and *hadar* (urbanized, mostly Sunni citizens) and *badu* (more recently settled Bedouin tribes). Other social identities cross-cut these divisions, but none are as salient politically. These affective divisions also reflect differences in wealth; class and communal identities overlap substantially. Shi'a citizens faced their most pronounced discrimination after the 1979 Iranian revolution but subsequently their situation improved. Nonetheless, problems remain. In 2016, for example, all nine Shi'a MPs boycotted a parliamentary session, protesting court rulings against 25 Kuwaiti Shi'a and one Iranian for membership in an Iran-linked terror group. Another divide is generational. Modern health care financed by oil wealth created a population explosion, and almost two-thirds of the population is now under 30, putting immense pressure on the government to create jobs. During the Arab Spring, this was an issue in Kuwait as well as in the other Arab Gulf states, given the central role played by youth activists in mobilizing protests, demanding democratic reforms, and highlighting corruption.

Rapid social change has also affected gender relations. The debate over the role of women in society has typically pitted Kuwait's Islamists against urbane women. For years this debate focused on women's suffrage. While the history of women's suffrage efforts goes back to the 1960s, women only received the vote in 2005, largely through the efforts of the prime minister and over the objections of Islamist MPs. (Sunni Islamists have been an established political force in Kuwait's parliamentary scene since the 1980s.) Once it became law, Islamists moved quickly to campaign for women's votes. In 2009 four women were elected to parliament, although in 2016 only one was. In the World Economic Forum's 2018 Global Gender Gap Report, Kuwait ranked second in the Arab world (after the UAE) on the status of women. Kuwait has a high level of female education and labor force participation; nearly 59 percent of Kuwaiti women enter the workforce, and female literacy is nearly 95 percent – almost equal to the overall adult rate.

Kuwait's economy is dominated by oil. The Kuwait Oil Company (KOC), originally jointly owned by British Petroleum and (the US-based) Gulf Oil Company. In 1938 it found oil in commercial quantities. After World War Two, the oil sector expanded dramatically. In 1970 the government nationalized the KOC, becoming the first Arab Gulf state to achieve total ownership of its oil industry. Most of Kuwait's oil comes from the Burgan oil field, the world's second largest. Burgan, however, has been in production for over 50 years, though some controversy exists over the actual level of remaining reserves. Today, as an archetypical rentier state, Kuwait taxes little and secures most of its official income from crude oil exports, which comprise almost all of its budgetary revenues. By most estimates, Kuwait possesses the world's sixth largest oil reserves, behind Venezuela, Saudi Arabia, Canada, Iran, and Iraq.

The government spent much of its new oil wealth on the public, first in direct handouts of cash and housing (and for the elite, inexpensive land). In time a large welfare state emerged, providing free education, health care, heavily subsidized utilities, and guaranteed state jobs (the constitution guarantees a right to work). Substantial oil revenues were also invested in the Reserve Fund for Future Generations beginning in 1976. By the early 1980s, Kuwait was earning more from its overseas investments than from oil exports. The oil glut of the mid-1980s placed some stress on the country, prompting it to pump oil beyond the quota mandated by the Organization of Petroleum Exporting Countries (OPEC). In this period, a political storm also arose over the collapse of the Suq al-Manakh, an unofficial stock market, whose bubble burst after many Kuwaitis, including ruling-family members, engaged in massive speculative stock purchases using postdated checks. When the market crashed in 1982, the government bailout was so politically charged that it was not finally resolved by Kuwait's National Assembly until 1998.

The 1990 Iraqi occupation was also a financial burden on the country. Financing the Desert Storm operation emptied Kuwait's Reserve Fund. Postwar rebuilding costs were high, although the pace of recovery was swift. These expenses, combined with controversy over the mismanagement of investment funds and lingering issues related to Suq al-Manakh provoked public calls for greater financial accountability. In 1993, Kuwait's National Assembly passed legislation enabling it to examine the financial records of all state-owned companies and investment organizations. For the decade's remainder, the government embarked on a major economic-liberalization initiative to encourage growth, cut government costs, and create jobs for younger Kuwaitis. The kingdom joined the World Trade Organization (WTO) in 1995. Many restrictions on foreign ownership were lifted in an effort to attract foreign direct investment. Major stakes in state-owned companies were privatized. In the energy sector, the government embarked on

Project Kuwait, an ambitious and controversial $8.5 billion plan to invite foreign oil companies to participate in the development of Kuwait's northern oil fields. The Kuwaiti business community, however, was ambivalent about this foreign participation. Much of the tension between the executive and the legislature leading up to the 2009 elections turned on the National Assembly's opposition to Project Kuwait.

When oil prices rose in 2005, the government budget jumped from a deficit to a $9 billion surplus. Much of this revenue was again spent on direct grants to citizens, infrastructure, and investment in the Reserve Fund (by law, 10 percent of Kuwait's revenues go into the fund). Virtually depleted by the 1991 Gulf War, by 2006 that account and its managing entity, the Kuwait Investment Authority (the country's sovereign wealth fund), had grown back to about $100 billion, generating $5 billion in income a year. Kuwait's economy remains dominated by the state-run energy sector. Kuwait benefited from the high oil prices of 2005 and has also suffered from the 2009 recession (it was the only Gulf state in which the government was forced to rescue a bank). When oil prices fell in 2016, after the government had made substantial financial commitments to quell discontent, the initial ruling bargain came into question. In 2016, following Assembly protests, the government backed down from a plan to remove gasoline subsidies. Still, in financial terms, the kingdom wound down the 2010s in solid financial footing, with the Kuwait Investment Authority holding well over $640 billion in assets as of 2018 – the fourth biggest in the world, and larger than any other Gulf country save the UAE.

Following the victory of conservative Islamists and pro-government parliamentarians in the 2016 general elections, opposition MPs began a coordinated pushback against newly announced privatization and austerity plans, which included removing subsidizes on utilities and fuel as a way to reduce financial pressures upon the government in an era of permanently depressed oil prices. Conversely, government officials and younger business elites desiring better international integration pushed new reform packages, such as the Kuwait 2035 Vision project, which like similar plans in the Gulf (such as Saudi Arabia's Vision 2030) proclaims to develop a huge private sector, wean the state from its oil addiction, incorporate high-tech innovation throughout the economy, and make the principality a financial hub for the world.

Opposition to this enormous economic upgrade proposal followed, not least because in the past, such expensive projects were often accompanied by massive corruption, poor commitment, and redistributions of investment from other politically sensitive projects. Another consequence of the pushback against austerity measures was to turn on expats, with some Kuwaiti elites accusing foreign workers of undermining economic growth; indeed, some MPs called for taxing their remittances sent back to home countries, and either curbing their numbers or further reducing their already minimal rights. Labor activists saw such attacks as ludicrous, not least because Kuwaiti citizens had become a minority in the country given the necessity of expatriate labor to staff every level of the economy that Kuwaitis with guaranteed government jobs would not operate – construction, retail, transportation, and other basic services. Moreover, advocates of change pointed out the kingdom's extreme vulnerability to disruptions in oil revenues. For instance, in April 2016 oil workers launched a three-day strike over pay, briefly cutting oil production nearly in half.

Political structures

Kuwait has been ruled since the eighteenth century by members of the Sabah family. Kuwait's modern history begins in 1899, when Mubarak the Great (who ruled 1896–1915) took power. Fearing pressure from the Ottomans, who exercised nominal suzerainty over the shaykhdom given its proximity to their Iraqi holdings, Mubarak entered into a protective relationship with Britain, establishing ties that would last beyond independence. Britain concerned itself primarily with foreign policy: first with regional security and later with oil. Internal affairs were left largely to Kuwaitis.

Oil revenues began to appear in significant quantities in the 1950s. Much of this was spent on infrastructure and the establishment of a welfare state. Oil also transformed Kuwait's political structure. Where once the ruler relied on business leaders for tax collection and political advice, rulers now began to rely increasingly on their ruling families, some of whose members joined the cabinet in its most important positions (known as the sovereign ministries). While bureaucrats held other positions, merchants as a group were marginalized politically. Moreover, dynastic monarchism, pioneered in Kuwait, was copied by the other GCC states in the following years. Dynasticism, here, means the practice of the royal head implanting fellow relatives – particularly brothers, uncles, and cousins – into offices of state power, such as the position of prime minister, senior roles heading other ministries, leadership of the armed forces, and the like, with the goal of both foreclosing internal opposition and securing more support from potentially jealous family members. Thus, in Kuwait, royal family members always occupy the most important offices relevant to decision-making, including the prime ministerial post, and until 2003, the crown prince was always also prime minister.

As elsewhere, the ruling family's deliberations are normally invisible, and take place through family councils and internal discussions that often obscure real jockeying for power. Occasionally, however, differences appear, as they did in 2006 following the death of Shaykh Jabir. Kuwait's ruling family continues to exercise predominant political power, and the Kuwaiti citizenry are generally supportive of the ruling family. Even during the Arab Spring, when the largest protests in its history erupted, no opposition groups called for its removal, although many called for a reduction in the emir's powers, an expansion of the assembly's powers, and some for an eventual constitutional monarchy.

Kuwait has the longest experience of the GCC states with public participation through elections. Prior to independence, its elite merchant families self-organized their own assemblies and councils, and in the late 1930s even temporarily forced the Sabah leadership to accept limits on absolutist powers. That tradition of mobilization continued through independence. The Kuwaiti constitution, adopted in 1962, is among the oldest in the region and in the Gulf. The country has had an elected unicameral National Assembly (Majlis al-Umma) since 1963, making Kuwait unique among GCC states in terms of its parliamentary history and conventions. The assembly's formal powers are limited when measured against the monarchy's authoritarian power. However, it does play an important and vocal role in shaping and challenging government policy. The assembly must approve all legislation. It can (and does) interpellate ministers (e.g., subject them to public questioning) and entertains votes of confidence for individual ministers. The assembly comprises 50 members elected for four-year terms. The country's 25 districts were gerrymandered in 1981 when the parliament was reconvened after a five-year suspension. These often oddly-shaped districts ranged in population from under 10,000 to under 3,000, making vote-buying feasible. Reformist MPs had long called for limiting the number of constituencies, and in 2006 a new election law reduced their number from 25 to 5, with each voter voting for up to four candidates.

Elections (except for the 1967 election) have been largely free and open. Cabinet ministers, one of whom must be elected, also vote. The Sabah emir has intervened unconstitutionally twice to suspend the assembly altogether, in 1976 and in 1986. In November 2011, demonstrators forced their way into the Assembly, demanding the prime minister's resignation; he resigned two weeks later. The emir then dissolved parliament and set elections for February 2012. In June 2012 Kuwait's constitutional court ruled the December 2011 suspension unconstitutional. The emir then unilaterally changed the electoral law, allowing voters in each district to vote for only one (not four) candidates. Widespread demonstrations over corruption and the emir's unilateral decision followed. The elections were boycotted by many Islamists, producing a pro-government assembly. In June 2013 the constitutional court dissolved the assembly on the basis of technicalities in the emir's elections decree. New elections held in July 2013 were also boycotted by some; the resulting assembly was pro-government and included more liberals. Elections in November 2016 gave Islamists 24 seats, and the Shi'a six.

Kuwait's small size precludes significant local government. Administratively, it is divided into six governorates. Elected local neighborhood cooperatives are an important element of Kuwait's political system and often the springboard to political careers. Kuwait's elected Municipal Council, which predates independence, has the power to approve building, construction, and road projects.

The legal system has been administered since 1996 by the Supreme Judicial Council, and is technically independent but in practice profoundly shaped by executive influence given the sweeping powers of the emir to appoint, dismiss, and oversee senior officials and judges. On personal-status matters, Kuwaitis are governed by Islamic jurisprudence (both Sunni and Shi'a); on most other civil and criminal matters, European codes (in particular, the French system) shape the conduct of trials, the nature of prosecution, and the content of law. That said, Kuwait has a mixed human rights record. As with the other GCC states, its primary weakness concerns maltreatment of foreign laborers. Shi'a Kuwaitis also experience some discrimination. The National Assembly has a Human Rights Committee.

Political dynamics

More so than other Gulf kingdoms, including Saudi Arabia, Kuwaiti political dynamics have been typified by a healthy degree of pluralism in which criticism of government performance and political issues has been understood as part of national political culture. Kuwaiti opposition has hence historically been vocal but non-revolutionary. The Arab Spring initially had less impact in Kuwait, in part because Kuwait's political system already allowed substantial room for dissent and in part because the government was quick to offer financial handouts to the population – $3,500 in cash grants and free basic foods for a year, in fact, thanks in part to plentiful financial reserves accumulated from the high price of oil. While Kuwaitis did not echo the call of revolutionaries elsewhere in the region for the overthrow of the regime, many did call for a reduction of the emir's powers. One exception was the bidun, who launched several protests and generally tended to demand the most radical changes given their highly marginalized status.

Suffrage is granted to most adult citizens (members of the police and military may not vote) aged 21 or older. Women gained the right to vote in 2005, after a sustained civil society campaign demanding greater gender equality. The constitution also bans ruling family members from running for office. Kuwaiti citizenship includes those who can trace their official ancestry in Kuwait back to 1921 – a contentious and arbitrary clause to many, because it meant that many local tribal communities that could not prove their historical residency through documentation were left without nationality during Kuwait's period of state formation after 1961; this contributed to the roughly 100,000 bidun living in Kuwait. At the same time, because the monarchy and its government could grant citizenship at will, many local Bedouin tribal communities perceived as supportive of the royal family were arbitrary naturalized in the 1960s.

The Kuwaiti parliament remains the forum that, for all its legislative weakness, allows public debates and political rivalries to play out in front of a national audience. In January 2006, the assembly played an unprecedented role in the succession crisis that followed the death of Shaykh Jabir. Unusually open discussion followed about the fitness of Crown Prince Shaykh Sa'ad Abdallah. As the ruling family continued to discuss the issue, the country grew impatient. In keeping with a constitutional provision, parliament voted unanimously to force Shaykh Sa'ad's abdication, prompting the royal family finally to name an appropriate successor, Shaykh Sabah al-Ahmad, prime minister since 2003 (when the posts of crown prince and prime minister were separated). The assembly's active involvement in a succession that might have played out as a bloodless palace coup in other GCC states emboldened it as an institution. Some MPs even called for the emir to appoint a prime minister from outside the ruling family. Emir Sabah, however, turned 90 in 2019, while the crown prince was born in 1937; succession remains uncertain, with talk often suggesting the power should transfer down to the next generation of Sabah princes.

Political parties are banned in Kuwait. However, party-like blocs (tribal, religious, and ideological) compete in elections and function openly in the assembly. Kuwait's Bedouins organize politically, often holding illegal tribal primaries. One important assembly bloc consists of generally pro-government and often tribal conservatives. Islamists include Salafis, the Muslim Brotherhood, and independent Islamists. The government had encouraged the growth of Islamism in the 1960s and 1970s to balance Arab nationalism. In

1976 and 1986, Islamists supported the government when it suspended the assembly. But by the 1981 assembly, the Islamists had clearly eclipsed the liberals, and as they found their own voice, the government turned increasingly to the tribal deputies for support. The Islamist base generally encompasses Kuwait's middle class, and also upwardly mobile urbanites shut out of money and power by the old economic elite. As elsewhere, their strength lies in their capacity to tap into an organized popular base, articulate a clear ideological agenda, and hence organize – to raise funds, take over associations, and form alliances (for example, at times with Shi'a Islamists).

Liberals, who have been losing ground steadily since the 2000s and desire democratic reforms, have their base in the old, urban, and Sunni *hadar* merchant families. Liberals began as Arab nationalists in the 1960s, but in the 1970s and 1980s, they reinvented themselves as a secular pro-democracy grouping. They now consist of many different voices; they include more tribal deputies who have markedly more pluralistic political views than their elders, and fewer merchant scions, who have generally turned back towards the regime. They have also garnered significant support from many of Kuwait's cosmopolitan youths, who often seek Western education, decry royal corruption, and desire more checks on the Sabah rulership.

Finally, with little interest in the predominantly Sunni Arab nationalism supported by the liberal Arab nationalists, the Shi'a aligned themselves with the ruling family in the 1960s and 1970s and were reliable supporters of government legislation. However, the Iranian revolution prompted the government to view Kuwaiti Shi'a as a potential threat, and the alliance weakened. Thousands of Shi'a were purged from government offices or subject to political scrutiny in the 1980s, when several terrorist attacks by Iranian-supported Shi'a Islamist networks struck the kingdom. More recently, however, the Kuwaiti Shi'a remain a staunchly pro-Sabah community and minority – far different than in most other Gulf kingdoms, where the Shi'a are both treated as a fifth column and often articulate the most political opposition against their royal autocracies.

Compared to other GCC states, Kuwait's civil society is vibrant. Kuwaitis feel free to criticize the government and the ruling family. Many civic associations exist, including trade unions, cooperative societies, professional groups, and a non-governmental human Kuwait Human Rights Society, granted a license in 2004. Broadcast media are largely state owned; however, print media are private and have, since independence, offered an opportunity for public debate and a lively forum for assembly candidates. Online news sites, social portals, and chat networks like WhatsApp proliferate. Today, social media plays an important role in political discourse. Kuwait also has an older institution that shapes political debate: the *diwaniyya*, a weekly meeting among men of the same extended family to discuss political and economic issues, and which is held as a culturally sacrosanct practice. At times – for example, during the 1986 suspension – these meetings became extremely politicized.

In recent years since the Arab Spring, and the wave of peaceful but ardent protests that followed, the Kuwaiti government has become more concerned with political dissent. Books, for example, are more often placed on the banned list (or in limbo). Hundreds are now banned a year, including books previously approved. Prevailing anti-terror and national security laws are deliberately ambiguous about what constitutes a threat to public safety or national interests. In 2014 the assembly passed a Unified Media Law which allowed the government to restrict a far greater degree of written and online speech, and created a body to oversee social media; in 2016, another round of laws regulated Internet publications, while a cybercrimes law effectively criminalized substantial electronic criticism of the government. Since then, hundreds of Kuwaiti journalists, writers, and activists have been arrested based upon Twitter posts and other online activities. Terrorism has also reared its head, both causing and justifying the government's increasing intolerance. In 2015 the country was shaken by a suicide attack on a Shi'a mosque which killed 27 people and injured over 200, for which ISIS took credit. The emir was quick to show his support for those attacked and his opposition to any efforts to incite sectarianism. Later, 15 people were convicted in connection with the attack.

One worrisome sign, which Kuwaitis fear may mean the reduction of their historical pluralism and royal climate of political tolerance, is the convergence of their regime with other GCC states in repressing dissent. Since the Arab Spring, police and security forces have clamped down on hundreds of citizens. In some cases, oppositionists have suffered relentless legal assault, as in the case of former MP Musallam al-Barrak, who has been repeatedly prosecuted and imprisoned for his tenacious criticism of the royal leadership. In other cases, repression takes creative form. For instance, the government began prosecuting citizens who criticized Kuwait's regional allies, whether Saudi Arabia's actions in Yemen, the Bahraini government's attack on dissidents, or in one case tweets deemed insulting to Dubai's crown prince. A former Kuwaiti MP, 'Abdul Hamid Dashti, was sentenced to prison in 2016 owing to his criticism of Saudi involvement in Yemen and Bahrain. In 2016, another former MP was fined and given a suspended sentence for insulting the

UAE. Most worryingly, courts also began levying a unique punishment that permanently undercut oppositionists – the revocation of Kuwaiti citizenship.

Once the Gulf's brightest beacon for pluralism and liberalization, Kuwait thus stands at a crossroads, its political system and monarchy caught between the historical traditions of toleration on the one hand and the pressures to preserve stability and order on the other.

KINGDOM OF BAHRAIN

Bahrain is a small archipelago located between Saudi Arabia and Qatar (Map 17.3). The largest island contains the capital, Manama. The second-largest island, Muharraq, is home to the state's second-largest city, also called Muharraq. The four main islands in the archipelago are joined by causeways. The population of Bahrain is the smallest of the GCC states, about 1.5 million; just under half are Bahraini Arabs, while the remainder are expatriates and foreign workers, primarily from Asia. Given the kingdom's tiny size and lack of arable land, almost the entirety of the population is considered urban.

The ruling family, the Khalifah, is a branch of the Bani 'Utub tribe that rules Kuwait. The Khalifah migrated from Kuwait to Zubarah, a settlement at the northwest tip of the Qatar Peninsula, and from there to Bahrain in 1782. They conquered the island and its Persian-backed rulers, and soon found themselves ruling over a mostly Shi'a population.

Social and economic environment

The Khalifah are Sunni; however, most Bahrainis are Shi'a. Between 70 to 75 percent of the population is Muslim, and of that number at least 70 percent are Shi'a. Every few decades, this communal imbalance caused major political challenges, and opposition uprisings in modern history are punctuated by Shi'a participation – from the leftist-inspired labor strikes and Arab Nationalist movement of the 1950s, to the political demands for liberalization in the mid-1970s after independence, to the post-Gulf War unrest of the 1990s, and finally to the massive unrest of the Arab Spring. In each of these periods, the Khalifah monarchy cracked down harshly.

More recently, the demographic question has caused new questions about Bahraini identity to be asked. Opposition leaders, including not just Shi'a elites but also Sunni liberals and critics, contend that the government has granted many Sunni Arabs (perhaps 50,000 or more) citizenship under a 2002 revision of Bahrain's citizenship law in order to shift the country's

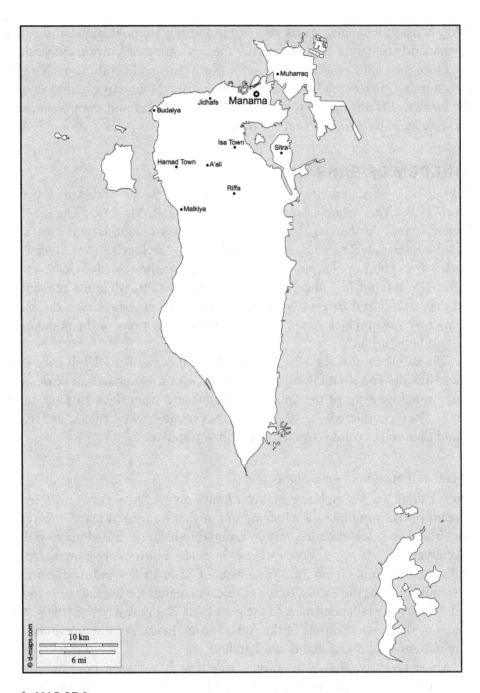

MAP 17.3
Kingdom of Bahrain. Major cities shown.

Source: D-Maps.

demographic balance. For their part, Sunni Bahrainis are divided between those of Arabian tribal origin and, somewhat lower in social status, the *hawwalah*, descendants of Arabs who migrated to Iran and later returned to Bahrain. The Shi'a are either *baharna*, indigenous to Bahrain, or *'ajam*, a smaller group of Persian origin and somewhat lower in social status. Bahrain's Shi'a, although mostly following the mainstream Twelver sect, look to many different clerical leaders, including those in Iran, Iraq, and Lebanon.

The Shi'a are, generally, poorer than the Sunni minority, and far less politically content. They have long faced discrimination in housing and education, while political discrimination has likewise left Shi'a largely out of positions of power. Fewer than 20 percent of senior government positions are held by Shi'a, and they are effectively barred from the security forces. The collective memory of Bahraini Shi'a remembers well episodes of past repression, when many were called Iranian agents and fifth columnists by paranoid Sunni elites. In the 1980s, for instance, the Shi'a experienced more exclusion than usual given the nervousness of the monarchy after the Iranian Revolution, as it feared its exporting of radicalism could mean their overthrow. Many Shi'a dissidents took refuge in Iran during this period. The Arab Spring was the most memorable and recent episode of uprising; at its peak, observers estimate almost one-fifth of the national citizenry at the time, or about 120,000 Bahrainis, openly protested in demanding political reform (and for some, an end to the Khalifah monarchy).

Before oil, Bahrain's economy was largely dependent on pearling – much like Kuwait's and Qatar's. Pearling and trading, given Bahrain's maritime position, gave rise to a modest but thriving class of merchant elites whose financial wealth made them logical partners for the Khalifah's political power. The relationship was not always smooth; in the late 1930s, for instance, much like Kuwait, Bahrain's merchant leaders demanded an elected assembly through which they could reduce the ruler's absolutist powers and participate in decision-making. Advised by the British and backed by British firepower, the regime refused. More than politics, though, what transformed this economic structure was the discovery of oil in commercial quantities in the 1930s. However, Bahrain's reserves were always modest, the lowest in the GCC. Bahrain was both the first Gulf state to develop an oil industry and the first to begin running out of oil. Production peaked at 76,000 barrels per day in 1970 and has been declining ever since. New recovery methods and the revenues shared with Saudi Arabia from a common offshore field ensured modest continuing revenues. Bahrain's large oil refinery has, since

1945, processed Saudi oil as well as its own; Saudi oil accounts for 80 percent of the throughput.

Despite its depleting reserves, oil production and refining still account for more than half of Bahrain's export and government revenues. In early 2018, Bahrain discovered significant oil reserves off its western coast, with the potential to significantly increase the country's production. While the kingdom's tiny population has made the slow decline of hydrocarbon rents less visible, Bahrain is still also the most vulnerable to diminishing returns. After its uprising was crushed in March 2011, for instance, the kingdom received billions of dollars in aid from its wealthier GCC neighbors to help replenish its treasury.

Bahrain's limited oil made it the first country to make serious efforts to diversify its economy, and in the late 1960s the state undertook several industrial projects. The largest was Aluminum Bahrain, which constitutes Bahrain's second major source of exports. Other projects included the major investments in shipbuilding, naval repair, and iron and steel production. Another diversification effort was the establishment of offshore banking units, designed originally to capture some of the financial business that had fled Beirut with the outbreak of Lebanon's civil war in 1975. Bahrain's tourism industry, weakened by the government response to the Arab Spring, was until 2011 a growing source of revenue, with Saudi visitors especially attracted by the ease with which they could travel to the island-kingdom.

Signifying its desire for greater economic globalization and integration with outside economic networks, Bahrain is a member of the WTO, having joined in 1995. In 2005 it signed a free-trade agreement with the United States and created a committee, headed by the chair of the Chamber of Commerce and Industry, to oversee its implementation and build public-private partnerships. The government has expanded Bahrain's financial sector to include over one hundred offshore banks and 28 Islamic banking institutions. The financial sector accounts for about one-quarter of Bahrain's gross domestic product (GDP). However, Bahrain faces strong competition in this sector from Dubai, leaving its economic future in an era of reduced hydrocarbon rents more uncertain than most other GCC kingdoms. Its sovereign wealth fund that invests surplus revenues and provides cash reserves in emergencies is the Mumtalakat Holding Company; it had the smallest of all GCC sovereign wealth portfolios, with just over ten billion dollars in assets as of 2018 (compared to, for instance, Kuwait's over $640 billion).

Political structures

Bahrain's ruling family, the House of Khalifah, has reigned since 1783. The country has four governates, each with an appointed governor, but in essence operates like a singular city-state given its tiny size and the supremacy of its incumbent monarchy. The ruling family has long been opposed by the majority of the Shi'a population. As a result, Bahrain's movements in the direction of political liberalization have been cautious. Bahrain's first attempt at political liberalization in the 1970s was short-lived. From 1961 to 1999, power was shared between Emir 'Isa bin Salman, and his brother and prime minister, Shaykh Khalifah bin Salman. (The latter had held the premiership since independence, and as of 2019 still holds the post, making him the longest-serving prime minister in the world.)

In an effort to create at least the image of popular participation somewhat like the Kuwaiti model, the monarchy upon independence in 1971 drew up a constitution promulgated in mid-1973. Then, he allowed elections in late 1973 for Bahrain's first National Assembly, a unicameral body. However, continuing protests against the government, led by labor organizations infused by Arab Nationalists, leftists, and Shi'a workers, prompted the ruler to issue the State Security Law in 1975, granting the government wide powers to detain and hold dissidents. The young assembly united in opposition to this law, which was never submitted for assembly approval. In August 1975 the government suspended the assembly and the constitution.

The early 1990s witnessed some efforts to introduce a degree of consultation as demands for political participation grew across the Gulf. In 1992, Bahrain's ruler announced plans for a new consultative assembly whose members would be drawn from business, professional, religious, and academic backgrounds. This initiative did little to assuage popular demands, however, and a 1994 petition calling for restoration of the National Assembly, signed by 20,000 Sunni and Shi'a professionals, prompted Emir 'Isa to increase the size and power of the consultative assembly. Shi'a protests over high unemployment and lack of political representation continued, however. Throughout the mid-1990s, large Shi'a demonstrations brought a harsh government response, including the arrest and detention of several hundred opposition activists. The violence ebbed and flowed until 1999.

In 1999 Emir 'Isa died and was succeeded by his son, Hamad. As new ruler, Hamad released political prisoners, welcomed back pro-democracy activists exiled in the 1990s, and promised a new era of reform. He called on Bahrain to vote on a new national charter that would reinstate an elected legislature, with real legislative authority. The bicameral National Assembly would consist of an elected lower house (Majlis al-Nuwaab) and an appointed upper house. He extended suffrage to women and promised to guarantee freedom of the press and religious belief. He won the tentative support of the Shi'a opposition by agreeing to amnesty four hundred political prisoners and repatriate over one hundred exiles. In February 2001, a popular referendum endorsed the new national charter. The State Security Law was abolished, and the state security police, which many blamed for past crackdowns, was replaced with a supposedly more accountable National Security Agency. However, the military, national guard, and police forces remained filled largely with Sunni expatriates from Jordan, Pakistan, Syria, and Yemen, a deliberative strategy to ensure no Shi'a representation in their ranks.

However, the underlying structure of royal autocracy never fundamentally shifted, likely for the same reason that Jordan's monarchy has always dithered when engaging the question of true democratization: democratic elections for parliamentary government would allow for demographic majorities to translate their numerical weight into political power. Much as the Palestinian majority in Jordan strikes fear in many non-Palestinians there about their fate in a democratic order, in Bahrain the notion of a political system where the majoritarian Shi'a could exercise political rights commensurate with their majority is a non-starter.

Hence, some signs of the limits to liberalization were visible early on. The old prime minister (the king's uncle), Shaykh Khalifah bin Salman Khalifah, retained his portfolio. Prime Minister Khalifah, a major powerholder since independence, was a key architect of the crackdown of the 1990s, and remained intractably opposed to empowering the Shi'a population. In 1999, the government issued a new Press and Publications Law that expanded the information ministry's censorship powers and mandated fines, publication closures, and even prison terms for journalists. It also issued blanket immunity for officials suspected of human rights violations. In place of the national charter, Emir Hamad promulgated a new amended constitution, which deprived the National Assembly of the right to introduce legislation directly, gave preponderant power to an unelected upper house, and ensured he had nearly limitless powers. In February 2002, Hamad changed the titular conventions of the monarchism, styling himself King Hamad.

People protested; nonetheless, elections went ahead. The first elections, held in May 2002, were for municipal councils. The opposition, with some reluctance, participated. A debate then emerged over the merits of participating in upcoming elections for the Chamber of Deputies in October 2002. In the end, four groups, headed by Bahrain's largest predominantly

Shiʻa opposition group, al-Wifaq National Islamic Society, boycotted, arguing that more constitutional reforms were needed and that gerrymandering had deprived them of any chance of winning a majority in the lower house. With slightly more than half the eligible voters participating, the outcome of the elections was a body dominated by Sunni Muslims, divided between Islamists and secularists but leaning toward the former. Six women ran, although none were elected. King Hamad then appointed a new parliament and cabinet, retaining his uncle as prime minister. Thus the lineaments of the new Bahraini political system were set – a weak parliamentary system where the Shiʻa could perhaps gain some symbolic voice but nothing more, ruled over by a powerful Sunni kingship.

Political parties are banned, but political societies, professional associations, women's groups, and other associations are permitted, allowing for a modicum of civil society. Before its 2016 suspension, al-Wifaq was the largest society with some 65,000 members, nearly all Shiʻa, but of many different political slants. Bahrain's Shiʻa ʻulama as elsewhere have long maintained independent institutions, and a degree of clerical autonomy unknown to Sunni clergy. However, in 2006 the government began implementing new legislation, paying salaries to some imams and prompting debate about the legitimacy and independence of state-salaried imams.

Bahrain's judiciary has two branches: civil law and shariʻa law. All courts under the 2002 constitution are overseen by the Higher Judicial Council, while an appointed constitutional court rules on constitutional issues. Like other GCC countries, however, the independence of the judiciary is suspect given that the appointment and tenure of judges is heavily determined by a single, unaccountable source – the monarchy. On a daily basis, Bahrain's civil law courts handle commercial, civil, criminal, and personal-status cases involving non-Muslims. Shariʻa courts have jurisdiction over personal-status matters for all Muslims (Bahraini and expatriate), with separate Sunni and Shiʻa courts. Women's groups have frequently criticized shariʻa court rulings. The Supreme Court, established in 1989, serves as the final court of appeal for the civil law courts and for personal-status case appeals for non-Muslims. However, during periods of crisis, such as the 1990s and the post-Arab Spring years, many everyday citizens accused of activism, opposition, and dissent end up being tried in military tribunals.

Political dynamics
Until the Arab Spring, one bright spot in Bahrain's other authoritarian landscape was the periodic ability of the National Assembly, through its elected

lower house, to highlight issues and cause embarrassment to the government. For instance, after the 2002 elections, news broke that the two government-managed pension funds, which held the savings of nearly all Bahrainis, were about to collapse. This brought out a streak of independence in the body despite that its domination by Sunni groups made it supposedly pro-government. Over Prime Minister Khalifah's objection, parliament formed a commission to investigate the fund's management, and in January 2004 the commission submitted a report detailing the extensive mismanagement and malfeasance of the fund managers, and recommending the interpellation of the ministers of finance, labor, and state to fully ascertain the extent of the corruption. To deter more radical steps, the government offered to rescue the pension funds, while royal emissaries sent thinly veiled warnings for parliamentarians to remember that the king's father had suspended the first National Assembly in 1975 with ease.

Moreover, Shi'a opposition did find ways to gain political audience through the legislature, giving some hope prior to the Arab Spring that Bahraini liberalization was not over. In the 2006 elections, al-Wifaq and the three other groups that had boycotted the 2002 elections participated. This decision led to a break in al-Wifaq's ranks, with the minority, which advocated continuing the boycott, leaving to form the al-Haq Movement. The 40-member elected lower house included 17 al-Wifaq MPs, eight Sunni Salafis belonging to al-Asalah Islamic Society, seven members of Minbar al-Watani al-Islami (National Islamic Forum, the local variant of the Muslim Brotherhood), four Sunni members of the secular pro-government al-Mustaqbal bloc), and various independent pro-government MPs. One woman was elected. During the election, the naturalization issue emerged as a result of publication of the Bandar Report by a government adviser, alleging a host of government improprieties. After entering parliament in 2006, al-Wifaq's main goal was amending the 2002 constitution. In 2008 al-Wifaq paralyzed parliament in an effort to question the government's naturalization of non-Bahraini Sunnis. Political divisions at the top of the ruling family also appeared in January 2008, when the king's cancer diagnosis and absence from the country created tension between the more reform-minded Crown Prince Salman bin Hamad, the king's eldest son, and Prime Minister Khalifah, who remained notoriously conservative and hardline on the issue of political liberalization.

The Arab Spring brought renewed conflict to Bahrain. In October 2010 flawed parliamentary elections and the arrest of opposition activists had already raised tensions. New protests began in February 2011 at Manama's

Pearl Roundabout, a major traffic site near the financial district, calling initially for reform, greater political participation, and protections of human rights. Although most of the protesters were Shi'a, the calls for reform were initially cross-sectarian, with many liberal Sunnis inspired by the Arab Spring also joining the call. These peaceful protests were met with a violent government response that killed dozens. The government took the opportunity to frame the protests in sectarian language, accusing the uprising as a Shi'a plot underwritten by Iran, although there was no evidence to support this. It also responded brutally: firing at the crowds and arresting and torturing many involved in the protests. When that failed to quell the opposition, the GCC sent a joint Saudi-Emirati military unit in March 2011 – on invitation of King Hamad, so as to not make it appear like an intervention – to assist Bahraini forces in smashing the uprising. Mass repression ensued, and collective punishment of the entire Shi'a population followed: the government destroyed Shi'a mosques, fired Shi'a civil servants, and launched continuing attacks on Shi'a neighborhoods.

The years since have witnessed the virtual closure of Bahrain's political dynamic, as the monarchy has taken advantage of regional tensions and sectarian acrimony to clamp down fully to a degree not witnessed since the 1970s. In 2016 the government stripped 'Isa Qassim, Bahrain's top Shi'a cleric, of his citizenship and suspended al-Wifaq (which boycotted the 2014 general elections to protest against the post-Arab Spring crackdown). Both al-Wifaq leaders and other prominent Shi'a oppositionists, including academics and youths, suffered campaigns of pursuit and detention. Periodic demonstrations were treated with arrests and beatings, with accusations of torture frequent. New anti-terror laws criminalized a broad range of speech and online activities; thus in 2018, courts sentenced Nabeel Rajab, a well-known human rights activist, to five years in prison over social media activity, while arresting dozens of others on terrorism charges. The December 2018 general elections, hence, were held under depressing circumstances; al-Wifaq and other opposition groups were barred from participating, and apart from al-Asalah's Salafi front no significant bloc won seats.

STATE OF QATAR

Qatar occupies a mitten-shaped peninsula that extends about one hundred miles northward into the Gulf and measures 50 miles across at its point of greatest width. The land is mostly low-lying and consists largely of sandy or stony desert, with limestone outcroppings and salt flats. The vast majority of the population lives in Doha, the capital, on the east coast (Map 17.4). It is divided administratively into ten *baladiyyat* (municipalities). However, since the majority of the population lives in Doha, local government has little practical importance.

Social and economic environment

Before oil production began in 1949, Qatar's population was among the poorest in the region. Most of its inhabitants lived at subsistence levels, with income derived from fishing and pearling. Today Qatar's per capita income is among the world's highest, owing largely to the development of its substantial gas reserves. Qatar also has a very small national population: of Qatar's population of around 2.7 million, just over 313,000 are Qatari citizens as of 2018; the rest are expatriate workers, mostly South Asians and Arabs. Most of the indigenous population is Arab, some originally from the peninsula but others hawwalah. Qataris are mostly Sunni Muslim and generally subscribe to a less conservative version of the Wahhabi interpretation of Islam practiced in Saudi Arabia.

Social cleavages exist in Qatar. Like other principalities on the Gulf littoral, the pre-oil era featured a merchant and trading elite that specialized in pearling, commerce, and shipbuilding. However, they historically exerted less political influence than their larger and older counterparts in Kuwait, Dubai, and even Bahrain, partly due to their small size and partly due to stronger political authority on part of the Thani family. As hydrocarbon rents made Qatar wealthy after independence, many ruling family members have become more involved in business themselves; thus the traditional separation of Thani-dominated government and merchant class-dominated business has become extremely fuzzy. Through a symbiotic process, the Thani and the business community have increased their collaboration in many areas relating to Qatar's economic growth. Beyond economic interests, tribal divisions remain important. Qatar has about 18 tribes linked through marriage. In 2005 the government stripped members of the al-Murrah tribe in southern Qatar of their nationality because of their alleged connection to Saudi Arabia and to the 1996 coup attempt; this act was reversed in 2006, but the episode reminded many of the fragility of citizenship and arbitrary nature of nationality imposed over tribal areas that, until the last century, were defined by nomadism, movement, and conflict.

The largest division is that between Qataris and foreign workers, who compose the vast majority of the populace and staff all echelons of the economy, and even the state, given the shortages of Qatari workers necessary

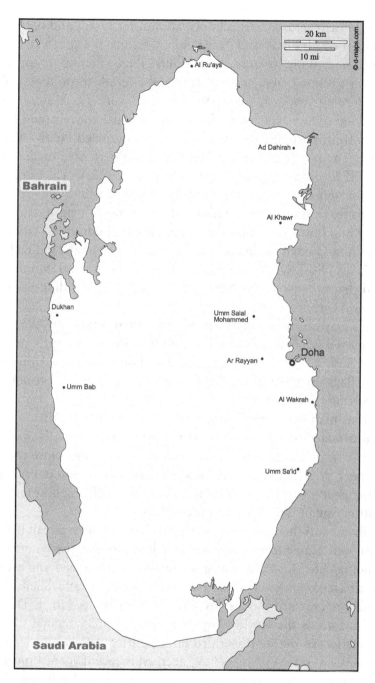

MAP 17.4
State of Qatar. Major cities shown.

Source: D-Maps.

to operate infrastructure, staff schools, administer retail, and perform other basic occupation. Indians and Nepalese constitute the greatest number of expatriates, and many assume lower-skilled jobs, such as in construction. While Qatar's human rights record is mixed overall, those most subject to abuse are foreign workers, especially domestic workers. A 2004 labor law excluded domestic workers (e.g., drivers and maids) entirely, and barred all expatriates from participating in any type of organized labor or collective bargaining. The plight of foreign labor received extensive media attention following FIFA's decision to have Qatar host the 2022 World Cup. In 2018, Emir Tamim signed a bill granting foreign workers some rights (e.g., allowing some to leave the country without their employer's permission). Qatar also signed into law a provision that would grant children of Qatari women married to non-Qataris permanent residence, as well as the Gulf's first refugee asylum law. Still, workplace abuses abound; in June 2019, investigators concluded that at least 1,400 Nepalese laborers died building the stadiums for the World Cup.

Women play an increasingly prominent role in Qatar. In 1955 the government opened the first girls' public school; by the 2000s, girls were graduating from high school at a higher rate than boys. At Qatar University, the kingdom's flagship institution, the disparity is even more pronounced, as over 70 percent of the students are women. In 2004 came a political breakthrough: a woman was named education minister while another woman was appointed president of Qatar University. Despite a conservative culture that still prizes patriarchy, there is a 94.2 percent literacy rate, close to the adult average; more than half of all eligible Qatari women attend college and university; and nearly 60 percent enter the workforce – the highest female labor participation rate in the region outside of Israel.

Initially oil and then natural gas exports have been responsible for much of the dramatic transformation that has taken place in the country's social and economic life. In 1975 the government nationalized the two major oil-producing companies, Qatar Petroleum Company and Shell. Although Qatar's oil reserves are modest by Gulf standards, its North Dome field, shared with Iran, is the world's largest deposit of unassociated natural gas. Its gas reserves are the world's third largest, after Russia and Iran, and so unlike other GCC states, its rents have accrued in recent years almost entirely from gas exports rather than crude oil production and refining. (The fact that it shares its enormous gas reserves with Iran also makes the kingdom less amenable to anti-Iranian geopolitical posturing than other Gulf kingdoms.) Exploitation of this large gas field began in 1991, and in 1997 the second phase of its development, construction of facilities for production and export of liquefied natural gas, was completed.

The government has invested these rents in a large welfare state that provides Qataris free education, health care, and guaranteed employment in a classic cradle-to-grave benefit system. By the late 2010s, Qatar's per capita GDP ranked among the world's ten most prosperous, and highest among all MENA countries. The profundity of these gas revenues enabled the regime to make vast investments in infrastructure; much like its Emirati counterparts of Dubai and Abu Dhabi, the skyline of Doha has completely revamped itself since the 2000s, boasting a density of skyscrapers and financial towers. However, the kingdom has also taken some steps toward economic diversification, beginning with the manufacture of fertilizer in the 1970s, then moving on to cement and steel plants, flour mills, and a shrimping industry, and finally by the 2000s embracing a financial and banking sector, including a large Islamic banking field. Tourism is small but growing. Higher education has become a major economic and social field thanks to government investments. In 2004 Qatar announced several education reforms, including the inauguration of a new Education City that presently hosts branches of major academic institutions, among them US-based Cornell, Carnegie Mellon, Texas A&M, Northwestern, and Georgetown universities, as well as HEC-Paris business school.

Economic liberalization and diversification have proceeded steadily over recent decades. Emir Hamad took power in 1995 with an agenda of economic reform, eager to deal with a problem of corruption so massive in the 1980s that it was undermining the country's economic growth. He clamped down on corrupt business practices and introduced standards for transparency and accountability in both the public and private sectors. These measures were accompanied by development programs to streamline and expand the economy. One target was the oil sector. The emir invited international oil companies to locate and develop new oilfield, and invested in advanced oil-recovery systems to extend existing fields and expanding production of the country's huge gas reserves. Qatar's oil exports more than doubled in a decade. Much of the additional income was invested in natural gas projects.

As a result, Qatar, which ran deficits in the 1990s, began experiencing some of the highest growth rates in the region, earning more from gas than from oil. It also invested in energy projects abroad, most notably in a $1.5 billion oil refinery in Zimbabwe. The drop in oil prices in 2008 (and again in 2014), coupled with the deepening global recession, reduced Qatar's budget surpluses, prompting the head of its sovereign wealth fund, one of the world's largest, to announce a six-month hiatus in March 2009. Nonetheless, Qatar remained in a far better financial situation than some of its neighbors, with well over $300 billion in its overseas investment portfolio managed by its sovereign wealth fund, the Qatar Investment Authority, as of 2018.

As the 2010s closed, the most serious challenge to Qatari prosperity was geopolitical. In June 2017, Saudi Arabia alongside the UAE and Bahrain imposed a commercial and travel blockade on Qatar. The crisis was the natural culmination of years of simmering rivalry and tension, with the Saudi government under King Salman and Crown Prince Muhammad bin Salman accusing the Qatari leadership of supporting terrorism, backing the Muslim Brotherhood, and growing too close to Iran. Rather than buckle into their expansive list of demands, Qatar simply found new trade partners, notably Iran and Turkey, developing new industries, lifting a moratorium on gas development (and increasing LNG production capacity), and strengthening its military. Indeed, the Turkish government under President Recep Tayyip Erdogan opened a military base in Qatar in 2016, and after the GCC crisis fast-tracked the deployment of 3,000 Turkish soldiers there to help guard the country against any internal or outside subversion.

Political structures

Qatar has been ruled since the nineteenth century by emirs from the Thani clan. Qatar's political system resembles those of the other GCC states. At the top is its ruling family, members of whom hold the sovereign ministries (and, in Qatar's case, usually several other ministries as well). They rule with advice from various mostly appointed councils and committees. In 2000 the emir formally established the Council of the Ruling Family, consisting of 13 family members. The constitution stipulates that rule be hereditary within the Thani family through the line of the emir's male offspring. In any case, the House of Thani is one of the largest ruling families in the region, numbering by some accounts into the many thousands. Divisions exist within the large ruling family, typically organized around relatives of previous rulers. One externality has been pluralism of interests and diversity of opinion within the royal stratum, which effectively constitutes its own social class. This explains, in turn, contradictory but simultaneous decisions – such as why Qatar hosts both a major American military installation and air base, as well as the sprawling Al-Jazeera media apparatus, which is usually critical of US policy.

Qatar's political system differs from those of the other GCC states in two important ways. The first is the largely unconsolidated nature of the country's government. While the emir is the country's leader, traditionally other powerful family members have run governmental fiefdoms with some independence and often different political agendas. Indeed, unlike other Gulf royal families, the Thani family never had a strong corporate identity; it never needed to unite itself against rival tribes and merchants (as in Kuwait) or conquer a hostile population (as in Bahrain). Thus, until the emir created the family council in 2000, the Thani clan never had an internal system of self-governance that could mediate disputes between warring branches. Such fragmentation only began to retrench in the 2010s, when the new Emir Tamim sought to better centralize his authority.

The second difference, a consequence of the first, is the relative instability the ruling family has experienced since independence. Emir Hamad came to power by overthrowing his father, Shaykh Khalifah bin Hamad, in a bloodless coup in 1995, then survived a countercoup attempt in 1996. His father, in turn, came to power in 1972 by overthrowing his cousin, Shaykh Ahmad Thani. Forced abdications in 1949 and 1960 also changed the path of succession, and until the 2000s every royal tenure carried with it violent conspiracies and internal squabbles. The current ruler, Emir Tamim, came to power after his father's voluntary abdication in 2013 – the first peaceful and unforced transfer of royal power in modern Qatari history. Among his first moves was to coup-proof himself; he continued to give senior princes positions of power, such as assigning the well-known Shaykh Abdullah bin Nasser as Prime Minister. Yet he also elevated his half-brother, Abdullah bin Hamad, as deputy emir – the closest Qatar has to a Crown Prince title, thus making him presumptive heir.

Whether causative of, or due to, such fractiousness within the ruling family, the pace of political liberalization in Qatar has been slow. The provisional constitution of 1970, which governed political life until it was replaced in 2003, provided for an appointed Council of Ministers and a largely-elected Advisory Council. However, after taking power in a coup in 1972, Shaykh Khalifah simply appointed an Advisory Council with little authority. In January 1992, 50 leading Qataris petitioned the emir to establish an assembly with legislative powers and to institute economic and educational reforms. His response was to expand the Advisory Council's membership. After Shaykh Hamad's ascension as Emir in 1995, tentative steps began toward political liberalization. In 1999, 2003, 2007, 2011, and 2015, Qatar held local elections, as it allowed citizen voters (including women) to elect a 29-member advisory Municipal Council, albeit one with few powers. Female suffrage was ensured despite modest opposition in the form of a petition signed by 22 Islamic scholars. Female candidates won seats in these contests.

In 1999 the emir established a constitutional committee, which submitted a draft constitution in 2002. In April 2003, the constitution was adopted by popular referendum; it came into force in 2004, replacing the provisional constitution drawn up at independence, and called for the creation of a partially-elected legislative body and offered protections for civil, political, and social rights. This proposed parliament-like institution, the Consultative Assembly, contains 45 seats of which 30 are to be elected through the country's first general elections. However, election dates for this body have been repeatedly set and postponed, leaving the future of Qatari electoral politics up in the air.

Qatar's state security forces are small but loyal to the crown. They were merged into one force in June 2003, and remain under the direct control of the emir. Qatar's military is the second smallest in the region, after Bahrain. Qatar also has a paramilitary royal guard in the Ministry of Defense and a regular police force. The presence of both American and Turkish military forces in the country is believed to help insulate the Qatari monarchy from major threats and thus subsume its insecurity. At a lesser level, everyday criticism and dissent is handled swiftly by the state. Anti-terror and cyber-crimes legislation starting in 2014 greatly broadened the range of speech and behavior that could be interpreted as threatening to public order and national security.

The Qatari judiciary is small but well-structured. Like other Gulf kingdoms, its independence from royal power is questionable. The legal system is an amalgam of Islamic law and European civil law. Shari'a is applied mainly as family law, based on the conservative Hanbali school of Islamic jurisprudence. In 1999, Emir Hamad established the High Judicial Council, which advises on judicial appointments and legislation concerning the judicial system. In October 2004, court reforms unified Qatar's dual court system (of shari'a and civil courts). In 2007, an Administrative Court and a Constitutional Court were established.

Political dynamics

By all accounts, Qatar ranks as one of the most closed states in the Gulf, given its paucity of electoral life, and lack of protection for associational and civic freedoms when used to criticize the government. No legislative body offsets the royal executive, political parties are banned, and few civil society organizations are truly independent of state influence or funding. Many petitions and applications to create non-governmental associations are denied.

Academics and writers regularly self-censor to avoid fines and punishment. Protests are rare, not least because organizers must obtain permissions to hold public events far in advance. Yet despite all these constraints, few Western observers associate the peninsular kingdom as being a repressive or despotic state simply because there has been no major public opposition against the Thani family in recent decades, apart from intellectuals and writers who have occasionally criticized the government. The Arab Spring had little impact in Qatar; there were no real protests, although the government detained some social media users.

Some ascribe this dearth of opposition and dissent to the tiny size of the citizenry, and the extraordinary level of wealth that exists. Poverty has been virtually eliminated among the Qatari national population. Others point to the presence of so many foreign workers, which may create an innate expectation for internal coherence among privileged citizens who stand atop the social hierarchy. More recently, Emir Tamim enjoyed an efflorescence of popularity after the Saudi-led blockade of the country in summer 2017. A campaign of open criticism from disgruntled members of the family backed by Saudi leaders, such as Shaykh Abdullah bin Ali, son of the ruler toppled in 1960, and Shaykh 'Abdulaziz bin Khalifah, the emir's uncle, gained no traction among the Qatari public.

This is not to say opposition historically only existed within the Thani family, given its past coups and conspiracies. In the 1950s, dissent was sharp and ideological, as the spread of Arab Nationalism and leftist movements instigated local analogues and supporters in Qatar. However, this faded over time. Terrorism exists, but is rare, as in a 2005 suicide car-bomb attack by an Egyptian on a theater popular with Western expatriates. (Perhaps preemptively, the country does host a number of conservative Islamist clerics, most notably Yusuf al-Qaradawi.)

One area of paradox lays in the media. Though Qatari journalists and writers are not free to criticize their government, much less royal power, the kingdom also hosts one of the most innovative and controversial media machines of the twenty-first century – Al-Jazeera. After Emir Hamad took power in 1995, he stopped formal news censorship, and dissolved the Ministry of Information. In 1995 he established Al-Jazeera as a satellite broadcast station, which was revolutionary at the time because it introduced frank and provocative news reports, commentaries, and debates. It was welcomed enthusiastically by a viewing public accustomed only to coverage of state visits and broadcasts of official speeches, and inspired a host of other satellite stations in the Gulf, including its Saudi-based competitor Al-Arabiya.

Al-Jazeera offended many other Arab governments, and notably stood on the frontlines of reporting during the Arab Spring with its coverage of the revolutionary uprisings in Tunisia, Egypt, Libya, and elsewhere. It also raised the ire of Bahrain for its sympathetic reporting on that kingdom's mass movement prior to its suppression in March 2011.

UNITED ARAB EMIRATES

The UAE, with a population of over 9.4 million, is a loose federation of seven emirates – Abu Dhabi, Dubai, 'Ajman, Fujayrah, Sharjah, Ras al-Khaymah, and Umm al-Qaywayn – located along the Strait of Hormuz (Map 17.5). The emirates vary in size and wealth. Abu Dhabi, the largest and wealthiest, covers nearly 90 percent of the UAE's territory and possesses most of the UAE's gas and oil reserves. Dubai, although running out of oil, has become an important regional business hub and tourist attraction, and is the second wealthiest emirate.

Social and economic environment

The most distinctive characteristic of the UAE's constituent shaykhdoms is tribal affiliation. Six principal tribal groups traditionally inhabited these territories when they were known by the British as Trucial States: the Bani Yas, a confederation of nearly a dozen different tribes, two branches of which (the Bu Falah and the Bu Falasah, respectively) provide the ruling families of Abu Dhabi and Dubai; the Manasir, who range from the western reaches of the UAE to Saudi Arabia and Qatar; the Qawasim, two branches of which rule Sharjah and Ras al-Khaymah; the Ali of Umm al-Qaywayn; the Sharqiyyin in Fujayrah; and the Nu'aim of 'Ajman. All are Sunni. Though many of these tribal groupings were nomadic, today over 86 percent of the Emirati population has become urbanized. From these tribal groupings have emerged the six ruling families of the UAE today – the Nahyan in Abu Dhabi, the Maktum in Dubai, the Qasimi of Sharjah and Ras al-Khaymah, the Nu'aimi of 'Ajman, the Mu'alla of Umm al-Qaywayn, and the Sharqi of Fujayrah.

Other cleavages are politically less salient. Dubai, with its long history as a trading center, has a powerful merchant class with a network linked to the Indian subcontinent and Iran. Before the emergence of oil as the dominant factor in the region's economy, Dubai's merchants were major traders, smuggling gold and other luxury items from picturesque ships (called *dhows* in Arabic) that concealed powerful engines capable of outrunning coast guard vessels. Oil transformed the class structure of these emirates, as it has those

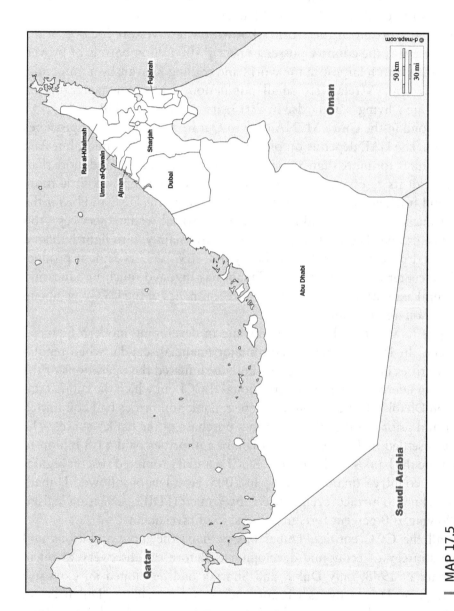

MAP 17.5
United Arab Emirates. Seven constituent emirates shown.

Source: D-Maps.

of the other Gulf states. The most important demographic impact has been the influx of foreign workers. Today, Emirati citizens constitute between 16 to 19 percent of the population, with that percentage lower still in the wealthier emirates of Abu Dhabi and Dubai.

Nearly 10 percent of the world's known oil reserves are located in the UAE; as of 2018, the country possesses nearly 100 billion barrels of proven reserves, the seventh largest in the world and trailing Kuwait by a miniscule. Given the country's relatively small population, rentierism has furnished extremely high living standards. In 2018, its per capita GDP of $41,711 ranked second in the entire MENA only to Qatar; adult literacy approaches 94 percent. The UAE depends on oil for 80 percent of its revenues, but Abu Dhabi accounts for more than 85 percent of all oil production and more than 90 percent of its reserves. Before oil, Abu Dhabi township was little more than a mud-brick village. Today it is the largest city in the UAE and by far the most advanced in terms of administrative and social welfare services. Abu Dhabi has also worked to diversify its economy, mainly with light industry, such as food processing, and some heavy industry, such as cement production. As a center of prosperity, Abu Dhabi has invested much in education and cultural exhibitions. It has, for instance, branches of the US Guggenheim and Paris Louvre museums.

Despite its wealth, Abu Dhabi was late in developing modern financial institutions. In 1991 it experienced a major financial scandal when regulatory authorities in seven countries abruptly terminated the operations of the Bank of Commerce and Credit International (BCCI), in which the ruling family of Abu Dhabi held a controlling interest. Bank authorities had committed major fraud prior to the Nahyan family's purchase of the bank's shares. The affair was settled in 1998 when Abu Dhabi authorities paid $1.8 billion to compensate the bank's creditors. The BCCI scandal prompted stricter regulation of the country's financial sector. In 2005, Abu Dhabi followed Dubai's lead in seeking to attract foreign direct investment (FDI) by enacting legislation allowing 100 percent foreign ownership of investments.

Of all the GCC entities, Dubai has perhaps the most ambitious and unusual strategy of economic development. Before the discovery of oil in Abu Dhabi in 1958, only Dubai and Sharjah had developed an extensive entrepôt trade. Driven by its vibrant traders and merchants, Dubai began to eclipse Sharjah both politically and commercially by World War Two. Indeed, the merchant class of Dubai in the late 1930s – much like in Kuwait and Bahrain – demanded that the ruling shaykh create a legislative assembly to enshrine their participation; it took some months, and British intervention, for the Maktum leadership to suppress the challenge. Starting in the 1940s, Dubai succeeded in dredging its own inlet (or "creek," as it is called locally), allowing larger ships to make Dubai a port of call. Dubai's merchants then reinvented themselves as modern business executives in a global economy. Dubai thus became a cosmopolitan entrepôt for goods and services, based on a local economy that approximated competitive market-based conditions. The other emirates have business communities that are tied more closely to the state. Building on its history as a trading hub, it created a niche for itself as a regional banking and tourism center. In 1979, it began building the world's largest man-made harbor at Jabal Ali, and in the 1980s it became an important source of connections for Iranian financing, despite the obvious conflict of interests given the generally GCC-wide antagonism to the Islamic Republic shown that decade amidst the Iran-Iraq War.

Today, despite Abu Dhabi's preeminence, Dubai has received more attention abroad because of its grandiose development projects. Its skyline and skyscrapers have become globally renowned for the sheer speed and density by which they were constructed over the past two decades (Photo 17.1). Tourists flock to Dubai's indoor ski slope and the world's largest mall, as well as the Burj Khalifah, the tallest structure and building in the world at nearly 2,722 feet. Dubai's location at the halfway point between Asia and Europe and its open economy have enabled it to become a premier upscale winter tourist center. To encourage more Western, Arab, and Asian visitors, Dubai hosts international tournaments in Dubai Sports City. It has also built a shopping and entertainment project called Dubai Festival City. As of 2019, future projects include Dubailand, a theme park twice the size of Disney World.

A key to Dubai's success as a center of banking, real estate, and services was modern financial standards of transparency and accountability to replace traditional, unregulated transactions. This has been an evolutionary process. In 2002, the government hired a retired Bank of England regulator to help draw up a financial regulatory system. And in 2004, the Dubai government established the Dubai International Financial Center (DIFC) to attract FDI. Licensed firms operating in the DIFC and other enclave free-trade centers benefit from no taxes on profits; no restrictions on foreign ownership, foreign exchange, or repatriation of capital; and access to operational-support and business-continuity facilities. In addition, Dubai aims to become a regional sales, distribution, and trading center for goods sold over the Internet. It also suffered the most from the 2008 recession, which hurt the financial and investment sectors, caused some dramatic declines in property values, and

PHOTO 17.1
Dubai Skyline

Source: Pixabay. Public domain.

forced the suspension of many domestic construction projects. In 2009 Abu Dhabi began taking steps to rescue financially-strapped Dubai.

Sharjah produces modest quantities of gas and condensate and, like Dubai, has undertaken extensive development projects, most recently focusing on centers of higher education. The contrast between these three affluent shaykhdoms and the other four remains substantial. The sovereign wealth funds of Abu Dhabi and Dubai possessed several hundred billion dollars of investments and assets as of 2018, while those of Sharjah and Ras al-Khaymah were miniscule in comparison. However, this gap has decreased somewhat as the federal government, financed by Abu Dhabi, has funded numerous development projects in the poorer emirates. However, the abundance of new income, the lack of a strong centralized planning authority with the power to veto or modify individual development ventures, and, most importantly, the continuation of intense competition among the various rulers for prestige have resulted in the duplication of many facilities, such as international airports. One area in which Abu Dhabi and Dubai have taken the inarguable lead has been, like Qatar, in hosting branches of major global universities in order to better brand themselves. Abu Dhabi, for instance, has campuses of New York University, Paris-Sorbonne University, and INSEAD, the European graduate school of business. Dubai has campuses of many British and European institutions, among them the University of Exeter and the London School of Business.

Despite differences between constituent emirates and the disparity of wealth between Dubai and Abu Dhabi and the rest, the UAE government has been able to create some baseline of unified development planning in certain areas. For instance, one of the most important innovations by the UAE federal government was the establishment of the UAE Offsets Group in the early 1990s, which mandates that foreign firms winning defense contracts must invest a percentage of their contract's value in joint ventures with local partners. In this way, a number of significant projects, ranging from a shipbuilding company to a health-care center, have been undertaken. The UAE, with Abu Dhabi in the lead, has also developed a vast network of global investments. Nonetheless, planners in Abu Dhabi recognized in the past decade looming economic problems similar to those confronting the other GCC states: youth unemployment (the 2018 rate was 7.8 percent, far higher than the overall jobless figure of 2.6 percent), housing shortages, and above all fluctuating oil prices that undermined the ability of the government to provide its social services and employment guarantees. In January 2018 it introduced a five percent Value Added Tax as a way to provide additional revenue during future oil price perturbations.

Political structures

Each of the UAE's seven emirates has its own dynastic ruler, the emir, hailing from six ruling families. The internal politics of the emirates' six ruling families have historically been replete with intrigue, with plenty of contention, conspiracy, and rivalries distinguishing relations between different branches and princes vying for power. Before the establishment of the UAE, many local rulers fell victim to assassination at the hands of brothers, cousins, or sons.

Abu Dhabi has been ruled by the Nahyan clan for over three centuries. In 1966, a palace coup brought Shaykh Zayed to power. He had the broad support of many who thought that his brother and predecessor, Shaykh Shakhbut, was not up to the task of ruling. In 1972 the UAE's new minister of education, Shaykh Sultan bin Muhammad al-Qasimi, assumed the position of ruler in Sharjah following an abortive palace coup in which his predecessor was murdered. In 1987, Shaykh 'Abd al-Aziz bin Muhammad al-Qasimi tried to seize power from his brother, the ruler of Sharjah; the event threatened the union's integrity, both because it raised the question of the legitimacy of all the rulers in the UAE and because Abu Dhabi initially backed the usurper and Dubai backed the incumbent. The UAE's Federal Supreme Council (FSC) temporarily defused the crisis by arranging a compromise sharing of power, with Shaykh Sultan remaining ruler.

Recent successions have been smoother, however. In 2004, Abu Dhabi's ruler, Shaykh Zayed, was succeeded on his death by Shaykh Khalifah, the crown prince and oldest of Zayed's 19 sons. However, since he suffered a serious stroke in 2014, Khalifah's brother Shaykh Muhammad administers much of the day-to-day business of Abu Dhabi and the UAE. In 1990 the ruler of Dubai, Shaykh Rashid bin Sa'id Maktum, was succeeded peacefully on his death by his son Maktum, who appointed his brother Muhammad, the de facto ruler, crown prince. When Maktum died in 2006, his brother Muhammad took over as new emir of Dubai. The current rulers of the other emirates are Shaykh Sultan bin Muhammad al-Qasimi (Sharjah), Shaykh Sa'ud bin Saqr al-Qasimi (Ras al-Khaymah), Shaykh Humayd bin Rashid Nu'aimi ('Ajman), Shaykh Hamad bin Muhammad al-Sharqi (Fujayrah), and Shaykh Sa'ud bin Rashid Mu'alla (Umm al-Qaywayn). In October 2010 Shaykh Saqr bin Muhammad al-Qasimi, ruler of Ras al-Khaymah, died, and a brief succession struggle ensued when his eldest son, Crown Prince Shaykh Khalid, returned from exile attempting to wrest leadership from his half-brother Shaykh Sa'ud, whose bid was recognized by the government of the UAE.

The UAE is ruled as a federation of these families. The UAE's constitution, drafted in 1972 and made permanent in 1996, provides for federal-level executive, legislative, and judicial bodies. The head of state, the president, is chosen by the seven members of the FSC for a five-year term. The first president and architect of the federation, Shaykh Zayed, served as president from independence until his death in 2004. His son and successor, Shaykh Khalifah, was chosen shortly afterward to be president of the UAE; thus the emir of Abu Dhabi is the head of state for the federation. The ruler of Dubai is the vice president.

There is little by way of pluralism or competition in politics. The Federal Supreme Council is the highest body of the state, and consists of the seven emirs of the country. It combines legislative and executive functions and meets four times a year. It is charged with formulating and supervising all federal policies, ratifying national laws, approving the country's annual budget, ratifying international treaties, and approving several appointments.

In procedural matters, a simple majority vote is sufficient for passage of any resolution. However, on substantive issues, Abu Dhabi and Dubai have veto power. The allocation of a preponderance of political power to Abu Dhabi and Dubai has been a major point of contention among the other shaykhdoms.

At the legislative level, there are no directly elected bodies. At the national level functions the Federal National Council (FNC), which is a consultative assembly with advisory powers. Half of its 40 seats are appointed, and the other half are elected for four-year terms by an electoral college chosen exclusively by the seven emirs of the country. In the absence of direct elections, turnout is low; in the 2015 contest, just 35 percent of eligible voters in the electoral college cast ballots. In terms of composition, in accordance with the relative size of their constituent populations, eight seats each are apportioned to Abu Dhabi and Dubai, six each to Ras al-Khaymah and Sharjah, and four each to the remaining three members. The FNC's duties are limited mainly to discussing and approving the budget, drafting some legislation, and serving as a forum for discussion and debate of policies and programs under consideration by the government. This last duty is of no small significance given the absence of political parties, trade unions, and many other kinds of voluntary associations, which are all banned. Theoretically, the constitution would permit the FNC's evolution into an elected body exercising real legislative functions if the ruling emirs allowed it.

Although the powers of the presidency are subordinate to those of the FSC, Shaykh Zayed was relatively successful in keeping together what has been the Arab world's foremost example of regional political integration. His success was due in part to Abu Dhabi's preeminence as the most pro-federation state in the union but also to his own strong personal dedication to the UAE's development. Abu Dhabi has thus far been a willing hegemon: many of the federation's operations are almost completely funded by Abu Dhabi.

Nonetheless, even without Shaykh Zayed's influence, the kinds of economic and security concerns that initially helped bring the seven shaykhdoms into a federation endure. The habits of working together are well established, and the advantages of doing so demonstrable. Each emirate exercises a degree of independence. Each has its own independent police force. The intelligence services, while formally under one umbrella, operate largely independently. The UAE military is not completely unified. In 1976, several Emirati military forces were formally united and placed under the single command of the Union Defense Force. However, the two principal shaykhdoms, Abu Dhabi and Dubai, did not fully integrate their defense forces into the union; indeed, the latter has created its own central military region command. Moreover, Fujayrah, Ras al-Khaymah, Sharjah, and Umm al-Qaywayn maintain their own national guard units. The UAE's military forces number about 70,000. As in other GCC states, many of the nationals working in the police and military are from more recently settled Bedouin families, or else are expatriates from other countries.

The UAE's federal judiciary was established in 1971, but judicial structures emerged only slowly. In 1973 a Supreme Federal Court was established, and in 1983 a comprehensive law governing the federal judiciary was issued, although individual emirates retained varying degrees of autonomy. Ras al-Khaymah and Dubai chose not to cede any jurisdiction to the federal courts, and so retained their own independent legal systems. The other emirates ceded most, but not all, jurisdiction. All the emirates retained their own shari'a courts with jurisdiction over personal-status matters. In 1983 a Federal Supreme Judicial Council was created to oversee administrative matters. The federal system is three-tiered, with primary courts, appeals courts, and a supreme court. The Supreme Court serves as the highest court of appeal and also determines the constitutionality of federal or Emirati laws when challenged. Like other GCC kingdoms, the independence of the judiciary is tenuous given the ease to which royal leaders can interfere and pressure courts to make particular rulings.

Political dynamics

Evaluated as one of the most closed autocratic states even by GCC standards, the UAE unsurprisingly has a mixed record on human rights. Foreign workers, as in other Gulf kingdoms, receive attention as an especially neglected and abused segment of the population. Higher wages attract expatriates, but many are subjected to unsafe working conditions, non-payment of wages, long hours, and poor living conditions. Many of the workers are in virtual debt bondage to recruiting agencies. As in the other Gulf countries, female domestic workers are at particular risk. In 2006, the government announced it would amend the labor law to improve the conditions of foreign labor after public protests in Dubai and a Human Rights Watch report critical of the problem brought unwanted international attention. The employment and abuse of young boys working as camel jockeys was formally banned in 2005; the boys were replaced with robot jockeys. Yet it has taken some time for the Emirati regime to recognize this issue, and only after considerable global pressure. Foreign workers continue to stage public protests, typically over non-payment of wages or workplace exploitation; in 2016, protesters opposed to abusive labor practices held demonstrations at Abu Dhabi's branch of the Guggenheim Museum.

Other incidents suggest the rule of law stops at the domain of royal interests. In 2009 an incident involving the videotaped torture, apparently by Shaykh 'Issa bin Zayed, brother of Abu Dhabi's crown prince, of an Afghan business partner brought the human rights issue to international attention. As in other GCC states, allegations of torture, mistreatment, and other abuses of those detained by the government on security-related charges are seldom investigated to the satisfaction of global monitors. In following the trend of the Gulf, in 2014 the UAE government began introducing tougher anti-terror laws that so drastically expanded the boundaries of criminal speech, behavior, and thought that they prohibited any form of political discourse deemed questionable by authorities. The government is not a signatory to most human rights treaties, and suspects wanted by the police and security forces for any reason – from foreign workers believed to be agitators to Emirati citizens who openly criticize their emir – are swiftly detained and prosecuted.

More like Qatar and less like Kuwait and Bahrain, the UAE has resisted regional trends toward political liberalization, including the toleration of meaningful opposition. Politics within the shaykhdoms historically have been tribal and authoritarian, although tempered by consultation and consensus. Debate over the development of a more responsive participatory system of government has been extensively covered in the press. In 2003 Dubai formed municipal councils to encourage some public participation. In 2005, Emir Khalifah as UAE President decreed that half the FNC's 40 seats would be subject to election rather than appointment, but the outcome was indirect selection, as instead an appointed electoral college voted on those seats. The next FNC "election" is due in 2019; with political parties, trade unions, and most other independent groups prohibited, Emiratis do not expect much competition.

Most associational life is banned in the UAE. All private associations must be licensed by the government, which rejects most applications, and large public organizations such as professional associations and student organizations typically rely upon official funding or other connections that render them vulnerable to shutdown. In 2005, the Abu Dhabi Chamber of Commerce and Industry, in an experiment with limited democracy, elected 15 of its 21 seats, but such examples of civic innovation are rare. For its part, the media is relatively free of formal censorship, but considerable self-censorship occurs. The government has blackballed journalists whose views it does not like, and has used the Anti-Terrorism Act of 2004 to restrict freedom of expression. New media laws since then have expanded the scope of speech monitoring to the online realm, with social media and chat groups now viable grounds for prosecution.

Interest groups and civic circles must typically rely upon royal allies to have any input into decision-making. Women, for instance, relied upon successful lobbying from sympathetic royals within the UAE's dynastic families to ensure that in the inaugural 2006 selection of the FNC's 20 non-appointed seats, they could vote alongside men – albeit in tiny numbers, as the electorate determined that year included just 6,500 voters. Female representation rose, however; in the 2015 round, 78 of the 252 candidates running for the 20 non-appointed seats were women.

The Arab Spring had a modest impact in the UAE, much like Qatar. There were no demonstrations; opposition consisted largely of some dissent in the poorer northern emirates, criticism via social media by youths and other rebellious voices, and a fair number of Emiratis signing a petition calling for the FNC to be directly elected and granted greater power. What was notably different was the government response – with both carrots and sticks. The carrots, though modest, came early. In February 2011 the government announced it would expand the electoral college for the FNC from its paltry size of 7,000 to almost 80,000. In March, officials announced they would invest $1.6 billion in the poorer emirates, and by the fall, public salary raises and other benefits were issued for all government employees.

The sticks soon followed. In March 2011, 160 Emiratis signed a modest petition calling for democratic elections and reform of the FNC. The government responded by dissolving the boards of the lawyers' and teachers' associations, after they issued a joint statement calling for the same reforms. It arrested five pro-democracy activists and sentenced them to several years' imprisonment. The regime also contracted with US-based private security contractor Blackwater (now known as Academi) to create more effective security organs. Throughout the next few years, the empowered government began detaining numerous individuals, from liberal activists to suspected Islamists with ties to the Muslim Brotherhood, which it regarded (much like Saudi Arabia) as a threat. The dragnet resulted in hundreds of arrests, with punishments ranging from fines and imprisonment to the revocation of citizenship, and by the late 2010s any credible threat of opposition was over. In 2018, authorities controversially sentenced a British graduate student conducting academic research to life imprisonment on charges of spying, though he was later released and deported after intense Western pressure.

SULTANATE OF OMAN

Located on the southeastern reaches of the Arabian Peninsula, the Sultanate of Oman has an area significantly greater than Kuwait, Bahrain, Qatar, and the UAE combined: 82,000 square miles (Map 17.6). Within it reside over 4.6 million people. A major portion of Oman's population lives in the Greater Capital Area, which includes Muscat, the capital; Matrah, a major port; and Ruhi, the country's commercial hub. The main city of inner Oman is Nizwa, the traditional religious center of the sultanate's interior. Sur, south of Muscat, is an important fishing port, and Salalah is the largest city and principal port of Dhufar, the southernmost province. Dhufar consists of three ranges of low mountains surrounding a small coastal plain and is separated from the rest of Oman by several hundred miles of desert. Inner Oman contains a fertile plateau and the oldest towns in the country. Separating this region from the Batinah is the Hajar mountain range, stretching in an arc from northwest to southeast and reaching nearly 10,000 feet in altitude at the Jabal al-Akhdar (green mountain). Much of Oman's population is found along the Batinah coast, which has the country's greatest agricultural potential.

Social and economic environment

A little over half of Oman's population consists of Omani nationals. While almost all are Muslim, half follow the Ibadhi sect – a little-known denomination that predates the Sunni-Shi'a split, and which is only found elsewhere in parts of North Africa. Much of the remainder of the population is Sunni, including many Baluchis, a people originally from the coastal area of Iran and Pakistan. Many of Oman's coastal merchants are Indians, either Hindus or Khojas (a community of Shi'a Muslims). There are also Persians and other Shi'a Muslims. Dhufar and the surrounding desert are home to several groups whose primary language is South Arabian, ancient Semitic tongues that predate Arabic. Shihuh tribes, a group of mixed Persian-Arab ancestry, inhabit the northern, strategically important exclave of the Musandam Peninsula at the Strait of Hormuz.

Like the other GCC states, Oman has experienced an influx of migrant labor, principally from South Asia. Oman's modest level of wealth has enabled it to avoid the situation of Kuwait, Qatar, and the UAE, where

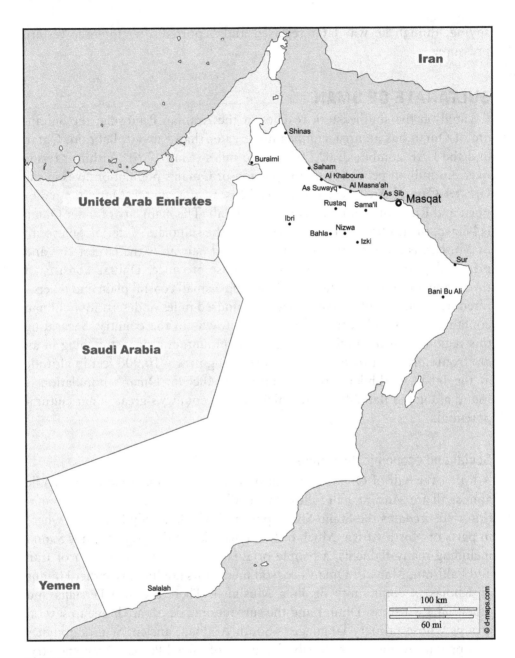

MAP 17.6
Sultanate of Oman. Major cities shown.

Source: D-Maps.

foreigners vastly outnumber the indigenous population, although by the mid-2010s Omani citizens found themselves as a minority for the first time. The sultanate has experienced rapid development in recent decades. Economic development was almost totally neglected in Oman until the accession of Sultan Qabus in 1970. Since then it progressed steadily, with a boom of modernization in subsequent decades. Oman's GDP annually grew by nearly 14 percent throughout the 1970s, and even in the turbulent 1980s managed an 8.7 percent annualized average growth rate, bucking the trend of other hydrocarbon exporters smarting from diminished energy markets. In the early 1980s construction was completed on copper mining and refining facilities, and in 1984 two cement plants began operations. Since the mid-1980s Omani development policies emphasizing light industry (e.g., food processing) have been promoted at industrial zones in Muscat, Sohar, and Salalah. Agriculture generates less than 3 percent of GDP but employs a significant portion of the labor force.

As a rentier state, Oman's economic lifeblood remains its oil revenues. Oil and gas account for about 80 percent of Oman's revenues. Oil exports began in 1967, and in the 1970s the large oilfield of Qarn Alam was discovered at the edge of the Empty Quarter. Oman, the largest non-OPEC producer in the region, typically produced about 1,000,000 barrels a day. However, oil in Oman is difficult to extract, and it also has relatively modest reserves compared to Kuwait and the UAE. Natural gas production has added to national revenues in recent years. Reflecting its worries about long-term economic prosperity, in the 2000s the government accelerated its economic diversification strategy while also encouraging Omani citizens to replace foreign workers. The latter was only modestly successful given the problems found in other similar campaigns in Saudi Arabia and Kuwait: in rentier states, citizens accustomed to guaranteed public employment, such as educational positions or privileged government offices, have little incentive to work instead in less glamorous occupations in the private sector, such as construction or retail services. Yet the commitment to "Omanization" remains; in 2018, the government imposed a six-month ban on expatriate work visas in dozens of professions.

Meanwhile, economic development funds for various projects have been carefully spread across the regions, with industrial poles in Salalah, Sohar, and Sur. A $15 billion tourism project has begun in Madinat al-Zarqa, and Vision 2020, Oman's long-term development plan, envisions opening nearly a dozen resorts across the country in coming years, developing a niche in heritage and ecotourism. In 2004, the Sultan permitted foreign ownership of land in some designated tourist areas. Such investments are sorely needed given the demographic context. Oman has one of the youngest populations in the Gulf, with nearly 22 percent of its society falling under 15 years of age, and nearly 55 percent in total under the age of 30. Youth literacy is nearly 99 percent, but youth employment nearly eclipsed 14 percent in 2018 – far higher than the overall national jobless rate of 3.1 percent. Oman's sovereign wealth fund had less than $20 billion in 2018, making the country's rentier dependence and future affluence questionable.

Political structures

The Bu Sa'id dynasty has ruled Oman since the eighteenth century. In the early twentieth century, a movement to restore an Ibadhi imamate led to substantial autonomy for the interior of the country. Qabus's father, Sultan Sa'id bin Taimur (r. 1932–70), with the assistance of British forces, largely reunified the country in the 1950s. This reunification was completed under Sultan Qabus, who took power in a nearly bloodless coup in 1970 and changed the name of the country from the Sultanate of Muscat and Oman to the Sultanate of Oman. In 1996, Sultan Qabus issued a Basic Statute of the State, in effect, the sultanate's constitution. The document vested substantial authority in the sultan but also set out a legislative and a judicial branch. In principle, it also guaranteed citizens a set of basic civil rights. In practice, Sultan Qabus wields uncontested executive and legislative powers; he is not only head of state but also prime minister, and also heads the ministries of foreign affairs, finance, and defense. No other Gulf monarch possesses so many formal responsibilities. Laws are often issued by decree.

The southernmost province of Dhufar, annexed in the late nineteenth century after it had been quasi-autonomous for years, became the site of armed insurrection in the early 1960s. By 1968, leadership of the rebellion had been seized by a Marxist-oriented group. Supported by Soviet and Chinese foreign aid and military assistance channeled through the Marxist government of South Yemen, the civil war consumed large areas of the province by the early 1970s. The rebellion was finally put down in 1975, with British advisers and Iranian troops playing key roles in assisting Omani troops and tribal militia forces. Sultan Qabus assured Dhufari loyalties thereafter by dispensing generous development funds to the province.

There are four politically important groups in Oman: the ruling family, tribes, expatriate advisers, and merchant class. Members from each of these groups occupy key ministerial and other government posts. Historically, the tribes have also played a significant role in the Omani political process. Under Qabus's father, Sultan Sa'id bin Taimur, manipulation of tribal rivalries was a major element in ruling the country. Qabus has tried to decrease the power of the tribes through development of local administration, such as local government councils. Although the tribes' influence may be reflected in the election of council candidates, especially in rural areas, their power has declined considerably.

As in the other GCC states, the sultan relies on his relatives, who control many (although not always the most important) governmental posts. The childless sultan has named no heir apparent, leaving Oman alone among the Gulf kingdoms with no clear successor or intra-familial mechanism for resolving competing claims, setting the stage for a potentially difficult transition. It is known that Sultan Qabus has asked his family to choose a leader from two candidates he has selected, to be revealed upon his death. They are suspected to be sons of Qabus's uncle, Sayyid Tariq bin Taimur, who has played an important role in government for years.

Oman's political structure has gradually evolved toward limited participation in government through narrow liberalization. In 1981, Oman established an appointed consultative assembly to advise the sultan on social, educational, and economic policy (defense and foreign policy were excluded). Members were drawn from the tribal and merchant communities as well as from government. Initially, 45 members served on the council; the total was raised to 55 in 1985. In November 1990 the sultan established a new Consultative Assembly (Majlis al-Shura) to replace the 1981 body. Regional representatives from each of the 59 districts would nominate three candidates, and the deputy prime minister for legal affairs would select one to serve, subject to the sultan's approval. In 1994 the Consultative Assembly's membership was expanded from 59 to 80, and women could for the first time be nominated (two were selected in 1995). In the 2015 elections, one woman was elected, as in 2011.

Although lacking legislative powers, and with no real authority to check Sultan Qabus' all-encompassing powers, the Consultative Assembly was empowered to review social and economic legislation, to help draft and implement development plans, and to propose improvement in public sectors. Ministries were required to submit to its annual reports on their performance and plans and to answer questions from assembly members. As the closest approximation to a parliament, the assembly could summon ministers to discuss any issue within the purview of their respective ministries. Moreover, it was required to refer questions and suggestions from citizens on public issues to appropriate committees. Voting turnout is modest, with 57 percent of Omanis casting ballots in the 2015 elections. Female suffrage has been in place since 2002.

Oman is large enough for meaningful local government, and a military that is larger than most other Gulf kingdoms' armed forces. In 1976 a government reorganization established 37 (later 59) districts (*wilayat*), one province (Dhufar, historically a separate sultanate that enjoys more local autonomy than other regions), and a municipality that embraces the capital. The districts are administered by appointed governors. They collect taxes, provide local security, settle disputes, and advise the sultan. Oman's armed forces also number about 70,000 troops. Its domestic security apparatus consist of the Royal Police, a small tribal national guard, and a modest intelligence directorate that reports directly to the sultan's palace.

Oman's judiciary is supervised by the Ministry of Legal Affairs, established in 1994. A 1999 Judicial Authority Law restructured the judicial system. Shari'a courts have jurisdiction over personal-status matters; other cases (civil, criminal, and commercial) go to the regular courts. Oman has a three-tiered court system: courts of first instance, six appeals courts, and a supreme court. The sultan is the final court of appeal. State security courts have been used on occasion for political dissidents.

Political dynamics

Given the extreme concentration of power in Sultan Qabus, it is not surprising that political competition and pluralism are lacking. The ban on political parties means that elections for the Consultative Assembly are waged by independent candidates who wish to largely maintain the status quo. There is somewhat more spirited competition for local elections regarding municipal councils; for instance, in 2016, seven women won seats on these local bodies, as opposed to the single woman serving in the Consultative Assembly.

Articles 32 and 33 of the 1996 Basic Statute guarantee free association, but the 1984 Press and Publications Law allows the government to censor publications. The Consultative Assembly approved a new Press and Publications Law in 2002, but as in other authoritarian countries, journalists and academics readily practice self-censorship to avoid detention, fines, and worse punishment. A number of websites and critical news outlets have been shuttered in the 2010s. Some professional and other associations exist, among them the Chamber of Commerce and Industry, but often have close ties with the state. Formally, public gatherings such as peaceful demonstrations require advance permission. In 2018, the government tightened its penal code to increase punishment for unauthorized protests and criticism of the sultan.

The Omani regime thus has a mixed human rights record regarding its own citizens. In 1994, state security forces arrested hundreds of regime opponents, including higher-ranking government officials and members of prominent families, alleging they were Islamists (a claim others dismissed since many were Shi'a or Ibadhi). They were charged with sedition but later pardoned. In 2005 the government again arrested dozens of dissidents (academics, civil servants, and Islamic scholars). They were convicted of sedition in May 2005 by a state security court. In June 2005 the sultan again pardoned 31 of them. More arrests occurred during the Arab Spring protests, but ongoing detentions and punishments continue; in 2016, for instance, a prominent writer was jailed due to making several controversial Facebook posts advocating democratic reforms.

The Arab Spring arrived in Oman in earnest in February 2011, when thousands of typically quiescent Omanis protested peacefully over material issues such as jobs, wages, inflation, and corruption. Demonstrations began in Sohar, and spread to Muscat and beyond. While hardly constitutive of a national movement, these were the largest demonstrations in decades, and continued for months. Much like in Kuwait, the youth activists and civic organizers behind these protests did not desire revolution, but instead called for reforms. The government's response was mixed. At times it acted forcefully, with the police unleashing violence on the crowds. However, Sultan Qabus also introduced modest changes in explicit deference to the demonstrators, such as a cabinet reshuffle and promises of more lucrative public employment. In October 2011, Sultan Qabus issued a royal decree expanding the powers of the Consultative Assembly, requiring the government to refer draft laws to the assembly prior to promulgation.

Economic reforms also followed, such as raising the minimum wage, introducing unemployment benefits, increasing government pensions, and hiring 50,000 new state employees. The government also created a new Public Authority for Consumer Protection. Much like Bahrain, Oman also earned the promise of billions of dollars in foreign aid from the wealthier GCC kingdoms given its lower financial reserves and hydrocarbon rents. Dissent eventually petered out, but not before several notable events, such as a hunger strike by imprisoned protesters in December 2011, and a May 2012 wave of strikes in the oil sector. A small outburst of protests related to employment difficulties took place in January 2018, resulting in selective arrests.

This pattern of mild opposition and mild repression encapsulates well the dynamic of Omani politics outside the extraordinary realm of royal decision-making as monopolized by Sultan Qabus. Going forward, the most important political issue will be succession.

FOREIGN POLICIES OF THE GULF STATES

The Gulf kingdoms have historically shared similar foreign policy concerns, leading to a degree of coordination, managed traditionally through the GCC as guided by Saudi Arabia. The GCC states differ, however, in many ways, perhaps most notably in the power imbalance between Saudi Arabia and the other states.

The Gulf states have long understood that their security lies outside their direct control. They are small in size, have diminutive citizenries flanked by much larger populations of foreign workers, and are militarily weak; yet their wealth draws often-unwanted attention from the outside world. As a result, they have a common strategic outlook: generally shy away from interventionism, band-wagon against outside aggressors, maintain cordial ties with other Arab countries, and seek larger, more powerful global allies for security. Following its involvement in the Iran-Iraq War, the US took over the role of regional hegemon once played by Britain. The US currently maintains major military facilities in several states, the product of a major buildup after the 1991 Gulf War – a critical turning point that marked the rise of the US as the primary protector of these states' sovereignty, especially against the threats from Iraq or Iran. Today Kuwait hosts a major American army base, which helped US troops rotate throughout Iraq and Afghanistan after 2003, and supported efforts to contain ISIS in Iraq after 2012. Bahrain hosts the Fifth Fleet, a major naval battle group which dominates the Gulf. Qatar's Al-Udeid Air Base hosts major US and allied air forces, and was heavily utilized during the 2003 invasion of Iraq and the air campaign against ISIS.

This asymmetrical relationship – local client, global protector – is not without tension, however, due to different approaches to Iran and to fear that the US will withdraw from the region, as some feared when the Obama administration announced the need for a grand strategic pivot of American interests towards Asia. The absence of the US could well put these states at the mercy of Iranian and Saudi expansionist ambitions, similar to the anxieties felt by these monarchical rulers when Britain announced, in the 1960s, that it would withdraw its forces from the Gulf. Thus, while the Gulf states rely to a great extent on the United States for their security, they try to temper that dependence, in part by diversifying arms purchases.

Regional cooperation has historically taken place through the GCC, with defense and security issues dominating its periodic summits, meetings, and coordination committees. Seen geographically, the GCC effectively is a club of the Arabian Gulf kingdoms, encompassing a collective space rich in hydrocarbon resources but highly vulnerable to external predation given the countries that neighbor it (Photo 17.2). As part of its security purpose, the GCC discussed installing an Internal Security Agreement in 1982 that might create common standards of policing and security (i.e., repression), in part over a growing concern about Iran, but also because some of the suspects in the 1979 Mecca Mosque takeover had fled to Kuwait. The agreement largely languished, particularly after the Gulf War exposed the GCC's inability to protect its membership from outside predation. It was amended in 1994. On the external front, in 1984 the GCC created a joint military called the Peninsula Shield Force consisting of 10,000 troops, based in Saudi Arabia. In 2000 the GCC concluded a Joint Defense Agreement to provide a framework for collective defense, but until the Arab Spring and the Bahraini intervention, the Peninsula Shield Force was little more than symbolic.

When the Arab Spring occurred, Saudi Arabia was among the most conservative critics of the democratic uprisings occurring across the region. The smaller Gulf states initially rallied behind Saudi efforts to expand the GCC into a more coherent political and security bloc. However, a 2011 Saudi Arabia proposal that the GCC form a political confederation was welcomed only by Bahrain, which had relied on Saudi Arabia to lead the GCC intervention in March 2011 to crush its revolutionary challenge. For the other principalities, the prospect of a confederation meant being absorbed into a much larger Saudi entity. In 2012, Saudi Arabia proposed a more draconian version of the old Internal Security Agreement; and though the Kuwaiti parliament refused to ratify the pact, the other states began implementing its mandates. This marked a new era in coordinating repression across borders. In 2013, Saudi Arabia proposed a unified GCC military command of 100,000 (half of which would be Saudi), but other GCC members opposed this. In 2014 the Interior Ministers of the GCC states did agree to establish a Gulf police force, headquartered in Abu Dhabi, and also floated the idea of a Gulf-wide biometric database that could track every single citizen in their countries, thereby turning the entire littoral into a contiguous security zone.

However, the Gulf kingdoms also showed divergent interests in their foreign policies – enough to fracture the GCC and cause geopolitical tensions

PHOTO 17.2
Gulf Cooperation Council membership.

Source: iStock.

easily apparent to outside powers. In the past, common collective threats to
state sovereignty were enough to pull these states together into a united front
– e.g., the Iran-Iraq War in the 1980s, the Gulf War of 1990–91, the Iraq War
of 2003, and later the Arab Spring and the perceived danger of Iranian meddling within their societies. When such crises pass, however, strategic differences divide these countries. Since the Arab Spring, the most visible became
the rivalry between Saudi Arabia (backed by Bahrain and the UAE) and Qatar.

While the Gulf kingdoms have sometimes had minor territorial disputes with one another, tensions between Saudi Arabia and Qatar had been building for some time, and burst into the open with differing viewpoints on regional issues after 2011. For instance, Saudi Arabia opposed the Muslim Brotherhood, which Qatar supported; thus they found themselves on opposite sides of the Egyptian coup in July 2013. Qatar also played an early and active part in supporting Libya's rebel forces, sending air and ground support for NATO's military campaign there. Relations reached a low point in 2013 when Saudi Arabia, the UAE, and Bahrain recalled their ambassadors in response to Qatar's granting refuge to Muslim Brotherhood members. These tensions were assuaged when Qatar agreed to expel seven leading Muslim Brothers, while Kuwait and Oman preferred to act as mediators in attempting to also enhance GCC unity.

However, in June 2017, Saudi Arabia and its allies imposed a land, air, and sea blockade on Qatar in what amounted to a non-militarized siege. While Saudi Arabia accused Qatar of sponsoring terrorism, the decision was also prompted by Qatar's increasingly independent foreign policy, including Emir Tamim's openness to cultivating modest ties with Iran, whom its neighbors still saw as an existential danger. Saudi Arabia issued a series of demands considered so outrageous by Qatar – such as shutting down Al-Jazeera, and closing the newly opened Turkish military base – that it had little choice but to ignore them. Kuwaiti mediation efforts failed, and the next several GCC summits were poorly attended by the royal leaders of the kingdoms. Oman remained neutral, and benefited to a degree from the conflict as cargo which once moved through Dubai now went through its ports. In 2018, Qatar's decision to leave OPEC deepened the rift, while bolstering its increasing inclination towards Turkey and Iran rather than traditional Arab allies.

The Arab Spring also affected the regional cold war between Saudi Arabia and Iran. Although this regional power struggle dated back at least to the Iranian Revolution, it had deepened in the 2000s, with the destruction of Saddam's regime in Iraq and the expansion of Iranian interests in the region. The Saudi monarchy increasingly framed the conflict in sectarian terms, a position not universally embraced by the Gulf states. The intervention and war launched by Saudi Arabia, and backed by Bahrain and the UAE, in Yemen in 2015 introduced a devastating conflict to the Arabian Peninsula, further securitizing the regional space and heightening tensions. Breaking from its past positions of foreign policy caution, the UAE acted more aggressively by sending some military forces to the country in joint efforts to roll back the Houthi movement. Not surprisingly, Qatar opposed the intervention, while Kuwait and Oman tried to maintain a low profile.

FUTURE PROSPECTS

For decades observers have predicted the imminent fall of the Gulf monarchies, described famously by one regional observer as "tribes with flags." Yet their relative success, compared to the authoritarian republics of the region, in weathering the Arab Spring indicates an underlying resilience rooted in different sources – political flexibility, dynastic leadership, small populations, rentier wealth, and adroit use of repression. Thus the prospects for political stability for these littoral autocracies are good. Absent a very long and deep drop in hydrocarbon rent and the complete exhaustion of their sovereign wealth funds, the GCC states are better positioned than most to survive internal challenges. They will also remain dependent on foreign labor, even as they continue to expand employment for nationals and attempt to diversity their economies. There is also important variation: whereas Bahrain's Khalifah monarchy was deeply shaken by the public spectacle of revolutionary unrest in the Arab Spring, in Oman the most salient crisis rests in whether Sultan Qabus has decided upon a viable successor behind closed doors. Foreign policy, too, exhibits real divergence with the Saudi-Qatari rift and insecurity wrought by Iranian conflict and outside interests raising stakes for all involved.

There are two sources of future change. One is youth. Echoing a trend seen elsewhere in the MENA, most of the Gulf kingdoms have youthful citizenries. In Kuwait and Bahrain, youth activists led the defining protests and marches of the Arab Spring. In Oman, and even the UAE and Qatar, young citizens are more likely to desire democratic reform, confront royal corruption, call for government transparency, and move to liberalize politics. How these ruling families – headed by extremely old kings, emirs, and sultans who are often more than triple the median age of their societies – deal with this will be critical. The second source is the rentier bargain. That bargain is a hyperbolic version of the classic authoritarian social contract in state-led developmental contexts: the promise of not just survival, but affluence and privilege in exchange for not just obeisance, but withdrawing from politics altogether. If either population growth exceeds rentier revenues or else volatility in global hydrocarbon markets continue, then these regimes will need to carefully rethink whether that bargain will remain viable in future decades.

NOTE

1 It is customary for members of each Gulf royal house to have the ceremonial title of *Shaykh* (for men) or *Shaykha* (for women), signaling their membership in the ruling family and thus their high position within the understood local hierarchy of familial rank, tribal status, and political custom.

FURTHER READING

For an historical introduction to the region, see Lawrence G. Potter, ed., *The Gulf in Modern Times: People, Ports, and History* (Palgrave Macmillan, 2014). In keeping with recent research on the area, the book is particularly attentive to trade and other links across the Gulf.

Historical overviews of the formation of the Gulf kingdoms across the twentieth century that link colonial politics to postcolonial sovereignty include: Rosemarie Said Zahlan, *The Making of the Modern Gulf States: Kuwait, Bahrain, Qatar, the United Arab Emirates and Oman* (Ithaca Press, 1998); Simon C. Smith, *Britain's Revival and Fall in the Gulf* (Routledge, 2013); Shaul Yanai, *The Political Transformation of Gulf Tribal States: Elitism and the Social Contract in Kuwait, Bahrain and Dubai, 1918–1970s* (Sussex Academic Press, 2015); and J.E. Peterson, *The Emergence of the Gulf States: Studies in Modern History* (Bloomsbury, 2016). A highly stylized narrative is found in Rory Miller, *Desert Kingdoms to Global Powers: The Rise of the Arab Gulf* (Yale University Press, 2016). A sweeping analysis of dynasticism as a mechanism of long-term monarchical survival rests in Michael Herb, *All in the Family: Absolutism, Revolution, and Democracy in Middle Eastern Monarchies* (State University of New York Press, 1999).

The Gulf's rentier basis, and the nature of its unique political economy, is accessibly reviewed and problematized in Giacomo Luciani, Steffen Hertog, Eckart Woertz, and Richard Youngs, *The Gulf Region: Economic Development and Diversification* (Gerlach Press, 2012). A classic view on the region's oil dependency is F. Gregory Gause III, *Oil Monarchies: Domestic and Security Challenges in the Arab Gulf States* (Council on Foreign Relations, 1994). An alternative critique on the excesses and distortions of rentier dependency is found in Adam Hanieh, *Money, Markets, and Monarchies: The Gulf Cooperation Council and the Political Economy of the Contemporary Middle East* (Cambridge University Press, 2018). An earlier criticism of how oil wealth has undermined the natural evolution of social class and healthy civil societies is Khaldoun al-Naqeeb, *Society and State in the Gulf and Arab Peninsula* (Routledge, 1990). A popular and well-cited work on the relationship between merchants, rulers, and oil rents is Jill Crystal's *Oil and Politics in the Gulf: Rulers and Merchants in Kuwait and Qatar* (Cambridge University Press, 1995).

Contemporary assessments of the Gulf monarchies tend to focus upon politics, but many studies emphasizing social issues of cultural adaptation, national identity, tribalism, and popular discourse have arisen. These include: Alanoud Alsharekh, ed., *The Gulf Family: Kinship Policies and Modernity* (Saqi, 2007); Alanoud Alsharekh and Robert Springborg, eds., *Popular Culture and Political Identity in the Arab Gulf States* (Saqi, 2008); Sean Foley, *The Arab Gulf States: Beyond Oil and Islam* (Lynne Rienner, 2010); Miriam Cooke, *Tribal Modern: Branding New Nations in the Arab Gulf* (University of California Press, 2013); Paul Dresch and James P. Piscatori, *Monarchies and Nations: Globalisation and Identity in the Arab States of the Gulf* (IB Tauris, 2013);

Omar AlShehabi, Adam Hanieh, and Abdulhadi Khalaf, eds., *Transit States: Labour, Migration and Citizenship in the Gulf* (Pluto Press, 2015); and Uzi Rabi, ed., *Tribes and States in a Changing Middle East* (Hurst, 2016).

Comparative evaluations of domestic politics and authoritarian stability in the Gulf kingdoms have been plentiful, especially the Arab Spring. Samplings, which generally tend to take a pessimistic note about the ability of these regimes to adapt to popular demands and rentier decline, include: Abdulhadi Khalaf and Giacomo Luciani, eds., *Constitutional Reform and Political Participation in the Gulf* (Gulf Research Center, 2008); Christopher M. Davidson, *After the Sheikhs: The Coming Collapse of the Gulf Monarchies* (Hurst, 2013); Fred Wehrey, *Sectarian Politics in the Gulf* (Columbia University Press, 2014); Michael Hudson and Mimi Kirk, eds., *Gulf Politics and Economics in a Changing World* (World Scientific Publishing, 2014); Yoel Guzansky, *The Arab Gulf States and Reform in the Middle East: Between Iran and the Arab Spring* (Palgrave Pivot, 2014); and May Seikaly and Mattar Khawla, eds., *The Silent Revolution: The Arab Spring and the Gulf States* (Gerlach Press, 2014). A more optimistic outlook is Yousef Khalifa Al-Yousef, *The Gulf Cooperation Council States: Hereditary Succession, Oil and Foreign Powers* (Saqi, 2017). Analysis of the Muslim Brotherhood and Islamism is found in Courtney Freer's *Rentier Islamism: The Influence of the Muslim Brotherhood in Gulf Monarchies* (Oxford University Press, 2018).

Security analysts and international relations scholars have long dissected the Arabian Gulf zone as a site of titanic struggle and realist clashes. Studies of Gulf security, including the GCC and beyond, include the following entries: F. Gregory Gause III, *The International Relations of the Persian Gulf* (Cambridge University Press, 2009); Matteo Legrenzi, *The GCC and the International Relations of the Gulf: Diplomacy, Security and Economic Coordination in a Changing Middle East* (IB Tauris, 2015); Geoffrey Gresh, *Gulf Security and the U.S. Military: Regime Survival and the Politics of Basing* (Stanford University Press, 2015); Khalid Almezaini and Jean-Marc Rickli, eds., *The Small Gulf States: Foreign and Security Policies before and after the Arab Spring* (Routledge, 2016); Kristian Coates Ulrichsen, ed., *The Changing Security Dynamics of the Persian Gulf* (Oxford University Press, 2018); and Mehran Kamrava, *Troubled Waters: Insecurity in the Persian Gulf* (Cornell University Press, 2018). The Saudi-Qatari rivalry described in this chapter is unfurled in Andreas Krieg, ed., *Divided Gulf: The Anatomy of a Crisis* (Palgrave Macmillan, 2019).

In addition to this general literature, each of the countries examined in this chapter have been studied in close detail by scholars.

Kuwait has produced a dense, rewarding literature. An accessible historical overview is Michael S. Casey, *The History of Kuwait* (Greenwood, 2007). More particular analyses of Kuwaiti development, institutions, and political struggles include Ahmad Mustafa Abu-Hakima, *The Modern History of Kuwait, 1750–1965* (Luzac, 1983); Miriam Joyce, *Kuwait, 1945–1996: An Anglo-American Perspective* (Routledge, 1998); Mary Ann Tétreault, *Stories of Democracy: Politics and Society in Contemporary Kuwait* (Columbia University Press, 2000); Pete W. Moore, *Doing Business in the Middle East: Politics and Economic Crisis in Jordan and Kuwait* (Cambridge University Press, 2004); Lori Plotkin Boghardt, *Kuwait Amid War, Peace and Revolution: 1979–1991 and New Challenges* (Palgrave Macmillan, 2006); Sean Yom, *From Resilience to Revolution: How Foreign Interventions Destabilize the Middle East* (Columbia University Press, 2016); and the volume by Jill Crystal, aforementioned.

Social issues in Kuwait, such as urbanization, identity, and gender, come through in these excellent works grounded in ethnographic insights and careful historical review: Anh Nga Longva, *Walls Built On Sand: Migration, Exclusion, and Society in Kuwait* (Perseus, 1999); Meshal al-Sabah, *Gender and Politics in Kuwait: Women and Political Participation in the Gulf* (IB Tauris, 2013); Farah al-Nakib, *Kuwait Transformed: A History of Oil and Urban Life* (Stanford University Press, 2016); and Claire Beaugrand, *Stateless in the Gulf: Migration, Nationality and Society in Kuwait* (IB Tauris, 2018). The best recent entry on how rentierism has shaped not only social relations, but also political interactions and economic markets in Kuwait is Michael Herb, *The Wages of Oil: Parliaments and Economic Development in Kuwait and the UAE* (Cornell University Press, 2014).

Bahrain has evoked a flurry of impressive recent work, which combine with an older academic tradition to create sizable resources for further study. One of the rare English-language histories is Miriam Joyce's *Bahrain from the Twentieth Century to the Arab Spring* (Palgrave Macmillan, 2012). For more specific takes, older volumes include Fuad Ishaq Khuri, *Tribe and State in Bahrain: The Transformation of Social and Political Authority in an Arab State* (University of Chicago Press, 1980); Jeffrey J. Nugent and Theodore Thomas, eds., *Bahrain and the Gulf: Past Perspectives and Alternative Futures* (Palgrave Macmillan, 1985); and Angela Clarke, *Bahrain: Oil and Development, 1929–1989* (Immel Publishing, 1991). The last decade has seen something of a renaissance in Bahraini studies, with the best entries including Nelida Fuccaro, *Histories of City and State in the Persian Gulf: Manama since 1800* (Cambridge University Press, 2012); Toby Matthiesen, *Sectarian Gulf: Bahrain, Saudi Arabia, and the Arab Spring that Wasn't* (Stanford University Press, 2013); Justin Gengler's *Group Conflict and Political Mobilization in Bahrain and the Arab Gulf: Rethinking the Rentier State* (Indiana University Press, 2015); and Omar AlShehabi, *Contested Modernity: Sectarianism, Nationalism, and Colonialism in Bahrain* (OneWorld, 2019).

Qatar has elicited a smaller library of work. The best English-language modern history is Allen J. Fromherz, *Qatar: A Modern History* (Georgetown University Press, 2017). Otherwise, these entries stand out in their scholarly exploration of the kingdom's historical development, political institutions, and foreign policy: Mehran Kamrava's *Qatar: Small State, Big Politics* (Cornell University Press, 2015); Matthew Gray, *Qatar: Politics and the Challenges of Development* (Lynne Rienner, 2013); Kristian Coates Ulrichsen, *Qatar and the Arab Spring* (London: Hurst, 2014); M. Evren Tok, Lolwah R. M. Alkhater, and Leslie A. Pal, eds., *Policy-Making in a Transformative State: The Case of Qatar* (Palgrave Macmillan, 2016); David Roberts, *Qatar: Securing the Global Ambitions of a City-State* (Hurst, 2017); and Cihat Battaloglu, *Political Reforms in Qatar: From Authoritarianism to Political Grey Zone* (Gerlach Press, 2018). More focused studies of Qatar's economic structure and human development are found in Zuhair Ahmed Nafi, *Economic and Social Development in Qatar* (Bloomsbury, 2014), and Ragaei al-Mallakh, *Qatar: Development of an Oil Economy* (Routledge, 2018).

The UAE was, until recently, only studied peripherally as an appendage to other Gulf countries. The last two decades, however, have seen a burst of social scientific research. Two accessible introductions to Emirati history are Michael Quentin Morton, *Keepers of the Golden Shore: A History of the United Arab Emirates* (Reaktion, 2016), and Mohammad Morsy Abdullah, *The United Arab Emirates: A Modern History* (Routledge, 2017). Other excellent surveys on specific emirates include Christopher Davidson,

Dubai: The Vulnerability of Success (Columbia University Press, 2008), as well as his *Abu Dhabi: Oil and Beyond* (Columbia University Press, 2009). Others that pay close attention to royal politics, hydrocarbon rents, and foreign policy are Khalid S. Almezaini, *The UAE and Foreign Policy* (Routledge, 2014); Kristian Coates Ulrichsen, *The United Arab Emirates: Power, Politics, and Policymaking* (Routledge, 2017); Karen Young, *The Political Economy of Energy, Finance and Security in the United Arab Emirates: Between the Majilis and the Market* (Palgrave Macmillan, 2014); and the aforementioned Michael Herb volume.

Oman's politics are the least-studied of the Gulf kingdoms, despite excellent historical studies of its pre-1970 decades. The best overviews of its modern political development include Marc Valeri, *Oman: Politics and Society in the Qaboos State* (Oxford University Press, 2013); Jeremy Jones and Nicholas Ridout, *A History of Modern Oman* (Cambridge University Press, 2015); Linda Pappas Funsch, *Oman Reborn: Balancing Tradition and Modernization* (Palgrave Macmillan, 2015). Enlightening analyses of its past historical junctures and policies include Joseph Kechichian, *Oman and the World: The Emergence of an Independent Foreign Policy* (RAND, 1995); Calvin H. Allen and W. Lynn Rigsbee II, *Oman Under Qaboos: From Coup to Constitution, 1970–1996* (Routledge, 2000); and Abdel Razzaq Takriti, *Monsoon Revolution: Republicans, Sultans, and Empires in Oman, 1965–1976* (Oxford University Press, 2016).

Online sources

Each of the countries examined here carries its own unique media sphere, including social media, broadcast stations, daily newspapers, and blogs. English-language sources abound, but many official media are not independent despite being quite readable, such as *The Kuwait Times* (https://news.kuwaittimes.net/website/) and the UAE's *Gulf News* (https://gulfnews.com/). Al-Jazeera is the biggest media player in the Gulf, and is highly regarded by many global readers despite its inability to scrutinize politics inside Qatar itself (www.aljazeera.com/).

For general Gulf news and information, the Gulf2000 portal provides an excellent introduction (http://gulf2000.columbia.edu). The Association for Gulf and Arabian Peninsula Studies (AGAPS) has a range of scholarly resources on its website (http://agaps.org/), as does the RAND Corporation's Gulf portal (www.rand.org/topics/persian-gulf-region.html). The World Bank's Gulf Economic Monitor contains statistics, data, and briefings on all aspects of development (www.worldbank.org/en/country/gcc/publication/gulf-economic-monitor). The Gulf Cooperation Council itself maintains a web presence, with a growing number of English-language resources, such as meeting minutes and official policies (www.gcc-sg.org/en-us/Pages/default.aspx). On the economic and social front, the Gulf Research Center's GLMM Programme specializes in tracking demography, labor migration, and populational trends in the Gulf kingdoms (https://gulfmigration.org/). The Gulf Research Center itself is also a treasury of useful research publications (www.grc.net). For business and financial news, consult with Gulf Business (https://gulfbusiness.com/), Arabian Business (www.arabianbusiness.com/gcc), and the business portal of *Gulf News* (https://gulfnews.com/business).

Please note that URLs may change far more quickly than books can be printed; so if these exact URLs do not work, simply search Google or another engine by the titles of these websites and online resources.

Republic of Yemen

Stacey Philbrick Yadav

INTRODUCTION

Over three civil wars in a half-century, Yemen remains a republican anomaly alongside its monarchical neighbors on the Arabian Peninsula. Its location on the geographic periphery of the region belies its relationship to many of the most central intellectual, political, and economic trends in the MENA. Its past was defined by the divergent trajectories of the Yemen Arab Republic in the north and the People's Democratic Republic of Yemen in the south. Following unification, two decades of authoritarian rule by a dominant party and president – accompanied by economic tumult and social unrest – ended with the Arab Spring. There, protests and hope both congregated around the possibility of democratic change.

Yet while the underlying structure of autocracy was shaken by the uprisings of 2011–12, so too was political order and stability. Different centrifugal pressures, from the Houthi movement in the northern highlands to the separatist Southern Movement in the south, as well as missteps and abuses by the transitional government installed in 2012, scuttled the nascent effort to craft a new constitution and move towards a new era. Instead, civil war has unfolded, implicating a long array of competing militias, insurgents, brigades, politicians, and terrorists that each have a different vision for the future. Compounding violence has been the Saudi-led military intervention that began in March 2015, which has destroyed what little remained of infrastructure and placed much of the populace in danger of disease and starvation. It is unclear whether and in what form(s) Yemen will emerge from its latest conflict, but challenges ahead will be generational in scope for one of the Arabian Peninsula's most populous, but also poorest, countries.

Box 18.1 provides vital data on this country.

BOX 18.1 VITAL DATA – REPUBLIC OF YEMEN

Capital	Sana'a
Regime type	Authoritarian (presidential republic)
Head of state	President 'Abdu Rabbu Mansour Hadi (since 2012)
Head of government	Prime Minister Maeen Abdulmalik Saeed (since 2018)
Legislative institution	Bicameral parliament, with elected 301-seat lower house (*Majlis al-Nuwaab*, or House of Representatives)
Female quota	No
Percentage of seats held by women	0.3%
Major political parties or coalitions (share of seats in most recent general elections, 2003)	General People's Congress (79%), Yemeni Congregation for Reform (15.3%), Yemeni Socialist (2.7%) [note: general elections not held since 2003]
Population	28,250,420
Major ethnic groups	Arab (93%), African (4%), Other (3%)
Major religious groups	Sunni Muslim (54%), Shi'a Muslim (45%), Other (1%)
GDP per capita	$873 ($2,377 at Purchasing Power Parity)
Unemployment rate	12.9%
Youth unemployment rate	23.7%
Major economic industries	Petroleum, refining, textiles, leather goods, cement, food processing (including fish)
Military spending as % GDP	5%

HISTORICAL BACKGROUND

Occupying the southernmost corner of the Arabian Peninsula, Yemen's location on the world's busiest sea lane and its position at the entrance to the Red Sea where Asia meets Africa has long given this land immense strategic importance. From roughly 1000 BC to 500 AD, the part of southern Arabia that now comprises Yemen was central to pre-Islamic trading kingdoms along the "frankincense trail." Occupying what Roman cartographers called Arabia Felix, the ancient kingdoms of Saba and Himyar especially depended for their prominence and prosperity upon their ability to protect and tax the passage of prized goods. The Islamic era, beginning in the seventh century AD, initiated many events critical to the making of today's Yemen. As Islam spread out of the nearby Hijaz region, Yemenis were among its earliest adopters, providing many of the first soldiers who helped to spread the new religion north and then west across North Africa. In the late ninth century, the establishment in Yemen of an indigenous Zaydi (Shi'a) tradition of governance ended 'Abbasid rule from distant Baghdad, facilitating its development in relative isolation from the Arabo-Islamic core.

The occupation of Yemen by the Ottoman Empire in the sixteenth century, followed by its expulsion after a long struggle led by the Zaydi leadership over the next century, served to deepen an indigenous, if nascent, sense of localized Yemeni identity. From the mid-seventeenth to the mid-nineteenth centuries, the interior highlands remained largely cut off from and unknown to the rest of the world, even as European powers came to exercise control over much of the rest of the region in ways that would leave a lasting impact on Yemen and its peoples.

The two Yemens: 1839–1990

The process by which one Yemen, albeit still vaguely defined, became two began with the dual effects of Great Britain's seizure of coastal Aden in 1839 and the Ottoman reoccupation of northern Yemen in 1849. By the time the Ottomans and the British had delineated a border between their domains in 1904, the practical bifurcation of Yemen and the development of two polities and political cultures were well under way. In the north, there was a tense and contested relationship of suzerainty granted to the Zaydi imamate, corresponding roughly to a dynastic territory, by the occupying Ottomans, whereas in the south the British built decentralized relationships with local tribal and communal elites outside of Aden. It governed the port city – central to its maritime access to and control over its imperial crown jewel, British India – as a protectorate.

Northern Yemen underwent a pathway defined by struggle and conflict. Defeat in World War One forced Ottoman withdrawal from north Yemen but left in place two ambitious imams – Yahya Hamid al-Din and his son, Ahmad – who were keen to transform the Zaydi imamate into a more rigidly monarchical state. In the process of centralizing their control, Imams Yahya and Ahmad fed Yemen's nascent nationalism, even as they inspired considerable resistance. (While the Arabic term *imam* generically means prayer leader, in Shiʻa Islam it is also a title given to political leaders of exalted status.) In "defending" Yemen from outsiders, the two imams isolated north Yemen's culture and society, generating discontent among the small but growing number of Yemenis who traveled abroad for education or work. Some exposure came, too, through travel to south Yemen, where British rule provided greater educational and economic opportunities, though few political freedoms. The Free Yemeni movement, which drew leaders from north and south influenced by nationalist and republican thinkers throughout the region, laid the intellectual groundwork for a revolution in 1962 that overthrew the Zaydi monarchy, and in the spirit of Arab Nationalist republicanism established the Yemen Arab Republic (YAR).

The history of the YAR can be divided into three periods. The first was the wrenching tenure of President Abdullah al-Sallal (1962–67), which was marked by military rule, a long civil war – during which Arab Nationalist-republican and Zaydi royalist factions were supported by Egyptian and Saudi military interventions, respectively – and a period of sudden, irreversible political and economic change. The second was a ten-year period distinguished by republican-royalist reconciliation, adoption of the 1970 constitution and elections under President ʻAbd al-Rahman al-Iryani, and the brief attempt by President Ibrahim al-Hamdi, who overthrew al-Iryani in a 1974 coup and ruled until his assassination in 1977, to build a genuinely developmental state. The third was the 12-year tenure of President Ali Abdallah Salih, who began his reign in 1978. His rule of the YAR was accompanied by the discovery of oil and the prospect of oil-driven prosperity; but also beset by many of the political challenges that often accompany rentierist incentives and hydrocarbon wealth. Salih also established his ruling party, the General People's Congress (GPC), which subsequently dominated northern Yemeni politics. Many of the patterns of rule that would come to characterize the new Republic of Yemen after unification in 1990 had been established by Salih during his tenure as president of its northern component, though they cannot be considered in isolation from dynamics developing simultaneously in the south.

Southern Yemen's history took a different trajectory. The north's political system differed from the south – its Zaydi imamate, for instance, fused monarchism with a unique Shiʻa denominational doctrine. Within the south, governance was fragmented. Aden had come under direct British occupation in 1839, but surrounding it were dozens of semi-autonomous "statelets" in the southern hinterland that had been governed by tribal dynasties and elite clans through indirect relationships to the

British, resembling patterns seen elsewhere in the Arabian Peninsula. As a consequence, there was no single polity in the south. Realizing Aden's geopolitical importance, Britain designated Aden as a Crown Colony in 1937, a status it would hold until 1963, when social unrest and political demands for independence compelled the British to withdraw its imperial hand by 1967. At that point, southern Yemen consisted of the former Aden Colony – a modernizing city-state and world-class port – and its vast, remote, politically fragmented periphery. Indeed, that periphery between 1964 and 1967 consisted of 17 different statelets, which briefly banded together to become the Federation of South Arabia, before folding into the new southern Yemeni republic after the British departure. They were woefully underdeveloped, connected only by a dispersed network of unpaved roads, airstrips, and telegraph lines.

The history of south Yemen as a republic following independence has four periods. The first was the period of takeover and consolidation (1967–69), a phase in which the Marxist group National Liberation Front (NLF) established control over the country, while power within the NLF passed from the nationalist to the socialist wing. This made the republic, now retooled as the People's Democratic Republic of Yemen (PDRY), the only Marxist state in the Arab world. The second was the period of uneasy co-leadership by Salim Ruba'i Ali and 'Abd al-Fatah Isma'il (1969–78), distinguished by the efforts of these two rivals to transform the Yemeni Socialist Party (YSP) into a vanguard party and organize the country around "scientific socialism" in alignment with the international socialist camp and radical liberation movements. The third was the era of Ali Nasir Muhammad (1980–85), which saw the consolidation of power by a single leader and growing moderation in both domestic and external politics. After a violent, month-long struggle between rival party factions, the fourth (1986–90) was a period of collective leadership in which a weak, decapitated YSP faced worsening economic conditions and declining aid from the Soviet Bloc.

The era of the PDRY was marked by considerable conflict and violence, as well as limits on free expression and organized religion. Alongside this, however, there were notable successes in state-building. The institutions of the party-state helped to bridge the vast gap between Aden and the hinterland and made good use of limited resources to advance literacy, health care, and women's rights. Thus, by the time of unification, north and south Yemen had developed two distinct polities, and their citizens had very different experiences and expectations regarding the role of the state, ensuring that the union would be uneasy at best.

Unification, conflict, and autocracy: 1990–2011

Despite these differences, northern and southern elites had debated unification for many years before it finally occurred in May 1990. Characterized as a "democratic opening" by many outsiders, today there is wider recognition that democratic institutions were used as a technique to manage unification and regime consolidation, rather than as long-term commitments. Neither the YAR nor the PDRY had well-established representative institutions going into the unification process, but new political parties, organizations, newspapers, and magazines sprang up quickly and occupied a genuinely vibrant public sphere in the early 1990s. Under the terms of unification, old elites and extant parties continued their leadership. Thus Ali Abdullah Salih became president, who in turn brought his GPC party into the new political arena; and Ali Salim al-Baydh, the YSP's secretary-general, became vice president. Their two cabinets merged, with positions shared equally between the GPC and YSP, and the two existing consultative bodies – neither of which had been freely elected – merged to create a single national parliament with 301 elected seats.

In the 1993 elections, the GPC won about twice as many seats as either of its main opponents, the YSP and the Yemeni Reform Grouping (*Islah*), a new party composed of conservative Islamists, northern tribal leaders, and younger Muslim Brotherhood members. As the YSP had preserved significant formal power under unification, its third-place finish came as a shock. The GPC, YSP, and Islah formed a "grand coalition" cabinet, and other top positions were allocated among these parties roughly on a 2:1:1 basis. Shaykh Abdullah bin Husayn al-Ahmar, a senior Islah leader, tribal heavyweight, and ally of President Salih, became parliament's speaker.

In addition to their diminished position, YSP leaders had to contend with the political conflict that accompanied rapidly worsening economic conditions in the early 1990s. This was driven by two interrelated regional developments: the suspension of foreign aid from the US and the wealthy kingdoms of the Gulf Cooperation Council (GCC) after President Salih's siding with Iraq during the Gulf War, and the consequent repatriation of about 800,000 Yemeni workers from mostly Saudi Arabia (and a few other Gulf kingdoms) as punishment for its alignment with Saddam Hussein. This second development cut off vital remittances, upon which the Yemeni economy depended, created unemployment and housing crises for which the state was unprepared once its expatriates were forcibly returned home. The effects of these events were particularly significant in the south, where the social safety nets of the socialist regime were being dismantled in favor of a unified, more liberal economy.

Many efforts at north-south reconciliation failed in this period, and because the armed forces of the two former states had not been fully integrated, a four-month civil war occurred in 1994. While this war was fought mainly between and on behalf of factions of the elite, many southerners viewed the use of Islamist irregulars as part of a broader effort to impose northern hegemony over the south. While the Republic of Yemen survived as a territorial unit, politics following the civil war were characterized by a consistent effort to consolidate power in the hands of a narrow northern elite centered around President Salih. The victorious regime acted quickly to reintegrate the defeated south, granting amnesty and urging those who had fled abroad to return to Yemen. Yet it also unleashed new economic and political initiatives that left many southerners angry and paved the way for the emergence of the *Hirak*, or Southern Movement, within little more than a decade. Grievances dating from this period include the forced retirement and delayed pensions of many south Yemeni officers, the expropriation of land and other property belonging to southerners, the appointment of northerners throughout the bureaucracy, and the promotion of Islamists from Islah to positions of leadership in the education and legal sectors. Collectively, southerners proud of their (perhaps exaggerated) cosmopolitan heritage interpreted these moves as tantamount to the "retribalization" and "Islamization" of the south.

Meanwhile, Yemen's economy as measured by GDP was halved by the costs of unification, civil war, and loss of remittances. Massive unemployment and rising poverty ensued. In mid-1995 the regime adopted major economic reforms in line with neoliberal expectations, with the International Monetary Fund contributing funds through the late 1990s. However, these produced inequality and corruption associated with crony capitalism. When President Salih was reelected in late 1994 by parliament (direct elections would not come for another five years), he appointed 'Abdu Rabbu Mansour Hadi, a southern general who had opposed secession, as his vice president. Together they were backed by a new, narrower coalition composed mainly of the GPC and Islah. In 1997, a still-reeling YSP boycotted parliamentary elections. Winning a huge majority, Salih's GPC then chose to rule alone, leaving Islah as opposition. Shaykh al-Ahmar remained speaker, demonstrating his (and Islah's) ambiguous relationship to President Salih. By 1999, the GPC had used its dominance to amend the constitution, expand the president's powers, and prevent the YSP from competing in the first direct presidential elections. Virtually unopposed and endorsed by Islah, Salih was elected to a new term.

Though elections became routinized, politics grew increasingly acrimonious through the early 2000s. Moreover, economic conditions were increasingly grim for most Yemenis, with unemployment persistently holding at about 40 percent and malnourishment and poverty remaining very high. The middle class was pauperized. Despite this, the GPC reaffirmed its dominance in the 2003 parliamentary elections, taking more than two-thirds of the seats, amid overt electoral manipulation. Islah remained in second place, but with fewer seats than before, while the YSP made a very modest comeback. As the Salih regime tightened its control of Yemen's political institutions and other aspects of daily life, these former adversaries began an alliance of necessity. To date, that 2003 contest remains the last general election held.

Beginning in late 2002, several opposition parties – led by Islah and the YSP – created what became known as the Joint Meeting Parties (JMP), which also included smaller factions associated with Zaydi nationalists and leftist movements. The JMP put forward its own candidate for the 2006 presidential election and drew up a political platform for local municipal council elections scheduled at the same time. This platform critiqued the regime's economic performance and outlined procedural reforms designed to promote economic and political transparency and accountability. The JMP chose a credible candidate – Faisal bin Shamlan – who waged a vigorous campaign. While President Salih again won decisively, he was compelled to campaign more earnestly and make policy concessions. Despite its relatively poor showing in local council elections, the JMP remained intact, pledged to hold the regime accountable, and began planning for the parliamentary elections in 2009 and the next presidential contest in 2013.

Before the JMP would again have the chance to compete at the ballot box, a number of more confrontational movements challenged President Salih and his regime. Their grievances shared a critique of the regime's exclusionary politics of patronage and came from the country's geographic and political periphery. The first of these movements emerged from the far northern governorate of Sa'da, where the Zaydi faith historically predominated. Aggressive evangelism from Sunni Salafis aimed at recruiting converts had accelerated throughout the 1980s and 1990s, producing cultural conflict. This implicated the government, given its complicated role regarding the expansion and (lack of) supervision of Salafi religious schools, as well as a Zaydi revivalist movement led by Husayn al-Houthi. When Houthi's followers pressed their demands by force beginning in 2004, the army's response was severe and led to the destruction of many homes and a wave of internal displacement. Humanitarian aid was siphoned off by the regime or Islah's charity, further fueling claims of discrimination against Zaydis. This was accompanied by an increasingly sectarian discourse among both the Zaydi followers of Houthi – the Houthis – and their critics. All-out war detonated in 2009 and continued thereafter, leading President Salih to name his response Operation Scorched Earth. In 2010, Saudi Arabia contributed air cover for Yemen's military, furthering the scale of destruction and establishing a precedent for its later intervention.

Yet anti-government mobilization was not limited to Sa'da or the conflict between Salafis and Zaydi revivalists. Starting in mid-2007, a rash of protests and demonstrations occurred across south Yemen. Beginning as a series of peaceful protests related to military pensions, this movement quickly broadened to include civil servants, lawyers, teachers, professors, and unemployed youth protesting the north's systematic exploitation of the south since 1994. As in Sa'da, the regime responded with violence. Some protesting southerners, moving beyond charges of unfairness, began asserting that unification was occupation and called for secession. Under the moniker of Hirak, these secessionists in the Southern Movement mirrored the Houthi movement in creating new committees, structures, and platforms in order to challenge the legitimacy of the Salih regime and the terms of unification.

The state's response to these movements both absorbed and divided its attention, leaving pockets of the country ungoverned. After being forced out of Saudi Arabia by 2009, Al-Qa'ida took advantage of these gaps to reconstitute its Saudi and Yemeni branches as Al-Qa'ida in the Arabian Peninsula (AQAP), claiming responsibility for terrorism targeting tourists, diplomats, and Yemeni troops. AQAP declared jihad against the regime, partly in response to Salih's eager counterterrorism cooperation with the US. As these crises escalated, the country's political opposition parties were mired in negotiations with the GPC over electoral and other procedural reforms. In February 2009, with the violence continuing on all fronts and the threat of a JMP election boycott looming, the GPC and JMP agreed to a two-year postponement of elections. Violence continued through 2010, despite President Salih's warning that conflict with the southern secessionists, AQAP, and the Houthis could result in many – not just two – Yemens.

Arab Spring and war: 2011–present

Influenced by developments in Tunisia and Egypt but fueled by domestic grievances specific to Yemen, early 2011 saw a period of widespread popular mobilization for change. Beginning in late January, unarmed protests by Yemeni youths erupted throughout the country. Moribund civil society

PHOTO 18.1
Protest in Sana'a, March 2011.

Source: Photo by Sallam, Flickr.

organizations revived, and new ones were created. The JMP participated, but struggled to connect with young non-partisans. President Salih ordered the peaceful protests to be squashed by force. In March, marches and protests virtually paralyzed Sana'a, capturing international headlines away from the uprisings in other countries (Photo 18.1). Security forces responded brutally. However, at that point, the regime itself began to fracture, as the military split and tribal leaders with powerful militias defected. Particularly demoralizing for regime loyalists was the decision of General Ali Muhsin al-Ahmar, a close confidante of Salih and core member of the GPC, to command his First Armored Division to stand down and side with the protesters.

In response to the unrest, Saudi Arabia and the GCC proposed a transition plan in April 2011 under which President Salih would resign in exchange for immunity for himself, his family, and his closest associates; taking his place would be Vice President 'Abdu Rabbu Mansour Hadi, who would appoint a unity government drawn from the GPC and JMP and thereafter plan for fresh elections, national dialogue, and a new constitution in a gradual transition that would complete by 2014. Very little of this came to pass. Over the next several months, President Salih agreed and reneged to the transition several times, while heavy fighting between militias, the army, and rebel groups raised fears that Yemen was on the verge of slipping once again into civil war. In June 2011, President Salih was severely injured in an assassination attempt, and under great domestic and international pressure, finally signed the transition agreement on November 23. Vice President Hadi assumed power and, in early December, appointed the GPC-JMP national unity government as stipulated. In February 2012, Yemenis turned out in large numbers to vote for Hadi in a single-candidate election in the hope that he would finish the transition.

Yet the remnants of the old autocracy began to recalibrate and reform. Just days after the election, out of office but not out of the picture, former president Salih claimed leadership of the GPC. His son, Ahmad, remained commander of the powerful Republican Guards; his half-brother remained head of the air force; and three of his nephews continued in top security and military positions. As importantly, many family members and others close to Salih retained control of major economic entities dominated by the military. Meanwhile, the JMP had now become part of the cabinet and thus ceased to function as opposition.

Throughout 2012, the transition became bogged down. President Hadi created a National Dialogue Conference (NDC) and ousted some of Salih's allies; but tensions among different factions emerged, while the southern Hirak and northern Houthi movements repeatedly imposed, removed, and changed the conditions for their participation on the NDC. Internal factionalism was tearing the JMP apart, while many GPC stalwarts – still led by Salih – intently dragged their feet. While the unity government and international mediators struggled to maintain progress, a security vacuum engulfed much of southern Yemen outside Sana'a. This resulted in the growth of the militant Ansar al-Shari'a, a local organization bringing together Yemeni members of AQAP and local Salafis in an effort to establish territorial control and impose order in Abyan and Shabwa Provinces. In ways that differed from AQAP and foreshadowed the rise of the Islamic State of Iraq and Syria (ISIS), Ansar al-Shari'a appeared less interested in becoming a global network than governing local spaces and imposing its will upon its immediate political context. Tenacious fighting between these militants, competing groups, and President Hadi's forces raged on.

Preoccupied with transition politics and its conflict with militant Islamists, the Hadi government neglected the growing humanitarian crisis and economic issues. As conditions worsened and political paralysis set in, public safety and order broke down. Kidnappings, theft, and random violence increased in many parts of the country as shortages of electricity and water persisted. Under these conditions, groups outside the governing coalition, such as the Houthis and the Hirak, remained not only politically relevant but also well-positioned to articulate the exclusion and alienation left unresolved – and arguably worsened – by the transitional process. By mid-2013, however, another issue loomed. As the NDC proved unable to fulfill its "outreach" mandate, and was rapidly bleeding credibility, conflict burst forth again between Houthis and Islah-affiliated militias in the city of Dammaj, and later throughout Sa'da and Amran Provinces. By September 2013, the NDC ground to a halt. Still, it issued a report in January 2014 that included an extension for the transitional government to allow time for implementation.

However, conflict and tensions persisted. Because the NDC had been the only real institutional channel for the Hirak and Houthis to participate in the transition, this extension and the NDC's conclusion constituted a return to political exclusion for both movements. Paired with the limited effectiveness of President Hadi and the government, the Houthis continued to mobilize around issues of corruption and political exclusion. They notably attracted some significant Sunni leaders to their political wing, Ansar Allah, and began their own campaign of protest and seizure. In September 2014, the Houthi movement captured Sana'a, while President Hadi narrowly side-stepped a coup by renegotiating the terms of the transitional government in the National Peace and Partnership Agreement (NPPA). The Yemeni military and security forces did not oppose the Houthis, nor did they prevent the Houthis from targeting prominent members of Islah afterward. Indeed, military units and militia groups affiliated with Salih threw their loyalties to the Houthi movement.

The transition essentially ended in January 2015, when President Hadi resigned. That month, the NDC exposed the lineaments of a new constitutional framework by issuing a proposal for a six-state federal system. However, the proposed boundaries isolated the 'Azal region (effectively, the Houthi stronghold) from the sea and from natural resources. Frustrated by an opaque political process that had often excluded them, Houthi members of the government intensified their pressures upon President Hadi, who in turn left office and fled to Aden, where he established a government-in-exile.

Conditions of civil war ensued, as the struggle between the Hadi-led government and the Houthi movement in control of Sanaʿa began to gain more global attention. In March 2015, the Houthis launched a new offensive to take all of southern Yemen, and soon reached the outskirts of Aden, at which point Hadi fled to Saudi Arabia. For their part, the southern Hirak remained loyal to the Hadi government, but frictions remained.

At that point, Saudi Arabia – with some assistance from the UAE, and mostly symbolic support from Morocco and Sudan – launched a military intervention in support of President Hadi, who despite his resignation still claimed presidential authority. That escalated this civil war into a full-fledged internationalized conflict, with many regional powers and players throwing their hats into the arena. The Houthis receive modest support and training from Iran and Lebanon's Hizbullah, but are not (or at least not simply) a "proxy" in the sense that they assert their own priorities, negotiate in their own name, and express grievances deeply grounded in their own history. Similarly, the myriad militias that work with (and sometimes against) the Saudi-backed coalition attempting to restore the Hadi government are not extending the interests of Saudi Arabia in an uncomplicated proxy relationship. This is most pronounced in the south, where secessionists have courted and received support from the United Arab Emirates, which is a nominal ally of Saudi Arabia and supporter of President Hadi, as well as in Hadhramaut, where the UAE and US forces have fought AQAP without Saudi support.

The face of Yemen by the late 2010s had thus irrevocably changed, as the notion of a unitary state had all but collapsed into fantasy, with even newer twists in the geopolitical narrative. In January 2017, former President Salih was killed while attempting to flee Sanaʿa; his loyalist forces, previously allied with the Houthi movement, had turned against their partners, resulting in a brief but intense struggle over the city. In January 2018, the southern Hirak turned against its partner, the Saudi-backed Hadi government; it seized its headquarters in Aden, threatening President Hadi during a fiery battle in urban quarters. Saudi airstrikes, meanwhile, had become indiscriminate to all involved; a gruesome incident in April 2019 that killed a number of school children drew global condemnation. At the same time, officials from the Hadi government, representatives from the Houthi movement, and international observers began to hold peace talks in Sweden, resulting in stop-and-start ceasefires and allowances for basic governance to occur – but not yet peace. Thus, the civil conflict raged on throughout the remainder of 2019. Both the Saudi-led coalition supporting the Hadi government and its Houthi opponents were responsible for an escalating number of civilian casualties, due to both collateral damage and deliberate targeting. Many international observers believe war crimes have been committed by both sides.

SOCIAL AND ECONOMIC ENVIRONMENT

The Republic of Yemen has over 28 million people living across six major regions, which differ substantially in climate and population. The northern highlands include much of the upper half of north Yemen and are bound on the west by mountains. The southern uplands consist of the lower half of north Yemen and include Taizz and Ibb Provinces. The coastal Tihama runs the length of north Yemen, between the Red Sea and the mountains. The arid east, on the edge of the desert, consists of the remote provinces of Marib, al-Jawf, and Shabwa. Far to the south are Aden and the area running from the Arabian Sea up to the mountains between the two Yemens. To the east is large, arid Hadhramaut Province and Wadi Hadhramaut. Finally, farther to the east are the culturally distinct Mahra region, bordering Oman, and the island of Socotra. Its biggest cities are the capital, Sana'a, followed by al-Hudaydah, Taizz, Aden, and al-Mukalla (Map 18.1).

Along with Sudan, Yemen is the only country in the MENA with less than half of its population living in urban centers (about 36 percent), a condition furthered by the war's dynamics of internal displacement. The bulk of Yemeni urban dwellers live in the major cities of Sana'a, Aden, al-Hudayda, and Taizz. The population of south Yemen is highly concentrated in a few places – in Mukalla and the towns of Wadi Hadhramaut, in the highlands northeast of Aden, and, above all, in Aden and its environs. By contrast, north Yemen's much larger population is also more widely dispersed across many towns, villages, and hamlets. Still, Taizz and al-Hudayda have experienced much growth, aside from the metropole of Sana'a. The age distribution of Yemen's population is remarkable: with 40 percent of the population aged 14 or under, and another 30 percent between the ages of 15 and 29, the country has among the youngest citizenries in the world, making the demand for education, housing, and other infrastructure pressing issues of national significance. As of 2019, the destruction of educational infrastructure from war means that a quarter of all Yemeni children are out of school.

The civil war has obliterated living standards, with the worst decline occurring since fighting escalated in spring 2015. The effect of endemic warfare has been the fracturing of Yemen into spatially and practically isolated islands. In 2019, the World Health Organization announced that the country

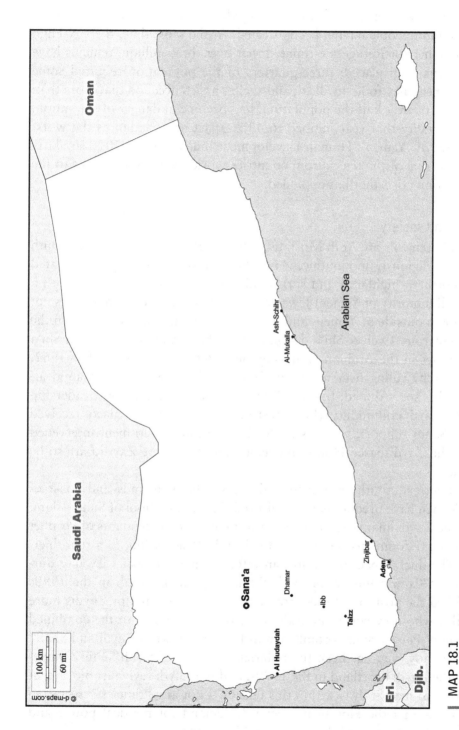

MAP 18.1
Republic of Yemen. Major cities shown.

Source: D-Maps.

was suffering one of the worst cholera epidemics in recorded history, with over a million people having been affected. At the same time, the UN High Commissioner for Refugees estimated that over three million Yemenis have been internally displaced; three-quarters of the population required some form of emergency food, medical, and shelter assistance; and that more than 15 million, or over half the population, had become in danger of starvation. Infant mortality that year jumped to 43.2, apace with Sudan as the worst in the MENA. Yemen's Human Development Index score in 2018 similarly paced it as one of the ten bottom countries worldwide – a testament to the humanitarian crisis that has exploded.

Culture and society

Nearly all Yemenis are Arab Muslims. While neither the north nor the south was ever religiously monolithic, Zaydi Shi'a have generally predominated in the northern highlands and surrounding towns and tribes, along with a very small minority of Yemeni Jews and Isma'ili Shi'a. The Zaydi faith is not well known outside of Yemen, and differs substantially in doctrine from the more numerous Twelver Shi'a denomination that prevails in Iran and Shi'a communities in the Arabian Gulf kingdoms. Before its deposal after 1962, the monarchy ruling over northern Yemen under Imam Yahya Hamid al-Din and his son, Ahmad, fused political authority and religious leadership over the Zaydi community. (In an historic inversion, that dynasty received profuse Saudi support, whereas in 2015, the Saudi government intervened against the Zaydi-based Houthi movement, declaring the Zaydi faith to be heretical.)

By contrast, southern Yemen and the southern uplands and coast of north Yemen have predominantly followed the Shafi'i school of Sunni Islam. Under the Zaydi imamate, a narrow stratum of *sada* (descendants of Prophet Muhammad) dominated politics and cultural life according to a rigid hierarchy. The dual impact of republican reforms aimed at social leveling during the 1970s and unification with the largely Shafi'i south in the 1990s diminished the position of these traditional authorities and of Zaydis more generally, who now constitute little more than 20 percent of the combined population. Far more important than differences between Zaydi and Shafi'i doctrines, however, has been the polarizing impact of Salafi Sunni evangelism in the Zaydi heartland in the 1990s, and the Zaydi revivalist movement that arose to meet it. It is within this tension – not any "timeless" sectarian animosity – that the Houthi movement's demand for political power and eventual effort to secure it by force should be understood.

That said, tribal ties more than sectarian affiliation have long been an important basis of social organization and identity in the northern highlands, in the mountainous region between the two Yemens, and in remote parts of the Hadhramaut, though they are of less significance in other parts of the country. Other forms of solidarity are significant as well, including family, locality, class, and caste-like occupational identities.

In addition to the privileged position of both Zaydi and Shafi'i *sada*, Yemenis recognize the significance of the *qadi* class – learned men who serve as judges, administrators, teachers, and religious figures. At the bottom are two groups: the *muzayyin* class that traditionally provided the butchers, barbers, and others to perform "demeaning" tasks, and the *akhdam* class of servants, street sweepers, and popular musicians. While the republican values of the state preclude formal discrimination on any of these grounds, the salience of such categorical distinctions in everyday life varies but is not irrelevant. In the middle are a relatively large, varied class of peasants, merchants, shopkeepers, and artisans. More recently, urban professionals have also made themselves known as a distinctive group of political significance, particularly as urban Sana'a grew to eclipse four million people by the time of the Arab Spring. The youths in that city who helped author the first peaceful protests against the Salih regime were, and are, Yemen's equivalent to the youth activist segment that has shaken politics in other MENA countries.

Rugged terrain, widely separated population centers, and limited means of transportation and communication have also contributed to diversity among the Yemeni people. Although Arabic is spoken by nearly all, there are several dialectical differences, as well as other sociocultural and regional differences. Among the most important is the difference between northerners from the highlands, as opposed to those from Aden and the southern half of north Yemen. The former are stereotyped as having strong tribal ties, claiming a warrior tradition, and, at least in the past, being more parochial. The latter are stereotyped as having non-tribal peasant origins and being docile or effete, engaged in commerce, and more traveled and cosmopolitan. In the east, many people in Wadi Hadhramaut reflect the cultural influence of Southeast Asia, with which they have long social and commercial ties. The people of Mahra and Socotra share a non-Arab language and culture. Finally, the people of the coastal desert and ports reflect the long racial and cultural influences of nearby Somalia and Ethiopia, and communities around Aden still carry some cultural markers of India and the British Raj. The Somali community today in Yemen represents the largest non-Arab group, and largely consists of refugees who have fled their own war-torn country since the 1990s.

Economic conditions

Yemen has long been, and remains, an extremely poor country. For centuries its economy was largely self-sufficient, based mainly on subsistence agriculture. While farming and animal husbandry remain chief sources of livelihood for a majority of the population, they contribute only a small percentage of Yemen's GDP, and shifts toward cash-crop agriculture over several decades have left the country heavily reliant on food imports, especially wheat. Modern industry outside the oil sector remains rare, marginal, and small, concentrated in textiles, leather, and crafts. The viability of the economy typically relies upon remittances from Yemenis working abroad, which in turn depends upon regional political and economic factors – such as the willingness of nearby prosperous kingdoms like Saudi Arabia to allow Yemeni expatriates to seek jobs there.

In 1987, modest amounts of oil were discovered in the north, in Marib, and first exported. At the time of unification in 1990, larger amounts of oil were discovered in Masila, an area northeast of Mukalla in the Hadhramaut. Oil production peaked at 465,000 barrels per day in 2003, then began to decline; experts predicted in 2009 that reserves would be depleted by the early 2020s. Liquefied natural gas exports began in late 2009. The share of Yemeni oil and gas in world markets is very small, but prior to the war it comprised a substantial part of government revenues. Yemen therefore exhibited some of the negative characteristics associated with rentierism (e.g., corruption, repression, autocracy), but enjoyed few of the benefits. Moreover, resource wealth was concentrated in the hands of government elites and their clients. Oil and gas revenues were not used to create strong welfare institutions or other sources of societal support. The paucity of domestic resources and government investments in services like education resulted in lower adult literacy rates, which in 2018 measured just 70 percent – one of the lowest in the MENA. Some elites even siphoned off subsidized diesel to sell along lucrative smuggling routes to East Africa.

Historically, for all these reasons, the modern Yemeni economy has suffered from poor periods of historical stagnation with only a few phases of real growth. In the unified republic, even modest expansion was stymied by unsuccessful reforms that sought to emphasize market-oriented competition but instead allowed for massive corruption. In 1994, Yemen's economy was in free fall, as GDP decreased by 50 percent in the first five years following unification. The value of the Yemeni riyal plunged, raising the cost of goods, especially essential imports. Because of massive unemployment and the loss of remittances from the nearly million expatriate Yemenis forcibly returned from the Arab kingdoms after the Gulf War, gross inequality and abject poverty increased at alarming rates. In mid-1995, the Salih regime agreed with the International Monetary Fund and World Bank to a program of economic stabilization, structural reforms, and concessional loans. This neoliberal commitment envisaged a future filled with private investment and capital so long as the government, in the short term, cut spending from key items like subsidies. Military expenditures were seldom touched, by contrast.

At first, stabilization measures and structural reforms helped rein in inflation and produce a brief spurt of growth; by the late 1990s, the IMF and World Bank had given Yemen several billion dollars to support its economic transformation. New measures designed to fight corruption, increase transparency, improve the fairness and efficiency of the courts, and reform the banking and financial sectors entered the agenda. However, the reforms faltered for familiar reasons witnessed elsewhere in the region: politically charged protests from citizens hurting by the rising cost of goods and services, and insufficient revenues from aid and oil rents to allow the government to maintain its composure. Another round of multilateral reforms in 2000, which again required ceasing subsidies and downsizing public employment in return for future aid and loans, was abandoned due to the political cost of following through with such eviscerating changes. Many foreign investors decided that the risks relative to potential gains were too great, given well-publicized cases of corruption, nepotism, and political favoritism that sprang up.

Despite higher oil revenues by 2005, the overall performance of the economy did not improve. Levels of unemployment, malnourishment, and those living below the poverty line persistently held at about 40 percent. The pauperization of the middle class continued, and the gap between the few rich and the many poor widened visibly. The education system declined, and medical services were in shorter supply and of poorer quality. On the personal level, Yemenis were increasingly ground down; they had borne the costs of subsidy cuts and other reforms without reaping the benefit of more accountable government and reduced corruption. More and more people were openly expressing anger and seemed ready to act on it. Thus, by the time the Arab Spring occurred, many observers argued the economy had already ceased to be viable. The Salih regime seemed to lack the will and capacity to adopt and implement reforms. Behind this were Yemen's oligarchs – its kleptocrats, really, whose wealth derived from control over state resources or small economic sectors – and the patronage pyramid they had come to depend upon.

In the 2010s, what little economic logic existed collapsed under the weight of violence and conflict, much like the country's failing infrastructure and health care institutions. In 2013, before the onset of the current war, Yemen's estimated annual GDP per capita was well under $1,500; in 2018, it had fallen to $873. Unemployment was nearly 13 percent in 2018, a number that heavily underestimated the difficulty of tracking job-seeking in a country in which reliable data are scarce. More worrisome, youth unemployment was nearly 24 percent. All told, the Yemeni GDP declined during 2011–18 by an average negative rate of almost 6 percent – it essentially shrunk by more than a half. Moreover, the wartime economy of Yemen settled into a perversely self-sustaining system of checkpoints and militia taxation that has profited the few at the gross expense of the many.

POLITICAL STRUCTURES

The Yemeni constitution was effectively suspended with the adoption of the GCC transitional framework after 2012, and has not yet been replaced by a new version despite proposals offered in 2015 by the NPC. But because the large majority of Yemenis are currently under the age of 29, most of the population has lived only under this constitution, and it thus forms an important benchmark against which any future system will be measured. Ratified by the people in a 1991 referendum, the constitution closely resembles the northern YAR's 1970 constitution. However, in the absence of a tradition of constitutional government in Yemen, the new constitution neither closely reflected political reality nor tightly constrained the use of power. Free speech, the right to organize, and the other rights it enshrined were largely aspirational, and the system of courts and appointed judges that came to populate the Yemeni judiciary in the 1990s never functioned independently of the regime. The desire of the majority of Yemenis to realize the rights and values of this constitution, or any constitution that guarantees equal recognition of disparate communities while also guaranteed fair and elected governments, should not be underestimated.

The constitution ratified in 1991 originally called for a plural executive, a feature that was amended twice – in 1994 to provide a singular president chosen by parliament, and in 1999 to provide a directly elected president. These amendments were part of Salih's consolidation of power and were enabled by the GPC's growing parliamentary majority and cooperation with Islah. According to the constitution, the 301 members of parliament were to be chosen by voters in single-member constituencies, though the last regularly scheduled election was held in 2003. The terms of office for legislators and the president were originally four and five years, respectively, and were amended to six and seven years in 2001. An upper chamber, the *Majlis al-Shura* (Consultative Council), appointed by the president and with mostly advisory powers, was created in 1997, thereby making the parliament a bicameral assembly. The constitution also provides for provincial and local council elections and for the appointment of provincial governors by the president. Delayed by a decade, local elections were held only in 2001 and in 2006. Under popular pressure, the Salih regime agreed that governors would be elected beginning in 2008, but since the Arab Spring there has been a reversion to appointment.

Opponents of the Salih regime persistently demanded constitutional changes throughout his presidency, and these demands were central in the post-2012 transitional period prior to the disintegration into civil war. Key proposals have included increasing legislative power at the expense of executive power, the adoption of some form of federalism, and greater devolution of power to local governments. If a negotiated end to the current war includes any reimagining of Yemen's political institutions, this might be expected to include more sweeping reforms such as replacement of the presidential system with parliamentary government, competitive national elections based on proportional representation, or the elevation of the Shura Council to legislative status equal to that of the lower chamber, the House of Representatives.

The constitution also established a multi-party system. The GPC came to dominate post-unification elections, though Islah has always posed some challenge – which explains the GPC's concerted efforts to retain Islah as an ally in the 1990s and foment internal divisions within Islah once it joined the opposition. The YSP has remained ideologically and organizationally coherent, with a small base of support in the south and in a few pockets of the north. Smaller parties have had little popular support, serving more often as vehicles for particularly influential individuals, but have played an important role in opposition dynamics since the JMP was formed. The post-Salih era has been marked by the dissipation of the traditional role of these parties, which were to distribute patronage and mobilize voters in an authoritarian republic.

Today, major parties (and especially the GPC) have fragmented and declined. Elites may retain titles associated with these organizations, but with President Hadi and his cabinet members dispersed, internal party mechanisms disabled for nearly a decade, and the enormous generational divide, the post-war period is likely to see the reconstitution of a new partisan landscape.

POLITICAL DYNAMICS

Yemen's political dynamics since the Arab Spring, as discussed before, have revolved around an overlapping set of conflictual issues: demands from social forces, each anchored in a geographic, cultural, or political context of grievances, for recognition and power; the inability of a transitional government, one installed largely by outside actors and inheriting the machinery of a party-based republican autocracy, to secure popular acceptance and steer the country into a new political order; and the interests of foreign interveners, in particular Saudi Arabia, in ensuring that their favored domestic partners emerge victorious. Against this backdrop is the rising noise of Salafi-jihadi militancy, regional separatism, and humanitarian disaster.

Beyond this, however, two deeper issues animate the political interactions that, in the past and present, shape major decisions. The first is the nature of competition over scarce resources, and the distribution of power based upon those resources. The model of politics that the unified republic implicitly reproduced was oligarchy. Salih's regime that took shape in the northern YAR in the 1980s featured, within the ruling GPC and within the president's inner circle, a small number of elites who got the little there was to get – be it political power or economic well-being – from the northern highlands. Often, these were *shaykhs* (chieftains) of well-known tribes, high-ranking military officers, or financial cronies of Salih's clique, the latter drawing disproportionately and deliberately from the far north at the expense of the traditional merchant class in and around Taizz.

Until 1994, unification interrupted this trend toward the concentration of power in the hands of northern oligarchs, given the extent to which the new government was forced to allocate its attention and efforts to southern problems. However, it resumed and intensified after the 1994 war, when increasing oil revenues and foreign aid made the state the principal source of wealth and private gain for the well-placed and fortunate few, who were disproportionately regime loyalists linked to the GPC. This transformation of a republican state into a source of private wealth had begun modestly when foreign aid flowed into the YAR in the mid-1970s, but the trend was countered by remittances that were spread widely and did not pass through the state. By the end of the 1990s, occupants of key government offices were able to use their positions in the bureaucracy to extract a price for providing services or permissions. This *nouveau* aristocracy of shaykhs, military officers, and businessmen had a strong sense of entitlement. By the end of the Salih era, its second generation had slipped into key positions and seemed to question the system even less. The GPC was intricately intertwined in this political economy; though nominally a dominant party designed to ensure victory for the president in manipulated elections, it also helped redistribute, channel, and enshrine favoritism and patronage among loyalists.

While the political struggles of the last two decades cannot be simplified purely to the battle over economic equity, it helps explain why so many groups outside the government have concluded that only by seizing power or separating can they achieve a political order that best satisfies their grievances. However, institutional inertia and the dissolution of governance has made this all but impossible. For instance, before the war, the broad base of this pyramid of corruption included the hundreds of thousands of government employees who were paid such low salaries that they were compelled to take petty bribes to make ends meet. They did not define or drive the kleptocratic order, but were essential to its maintenance. While the war has shown that the Houthis are not immune to the temptations of power – reports, for instance, have exposed the pilfering of humanitarian aid by some Houthi militia units – their anti-corruption demands, which they made from 2012, were central to their ability to mobilize widespread support, even among those antipathetic to the Zaydi faith. The movement of Yemen's Central Bank to Aden in 2016 has led to the collapse of even meager civil servant salaries in many parts of the country. As such, the specific structure of Yemen's kleptocratic order, much like its party system, is unlikely to emerge from the war intact, though the opportunities that will come with post-war reconstruction suggest that Yemeni elites will find profits in the ashes.

The second issue shaping political dynamics is pluralism, as it intersects with religion and civil society. Prior to unification, northern Yemen had little by way of a tolerated civil society or media scene that could express a plurality of social interests. The same held true for the south, where both the British and the PDRY governments sought to limit any kind of autonomous organizing by associations they could not control. After unification, the new constitution enabled the freedom and explosive growth of newspapers and magazines, though radio and television remained government monopolies. Organized interest groups – civil society or non-governmental organizations – sprang up by the hundreds and openly voiced their concerns.

Over time, however, the Salih regime learned over the years how to sub-vert its critics through an array of carrots and sticks, including the establish-ment of a special court for journalists in 2009 and the use of anti-terror laws to selectively prosecute those who reported on embarrassing news, such as when army units were defeated by militia groups. During the Arab Spring, a reinvigorated press and associational sector emerged from the initial wave of protests against Salih, but the political violence and repression that fol-lowed after 2012 marked a deterioration in press freedoms. Indeed, the war has made Yemen a deadly place for journalists, who face significant threats from all armed actors – the Hirak, the Houthis, the Hadi government, Salafi militants, and smaller belligerents – who seek to quiet critics and squelch negative reportage.

Infusing these state-society interactions, including spaces of rebellion, has been Islamism. The "Islamist" category is broad, encompassing groups and organizations that overlap in some ways but are at odds in others. In Yemen, they range from members of militant organizations of both Salafi and Zaydi revivalist persuasions, to radical extremists who aim to capitalize on the state's weakness, to reform-oriented affiliates of the Muslim Broth-erhood who participate in governing coalitions and direct social welfare toward Yemen's poor. Like some other MENA countries undergoing spasms of political reformation after the Arab Spring, the future of Yemeni politics requires institutional engagement with political actors whose broader world-view and governance objectives reflect religious commitments and identities.

In the north, the earliest Islamists drew intellectually and organization-ally from their Muslim Brotherhood counterparts in Egypt, but were also firmly aligned with nationalist and republican trends in Yemen through the 1962 revolution that created the YAR. By the 1970s, having survived the revolution and the years of civil war that followed, Yemeni Islamists turned increasingly away from Cairo and toward Saudi Arabia, coming particu-larly under the influence of influential figures like 'Abd al-Majid al-Zindani, who played a role in the northern Yemeni bureaucracy and would become a major figure in Islah after 1990. At the same time, the growth of Islamism in unified Yemen and the role of al-Zindani in that process were largely the result of Saudi Arabia's systematic use of Islam for foreign policy purposes. The rise of Salafi organizations in Yemen was heavily inflected by Saudi assis-tance given in past decades to advance Wahhabi Islam and its conservative strictures, particularly in the Zaydi-dominated northern highlands. In the 1980s, the Saudi government also recruited a large number of Yemenis for the "jihad" against Soviet forces in Afghanistan, a struggle that served as the incubator for the next generation's global revolutionary Islamists. When Soviet forces withdrew from Afghanistan in 1989, many radicalized, battle-hardened Yemenis came home.

As political conflict between the GPC and YSP escalated after 1991, President Salih often ignored the vigilante killing of southern leaders by militants returning from abroad with old scores to settle. As a loyalist general then, Ali Muhsin al-Ahmar folded many of these veterans into units of the northern army under his control, and many participated in the 1994 war with Muhsin's troops or as irregulars, leaving the Salih regime in debt to them. Thereafter, when the regime balked at their demands, armed conflict occasionally occurred between these militants and the security forces. This conflict became more complicated as it attracted international attention, especially after militants from Al-Qa'ida bombed a US naval ship in Aden in fall 2000. Yemeni intelligence and security forces collaborated with the US after 9/11 in counterterrorist operations, while major events rocked the regime in 2002: the suicide bombing of the French oil tanker *Limburg* off Yemen's southern coast, the killing of an Al-Qa'ida leader in an American drone strike, the assassination of YSP's thinker-activist Jarullah Omar, and the murder two days later of three American medical missionaries by a colleague of Omar's assassin.

Alongside this engagement with militant Salafis, President Salih found himself on increasingly shaky ground with Islah, which had begun in earnest to embrace its position as the largest opposition party. Different factions in Islah opposed Salih for different reasons. Salafis within the party resisted his efforts to curtail the evangelical and educational freedom of the "scientific institutes," which Salih tried to bring under government control in 2002. Some scholars and jurists were removed from their mosques and replaced with more moderate figures. At the same time, more centrist Islamists from the Muslim Brotherhood faction of Islah were concerned about Salih's consolidation of power. JMP members criticized his close ties to some Salafis in the party (especially al-Zindani), who they claimed used the language of *takfir* (allegations of disbelief) to discipline fellow party members at the behest of the Salih regime.

One effect of the state's ambivalence was the development of a Zaydi revivalist movement in Sa'da. Long before the Houthi movement emerged as an insurgency, its foundations were laid in the Believing Youth, a network of youth groups and summer camps designed to reinvigorate the Zaydi community in the face of Salafi evangelism. While Husayn al-Houthi played a leading role in this movement, its populist mobilization relied less on his traditional authority than on his charismatic leadership and more inclusive organization-building. President Salih initially supported al-Houthi's efforts, having become concerned about the assertiveness of the Salafis once they were no longer needed to help rein in the socialists in the south. But when the Houthis began challenging the regime directly, it cracked down on the movement; this turned the movement into an insurgency.

The resolution of a meaningful political transition in war-torn Yemen, thus, requires not just dialogue about the organizational structure of a new order and the distribution of resources between actors, but also deeper questions about how religious identity, incomparable faiths, and pious alignments will play into the desiderata of democratic politics – political parties, civil society, and everyday associations. What complicates this struggle is the threat of radical Salafi organizations, whose suppression is often a rare point that approaches consensus. After the struggle to oust President Salih in 2011, Ansar al-Shari'a in the south waged an intense struggle to capture a territory it proclaimed as a self-styled caliphate. The Saudi-backed Hadi government waged war alongside local militias to recapture this territory in 2012, triggering lethal AQAP suicide attacks in Sana'a and elsewhere. After the civil war escalated with Saudi intervention in March 2015, AQAP took control of the port of Mukalla and other areas of Hadhramawt, and by mid-summer ISIS had launched its own campaign. While combined efforts by a multitude of actors – Yemeni army units, US assets, Emirati forces, and local allies – contained and blunted this tide by 2018, many Salafi militants were simply reabsorbed into provincial militias. ISIS attacks rose during the spring and summer of 2019, as extremists took advantage of the overall climate of insecurity and disorder created by the civil conflict.

FOREIGN POLICY

The foreign relations of Yemen have always been filtered through its location, and overshadowed by its ever-involved neighbor of Saudi Arabia. Unified Yemen spent the early 1990s diplomatically and economically isolated by the GCC given Salih's decision to back Iraq during the Gulf War. Its foreign policy thereafter focused on restoring good relations with Saudi Arabia, and the other Gulf kingdoms, as well as the US. From Yemen's perspective, good relations meant foreign aid and the possibility of jobs and remittances; for all countries involved, amity meant a neighborhood safer for investment and tourism, and less likely to destabilize into future conflict. Among the Arab Gulf states, Kuwait was the most reluctant to forgive, but Yemeni persistence finally resulted in diplomatic relations being restored in 2000. Over the second half of the 1990s, relations with Qatar, the United Arab Emirates, and Oman also improved. As for Saudi Arabia, the biggest obstacle to maintaining stable ties is their long, permeable, and insecure border rife with territorial claims and counterclaims. This thorn in the side of Saudi-Yemeni relations was removed in a June 2000 agreement covering the entire border, in which Yemen gave up all claims to the provinces seized by Saudi Arabia in 1934 and the Saudis made some concessions along the long desert border east to Oman. Thereafter, some Saudi aid began to flow, and some Yemeni workers were allowed to return to the kingdom.

By the end of the 2000s, Saudi Arabia found itself in the position of playing major patron to the Salih regime. Faced with the growing Houthi movement, the creation of AQAP, and the possibility of Yemen's collapse, the Saudi government reportedly provided at least $2 billion in 2009 alone to cover the Yemeni budget shortfall caused by declining oil revenues. Beginning in November 2009, moreover, the Saudis responded to cross-border military action by Houthi militants, who had sought to escalate their campaign by attacking Saudi targets, by targeting them with sustained air strikes and some ground actions. This has culminated in the current war begun in March 2015, in which Saudi Arabia – in a campaign it dubbed Operation Decisive Storm – led its coalition against the Houthi movement. Much like Salih before him, President Hadi and his government have become reliant upon Saudi patronage and protection; when the Hirak seized government offices in Aden in 2018, Hadi fled to the kingdom, reconstituting his government-in-exile within Riyadh. The downside is that if and when the Hadi government is restored to something approximating stable power, Saudi interests will weigh heavily upon all decision-making.

Of the other Gulf kingdoms, the UAE has the largest footprint in Yemen, as it has also participated in the military intervention – but in surprising ways. Saudi Arabia and the UAE back different factions, despite ostensibly both opposing the Houthi movement given their belief that it operates as a proxy for Iran, their shared existential threat. Yet Saudi Arabia provides air support to militias aligned with Islah, while UAE troops work with Salafi allies who oppose Islah; indeed, Islah members have been detained and killed by Emirati security forces in the south. The UAE also supports the Hirak, and has gone so far as to recognize the quasi-governmental institutions created by the Hirak's political wing in Aden, the Southern Transitional Council, even though doing so contravenes the legitimacy of the Saudi-backed Hadi government. Indeed, during summer 2019, the UAE-backed Hirak increasingly clashed with the Saudi-backed forces supporting the Hadi government. At the same time, the Emirati government began strategically withdrawing some of its military forces, adding another geopolitical wrinkle to this complex war.

From Salih to Hadi, Yemeni foreign policy has followed one constant: official cooperation with, and often deference to, US interests. In the late 1990s, the Clinton administration enthusiastically backed the IMF and World Bank economic programming in the country. What made the country even more valuable was the specter of terrorism, as embodied in the 2000 bombing of the USS Cole and the 9/11 attacks in America. Days after those Al-Qa'ida strikes, President Salih flew to Washington, DC and pledged full support for the newly announced global war on terror. US military aid increased significantly, and Yemen participated in the CIA's controversial torture and renditions program. Salih also did not oppose the US invasion of Iraq, despite its unpopularity among many Yemenis. This put his regime in a more precarious situation; strategically, bolstering American grand strategy in the MENA made sense as it could secure more aid, protection, and resources, but it also further alienated Yemeni society. It also fueled the mobilization of some Islamists accustomed to labeling the US as a mortal threat.

At the same time, human rights became a weak point in Yemen's efforts to frame itself as a moderate and supportive country. By the mid-2000s, a growing number of donors had begun to criticize Yemen over economic reform and governance – and to act on the criticism. Multilateral financial institutions warned that aid remained contingent on Yemen's keeping its part of the aid-for-reform bargain. In October 2005, the US ambassador flatly asserted that Yemen's progress toward democracy had stalled. A month later, President Salih was surprised in Washington when he was told that Yemen was no longer eligible for a Millennium Challenge grant – a special foreign aid program created to assist countries deemed on the cusp of political transition – because of failures regarding corruption and repression. Shortly thereafter, the World Bank announced a one-third reduction of its aid to Yemen for the same reasons. The European Union applied similar pressure.

However, in the end, shared fear of extremist violence and radical Islamism realigned Yemeni foreign relations with Western interests, particularly with AQAP in the late 2010s and ISIS not long after. US military assistance in 2009 was nearly double that of 2007; that year, special antiterrorism specialists and Special Forces teams were dispatched from the US to train Yemeni forces, while the State Department rolled out a $120 million stabilization package to create immediate jobs and improve social services.

(Because of the structure of Yemen's military and security services, however, much of this aid went through the hands of Salih's family members or closest associates and was used to suppress regime critics.) US drone strikes in Yemen targeting militant and terrorist targets, used rarely by the Bush administration, accelerated under the Obama administration. The Arab Spring did not interrupt this pattern, nor did the Trump administration. Though data vary, reliable estimates suggest that the US undertook, through 2019, well over 300 drone strikes in the country, resulting in thousands killed (including several hundred civilians). Similarly, American demands for democracy were muted after 2015, as the imperative of halting radical Islamist actors became all-encompassing. The Hadi government has, dutifully, given open and unambivalent support to American actions in the country, banking on the possibility that sustained US interests will help reinstall its authority.

FUTURE PROSPECTS

Yemen's political transition since the Arab Spring has bogged down in civil war, fueled in equal parts by domestic grievances, obstinate political elites, and Saudi interventionism. As this book goes to press, that conflict enters its fifth year. With no new constitution, the Hadi government displaced, and extant institutions ruptured, the Yemeni state is collapsing – but not at the same time, and in different ways across the many different social forces and competing actors. Complicating matters, much like Syria's civil war and the ongoing Libyan conflict, is the splintered nature of the territorial situation. Loyalist militias linked to the late President Salih supported the Houthis before the alliance ended, resulting in a costly battle. The Hirak in the south allowed the Hadi government to relocate there after the Houthis conquered Sana'a, only to end the partnership and drive that government into Saudi exile. The UAE has many competing interests, and seems bound only by its common agreement with Saudi Arabia that the Houthi movement – understood, too simplistically, as an Iranian proxy – must be stopped.

One certainty about Yemeni politics today is that its paralysis and descent into civil war has produced a humanitarian catastrophe in which extensive urban combat, high civilian casualties, and a near-total blockade of food and medical aid to civilians has traumatized a national populace. International aid agencies have warned repeatedly that the fallout of this war will be unprecedented. The extent of food insecurity and starvation, critical shortages of water, the entirely preventable cholera epidemic, and breakdown of basic public safety underline that even if a compromise can be struck to create a more pluralistic and peaceful political system in the coming years, the generation expected to embrace this will be one scarred by violence. Peace talks have begun, but any long-term provisions have yet to be laid out. The future of Yemen is far from clear, but catastrophe seems certain at the close of the 2010s.

FURTHER READING

An accessible (if dated) introductory history of Yemen that touches upon all major trends until the twenty-first century is Paul Dresch, *A History of Modern Yemen* (Cambridge University Press, 2001). A stylized, journalistic account of Yemen's uniqueness comes from Victoria Clark, *Yemen: Dancing on the Heads of Snakes* (Yale University Press, 2010). Two excellent modern primers that summarize the past and contextualize the present for newcomers are Helen Lackner, *Why Yemen Matters* (Saqi, 2014) and Sheila Carapico, *Arabia Incognita* (Just World Books, 2016).

For economic and political histories of north and south Yemen, prior to unification, see Fred Halliday, *Arabia without Sultans* (Penguin, 1974); Robert W. Stookey, *Yemen: The Politics of the Yemen Arab Republic* (Westview Press, 1978) and *South Yemen: A Marxist Republic in Arabia* (Westview Press, 1982); John E. Peterson, *Yemen: The Search for a Modern State* (Croom Helm, 1982); Joseph Kostiner, *The Struggle for South Yemen* (Croom Helm, 1984); Ragaei El-Mallakh, *Economic Development of the Yemen Arab Republic* (Routledge, 1986); Robert D. Burrowes, *The Yemen Arab Republic: The Politics of Development, 1962–1986* (Westview Press, 1987); Noel Brehony, *Yemen Divided: The Story of a Failed State in South Arabia* (IB Tauris, 2011); and John M. Willis, *Unmaking North and South: Cartographies of a Yemeni Past* (Columbia University Press, 2013).

Politics since unification encompass a strong variety of works, which touch upon both strategies of authoritarian governance by the Salih regime and countervailing forms of social resistance. See, for example: Sheila Carapico, *Civil Society in Yemen* (Cambridge University Press, 1998); Lisa Wedeen, *Peripheral Visions: Publics, Power, and Performance in Yemen* (University of Chicago Press, 2008); Sarah Phillips, *Yemen's Democracy Experiment in Regional Perspective: Patronage and Pluralism* (Palgrave Macmillan, 2008) and *Yemen and the Politics of Permanent Crisis* (Routledge, 2011); Isa Blumi, *Chaos in Yemen: Societal Collapse and the New Authoritarianism* (Routledge, 2012); and Uzi Rabi, *Yemen: Revolution, Civil War, and Unification* (IB Tauris, 2015).

For Yemen's external relations in historical perspective, see Fred Halliday, *Revolution and Foreign Policy: The Case of South Yemen, 1967–1987* (Cambridge University Press, 1989); F. Gregory Gause, *Saudi-Yemeni Relations: Domestic Structures and Foreign Influence* (Columbia University Press, 1990); and Asher Orkaby, *Beyond the Arab Cold War: The International History of the Yemen Civil War, 1962–68* (Oxford University Press, 2017). On the relationship between Yemen's domestic and international politics, see Laurent Bonnefoy, *Yemen and the World* (Oxford University Press, 2018). The US-Yemeni connection is unpacked in Gregory Johnsen, *The Last Refuge: Yemen, al-Qaeda, and America's War in Arabia* (W.W. Norton, 2014).

Yemen's civil conflict since 2012, and particularly its escalation with outside military intervention, requires careful analysis. A good collection that helps explain the origins and dynamics of this civil war is the special issue of *Middle East Report* entitled *The Fight for Yemen* (No. 289, Spring 2019). See also Marieke Brandt, *Tribes and Politics in Yemen: A History of the Houthi Conflict* (Oxford University Press, 2017); Ginny Hill, *Yemen Endures: Civil War, Saudi Adventurism, and the Future of Arabia* (Oxford University Press, 2018); Isa Blumi, *Destroying Yemen: What Chaos in Arabia Tells Us about the World* (University of California Press, 2018); Helen Lackner, *Yemen in Crisis: Autocracy, Neo-Liberalism and the Disintegration of a State* (Saqi, 2018). Major insights can be gleaned by exploring the Islamist dynamic, and how Islamism has shaped social and political interactions. The best studies of this are Laurent Bonnefoy, *Salafism in Yemen* (Oxford University Press, 2012), and Stacey Philbrick Yadav, *Islamists and the State: Legitimacy and Institutions in Yemen and Lebanon* (IB Tauris, 2013).

A closer look at social forces, particularly tribalism and provincial identities, are provided by these excellent works: Paul Dresch, *Tribes, Government, and History in Yemen* (Oxford University Press, 1989); Steven C. Caton, *Peaks of Yemen I Summon: Poetry as Performance in a North Yemeni Tribe* (University of California Press, 1990); Shelagh Weir, *A Tribal Order: Politics and Law in the Mountains of Yemen* (University of Texas Press, 2007); and Noel Brehony, ed., *Hadhramaut and its Diaspora: Yemeni Politics, Identity and Migration* (IB Tauris, 2017). For law, religion, culture, and society, see Brinkley Messick, *The Calligraphic State: Textual Domination and History in a Muslim Society* (University of California Press, 1993); Bernard Haykel, *Revival and Reform in Islam: The Legacy of Muhammad al-Shawkani* (Cambridge University Press, 2003); and Steven C. Caton, *Yemen Chronicle: An Anthropology of War and Mediation* (Hill and Wang, 2005).

Online sources

Though Yemen has one of the lowest Internet penetration rates in the MENA, researchers can still find substantial resources online that provide insight into contemporary Yemeni events. Some English-language news websites are Yemen Post (www.yemenpost.net/) and Yemen Online (www.yemenonline.info/). Excellent analyses can be also found on the country portals provided by think tanks like Chatham House (www.chathamhouse.org/research/regions/middle-east-and-north-africa/yemen), the Atlantic Council (www.atlanticcouncil.org/yemen), the Brookings Institution (www.brookings.edu/topic/yemen/), the Middle East Institute (www.mei.edu/regions/yemen), and International Crisis Group (www.crisisgroup.org/middle-east-north-africa/gulf-and-arabian-peninsula/yemen). In addition, international monitors and organizations have maintained close contact with Yemeni actors in highlighting the ongoing conflict. The best source for data on the Yemeni war, including interventions and airstrikes by outside actors, is the Yemen Data Project (http://yemendataproject.org/). The Civilian Impact Monitoring Project has an excellent country page (http://civilianimpactmonitoring.org/index.html). The UN Office for the Coordination of Humanitarian Affairs provides a useful site as well (www.unocha.org/yemen). Finally, the Yemen Peace Project is an advocacy organization delivering information about the Yemeni conflict (www.yemenpeaceproject.org).

Please note that URLs may change far more quickly than books can be printed; so if these exact URLs do not work, simply search Google or another engine by the titles of these websites and online resources.

INDEX

THE SOCIETIES OF THE MIDDLE EAST AND NORTH AFRICA

Structures, Vulnerabilities and Forces

THE SOCIETIES OF THE MIDDLE EAST AND NORTH AFRICA

STRUCTURES, VULNERABILITIES, AND FORCES

Edited by Sean Yom

Edited by Sean Yom

Exploring the societies and populations of the Middle East and North Africa, this new textbook provides the historical and cultural context necessary for understanding the peoples inhabiting Arab world, Israel, Turkey, and Iran, since the early twentieth century.

Hb: 9781-138580480 • Pb: 9781138580503 • eBook: 9780429507311

Routledge
Taylor & Francis Group